Child Language Acquisition

Contrasting Theoretical Approaches

Is children's language acquisition based on innate linguistic structures or built from cognitive and communicative skills? This book summarizes the major theoretical debates in all of the core domains of child language acquisition research (phonology, word learning, inflectional morphology, syntax and binding) and includes a complete introduction to the two major contrasting theoretical approaches: generativist and constructivist. For each debate, the predictions of the competing accounts are closely and even-handedly evaluated against the empirical data. The result is an evidence-based review of the central issues in language acquisition research that will constitute a valuable resource for students, teachers, course-builders and researchers alike.

BEN AMBRIDGE is Lecturer in Psychology at the University of Liverpool. He has published numerous articles on child language acquisition with a particular focus on the acquisition of syntax and morphology, and the retreat from overgeneralization error.

ELENA V. M. LIEVEN is Professor and Senior Researcher at the Max Planck Institute for Evolutionary Anthropology, Leipzig, and Director of the Max Planck Child Study Centre, University of Manchester. She is best known for her work on naturalistic corpus data, and is a former editor of the *Journal of Child Language*.

Child Language Acquisition

Contrasting Theoretical Approaches

Ben Ambridge

Elena V. M. Lieven

CAMBRIDGE
UNIVERSITY PRESS

CAMBRIDGE UNIVERSITY PRESS
Cambridge, New York, Melbourne, Madrid, Cape Town,
Singapore, São Paulo, Delhi, Tokyo, Mexico City

Cambridge University Press
The Edinburgh Building, Cambridge CB2 8RU, UK

Published in the United States of America by Cambridge University Press, New York

www.cambridge.org
Information on this title: www.cambridge.org/9780521745239

First published 2011

Printed in the United Kingdom at the University Press, Cambridge

A catalogue record for this publication is available from the British Library

Library of Congress Cataloguing in Publication data
Ambridge, Ben, 1977–
Child language acquisition : contrasting theoretical approaches / Ben Ambridge,
Elena V. M. Lieven.
   p.   cm.
Includes bibliographical references and index.
ISBN 978-0-521-76804-7 (hardback)
1. Children – Language.   2. Language acquisition.   3. Language arts (Early
childhood)   4. Verbal ability in children.   I. Lieven, Elena V. M.   II. Title.
P118.A47   2011
401'.41 – dc22   2010048067

ISBN 978-0-521-76804-7 Hardback
ISBN 978-0-521-74523-9 Paperback

Contents

Figures

Tables

Boxes

Summary tables

Preface

How do children acquire their native language? This question has prompted a lively theoretical debate and a great deal of empirical research, much of which explicitly tests the predictions of the various competing accounts. In our view, it is therefore unfortunate that most previous child language textbooks and monographs barely cover this debate at all. Instead, most authors, whether implicitly or explicitly, adopt a particular theoretical position and largely discuss only research conducted within the relevant paradigm. If proposals that derive from an opposing theoretical viewpoint are discussed at all, it is generally only to dismiss them, with no serious consideration of their strengths and weaknesses.

We want to change all that with this textbook. Our goal is to identify the key debates in each of what we consider to be the 'core' domains in language acquisition (by monolingual, typically-developing speakers) and to outline the empirical evidence for and against each theoretical proposal, in an even-handed, systematic and (as far as space permits) comprehensive manner. We aim to hold every proposal to an equally high standard of proof – making no prior assumptions with regard to parsimony or psychological plausibility – and, in so doing, to provide detailed challenges to all researchers, of all theoretical standpoints.

This focus on theoretical debates has three important consequences. The first is that, although we seek to be comprehensive in covering all the major domains of acquisition (speech perception/segmentation and production, word learning, inflectional morphology and syntax), this textbook does not constitute a descriptive account of what children's language looks like at each age (there are many other textbooks that fulfil this function). Whilst the reader will, nevertheless, build up a detailed picture of the timecourse of key acquisition phenomena, areas which have attracted rather less theoretical debate are not covered.

The second consequence of our theoretically oriented approach is that when selecting studies to include, we have focused, as far as possible, on quantitative experimental or naturalistic-data studies that have been published in peer-reviewed journals, and that include appropriate statistical analyses. Whilst descriptive accounts of children's language (in terms of one or other theory of adult linguistics) play an important role in the development of theories of language acquisition, they are generally not an appropriate basis on which to compare competing theoretical accounts (which, for the most part, make precise quantitative predictions).

The final consequence of organizing this textbook around theoretical debates is that it is relatively modular in its structure. Each chapter covers a particular domain of language acquisition, meaning that readers who are interested in a particular topic will be able to 'dip in' at the relevant chapter. The internal structure of each chapter is also relatively modular, with each focusing on two, three or four key debates. Our intention is that researchers who are interested in a particular debate will be able to read the relevant section without having to consult the rest of the chapter, and that course leaders can base lectures around individual debates. Whilst the division of language acquisition into a number of relatively self-contained (and inevitably somewhat arbitrary) domains is, of course, artificial, our goal in doing so is to provide an ordered set of topics around which an undergraduate or postgraduate course can be based.

Because the debates are often complicated and draw on a great deal of empirical research, we end each with a summary table that summarizes the evidence for and against each of the proposals (and that will hopefully serve as a useful guide for revision, coursework projects etc.). We certainly do not wish to imply that one can choose between the rival accounts by counting up the relative numbers of 'for's and 'against's (not least because one critical shortcoming can trump any number of advantages). Rather, these tables reflect the approach that we adopt throughout this book: our aim is not to choose a 'winner' in each debate, but simply to bring together the relevant findings, in order to allow the reader to draw his or her own conclusions. We hope that we have succeeded in our aim to be fair to – and appropriately critical of – researchers from all theoretical persuasions.

Acknowledgements

We thank the many people who have read and commented on drafts of this book, a reviewer for Cambridge University Press and our students, friends and families. We thank Nicole Lorenz for preparing the author index and Kay McKechnie for copy-editing. Special thanks are due to Siu-Lin Rawlinson for redrawing Figures 8.3, 8.5 and 8.10–8.13 by hand from the originals, at extremely short notice. Ben Ambridge's own research discussed in this book was supported by grants RES-062-23-0931, RES-000-22-1540 and PTA-026-27-0705 from the Economic and Social Research Council; Elena Lieven's by grants RES-000-22-1285, RES-000–23-6393 and RES-000-23-7911 from the Economic and Social Research Council, and by the Max Planck Institute for Evolutionary Anthropology.

1 Introduction

In this introductory chapter, we briefly outline (1) the major theoretical approaches to child language acquisition research, (2) the domains and debates to be covered in the rest of the book and (3) the major methodological paradigms used in the field.

1.1 The major theoretical approaches

Although there are a few exceptions, for the majority of the debates that we will encounter in this book, each of the competing proposals will generally be aligned with one of the two major theoretical approaches to language acquisition. These are (a) the **nativist, generativist, Universal Grammar (UG)** approach and (b) the **constructivist, emergentist, socio-pragmatic, functionalist, usage-based** approach. As outlined below, which terms are most appropriate depends on the precise nature of each proposal, and the domain under investigation.

1.1.1 Nativist/generativist/Universal Grammar (UG) proposals

- A theoretical proposal that is **nativist** assumes that some important aspects of children's *linguistic* knowledge are not acquired, but **innate** (present from birth and, for at least some researchers, encoded in the genome).
- A theoretical proposal that is **generativist** assumes that children's knowledge of grammar (encompassing syntax, inflectional morphology and, in some approaches, phonology) consists of knowledge of formal 'rules' or operations that operate on abstract linguistic categories (e.g. VERB, NOUN) and phrases (e.g. VERB PHRASE, NOUN PHRASE). For example, oversimplifying somewhat, one operation for forming an English sentence combines a NOUN (e.g. *John*) and a VERB (e.g. *danced*) in that order (e.g. *John danced* not *Danced John*). This is an example of a **syntactic** operation (a 'rule' of **syntax**; see Chapters 4 and 6). An example of a **morphological** operation (a 'rule' of **inflectional morphology**) is the process by which the past-tense

-ed inflectional morpheme is added to a regular English VERB (e.g. *kiss* → *kissed*; see Chapters 4 and 5).

- All the **generativist** approaches that we will meet in this book are also **nativist** approaches, in that they assume that knowledge of (at least some of) these categories, phrases and operations is innate. Approaches that are both nativist and generativist are also termed **Universal Grammar** (UG) approaches, because this knowledge is held to be part of a Universal Grammar (a general grammar that applies to all the world's languages), which is innately specified (i.e. children have knowledge of UG from birth). In principle, it would be possible to have a proposal that is **generativist** (i.e. couched in terms of formal rules/operations on syntactic categories and phrases) but not **nativist** (these rules/operations, categories and phrases are learned as opposed to innate). However, none of the generativist accounts discussed in this book are of this type (and indeed, we are aware of no such proposals in the child language acquisition literature).

- It is also possible for a proposal to be **nativist** (i.e. to assume that children have some innate linguistic knowledge) but not **generativist** (because this knowledge pertains to some area of language other than grammar). For example, a strong version of the lexical-principles account of word learning (see Chapter 3) assumes that children are born with the assumption that new words are most likely to refer to whole objects (as opposed to parts or properties of objects). Such a proposal is nativist (it assumes innate knowledge) but not generativist (this knowledge pertains to word meanings, not grammar). Although we will encounter some proposals that are nativist but not generativist (though not vice versa), the two almost always go hand in hand, and some authors use the terms interchangeably. We will endeavour to be precise in our use of these terms, though we will sometimes refer to generativist–nativist approaches where appropriate.

1.1.2   Constructivist/emergentist/socio-pragmatic/functionalist/ usage-based proposals

- A theoretical proposal that is **constructivist** assumes that children do not have any innate knowledge of grammar (i.e. it is a **non-nativist** proposal). Of course, the *ability to learn* language is held to be innate (and specific to humans), but, to again take an example from the domain of syntax, the approach assumes that children are not born with grammatical categories such as VERB and NOUN, but must acquire them by generalizing across the adult speech that they hear. Hence, most constructivist approaches are **input-based** approaches, in that they assume that characteristics of the input are a driving force in children's acquisition (for instance, that they will most easily acquire the words and constructions that they encounter most frequently).

- Constructivist proposals are **non-generativist** in that they do not see the adult end state as a system of formal rules or operations that act on categories such as VERB. For example, in Chapter 5, we will see how a constructivist account of past-tense formation argues that forms such as *kissed* are *not* produced by a formal operation (or 'rule') that adds *-ed* to the verb (*kiss → kissed*), but by analogy with similar sounding pairs such as *miss → missed*. The differences between generativist and constructivist approaches to morphology and syntax are outlined in detail in Chapter 4.
- Because, under this view, the categories and procedures for sentence formation are not innate but emerge from the generalizations that children form, **constructivist** proposals are also sometimes termed **emergentist** proposals.
- A theoretical proposal that is **functional** or **usage-based** (we will use these terms interchangeably) assumes that children's language acquisition is driven by – and hence cannot be explained without reference to – their desire to **use** language to perform communicative **functions** (such as requesting an object or activity, commenting on a situation etc.) and to understand the utterances of others. For example, the finding that children produce more sentences beginning with *I* than *You* most likely demands a functional, usage-based explanation (e.g. children are more interested in talking about themselves than a conversational partner). Constructivist proposals are sometimes described as **emergentist** in the sense that children's grammar **emerges** from their **use** of language in this way (as opposed to the related, but different, sense discussed above).
- A theoretical proposal that is **socio-pragmatic** assumes that crucial to children's ability to learn language is the ability to make social-pragmatic inferences regarding a speaker's focus of **attention** and his or her **communicative intentions**. For example, social-pragmatic accounts of word learning (see Chapter 3) assume that children know that a speaker who produces a word whilst looking at an object (a) is attending to that object and (b) intends to label that object for the child.
- Most **constructivist** proposals are also **functional/usage-based** and **social-pragmatic** in nature. However, we will also encounter constructivist proposals that do not make reference to language use or to social-pragmatic understanding. For example, in Chapter 6, we will discuss constructivist proposals under which children form grammatical categories by grouping together words that appear in similar sentence positions (e.g. *the X*), without regard to meaning. Thus though some authors use all of the terms discussed in this section interchangeably, we will again endeavour to be precise in our use of the relevant terms.

1.2   The domains and debates

- Chapter 2 investigates speech perception, segmentation and production. The debates here concern how children develop an inventory of the phonemes of their language (in perception), how they segment the continuous speech stream that they hear into words, phrases and clauses, and how they arrive at an adultlike capacity for speech production. In each case, the debate is between one constructivist position and one or more positions that posit some innate knowledge (e.g. of distinctive phonological features, stress cues to word segmentation and rules or constraints on production).

- Chapter 3 investigates how children learn the meanings of words. The debate here is between one account that (at least in its strong form) makes certain nativist assumptions (the lexical constraints/principles approach), one constructivist account (the social-pragmatic account) and one account that is neither constructivist nor nativist, and rejects both innate principles and the importance of social-pragmatic understanding (the associative-learning account). We also evaluate a proposal under which children use syntax to learn word meanings (syntactic bootstrapping), which is potentially compatible with both approaches.

- Chapter 4 does not present empirical data but sets out the positions of the two competing theoretical approaches with respect to inflectional morphology (Chapter 5) and syntax (Chapters 6–8). This chapter can be skipped by readers who are already familiar with both approaches.

- Chapter 5 discusses three debates in the acquisition of inflectional morphology: root infinitive errors, productivity and rules versus analogy in inflectional morphology (with special reference to the English past-tense debate). In each case, the debate is between one or more generativist accounts (e.g. the Agreement/Tense Omission model; the variational learning model; the dual-route model) and one constructivist account (e.g. lexical-learning approaches; the single-route model).

- Chapter 6 also discusses three debates, in this case, relating to the acquisition of basic syntax: acquiring syntactic categories, learning basic word order and the retreat from overgeneralization error. Again, in each case there is a debate between one or more generativist accounts (e.g. semantic bootstrapping, prosodic bootstrapping, parameter setting) and one or more constructivist accounts (e.g. distributional learning), though (particularly for the first and third debates) we will also encounter some proposals that combine elements of both approaches.

- Chapter 7 (movement and complex syntax) discusses the acquisition of passives, questions, relative clauses (and questions containing relative clauses, with special reference to the 'structure dependence' debate) and sentential complement clauses. For each topic, the debate is a relatively straightforward contrast between generativist movement-based approaches and constructivist approaches which assume that children acquire constructions by abstracting across exemplars of the relevant constructions in the input (and also by combining these acquired constructions).

- Chapter 8 discusses three debates regarding children's acquisition of adultlike interpretations of pronouns (binding), quantification (quantifiers such as *each* and *every*) and control (null or omitted arguments). Although most of the proposals and experimental studies in this area stem from the generativist approach (e.g. innate binding principles), we will also discuss constructivist approaches based on the notion of construction learning and social-pragmatic understanding.
- Chapter 9 briefly highlights some debates that are not considered in detail elsewhere, but that bear on the wider debate between generativist–nativist and constructivist approaches: modularity/domain specificity, atypical language development (SLI, Williams syndrome, autism), the critical-period hypothesis (early language deprivation, children 'inventing' languages, second language learning), the genetic basis of language and its evolution, and language change. We end by drawing together some conclusions based on the research discussed throughout the book, and by presenting some future challenges for both approaches.

For each debate in each domain, our goal is to *contrast* the competing theoretical proposals, and to investigate which is better supported by the data. Although, as we shall see, both the generativist and constructivist approaches have their own strengths and weakness, we should emphasize that our goal is *not* to advocate a 'third-way' or 'radical middle' account of language acquisition that seeks to reconcile the two approaches. It is becoming increasingly common to see statements such as 'all theories of language acquisition posit some learning and some innate knowledge'. This is true, but only trivially so. The point of disagreement between the two theories is whether or not children are born with distinctive features (e.g. voiced/unvoiced), grammatical categories (e.g. VERB, NOUN), phrase structure (e.g. VP = VERB, NP), principles (e.g. structure dependence, the binding principles), parameters (e.g. the head-direction parameter), default assumptions (e.g. an object in the world has only one label), linking rules (AGENTS of ACTIONS are SUBJECTS of sentences) and so on (depending on the particular domain). The challenge for generativist approaches is to provide evidence that children have this innate knowledge, and/or evidence against the claim that it can be acquired on the basis of experience. The challenge for constructivist approaches is to provide evidence against the claim that children have this innate knowledge, and/or evidence that it can be acquired from experience. But this highly abstract, specifically linguistic knowledge is either present at birth or it is not. There can be no compromise position.

1.3   Methodologies

Since it is, of course, impossible to investigate speakers' linguistic knowledge directly, various methodologies are required to infer their knowledge from observable behaviour. This behaviour includes not only production of language but also performance on tasks designed to reveal comprehension (e.g. acting out a sentence with toys) and speakers' intuitions regarding possible interpretations or grammatical acceptability (i.e. judgment tasks). It is important to bear in mind that no methodology (even simply recording children's spontaneous speech) provides a 'pure' measure of linguistic knowledge. Children's performance will always reflect not only their knowledge but also factors such as attention and memory (e.g. the ability to keep an entire sentence in mind) and the ability to meet the particular task demands of a particular study (e.g. the ability to repeat a sentence or to manipulate toys).

There are two ways around this problem. The first is to seek converging findings from different methodologies. For example, if we want to know whether children understand that English uses SUBJECT VERB OBJECT (AGENT ACTION PATIENT) word order (as in *The dog kicked the cat*), we could look to see whether children produce such sentences in their spontaneous speech, whether they produce them in an experimental setting with novel verbs, and whether they show understanding of such sentences when they hear them (e.g. when asked to enact the sentence with animal toys).

The second approach is to build suitable controls into our investigations. For example, if a child cannot correctly enact *The dog meeked the cat* (where *meeking* is a novel action taught in an experiment), one possibility is that she does not have verb-general knowledge of SUBJECT VERB OBJECT word order. Another possibility is that the child is failing the task because she is unable to remember the sentence, does not understand what is required in the task, and so on. A possible control condition here would be to have the child enact a sentence with a familiar verb. For example, if she can correctly enact *The dog hit the cat*, then this allows us to rule out (at least) the possibility that the child simply does not understand the task (or does not wish to 'play'). Suitable controls must also be built into investigations of children's spontaneous speech. For example, if a child produces the form *her* in subject position (e.g. **Her is playing* vs *She is playing*), one possibility is that she does not have the correct system for marking case. Another possibility, however, is that the child has yet to learn the form *She*. A suitable control in this case would be to see if the child continues to produce such errors after she has produced the *She* form in her spontaneous speech.

Table 1.1 *Major paradigms in child language acquisition research (the focus here is on paradigms that will be frequently encountered in subsequent chapters, in particular those that produce quantitative data that can be analysed statistically)*

Paradigm	Examples	Advantages	Disadvantages
Naturalistic data studies			
Recording children's **spontaneous speech**, often longitudinally	Speech perception, segmentation and phonology (Ch. 2); inflection (Ch. 5); simple and complex syntax (Chs. 6–7)	Naturalistic vs artificial (e.g. lab studies); can also record caregivers to investigate role of input; single corpus can test many different predictions	Very time consuming; consequently, sampling often thin (e.g. 1hr per week), leading to unreliable estimates of productivity/error
Caregiver diary (often combined with longitudinal recordings of spontaneous speech)	Speech perception, segmentation and phonology (Ch. 2); simple and complex syntax (Chs. 6–7)	Very detailed data on a particular structure (e.g. coarticulation, *wh*-questions); often attempt to record *all* instances	No data on acquisition of other structure; can be used in only one domain
Caregiver checklists (e.g. *McArthur Communicative Development Inventory*)	Word learning (Ch. 3); inflection (Ch. 5)	Can collect large volumes of data quickly; generally good reliability (e.g. high correlation between reported and experimentally assessed vocabulary)	Can exhibit particular biases (e.g. parents may recall more nouns than verbs for vocabulary checklist); cannot be used to test fine-grained predictions (e.g. different error rates for different auxiliaries)
Experimental production studies (elicited production/repetition studies are sometimes conducted longitudinally)			
Elicited production: child asked to describe scene (e.g. *Ernie meeking Bert*) or 'fill in the gap' (e.g. *Ernie always meeks, so yesterday he . . .*), often using novel verb	inflection (Ch. 5); simple and complex syntax (Chs. 6–7)	High degree of control over variables of interest; useful for collecting data on structures rarely produced in spontaneous speech (e.g. complex questions)	Relatively difficult for children; problems with memory, utterance-planning etc. may obscure competence; children may still avoid very low frequency/complex structures

(*cont.*)

Table 1.1 (*cont.*)

Paradigm	Examples	Advantages	Disadvantages
Repetition (or '**elicited imitation**'): child asked to repeat experimenter's utterance, with deviations analysed. Sometimes the utterance is ungrammatical (e.g. *I pretend her playing*) and/or particular items (e.g. auxiliaries) may be replaced with novel items, or a cough (e.g. *She fep playing*; *She [cough] playing*); Correction or substitution of the missing item constitutes evidence for knowledge	Simple and complex syntax (Chs. 6–7); inflection (Ch. 5)	Can be used to elicit attempts at structures that children would normally avoid (e.g. complex relative clauses). Perhaps surprisingly, errors do seem to reflect children's knowledge	Too 'easy' for very short sentences and/or older children (though using time taken to repeat as dependent measure can be a solution)
Syntactic priming: experimenter describes scene using particular structure (e.g. passive). Child then describes new scene. Use of same structure as opposed to alternative (e.g. active transitive) suggests prior knowledge of structure	Complex syntax (Ch. 7); occasionally simple syntax (Ch. 6) though can be problematic	High degree of control over target structure without drawbacks of imitation paradigm; does not require use of novel verbs, reducing memory demands	Use of a structure does not necessarily reflect prior knowledge as children can be 'primed' to use ungrammatical structures that they have never encountered (see below and Ch. 5)

Weird word order: experimenter describes scene using an ungrammatical structure with a novel verb (e.g. SOV *Ernie the car gopping*). Child then describes new scene (with same verb). Use of ungrammatical word order suggests verb-specific learning	Simple syntax (Ch. 6)	Since WWO studies contain a condition in which conventional word order (SVO for English is primed), they can be seen as priming studies (sharing their advantages) with added advantage of WWO 'control' condition	Like other production paradigms, can be relatively difficult for children, particularly since novel verbs are generally used

Comprehension studies (again, these can be – though in practice rarely are – conducted longitudinally)

Act-out tasks: child asked to enact scene described by experimenter, usually using novel verb (e.g. *Ernie is meeking Bert*) or conflicting cues to meaning (e.g. *Him are pushing the girls*)	Simple syntax (Ch. 6); occasionally complex syntax (Ch. 7)	Easier than production studies (particularly for very young children who produce only very short utterances) – better measure of knowledge	Surprisingly difficult for young children, perhaps due to memory demands involved in planning an action
Preferential looking: child hears sentence, usually with novel verb (e.g. *Ernie is meeking Bert*) and can watch either of two scenes; one matching (e.g. Ernie performing novel action on Bert) one mismatching (e.g. Bert performing action on Ernie)	Word learning (Ch. 3); simple syntax (Ch. 6)	Easier than act-out tasks, thus suitable for use with children as young as 1;10 (simple syntax) and 6 months (word learning); eye tracking can be used to investigate knowledge at a fine-grained level	Relies on assumption that children will always look longer at the matching than mismatching screen (in fact, may identify matching screen, then look away); controversy regarding training (see Ch. 5); unsuitable much above 2;6
Pointing: as preferential looking, with children asked to point to the matching scene, display or (for word learning) object	Simple syntax (Ch. 6); word learning (Ch. 3)	Produces unambiguous binary outcome measure (compare preferential looking above)	Slightly harder than preferential looking tasks, thus generally unsuitable for children younger than 2;0

(*cont.*)

Table 1.1 (*cont.*)

Paradigm	Examples	Advantages	Disadvantages
Conditioned head-turn preference procedure: children trained that (for example) English audio is looped when they fix gaze on one loudspeaker; Russian audio another loudspeaker	Speech perception, segmentation and phonology (Ch. 2); simple syntax (Ch. 6)	Can be used with very young children (e.g. 4 months)	Interpretation can be problematic; listening time difference means children can *tell the difference* between two stimuli, but not necessarily anything more
Habituation: used together with some looking/listening time measure; children become bored with repeated presentations of similar stimuli (e.g. dog, cow, horse) and looking/listening times decrease; if a stimulus from a different category (e.g. hammer) causes recovery of looking times, this is evidence that children have formed the two categories	Speech perception, segmentation and phonology (Ch. 2); word learning (Ch. 3)	Can also be used with very young children	If some children show habituation (novelty preference) and others a familiarity preference, these may cancel each other out when group means are taken, potentially hiding effects
High-amplitude sucking/kicking: similar to head-turn preference procedure above, except that playback controlled by sucking or (pre-natally) kicking rate	Speech perception, segmentation and phonology (Ch. 2)	Can be used with children only a few days old (or even unborn)	Can be used to investigate knowledge of language only at a coarse level (e.g. do infants prefer mother's voice to that of another speaker?)
Event-related potentials (ERPs): recorded from scalp electrodes in a cap	Speech perception, segmentation and phonology (Ch. 2)	Can be used with very young infants; good at detecting relationship between stimulus and response	Bad at detecting localization; problems with relating infant measures to better-specified adult measures

Technique	Used to investigate	Advantages	Disadvantages
Functional magnetic resonance imaging (fMRI): measures changes in blood flow relating to neural activist in the brain	Speech perception, segmentation and phonology (Ch. 2)	Good at detecting localization	Difficult to use with infants; hence usually carried out when infant asleep or sedated, but can be done on waking infants with careful protection procedures; poor temporal resolution, so hard to distinguish responses that occur within a short time window

Judgment studies

Technique	Used to investigate	Advantages	Disadvantages
Yes/no judgment tasks: children shown a picture (e.g. Mama bear washing herself) and asked a *yes/no* question (e.g. *Is Mama bear washing her?*). In **truth-value judgment** version, question is asked by a puppet, not experimenter (NB: some authors use the terms 'yes/no judgment task' and 'truth-value judgment task' interchangeably)	Binding, quantification and control (Ch. 8); complex syntax (Ch. 7)	Require little/no verbal response, so suitable for use with young children; arguably only appropriate method for investigating which possible sentence interpretations children will *allow* (as opposed to which they prefer; or which sentence types they produce themselves)	Children often show a *yes*-bias (can be corrected for statistically, provided child gives *some* 'no' responses); children may reject descriptions for reasons unrelated to grammar (e.g. picture does not accurately depict verb) or accept 'close enough' descriptions that they do not in fact consider 'correct' (see Ch. 7)
Grammaticality judgment tasks: children hear a sentence (e.g. *The magician disappeared the rabbit*) – illustrated with scene or picture and rate acceptability ('said it right' vs 'said it a bit silly') on binary or graded scale; sentences often spoken by puppet	Simple syntax (Ch. 6); inflection (Ch. 5)	Arguably only appropriate method for investigating whether children consider particular utterances to be (un)grammatical – Avoidance of a form does not necessarily equate to perceived ungrammaticality: speakers can enact (and sometimes produce) utterances they know to be ungrammatical	Unsuitable for use with very young children (who may base judgments on truth value or semantic factors); binary version used with 3–4-year-olds, graded 4–5-year-olds

An important implication is that we should be wary of studies that are designed to show that children do not have certain knowledge until a particular age. The problem is that we can never be certain whether children do not have the knowledge in question, or are simply unable to display this knowledge due to the demands of the task. A better question than *Do children succeed at this task at age X?*, then, is *What are the conditions under which children at age X pass and fail this task?* Finding the answer to such questions will allow us to make inferences regarding *how* children acquire particular aspects of language, as opposed to simply *when* they do so.

With these considerations in mind, in Table 1.1 we outline the most commonly used methods (or **paradigms**) used in child language acquisition research, along with their associated advantages and disadvantages. These will be described in greater detail when they are subsequently encountered (for a detailed description and discussion of all the major paradigms used in child language research, see Hoff, in press.)

2 Speech perception, segmentation and production

2.1 Introduction

When we hear speech, a stream of sound enters the auditory system. From this stream, any adult who is a native speaker of that language can virtually instantly identify sound sequences that allow them to understand what is being said. They can also produce these sounds to convey meaning. The question of how this is done is by no means resolved for adult speech perception. But explaining how an infant learning a first language identifies and produces the units of that language presents even more difficulties. This issue divides into two main questions. First, how does the infant work out what are the meaningful sounds of the language and second, how does the infant connect these same meaningful sounds to the movements of the articulators (e.g. tongue, lips) needed to produce them? In this chapter, we first outline the basic acoustic and articulatory features of speech and then, in Section 2.3, children's learning of the sounds of their language. Here, the main debate we consider is whether or not children build the **phonemic inventories** on the basis of **innate distinctive features** – a clearly **nativist** position. The **constructivist** alternative is that the acoustic variability between phonemes that are analysed as having the same features means that the phonemic inventory, and the **articulatory contrasts** that underpin it, have to be built bottom-up from the input. Section 2.4 considers how children **segment** the speech stream into **words, phrases and clauses**. This is a major issue for all theoretical positions since there are no absolute cues to segmentation in the speech stream, and these categories are ultimately crucial to every theory of language development. With regard to word segmentation, whilst most authors agree that cues such as stress patterns and transitional probabilities will be useful at some point, the question is whether these must be supplemented by an innate constraint (a nativist position) or knowledge of the meanings of particular strings (a constructivist, usage-based position), in order for segmentation to get off the ground. In addition, since the

We are indebted to Marilyn Vihman, Juliette Blevins, Thomas Grünloh and Martin Haspelmath for help with this chapter and, of course, take full responsibility for remaining errors and lack of clarity.

early **identification of syntactic phrases and clauses** is crucial to generativist accounts of grammar acquisition (see Chapters 5–6), there are proposals for how these might be identified using acoustic cues in the speech stream. For **constructivists**, this is less of a problem. Since syntax is seen as being emergent from meaning, phrasal and clausal structure can be built gradually, rather than being a prerequisite for grammar acquisition. In Section 2.5, we look at children's **speech production**. **Generativist–nativist theories** tend to start from the position that children have a **full representation of the adult system** and, to account for the fact that children's productions do not sound like those of adults, propose a set of **innate rules, processes or constraints** that operate on the underlying representation. By contrast, constructivists maintain that children have only **partial representations of words tied to child-identified meanings** and that, in producing these words, the contrastive system develops.

2.2   Characteristics of speech

We produce speech through a combination of movements of the articulators and control of airflow. Languages differ in the sets of sounds they use (**segments**). No pronunciation of the 'same' sound by the same speaker on different occasions or by different speakers is *exactly* the same – these differences between sounds are called **phonetic**. A group of concrete phonetic segments that are perceived by speakers as being functionally equivalent (e.g. all the slightly different phonetic pronunciations of a particular sound such as /p/, see below) is called a **phoneme**. For instance, the difference between /r/ and /l/ is **phonemic** in English (i.e. if /r/ is changed to /l/ a different word is perceived; e.g. *rap* → *lap*) but not in Japanese (i.e. Japanese speakers perceive /r/ and /l/ as phonetic variations of the same phoneme).[1] For most English speakers, stressed syllables starting with initial stops like the /p/ in *pun* are **aspirated** (a strong burst of air occurs at the release of the segment), while they are relatively unaspirated in unstressed syllables, e.g. the /p/ in *petunia*. The two *p*s are written the same, and perceived as phonetic variations of the same phoneme, /p/ (termed '**allophones**' of /p/). Thus English makes use of the phonetics of aspiration, but aspiration is not phonemic. In other languages such as Nepali, aspiration can be phonemic, for instance /pul/ with unaspirated *p* means 'bridge', while /pʰul/ with aspirated *p* means 'flower' (see below for further details).

The problem of speech perception would be a lot simpler if each segment and word could be identified uniquely in the acoustic stream. However, this is not the case. We can see this for word boundaries in Figure 2.1, which shows a spectrogram for the utterance *There are really a lot of words to learn*. Spectrograms show how the **spectral density** of a signal, which results from changes in airflow turbulence caused by movements of the tongue, varies with time. The bar at the top of Figure 2.1 show the approximate boundaries between

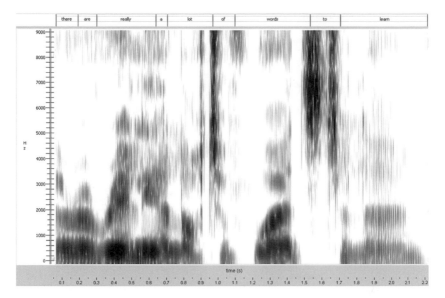

Figure 2.1 A sound spectrogram of the utterance *There are really a lot of words to learn* (from Jusczyk, 1997: figure 1.1. © 1997 Massachusetts Institute of Technology; reproduced by permission of the MIT Press)

words. We can see that there is a pause in the middle of *really* and no pause between *there* and *are* – so pauses are not a fully reliable guide to individual words.

When sequences of segments are produced in continuous speech, their characteristics are affected by the context. For example, in **coarticulation** the acoustic characteristic of a segment can vary depending on the preceding or the succeeding segment, or both. Thus the phoneme /p/ in *pat* and *pet* will not have an identical acoustic picture since it is subject to **phonological processes** that govern its production in different phonological environments – the /p/ is produced differently depending on the following vowel. Languages also differ in the sequences of segments that are allowed, called the **phonotactics** of the language: for instance, the sequence /zd/, which is possible at word onset in some languages, is not allowed in this position in English, though it can occur across word boundaries.

One important method of analysing segments is by measuring the main concentrations of acoustic energy produced during speech (called **formants**) and the frequencies at which they occur, in a spectrogram. Usually frequencies of the first and second formants are enough to identify differences between vowels in isolation, while the third and fourth formants tend to identify characteristics of the speaker: his or her anatomy and speech timbre. Thus comparing open

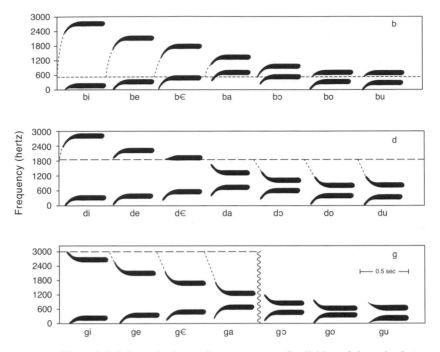

Figure 2.2 Schematized sound spectrograms of syllables of the voiced stop consonants [b], [d] and [g] before seven different English vowels (from Jusczyk, 1997; reproduced by permission of the MIT Press)

and closed vowels (e.g. with the jaw relatively open as in [a] or closed as in [i] or [u]), the first formant f_1 has a higher frequency for open vowels and a lower frequency for closed vowels. If we compare front and back vowels (e.g. with the tongue positioned relatively forward in the mouth in [i] and further back in [u]), the second formant f_2 has a higher frequency for the front vowel and a lower frequency for the back vowel.

Characteristics of consonants can also be identified in spectrograms (for instance, a period of silence in stops [d], or an aperiodic spread of sound across part of the spectrum in fricatives [s]). However, when consonants and vowels occur together in a syllable, this can affect the formants in the surrounding vowels (for instance, lowering the frequencies or bringing two formants closer together). The time courses of these changes are called **formant transitions**. Figure 2.2 shows the first and second formant transitions for three sequences of syllables beginning respectively with the consonants [b], [d] and [g].

The thing to notice in this figure is the way that the second formant of the consonant changes as a function of the vowel that it is paired with, meaning that

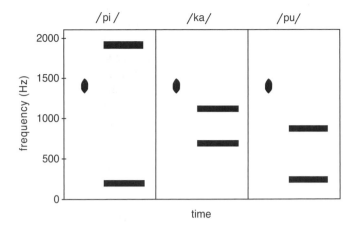

Figure 2.3 Schematic spectrograms of the syllables [pi], [ka] and [pu] (from Jusczyk, 1997; reproduced by permission of the MIT Press)

the consonant and vowel cannot be separated into two segments in which the initial consonant has a uniquely identifiable shape across all vowel contexts. Figure 2.3, from a study by Liberman, DeLattre and Cooper (1952), illustrates this further. Here schematic spectrograms for three synthesized vowels [i], [a] and [u] are shown. When an *identical* burst of noise was placed before these vowels (the oval burst in Figure 2.3), listeners identified two different consonants /p/ and /k/. Thus although there are cues to sound segments in the acoustic signal, in actual speech these cues vary as a function of the phonological context in which the segments are produced.

Two other factors are central to the acoustic properties of the signal produced. First, speech has **suprasegmental features**, such as **accent, intonation** and **rhythm**, which operate across a syllable, word or utterance and these, too, strongly affect the production of the segment. Unstressed syllables can virtually disappear from the acoustic signal, and languages differ in the patterns of stress that operate at the level of the word, syllable and utterance. Finally, hearers must be able to ignore phonetic differences between speakers (for instance, between the pitch of male and female voices) and pick up on those characteristics that signal the segments that are relevant for meaning differences in their language.

Thus, again, although there are cues to both segments and words in the acoustics of the speech stream, these are complex and vary with different aspects of context and speaker. Clearly children must have biologically evolved capacities that enable them to decode the speech that they hear. The issue is how specific to language itself these abilities are, and the extent to which more general capacities of the auditory system, on the one hand, and of human cognition, on the other, might be able to solve the problems involved.

2.3   Developing a phonemic inventory

The central question in the study of infant speech perception and production is how the infant works out what are the meaning-bearing sounds of the ambient language. The widely held **nativist** assumption is that there is a small set of features from which the sound segments of all the world's languages can be described, and which form the basis of children's phonological acquisition since they are innate. The **constructivist** view is that children acquire phonological contrasts during development.

What infants have as evidence of the meaning-relevant sounds of their language is the acoustic pattern of the sounds heard, on the one hand, and, on the other, the relationship between the sounds they produce and the motor movements involved in this production. The lungs, vocal cords, oral and nasal cavities and articulators in the mouth (tongue, lips) constitute the **vocal tract** and are all involved in this. The lungs determine whether the speech sound is produced on an egressive (in most sounds) or ingressive breath (e.g. clicks). The vocal cords control the type of voicing. The sound can then travel through the nasal or oral cavity, and is affected by the precise position and movement of the articulators against different parts of the mouth (e.g. teeth and palate). Below we give some examples of the factors that give rise to different speech sounds:

- **Consonants** involve full or partial restriction of the airflow, while for **vowels** the airflow remains open. Acoustically, vowels and some consonants can be identified by formant frequencies.
- **Place of articulation**: the position in the mouth where the vocal tract is closed (e.g. for labials [p] and [b], the lips come together; for alveolars [t] and [d], the tongue is placed against the alveolar ridge behind the teeth).
- **Manner of articulation** refers to how the vocal tract is closed (e.g. in stops, such as English /p/, /b/, /t/, /d/, the airflow is fully stopped, while in fricatives such as English /s/, /z/ and vowels it is not). In nasals (e.g. English /m/ and /n/), the airflow is through the nose, for other speech sounds it is oral.
- **Voicing**: this refers to the vibration of the vocal cords. When they vibrate, voiced consonants (e.g. English /b/) and vowels are produced. When they are fully open, unvoiced consonants are produced (e.g. English /p/). The timing of the voicing in voiced consonants is called the **voice onset time**. If the vocal cords start to vibrate before plosive closure is released (i.e. when the lips open, negative voice onset time), the plosive is voiced (e.g. /b/ in *beer*); if they start to vibrate at around the same time as release, the consonant is voiceless (e.g. /p/ in *spy*). If they start to vibrate considerably after release (positive voice onset time), the undisturbed airflow before release produces an **aspirated** consonant (e.g. [pʰ] in *pear*). As noted above, for some languages, aspiration is phonemic – it changes meaning – while in others, such as English, it

is phonetic – it does not change meaning: initial plosives in English are aspirated; medial and final plosives are not.

It is crucial to keep in mind this distinction between phonetics and phonemics. **Phonetics** refers to the actual sounds produced in speech in terms of both the articulation required to produce them and the acoustic correlates of this. **Phonemes** are linguistic abstractions. For instance, the *p* in *pan and span* is the same phoneme /p/ but phonetically they are different sounds, the first [pʰ] is aspirated and the second [p] is not. For adults (at least if literate) phonemes have some psychological reality: people can produce contrasting pairs such as *pan/ban, pad/pat* and *pan/pen* and identify the differences. However, it is a much disputed theoretical question as to what this reality consists of and, as we shall see, even more so, at what point it becomes available to children.

Within a language, sets of sounds that can be described by one or more phonetic features that they have in common are called **natural classes**. For instance, in English, /p/, /t/ and /k/ form the natural class of voiceless stops with two features in common ([−voicing] and [+stop]) but they differ on a third feature ([+bilabial], [−alveolar] and [+velar] respectively). Another characteristic of a natural class is that the sounds within it have similar effects on sounds in the surrounding context. Thus voiceless plosives (the final segment in *map*, *hit* and *tick*) have the same effect on a following English plural morpheme which is realized as [s] in *maps*, *hits* and *ticks*, while voiced plosives (the final segment in *tab*, *bid* and *leg*) form another natural class producing a voiced fricative [z] in *tabs*, *bids* and *legs*. Because these natural classes share phonetic properties and because many of the same groupings of sounds can be found in languages that are unrelated, most phonological theories take these properties (e.g. place and manner of articulation, type of voicing) as the underlying units upon which phonological alternations operate. These are called **distinctive features (acoustic features** in the case of Jakobson, 1968 or **articulatory features** for Chomsky and Halle, 1968; cf. Gussenhoven and Jacobs, 1998: ch. 5). Because this is an abstraction from the actual characteristics of the speech sounds, there is much debate about the precise definition of these features and, again, whether they have psychoacoustic reality or, rather, are convenient shorthand for some levels of analysis. For **generativists**, the set of distinctive features is innate and the phonemes in the inventories of all languages result from combinations of these features. For **constructivists**, the contrasts identified in distinctive features form a useful descriptive tool and clearly reflect some articulatory realities, while being language-specific and emergent.

2.3.1 *Generativist–nativist approaches*

The long-standing nativist solution to the question of how the child discovers the meaningful sounds of the language is to propose that there is a small set of **innate distinctive features,** and that the child analyses the incoming sound to determine which values and combinations of these features are relevant for the language being learned. Thus the child can perceive the speech signal in terms of a pregiven and universal set of **feature contrasts** (for instance, in place of articulation) and the task is to discover which ones matter for the particular language, i.e. to develop an abstract inventory of phonemes for the language which are independent of (a) position, (b) suprasegmental factors (e.g. patterns of stress) and (c) individual speakers. Depending on the theory, rules, processes or constraints then determine how these phonemes are realized and sequenced in the actual speech stream; for instance, as mentioned above, in English, whether a final plosive is voiced or not determines whether a following /s/ is realized as [s] or [z] (see Section 2.5).

Relevant to the viability of innate distinctive features, much research has been devoted to investigating precisely what infants can detect in terms of the acoustic and articulatory features of particular segments. In what follows, we summarize this research. As we shall see, many of those who have conducted this research do not fit straightforwardly into one or other end of the nativist–constructivist dimension, almost all taking up positions somewhere in between.

2.3.1.1 Phonetic and phonemic contrasts   Many phonetic contrasts that occur in the languages of the world can be discriminated by infants from as early as they have been tested, although there are a few (for instance, some **fricatives –** sounds made by forcing air through a narrow channel, such as English /sa/ versus /za/) that may be initially more difficult to discriminate. Very young infants are usually tested using the **high-amplitude sucking** procedure (see Chapter 1). In experiments using this methodology, infants suck on a non-nutritive teat. After a sucking base rate (usually around 25 sucks per minute) is established, the presentation of the stimulus is made dependent on the infant's maintaining a high-amplitude sucking rate of around 45–60 sucks per minute. After some time of hearing the same stimulus (about 3 minutes), sucking rates decrease. Once this decrease is consistent (e.g. of at least 20 per cent over 2 consecutive minutes), a new stimulus is introduced for the experimental group, while for the control group the same stimulus continues without interruption. If infants are able to discriminate between the two stimuli under investigation, the sucking rate of the infants in the experimental group (though not the control group) will recover to the high-amplitude rate, in response to the presentation of the new stimulus.

Infants tested with this procedure can detect differences in voice onset time, contrasts in place and manner of articulation, in some cases both at the beginning and the end of syllables (see Jusczyk, 1998). Crucially, these contrasts are perceived **categorically**. Categorical perception refers to the perception of a changing stimulus as divided into two clear categories when, in fact, the underlying acoustical characteristics of the stimulus are continuous. This is important because it makes a continuous acoustic stimulus categorical and therefore provides a potential basis for phonemic categories. Categorical perception has been shown for a number of phonetic contrasts in experiments with adults (Liberman, Harris, Hoffman and Griffith, 1957; Lisker and Abramson, 1964). In the classic first experiment with infants, Eimas, Siqueland, Jusczyk and Vigorito (1971), using the high-amplitude sucking procedure, found that 1- and 4-month-old infants could discriminate speech sounds which allow adults to discriminate between voiced and voiceless stop consonants (/p/ and /b/). For English, if voice onset time is less than 25 msec, adults report hearing /ba/, while if the voice onset time is more than 25 msec, /pa/ is perceived.

In this experiment, the stimuli were synthesized speech sounds: three variations of the **bilabial**[2] voiced stop /b/ and three of /p/, the voiceless version. Three groups of infants were tested in different conditions: one group was exposed to a 20 msec difference in voice onset time that crossed the category difference between /b/ and /p/; a second group was exposed to 20 msec differences that did not cross the category boundary; the third group was a control group in which the stimulus did not change. The six stimuli had the voice onset times of −20, 0, +20, +40, +60 and +80 msec. One of the two experimental groups heard stimuli with voice onset times of +20 and +40 msec − the first is perceived by adults as /ba/, the second as /pa/; i.e. a difference in phonemic category. The second group heard stimuli with voice onset times of either −20 and 0 msec (both perceived as /ba/ by adults) or +60 and +80 msec (both perceived as /pa/ by adults); i.e. perceived by adults as within the same phonemic category. The results showed that the infants in the cross-phonemic category group increased their sucking rate after the introduction of the second stimulus significantly more than did those in either the within-category group or the control condition, while there was no difference in recovery rate between the control group and the within-category group. Thus infants show basically adultlike performance − they show categorical perception even though the differences in voice onset time were the same for each stimulus.

Since this original experiment of Eimas *et al.*, there have been many studies exploring infant sensitivity to a range of phonetic contrasts. One much-studied contrast is in place of articulation (for instance, between the voiced stop consonants [b], a **bilabial**, and [d], an **alveolar**, which is articulated with the front part of the tongue against the alveolar ridge behind the teeth). This is particularly interesting because, depending on where in the syllable these sounds appear (in initial, medial or final position), the acoustic cues differ. Studies using the high-amplitude sucking procedure have shown that newborns and very young children can discriminate between these consonants (Morse, 1972), and that they can do so independently of where they appear in the syllable (Jusczyk, 1977; Jusczyk and Thompson, 1978). For instance, in Jusczyk (1977), synthetic stimuli were prepared from actual speech and then digitized. Stimuli were matched for overall duration, but when [d] and [g] appeared syllable-finally (/bad/, /bag/ or /ad/, /ag/), the second and third formants differed in their terminal frequencies, while when they appeared syllable-initially (/dab/, /gab/), they differed in their starting frequencies.

Early experiments on infants' capacity to discriminate these types of contrasts tested English-hearing infants on English contrasts, but a series of subsequent experiments showed that infants could also discriminate phonetic contrasts that were not phonemic for their native language. For instance Aslin, Pisoni, Hennessy and Perey (1981) showed, using the conditioned **head-turn preference procedure** (see Chapter 1), that English-learning infants, aged 6 months, presented with synthetic consonant–vowel sequences, could discriminate the prevoiced–voiced contrast that differentiates stop consonants in Thai. This procedure involves conditioning children to turn their head in the direction of a visual reinforcer (e.g. a moving mechanical animal) in response to one particular audio stimulus, but not to another. Once conditioning has been established (for instance, to 9 out of 10 'correct' head turns to the reinforced stimulus), children are presented with a second, non-reinforced stimulus. If they turn their heads to this new stimulus, the inference is that they cannot discriminate it from the previously reinforced stimulus. Thus their ability to discriminate the previous from the newly introduced stimulus can be assessed from whether or not they turn their heads.

Although vowels show graded, rather than categorical, contrasts in perception, speakers can, of course, distinguish between the different vowels of their native language. Using the high-amplitude sucking procedure, and tokens recorded by a speaker (rather than artificially constructed), Trehub (1973) showed that English-hearing infants aged between 1 and 4 months could discriminate vowel contrasts both in isolation ([a] vs [i]) and in syllables ([pa] vs [pi]). Similar to the above experiments on non-native consonant contrasts, Trehub (1976) also showed that 1–4-month-old infants from non-French speaking homes could discriminate the oral–nasal vowel distinction [pɑ] and [pɑ̃] produced by a French speaker. This contrast appears in French (and other languages such as Polish) but not in English.

Kuhl (1979, 1983) showed, using head-turn preference, that older, American-English-hearing infants (6-month-olds) could discriminate [a], as in *pop*, from [i], as in *peep*, and [ɑ], as in *cot*, from [ɔ], as in *caught*. Within a vowel category, native speakers will judge some stimuli as more typical examples of that vowel than others (i.e. they show a **prototype categorical structure** for the vowels of their language). Grieser and Kuhl (1989) showed a similar effect for American-English-hearing 6-month-olds. The infants were trained on a discrimination between good exemplars of [i] and [ɛ] (as in *peep* and *pep*), as judged by adults. Children were conditioned with a visual reinforcer (a moving mechanical animal) to turn their head in the direction of the reinforcer in response to one vowel and not to turn in response to the other. Once conditioning had been established (9 out of 10 head turns on test trials), children were presented with other exemplars of these vowels. Grieser and Kuhl synthesized 32 exemplars of each vowel stimulus which varied the first and second formants in equal steps from the central vowel, and found that the infants could reliably discriminate these exemplars into the two vowel categories.

In their second experiment, Grieser and Kuhl tested infants to see whether, like adults, they were sensitive to 'good' and 'bad' exemplars of vowel categories, which would count as evidence for the formation of a prototype. Two groups of 6-month-old infants were initially familiarized either with the good exemplar of the vowel /i/ or with the poor exemplar. To produce these exemplars, the researchers synthesized stimuli covering the whole range of formant frequencies produced by typical male speakers for this vowel. They then selected a /i/ vowel that adults consistently judged a good exemplar of the vowel (the prototype) and another that was consistently judged as a relatively poor exemplar (the non-prototype). The groups of infants in the prototype and non-prototype conditions were tested with the 16 synthesized variants. The prototype group was presented with the 16 variants synthesized around the good exemplar and the non-prototype group with the 16 variants synthesized around the non-prototype. Infants trained on the prototype generalized further along gradients of distance from the prototype than did infants trained on the non-prototype. Grieser and Kuhl interpret this as a prototype effect where 'the real psychophysical distance . . . between the prototype and surrounding members is effectively decreased . . . and the prototype's functional role as a perceptual magnet for the category serves to strengthen category cohesiveness' (Kuhl, 1991: 99). This is termed **the perceptual magnet model**.

2.3.1.2 Phonetic stability   Not only do the acoustic features of particular segments vary as a function of their position, but the acoustics of the same segment produced by different speakers or by the same speaker on different occasions also vary. As we saw above, at 6 months, infants treat vowels spoken by different speakers as equivalent. For consonantal phonetic contrasts, infants show some phonetic stability at an earlier age. Using the high-amplitude sucking procedure, Jusczyk, Pisoni and Mullenix (1992) familiarized 2-month-olds with 12 different tokens of /bug/ produced by different speakers and then, for the experimental group, shifted the presentation to different exemplars of /dug/ by the same speakers. The infants could detect the change. Note that this is an important finding because the ability to see tokens of the same segment produced by different speakers as the same shows that infants have formed some kind of category across these different tokens.

Changes in speaking rate can affect the acoustic characteristics of a segment, particularly for segments that depend on the rate of change in formant transitions reflecting the effect of the preceding consonant on the vowel formants. For instance, [ba] and [wa] differ on this dimension, but changes in speaking rate will affect the duration of the formant transition; thus a fast [w] will have the same formant transition as a slow [b]. This will affect, therefore, whether speakers hear [w] or [b]. Miller and Eimas (1983, experiment 2) showed that 3–4-month-old infants can perceptually compensate for differences in the formant transition durations relative to overall syllable duration. Again, this is important because it shows that some mechanism is in place that allows for 'trading relations' between different acoustic aspects of the stimulus, allowing for phonetic categories to remain stable under changes in one or other aspect of the acoustic stimulus.

2.3.1.3 Developmental changes in perception   Despite very early perceptual abilities, research has also shown that there are developmental changes in speech perception over the first year of life. Some studies show increasing sensitivity to the phonotactic features of the ambient language. When tested with consonant clusters that are permissible in their ambient language, infants of 9 months preferred to listen to them (as opposed to illegal clusters), but infants of 6 months did not (see also Best, McRoberts and Sithole, 1988). The vowel prototype discussed above also seems to be developmental. Thus 4-month-olds tested with the same stimuli as in the Kuhl experiments did not show the prototype effect (Polka and Werker, 1994). Unlike the results on categorical perception, which show the effect so early that this is unlikely to be affected by the ambient language, these results seem to indicate the development of a category from a continuous acoustic stimulus as a result of experience with the ambient language at around 6 months.

Infants also show loss of sensitivity to contrasts that were previously present, under the influence of the ambient language. Some of these studies have included comparisons with infants being raised learning languages other than English. Studies by Werker and Tees (1983, 1984) showed that a group of infants aged 6–8 months could discriminate both native and non-native consonant contrasts, while a group of 11–12-month-olds and adults could only discriminate native contrasts. Using the head-turn procedure, Werker and Tees (1984) conditioned English-learning, Canadian infants to turn their heads to a change in stimulus either from /ba/ to /da/ (a native contrast) or one reflecting a non-native contrast.[3] The criterion for correct responding was 8 out of 10 head turns on 'change' trials and not more than 2 incorrect head turns on 'non-change' trials (for the adults tested, a button press was the required response). Eight out of 10 of the infants aged 6–8 months discriminated the non-native contrast and, in a second experiment, 8 out of 14 of the infants aged 8–10 months could also do so. However, only 1 out of 10 of those aged 10–12 months could make the discrimination.

Neurocognitive research with **event-related potentials** (see Chapter 1), in which brain responses to stimuli are measured from electrodes placed on the scalp, broadly supports this picture, with discriminations of phonetic features in different languages by 1–4-month-olds and of phonemic features by 6–7-month-olds independent of their ambient language. Older infants of 11–12 months displayed discriminations only for phonemic contrasts relevant to their own ambient language (see Friederici, 2009).

In summary, there is clear evidence for discrimination of most of the major articulatory contrasts used in languages from as early as they can be tested and, at the same time, of developing sensitivity to the categories of the ambient language. But do these discriminations start from an innate set of distinctive features or, alternatively, do the features that form the basis of differences between meaning-bearing sounds in a particular language develop from the interaction between the properties of the mammalian auditory system, the language the infant is hearing and general properties of infant cognition?

2.3.1.4 Innate categories as the basis for a segmental inventory
When it was shown that infants behaved as adults and discriminated the acoustic correlates of many consonant distinctions categorically, this was at first taken as indicating a human-specific and innate inventory of phonological features. Under the motor theory of speech perception (Liberman, Harris, Hoffman and Griffith, 1957), it was argued that humans possess an innately specified set of feature detectors which map from the acoustics of a speech sound to the positions of the articulators, giving rise in processing to a loss of phonetic detail and early abstraction of phonemes. However, subsequent research has called this into question on a number of fronts.

First, it seems that a number of non-human and even perhaps non-mammalian species also show categorical perception for the same speech sounds (Kuhl and Padden, 1980). Second, there are experiments suggesting that categorical effects can be found in non-speech stimuli such as tones (Aslin and Pisoni, 1980) and vision (Bornstein, 1987). This suggests that categorical perception is a feature of the mammalian perceptual system which has been utilized for speech in evolution rather than having arisen purely in the course of language evolution. This is supported by the fact that the phonemes of sign languages, which are transmitted through visual rather than auditory processes, can also be analysed in terms of discriminable distinctive features. Thus categorization of speech, auditory or visual, is likely to be very important in the development of phonetic contrasts, and may indeed be one of the bases on which the phonological structures of language have been built, despite having evolved prior to human speech.

These results mean that, for most researchers, initial discriminations are no longer seen in terms of a direct connection between acoustics and phonetic features. Rather the basis for discrimination is seen as residing in the acoustic signal itself. Thus Aslin and Pisoni (1980) and Aslin, Werker and Morgan (2002) suggest that infants are able to make these discriminations by using general auditory mechanisms that are categorical in nature, innate in the mammalian system and independent of linguistic experience. These authors see part of the development of a phonemic inventory being underpinned by what is termed '**maintenance**', i.e. the ambient language maintains those initial acoustic contrasts perceived by the auditory system that are relevant to the language being learned. This is termed the '**universal theory**'. An argument for an initial capacity for distinguishing the universal range of phonetic contrasts comes from the evidence of loss of non-native speech contrasts during the second half of the first year as outlined above.

While Aslin and Pisoni (1980) propose that universal categories, followed by loss, is part of the story, they also suggest other mechanisms through which language experience could mould the phonetic categories. One example is Kuhl's (1991) 'perceptual magnet' model of the development of vowel prototypes. When Kuhl tested rhesus monkeys with the same stimuli, she found no prototype effect: the monkeys discriminated simply as a function of the distance between referent and comparison stimuli regardless of whether the referent was a 'good' or 'bad' exemplar of the vowel (Kuhl, 1991), which suggests that this may be a human-specific development. An interesting issue here is whether this development of a prototype reflects infant cognitive development more generally, rather than being confined to the categorization of speech.

Jusczyk (1997) also proposes that learning is innately guided. He sees infants' innate capacities as allowing them 'to perceive similarities involving phonetic segments and to discriminate subtle distinctions among different syllables' (pp.108–9). But he adds 'the acquisition of phonemic categories and phonemic distinctions falls out of learning to segment and recognize words in the fluent speech of one's native language' (p. 109). So Jusczyk's model seems to be one in which, while the acoustic distinctions are available to infants and are sharpened by extensive experience with the ambient language, they only start to become part of a *contrastive* phonemic inventory with the onset of communicative intent and word learning.

2.3.2   Non-nativist approaches

The theory of a small set of innate distinctive features aims to describe most or all of the natural classes of the meaning-bearing sounds of human languages. One challenge to this is presented by Mielke (2008), who has conducted a large-scale crosslinguistic survey of 628 language varieties and found that unnatural classes (i.e. classes that are not defined by any proposed distinctive feature) are common. He concludes that the natural classes and distinctive features in human languages can be described in terms of historical sound changes and similarity generalizations (see also Blevins, 2004) and therefore that phonological distinctive features are language-specific and emergent. Similarities across languages derive from the articulatory and acoustic factors that drive the phonetics of speech and from the social and cognitive factors that drive language change and language learning. Support also comes from computer-modelling experiments in which interacting 'agents' develop speechlike categories (de Boer, 2000; Steels and de Boer, 2007).

The most telling developmental argument for a non-nativist approach to the phonemic inventory is that it would, in fact, be impossible to build such an inventory from an innate and fixed set of acoustic features. This is the position taken by Pierrehumbert (2003). She points out that extensive acoustic variability exists even in the production of phonemes analysed as bearing the same distinctive features. As a result, her claim is that the phonemic inventory of the language and the relevant articulatory contrasts must be built bottom-up from the actual input.

A crucial point is that all experiments on infant speech perception test with isolated exemplars while holding all other factors constant. These experiments are concerned with particular phonetic contrasts, and the stimuli (both synthesized syllables and tokens extracted from natural speech) are presented repeatedly. It is not clear, therefore, how closely related the contrasts are to those that the infant might make when listening to normal speech, where the articulatory gestures involved in producing a sequence of segments – and their acoustic correlates – are affected by the preceding and following context of each segment as well as by suprasegmental features.

A number of experiments have attempted to deal with this problem by investigating 'trading relationships' between different aspects of the speech signal. An example is Miller and Eimas' experiment (1983; see above) on whether infants can compensate for the interaction between speech rate and formant transitions. Another is Fowler, Best and McRoberts' (1990) experiment which showed that 4-month-old infants could compensate for coarticulation in discriminating contrasts in place of articulation. But even here, the experimental conditions present stimuli under ideal and isolated conditions. Although infants can make the distinctions outlined above under these conditions, it is not clear that they could identify them in the actual speech that they hear.

Pierrehumbert (2003) argues that there is no alternative to identifying the relevant phonetics of a language and, subsequently, its phonemic inventory from bottom-up distributional analysis of the statistics in the speech stream. On her account, the major problem with the idea of the development of phonetic and phonemic categories on the basis of any kind of pregiven acoustic (or articulatory) distinctions is the language-specific nature of these categories. She gives the example of voiced and voiceless stops in American and Indian English. In

American English word-final stops are often unreleased, which would remove the voicing distinction, but this is maintained because the preceding vowel is lengthened (e.g. in /pub/ as opposed to /pup/). In Indian English, preceding vowels are not lengthened but word-final stops are always released. Thus the phonetics of voicing has to be learned for the particular language since seemingly similar categories in different languages in fact show different quantitative spectral characteristics.

Because the concept of a phoneme involves identity across contexts (e.g. the /t/ in *tab* and *bat*), rather than the actual acoustic signal, which will be different for allophones of the same phoneme, phonemes play no part in the model, except as a possible later outcome of bootstrapping after the development of a lexicon. Pierrehumbert (2003) reports that the probability distributions that contrast different segments in a particular position are fairly well distinguished, but less so when measured across different contexts. She gives the example of the /s/, /z/ distinction in English. The acoustics of the /z/ in *matches* is similar to the /s/ in *sit*. Thus the distinction first has to be made between these segments in initial position or in final position before it is possible to relate initial and final /s/ or /z/ to their allophones. This undermines the idea of a universal set of phonetic contrasts from which children have to prune those that are irrelevant to the language they are learning:

> The extent of such variability means that the relationship of phonetic cues to the hierarchical prosodic and intonational representation must be learned in each individual language. (Pierrehumbert, 2003, p. 126)

But there is then the problem of how children actually do develop an inventory of the contrastive sounds in their language.

Some relationships between acoustics and segmentation within a language are relatively straightforward and some categories could perhaps be learned bottom-up from the input. Pierrehumbert (2003) gives the examples of experiments by Maye and Gerken (2000) and Maye, Werker and Gerken (2002) which showed that whether infants could identify a contrast between stimuli depended on the statistical distribution of phonetic variation in the signal. English-hearing infants aged 6–8 months were presented with 8 speech sounds from a synthesized continuum between voiced and voiceless unaspirated velar stops [d] and unaspirated [t] (the /t/ that comes after /s/ in *stop*). In a preferential-looking paradigm, two groups of infants were presented with six blocks of 24 syllables each. The difference between the groups was in the frequency with which syllables from different parts of the continuum were presented. One group heard a unimodal distribution with stimuli from the centre of the continuum presented more frequently, while the other group heard a bimodal distribution with stimuli from the end points of the distribution occurring more frequently. At test, the bimodal group discriminated a list in which stimuli 1 and 8 alternated from a non-alternating list. Thus if there are clear acoustic correlates of categories, such as the bimodal distribution in this experiment, children may be able to extract them.

However, Pierrehumbert points out that this applies not to idealized phonemes abstracted from position and stress, but to their **positional variants** (i.e. the versions that appear in particular contexts, since changes in context change the acoustic 'signature' of a particular phoneme). Pierrehumbert makes it clear that this type of direct link between acoustics and segmentation, giving rise to the categorization of segments in particular positions, will not solve the whole problem of children's development of phonemic categories.

Pierrehumbert's (2003) solution is an exemplar-based model that operates over 'the parametric phonetic space ... (which) can be understood as a high-dimensional cognitive map on which a metric of proximity or similarity is defined' (p. 128). Each stimulus is categorized through a statistical-choice module which compares it to competing distributions in its neighbourhood and selects the most probable. In the model, phonological categories initially emerge as density distributions in multidimensional space from the statistics of the speech stream. These distributions are refined by feedback loops which are both internal and external (i.e. feedback from the child's own productions and from the environment). Anything that has phonetic correlates (e.g. syllables and metrical feet) is also a potential category. Crucial to her argument is that prosodic structure interacts with phonetic context, and thus the density distributions that underlie categories are of the range of phonetic properties of allophones, in relation to the range of prosodic variables, rather than arising from pregiven distinctions in universal grammar.

2.3.3   Developing a phonemic inventory: conclusion

In the field of infant speech perception, there is little argument over the facts. The issue is how to interpret them. Clearly there is some innate basis for speech perception shown in the early abilities of infants to discriminate contrasts relevant for speech, even those that do not occur in their ambient language. The question is how much of this is species-specific and how much is no more abstract than basic human (and mammalian) auditory perception. All would agree that the loss of some contrasts and the development of the ability to compensate for variability and for interactions between different aspects of the signal suggest an increasing refinement of these acoustic categories by the ambient language. Again the question is whether this takes place on the basis of a pregiven set of specifically linguistic distinctive features or whether these are emergent. Those who argue that the infant cannot start with an initial set of pregiven categories, because the variability inherent in speech is too great, would presumably see these developments in the second half of the first year as

Summary table 2.1 *Speech perception and distinctive features* (☑ *= supports theory;* ☒ *= counts against theory*)

Issue/phenomenon / Summary of position	Nativist/generativist theories	Constructivist theories
	Children are born with an innate and universal set of distinctive features (Chomsky and Halle, 1968, Stampe, 1979).	A pregiven set of distinctive features could not give rise to the contrasts within and across languages, therefore linguistic contrasts are language-specific and emergent (Pierrehumbert, 2003; Mielke, 2008).
Discriminating phonetic contrasts	☑ Can be discriminated by infants from as early as tested (summaries in Vihman, 1996; Jusczyk, 1998). ☒ Can be discriminated for contrasts that are not in native language (Aslin et al., 1981).	But discriminating a contrast does not necessarily depend on an underlying set of distinctive features (it may be learned). Ability to discriminate a contrast in isolated segments when all other factors are held constant may not translate in the ability to do so in real life.
Positional stability	☑ Very young infants can detect phonetic contrasts independent of position in syllable despite acoustic cues differing (Morse, 1972; Jusczyk, 1977; Jusczyk and Thompson, 1978).	☒ Suggests acoustic cues may not be sufficient to detect differences in place of articulation without some innate knowledge of possible contrasts.
Categorical perception	☑ Shown by infants (Eimas et al., 1971) but ☒ Also by non-human primates (Kuhl and Padden, 1982) and for non-speech stimuli (tones: Aslin and Pisoni, 1980; vision: Bornstein, 1987).	☑ Findings in left-hand column suggest categorical perception may be a feature of perceptual systems in general rather than specific to speech or even sound (Aslin and Pisoni, 1980).
Effect of ambient language	Loss of non-native contrasts (Werker and Tees, 1983, 1984; Friederici, 2009) and increasing preference for native contrasts (Best et al., 1988) could suggest a universal set of distinctive features gradually shaped by the ambient language (see Aslin and Pisoni: universal theory, 1980; ☑ nativist approach), but equally compatible with shaping of the child's emergent phonological system by ambient language (Pierrehumbert, 2003; ☑ constructivist approach).	
Development of a prototype structure for vowels		Part of shaping of universal features to ambient language (☑ nativist approach) but could equally suggest a more general human cognitive involvement in the categorization of speech (Kuhl, 1979, 1983, Grieser and Kuhl, 1989; ☑ constructivist approach).
'Trading relationships'	☑ Infants can compensate for interactions between different aspects of the speech signal (Miller and Eimas, 1983; Fowler, Best and McRoberts, 1990).	☒ Suggests early ability to perceive speech-relevant constancies despite coarticulation, changes in speech rate etc; acoustic signal may be insufficient without innate knowledge.
Statistical distribution of phonetic variation	Findings in right-hand box may reflect learning of positional variants, not of the idealized phoneme.	☑ Suggests that a bottom-up learning of some categories is possible (Maye and Gerken, 2000; Maye et al., 2002).

evidence for the slow building of the sound system of the particular language, which only becomes phonemic once the child starts to develop a lexicon in which the segments in words start to contrast meaningfully. More nativist and formalist approaches argue that the child comes equipped with a universal set of distinctive features and with rules or constraints that adjust these to the ambient language. As we shall see, these contrasting approaches to the question of exactly when and what the child can identify in the speech stream are also crucial for the issues covered in the next two sections: segmentation of the speech stream into higher-level units (clauses and phrases) in Section 2.4 and children's early speech production in Section 2.5.

2.4   Segmenting the speech stream into words, phrases and clauses

Consider a sentence such as *There really are a lot of words to learn*. When this sentence is written down, it is clear where one word ends and another begins, as the word boundaries are marked by spaces. However, when an infant hears spoken language (or an adult hears a foreign language), it is extremely difficult to determine where one word ends and another begins. One might imagine that spoken language (like written language) contains gaps (pauses) between the words. In fact, not only do pauses *fail* to occur between words, but they frequently occur within words (see Figure 2.2). The question, then, is how infants **segment** the continuous speech stream into words (units that are important for meaning). As we shall see, there are a number of cues in the speech stream which have been invoked by researchers of all theoretical persuasions as aids to morpheme and word segmentation. However, all of these cues are only probabilistic guides to where one word ends and another begins. This means that there is a problem as to how the child knows that what has been segmented actually is a word. We consider one **nativist** solution to this problem, the **unique stress constraint**. **Constructivists** see the identification of units in the speech stream as arising from a mapping between the **meaning,** inferred by the child from the communicative situation, and the string that has been segmented out, whether, initially, this is one word or a string of words.

To acquire grammar, children must also segment the stream into **clauses** (roughly equivalent to sentences) and **phrases** (e.g. VERB PHRASE, NOUN PHRASE (see Chapters 4 and 6). There are a number of potential cues to clause and phrase boundaries in the speech stream but the question is whether these are reliable enough to uniquely identify these units. For **generativists**, the rapid and reliable identification of these units is critical to the way in which the child must use innate universal grammar to identify the specific features of the language being learned (for instance, to set the head direction parameter). For **constructivists**, grammatical units such as noun phrase and verb phrase are emergent, that is, they are constructed during development. So the child is 'looking for' a mapping between an intonation unit (whether or not this actually is a syntactically defined phrase or clause) and an intended meaning.

2.4.1   Words

Despite the apparent difficulty of the task, experimental evidence suggests that children are able to extract at least some words from the speech stream as young as 7½ months. When infants were familiarized with passages containing a target word such as *cup* (e.g. *The cup was bright and shiny*, *A clown drank from the red cup*) they preferred (in a conditioned head-turn preference test session) to listen to repetitions of this target word than of a word that had not occurred in the passages. Infants aged 6 months did not show a listening preference when tested with exactly the same procedure (Jusczyk and Aslin, 1995). These results suggest that infants of this age are beginning to recognize words in fluent speech. There are a number of cues to word segmentation in the speech stream that infants might potentially make use of to do this. We will briefly outline these in turn before turning to research that investigates whether infants can actually use them.

2.4.1.1 Constructivist approaches

2.4.1.1.1 Isolated words   It would presumably be much easier to learn words that occur frequently in isolation. Brent and Siskind (2001) showed that 9 per cent of the utterances of eight mothers speaking to their 9–15-month-old children (1,800 utterances per mother) were single words. These were not just the names of objects; for instance, among the most frequent were *come*, *go*, *up* and *down*. Furthermore the frequency with which a mother used a particular word in isolation (though not the overall frequency of the word) was strongly correlated with when the child learned that word. But even if children were able to develop a small lexicon of highly frequent words that often occur in isolation, this is unlikely to be the way they learn the majority of words, which will almost always appear embedded in utterances.

One suggestion is that this lexicon of isolated words could be used to further segment the speech stream. Brent (1999), following Brent and Cartwright (1996), developed a computer model that did this, achieving success rates of around 70–80 per cent in identifying words in corpora of child-directed speech. The model produces a number of possible lexicons and then uses these to derive the words in the corpus. Each derivation is compared in an algorithm that measures the length of the derivation and takes the shortest. However both Gambell and Yang (2005) and Swingley (2005a) point out that the Brent model involves storing the whole corpus at once and running the model to produce better and better lexicons. This is highly unlikely to reflect the behavioural reality of infants' segmentation strategies.

2.4.1.1.2 Transitional probabilities   There is a great deal of statistical regularity in the speech stream, at many different levels. This can be measured in a variety of ways including co-occurrence frequency (the frequency with which particular units, for instance words or syllables, occur together) and the **transitional probability** between units (the probability of one unit given another). In speech, certain sequences of sounds are more likely to occur together within a word than they are across successive words. Thus the transitional probability between two syllables is generally higher within a word than at a word boundary. For instance, in the sequence *pretty baby*, the transitional probability from *pre* to *ty* is higher than from *ty* to *ba*, as *pretty* is a common word, whilst *tyba* is not a word at all (and thus this combination will generally occur only at word boundaries). The transitional probability of one sound (B) co-occurring with the other (A) is measured as follows:

$$\text{The probability of sound B, given sound A} = \frac{\text{Number of occurrences of A} + \text{B (e.g. } \textit{pretty})}{\text{Total number of occurrences of A}}$$

(e.g. transitional probability of *ty*- given *pre*-)

(*pre - tty, pre - dict, pre - cise* etc.)

In a classic experiment, Saffran, Aslin and Newport (1996) showed that 8-month-old infants can successfully identify such differences in transitional probabilities after listening for only two minutes to sequences of three-syllable pseudo-words run together in continuous speech (e.g. *bidakupadotigolabubidaku...*). Sequences of syllable pairs designed as 'word-internal' had transitional probabilities of 1.0 between the syllables, while transitional probabilities between syllables across 'words' were always lower (0.33). In the familiarization phase, infants heard a continuous stream of syllables spoken by a female speaker in a monotone, without pauses or any other intonational cues to word boundaries. In the test phase, infants were presented with repetitions of one of four 3-syllable strings. These were either 'words' (i.e. with transitional probabilities between the two pairs of syllables of 1.0), non-words (the same syllables but not in the order heard during familiarization) or part-words (3-syllable strings that had been heard in familiarization but in which the transitional probability between the second and third syllable was 0.33). To give an example, if in the continuous string *bidaku/padoti/golabu/bidaku* (slashes separate the strings that – on the basis of transitional probabilities – are 'words'), the probabilities between *ku* and *pa*, *ti* and *go*, *bu* and *bi* were set to 0.33 and all others to 1.0, infants listened significantly longer to the non-words or part-words (*kupado* or *dotigo*) than to the words (*bidaku, padoti* etc), showing that they were able to discriminate the difference.

This type of statistical learning seems to be domain-general. Saffran, Johnson, Aslin and Newport (1999) showed that it worked over sequences of non-linguistic tones and Kirkham, Slemmer and Johnson (2002) showed that 2-, 5- and 8-month-old infants are sensitive to sequences of visual shapes organized using similar patterns of transitional probabilities. As a result, there have been suggestions that this could be a way to segment the speech stream that does not depend on any mechanisms that are specific to language. However, as we shall see in Section 2.4.1.2 below, there are reasons to doubt that this kind of learning could scale up to the realities of the language-learning situation.

2.4.1.1.3 Phonotactic and allophonic regularities   As noted in Section 2.3 above, every language has **phonotactic constraints** on which sounds can co-occur within words. So *kt* cannot begin a word in English, though it can in Russian. But, of course, it can occur across word boundaries (*Back to the Future*). Children might be able to use this type of information to segment the speech stream when they hear a consonant sequence that is infrequent within words. Mattys, Jusczyk, Luce and Morgan (1999) played 9-month-old infants two sets of novel words, all with consonant (C) vowel (V) sequences of the form CVCCVC. In one set, the two central consonants frequently occurred within English words (e.g. *ft* in *beftok*) and in the other set, the two central consonants frequently occurred between words but not within them (e.g. *vt* in *bevtok*). The infants discriminated between the two lists and preferred to listen to the first set (i.e. to the set with within-word phonotactics). However, when a pause of 500 msec was inserted between the two CVC 'syllables', infants reversed their preference and listened longer to the set with CC sequences that were more frequent across words. Thus by this age, infants are sensitive to the phonotactics of word boundaries.

There are also allophonic constraints which affect production: for instance, the phoneme /t/ is produced with aspiration at the beginning of or within English words (e.g. *tab, nitrate*) but unaspirated at the end (e.g. *bat, night*). The two different sounds are two different **allophones** of the phoneme /t/. Children might therefore be able to use this information to identify a word boundary when they hear an unaspirated /t/.[4] Jusczyk, Hohne and Bauman (1999) tested infants in a preferential listening experiment in which they were first exposed to *nitrates* and subsequently listened to two passages, one containing the same word and the other containing *night rates*. The group of 9-month-olds could not distinguish the two lists but the $10\frac{1}{2}$ -month-olds did.

These results indicate a developing sensitivity to language-specific constraints which could, in principle, be guides to word segmentation. Although these results show that infants in the last three months of their first year are sensitive to the allophonic and phonotactic cues of their language, this does not necessarily mean that they actually use such cues.

2.4.1.1.4 Stress patterns   Languages also differ in the prosodic patterns of words such as stress and tone (Beckman, 1986). Cutler and Carter (1987) found that, in a large corpus of English utterances, most stressed syllables were either monosyllabic words or began a word (particularly content words). They concluded that the predominant stress pattern of English words is **trochaic** (strong–weak, e.g. *HAPpy*[5]) as opposed to an iambic stress pattern (e.g. *traPEZE*). Other languages show different patterns of word stress, or none.

Jusczyk, Houston and Newsome (1999), using the same paradigm as Jusczyk and Aslin (1995, outlined above, which showed that infants could identify monosyllabic words), showed that English-learning infants can identify bisyllabic words from at least $7\frac{1}{2}$ months, but only if they have the typical English trochaic stress pattern. Children were familiarized with pairs of words with trochaic stress (e.g. DOCtor, CANdle, then tested on four passages, two with the familiarized words and two with other words (KINGdom, HAMlet). The infants showed a familiarity preference for the target words and, in a second experiment, showed the same preference when they first heard the words embedded in passages, and were then tested on the words in isolation. Another group of infants of the same age were unable to recognise words with weak/strong stress (e.g. guiTAR), with which they had been familiarized, when they heard them in passages, but showed a tendency to match the strong syllables of these words to lists containing them in isolation. When familiarized with passages containing 'guiTAR is' they treated strong syllables as markers of word onsets in that, at test, they preferred to listen to lists of words containing TARis, than to lists containing non-familiarized words with the same stress patterns. However, experiments with older infants of $10\frac{1}{2}$ months showed that these children were able to segment words with weak/strong stress from the contexts of fluent speech in which they occurred. Thus the suggestion is that children might use these language-typical patterns of rhythmic stress to identify word boundaries.

Although some languages show more consistent word stress than English (for instance, in Finnish it is always on the first syllable and in Polish on the penultimate syllable), word-prosodic patterns would not be useful in identifying word boundaries for all languages. For instance, English is a stress-timed language: stressed syllables appear at a roughly even rate and unstressed syllables are shortened to fit in. But in other languages, syllables (e.g. Spanish) or mora (e.g. Japanese) are produced with equal emphasis. In French, stress falls on the final or next-to-final syllable of a string, rather than within a word. In Inuktitut, a polysynthetic language, there are a complex set of interacting factors determining whether and where stress falls within a word (syllable weight, length of vowels, presence and position of consonant clusters, number of syllables within the word).

2.4.1.2 Generativist approaches Yang (2004) and Gambell and Yang (2003, 2005) argue that word segmentation would be impossible without some innate mechanism to get it started. The position can be summarized as follows:

- To identify the (phonotactic, allophonic and prosodic) characteristics of words (as opposed to boundaries between words), the child must first learn some words (presumably by encountering them in isolation). However, it is not easy to see how the child could learn that a particular string (e.g. *Mummy*) is a word that is being presented in isolation, as opposed to two words (e.g. *Mum, Me*). Conversely, the child must learn that certain strings that are frequently presented in isolation are *not* words, but are multiword phrases (e.g. *wozzat* = 'what's that'; *seeda* = 'see the').
- Therefore to know that something is a word, some language-independent strategies are needed. Otherwise the problem becomes circular: children already need to know the language-specific characteristics of words, for instance the prosodic patterns, phonotactic or allophonic constraints for English, in order to segment them out (see also Swingley, 2005a).
- Statistical learning (identifying syllable pairs in a string that have lower transitional probabilities than other syllable pairs, and treating them as word boundaries) is the only language-independent strategy that has been proposed. All the others outlined above (metrical segmentation, phonotactics etc.) depend on knowing the specifics of the particular language and how this relates to words and word boundaries.
- The results of applying the transitional probability model to real corpora of child-directed speech resulted in very poor results for word segmentation (41.6 per cent **precision**, the number of correct words out of all the words extracted, and 23.3 per cent **recall**, the number of correct words extracted out of the total number of actual words; Gambell and Yang, 2005). The reason for this is that the corpora contained a very high proportion of monosyllabic words. The transitional probability model cannot work on monosyllabic words because there are no transitional probabilities within words to compare with those between words.
- Yang concludes that there must be some innate guide to word segmentation and proposes an innate **Unique Stress Constraint**: a word can have only one primary stress. This means that if two stressed syllables are adjacent, a word boundary is postulated. For instance, using his examples, we would know that ChewBAcca is one word and DARTH VAder is two even when we heard them for the first time because each word contains only one stressed syllable.
- When added to the local minima model, this results in much more successful word segmentation (over 70 per cent for both precision and recall; Gambell and Yang, 2003, 2005).

- More important is that a model that uses *no* transitional probabilities at all does much better again (about 95 per cent for both precision and recall). This model works as follows: the model has a lexicon which stores previously segmented words. No statistical training is used. The input is scanned from left to right. If a word that has been stored in the lexicon is recognized, the model puts the word aside and proceeds to the remainder of the string, thus enabling segmentation between the recognized word and what follows it. Gambell and Yang call this algebraic learning.

When applied to English, this model clearly does better than the transitional-probability model. The fact that English child-directed speech has so many monosyllabic words becomes an advantage rather than a disadvantage. There is no problem that children have to know what a word is before they can segment out further words – this is pregiven.

2.4.1.3 Segmenting words: conclusions Clearly, infants are sensitive to variations in transitional probabilities, but this does not necessarily mean either that they, in principle, can or, in practice, actually do use them to discover word boundaries in naturalistic contexts. Both Aslin and Newport (2009) and Gómez (2007) briefly address the problems with the transitional-probability model raised by Yang (2004). Swingley (2005a) also noted the problem for the transitional-probability model that English child-directed speech contains so many monosyllables. Similarly to Gambell and Yang (2003), he pointed out that it is not clear how an infant would 'decide' what the right 'cut-off' was for a within-word, as opposed to a between-word, boundary, nor the ways in strings that were mis-segmented by such a procedure would then be 'recovered'.

However, if the Unique Stress Constraint is indeed innate, then, as Yang (2004) says, it should work for all languages. However, as we have already seen, many languages do not have word-level stress (for instance, Japanese). A second issue, even for a word-stressed language like English, is whether initial mis-segementations such as *Mum me* as two words and *What's that* as one actually matter. It may be that much of the early lexicon is only roughly matched to that of the adult and consists in part both of unanalysed strings and mis-segmentations. As Yang points out, we know that there are the occasional mis-segmentations (*All the others are haive, you should be-have too*) but there is also evidence that infants are segmenting and remembering frequent strings as well as individual words (Bannard and Matthews, 2008).

An alternative to positing the Unique Stress Constraint as innate is to suggest that when children can pair a string with an entity that they know well (for instance, *Mummy* or their own name), they infer that it *is* a word regardless of how many syllables it has. Thus, meaning fixes the initial words as words and then allows the infant to identify the typical patterns of word stress (and also allophonic and phonotactic constraints) in the language. There is evidence that children can learn some words through frequent repetition: $4\frac{1}{2}$-month-old infants listen significantly longer to repetitions of their own name than to other names (Mandel, Jusczyk and Pisoni, 1995) and show a listening preference for *baby* (Mandel and Jusczyk, 1997) and some other very common words (*hands, feet*; Tincoff, 2001) at 6 months. Tincoff and Jusczyk (1999) showed, using a preferential looking procedure, that 6-month-olds can link the words *Mommy* and *Daddy* to videotapes of their parents and not to unfamiliar adults. In this experiment, infants were familiarized to the position of video displays showing their mother/father. During baseline trials, their looking preference for one or the other video was measured. In test trials, ten different variants in two blocks of *Mommy* and two of *Daddy* (spoken by a 10-year-old to neutralize for male/female voice) were played. Proportional looking times (for correct and incorrect looking to each video, adjusted for the infant's baseline preference) showed that the infants looked significantly more to the parent being named than to the unnamed parent (18 out of the 24 infants had a longer looking time to the 'correct' video). In a second experiment the researchers showed that infants did not look longer to a video of an unfamiliar woman when hearing *Mommy* or an unfamiliar man when hearing *Daddy*.

Meaning and intentional communication are perhaps the major factors left out of consideration in Yang's theoretical position. Once the child has some sense that the speech stream is being used for communication, this may start to provide an anchor for particular words (Behne, Carpenter, Call and Tomasello, 2005). Sensitivity to a variety of potential word-segmentation cues seems to be developing at around 8–9 months and it is around this time (or perhaps a few months later; see Chapter 3) that children start to develop an understanding of intentional communication (see also Bruner, 1975; Bates, Camaioni and Volterra, 1975). Although this is unlikely to explain all of early word learning (see Chapter 3), the fact that lexical development takes off around the beginning of the second year of life suggests that the development of communicative understanding that words have meanings may play an important part in children's ability to further segment words out of the speech stream (Tomasello, 2003).

It seems clear that word segmentation must take place through a combination of processes, the relative importance of which might change with development. There have been a number of studies which demonstrate this interaction of processes in infant speech perception experimentally. For instance, Johnson and Jusczyk (2001) used natural speech syllables combined into artificial 'languages' and replicated the findings of Saffran, Aslin and Newport (1996) on statistical learning. However, they also showed that when presented with conflicting stress and coarticulation cues, 8-month-olds weighted the coarticulation cues more heavily than the statistical cues. Thiessen and Saffran (2003) found that there were developmental changes in the cues to which infants gave more weight. Younger infants paid more attention to transitional probabilities, while older infants paid more attention to stress cues. However, prior to the Gambell and Yang model, there had not been an attempt to model such interactions between processes on real data.

It is interesting that the development of lexicon seems to take a considerable time. However, it does seem that, by at least 6 months, infants are starting to develop a small stock of words, given the results of the Jusczyk and Tinkoff studies cited above. There are also experiments showing that having a known word precede an unfamiliar word aids segmentation (Bortfeld, Morgan, Golinkoff and Rathbun, 2005), as does having a novel word preceded by a function word (Shi, Cutler, Werker and Cruickshank, 2006). It is possible that these initial segmentations could provide the basis for starting to identify the language-specific, prosodic, phonotactic and allophonic patterns associated with words.

Since all are agreed that segmentation must involve a number of factors, it seems particularly important to develop models that attempt to implement this interaction between processes. Both Swingley's (2005a) and Gambell and Yang's (2005) models do this. A model that used early word meanings as a way to bootstrap into metrical segmentation seems an obvious next step from a constructivist viewpoint.

2.4.2   Phrases and clauses

2.4.2.1 Generativist approaches   As we will see in more detail in Chapter 4, syntactic clauses and phrases are central to any theory of acquisition since they ultimately form the building blocks (constituents) for novel utterances. Roughly speaking, a clause corresponds to a sentence (e.g. *The man kicked the ball*), though some sentences may contain two or more clauses, each of which functions like a 'mini sentence', expressing one idea (e.g. *Sarah said / the man kicked the ball*). Syntactic phrases will also be outlined more fully in Chapter 4. For now, it will suffice to say that a simple sentence like *The man kicked the ball* contains two phrases: the Noun Phrase (NP) *The man* and the Verb Phrase (VP) *kicked the ball* (the VP contains a VERB, *kicked*, and a second NP: *the ball*).

As well as splitting up the speech stream that they hear into words, children must therefore also identify clauses (e.g. *The man kicked the ball*) and phrases (the VP *The man* and the NP *kicked the ball*). In addition, from within the generativist position, some researchers have argued that if clauses and phrases can be identified as units in the speech stream, this might allow infants to start to set various **parameters** of **Universal Grammar** before (necessarily) learning any of the individual words or identifying their syntactic categories. For example, the setting of the **head-direction parameter** (explained more fully in Chapter 4) governs whether a speaker would say *The man kicked the ball* (as in English) or (the equivalent of) *The man the ball kicked* (e.g. as in Korean). In Chapter 6, we discuss the evidence regarding whether children can use clauses and phrases extracted from the speech stream to set parameters. For our present purposes, however, the question is whether or not infants can indeed use acoustic cues to segment the speech stream into clauses (e.g. *Sarah said // the man kicked the ball*) and phrases (*The man // kicked the ball*). Particularly important is the issue of whether children can split a clause into a Noun Phrase (e.g. *The man*), which (in English) is the subject, and a Verb Phrase (e.g. *kicked the ball*), which contains the object (e.g. *the ball*). Potential acoustic cues to this **NP/VP split** have therefore attracted much research.

2.4.2.1.1 Are prosodic cues to syntactic phrase boundaries available and reliable in speech to children?   Studies of adult–adult speech have found that the following cues (summarized by Fisher and Tokura, 1996: 343) are associated with syntactic phrase boundaries (the same cues also mark clause boundaries, where they tend to be more pronounced):

- **Final-syllable lengthening**. Syllables that end phrases or clauses tend to be lengthened relative to syllables elsewhere in constituents (e.g. Cooper and Paccia-Cooper, 1980; Crystal and House, 1988; Klatt, 1976; Lehiste, 1972; Scott, 1982; Streeter, 1978).
- **Pauses**. Pauses are more likely to occur at major syntactic boundaries than arbitrarily within phrases (e.g. Goldman-Eisler, 1972; Scott, 1982) and pause length appears to reflect the hierarchical structure of phrases (e.g. Cooper and Paccia-Cooper, 1980; Gee and Grosjean, 1983).
- **Pitch contours**. Fundamental frequency (F0) [i.e. pitch] tends to decline and its range also narrows at the end of intonation units (which often correspond to major syntactic constituents), and then rises at the start of the next syntactic unit (e.g. Cooper and Sorenson, 1977). Final lengthening and pitch changes can lead to the perception of a subjective pause or break in speech by adults (e.g. Duez, 1993; Wightman, Shattuck-Hufnagel, Ostendorf and Price, 1992), even when there is no period of silence.

Fisher and Tokura (1996) conducted an analysis of spontaneous speech (directed to a child aged 1;0) to investigate whether these cues to syntactic structure were in fact present. Whilst these cues (particularly pauses) were excellent markers of clause boundaries, they were not statistically significant predictors of phrase boundaries, such as that between a SUBJECT NP and a VP (e.g. *The boy / is running*). The problem seems to be that 84 per cent of the full sentences analysed had unstressed pronoun subjects (e.g. *He kissed the dog*), in which there is no prosodic boundary between the subject NP and the VP (*He* and *kissed* form a single 'prosodic word' with stress on the second syllable: *'eeKISSed*; Gerken, Jusczyk and Mandel, 1994; Nespor and Vogel, 1986). Whilst Fisher and Tokura (1996) found that, for NPs greater than one syllable in length, final syllables were significantly longer at the NP/VP boundary than within a phrase, such sentences represent only 16 per cent of the total. The situation may be somewhat better for Japanese, where pitch-contour changes were significantly more common at phrase boundaries than within phrases.

A problem, however, is that Fisher and Tokura (1996) do not report availability or reliability figures for phrase-boundary cues. Thus, in English, although (for multisyllabic subjects), final syllables were significantly longer at phrase boundaries than phrase internally, *on average*, it is unclear how often a lengthened syllable is present when there is a boundary to be uncovered (**availability**) or how often a lengthened syllable, when one is present, actually does signal a phrase boundary (**reliability**). Furthermore, the impact of partially reliable cues would be unclear (Fernald and McRoberts, 1996: 379). For example, an arbitrary figure of 80 per cent reliability for a particular cue to a clause or phrase boundary may sound impressive, but it is not clear what would happen for the 20 per cent of sentences where the child positioned the boundary incorrectly.

In fact, the actual reliability figures for the proposed boundary cues appear to be rather low. For example, Fernald and McRoberts (1996: 368) cite an analysis of formal academic speech in which 116 pauses (1 sec or longer) occurred at clause boundaries, with 119 occurring clause internally (i.e. a reliability figure of lower than 50 per cent). Pitch contours and final syllable lengthening are likely to be even less reliable cues: pitch is affected by emphasis (stressed syllables are of higher or lower pitch than surrounding syllables), utterance type (questions tend to have a rising intonation) and meaning (tone languages such as Mandarin Chinese use 'the same' segment sequence, e.g. *ma*, to mean different things, e.g. *hemp/horse/scold*, according to the pitch contour). Similarly, syllable length is affected by speech rate, the speaker's mood and the inherent length of the vowel (e.g. a lengthened /i/ is shorter than a non-lengthened /e/). Another study of adult–adult speech (Klatt, 1976) found that only 65 per cent of lengthened syllables (defined as a syllable with a duration >1.2 its median) occurred at phrase or clause boundaries.

A possible objection to these criticisms is that the reliability figures cited are all from studies of adult–adult speech (Fisher and Tokura, 1996, study child-directed speech but do not provide reliability figures, or data for phrase as opposed to clause boundaries). Since infant-directed speech features exaggerated pitch contours, lengthening and pauses (e.g. Bernstein Ratner, 1996), it is possible that these cues may reliably mark phrase boundaries in speech to children, but not speech to adults. Future studies should investigate this possibility for a wide range of languages. However, the outlook is not promising, since the use of a universal child-directed-speech register with these characteristics may well not be universal (Lieven, 1994).

2.4.2.1.2 Are children sensitive to prosodic cues to syntactic phrase boundaries? Nevertheless, there exists some evidence that, where prosodic cues to phrase structure are available, children are sensitive to them. In a study conducted by Soderstrom, Seidl, Kemler Nelson and Jusczyk (2003), children aged 9 months (experiment 1) and 6 months (experiment 2) were familiarized with a pair of strings each extracted from longer sentences spoken by an adult using child-directed speech. The **strings** were identical except that one constituted a syntactic unit (an NP) whilst the other straddled an NP/VP boundary:

(a) At the discount store, **[new watches for men]** [are simple and stylish] (NP unit)
(b) In the field, [the old frightened **gnu] [watches for men** and women seeking trophies] (non-unit; NP/VP boundary)

Consequently, the non-unit string (b) contained a syntactic boundary (after *gnu*) marked by the cues of final-syllable lengthening and pitch drop, as confirmed by acoustic analysis (though no pause was detected). The unit string (a), though identical when considered as a series of phonemes, did not contain a syntactic boundary after *new* (and hence no prosodic cues to such a boundary).

At test, two passages were available for listening (presented repeatedly): one contained the relevant string as a complete noun phrase (*At the discount store, **new watches for men** are simple and stylish. In fact, some people buy the whole supply of them*) whilst the other contained the string as a syntactic non-unit (*In the field, the old frightened **gnu watches for men** and women seeking trophies. Today, people by the hole seem scary*). In other words, the passages available for listening at test were those from which the familiarization strings were extracted. This study used a version of the conditioned head-turn paradigm (see Chapter 1). The infant controls playback of each passage (i.e. determines how many times it is repeated) by looking at a flashing light located above the relevant loudspeaker. Note that in this version of the paradigm, only one of the two passages is available on each trial; thus (unlike in the studies of Jusczyk *et al.*, 1992, and Gerken, Jusczyk and Mandel, 1994) infants decide how long to listen to *each passage independently*, as opposed to 'choosing' one of the passages over the other.

The rationale behind the paradigm is that if infants do indeed parse their input into syntactic phrases on the basis of prosodic cues, then they should prefer to listen to the passage where the familiarized five-syllable string constitutes a unit (*new watches for men*) than the passage where the familiarized five-syllable string constitutes a non-unit (*gnu watches for men*) as they will be better able to recognize the unit than the non-unit as having been presented previously.[6] If they do not, there is no reason to prefer one over the other.

The prediction of the prosodic bootstrapping hypothesis was supported for both age groups. The authors ruled out the alternative possibility that infants simply preferred one test passage over the other by showing that the preference was reversed for infants who heard *people by the hole (seem scary)* as a unit and *people buy the whole (supply)* as a non-unit. Neither did infants listen longer to the NP-unit than the non-unit string during familiarization. The effect does not appear to be specific to NP units. In a third study, infants aged 6 months showed a similar pattern for VP units (*Inventive people design telephones at home*) versus non-units (*The director of design telephones her boss*).

Similar studies have shown that 6-month-olds are also sensitive to final-syllable lengthening, pauses and pitch contours as cues to clause (as opposed to phrase) boundaries (Nazzi, Kemler Nelson, Jusczyk and Jusczyk, 2000; Seidl, 2007).

Sensitivity to these cues has also been demonstrated by studies that use a pause-insertion paradigm (Hirsh-Pasek *et al.*, 1987 for clause boundaries; Jusczyk *et al.*, 1992; Gerken, Jusczyk and Mandel, 1994, for phrase boundaries). Children prefer to listen to passages where an artificial pause is inserted at an NP/VP boundary (e.g. *Many different kinds of animals / live in the zoo*) rather than within a phrase (e.g. *Many different kinds / of animals live in the zoo*). However, whilst such studies demonstrate that children know there is *something* odd about such sentences, they do not demonstrate that children actually use prosodic cues to identify phrase boundaries. The findings of Soderstrom *et al.* (2003) are more compelling because they do not require stimuli to be artificially manipulated in this way.

2.4.2.2 Constructivist approaches For generativist approaches, the question of whether children could use acoustic properties of the speech stream to segment it into clauses and phrases is vital. This is because, under 'phonological bootstrapping' approaches to syntax acquisition (see Chapter 6), children must be able to segment their input into phrases to set the syntactic parameters of their language, regardless of whether or not they understand the meanings of the words and phrases. Indeed, unless innate semantics–syntax 'linking rules' are posited (see Pinker, 1989), knowing the meaning of the words will not help children to set the parameters anyway.

Under constructivist approaches to syntax acquisition (e.g. Tomasello, 2003), children will presumably use cues such as pitch contours and pauses to split the input that they hear into chunks. However, the question of whether children can identify these chunks as syntactic constituents such as NP and VP on the basis of purely acoustic properties does not arise for two reasons. First, under constructivist accounts, children's early grammars do not contain these types of constituents but consist of a set of low-level lexically specific slot-and-frame patterns with functional, as opposed to syntactic, slots (e.g. *I wanna ACTION*). Second, there is no issue of whether children can identify clauses and phrases without knowing their meaning, because the assumption is that they do not.

Summary table 2.2a *Segmenting speech into words* (☑ = *supports theory;* ☒ = *counts against theory*)

Note that the position of the columns in Tables 2.2a and 2.2b (non-nativist on the left, nativist on the right) is reversed with respect to the other summary tables that contrast these positions. This reflects the fact that the studies discussed have generally been taken as evidence that there are cues to word segmentation in the input, with the, sometimes implicit, assumption that, in combination, these would be sufficient. The nativist proposal on the right challenges this assumption.

Issue/phenomenon	Non-nativist approaches: probabilistic cues to word segmentation	Nativist theory: the Unique Stress Constraint
Summary of position	There are many cues to word segmentation in the speech stream. Words (and strings) will be segmented as the child starts to take part in communication and to map sound to meaning (Jusczyk, 1997; Tomasello, 2003).	Although there are cues to segmentation in the speech stream (a) these are all probabilistic and could lead to mis-segmentation and (b) the child has to know that what has been segmented is a word. Therefore there is no way to get word segmentation off the ground without some innate principle (Yang, 2004; Gambell and Yang, 2003, 2005).
Some words can be learned in isolation, and then used to segment the speech stream further (e.g. Brent and Cartwright, 1996)	☑ 9% utterances in English CDS are isolated words (Brent and Siskind, 2001). ☑ Frequency of CDS use in isolation predicts age of acquisition (Brent and Siskind, 2001). ☑ Infants aged 4–6 months already know some words (e.g. own name, *baby, feet;* Mandel *et al.,* 1997; Mandel and Jusczyk 1997; Tincoff, 2001) and can recognize them when presented in stream (Jusczyk and Aslin, 1995). ☑ Computational model using isolated words had 70–80% success (Brent, 1999). ☑ Having a known word or function word precede an unfamiliar word aids segmentation (Bortfield *et al.,* 2005, Shi *et al.,* 2006).	☑ Though children can presumably learn some words by hearing them in isolation, many words (e.g. *the*) cannot be learned in this way. ☑ Children would need some way of knowing that a multisyllabic word presented in isolation *is* a single word (Gambell and Yang, 2005). ☑ Brent's model (left-hand column) achieves success by storing whole corpus at once – psychologically implausible.
Phonotactic constraints within/across words could aid segmentation	☑ 9-month-old infants are sensitive to phonotactic constraints (Mattys *et al.,* 1999).	☑ Infants would already have to know some words to learn which clusters appear within vs across words in the target language (Gambell and Yang, 2005).

Allophonic constraints within and across words could aid segmentation	☑ 10½-month-olds are sensitive to allophonic constraints (Jusczyk et al., 1999).	☑ Infants would already have to know some words to learn which allophones are characteristic of word beginnings/endings/boundaries in the target language (Gambell and Yang, 2005).
Stress patterns (e.g. Jusczyk, Houston and Newsome, 1999)	☑ English-hearing 7½-month-olds are sensitive to the predominant trochaic pattern of English words (Jusczyk et al., 1999). ☒ But some languages do not have word stress (Beckman, 1986).	☑ Infants would already have to know some words to learn which stress pattern is typical in the target language (Gambell and Yang, 2005).
Transitional probabilities (e.g. Saffran et al., 1996)	☑ 8-month-olds can identify differences in transitional probabilities after 2 minutes listening (Saffran et al., 1996). ☒ Not confined to speech sequences, so a possible universal strategy (Saffran et al., 1999; Kirkham et al., 2002).	☑ English child-directed speech contains a high proportion of monosyllabic words for which there are no within-word transitional probabilities between syllables. ☒ Results of applying model to CDS gave very poor results (Gambell and Yang, 2005).
The Unique Stress Constraint: a word is a string with unique stress	Children could use meaning to identify cues to segmentation (see below), then subsequently identify the typical pattern of word stress in the language.	☑ Like transitional probabilities is proposed to be independent of any particular language. ☑ Does much better than TP model on segmentation (Gambell and Yang, 2005). ☒ Will not work for all languages, e.g. languages without word stress or with complex stress patterns.
Mapping strings to meaning is essential to word segmentation	☑ The development of a lexicon is closely correlated with the development of intentional communication (Carpenter et al., 1998; Tomasello, 2003). ☒ Children are probably starting with strings of different length mapped to meaning as well as words (Lieven et al., 2009).	Presumably would not deny that meaning aids word segmentation, but includes no role for meaning in proposal.

Summary table 2.2b *Segmenting speech into phrases and clauses* (☑ = *supports theory*; ☒ = *counts against theory*)

Issue/phenomenon / Summary of position	Constructivist theory	Nativist theory
	Children will identify intonation units mapped to child-identified meanings, with syntactic units emergent from this process.	Children can identify syntactic phrases (e.g. noun phrase and verb phrase) and clauses using acoustic cues in the speech stream.
Are there cues to phrases and clauses in adult-to-adult speech?	Once children have identified phrases and clauses using meaning, they can begin to learn which acoustic cues are characteristic of boundaries.	☑ Final-syllable lengthening (e.g. Cooper and Paccia-Cooper, 1980; Klatt, 1976). ☑ Pauses (e.g. Goldman-Eisler, 1972; Scott, 1982; Gee and Grosjean, 1983). ☑ Pitch contours (e.g. Cooper and Sorenson. 1977; Duez, 1993).
Are final-syllable lengthening, pauses and pitch contours good cues to clause and phrase boundaries in child-directed speech?	Findings that they are generally not (see right-hand box) are not problematic for this approach: children's early grammars do not contain these syntactic units, instead they learn meaningful 'chunks' (Tomasello, 2003; For evidence see ☑ Bannard and Matthews, 2008; Bannard et al., 2009).	☑ Pause cues were good guides to clauses but ☒ Not to phrases (Fisher and Tokura, 1996), particularly as 84% of full sentences had unstressed pronoun subjects, so no pause between subject NP and VP (Gerken et al., 1994; Nespor and Vogel, 1986). ☒ Though final-syllable lengthening is a cue to NP/VP boundary for NPs longer than one syllable, only 16% of sentences are of this type (Fisher and Tokura, 1996). ☒ Cues have low reliability (50–65%) and unclear whether more reliable – but still far short of 100% – cues would help or hinder (Fernald and McRoberts, 1996; Klatt, 1976).
Are children sensitive to prosodic cues in child-directed speech?	Studies in right-hand box show that children can *detect* final syllable lengthening, pause insertions and pitch changes, but not necessarily that they know that they are cues to phrase and clause boundaries.	☑ 6- and 9-month-old infants can detect a NP/VP boundary which is correlated with pitch drop and final syllable lengthening (Soderstrom et al., 2003). ☑ 6-month-olds are sensitive to these cues to clauses (Nazzi et al., 2000; Seidl, 2007). ☑ Infants prefer to listen to sentences where artificial pauses are inserted between syntactic units than within them (for clauses: Hirsh-Pasek et al., 1987; phrases: Jusczyk et al., 1992; Gerken et al., 1994).

On the contrary, children's 'way in' to phrase structure is through learning *meaningful* chunks (e.g. *John*; *The boy*; *The boy who is smoking*) and noticing the ways in which these can be substituted for one another across utterances (eventually yielding – in this case – constructions with NP slots). This process is discussed in detail in Chapter 6 and – for complex sentences – Chapter 7.

2.4.2.3 Segmenting phrases and clauses: conclusion

- While final syllable lengthening, lowered pitch contours and pauses are statistical guides to clauses (reasonably reliable) and phrases (less reliable), it is not clear that they are good enough guides to allow the child to bootstrap from them into principles of syntactic organization.
- This could be tested in a modelling study that varied the reliability of these cues and measured the success of the model at segmenting a real speech stream into clauses and phrases.
- An analysis of prosodic cues to segmentation in the child-directed speech of typologically different languages would be very interesting.
- The issue of whether children can identify phrases (e.g. Noun Phrase, Verb Phrase) and clauses on a purely acoustic basis is crucial to 'prosodic bootstrapping' generativist approaches, under which this knowledge is needed to kick-start syntax acquisition. For constructivist approaches, children do not need to be able to parse their input into phrases and clauses on the basis of purely acoustic properties, as the route to syntax is through meaning.

2.5   Speech production

2.5.1   Introduction

Children's early speech does not sound like that of adults, and it takes a very long time to do so fully, with some contrasts not appearing until well into the school years. The main contrast between the **nativist** and **constructivist** approaches that we present here is that the former see children's productions as starting from a full representation of adult word forms while the latter see children as having their own phonemic systems which develop into the adult system. Nativist approaches differ in the ways in which children's actual productions are derived from the full underlying representations. In **generative phonology** (e.g. Smith, 1973), it is by rules which the child has to unlearn in order to arrive at the adult system. In **natural phonology** (Stampe, 1979) the child's simplifications occur through processes that are common to both children and language change. Development consists in the child then learning which processes must be abandoned for the language being learned. **Optionality theory** is an alternative nativist theory (at least in its original formulation): speech production is subject to a number of competing **universal constraints** which are ranked differently in priority depending on the language. The proponents of all these theories would see the results on perceptual discrimination discussed above as providing support. Finally, there is the **constructivist** position that children start to make use of the **underspecified vocal patterns** that they already have and match these to similar adult input patterns (e.g. Waterson, 1971; Menyuk and Menn, 1979), the theory of **templatic phonology**. In doing so, phonological contrasts in terms of articulatory features emerge. As we shall see, more recent approaches are considerably less polarized than this summary would suggest and most approaches fall somewhere along a continuum between the two extremes.

During the first year of life, babies move from early vegetative sounds of crying, grunting etc. through the development of cooing and laughter, to babbling and the production of first words (Oller, 2000). Jakobson ([1941] 1968) claimed that there was a complete discontinuity between babbling and the beginnings of word production. He proposed that when infants start to produce words they work through a series of universal phonological **contrasts** (**oppositions** or **distinctive features**) starting from the most common in the languages of the world which, he hypothesized, were also the easiest to produce (e.g. the earliest syllable to be produced will include a vowel and a front consonant, usually labial, hence /ba/; the first consonant opposition is oral vs nasal: /ba/ vs /ma/). These are the most common contrasts across the languages of the world and the idea is that the least common will be acquired last by children learning languages in which they appear. This suggestion of an initially limited core of sound types produced by infants and their relationship to the most frequent sound contrasts found across languages seems to be correct, and many theories espouse some version of this position, usually explained in terms of ease of articulation both for the infant and (crosslinguistically) adults. However, because Jakobson saw this as the innate unfolding of universal contrasts, he maintained that babbling was irrelevant to the development of speech. More recent research has shown that although early babbling is quite similar across babies learning different languages (due to the anatomy of the articulators and consequent ease of production), the sounds in babbling are, in fact, increasingly influenced by aspects of the ambient language (Oller, Wieman, Doyle and Ross, 1975; Boysson-Bardies and Vihman, 1991). It has also been shown that the sounds that the child produces in late babbling are also the sounds produced in the first words (Locke, 1983; Vihman *et al.*, 1985), suggesting that, in fact, babbling and speech production are part of a continuous development.

Although when children start to produce their first words, some of the very earliest can sound quite similar to those of the adult language, they go through a long period in which their productions vary from the adult language in systematic ways (see Hoff, 2001: 126–7; Vihman, 1996: appendices B and C;

Table 2.1 *Types of differences from the adult model in words produced by children*

Name	Description	Example
Syllable deletions	– from multisyllabic forms (often weak syllable deletion)	[nænə] for *banana*
Final-consonant deletion		[da] for *that*
Reduplication	– of one syllable of a word instead of producing two different syllables	[baba] for *bottle*
Consonant harmony	One consonant in a word takes on features of another	[gʌk] for *duck* (starts and ends with a velar rather than starting with the alveolar /d/)
Reduction of consonant clusters	– to one consonant	[kæk] for *cracker*
Metathesis	Transposition of sounds	[bais] (rhymes with *spice*) for *spade*
Epenthesis	A sound is inserted	[belu] for *blue*
Segment substitutions		[ti] for *key* (a front velar /k/ is replaced by a dental /t/)

Lust, 2006:164). Some of the changes from the adult model in words produced by children are set out in Table 2.1.

There have been a variety of explanations for these changes, including memory and articulatory limitations. Traditionally, the differences have been described in terms of **phonological processes** which alter the underlying representation of the segments in the adult word into what the child produces. This, of course, assumes that the child represents the word to be produced in terms of its underlying sequence of segments. The main theoretical issue is, therefore, whether children are producing words on the basis of a full adultlike representation of the word's segmental phonology or whether this is emergent from the child's attempts to produce words. It is to this debate that we now turn.

On the one hand, we know from the evidence cited in Section 2.3 above that infants can detect a wide range of phonologically relevant distinctions in isolated syllables from an early age, and become increasingly sensitive to the particularities of the ambient language over the first year of life. On the other hand, there is somewhat conflicting evidence about their ability to detect phonemic contrasts in words, in some cases until the middle of the second year. As we saw above, Jusczyk and Aslin (1995) found that $7\frac{1}{2}$-month-olds (but not 6-month-olds), tested in the head-turn preference procedure, listened longer to passages containing words with which they had been familiarized (e.g. *dog*).

However, when familiarized on the real word and then exposed to passages with a change in onset (*bawg*), they did not show this preference, suggesting that they had encoded a considerable level of phonetic detail in the memorized word.

In a detailed extension of this experiment, Swingley (2005b) tested 11-month-old Dutch-hearing infants on their discrimination of real words from a number of manipulations. These involved changes in onset, codas (final segements of syllables) and other mispronunciations. For example, for the stimulus [hɑnt] (Dutch *hand* 'hand'), related changes were: in onset, [xɑnt], offset, [xɑŋk] or 'mispronunications' with the same onsets and codas but different vowels [hɑːk]. The results showed that the infants were sensitive to mispronunciations and to changes in onsets, though not to codas (see also Vihman, Nakai, DePaolis and Hall, 2004). However, a smaller group of infants with larger receptive vocabularies, measured later at 1;4, did show sensitivity to codas.

On the other hand, in studies using the 'switch task', where infants have to pair a word to an object before hearing a change in the phonetic detail of the word, they do not succeed in discriminating phonetically similar 'words' until 17 months, though they can discriminate phonetically different words at 14 months (Stager and Werker, 1997; Werker, Fennell, Corcoran and Stager, 2002). The 'switch' task involves training children on two different word–object pairings (e.g. *bih* for one object and *dih* for the other) until they habituate. At test, there are two types of trial: 'same' trials on which the infants hear the familiar word–object pairing and 'switch' trials where they hear the opposite pairing. If children can tell the difference between the two words, they should show surprise in the 'switch' trials. Infants of 14 months can do this task (Curtin and Werker, 2007). At this age, children do not discriminate words with minimal phonetic differences, e.g. *bih* and *dih*, though they do show discrimination between two phonetically very different words (e.g. *ilf* and *nim*). Curtin and Werker explain this in terms of task demands, suggesting that mapping a word to a referent is a more complex task than simply discriminating between two auditory stimuli, and that infants' attentional resources are limited.[7]

2.5.2   *Generativist approaches*

   2.5.2.1 Universal rules/processes   Generativist approaches tend to be characterized by an assumption that representation in perception is adultlike and the problem to be explained is children's failure to reproduce this in their early production. There tends to be an emphasis on universal phonological representations (based on innate distinctive features), which are then modulated by the language being learned. These approaches focus on the sequencing of segments, and rules or constraints are proposed for why these are so different from adult production.

Thus Smith (1973), in an in-depth analysis of his son, Amahl's, development, posited a series of **realization rules** working on the **distinctive features** of a fully represented adult system to generate the child's actual utterances (**Generative phonology**). An example would be that the child has a rule which converts the value of the initial consonant in the underlying adult representation to a [+coronal] feature (the [+coronal] feature refers to the place of articulation; e.g. the initial consonant in *zoo* and *that*). Smith postulates that at one point his son had a rule that changed initial consonants to the feature [+coronal] (*shut*, *touch*, *yes* and *yawn* all started with a [d] sound). These rules have to be unlearned as the constraints on production lessen.

Donegan and Stampe (1979) see the child's system as containing a universal set of natural phonological processes (thus, **Natural phonology**) that occur in the production of sequences of phonemes (e.g. deletion of unstressed syllables, simplifications of clusters; see Table 2.1). In this approach, the child has to learn which of these processes apply to the ambient language. So the idea is that the child has a system that allows the production of an approximation to every adult form and, as development proceeds, the child has to learn which of these rules to abandon.

These rule-based and universalist theories face two types of problem. First, there does seem to be something rather unparsimonious in positing that children start with sets of rules (such as [+coronal]) or processes (such as cluster simplification) which have to be unlearned, as opposed to building up from a less specified representation. Second, as we have seen from the discussion of Pierrehumbert's position above, it seems that the articulatory features associated with the production of particular phonemes differ between languages, between speakers, and as a function of position in the word and utterance, rendering the idea of a universal set of distinctive features and realization rules difficult to support.

2.5.2.2 Optimality theory   One theoretical direction has been to abandon the rule-based approach for one based on the idea of competition between constraints on the surface form (**Optimality theory** or **OT**; Prince and Smolensky, 1993, 2004). Competition between constraints is resolved by ranking, which differs between languages (see Gussenhoven and Jacobs, 1998: 45–53 for a brief outline). The constraints fall into two categories: **markedness** and **faithfulness**. Markedness constraints are aimed at making the output 'unmarked', which would have the effect of generating a simpler-to-produce output (similar to the universal phonological processes of Donegan and Stampe's 'natural phonology'), while faithfulness constraints aim at reproducing the input structure as closely as possible. Thus, like the approaches outlined above, the target representations are seen as adultlike: but now instead of a sequence of rules that are applied, there are ordered constraints. These constraints are ranked differently in the adult system and the early language learner, since children's immature production systems force them to rank markedness constraints above faithfulness constraints. The learner reorders these constraints as a consequence of exposure to the particulars of the language being learned. With development, faithfulness constraints come to outrank markedness, bringing the child's productions into line with the adult's. In the original versions of OT (Prince and Smolensky, 1993) these constraints were innate, as was their ranking. More recently, not all theorists working with Optimality theory necessarily see the constraints as innate (Fikkert and Levelt, 2008). In output every possible version of a target is generated and the ranking of constraints determines which target wins. Development then consists of learning the particular ranking of constraints in the child's ambient language.

We present a simplified example from Kager, Pater and Zonneveld (2004: 36, based upon Gnanadesikan's chapter in the same volume). The child analysed by Gnanadesikan produced [piz] for *please*, but correctly produced [læb] for *lab* (i.e. omitted the liquid [l] in the first word but produced it in the second). OT explains this apparent contradiction in terms of the ranking of constraints in development. The posited constraints operating here and their relative rankings in the adult system are as follows (note that negative constraints – i.e. constraints that work *against* certain productions – are marked with an asterisk *):

(1) MAXIMIZE INPUT–OUTPUT (MAX-IO): a faithfulness constraint that **requires** every segment in the input to have a corresponding output. Thus segments cannot be deleted (see Table 2.1)
(2) AVOID LIQUID ONSETS (*L-ONS): a markedness constraint **against** liquid onsets (e.g. /l/ in *love* and /r/ in *run*)
(3) AVOID COMPLEX CLUSTERS (*COMPLEX): a markedness constraint **against** clusters (see Table 2.1)

For the child, the situation is as follows. When the target is [læb], the fact that the faithfulness constraint MAX-IO is ranked above the markedness constraint *L-ONS rules out the deletion of the initial liquid [l]. When the target form is [pliz], the constraint *COMPLEX becomes relevant as follows (see also Table 2.2):

• The markedness constraint *COMPLEX against clusters is the highest ranked (presumably because of the difficulty of producing them).
• Consequently, the faithfulness constraint to observe a match between input and output segments (MAX-IO), which would give [pliz], is violated anyway by all possible outputs in Table 2.2. Thus the correct adult form [pliz] cannot be produced.

Table 2.2 *Constraint ranking for [pliz] in one child's speech (adapted, with permission, from table 40 in Kager et al., 2004, which is in turn based on Gnanadesikan, 2004)*

Input: /pliz/	Constraints	Markedness: no complex clusters *COMPLEX	Faithfulness: input segments match output segments MAX-IO	Markedness: no liquid onsets *L-ON
Possible outputs				
pliz		*! Ruled out because highest ranked constraint		
iz			**! Missing 2 segments	
liz			* Missing 1 segment	*! Liquid onset
☞ piz			* Missing 1 segment	

- The solution [iz] (i.e. [pliz] with the complex cluster [pl] removed) violates the MAX-IO, segment matching, faithfulness constraint twice, as both [p] and [l] are missing.
- The next possibility is [liz]. This constitutes only one violation of the faithfulness constraint (all that is missing is [p]) but also one violation of the higher-ranked constraint against liquid onsets (*L-ONS).
- The next possibility is [piz]. This does not violate either the no complex clusters constraint (top ranked) nor the no liquid onsets constraint (*L-ONS – second ranked). This form does constitute one violation of the faithfulness constraint (MAX-IO) since [l] is missing. However, since this is the lowest number of violations associated with any of the possible outputs considered, this form 'wins' and so is produced (shown as ☞ in Table 2.2).
- The 'adult' target [pliz] will be produced when the child reranks the markedness constraint against complex clusters so that it is lower than the faithfulness constraint.

There are a number of potentially problematic points to note about the original versions of OT. First, and most importantly, there is the assumption (embodied in the MAX_IO constraint) that there is a full representation in terms of distinctive features at the segmental level of the adult input (see Section 2.3.1 above). Second, all possible solutions to every ranking of constraints are generated before the one that minimally violates the constraints is chosen. Third, there is the question of how the child deduces the correct ranking of constraints in the language from the adult input, since sometimes the same solution could be reached by a number of different routes. Finally, there may be a problem with the proliferation of constraints as new crosslinguistic, diachronic and developmental data are considered (cf. Blevins, 2004: 217–58).

More recent work within the OT framework has maintained a constraint-based approach but is not necessarily committed to the innateness of the constraints (Kager *et al.*, 2004; Fikkert, 2007). Some approaches see the constraints as grounded in articulatory or acoustic factors, with what is easy to perceive or produce appearing earlier, and faithfulness to phonological categories starting to appear once these have emerged. Another approach, quite close to Pierrehumbert's position, sees constraints as deriving from generalizations over the lexicon rather than necessarily being universal and innate (Fikkert and Levelt, 2008). The difference seems to lie in whether input frequencies (Pierrehumbert, 2003) or generalizations over the child's own lexicon (Zamuner, 2003; Fikkert and Levelt, 2008) underlie the child's productions. As we shall see in subsequent chapters, this contrast between an emphasis on frequency and one on the internal development of the child's system (along a path more or less related to universals) is also fundamental to theoretical divides in the learning of word meanings and of syntax.

2.5.3 Constructivist approaches

A long-standing alternative to explaining the child's production as the result of rules or constraints operating on a representation of the sequence of segments in the adult model has been the **whole-word approach**. Instead of rules operating to segments to produce harmony, metathesis etc. (see Table 2.1), children are trying to produce words with meanings. These have been stored as a whole but in underspecified detail. The child then fits them to individually developed templates. An example comes from appendix C in Vihman (1996: 251). Alice, aged 16 months, developed a *Cæ* (Consonant +[æ]) template. Examples of her productions with this template are [ʔæ] for *apple*, [tæʔ] for *duck*, [mæ̃] for *man*, [næ̃] for *no* and [næ] for *nose*. The templates are formed on the basis of prosodically and phonetically similar word patterns in the adult language and the child's own productions (Waterson, 1971; Macken, 1979). We shall see a related constructivist approach to early multiword utterances in Chapter 6.

Thus constructivist approaches see the phonemic inventory being built up through the development of the lexicon. While it is clearly the case that physical factors and motor skills affect children's production, the issue is whether they 'lie on top of' a pre-specified set of phonological contrasts (as under the generativist approaches discussed in the previous section) or whether these are built up through mutual refinement of both perception and production. The constructivist claim is that the child is initially operating with underspecified whole words. Initially, there are very few of these and they often sound pretty accurate – probably, it is suggested, as a result of selection based on articulatory possibilities, which explains why the first productions of children are often similar both within and across languages. However, children then often seem to 'regress' and to produce words which are 'read through' individual production templates. This results in many of the words produced by a particular child sounding very similar, while there are major individual differences between children, depending on each child's particular inventory of production templates (Braine, 1976; Waterson, 1979; Menn, 1983; Vihman and Velleman, 2000). For instance, in the following examples taken from Vihman and Croft (2007), at 18 months, Waterson's son, P, learning English, had a template with an initial 'optional' stop, followed by a vowel followed by [ʃ]. He produced the following: [byʃ] (*brush*), [diʃ], (*dish*) [iʃ] (*fetch*) [iʃ] or [uʃ] (*fish*) and [uʃ] (*vest*) (Waterson, 1971). Madli, learning Estonian, had a template that started with an 'optional' /p/ or /t/ followed by a vowel and ending with /s/. She produced [is:] (for *isa, issi* 'Daddy'), [as:] (for *kass* 'kitty'), [pis:] (for *piss* 'pee'), [us:] (for *suss* 'slipper'), [tis:] (for *tiss* 'teat') and [us:] for (*uss* 'snake') (Kõrgvee, 2001). Vihman and Croft (2007) summarize the evidence for this position as follows:

- A child can produce sounds that are the same in the adult target differently in different words.
- It is difficult to account for the relationship between the adult target and the child production on a segmental basis.
- A child's words may be more similar to each other than is reflected in the differences between the adult targets.

One of the fundamental ideas in these approaches is that the infants both implicitly select words to produce that match their current vocal patterns and adapt the production of adult targets to vocal patterns that they can produce. Selection is evident in the similarity in the very early lexicons of children learning different languages, and derives from phonetically accessible forms based in articulatory possibilities (e.g. reduplicated syllables of **labials** with **open vowels**, which are produced with the tongue in low position in the mouth, and are used in nearly all languages: *mama, baba*). Vihman and Croft argue that this template of initial words is very similar for children learning different languages, and is difficult to account for on any segmental substitution account.

Subsequently, children develop word templates which reflect not only differences in the languages being learned (for instance, in number of syllables, rhythmic patterning), but also individual differences between children learning the same language. In a study of somewhat later productions, Vihman and Croft (2007) analyse initial consonant omission in children learning five different languages (English, French, Welsh, Estonian and Finnish). They showed that, across languages, between 12 and 24 per cent of the children's *selected* forms were based on adult forms without a consonant onset (i.e. *uh-oh* in English) and that the proportion was roughly similar, independent of the language being learned). However, the proportion of *adapted* words that omitted an onset consonant was similar and roughly the same for the other four languages with English being very much lower at only 4 per cent. So why do children learning English provide so many more onset consonants than children learning the other four languages? Vihman and Croft discuss this in terms of the rhythmic patterns of the languages and how this is manifested. English has a trochaic pattern that manifests itself in a longer and louder first syllable. This is not the case for the other languages, despite the fact that three (Welsh, Finnish and Estonian) are also trochaic (with stress on the initial syllable of the word); French has a dominant iambic pattern, with stress on the final syllable). However, despite being trochaic, other phonetic features of these languages (such as lengthening of the medial consonant in Finnish geminates or long consonants in Welsh stressed syllables) mean that children extend the no-onset pattern to words that have onsets, except in English where the phonetic characteristics of the rhythm and loudness mean that children develop a word template which preserves onset consonants.

The major contribution of this approach to phonological theory is that it also sees the segmental phonological structure of words in the adult system in terms of language-specific phonotactic templates, radically revising the Universal Grammar notions of 'continuity' and 'universality'. In its emphasis on language-specific segment categories, this approach is similar to that of Pierrehumbert, but, interestingly, in its emphasis on child-selected templates, it has some resonance with the more recent versions of constraint-based theoretical approaches outlined above. Even the emphasis on word templates rather than words built up from segments seems to be acknowledged – if not fully accepted – by some constraint-based theorists (Fikkert and Levelt, 2008). However, the strong emphasis on children's own phonemic systems does seem to contrast with their ability to recognize words that differ in sounds that they do not produce. One possible implication is that different representations for production and perception might be a consequence of this approach.

2.5.4   Speech production: conclusion

The different traditions in phonological theory based around the opposition between pregiven rules, categories and constraints, on the one hand, and an emergent phonology based on language use and the language the child is learning, on the other, continue in various ways. However, the strong impression from the literature is that, among researchers who engage with empirical data, there is quite close agreement on a number of fundamental issues. These are as follows:

- Early perceptual sensitivity does not necessarily mean that infants either start with, or develop, a fully segmental phonology in advance of production.
- Acoustic and articulatory factors impose a similar structure across infant utterances in different languages in the earliest stages of perception and production.
- Despite this, infants are sensitive to certain aspects of their ambient language such as its prosodic patterning from birth.
- While some basic contrasts (consonant contrasts and vowel contrasts) and prosodic patterns are perceived in early infancy, more complex contrasts (consonant clusters, the identification of familiar words, pattern extraction) develop.
- The point at which infants connect the sounds they are hearing to communicative function (roughly at 7–9 months) is crucial to the emergence of language-specific phonological contrasts.
- Full adult phonology is very slow to develop – some contrasts are only mastered in late childhood.

2.6 Speech perception, segmentation and production: conclusion

It seems fairly clear that crucial changes take place when children start to connect speech to meaning and to learn words. But this still leaves open the process by which the relationship between perception, production and the phonemic inventory builds up. Most recent discussions point to the necessity of more experiments that test perception and production in the same child – to see whether the distinctions made in perception change in relation to those produced. However, an innate inventory of contrasts seems unlikely given the crosslinguistic data (Mielke, 2008).

Despite widespread assumptions to the contrary, it is not yet clear how children can segment words purely on the basis of transitional probabilities and other cues to which they have been shown to have, or develop, sensitivity to in the first year of life.

As we shall also see in Chapters 5 (Inflection) and 6 (Basic syntax), it seems that generativist approaches will be forced to posit some constructional templates in children's representations. Presumably, in principle, there is no necessary conflict between accepting this and continuing to maintain that children also produce or comprehend speech in terms of a (developing) featural representation with rules or constraints operating upon them. However, it is interesting that there is considerable rapprochement between some versions of OT and templatic approaches, which is certainly not the case for theories of syntactic development.

Summary table 2.3 *Speech production* (☑ = *supports theory*; ☒ = *counts against theory*)

	Generativist approaches		Constructivist approaches
	Generative phonology (e.g. Smith, 1973) Natural phonology (e.g. Stampe, 1979)	Optimality theory (e.g. Prince and Smolensky, 1993; Kager, Pater and Zonneveld, 2004)	Whole-word approach (e.g. Waterson, 1979; Menn, 1983; Vihman and Croft, 2007)
Summary of theory	Production generated by rules or processes operating on full underlying representation in terms of distinctive features.	Production on the basis of competing universal constraints operating on adult segment sequences. Constraints are ranked differently in the child system than in the adult.	Children use their own underspecified vocal patterns and match them to adult input patterns. The phonological inventory is emergent.
Issue/phenomenon			
Rules/processes have to be unlearned/lost as production constraints lessen	☒ Unsatisfactory to have to unlearn rules (Kager *et al.*, 2004; Fikkert and Levelt, 2008).	☑ Constraints are reordered, there are no rules but ☒ Possible proliferation of constraints (Blevins 2004).	Not a problem for this approach (no rules or constraints are posited).
Is there evidence for full adult representations in young infants?	☑ Yes – Smith (1973) reports that his son could produce – supports full adult representation. ☒ Not fully – see right, but ☑ might be due to task demands rather than failure to discriminate on basis of distinctive features (Curtin and Werker, 2007). ☒ Acoustic evidence does not support universal distinctive features (Pierrehumbert, 2003).	☑ Smith (1973) reports that his son could detect differences that he could not	☒ No, 7$\frac{1}{2}$-month-olds familiarized on /dog/ did not detect change to /bawg/ (Jusczyk and Aslin, 1995). ☑ 11-month-olds (Swingley, 2005b) and 16-month-olds (Vihman *et al.*, 2004) could detect some changes (e.g. to onsets but not offsets). ☑ Developmental changes in 'switch task' – infants do not fully succeed on discriminating phonetically similar words until 17 months (Stager and Werker, 1997; Werker *et al.*, 2002).

Do very early productions sound similar across languages?	Yes (Vihman, 1996), but this can be explained as innate unfolding of contrasts between distinctive features (Jakobson, 1941; ☑ universal rules), innate initial universal ranking of constraints (Kager *et al.*, 2004; ☑ Optimality theory) or as arising from limitations of children's anatomy (Vihman and Croft, 2007; ☑ constructivist approach)		
Is there an influence of ambient language on babbling and early words?	☒ Yes (Oller *et al.*, 1975, Vihman *et al.*, 1985; Boysson-Bardies and Vihman, 1991). Does not support universal distinctive features.	☒ Findings in left-hand column do not support an initial universal ranking of constraints.	☑ Results from 'adaptation' of what child can produce to what is heard (Waterson 1971; Macken, 1979).
Are there individual differences between children's word forms?	☒ Yes (Braine 1976; Waterson, 1971; Macken 1979; Menn 1983). Counts against the account as universal rules/processes should produce the same outcome, unless there are differences between children's articulatory capacities (natural phonology; Donegan and Stampe, 1979).	Compatible with the account under the assumption that individual children rank constraints differently (Fikkert and Levelt, 2008).	☑ Patterns derive from the child's selection of adult models and adaptation of them to fit the individual child's word templates (Vihman and Croft, 2007).
Children take many years to develop a full phoneme inventory	Possibly more compatible with an emergent phonology than one based on innate distinctive features.		

In terms of future research, there needs to be a major effort to establish the developments that take place in children's perceptual and productive development when they are exposed to polysynthetic and agglutinative languages in which words are much longer and have meaningful internal structure. We also see computational modelling as essential to working out how different aspects of infant perceptual abilities might combine to aid in segmenting the speech stream into meaningful units such as words and phrases.

3 Learning word meanings

3.1 Introduction

At the same time as they are parsing the continuous speech stream into individual words (Chapter 2), children must learn the meanings of these words. This chapter investigates different proposals for how they do this.

Initially, it may seem as if there is no question to answer. One might imagine that the child's caregiver simply produces a word (e.g. *rabbit*) and points out the object that this word denotes (e.g. a rabbit that is running past). A problem with this account is that such 'teaching' is virtually impossible for word types such as abstract nouns (e.g. *happiness*), non-actional verbs (e.g. *watching*), prepositions (e.g. *in*) and determiners (e.g. *the*) (Tomasello, 2003). Another problem (Quine, 1960) is that if a child's mother (or a speaker attempting to teach his or her own language to a foreign linguist) produces a word (e.g. *gavagai*) as a rabbit runs past, the range of potential meanings is virtually infinite. Of course, *gavagai* could mean *rabbit*, but it could equally mean *leg*, *white*, *furry* (a part or property of the rabbit), *animal*, *rodent*, *Flopsy* (an object name, but at a different level of specificity), *running*, *fleeing*, *chasing* (the action of the rabbit), *pointing*, *looking*, *catch it!* (actions involving the speakers) or even *grass*, *field* or *Today is Tuesday* (something not connected to the rabbit at all).

The debate over learning word meanings is not a generativist–nativist versus constructivist debate of the type that we will encounter in subsequent chapters on grammar: whilst generativist accounts assume that certain knowledge of grammar can be innate, nobody would argue that children can be born knowing word meanings (as, of course, different languages have different words for the same referent). In the domain of word learning, there is instead a three-way debate between **lexical-constraints, social-pragmatic** and **associative-learning** accounts.

Under **lexical-constraints** or **lexical-principles** approaches, children's word learning is guided by a number of 'default assumptions' regarding how words map onto their meanings (e.g. that words are more likely to label objects, e.g. *rabbit*, than properties or actions, e.g. *furry*, *running*). As discussed in more detail below, these accounts are rather equivocal with regard to whether these constraints or principles are innately specified (as is the claim for certain grammatical principles under generativist accounts) and specific to word learning, or acquired, and have their origins in non-linguistic cognition.

Under a **social-pragmatic** account, the child uses cues such as eye-gaze to infer (i) the entity that is the object of the speaker's attention (e.g. the rabbit as opposed to the grass) and (ii) the speaker's intentions towards that entity (e.g. to name it, as opposed to suggesting that it would make a good meal). This approach does not posit any principles that are innate and specific to word learning, though children may learn to behave in accordance with purely *descriptive* pragmatic principles of communication (e.g. they may notice that speakers do not typically use two different words to refer to precisely the same entity). In its rejection of innate, domain-specific constraints, this approach shares close conceptual ties with constructivist accounts of grammar acquisition.

Associative-learning accounts have essentially no parallels in other domains of acquisition research, as nobody would argue that grammar can be learned in this manner. Under this approach, which assumes neither lexical-constraints nor social-pragmatic understanding, the child might associate the word *gavagai* with the rabbit (as opposed to, say, the grass) simply because it is the most salient entity present (e.g. having just run into the scene, it is novel and moving, whilst the grass is old and stationary), at the time that the word is produced.

Having considered the three major theoretical accounts of word learning, we end the chapter by discussing the debate over **syntactic bootstrapping**. This is the claim that children can use the syntax (grammar) of the sentence to learn word meanings. For example, the child may know that the sentence frame *This is a . . .* most likely introduces a noun (e.g. *rabbit*) rather than a verb (e.g. *running*). This claim is compatible with all three theoretical accounts of word learning discussed above. However, because syntactic bootstrapping (at least in its original conceptualization) relies on knowledge of abstract sentence structure, it is generally accorded more importance by researchers who take a generativist rather than a constructivist approach to grammar acquisition. This is because the latter approach assumes that the requisite knowledge of sentence structure is not acquired until relatively late in development (i.e. after the point at which children are already expert word learners).

3.2   The constraints or 'principles' approach

Constraints accounts assume that 'children's word learning is guided by a set of default assumptions or constraints on hypotheses' (Woodward and Markman, 1998: 379). These serve to rule out (or at least, make the child consider unlikely) a number of possible hypotheses with regard to the word's meaning. For example, the **whole-object assumption** would rule out the hypotheses that *gavagai* means *leg* (a part of the rabbit), *furry* or *white* (properties). The claim is not that such constraints can entirely solve the word-learning problem, as a number of possible hypotheses will always remain, but that a handful of constraints can sufficiently restrict the number of hypotheses to allow each to be tested against future observation data.

Is the constraints approach a nativist approach (i.e. does it assume that these constraints are present from birth)? Its proponents are sometimes unclear. For example, Hollich, Hirsh-Pasek, Golinkoff and Bloom (2000: 10) claim that 'The solution [to Quine's problem] rests within the head of the child. The child is predisposed to make certain hypotheses over others about word-meaning.' Yet elsewhere (2000: 17) they claim that 'principles . . . are the *products* of attentional/associationistic factors in early development, which then become the *engines* on subsequent development'. Accordingly, in this section, we present constraints approaches as claiming simply that (at least some) constraints or principles exist in the mind of the child before significant word learning has taken place, whatever their ultimate origin.

3.2.1 The whole object assumption

The **whole-object** (or **object-scope**) **assumption** is that new words name whole objects (e.g. *rabbit*) as opposed to their parts (e.g. *leg*) or properties (e.g. *furry*). Under some versions of the account, it additionally includes the assumption that words 'refer to objects over actions or events' (Hollich *et al.*, 2000: 7) and also over 'spatial relations and other non-objects' (Golinkoff, Mervis and Hirsh-Pasek, 1994; Woodward and Markman, 1998: 380; Hollich *et al.*, 2000).

The classic study demonstrating that children associate new words with whole objects as opposed to parts of objects was conducted by Markman and Wachtel (1988, study 2). Children aged 3;0–4;3 were shown unfamiliar objects (e.g. a lung) and given an unfamiliar (though real) word (e.g. *trachea*) as a label. When asked (for example) 'Which one is the trachea? The whole thing [experimenter circles whole lung] or just this part [points to the trachea]', children chose 'the whole thing' on 80 per cent of trials. Thus it can be argued that children showed a bias or default assumption towards assuming that new words label whole objects as opposed to their parts.

Similar experimental evidence has been used to support the claim that children assume that a new word refers to an object as opposed to a property of that object. For example, in a study by Hall, Waxman and Hurwitz (1993), children (aged 2;2–2;11, $M = 2;7$ and 4;1–4;11, $M = 4;5$) were shown an unfamiliar object made of a distinctive substance. Although the novel word was introduced in a sentence frame more commonly associated with adjectives (properties) than nouns (objects) – e.g. *This is a fep one* – when asked to 'find another one that is fep' children chose an object with the same shape as the first (made from a different substance) over an object made from the same substance as the first (with the same shape). That is, children interpreted 'That's a fep one' as meaning something like *That's a vase* as opposed to *That's a clay one* (see also Soja, Carey and Spelke, 1991), despite the fact that the sentence frame in which the novel word appeared (e.g. *That's a _ one*) typically specifies properties, as opposed to objects (e.g. *That's a clay one; *That's a vase one*). This provides support for the claim that children are predisposed to treat new words as labelling objects, rather than their properties (overruling syntactic bootstrapping information; see Section 3.5).

3.2.2   Mutual exclusivity

If Quine's (1960) linguist had already learned that the word for rabbit in the language under investigation was (for example) *lapin*, a reasonable assumption would be that a native who uttered *gavagai* in the presence of the rabbit was labelling not the rabbit itself (or else he would have said *lapin*) but a part (e.g. *leg*), property (e.g. *white*) action (e.g. *running*) etc. . . . This is the assumption of **mutual exclusivity** (or **novel name–nameless category**) which 'leads children to prefer only one label per object' (Golinkoff *et al.*, 1994; Woodward and Markman, 1998; Hollich *et al.*, 2000).

The study of Markman and Wachtel (1988) discussed above also provides evidence that young children operate with this constraint. Recall that, when given unfamiliar labels (e.g. *trachea*) for unfamiliar objects (e.g. *lung*), children aged 3 and 4 interpreted the novel word as referring to 'the whole thing' (e.g. the entire lung). In a follow-up study, exactly the same procedure was used, except that children were initially taught a name for the unfamiliar object as a whole. For example, during initial training, children were told 'This is a lung. We all have two lungs in our chest and we use them to breathe', and were shown a picture of an entire lung. At test, children were shown the same picture and asked 'Which one is the trachea? The whole thing [experimenter circles whole lung] or just this part [points to the trachea].' According to the mutual-exclusivity assumption, children should reject *trachea* as a second label for the entire lung, and so should assume that the new word refers to something else (e.g. a part of the lung). This prediction was confirmed with children choosing the subpart as the referent for the novel word on 85 per cent of trials. This study therefore provides evidence not only for the mutual-exclusivity assumption, but also for the claim that this assumption overrides the whole-object assumption.

Similar findings were observed in the studies of Carey and Bartlett (1978) and Dockrell and Campbell (1986). In the first, children aged 3;0–3;10 ($M =$ 3;6) were shown two trays – one red and one an olive green colour – and asked to 'give me the chromium tray, not the red tray, the chromium one'. In support of mutual exclusivity, children assumed that *chromium* was not an additional label for 'red', but a label for the as-yet-unknown colour, and correctly handed the experimenter the chromium tray. Although children could succeed at this part of the task without paying attention to the word *chromium* (interpreting the request as 'bring me the tray . . . not the red one'), subsequent testing one week later revealed that most children had indeed learned the word *chromium*, as they were able to choose this colour from an array. In the second, children were simply shown (for example) a cow, a horse and a novel animal and asked to pass the experimenter 'the gombe'. Again, in accordance with mutual exclusivity, children took *gombe* to be a label for the novel item, not a second label for cow or horse.

3.2.3   The taxonomic assumption

Having acquired a word (e.g. *shoe*) and a referent for it (e.g. the child's own shoe), the child must learn to extend this word to other instances of shoes (e.g. her mother's shoe). This is not as simple as it may at first appear. The child must learn that items that are 'of the same kind' may be referred to with the same word, even though (as in this case) they may look very different (e.g. baby booties and a high-heeled shoe). The notion that words extend to (or 'group') items that are *taxonomically related* ('of the same kind') is so central to language that it is hard to imagine that it could be otherwise. In principle, though, it is logically possible that words might, instead, 'group' items that are *thematically* related (e.g. shoes and feet, babies and bottles). According to constraints approaches, children do not do this because they are constrained by the **taxonomic assumption** (or **extendibility**) to extend object labels to members of a class, not to thematically related objects (Golinkoff *et al.*, 1994; Woodward and Markman, 1998; Hollich *et al.*, 2000).

Markman and Hutchinson (1984, experiment 1) introduced children to a puppet who spoke 'puppet talk' (i.e. used novel names for familiar items). Using this procedure, children were taught a new name (e.g. *sud*) for a familiar item (e.g. a police car) and then asked to 'Find another sud that is the same as this sud.' On around 80 per cent of trials, children aged 2;5–3;11 chose a taxonomically related object (e.g. a regular car) over a thematically related object (e.g. a policeman). However, in a condition where children were not given a new word (e.g. they were shown the police car and asked to 'find one the same as this') they selected the thematic match (e.g. the policeman) just as often as the taxonomic match. Various follow-up studies have confirmed that the effect holds when children must form entirely new categories such as 'blob-like things' (e.g. Booth and Waxman, 2002, for children as young as 1;6) but disappears when objects are 'labelled' with a tone (Balaban and Waxman, 1997) or with a different label for each category member (Waxman and Braun, 2005).

There is a certain amount of controversy in the literature over whether these effects are characteristic of a 'shape bias' (i.e. a bias to extend labels to items of the same shape) as opposed to a true taxonomic constraint (e.g. Baldwin, 1992; Imai, Gentner and Uchida, 1994; Golinkoff, Suff-Bailey, Olguin and Ruan, 1995; though see Cimpian and Markman, 2005). There is also some evidence that children form classes of items that have a common function (e.g. 'things that can be used as covers'; Booth and Waxman, 2002). Nevertheless, it certainly seems that children have a tendency to extend labels to items that are 'of the same kind' (however this may be characterized) rather than to items that are thematically related.

3.2.4   Problems for constraints accounts

A problem for constraints accounts is that children seem to frequently violate the proposed constraints. With regard to the whole-object assumption, it has often been pointed out (e.g. Bloom, Tinker and Margulis, 1993; Nelson, Hampson and Shaw, 1993) that children do not seem to have difficulty learning words that refer to parts of objects (e.g. *leg*), actions (e.g. *get*), spatial relations (e.g. *in*) and so on. Indeed, the whole-object assumption would not only hinder the learning of action words such as *get*, but incorrectly predicts that children will make word-class errors (e.g. assuming that *get* is the label of the object received). Neither – in violation of the constraint of mutual exclusivity – do children seem to have difficulty learning that a particular item can, at the same time, be *Fido*, a *dog*, an *animal, he* or *it* (again, the constraint would actively hamper learning), as demonstrated in a number of experimental studies in which children successfully learn multiple names for objects (e.g. Mervis, Golinkoff and Bertrand, 1994; Deak and Maratsos, 1998; Clark and Svaib, 1997).[1] Whilst there is some evidence that, as predicted by the taxonomic assumption, children may overextend noun labels, the data are far from clear (see Box 3.1). Certainly, children do not seem to make the kinds of underextension errors that the assumption would predict (e.g. hearing *it* used to refer to a shoe, and extending this word only to other shoes; Tomasello, 2003).

3.2.5   The developmental lexical principles framework

Partly in response to these problems, Golinkoff *et al.* (1994; see also Hollich *et al.*, 2000) proposed an emergentist coalition model of word learning. Constraints or **lexical principles** are retained, but operate alongside (and may be overridden by) social and attentional cues (see Sections 3.3 and 3.4). A second modification is that at least some principles are explicitly learned rather than innate (Hollich *et al.*, 2000: 17).

However, it is not clear that these modifications satisfactorily address the problems facing constraints/principles accounts. One problem is that some constraints may have to be overridden more often than not (e.g. with regard to the whole-object assumption, it is not the case that the majority of words refer to whole concrete objects; Bloom, 2000). If this were the case, then children could presumably use whatever cue they are using to override the putative constraint (e.g. eye-gaze/salience) to learn words directly. This modification also makes constraints accounts difficult to falsify: any experimental finding that children do not seem to respect a particular constraint does not constitute evidence against the existence of the constraint.

The modification that many important constraints or principles are learned rather than acquired is also problematic. If a 'constraint' is a product of learning, then it is nothing more than a descriptive label that serves no purpose, other than to serve as a mnemonic for the outcome of these factors (Deak, 2000). Suppose that, given the choice, a child prefers to sit on a chair rather than the floor. One *could* say that the child's experience of comfortable chairs and uncomfortable floors has given rise to a 'chair-preference constraint' that explains her behaviour in a subsequent forced-choice test.[2] But the positing of the constraint adds nothing to the explanation: the child has simply learned that chairs are more comfortable than the floor.

Another remaining problem (Deak, 2000) is that, unless there are a virtually infinite number of constraints, they do not in fact significantly narrow the hypothesis space. For example, whilst the whole-object assumption may help the learner to rule out several incorrect hypotheses (e.g. *gavagai* means *leg* or *furry*) there are, in principle, an *infinite* number of incorrect hypotheses, each of which will require a constraint to rule it out. For example, another logically possible hypothesis that the learner might entertain is that *gavagai* means 'rabbit' if it is a Tuesday, and 'dog' if not. Following the logic of the constraints approach, a researcher could posit a 'naming consistency constraint' which specifies that children do not entertain the hypothesis that words change their meanings based on the day of the week, and conduct an experimental study to show that children respect this constraint. Although, of course, this example is intentionally facetious, it is hard to make a convincing argument that a language whose words change their meanings periodically is less feasible than a language that uses the same word to refer to dogs, bones and leads but a different word to refer to different dogs (a possibility that children would apparently consider, were it not ruled out by the taxonomic assumption or similar). Thus, at least if we take Quine (1960) at face value, constraints cannot narrow the hypothesis space. If there are an infinite number of possible hypotheses for a word's meaning, some of which are then ruled out by constraints, there are still an infinite number (infinity minus something is still infinity).

Box 3.1 Controversies in word learning

Note: This section is based largely on Bloom's (2004) chapter 'Myths of word learning'.

(1) **The 'vocabulary spurt'.** Most child language textbooks note that after learning about fifty words, the rate at which children learn new words increases dramatically. This phenomenon, known variously as the *vocabulary spurt*, the *vocabulary burst*, or the *naming explosion* (L. Bloom, 1973; Dromi, 1987; McCarthy, 1954; Nelson, 1974), has been attributed to the 'naming insight' (i.e. the insight that words refer to objects in the world; McShane, 1980), the coming-online of word-learning constraints (Behrend, 1990) and the attainment of adultlike categorization abilities (Gopnik and Meltzoff, 1992). However, for most children, the phenomenon is almost certainly nothing more than a statistical artefact. If a graph is plotted of the rate of cumulative vocabulary (number of words; x-axis) versus the rate of word learning (new words per day; y-axis), there *appears* to be a 'spurt' at around fifty words. However, when Ganger and Brent (2004) used regression analysis to fit curves to the data, they found that the vast majority of children displayed smooth acceleration in the rate of learning, with a mathematical function that included a 'spurt' achieving less accurate coverage of the data.

(2) **Do children learn ten words per day?** On even a conservative estimate of the number of words known by a young adult (say 60,000 at age 17), it is true to say that – *on average* – learners acquire around ten new words per day from 1 year of age. However, this figure is misleading because, as we saw above, the rate of new-word learning is not constant but ever-increasing. Thus between the ages of 1 and 2 years, most children will learn less than one word a day (Fenson *et al.*, 1994), whilst a 17-year-old will learn around 10,000 new words per year, mostly from reading (Nagy and Herman, 1987). The theoretical implication is that there is no need to posit a qualitative change in learning or a specialized word-learning system to account for the 'remarkable' rate at which young children learn words: one could even argue that, given the number of new words to which they are exposed daily, infants' word learning is remarkably slow.

(3) **Children's overextension errors.** Many authors have recorded examples of errors where a child overextends a word to refer to an object that is not, in fact, of the relevant category (e.g. *doggie* to refer to all four-legged animals; Clark, 1973). Other examples (from Bloom, 2004) include *hot* to denote an oven (Macnamara, Cleirigh and Kellaghan, 1972), *sock* to denote a shoe. (Dromi, 1987) and *pee-pee* to denote

an ice-cream cone (Bloom, 2000). However, there is controversy over whether these reflect (a) an immature understanding of word meanings – i.e. the child *actually thinks* that the word for cow is *dog* – (as is usually claimed, or at least implied, in most textbooks) or (b) the child's attempt to communicate her intended meaning as best as possible, using only a small vocabulary (Clark, 1978). Central to this question is the debate over whether such errors are observed in comprehension as well as production (e.g. Thomson and Chapman, 1977; Fremgen and Fay, 1980). In a combined production and comprehension task, Kuczaj (1982) found that, when asked to choose all the exemplars of an item (e.g. *doggie*) from an array, children always first chose the correct item, before sometimes selecting an item to which they had overextended this word in production (e.g. *cow*), but rarely selecting an unrelated item (e.g. *ball*). This suggests a prototype structure to children's word meanings: children know that the 'best' referent for *doggie* is a dog, but at the same time will apply this term more broadly, even in comprehension.

(4) **Is there a dedicated system for word learning?** Children acquire word meanings from only a few incidental exposures and with few apparent errors, yet retain this knowledge over a long period of time. The claim is that such (apparently) effortless, rapid and error-free learning is possible only with the aid of a dedicated **fast-mapping** system for word learning (Carey and Bartlett, 1978). In a challenge to this claim, Markson and Bloom (1997) showed that children could 'fast-map' not only a novel word, but also a novel fact. After a one-month delay, children aged 3–4 were equally able to select (from a choice of ten objects) the one that they had been told was called a *koba* (novel word condition) or the one about which the experimenter had said 'my uncle gave that to me'. Whilst the debate continues (Waxman and Booth, 2000, 2001; Bloom and Markson, 2001), Markson and Bloom's (1997) finding suggests that it makes little sense to posit a dedicated system for every aspect of language learning for which children are – by some arbitrary criterion – 'impressive'.

(5) **Do nouns have an advantage over verbs in early word learning?** This is a popular claim, but one that would seem to be trivially true in its weak form, yet false in its strong form. The idea is that nouns pick out 'cohesive packages [such as] concrete objects and individuals' (Gentner, 1982: 324), whereas verbs and other relational terms 'have a less transparent relation to the perceptual world' (p. 328). Certainly, for noun–verb pairs for which this is true (e.g. *ball* vs *think*) the noun will be easier to learn than the verb. Yet it is easy to think of noun–verb pairs for which the verb is more concrete and hence easier to learn (e.g. *situation* vs *eat*). Thus a strong form of the claim (all nouns are easier to learn

than verbs) is untrue, whilst a weaker form – that it is easier to learn the meaning of words that have more transparent meanings – is trivially true. Although the 'noun-bias' is often presented as a fact in textbooks (and research articles), the empirical support for the claim is actually rather weak. It is true that many studies have shown that nouns outnumber verbs in children's early vocabularies (e.g. Au, Dapretto and Song, 1994; Gentner and Boroditsky, 2001; though even this does not seem to be true across all languages; see Gopnik and Choi, 1995; Tardif, 1996; Childers, Vaughan and Burquest, 2007; Brown, 1998; de Léon, 1999), but many do not correct for the simple fact that most parental checklists (the most commonly used measure) list more nouns than verbs. However, nobody seems to have considered the fact that nouns outnumber verbs in the adult language (at least in the *Oxford English Dictionary*; see Ambridge, 2009) by almost exactly the same ratio (5:1) that is taken as evidence for a noun-bias in children (e.g. by Gentner, 2006). Presumably, languages simply 'need' more different nouns than verbs. Consider a simple action such as *giving*. There are only a few different ways in which one can *give*, and hence only a few alternative verbs (e.g. *donate, bequeath, proffer*). On the other hand, the number of different things that one can give (e.g. *money, advice, a cake*) is virtually infinite.

Most experimental studies that have compared the success of teaching novel nouns and verbs to children find a noun advantage (e.g. Leonard, Schwartz, Morris and Chapman, 1981; Schwartz and Leonard, 1984; Childers and Tomasello, 2002; Grassmann and Tomasello, 2007; though see Oviatt, 1980). However, because these studies look only at *object* nouns (and *action* verbs), they provide evidence only for the weak (and perhaps trivial) version of the claim discussed above.

3.3   The social-pragmatic approach

The central claim of the social-pragmatic approach (e.g. Bruner, 1978; Nelson, 1985; Clark, 1993; Tomasello, 2003) is that 'the process of word learning is constrained by the child's general understanding of what is going on in the situation in which she hears a new word' (Tomasello and Akhtar, 2000: 5). Returning to Quine's (1960) *gavagai* example, if the child and the speaker are sharing **joint attention** to the rabbit (i.e. both are attending to the rabbit, and know that the other is doing so), the child will know that the new word refers to at least something to do with the rabbit (e.g. as opposed to the grass). Suppose now that the child understands the **communicative intention** of the speaker (i.e. what the speaker is trying to accomplish with her utterance). If the intention is to prompt the child to catch the rabbit, then *gavagai* probably means 'catch it!'. If it is to label the object for the child (as part of a familiar 'naming game' played by many Western parents), then *gavagai* probably means rabbit. (In fact, Quine himself acknowledged that, in a real-life situation, the learner in his parable would also be able to make use of such social-pragmatic cues). Proponents of the social-pragmatic approach argue that the advantage of this approach over constraints approaches is that there is independent evidence for the prerequisite skills of sharing **joint attention** and understanding others' **intentions** from studies of non-linguistic learning; the type of evidence that cannot, in principle, exist for purely lexical constraints (e.g. the whole object assumption).

Other researchers adopting a social-pragmatic approach (e.g. Clark, 1993; Bloom, 2000; Diesendruck and Markson, 2001; Diesendruck, 2005) have argued that children make use of the pragmatic principles of **conventional- ity** – the assumption that for many meanings there is a conventional form that is agreed upon by all speakers in a particular community – and **contrast**: the assumption that any difference in form reflects a difference in meaning. Whilst these may look similar to the lexical principles outlined in Section 3.2 (in par- ticular, *contrast* appears very similar to *mutual exclusivity*), the claim – as we will see below – is that these pragmatic principles rely on an understanding of speakers' communicative intentions. A number of researchers (e.g. Clark and Grossman, 1998; Bloom, 2000) have also emphasized the importance of the **pragmatic directions** (e.g. phrases such as *looks like*, *part of* and *is a kind of*) that adults often use to provide children with information regarding word meanings.

3.3.1   *Joint attention in word learning*

A large-scale longitudinal study conducted by Carpenter, Nagell and Tomasello (1998) found a correlation between the amount of time spent by mothers engag- ing in joint attention with their children (as coded from videos by independent observers) and the level of children's word comprehension up to a year later. Childers, Vaughan and Burquest (2007) report similar findings from a study of children learning the Nigerian language Ngas. However, a shortcoming of these studies is that they do not control for confounding variables (variables which may be correlated with both joint attention and children's comprehension), such as the caregivers' interest in promoting their children's language development. Social-economic status is another confounding variable that, ideally, should be controlled for, though each of these studies was conducted within a relatively homogeneous group.

The classic experimental study of joint attention in word learning was con- ducted by Baldwin (1993a; see also Baldwin, 1991, 1993b; Baldwin *et al.*, 1996). In this study, children were first shown two toys, then were given one to play with whilst the experimenter held the other. In one condition, the experimenter established joint attention with the child to the toy that the child was playing with, before labelling it (e.g. *It's a toma*). In a 'discrepant labelling' condition (with different children), the experimenter looked at her own toy when producing the object label (having ensured that the child was attending not to the experimenter's toy, but to her own). If children learn words simply by pairing a label with the item that they are attending to when they hear that label (i.e. on the basis of **temporal contiguity**), children in the discrepant labelling condition would incorrectly assume that their own toy (as opposed to the experimenter's) was the *toma*. However, if they understand joint attention (i.e. that adults use words to share attention to some entity with them) children in this condition would not assume that their own toy was the *toma* (they would assume, by process of elimination, that the experimenter's toy was the *toma*).

In a test phrase, children were shown both toys and asked questions such as 'where's the toma?' In the joint-attention condition, children correctly chose their own toy as the *toma* significantly more often than would be expected by chance at 1;4–1;5 and 1;6–1;7, but not at 1;2–1;3. In the discrepant-labelling condition, the youngest group were significantly below-chance (i.e. they incorrectly selected their own item as the *toma*, despite the fact that the experimenter had been playing with a different toy when she produced the label). The group aged 1;4–1;5 were at chance, perhaps indicating that they understood enough about joint attention to block the learning of an incorrect label (if not to infer the correct label). The oldest children (1;6–1;7) were significantly above chance, choosing the experimenter's toy as the *toma* on 77 per cent of trials.

One possible objection is that the children who succeeded at this task looked up and saw the experimenter's toy when they heard the novel label. Thus it is not clear that a 'temporal contiguity' account (children attach the label to the item that is presented as close as possible in time) cannot explain children's success. In a modified version of the study (Baldwin, 1993b: study 1) two toys were hidden in separate opaque buckets. The experimenter then looked into one and said 'there's a modi in here' before giving the child the toy from the *other* bucket. Nevertheless, children (aged 1;7–1;8) knew that the *modi* was the toy that the experimenter was looking at when she produced the word, not the first toy that the child saw after hearing the word.

Another possible objection is that children may be using the speaker's behaviour or gaze to focus *their own* attention onto a particular object, not to make inferences regarding the speaker's attentional focus. If this is the case, then children could succeed at the task by pairing the novel label with the item that was most 'active' in their own attentional focus without understanding 'joint attention' (i.e. that speakers use words to share attention to an entity). In a modified version of the last study discussed, Baldwin (1993b: study 2) had the experimenter attract the child's attention to one of the buckets by adjusting its lid (without looking at it) before producing the novel label. Although children did focus their attention on this bucket, they did not assume that the item contained within was the *modi*, performing at chance levels. Another study (Moore, Angelopoulos and Bennett, 1999) showed that children aged 2;0 associated a novel label with a toy that the speaker who produced the label was looking at, even if their attention was directed to another toy that was lit up and spinning around (children aged 1;6 learned neither the correct nor the incorrect mapping).

The authors of the studies discussed above interpret their findings as demonstrating that children use an adult's eye-gaze not simply to focus their own attention, but to make inferences about which entity the adult is attempting to share joint attention to (and hence is labelling). One possible objection to this conclusion is that children may have simply noted that adopting the assumption that 'the best candidate for a referent is the item that the speaker's eyes are pointing at when she produces the word' produces relatively stable word–item pairings (or at least better pairings than selecting a referent at random). On this account, children would be using eye-gaze not to make inferences about joint attention, but simply as a cue in associative learning.

Evidence against this view comes from studies which show that children know that an adult label refers to the object to which the adult and child are both *thinking about*, even if it is not visible. In the studies of Akhtar and Tomasello (1996: study 1) and Tomasello, Strosberg and Akhtar (1996: study 2), children (aged 2;0 and 1;6 respectively) first watched several rounds of a finding game where an experimenter retrieved a different novel toy (none of which were labelled) from each of four hiding places (one of which was a toy barn). The experimenter then said 'let's find the toma' and attempted to open the toy barn; but the barn turned out to be locked, so the toy was never retrieved. At both ages, children were able to select the *toma* as often as children who had seen it successfully retrieved. Similar results were found in an analogous study (with children aged 2;0) in which the novel word labelled a novel action, as opposed to an object (Akhtar and Tomasello, 1996: study 2). That is, children knew that the novel word (*meeking*) referred to an action that the experimenter *had in mind* when she produced the word (having demonstrated it previously), though it was never subsequently performed. Indeed, it would seem likely that most verb learning takes place in this kind of scenario. In a diary study, Tomasello and Kruger (1992) found that 70 per cent of the mother's verb uses referred to past or future rather than ongoing events.

There is also some evidence that children know that adults' attention is captured by (and hence their utterances most likely refer to) objects that are new to them (even if they are not new to the child), even when eye-gaze cannot be used as a cue. In the study of Akhtar, Carpenter and Tomasello (1996: study 2), children (aged 2;0) played with three novel objects with their mother and two experimenters. The mother and one experimenter then left the room, whilst the child and the remaining experimenter played with a fourth novel object. The mother and experimenter then returned to the room and said (for example) 'Look, I see a modi!' (or in a control condition simply 'Look at that!'), whilst looking in the general direction of all four objects. When asked to 'show me the modi', 10 out of 24 children in the experimental condition (as opposed to only 4 in the control condition) were able to select the item that had been new for the speaker, though not for the child.[3] Interestingly, an older study (Tomasello and Akhtar, 1995: study 1) demonstrated that children would interpret a novel word as referring either to a novel item or a novel action, depending on which was new for the speaker (though, in this case, new for the child as well).

3.3.2   Joint attention in non-linguistic contexts (origins of joint attention)

An important claim of the social-pragmatic approach is that joint attention is important not only for word learning, but for all kinds of cultural learning. One non-linguistic study (Liszkowski et al., 2004) investigated infants' (aged 1;0) own attempts to establish joint attention to an outside entity with an adult. In this study, a series of brightly coloured puppets appeared behind windows. Infants who pointed towards the puppets did not appear to be satisfied (i.e. they repeated the points) if an adult oriented her attention either solely to the puppet (looking at it silently) or solely to the child (e.g. saying 'Oh, I see you are in a good mood!'). Children were satisfied (producing a single point of longer duration) when the adult shared attention to the puppet with them, alternating her gaze[4] between the child and the puppet making relevant comments (e.g. 'Oh wow! What's that?').

Studies have been designed specifically to test the claim of the social-pragmatic approach that the strategies that children seem to be using in word-learning studies (whether or not they are described as 'constraints') have their roots in non-linguistic social cognition. First, Tomasello and Haberl (2003) conducted a non-linguistic version of the study of Akhtar et al. (1996). In this previous study, children inferred that a label produced by an adult most likely referred to an item that was new to her (though not the child) in the context of the experiment. In Tomasello and Haberl's (2003) study, a returning experimenter (who had left the room before the toy was brought out) did not ask for the toy by name, but simply said 'Wow! Look at that . . . Give it to me please!' The children (aged 1;6) were able to infer that the experimenter would be excited about the item that she had not seen.

Moll, Koring, Carpenter and Tomasello (2006) used the findings from a similar study to argue that the proposed linguistic constraints of 'mutual exclusivity' and the 'whole-object assumption' are best understood as non-linguistic strategies. Echoing the findings of Markman and Wachtel (1988: study 2), children aged 1;2 and older inferred that a speaker's utterance referred to the whole toy when she had not previously encountered the toy (in line with the whole-object assumption) and to a specific part of the toy (or to a different toy entirely) when she had (in line with mutual exclusivity). The twist is that in the study of Moll *et al.* (2006), the experimenter did not name the toy (simply saying 'Oh great! Look!'), meaning that no word-learning constraint could be operational (see also Moll and Tomasello, 2007; Moll, Carpenter and Tomasello, 2007; Grassman, Stracke and Tomasello, 2009).

These findings support the view that the principle of mutual exclusivity has its roots in non-linguistic pragmatic understanding. In fact, this assumption is also shared by current constraints-based approaches (e.g. Hollich *et al.*, 2000): The disagreement is whether positing linguistic constraints adds anything to the explanation, with proponents of the social-pragmatic approach arguing that it does not (e.g. see Tomasello and Akhtar, 1995: 221).

3.3.3   Understanding the speaker's communicative intentions in word learning

Returning, again, to Quine's (1960) *gavagai* example, whilst the ability to establish joint attention may be sufficient to infer that the word means *something* to do with the rabbit, to understand precisely what (e.g. 'rabbit', 'catch it!'), it is necessary – according to the social-pragmatic approach – to understand the communicative intention of the speaker.

One study (Tomasello and Akhtar, 1995) placed children in a situation that maps fairly directly onto Quine's (1960) parable, in that they had to decide whether a novel utterance labelled an object (e.g. 'rabbit') or requested an action (e.g. 'catch it!'). Children (aged 2;3) were familiarized with a game in which a spinning action was performed with a novel toy on a turntable. The novel utterance – chosen to be ambiguous between an object label (*widget*) and a request for a action (*widge it!*) – was produced in identical form (e.g. *Widget, Jason. Widget!*) in two different conditions: In an 'action-highlighted' condition, the experimenter readied the turntable for the action, placed the toy on it and alternated her gaze between the child and the apparatus. In an 'object-highlighted' condition, the experimenter picked up the toy and alternated her gaze between the child and the toy.

In a test phase, the experimenter simply asked the child 'can you show me widget': The question was whether the child would demonstrate the novel action or pick up the novel toy. As predicted, 9 out of 12 children in the 'action-highlighted' condition performed the novel action (seven of these with a different novel toy) whilst 7 out of 12 in the 'object-highlighted' condition showed the novel toy to the experimenter). This provides support for the claim of the social-pragmatic approach that the child can solve Quine's (1960) conundrum by inferring whether the communicative intention of the speaker is to label an item, request an action, express annoyance etc.

A possible objection to this conclusion is that children in the 'action-highlighted' condition may have interpreted *widget* as an object name referring to the apparatus used to perform the action. The authors argue against this possibility on the grounds that – despite previously seeing the apparatus used to perform a different action – children in the action-highlighted condition never performed this alternative action (or simply held up the apparatus) when asked to 'widget'.

Although this seems plausible, it is always difficult to make inferences regarding what children will and will not do if they do not understand an experimental task. Future studies should therefore aim to test this possibility more directly, and to investigate whether (as predicted) children are able to use their understanding of communicative intentions to match a novel word with the correct referent when many are possible (e.g. an object label, a request for action, a greeting, an expletive etc.).

3.3.4   *Prerequisites for understanding speakers' communicative intentions*

In a number of word-learning studies, children seem to use both their understanding of a speaker's *communicative* intentions, and her intentions more generally. For example, Tomasello and Barton (1994, study 4) had an experimenter announce her intention to 'find the toma'. In the crucial condition, the experimenter initially examined and frowned at two novel toys (producing no language) before picking up a third with a gasp and a 'wide-eyed' expression. In a test phase, children (aged 2;0) were asked by the experimenter to 'give me the toma', and given a choice of five objects (all of which they had seen before). Ten out of the fifteen children in this condition were able to correctly identify the *toma* even though two other toys had been presented in the period between hearing the label and seeing the target toy. Tomasello *et al.* (1996: study 1) replicated this finding for children aged 1;6. Tomasello and Barton (1994: study 3) conducted a similar study with action as opposed to object labels. Children (aged 2;2) imitated an action that the experimenter marked as deliberate ('there!'), but not one that she marked as accidental ('whoops!'), even though the accidental action was performed immediately after the label ('I'm gonna meek Big Bird').

If, as the account claims, understanding others' intentions is a prerequisite for word learning, children should demonstrate this ability outside a word-learning context. Carpenter, Akhtar and Tomasello (1998) found that children aged 1;2 and above imitated deliberate actions ('there!') twice as often as accidental actions ('whoops!'), even though neither were named (a 'non-word-learning' version of the study of Tomasello and Barton, 1994). Similar findings are observed when the experimenter uses no relevant language at all. When asked to imitate a task such as making a toy mouse go into a house (Carpenter, Call and Tomasello, 2005) or turning on a light switch (Gergely, Bekkering and Király, 2002), children (aged 1;0–1;2) imitate the 'goal' or end result (i.e. the mouse arriving at the house, or the light illuminating), not the means by which it was achieved (e.g. the mouse sliding across the mat, or the experimenter pressing the switch with his head because his hands were full). Similar findings with slightly older children were reported by Meltzoff (1995) and Bellagamba and Tomasello (1999). The study which demonstrates the earliest understanding of adults' intentions is perhaps that of Behne, Carpenter, Call and Tomasello (2005). Children aged 0;9 became frustrated and upset when the experimenter refused (i.e. was able but unwilling) to pass them toys, but not when she was unable to do so (e.g. because she could not reach). However, a younger group aged 0;6 did not differentiate.

Finally, a number of studies have investigated children's understanding of adults' intentions behind a special form of non-linguistic (though certainly communicative) behaviour: pointing. Perhaps surprisingly (given that children themselves point at a younger age), children aged 1;2 were able to choose the correct location of a hidden toy (from a choice of two) when an adult pointed towards it on only 64 per cent of trials (though this is better than chance as a group, only 7 per cent of children met this criterion individually).[5] However, when children do succeed at this task, they seem to do so by understanding the communicative intention behind pointing ('the object that you want is there'), as opposed to by merely following the direction of the hand: children aged 1;6 were able to choose the correct location of a hidden toy to which the experimenter pointed (from a choice of two) when the experimenter alternated her gaze between the container and the child whilst pointing, but not when she gazed blankly whilst pointing (Behne, Carpenter and Tomasello, 2005). This conclusion is supported by the findings of a study showing that children aged 1;0 will point to inform the experimenter of the location of an item that she has lost, even when the item is uninteresting to the children (e.g. a hole punch) and a more attractive toy is present (Liszkowski, Carpenter, Striano and Tomasello, 2006).

3.3.5 *Pragmatic principles and pragmatic directions*

Clark (1988: 319) defines the pragmatic principles of **conventionality** and **contrast** as follows:

For certain meanings, there is a **conventional** form that speakers expect to be used in the language community, that is, if one does not use the conventional form that might have been expected, it is because one has some other, **contrasting** meaning in mind.

At first glance, this may appear very similar to the lexical principle of **mutual exclusivity** (or **novel name-nameless category**) which 'leads children to prefer only one label per object' (Golinkoff *et al.*, 1994; Woodward and Markman, 1998; Hollich *et al.*, 2000). However, there are a number of important differences. First, because the proposal makes reference to *meanings* as opposed to *objects*, it does not incorrectly predict that children should have difficulty in referring to the same entity as (for example) *dog* and *Fido*. Mutual exclusivity conceptualizes *dog* and *Fido* as different labels for a single *object*, meaning that children should show at least some difficulty learning both. Under Clark's (1988) formulation, the two words have different *meanings* – *dog* refers to dogs in general (e.g. as opposed to cats), whereas *Fido* refers to my pet dog (e.g. as opposed to somebody else's) – even though they can both be used to refer to the same entity. Thus if the speaker refers to a dog not by using the conventional form *dog* but another form, *Fido*, instead, it is because she has a contrasting meaning in mind (not dogs in general but my dog). Another way in which conventionality and contrast are different to mutual exclusivity (at least in its original formulation) is that the former are explicitly claimed to be learned:

Presumably, early on in development, children realize that certain forms are more frequently used to express certain meanings [and] that many speakers use that same form. (Diesendruck, 2005: 452)

A third difference between contrast and mutual exclusivity is that the former requires some understanding of the **communicative intention** of the speaker (e.g. 'the speaker must have said *Fido* instead of *dog* because **her intention** is to refer to this entity as her dog in particular, and not as a member of the dog species in general'). In contrast, a learner could apply the principle of mutual exclusivity without any understanding of the speaker's intention (e.g. 'I already have a word for cow, so *gombe* must label this other animal'). Thus the evidence for children's understanding of the communicative intentions of others reviewed above constitutes support for the pragmatic principles over the lexical principles approach.

Finally, and relatedly, the principle of contrast (like the understanding of others' intentions) is argued to apply to general acts of reference (e.g. stating a fact about an object) as opposed simply to naming. Mutual exclusivity (or novel name–nameless category) is a lexical principle, and hence (at least in its strong form) applies only to word learning.

This point is illustrated by a study conducted by Diesendruck and Markson (2001: experiment 1). Children aged 3;1–4;1 ($M = 3;6$) were shown two unfamiliar objects and taught the name (e.g. *mef*) for one. When asked (for example) 'Can you give me the wug?', children overwhelmingly (82 per cent of trials) selected the previously unlabelled object, as predicted by both the mutual exclusivity and contrast approaches. In another condition, children were shown two unfamiliar objects, and told an arbitrary fact about one (e.g. 'This is from Mexico'). The experimenter then asked (for example) 'Can you give me the one that my dog likes to play with?' Children overwhelmingly (73 per cent of trials) selected the object about which no fact had previously been given (though there is no reason, in principle, why the two facts could not be true of a single object). Mutual exclusivity, as a proposal about word learning, cannot explain this finding (note that children in the 'fact' condition were never taught the names of the objects). Rather, children seem to be using the principle of contrast – operating over facts as opposed to words – to reason about the communicative intentions of the experimenter (e.g. 'She knows that I know that Object A is from Mexico, so if she wanted Object A she would have asked for the one from Mexico. Therefore she must want Object B').

Evidence that children were, in fact, engaging in such reasoning was provided by a follow-up control study (experiment 3). This followed the same procedure as the 'fact' condition of experiment 1, except that a new speaker (a puppet who had been absent when the first fact – e.g. *This is from Mexico* – was given about Object A) made the request (e.g. 'Can you give me the one that my dog likes to play with?'). Because this speaker was absent when the first fact was given, the contrastive reasoning process outlined above cannot be followed. Accordingly, children chose at random (Objects A and B were chosen on exactly 50 per cent of trials each).

These studies provide evidence for the pragmatic principle of contrast, but do not investigate knowledge of conventionality; the principle that many meanings have a conventional form used by all speakers of a particular language community (e.g. *dog* for the meaning of 'generic dog'). Diesendruck (2005: experiment 1) investigated whether children (aged 3;5–5;0, $M = 4$;5) behave in accordance with this principle. The experimenter taught children either a common noun (e.g. 'This is the teega. Teegas are like this. Have you ever seen teegas?') or a proper noun (e.g. 'Here's Teega. His name is Teega. He's called Teega') to label one of two novel creatures present (Character A). In the test phase, a puppet who had been absent when Character A was labelled requested a character using a new novel word (e.g. *melloo*), presented either as a proper noun (e.g. 'Can you show me Melloo?') – for children who had learned *teega* as a common noun – or a common noun (e.g. 'Can you show me the melloo?') – for children who had learned *Teega* as a proper noun (i.e. a switch design was used).

Children who had heard Character A introduced as *a teega* (common-noun condition) handed the puppet Character B (at above-chance levels) when he asked to see *Melloo*. Presumably, they reasoned as follows: 'The puppet – as a member of the speech community – knows that Character A is a teega. So if he had wanted Character A, he would have used that word.' However, children who had heard Character A introduced as *Teega* (proper-noun condition) selected at random when the puppet asked for *the melloo*. Presumably, they reasoned as follows: 'The puppet does not (or may not) know the name of Character A. So when he asked for *the melloo*, he could equally well have been referring to Character A (using the species name because he does not know the individual's name) or Character B.' In other words, children appear to know that common nouns (e.g. *dog*) are conventional (i.e. all speakers know them), whilst proper nouns (e.g. *Fido*) are not (i.e. only speakers who have heard the dog introduced as *Fido* know this name). Thus this study provides strong evidence that children are in possession of the principle of conventionality, as well as contrast.

Clark (1993) emphasizes the importance of what she terms **pragmatic directions** in word learning. In many cultures, when talking to children, caregivers will explicitly set out the relationship between words using phrases such as *looks like*, *part of* and *is a kind of*. These are presumably very useful for learners. For example, without pragmatic directions, if a child were to hear the word *animal* used to refer to a cat and *dog* to refer to a dog, she may incorrectly assume that the word *animal* is the basic-level term for 'cat' (in the same way that *dog* is the basic-level word for 'dog'). On the other hand, if the child were to hear a caregiver say 'a dog *is a kind of* animal', and correctly interpret this statement, she should be able to subsequently refer correctly to both cats and dogs as *animals*.

Clark and Grossman (1998) conducted a study designed to investigate whether young children are able to make use of the information provided by the phrase *is a kind of*. Children aged 2;0–2;6 ($M = 2;2$) were taught a novel label (e.g. these are *ruks*) to refer to the members of a set of items (e.g. plastic cups). Children were then taught another novel label (e.g. these are *dobs*) for a second set of similar, but different, items (e.g. plastic shuttlecocks),with the experimenter providing, just once, the pragmatic direction 'a dob is a kind of ruk'. At test, children were shown all the items (and various distracter items) and asked to identify the *ruks*. The majority of the children tested (11 out of 18) correctly identified all of the cups and shuttlecocks as *ruks*, but picked out only the shuttlecocks when asked for the *dobs*. In another condition, many children who were taught a novel label for an item (e.g. *ruk* for a plastic cup), which the experimenter then retracted (e.g. 'Oh, I was wrong. That's not a ruk, it's a dob') were able to learn that the terms *ruk* and *dob* are mutually exclusive (though children found this type of learning more difficult, presumably due to the uncertainty caused by the experimenter's 'mistake').

Nevertheless, whilst this study demonstrates that children are able to make use of the pragmatic directions provided by caregivers, it seems unlikely that they play a crucial (i.e. necessary) role in word learning for two reasons. The first is that, whilst caregivers in many cultures engage in this type of explicit teaching, many do not, and indeed rarely directly address children at all (Heath, 1983; Schieffelin and Ochs, 1986; Lieven, 1994). There is no reason to believe that children who do not receive this type of teaching do not arrive at an adultlike set of word meanings. The second is that children can only make use of a pragmatic direction such as *is a kind of* once they have learned the meaning of this phrase itself. Presumably, the learning mechanisms that were used to acquire the meaning of this complex and abstract phrase are sufficient to acquire the rather more transparent meanings of words such as *dog* and *animal*. Thus, whilst this type of explicit teaching is no doubt useful for helping older learners to hone their word meanings, it would seem unlikely that it necessary for early word learning to proceed.

3.3.6   Evaluating the social-pragmatic account

One advantage of the social-pragmatic account is that necessary skills – establishing joint attention and reasoning about speakers' intentions – are observed in other domains of learning. Thus the account is more parsimonious, and enjoys more independent support, than lexical-constraints approaches. It is also claimed (e.g. Tomasello, 2003) that this approach offers some account of why word learning seems to begin at around 1;0: it is at this age that the skills of establishing joint attention and understanding others' communicative intentions begin to emerge.

One problem for the account is that, whilst many studies have provided evidence that children understand adults' intentions in non-linguistic domains, only a handful have directly shown that they are able to use their understanding of the speaker's intentions to choose between multiple possible referents for a word (Tomasello and Akhtar, 1995; Diesendruck and Markson, 2001; Diesendruck, 2005). Future studies conducted along similar lines are therefore needed.

A second weakness of the account is that it remains vague with regard to the means by which a whole utterance, of which the child has identified the meaning, is broken up into its component parts. For example, Tomasello (2003) discusses the example of a child hearing 'put your hat on', whilst the mother holds the hat and gestures towards the child. The child understands what the mother is trying to achieve with the utterance (i.e. her communicative intention) and may already know the meaning of some of the words (e.g. *hat*). The idea is that the child can use this knowledge to somehow work out the meaning of the rest of the words in the sentence (e.g. *put*, *your* and *on*). Presumably, the child does this by recognizing differences and similarities behind the meanings of other utterances containing some of the same words (e.g. *take* your hat *off*, *That is* your *hat and that is* his *hat*). However, if the child has to compute these cross-situational distributional regularities anyway, then this at least raises the possibility (discussed in Section 3.4) that this procedure alone might be sufficient for word learning, without the need for social understanding.

Indeed, the final – and greatest – problem facing the social-pragmatic account is evidence that simple associative learning (discussed in Section 3.4) – i.e. the learned pairing of a word (e.g. *gavagai*) and an entity in the world (e.g. a rabbit) – may be sufficient for word learning, with no social-pragmatic under-standing required. This evidence comes from three groups of studies. First, children aged 1 year and older show some evidence of word learning in studies where a novel object displayed on a screen is labelled by a disembodied voice, played over a loudspeaker; a context that is arguably devoid of social cues (e.g. Schafer and Plunkett, 1998; Houston-Price, Plunkett and Harris, 2005; Werker *et al.*, 1998; Smith and Yu, 2008).

Second, as noted in Chapter 2, some studies have shown that children aged 0;6 are able to recognize highly familiar words such as *Mommy* and *Daddy* (Tincoff and Jusczyk, 1999), their own name (Mandel, Jusczyk and Pisoni, 1995) and very common words such as *feet* (Tincoff, 2001). Similarly, infants learning 'baby sign' (see Johnson, Durieux-Smith and Bloom, 2005) are even able to *produce* 'words' (i.e. hand signs) to request food, drink, activities etc. from around the same age. The significance of the age of these children (0;6) is that studies of joint attention and intention reading have found no evi-dence for these skills in children under around 1;0 (indeed, it is not until around this age that children are able to systematically check an adult's gaze; Franco and Butterworth, 1996). Studies illustrating that children can choose between possible referents for a word by reasoning about the speaker's communicative intentions have typically focused on children aged 2 (Tomasello and Akhtar, 1995) or even 3–4 (Diesendruck and Markson, 2001; Diesendruck, 2005). The implication is that whilst word learning is surely facilitated by an understanding of the speaker's communicative intentions, it may well be the case that a good deal of word learning takes place before children acquire this ability, calling into question the claim that it is a prerequisite.

Third, autistic children, who have severely impaired social understanding, arguably do not perform as poorly at word learning at the social-pragmatic account would predict. A replication of the studies of Baldwin (1991, 1993a) found that autistic children made mapping errors on 70 per cent of trials (Baron-Cohen, Baldwin and Crowson, 1997). That is, these children associated the novel word with the object that they – but not the speaker – were looking at, at the time of labelling. However, this high error rate does not seem to be observed in more naturalistic contexts. Although many autistic children speak little or not at all, most who do speak seem to use the correct meanings for most of the words that they use, though we need to know more about the conditions under which these words are learned and used.

3.4   The associative learning approach

The associative learning approach to word learning is sometimes caricatured as a behaviourist approach, under which children learn words by classical conditioning, associating sounds and objects in the same way that Pavlov's dog learned to associate a bell (conditioned stimulus) with food (unconditioned stimulus). Proponents of the approach (e.g. Smith, 2000: 170) argue that this characterization is unfair and that 'classical conditioning is not the only form of associative learning, and it is *not* a candidate model for word learning'. But why? What is the difference between a dog learning the association between a bell and food and a child learning the association between the word *rabbit* and a rabbit in the world (or the thought of one)?

The answer is that the associative learning performed by Pavlov's dog is 'dumb': all that drives the pairing is repeated presentation of the bell and the food. In contrast, children's associative learning is 'smart' in that they can make use of various 'general processes of perceiving, remembering and learning' (Samuelson and Smith, 1998: 95) to infer which of several possible entities a word is paired with. These general processes (which will be defined as we subsequently encounter them) include **context dependency** in **remembering**, **blocking** and **cross-situational analysis** in **learning**, and the **perceptual** phenomenon by which children's visual attention is drawn to stimuli that are **novel** or **salient**.

Thus the claim of the approach is that it is possible to build an associative learning version of each of the alternative explanations [including] the social-pragmatic [and] . . . constraints accounts (Samuelson and Smith, 1998: 95). In this section, we investigate the evidence for this claim.

3.4.1   Associative-learning accounts of 'constraints' and 'social-pragmatic' phenomena

It is not difficult to see how these general learning phenomena can provide alternative accounts of constraints such as mutual exclusivity (the constraint whereby children avoid assigning a novel word to a referent that already has a name, preferring to assign it to a currently nameless object or object-part). Children's **attention** will be drawn to the novel object, meaning that they will be focusing on this object, at the expense of the other, when they hear the name. The general-learning phenomenon of **blocking** will also apply. If a learner (e.g. a dog or a child) has already learned that one cue (e.g. a bell or the word *lung*) is reliably associated with a stimulus (e.g. dinner or a picture of a lung), then it is more difficult to learn that an additional cue (e.g. a buzzer or the word *trachea*) is also associated with that stimulus. Indeed, proponents of modern constraints approach (e.g. Hollich *et al.*, 2000) agree that constraints have their origins in more general principles of associative learning.

It is more difficult to see how an associative-learning explanation can account for experimental findings that have been claimed to support the social-pragmatic approach. Nevertheless, Samuelson and Smith (1998) propose an account of the findings of Akhtar *et al.* (1996: experiment 2) in terms of **context dependency**. This is a phenomenon whereby remembering is most effective when it takes place in the same context as the original learning (e.g. Godden and Baddeley, 1975, showed that divers taught a list of words underwater recalled more words when tested underwater than on land, and vice versa). In the study of Akhtar *et al.* (1996) children inferred that a label produced by an adult most likely referred to an item that was new to her (though not the child) in the context of the experiment (she had left the room before the toy was brought out). This finding was taken as evidence that children know that adults' attention is captured by (and hence their utterances most likely refer to) objects that are new to them.

Samuelson and Smith (1998) argue that, given the phenomenon of context dependency, the object that is new to the speaker is therefore the most new to the child and, hence, will be the item on which the child's attention is focused when she hears the new word: the three distracter objects were presented in the same context (all adults present) during training and test, and hence were well recalled (i.e. seemed old to the child) at test. The target object was presented in a different context during training (two adults missing) and test (all adults present) and hence was less well recalled (i.e. seemed *newer* to the child) at test. In support of this interpretation, Samuelson and Smith (1998) showed that if that one item was presented in a different context to the other three without having anyone leave the room (this object was played with on a different table with a brightly coloured cloth), children still inferred that a new word referred to this item (in fact, children performed slightly better than in Akhtar's original study). The debate around this series of studies continues. Diesendruck, Markson, Akhtar and Reudor (2004) argued that having the child move to a special location to play with one of the toys might cause the child to infer that it is special to the experimenter and hence the toy that she had in mind when producing the novel name. In support of this social-pragmatic interpretation, these authors found that the effect disappeared when the move to the other table was presented as accidental (the experimenter dropped the toy and it rolled to the other table). However, in this study (unlike the previous two) the same 'game' was played with all four objects. Thus, one could argue, in defence of the associative learning account, that the 'context shift' was not sufficiently great to cause the context-dependent remembering effect on which this account hinges.

A different study (Houston-Price, Plunkett and Duffy, 2006) investigated a **salience**-based account of the (apparently) social-pragmatic phenomenon whereby children use joint attention with a speaker to determine the referent of her utterance. We have already met the objection that children may not understand joint attention, but that the speaker's head or eye movements towards an object may increase the salience of, and hence focus the child's *own* attention onto, that object at the time that a new word is presented. We have also discussed a study that provides some evidence against this view. Moore *et al.* (1999) showed that children aged 2;0 associated a novel label with a toy that the speaker who produced the label was looking at, even if a different toy was simultaneously made to light up and spin around (children aged 1;6 learned neither the correct nor the incorrect mapping).

Houston-Price *et al.* (2006) argue that this counts as evidence for the social-pragmatic over the salience-based account *only* if it is assumed that having a speaker look at an object (and ignore another) is less effective in increasing the salience of that object for the child than having it light up and spin around. Perhaps the reverse is true. To test this possibility Houston-Price *et al.* (2006) conducted a modified version of the study where two items were presented on adjacent screens, accompanied by a single word played over a loudspeaker (e.g. *gopper*). When a 'social' cue was presented (a video-recorded face turned towards one item) children associated this item with the novel word (i.e. when they heard *gopper* in subsequent trials with no cue, they looked at this item for significantly over half of the total looking time). However, when a 'salience' cue was presented (one of the items began to move), children associated the novel word with the non-moving item. This is an odd finding, as children were apparently using the salience cue, but not in the way intended.

Whether or not this interpretation is correct, this study suffers from a problem common to all those discussed in this section: any manipulation that is intended to increase the salience of one item over another (e.g. movement, illumination, a change in context) could be construed as an attempt by a (perhaps hidden) speaker to establish joint (conceptual if not visual) attention to that item with the listener. Thus it may never be possible to entirely tease apart salience-based versus social-pragmatic accounts of experimental phenomena.[6]

3.4.2   *Cross-situational learning*

Imagine that a child hears the word *ball* and sees a screen depicting both a bat and a ball. On a second trial, the child again heard the word *ball*, and this time sees a ball and a dog. By keeping track of cross-situational regularities, the

Summary table 3.1 *Learning word meanings* (☑ = *supports theory;* ☒ = *counts against theory*)

	Constraints/principles (nativist?)	Social-pragmatic (constructivist)	Associative learning
Summary of theory / Issue/phenomenon	'Children's word learning is guided by a set of default assumptions or constraints on hypotheses' (Markman and Woodward, 1998: 379).	'The process of word learning is constrained by the child's general understanding of what is going on in the situation in which she hears a new word' (Tomasello and Akhtar, 2000: 5).	Children use 'general processes of perceiving, remembering and learning' (Samuelson and Smith, 1998: 95) to infer which of several possible entities a word is paired with.
Do children assume a new word refers to a whole object as opposed to part or property of the object, actions, etc.?	☑ Yes – findings support whole-object assumption / object-scope (Markman and Wachtel, 1988; Hall *et al.*, 1993; Soja *et al.*, 1991). ☒ No – children easily learn words for parts, properties, actions etc. (e.g. Bloom *et al.*, 1993; Nelson *et al.*, 1993)	☑ Not necessarily – children interpret a novel word as referring to either an object or an action, on the basis of speaker's intentions (request object vs action) or object novelty (Tomasello and Akhtar, 1995).	Not necessarily – children assumed to interpret a novel word as referring to whatever is most salient (object, part, action etc.). We are aware of no studies that have tested this prediction.
Do children preferentially assign a new word to an object that does not yet have a name?	☑ Yes – findings support mutual exclusivity / novel-name nameless category (Markman and Wachtel, 1988; Carey and Bartlett, 1978; Dockrell and Campbell, 1986). ☒ No – children easily learn multiple names for objects (Mervis *et al.*, 1994; Deak and Maratsos, 1998; Clark and Svaib, 1997)	☑ Markman and Watchtel's (1988) whole-object assumption vs mutual exclusivity effect holds if no novel word is given (Moll *et al.*, 2006, 2007; Moll and Tomasello, 2007; Grassman *et al.*, 2009). ☑ Constraint is not necessary as children know that novel word refers to object that is new for the speaker, even if it is not new for the child (Akhtar *et al.*, 1996). ☑ Children know adult's attention drawn to new object, even if no label given (Tomasello and Haberl, 2003).	☑ Akhtar *et al.*'s (1996) finding (below, left) could be explained in terms of context-dependency (Samuelson and Smith, 1998) though Diesendruck *et al.* (2004) counter that children used social-pragmatic cue in Samuelson and Smith's study.

	☑ Effect applies for facts as well as words (Diesendruck and Markson, 2001). ☑ Children take into account whether word is novel to speaker (Diesendruck, 2005).		Not discussed.
Do children extend object labels to members of a class, not to thematically related objects?	☑ Yes – findings support taxonomic assumption / extendibility (Markman and Hutchinson, 1984; Booth and Waxman, 2002), though possibly due to a shape bias (Baldwin, 1992; Golinkoff et al., 1995; Imai et al., 1994; cf. Cimpian and Markman, 2005). ☒ No – some words (e.g. it) extended far more broadly (Tomasello, 2003).	☑ Children use adults' pragmatic directions (e.g. X is a kind of Y) to make inferences regarding word extensions (Clark and Grossman, 1998) but ☒ Pragmatic directions unlikely to be universal (Lieven, 1994; Schieffelin and Ochs, 1986; Heath, 1983).	
Establishing joint attention		NB: Primarily relates to social-pragmatic account, though a role for joint attention is also posited under current lexical-principles accounts. ☑ Evidence for joint attention in word learning (Carpenter et al., 1998; Childers et al., 2007; Baldwin, 1991, 1993a, b; Baldwin et al., 1996; Moore et al., 1999) – even if this is conceptual as opposed to visual (Akhtar and Tomasello, 1996; Tomasello et al., 1996) – and in non-linguistic contexts (Liszkowski et al., 2004; Moll et al. 2006, 2007).	Controversy as to whether ☑ salience cue trumps attentional cue (Houston–Price et al., 2006) or ☒ vice versa (Moore et al., 1999), when the two cues are placed in conflict. ☑ Children can learn some object words in a situation (relatively) devoid of these cues (Schafer and Plunkett, 1998; Houston–Price, Plunkett and Harris, 2005; Werker et al., 1998; Smith and Yu, 2008), and ☑ at an age at which these abilities are yet to emerge (Tincoff and Jusczyk, 1999; Mandel et al., 1995; Tincoff, 2001). Autistic children arguably make fewer mapping errors than one would expect.
Understanding others' (communicative) intentions		NB: Primarily relates to social–pragmatic account, though a role for understanding communicative intentions is also posited under current lexical–principles accounts. ☑ Evidence children use this to choose between possible referents for a novel word (Tomasello and Akhtar, 1995). ☑ Evidence for understanding others' intentions more broadly (Tomasello and Barton, 1994; Tomasello et al., 1996; Carpenter et al., 1998, 2005; Gergely et al., 2002; Meltzoff, 1995; Bellagamba and Tomasello, 1999; Behne et al., 2005; Liszkowski et al., 2006).	

child can learn that *ball* refers to the ball as opposed to the dog or the bat. All accounts of word learning assume some cross-situational learning of this type (it is really the only way in which children can learn words that do not stand in a straightforward relationship with entities in the world; e.g. *the, a, is, on*). The claim of the associative-learning account, however, is that such learning (along with the other general principles discussed above) can obviate the need for constraints or social-pragmatic knowledge.

Smith and Yu (2008) presented children aged 1;0 and 1;2 with a more complicated version of the scenario outlined above. On each of thirty training trials (lasting around four minutes in total) infants saw two novel objects (from a set of six), and heard one of six novel words (e.g. *gasser*) presented in isolation over a loudspeaker. Word-referent pairings were thus always ambiguous *within a given trial*, but, across the training as a whole, only one set of mappings was possible. Learning was assessed using preferential-looking test trials of the same format as the training trials with each novel object appearing twice as the target, and twice as a distracter. Children at both ages looked significantly longer at the target than the distracter.

Of course, one can quibble as to whether children were using *no* social-pragmatic knowledge here (versus knowledge of the conventional 'game' of object naming). Nevertheless, to put this finding in context, it is worth noting that no studies have demonstrated that children aged 1 year can use word-learning constraints (Section 3.2), social cues such as eye gaze (Section 3.3) or, as we will see in Section 3.5, syntactic bootstrapping to learn which of even *two* potential referents a word refers to (as opposed to six in this study). Although there is an issue regarding whether this procedure would scale-up to the much larger task of real-life vocabulary learning, Smith and Yu (2008) found that adults actually performed better with larger training sets, presumably because they provide better evidence against spurious correlations. In a similar, though smaller study, Akhtar and Montague (1999) found that children's ability to perform cross-situational learning (in this case of adjectives) increased between 2;5 (the youngest group tested) and 3–4. These authors speculated (probably incorrectly, in the light of Smith and Yu's result) that cross-situational learning is not available until the later stages of word learning.

Any controversy over distributional learning 'versus' other approaches is surely misplaced, however. Whatever theory of word learning turns out to be correct, some cross-situational learning will – given the way that words 'work' – be required, almost by definition. Consider, for example, how a child could learn the difference between words with similar meanings such *walk, run* and *go*. It is hard to see how this could be done other than by observing a range of different, but similar, situations involving *walking* but not *running*, *going* but neither *walking* nor *running* and so on (i.e. by performing cross-situational learning). Whether or not 'smart' associative learning of this type can obviate the need for constraints or social-pragmatic understanding is a question that we consider at the end of this chapter.

3.5   Syntactic bootstrapping

As we saw above, children aged as young as 1;0 appear to be able to acquire some words (e.g. object words, adjectives) solely by cross-situational learning. However, the **syntactic bootstrapping hypothesis** arose in response to the claim that it is impossible *in principle* to learn the meanings of certain items – in particular certain verbs – from cross-situational learning alone (Landau and Gleitman, 1985; Gleitman, 1990).

First, some verbs differ in meaning only on the perspective they take on events. For example, any event of *fleeing* is also an event of *chasing*; so a child could never learn which of these two meanings was associated with a verb used to describe a *chasing/fleeing* event. Other verbs describe the same event at different levels of specificity. For example, a child would have difficulty learning the difference between *seeing* and *looking*, as any event that involves the former also involves the latter. Also claimed to be problematic for cross-situational learning are verbs that do not refer to observable events at all (e.g. *think, know*; though this criticism seems a little odd, as distributional learning can presumably work over pairings of words and *abstract* entities or events, as well as concrete ones). These difficulties are compounded by the fact that caregivers rarely use verbs to describe ongoing events (Lederer, Gleitman and Gleitman, 1995), but more often to request that the child performs some action (though again, this problem may not be insurmountable as long as the child has the relevant action *in mind*).

As an experimental demonstration that cross-situational observation will not suffice for verb learning, Gillette, Gleitman, Gleitman and Lederer (1999) conducted a 'simulation' of vocabulary learning with adults. Participants watched videos of parent–child interactions with no soundtrack and had to guess which verb (or, as a comparison, noun) was being used by the mother at certain points in the interaction. Only 15 per cent of verbs were correctly identified, as opposed to 45 per cent of nouns.

3.5.1   What is syntactic bootstrapping?[7]

Consider the sentence *He blicked him*. Although this sentence does not convey much information, adult speakers of English are able to infer that *blick* is most likely an action that one entity performs on another (e.g. it might mean something like *hit*) as opposed to one that an entity performs alone (e.g.

dance). Conversely, a verb heard in a sentence such as *He meeked* is likely to denote a single-participant event (e.g. *dance*). How do adult speakers make these inferences? One possibility is that speakers have links between particular syntactic frames and semantic or conceptual structures, such as those shown below:

Syntactic frame	Example	Semantic structure
[NP] [VERB]	He danced	AGENT–ACTION
[NP] [VERB] [NP]	He hit him	AGENT–ACTION–PATIENT
[NP] [VERB] [NP] [NP]	He gave him a book	AGENT–ACTION–RECIPIENT–THEME

The claim of the *syntactic bootstrapping* hypothesis is that young children also have such links, and can use them to learn the meanings of words (in particular, verbs that would otherwise be problematic, as discussed above, but also nouns and other word types).

The issue of whether or not the syntactic bootstrapping hypothesis is a nativist–generativist theory is a difficult one. The links themselves are generally assumed to be 'acquired during the course of learning' (Gleitman, 1990: 41).[8] However, because syntactic bootstrapping requires children to recognize instances of syntactic frames (e.g. [NP] [VERB] [NP]), the claim that syntactic bootstrapping is an important process in early word learning sits more comfortably with generativist than constructivist accounts. Under generativist accounts, the ability to recognize syntactic frames comes 'early', because it is aided by innate knowledge of syntactic categories (e.g. NOUN, VERB) and sentence structure (e.g. Pinker, 1989a; Mintz, 2003; Christophe *et al.*, 2008; see Chapter 6). Indeed, Gleitman (1990: 37) herself argues that infants can parse a sound waveform into a 'rudimentary phrase structure tree' before they have necessarily learned any of the individual words (some evidence regarding this prosodic bootstrapping account was discussed in Chapter 2). Under constructivist accounts, the ability to recognize syntactic frames comes 'late' because it will not emerge until children have constructed categories such as NOUN and VERB (and can recognize constructional patterns such as NP VERB NP) on the basis of input-driven learning.

This means that both generativist and constructivist accounts agree that syntactic bootstrapping will be useful for word learning *at some point* in development. Where the accounts differ is in the importance accorded to the process. Generativist accounts usually assume that syntactic bootstrapping is available early in development and is a crucial component in word learning. For constructivist accounts, syntactic bootstrapping will not be possible until relatively late in development, when considerable word learning has already taken place, and thus – although useful – is presumably not a crucial process.

3.5.2   Evidence for syntactic bootstrapping

Naigles (1990) used a preferential-looking paradigm to test the syntactic boot-strapping hypothesis. In a training phase, children (aged 2;1) watched a video showing two characters performing two actions simultaneously (in a single scene). One was a causative action that one character performed on another (e.g. a duck pushing a bunny into an unusual bending position), whilst the other was a non-causative action performed independently, but in synchrony, by both characters (e.g. the duck and the bunny making arm circles). The manipulation was that half of the children heard a transitive sentence (e.g. *The duck is gorping the bunny*) and half an intransitive sentence (e.g. *The duck and the bunny are gorping*). The prediction from the syntactic bootstrapping hypothesis was that the children would use the syntactic frame in which the verb *gorp* was presented to infer its meaning. Specifically, the prediction was that children who heard the transitive ([NP][VERB][NP]) sentence would assume that *gorp* meant 'to push into a bending position' (i.e. the causative action), whilst those who heard the intransitive ([NP] [VERB]) sentence would assume that *gorp* meant 'to make arm circles' (i.e. the synchronous action).

This prediction was investigated in a preferential-looking test phase in which children were asked 'Where's gorping? Find gorping now!' One screen displayed the duck pushing the bunny into the bending position (with no arm-circling action). Children who, on the basis of the syntactic-bootstrapping training phase, had learned that *gorp* meant 'to push into a bending position' (i.e. children in the transitive- audio condition) would be expected to 'choose' (look longer at) this screen. The other screen displayed the duck and the bunny making arm circles (with no pushing-into-bend action). Children who, on the basis of the syntactic-bootstrapping training phase had learned that *gorp* meant 'to make arm circles' (i.e. children in the intransitive –audio condition) would be expected to 'choose' (look longer at) this screen. Figure 3.1 summarizes the complete procedure for one set of trials (each child completed four sets of this type with different novel verbs and actions).

Did children succeed at the task (i.e. could they perform 'syntactic bootstrap-ping')? The short answer is 'yes': 10 of the 12 children in each condition looked longer at the 'matching' screen (i.e. the screen that they would be predicted to 'prefer'). The long answer takes us into a digression into the controversy over how best to assess the results of preferential-looking studies (see Box 3.2).

Naigles and Kako (1993; see also Naigles, 1996) conducted a replication of the study of Naigles (1990) using slightly different methodology. Looking across the two studies, the authors compared the performance of children who heard intransitive and transitive frames (from Naigles, 1990) and children who heard the novel verb introduced in no syntactic frame (*Look, gorping!*). Only children in the transitive condition performed differently to those in the

Left screen	Right screen	Audio
 Duck pushes bunny down; both make arm circles		**Training trial 1** Look! The duck is gorping the bunny!
	 Duck pushes bunny down; both make arm circles	**Training trial 2** Look! The duck is gorping the bunny!
 Duck pushes bunny down; both make arm circles	 Duck pushes bunny down; both make arm circles	**Training trial 3** Look! The duck is gorping the bunny!
 Duck pushes bunny down	 Both make arm circles	**Baseline control trial (uninformative audio)** Oh! They're different now
 Duck pushes bunny down	 Both make arm circles	**Test trial 1** Where's gorping now?
 Duck pushes bunny down	 Both make arm circles	**Test trial 2** Find gorping!

Figure 3.1 An example trial from Naigles (1990) for a child in the *transitive-audio* condition. Stimuli are taken from a modified replication of this study conducted by Noble, Rowland and Pine (in press) (reproduced by permission of the authors)

Box 3.2 How should preferential-looking results be interpreted?

(1) **Raw looking times?** The simplest way to report preferential-looking results is simply to compare the mean total looking time to the two screens. Naigles (1990) reports that children looked significantly longer at the matching than the mismatching screen (e.g. children who had heard *gorp* presented in a transitive frame during training looked longer at the screen showing the duck pushing the bunny into the bending position than that showing the two making arm circles). This comparison (whilst it is often conducted) is statistically illegal as the two measures are not independent: any time the child spends looking at the matching screen necessarily decreases the time spent looking at the mismatching screen. This is like testing whether a coin is fair by illegally comparing 60 head tosses and 40 tail tosses (though it must be stressed that Naigles, 1990, also conducts a number of legal statistical analyses, discussed below, that are consistent with her conclusions).

(2) **Comparison to chance?** In the coin-toss scenario, the statistically legal test is to compare the number of heads (60) to the number of heads that one would expect by chance (50; given that there were 100 tosses in total). This is important as the choice of test can affect the outcome. For this example, this correct test (60 vs 50) reveals that there is no evidence that the coin is biased (i.e. $p > 0.05$), whilst the illegal test (60 vs 40) incorrectly leads us to conclude that there is (i.e. $p < 0.05$). For preferential-looking data, then, a legal test is to compare the mean looking time to the correct screen to the looking time that one would expect by chance. A problem with this test is that it assumes that if children have learned nothing, they will look for equally long at both screens. However, this is rarely the case. In practice, children generally find one video more appealing than the other *per se* (i.e. even when no directive audio is played), meaning that (unlike in the coin-toss example) the two outcomes are not equally probable beforehand.

(3) **Comparison to baseline?** The way to control for such a bias is to see if children look longer at the matching screen at test (i.e. after hearing the audio that directs them to this screen) than during a pre-test control trial, where the audio does not direct them to look at one screen over the other (e.g. 'Oh they're different now'). For example, Naigles (1990) reports such an analysis using 'difference scores'. She shows that children's looking-time preference for the matching screen (i.e. seconds looking at the matching screen minus seconds looking at the other screen) is significantly greater in the test than in the baseline control trial. A problem for the comparison-to-baseline measure is that children who 'prefer' one screen over the other in the baseline control

trial may switch their preference for the test trial, not because they are following the directive audio, but because they have become bored with the screen at which they looked longest during the baseline trial. Another issue is whether to perform this comparison for the two conditions (transitive audio and intransitive audio) separately, or whether to collapse across both. Naigles (1990) chooses the latter option. Whilst, statistically speaking, this is perfectly justified (as no interaction with audio condition was observed), ideally one would wish to see evidence that the effect holds for the intransitive- and transitive-audio conditions when analysed separately (there is nothing statistically illegal about conducting planned comparisons to test specific hypotheses, even in the absence of a statistically significant interaction).

(4) **Number of children looking longer at matching than mismatching screen?** The problem with all the measures outlined above (and other measures such as single longest look at each screen, looking time during the first N seconds and so on) is that they treat 'looking time' as if it can be meaningfully interpreted as a continuous variable. A true example of a continuous variable is 'items correct on a test'. This variable is continuous because somebody who scored 8/10 performed exactly twice as well as somebody who scored 4/10. Looking time to the matching screen does not fit this criterion: if one child looks for 8 seconds (out of a possible 10) at the matching screen and another looks for 4 seconds, this does not mean that the first child has learned the meaning of the word 'twice as well' (whatever this could mean). Probably the most appropriate measure, then, is the proportion of children who looked for longer at the matching than the mismatching screen. This can then be compared to the performance that would be expected by chance: 50 per cent of children look longer at the matching screen, 50 per cent at the mismatching screen (though again, the caveat that the two screens may not be equally appealing *per se* applies here). Naigles (1990) reports that 10/12 children in each condition looked longer at the matching than mismatching screen, a significantly greater proportion than would be expected by chance (6/12) at $p < 0.05$.

(5) **First look?** A problem for number-of-children measure is that it still uses gaze duration (looking time) as a measure of understanding. In fact, it is entirely possible that some children may quickly identify the matching screen and then inspect the other screen (or alternate between the two) for the remainder of the trial duration. A binary measure that does not suffer from this shortcoming is first look, whereby children are classified on the basis of the screen that they look at first. A problem with this measure is that children may need to look at both screens before 'choosing' one, so their first look may not be indicative of their

'choice'. Perhaps for this reason, many preferential-looking studies fail to show effects when looking-time data are reanalysed using this method (as in Naigles and Kako's, 1993, reanalysis of the data from Naigles, 1990).

(6) **Pointing?** One solution to these problems is not to use looking-time data at all. If children are taught (using unrelated practice trials) to *point to* the matching screen, this produces a binary measure (number of trials for which children pointed to the correct screen) that can be compared to chance. A disadvantage of this method is that it is unlikely to work for children younger than 2. A problem that the pointing method shares with other binary measures (number-of-children and first-look) is that it does not take into account any baseline preferences that children may have for one scene over the other.

Given that each analysis has its shortcomings, before concluding that children have 'succeeded' at a preferential looking task, one would ideally want to see significant effects on a continuous comparison-to-baseline measure (3) *and* a binary comparison-to-chance measure (4–6). Whilst the study of Naigles (1990) meets this criterion, a number of more recent studies do not. Another option is to use a more sophisticated analysis to investigate the time course of looking at each screen (Barr, 2008), though, as far as we are aware, this method has not yet been used in the syntactic bootstrapping or construction-learning literature. Ideally, one would also want to see success on both of these measures for each construction on which children are being tested (e.g. transitive and intransitive) when the data are analysed separately.

no-frame group. Thus whilst there is good evidence that children can perform syntactic bootstrapping with transitive frames (e.g. *The duck is gorping the bunny*), the evidence that they can do so with intransitive frames (e.g. *The duck and the bunny are gorping*) is more equivocal (a finding to which we return in Chapter 6).

A very similar pattern of findings emerged in a modified replication in which 2-year-olds (1;11–2;4, $M = 2;3$), 2½ year-olds (2;5–2;10, $M = 2;7$), 3-year-olds (2;11–3;10, $M = 3;4$) and 4-year-olds (3;11–4;10, $M = 4;3$) were asked to point to the matching screen (Noble, Rowland and Pine, in press). For the transitive audio condition (e.g. *The duck is gorping the bunny*), children in all age groups selected the matching (asymmetric) action at significantly above-chance levels. For the intransitive audio condition (e.g. *The bunny and the duck are gorping*) only the two older groups were able to select the matching (synchronous) action at above-chance levels. One possible explanation is that children in the intransitive condition (who heard *The duck and the bunny are gorping*) interpreted the novel verb as meaning something very general (e.g. similar to *playing*), in which case 'choosing' the causative action (the duck pushing the bunny into a bending position) is not necessarily incorrect. Another possibility is that children would be able to perform syntactic bootstrapping with more usual single-participant intransitives (e.g. to infer that *The duck is gorping* refers to a single participant action) but that they are confused by the conjoined subject (e.g. *The duck and the bunny*) into thinking that, because two participants are named, the action must be transitive.

This suggestion is consistent with the findings of a series of similar studies conducted by Hirsh-Pasek, Golinkoff and Naigles (1996). Whilst children aged 2;4 succeeded with transitive sentences (e.g. *Find Big Bird squatting*[9] Cookie Monster; experiment 5), they failed with conjoined-subject intransitives (e.g. *Find Big Bird and Cookie Monster squatting*). However, when these sentences were modified to highlight the conjoined nature of the subject (e.g. *Find Big Bird squatting with Cookie Monster*; experiment 7; and *See, Big Bird and Cookie Monster are squatting*; experiment 8) performance improved, with boys aged 2;4 and girls aged 2;1 succeeding in the *with* study, and children aged 2;0 (but not a group aged 2;5) in the *are* study (though the unexplained age and gender effects and interactions are a cause for concern). Similar results were reported by Kidd, Bavin and Rhodes (2001; see also Bavin and Growcott, 2000). Children (aged 2;6) succeeded in a transitive condition and an *are* intransitive condition, but narrowly failed in a *with* intransitive condition. (We are taking these results at face value here, though all these studies reported the illegal raw looking-times comparison).[10]

This raises the possibility (Fisher, 1996; 2002) that children perform 'syntactic' bootstrapping not on the basis of a full-blown syntactic analysis of the sentence ([SUBJECT][VERB][OBJECT) – or even a simpler [NP] [VERB] [NP] analysis – but may simply have a bias[11] to interpret all utterances with two participants as transitive. In some cases, this bias may be overridden by the presence of *and*, *are*, or *with*, which denotes a conjoined subject. Support for this claim comes from a series of studies conducted by Fisher (1996, 2002). In one study (Fisher, 1996: experiment 3 for children aged 3;6; and Fisher, 2002 for children aged 2;6) children in a transitive condition heard sentences such as *He's blicking him over there* whilst children in an intransitive condition heard *He's blicking over there*. The video (e.g. one monster pulling another along in a cart) was the same in both conditions. When asked to 'point to the one who's blicking the other one fast' (transitive condition) or 'point to the one who's blicking fast' (intransitive condition), children in the transitive condition selected the agent (i.e. the one performing a transitive action on the other), and those in the intransitive condition, the actor (i.e. the one performing an intransitive action such as moving) respectively. Though children were not actually required to perform syntactic bootstrapping to learn verb meanings (the meaning was already given; see footnote 10), this study shows that children do use the number of participants to guide their interpretations of sentences.

Another part of the study (Fisher, 1996: experiments 1 and 2) investigated whether children (aged 3;8 and 5;4) were able to use the prepositions to distinguish between giving and receiving events. Children who were asked to 'point to the one who's blicking the balloon *to* the other one' correctly selected the giver on around 80 per cent of trials. However, those who were asked to 'point to the one who's blicking the balloon *from* the other one' appeared to perform at random. This is problematic because verbs that denote symmetrical events such as *giving/receiving* are often cited as paradigmatic cases where syntactic bootstrapping would be required to learn verb meanings, with observation ineffective (e.g. Gleitman, 1990). Yet even 5-year-olds seem unable to use syntactic bootstrapping in exactly this scenario.

3.5.3 Problems for syntactic bootstrapping

One problem, of course, is that children often fail to show evidence of performing syntactic bootstrapping when they might be expected to do so (see studies reviewed above). A more fundamental criticism is that even when children are performing 'bootstrapping' to learn word meanings, it may be not be 'syntactic' (i.e. they may not be using abstract sentence structure). We have already discussed evidence that children may instead be using the number of participants (Fisher, 1996; 2002) and information provided by words such as *with, and* and *are*. Pinker (1994) goes further, arguing that virtually all of the information that helps children infer the meaning of an unknown verb comes from the other words in the sentence and real-world knowledge, not syntax. Pinker (1994: 382) illustrates the point with the example sentence *I filped the delicious sandwich and now I'm full*. A speaker who was presented with the key content words (e.g. *full*, *sandwich*, *delicious*, *filp*) in random order (i.e. with no syntactic information) would presumably have little difficulty in guessing the meaning of the missing verb.

Conversely, a speaker who was presented with only syntactic information (e.g. *[NP] filp [NP] . . .*) would have great difficulty in determining the meaning of the verb, beyond the fact that it denotes an action that involves two entities. The syntax alone would not differentiate the verb from those with very different meanings but similar syntactic properties (e.g. *kick, cost, read*). Indeed, it is precisely this information (which can be acquired from real-world observation, but not syntactic bootstrapping) that is normally taken to constitute a verb's 'meaning'. Pinker (1994: 405) goes on to argue that the crucial syntactic bootstrapping study (Naigles, 1990) was artificially set up to penalize observation, while letting syntax lead to the right answer by coincidence:

Consider what would have happened if the children had been shown a scene depicting [arm] circles without pushing . . . down or vice-versa. In that case, observation would have been sufficient to distinguish the two actions, with no syntax required. Now consider what would happen if the children had been shown an arm-circling rabbit causing the duck simultaneously to pop . . . down *and* to make arm circles . . . In that case, neither the sentence *The duck is gorping the bunny* or *The duck and bunny are gorping* would have distinguished the two kinds of motion.

Pinker (1994: 407) ends his critique with a challenge to proponents of the syntactic bootstrapping hypothesis:

There is an extremely simple experiment that could test whether children can learn a verb root's semantic content from multiple frames. There could be no TV screen, or content words, just syntactic frames. For example, children would hear only *She pilked; She pilked me something; She pilked the thing from the other things; She pilked the other things into the thing; She pilked one thing to another*, and so on. If children can acquire a verb's content from multiple frames, they should be able to infer that the verb basically means 'create by attaching' (Levin 1985).

A version of this study was later conducted by Sethuraman, Goldberg and Goodman (1997). Children were asked to enact sentences in which novel verbs were presented in various frames (e.g. *the tiger orks*; *the cow orks the tiger*). No definitions of the novel verbs were given; the question was whether, as the syntactic bootstrapping hypothesis predicts, children could use these frames to arrive at a meaning for each verb. In fact, children in both age groups (2;4–3;0; $M = 2;8$ and 3;1–4;1; $M = 3;8$) made no attempt to maintain a consistent meaning for a particular verb across different frames. For example, one child (aged 4;0) assigned *ork* a meaning similar to 'roll' when enacting *the tiger orks* and a meaning similar to 'stand behind' when enacting *the cow orks the tiger*.

3.5.4   *Syntactic bootstrapping: conclusion*

Despite these criticisms, there can be little doubt either that the syntactic structure of a sentence conveys at least *some* information regarding the verb's meaning, or that children are aware of at least *some* of the relevant syntax–semantics correlations (from as young as 2 years). Thus although we have no evidence of children actually performing syntactic bootstrapping in a real-world scenario, it would be odd to assume that they do not do so (given that they can, and that it would be useful).

The issue, then, is whether syntax is just one of the many sources of information that children use to learn verb meanings, or a source of information without which it is not possible to learn the meanings of verbs that denote different aspects of the same event (e.g. *give* and *receive*); the original claim of Landau and Gleitman (1985) and Gleitman (1990). In our view, Pinker (1994)

Summary table 3.2 *Syntactic bootstrapping* (☑ = *supports position;* ☒ = *counts against position*)

Issue/phenomenon	Summary of position	
	Syntactic bootstrapping is necessary for learning some word meanings (e.g. *give* vs *receive chase* vs *flee*; (e.g. Landau and Gleitman, 1985; Gleitman, 1990) and is syntactic in nature.	'Syntactic' bootstrapping effects mainly reflect real-world knowledge / cues provided by other words in the sentence (not syntax *per se*) and are merely helpful (as opposed to necessary) for learning word meanings (e.g. Pinker, 1994).
Adult simulation study	☑ True that it is difficult to guess word meanings purely from observation (Gillette et al., 1999), but see right-hand column.	Listeners in Gillette et al.'s (1999) study also deprived of cues normally provided by the other words in the sentence.
Children can use a sentence frame (transitive/intransitive) to infer something about the verb meaning (causal vs non-causal).	☑ Good evidence that 2-yr-olds can do this for transitive sentences, but ☒ mixed findings for intransitive sentences (Naigles, 1990; Naigles and Kako, 1993; Naigles, 1996; Noble et al., in press; Hirsh-Pasek et al., 1996; Kidd et al., 2001; Bavin and Growcott, 2000). ☒ Even 5-yr-olds fail to use syntactic bootstrapping information in a scenario (*give* vs *receive*) where it is claimed to be particularly crucial (Fisher, 1996).	Pinker (1994: 405) argues that syntactic bootstrapping studies (e.g. Naigles, 1990) are artificially set up to penalize observation, while letting syntax lead to the right answer by coincidence. ☑ In support of this claim, children show little evidence of being able to combine information provided by syntactic frames to arrive at a coherent verb meaning (Sethuraman et al., 1997).
	Some evidence that children use the number of arguments (as opposed to the syntactic frame *per se*) to make inferences regarding verb meaning (Fisher, 1996, 2002). Extent to which this 'bias' could be characterized as syntactic vs real-world knowledge is unclear.	

makes a compelling case that syntax is not only one of many sources of information that the child may use but, in fact, a relatively minor one (compared to observation, the meanings of the other words in the sentence and real-world knowledge). Given this state of affairs, the question arises as to whether it is necessary to posit a specific mechanism of syntactic bootstrapping at all. A learner that attempted to infer the meaning of unknown words by understanding the communicative intention of the speaker (a targeted kind of real-world observation), knowing many of the other words in the sentence and performing cross-situational distributional analysis would be performing 'syntactic bootstrapping' by default.

For example, consider the potentially problematic case of *give* and *receive* (or any pair of this type). Suppose that the information available to the learner is the content words of the sentence, with no order information (e.g. *VERB*, *John*, *Sue*, *present*) and real-world observation (John is the giver, Sue the recipient). If the learner understands that the intention of the speaker is to comment on John (e.g. the speaker is looking at John, he is the topic of prior discourse etc.), then she will interpret the verb as *give*. If the speaker has established (again using verbal or non-verbal cues) Sue as the person of interest (and it would be odd to comment on the situation with *receive* rather than *give* were this not the case), then the learner will interpret the verb as *give*.

In the spirit of Pinker (1994), then, we offer this challenge to proponents of the social-pragmatic and syntactic bootstrapping approaches respectively. Proponents of the former account should be able to demonstrate that children will interpret a novel verb as either *give* or *receive* (and *chase/flee* etc.), depending on the social-pragmatic cue of discourse context (with no word-order information given). Proponents of the latter should be able to demonstrate that children will interpret a novel verb as either *give* or *take* solely on the basis of word-order cues, when deprived of the cues to meaning provided by real-world knowledge and discourse context (but see Fisher, 1996).

3.6   Conclusion: how do children learn the meanings of words?

Whilst for object words (and perhaps verbs) children *look as if* they are in possession of constraints such as the whole-object assumption, most theorists (even many who advocate constraints approaches) would probably agree that such constraints can be reduced to more general principles of learning. Whether these are mainly socio-pragmatic or associative in nature is difficult to determine. On the one hand, children are able to learn at least some words by pure (cross-situational) association, in a situation that is (relatively) devoid of social cues and at an age (6 months) younger than that at which they have been shown to make use of social cues (even in non-linguistic tasks). On the other hand, when pure associative/attentional cues (e.g. an object lighting up and spinning around) and social-pragmatic/intentional cues (e.g. eye-gaze) are placed in conflict, it is generally the latter that win out. There is also evidence that, from about 1;2, children are good at monitoring others' attention and intentions in non-linguistic contexts. That said, children do not appear to be able to make use of these cues in the service of word learning until later in development. From around 2 years of age, children appear to make use of aspects of sentence structure (e.g. word order; number of participants) to make inferences about the meanings of new words (particularly verbs). However, the extent to which pure 'syntactic' information (as opposed to the information given by the other words in the sentence) is useful remains contentious.

In summary, then, a successful account of word learning will likely include roles for both social-pragmatic and associative learning. To our knowledge, the only current account that does so is the emergent coalition model of Golinkoff *et al.* (1994),which also posits independent roles for lexical principles or constraints (in our view, incorrectly) and syntactic cues. Although this account includes various suggestions regarding the ways in which cues are weighted differently at different points in development, it is not, in general, sufficiently detailed to make quantitative predictions (though it may well be correct in positing that associative/attentional cues are of greater relative importance than social-pragmatic cues early in development). A more successful model would not only make quantitative predictions in this area but also explain precisely how apparent 'constraints' and 'syntactic bootstrapping' effects can be shown by a social-pragmatic associative learner.

Finally, it is important to recognize that none of the approaches discussed in this chapter offers a satisfactory account of *development*, by which we mean both the development of a word's meaning within a child's lexicon and development of the child's word-learning system. The theories discussed here generally idealize word learning (usually implicitly) as a scenario in which the child uses lexical principles, pragmatic constraints, cross-situational learning or syntax to identify the referent of a novel word on the basis of a single exposure (or several exposures). The word is then seen as 'acquired' (though we have also discussed some studies that investigate how object labels can be extended to new exemplars). However, as a number of authors (e.g. Bloom, 2004; Fernald, Zangl, Portillo and Marchman, 2008) have noted, this scenario is not realistic. The situation in which a new word's referent is first identified represents not the end but the *beginning* of the acquisition process. The meaning of the word continues to be refined throughout childhood, and – for most words – presumably into adulthood. There is also a tendency to view the child as a static learner (or, at best, a learner who weights cues differently at different stages of development). This too, is likely to be too simplistic. The relative weighting of social-pragmatic, associative, statistical and syntactic cues will most likely vary from utterance to utterance, reflecting the child's prior knowledge of the other words in the utterance, the communicative situation, the child's own communicative goals, and so on.

In conclusion, a successful account of word learning will most likely integrate social-pragmatic factors, general-learning factors (e.g. salience, context-dependence) statistical (i.e. cross-situational) learning and some form of 'bootstrapping' based on knowledge of other words in the utterance. A successful account will also have to explain developmental changes in children's word learning. It would also be desirable to have an account in which improved performance on word-learning tasks is linked tightly to independent measures of the factors that are held to support learning (e.g. joint attention, social understanding, memory and statistical learning).

4   Theoretical approaches to grammar acquisition

The defining characteristic of human language is that it allows speakers to produce entirely new utterances (i.e. utterances that the speaker has never heard in precisely that form). Clearly in order to do so, speakers must be in possession of a **grammar**: a set of some kind of abstract 'rules' or 'schemas' used for combining words into sentences (**syntax**) and adding markers to words to express features such as tense (**morphology**). Two central questions in child language acquisition research are therefore: (1) what does this grammar look like? (i.e. what is the nature of the underlying system)? and (2) where does it come from (i.e. how is it acquired)? In this chapter, we outline two competing answers to the first question – the theoretical accounts of the adult endstate assumed by the **generativist** and **constructivist** approach respectively – and the implications of these accounts with regard to the second question. Although, in principle, one could imagine a non-nativist generativist account, all the actual generativist accounts that will be discussed in this chapter (and the remainder of the book) assume that at least some linguistic categories and principles regarding utterance formation are innate (i.e. present from birth). Constructivist accounts assume that whilst the *potential* to acquire language is of course innate, children are not born with innate knowledge of grammatical categories or principles, and construct their grammars on the basis of the input to which they are exposed.

4.1   Generativist approaches

4.1.1   Introduction

Students often have difficulty understanding discussions of generative grammar, because it is not always clear exactly what the (often highly abstract) theoretical descriptions are *for*. As you read this section, you should keep in mind that what is being outlined is no more or less than (one view of) **the knowledge that competent adult speakers have of their language.** Theoretical linguistics is a complex and rapidly changing field, with different researchers often proposing different analyses. Thus we do not attempt here to give a comprehensive outline of the state of the art in generative grammar. Rather, our goal is to outline only the aspects of the theory that are necessary for understanding child language acquisition research in the generative tradition. We do aim, however, to give sufficient detail to enable those with no prior knowledge of generativist syntax to read and understand not only the discussions of generativist language acquisition research in subsequent chapters, but also the relevant primary sources.[1] The version of generative grammar presented here is essentially that assumed by Guasti (2004) – perhaps the leading generativist language acquisition textbook (see also Radford, 2004; Carnie, 2006).

An early **non**-generativist view (Skinner, 1957) was that knowledge of language consists of a set of words (e.g. *Mummy*) and sentences (e.g. *I want it*) paired with their meaning. Skinner (1957) argued that children learn language through fine-grained selective reinforcement by parents or caregivers, in the same way that a rat in one of Skinner's famous animal-learning studies might learn to press a particular combination of levers to receive a food reward. For example, if a child attempts to imitate an adult saying the word *Mummy*, the parent may 'reward' correct or close attempts (e.g. with praise or smiles) but not clear errors (e.g. *baba*). Skinner's (1957) claim was that this type of selective reinforcement, operating over whole utterances (e.g. *I want it*) as well as single words, is sufficient to explain language acquisition.

Chomsky (1959) argued that Skinner's (1957) account cannot possibly be correct. If children learned imitatively in this way, their ultimate knowledge of language would consist of nothing more than a repertoire of rote-learned phrases. In fact both adults and young children produce sentences that they cannot possibly have heard before. In all likelihood, many of the spoken utterances that you have produced today had never been previously produced in exactly that form. Children's characteristic errors (e.g. **I sitted down*) constitute evidence that they too produce novel utterances that they have not acquired by directly imitating adults. Furthermore, a speaker's knowledge of a particular language allows her not only to produce novel utterances, but also to determine whether or not a particular novel sequence of words constitutes a possible sentence in that language. Chomsky (1959) famously illustrated this point with the following pair of sentences:

> Colorless green ideas sleep furiously.
>
> *Sleep green colorless furiously ideas.

Although (unless you are familiar with this example) you have probably never heard either of these sentences before, your knowledge of English allows you to determine that the first sentence is 'grammatical' (i.e. it is a possible sentence in

English), whereas the second is not.[2] Importantly, speakers cannot be making the decision on the basis of meaning (or 'semantics') as both sentences are meaningless.

4.1.2 A generative phrase-structure grammar

Chomsky (1959) therefore argued that speakers must possess a system or set of rules (i.e. a **grammar**) that is **generative** (i.e. that generates novel utterances): a **generative grammar** (or **generative syntax**). Suppose that these rules were formulated in terms of individual words (e.g. *The* goes before *boy*; *The* goes before *baby*; *A* goes before *boy*; *A* goes before *baby*). This would be problematic for two reasons. First, whenever a speaker learned a new word (e.g. *computer*), she would have no idea whether to place *the* before or after this word when producing a sentence (i.e. *computer the* vs *the computer*). Second, speakers would have to store an impossibly large number of rules (e.g. *The* goes before *boy*; *The* goes before *baby*; *The* goes before *computer*; *The* goes before *cup*; *The* goes before *man*; *A* goes before *boy*; *A* goes before *baby* etc.). The obvious solution is to propose that the rules that speakers possess (i.e. the grammar) are formulated in terms of **categories**. If we replace the various rules discussed above with the single rule 'a DETERMINER goes before a NOUN', both problems disappear. Speakers need store only one rule, and can use this rule whenever they learn a new noun such as *computer* (provided, of course, that they recognize it as a noun, and know which words are determiners). This rule is **abstract** because it is formulated in terms of categories, as opposed to individual items (a rule that is formulated in terms of individual items is termed **concrete**).

Generative syntax captures this generalization by positing the existence of a DETERMINER PHRASE (DP) consisting of a DETERMINER (D) and a NOUN PHRASE (NP). Adult English speakers are also in possession of the knowledge that the DETERMINER (e.g. *the*, *a*) precedes the NOUN PHRASE (e.g. *boy*, *baby*, *computer*, *cup*, *man*). This general knowledge can be summarized using a **phrase-structure tree** (Figure 4.1). When a researcher wishes to claim that a particular string (e.g. *the boy*) receives a particular syntactic analysis, each word is also shown on the tree diagram in the relevant position (Figure 4.2).

Phrase-structure trees are sometimes written out using bracketed notation. For example, the tree shown in Figure 4.2 can be represented as:

> [DP [D the] [NP boy]]

It is important to bear in mind that this notation is used purely as a space-saving measure: the structure assumed is identical in both cases.

Figure 4.1 A simple phrase-structure tree

Figure 4.2 A simple phrase-structure tree for the string *the boy*

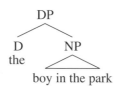

Figure 4.3 A NOUN PHRASE can be of any length

DETERMINER and NOUN are both examples of **syntactic** (or **grammatical**) **categories** (more examples will be discussed shortly). It seems, then, that we could have shown the DETERMINER PHRASE (DP) as containing simply a DETERMINER (*the*) and a NOUN (*boy*). What is the reason for the assumption that, in fact, the DETERMINER PHRASE (DP) contains a DETERMINER (D) and a NOUN **PHRASE** (NP)?

The answer is that the position that is filled, in Figure 4.2, by the single word *boy* (a NOUN) could alternatively be filled by a string such as *boy in the park* (a NOUN PHRASE or NP), as shown in Figure 4.3. As, for now, we are not concerned with the internal structure of the NP, this is not shown (as is conventional, a triangle is used to illustrate that the phrase has internal structure that is omitted from the diagram).

This highlights an important feature of generative syntax: the 'rules' for combining words to form utterances make reference not only to syntactic categories (e.g. DETERMINER, NOUN) but also to phrases (e.g. NOUN PHRASE). Thus the grammar that we are outlining here is a **phrase-structure grammar**.

4.1.3   *The internal structure of phrases*

As noted above, DETERMINER (e.g. *the*, *a*) and NOUN (e.g. *boy*, *baby*, *computer*, *cup*, *man*) are examples of **syntactic** (or **grammatical**) **categories**. Other common syntactic categories include VERB (e.g. *run*, *walk*, *kick*, *kiss*),

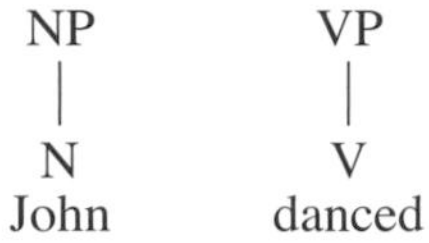

NP   VP
| |
N   V
John   danced

Figure 4.4 A simple NP or VP consists of a single NOUN or VERB

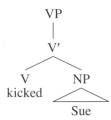

Figure 4.5 The three-level structure of VP: V′ contains the head (V) and its complement (an NP)

ADJECTIVE (e.g. *green*, *happy*, *sad*) and PREPOSITION (e.g. *into*, *along*). The syntactic category of each word (e.g. NOUN for *baby*, VERB for *kick*) is stored with the word's entry in the **lexicon** ('mental dictionary'). In the same way that a DETERMINER (D) always appears in a DETERMINER PHRASE (DP), and a NOUN (N) in a NOUN PHRASE (NP), a VERB (V), ADJECTIVE (A) or PREPOSITION (P) always appears in a VERB PHRASE (VP), ADJECTIVAL PHRASE (AP) or PREPOSITIONAL PHRASE (PP). The category that lends its name to the phrase in which it appears is termed the **head**.

The simplest possible NP contains the head NOUN (e.g. *John*) and nothing else. Similarly, the simplest possible VP consists solely of the head VERB (e.g. *danced*). This is illustrated in Figure 4.4 (a single vertical line | is used instead of two diagonal branches to indicate that the phrase contains only a single **constituent**).

On some occasions the VP requires not only a VERB (e.g. *kicked*) but also a phrase specifying (in this case) what was kicked (the difference is that **transitive** verbs such as *kick* require an object – one can say *John kicked Sue* but not **John kicked* – whereas **intransitive** verbs such as *dance* do not – one can say *John danced*).[3] In cases where a phrase (e.g. VP) requires not only the head (e.g. the VERB *kicked*) but another phrase (e.g. the NP *Sue*), the latter is termed the **complement** (informally, one can think of the complement as completing the VP). When a VP contains not just a VERB but an obligatory complement, this is represented as shown in Figure 4.5. The head (here V) and its complement (here NP) combine to form V′ (pronounced 'V-bar').

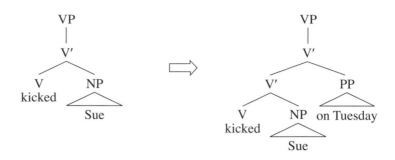

Figure 4.6 Expanding V′ to house an adjunct

Suppose that the speaker wishes to add the PREPOSITIONAL PHRASE (PP) *on Tuesday* to the VP *kicked Sue*. Whereas the NP *Sue* is an obligatory **argument** of the VERB *kicked* (i.e. it cannot be omitted without rendering the sentence ungrammatical), the PP *on Tuesday* is simply an **optional** add-on (the technical term for which is an **adjunct**). This is done by expanding the original V′ into a new V′ (containing everything that was in the original V′) and the adjunct (see Figure 4.6).

Expanding V′ into a new V′ plus something else is an example of **recursion**. Recursion allows speakers to generate infinitely long utterances. For example, the new V′ introduced in Figure 4.6 could again be split into another V′ and another PP to give *John kissed Sue* <u>*behind the bike shed*</u> *on Tuesday*. Applying this procedure again would give an utterance such as *John kissed Sue* <u>*after school*</u> *behind the bike shed on Tuesday*. The difference between arguments and adjuncts is critical for various generativist acquisition accounts of question acquisition (see Chapter 7) and the binding principles (see Chapter 8).

Thus for the category VERB, we have three levels: VERB itself (abbreviated to V), V′ and VP (occasionally written as V″). The three levels are sometimes referred to as **zero-bar phrases** (V), **one-bar (single-bar) phrases** (V′) and **two-bar (double-bar) phrases** (V″; i.e. VP). In fact, the assumption is that all syntactic categories have three levels (e.g. V, V′, VP; N, N′, NP; and so on). If we use X as a variable to stand for category names in general (e.g. VERB, NOUN, PREPOSITION and ADJECTIVE) we can say that all categories have three levels: X, X′ and XP. This is where the name for this theory of syntax, **X-bar theory**, originates.[4] Thus the head, regardless of its syntactic category, combines with any complement to form a single-bar phrase, as shown in Figure 4.7.

Before we move on, notice from Figure 4.7 that, for every phrase type, the head precedes (goes before) the complement. The claim (though there is debate over possible exceptions) is that a language will generally either place all heads before their complements (e.g. English) or all heads after their complements

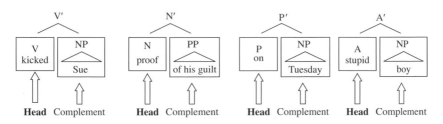

Figure 4.7 For every category, the head combines with any complement to form a single-bar phrase

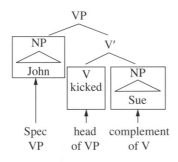

Figure 4.8 Initial structure of a simple transitive sentence

(e.g. Korean). For example, in Korean the V′ shown in Figure 4.5 would have the internal structure [$_{NP}$ Sue][$_V$ kicked], whilst the A′ would have the internal structure [$_{NP}$ boy][$_A$ stupid].

4.1.4   Combining phrases into sentences

Up to this point we have been examining only the internal structure of phrases (e.g. DP, NP, VP) and not how phrases are combined into sentences. Under the approach outlined here, all sentences start out as VPs (we see shortly what they subsequently become). This is achieved (see Figure 4.8) by assuming that VP contains not only V′ (as shown in Figure 4.6) but also a **specifier position** (**Spec VP**) that houses the sentence subject (in this case the NP John). In fact, the assumption is that every two-bar phrase (VP, NP, PP etc.) consists of a specifier position and a single-bar phrase (though these levels are not always shown if they are not important for a particular analysis).

4.1.5   Functional categories and functional phrases

So far, the discussion has focused mainly on **lexical categories** (NOUN, VERB, ADJECTIVE, ADVERB and PREPOSITION) and their related phrases (NP,

N′; VP, V′ etc.). Words that belong to lexical categories are known as **content words** as that they denote some entity (e.g. *John*, *baby*), activity (e.g. *sleep*, *kiss*), property (e.g. *colourless*, *green*; *quickly*, *slowly*) or relation (e.g. *under*) that has descriptive content (i.e. it would be possible to explain to somebody what each of these words meant). **Function words**, in contrast, are words that perform some **grammatical function** (i.e. do some grammatical 'work'). For example, one **functional category** (category of function words) that we have already met is that of DETERMINERS (e.g. *the*, *a*). These words do not have much meaning on their own (it would be very difficult to explain what they mean) but perform a grammatical function; specifying whether the relevant noun denotes something that is already under discussion (e.g. *the cat*), or something that is new to the conversation (e.g. *a cat*). Similarly, items that belong to the functional category of PRONOUN (e.g. *he*, *it*) carry little meaning of their own (what does 'it' mean?), but serve the grammatical function of referring back to something that is already under discussion (e.g. *Where is the book? John saw **it** yesterday*). Although they are somewhat more meaningful than determiners and pronouns, QUANTIFIERs (e.g. *most*, *many*, *every*) and NEGATION markers (e.g. *not*, *n't*) are also considered to be functional (as opposed to lexical) categories.

Two particularly important functional categories are **COMPLEMEN-TIZER (C)** (e.g. *that*) and **INFLECTION (INFL or I)**, the latter of which includes not only whole words such as auxiliaries (e.g. *is*, *was*, *has*, *had*) but **inflectional morphemes** such as the past-tense -*ed* and present-tense -*s* verb markers. In the previous section, we noted that sentences 'start out' as VPs. The reason that this somewhat odd terminology was used is that, in fact, it is standardly assumed that every sentence is a VP contained within an IP (with the usual levels of IP>I′>I) that is itself contained within a CP (with the usual levels of CP>C′>C). What this entails is discussed in the two following sections.

4.1.5.1 The Inflectional Phrase (IP)　We noted at the beginning of this chapter that the child's **grammar** consists not only of rules for combining words into phrases and sentences (**syntax**), but also rules for marking words or phrases for grammatical features such as tense (**morphology**). The process by which this marking occurs is termed **inflection** (see the next chapter for a detailed introduction). For now, we consider a simple case where a verb (e.g. *kick*) receives the past-tense maker -*ed* (an **inflectional morpheme**). Consider the example sentence *John kicked Sue*. Thus far we have glossed over the question of how the VERB *kick* receives its -*ed* past-tense marking. The process is illustrated in Figure 4.9.

The sentence starts out as a simple VP (*John kick Sue*). The past-tense marker -*ed* is a member of the category INFLECTION, and so appears at the

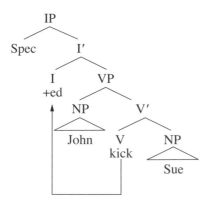

Figure 4.9 The verb moves from V to I to receive inflection

head of IP, within I′ (in exactly the same way that *kick*, for example, is a member of the category VERB, and so appears at the head of VP, within V′). However, since the head I comes before the VP, this creates a problem: the *-ed* marker is at the beginning of the sentence (*-ed John kick Sue*), instead of on the verb (*John kicked Sue*). The VERB (*kick*) therefore **moves** or **raises** from within the VP to the head I where it picks up the *-ed* marker (*kick+ed*). Under an alternative formulation (for our purposes essentially nothing more than a notational variant) the verb starts out as *kicked* in the VP. The **tense feature** (i.e. +PAST) of the *-ed* inflection is then **checked** (or **matched**) against an abstract tense feature at I.[5] Either way, the important point is that the verb raises to I where it receives/checks/matches its inflection.[6]

The sentence does not yet have the correct surface word order, however. As shown in Figure 4.9, whilst the *-ed* marker is now attached to the verb, because the verb has raised to I, it is now at the beginning of the sentence (*kicked John Sue*). The solution – shown in Figure 4.10 – is to have the SUBJECT (*John*) move to the specifier position of IP, giving the correct word order (*John kicked Sue*).

There is another motivation for this assumption. The abstract category of INFLECTION includes not only markers that specify tense on verbs, but also markers that specify the **case** of nouns. The case marking that a noun receives denotes its grammatical role in the sentence. For most case-marking languages a noun that is the SUBJECT (e.g. the AGENT of an active sentence) receives **nominative** case, with the noun that is the object (e.g. the PATIENT of an active sentence) receiving **accusative** case. In Russian, for example, if Veronika kicked Alexandra, the AGENT takes nominative case (*Veronika*), whilst the PATIENT takes accusative case (*Alexandroo*). English does not mark case on nouns, but does so for pronouns. However, English does not 'add' a marker

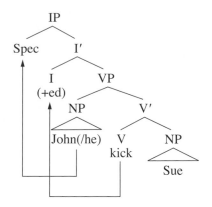

Figure 4.10 The subject moves to Spec IP to check nominative case (e.g. *he/*him*)

(e.g. *a*, *oo*) onto the noun. Rather English marks case by using different forms of the pronoun. For example, if John kicked Sue, we would say ***He*** (nominative case) *kicked **her*** (accusative case) and not *****Him*** (accusative case) *kicked **she*** (nominative case). Pronouns (and – in case-marking languages – nouns) receive or check the correct case marking at Spec IP.[7] Thus the pronoun raises to Spec IP (Figure 4.10) not only to ensure the correct word order, but also to receive/check its case marking (for this example to ensure that the subject pronoun is *He* as opposed to *Him*).

In some cases, tense will be marked not by a marker on the verb (e.g. kick-*ed*) but by an auxiliary (*is*, *was*, *have*, *does*, *do*, *will* etc.). Because auxiliaries are also members of the functional category of INFLECTION, they appear in the tree at I (Figure 4.11). As in Figure 4.10, the subject (*He*) raises from within the VP (a) to ensure the correct word order (*He will kick Sue* not **Will he kick Sue*) and (b) to receive/check nominative case (*He/*Him will kick Sue*).

There is one final aspect of IP that has not been covered. The functional category of INFLECTION morphemes contains not only morphemes that mark TENSE (e.g. *-ed*; *will*), but also morphemes that mark person and number AGREEMENT. **Agreement** is discussed in more detail in Chapter 5. For now it will suffice to note that a verb must 'agree' with its subject. Consider, for example, the sentence **John like Sue*, which is ungrammatical because the verb (*like*) needs to agree with its subject *John*: a 'third person singular' marker *-s* must be added to the verb: *John like-**s** Sue*. This marker (as well as marking present tense) marks third person (where the first person is the speaker, the second is the listener and the third person is a third party that the speaker and

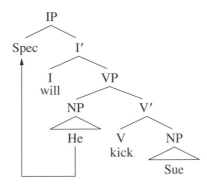

Figure 4.11 Auxiliaries (e.g. *will*) are directly generated at I *(John will kick Sue)*

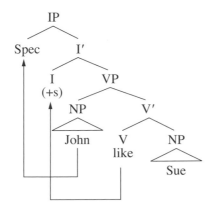

Figure 4.12 Verb Agreement is checked at I

listener are talking about) and singular (we are talking about a single person *John*, not a group of people such as *John and Bill*). Under the account we have been discussing up to this point, agreement markers on verbs are – in exactly the same way as tense markers – added (or checked) at I (Figure 4.12).

However, many modern generativist theories (including those discussed in Chapter 5) split INFLECTION into two further functional categories: TENSE (TNS) and AGREEMENT (AGR), which have the usual levels (TP>T′>T(NS); AGRP>AGR′>AGR). Tense markers on verbs (-ed) are added/checked at TNS. Verb markers (e.g. -s) that encode both tense (present) and agreement (third person singular) must be checked at both TNS and (subsequently) AGR. Case (which, in the simpler version of the theory, is checked at Spec IP) is instead

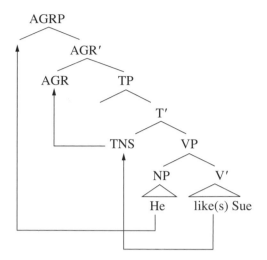

Figure 4.13 IP is split into AGRP and TNSP

checked at Spec AGRP (there is no room for it to check at AGR, since this is where the verb markers are checked). This process is illustrated in Figure 4.13.

Although this may seem unnecessarily completed, some theories of inflectional morphology to be discussed in Chapter 5 necessarily assume this split of TNS and AGR. You should be aware that different authors/researchers often make different assumptions. You may occasionally (e.g. Wexler, 1998) see AGR split into AGRs and AGRo, for subject and object agreement respectively (some languages require the verb to agree with its object). Conversely, some researchers (e.g. Chomsky, 1995; Radford, 2004) posit only TP, where tense and (subject and object) agreement are checked. It is also important to bear in mind that some textbooks (e.g. Guasti, 2004) show only a unitary IP purely as a simplifying measure (whilst acknowledging that IP is in fact probably split into AGRP and TP). We will follow this practice wherever possible (i.e. we will show only IP unless the theory under discussion requires a separate TP and AGRP).

4.1.5.2 The Complementizer Phrase   Consider a sentence such as *Bill said that John kissed Sue*. This sentence contains two **clauses** (roughly equivalent to a sentence), each expressing one idea or **proposition**: (a) Bill said *b*, (b) *John kissed Sue*. To capture this structure, whereby the second clause is **nested** within the first, generative syntax posits a **COMPLEMENTIZER PHRASE (CP or C″)**, with all the usual levels (C, C′ and CP). In the simplest case, the head C is an actual **complementizer** such as *that* (though this is often optional in English). The complement of the head C is the IP that contains the

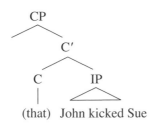

Figure 4.14a Structure of a complement clause

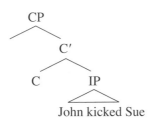

Figure 4.14b All 'sentences' are CPs

remainder of the clause. Ignoring, for now, the structure of the **main clause** (*Bill said X*), the structure of the **complement clause** (*John kissed Sue*) is therefore that shown in Figure 4.14a. Note that, as discussed above, we show a unitary IP as a simplifying measure, and – since it is not relevant for the present discussion – we do not show its internal structure.

In fact, as noted above, the assumption is that every clause has a CP, whether it is a complement clause (as in Figure 4.14a) or a main clause (Figure 4.14b), in which case the linguistic entity that we informally call a 'sentence' is more properly a CP.

What is the motivation for this assumption? That is, what aspect of an adult speaker's knowledge do we capture by assuming that every 'sentence' has (or, more accurately, *is*) a CP? The answer is the ability to perform **movement** operations. Movement will be discussed in more detail in Chapter 7. For now, we will illustrate the concept with a simple example. Under a generativist analysis, *yes/no* questions (questions which expect 'yes' or 'no' as an answer) are formed from the corresponding declarative statement by movement of the auxiliary (e.g. *is*). This process (see Figure 4.15) is known as **subject–auxiliary inversion**.[8]

Assume, for a moment, that we do not posit a CP. In this case, the entire sentence would be contained within an IP (or AGRP). This is problematic, because the only way that the auxiliary can move to the required location is to move outside the phrase structure tree altogether (Figure 4.16).

The boy is kicking the girl → Is$_i$ the boy t_i kicking the girl?

Figure 4.15 *Yes/no* questions are formed from declaratives by movement of the auxiliary

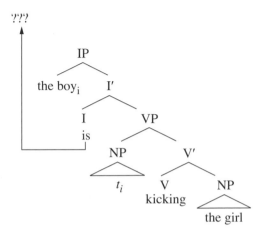

Figure 4.16 Illegal movement 'outside' the phrase structure tree

The solution to the problem is to posit that all sentences have a CP (with C and C′). Then if the sentence happens to involve subject–auxiliary inversion, the auxiliary has somewhere to go (it has a **landing site**), as shown in Figure 4.17. Furthermore, as we will see in Chapter 7, if the question requires a *wh*-word (e.g. *Who is the boy kicking?*), there is a place for that too (Spec CP). Whilst not all generative syntacticians would necessarily agree that questions are formed by movement in this way, this analysis forms the basis of all the leading generativist accounts of children's question formation (discussed in Chapter 7).

Similarly, the analysis of CPs presented here is assumed by the leading current generativist accounts of children's acquisition of multiple-clause sentences (see Chapter 7). The assumption is that each clause is a CP embedded within another CP (and so on, for sentences with more than two clauses). The full analysis for a sentence with a sentential complement clause (*Bill said [that] John kicked Sue*) is shown in Figure 4.18.

Relative clauses (again, see Chapter 7 for acquisition theories) are structured in the same way (e.g. *[CP The dog$_i$ [CP that t$_i$ jumps over the pig] bumps into the lion]*; with the internal structure of each CP not shown). Inserting a CP into another CP is another example of **recursion**. As we have already seen,

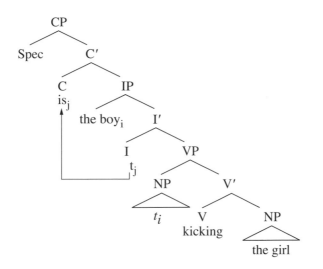

Figure 4.17 CP provides a landing site for subject–auxiliary inversion in questions

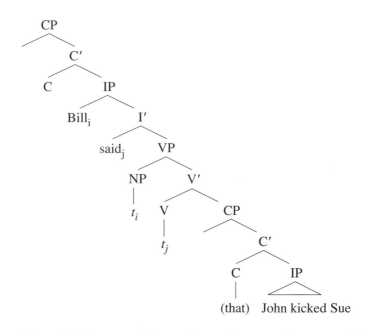

Figure 4.18 Sentences with a complement clause contain two nested CPs

recursion allows speakers to generate (in principle) infinitely long sentences, in this case by adding CPs:

> [CP James hoped [**CP that Sarah knew** [CP that Bill said [**CP that John kissed Sue**]]]]

Thus any successful account of an adult's linguistic knowledge must allow sentences to be embedded within one another in this way (a constructivist approach to embedded clauses is discussed in Section 4.2.5).

4.1.6   Sentence formation

We are now in a position to discuss the generativist approach to sentence formation. The first step in sentence formation is the selection of the appropriate verb (e.g. *kick*) from the **lexicon** ('mental dictionary'). The **lexical entry** for each item (e.g. *kick*) specifies its syntactic category (e.g. VERB) and the **arguments** (or **roles**) that the verb requires, both semantic and syntactic. The **semantic roles** required by *kick* are an **AGENT** (the kicker) and a **PATIENT** (the one being kicked). The **syntactic** roles required by *kick* are a **SUBJECT NP** (to express the AGENT) and an **OBJECT NP** (to express the PATIENT). Two related processes are at work here: **semantic selection** (also known as **theta-selection** or θ**-selection**) is the process by which a verb specifies the semantic roles that it requires (e.g. AGENT and PATIENT). **Category selection** (also known as **c-selection**) is the process by which the verb selects the syntactic roles that it requires (e.g. a SUBJECT NP and an OBJECT NP). Through these two processes, the verb is said to **project** its argument structure, thus determining the syntactic structure of the sentence. For example, because *kick* requires an AGENT and a PATIENT (theta-selection), it must project a tree structure that will house a SUBJECT NP and an OBJECT NP (c-selection), as shown in Figure 4.8. First, the VERB projects a V′ that includes the VERB itself (*kick*) and the OBJECT NP (*Sue*). Next, the VERB projects a VP that includes the SUBJECT NP (e.g. *John*) and V′ (*kicked Sue*). In this way, the verb determines the **argument structure** of the sentence. For example, whilst transitive verbs (e.g. *kick*) will project a tree that includes a SUBJECT NP and an OBJECT NP, intransitive verbs (e.g. *run*) will project only a SUBJECT NP.

Finally, as we have already seen, to allow for (a) checking of TNS and AGR and (b) any required movement operations, an IP (or AGRP and TNSP) and a CP respectively are projected for each sentence. Some theories also posit other functional categories, for example NEG (*not*; *n't*) to deal with negation, but the positioning of these additional phrases in the tree (as well as their existence) is generally controversial (NEGP is discussed rather speculatively in Chomsky, 1993, and omitted in Chomsky, 1995). Any other phrases that are posited will be projected somewhere in between the original VP and the CP.

4.1.7   *Innate principles and the poverty-of-the-stimulus argument*

Thus far, we have presented the generative account of syntax as an account of the set of rules for sentence formation (the 'grammar') possessed by competent adult speakers. We have not yet touched on the question that is the central concern of this book: how *children* acquire this system. In principle, one could imagine an account whereby children construct a generativist-style phrase-structure grammar from their input (i.e. the adult speech that they hear). In practice, most actual generativist accounts of language acquisition assume that much of this knowledge is not learned at all, but is present from birth (i.e. is **innate**). In other words, all actual generativist accounts are also **nativist** accounts.

Why do generativist accounts assume that knowledge of phrase structure is innate and not learned? The claim is essentially that the system is too abstract and complex to be acquired by a learner who came to the task with no knowledge of the way that language is structured. The problem is that, given a set of input sentences, there are an infinite number of possible rules that the learner could formulate, and no way of knowing which is the correct one. This **argument from the poverty of the stimulus** is often illustrated using the example of the rule for *yes/no* question formation.

As we have seen in this chapter, *yes/no* questions are formed by moving the auxiliary to the beginning of the sentence (subject–auxiliary inversion):

> The boy is crazy → Is the boy crazy?

Imagine that (counter to the generativist claim) a child was attempting to formulate a rule for question formation purely on the basis of the input, with no prior knowledge of phrase structure. On the basis of declarative/question pairs such as this one, the child could set up the rule 'move the auxiliary to the start of the sentence'. However, this child would run into trouble as soon as she encountered sentences with more than one auxiliary:

> The boy who is smoking is crazy → Is the boy who is smoking crazy?
>
> The girl is kissing the boy who is smoking → Is the girl kissing the boy who is smoking?

If the child reformulated the rule as 'move the *first* auxiliary to the start of the sentence' it would work for the second example, but not the first (it would give **Is the boy who smoking is crazy?*). If she reformulated the rule as 'move the *last* auxiliary to the start of the sentence', it would work for the first example, but not the second (it would give **Is the girl is kissing the boy who smoking?*). Worse still, these are not the only possibilities that a child who started out with no knowledge of sentence structure must consider. In principle, the rule could turn out to be 'move the auxiliary that is spoken the loudest', 'move the auxiliary that is closest to the word *the*' and so on.

The poverty-of-the-stimulus argument is sometimes (mistakenly) characterized as an argument that the input is 'deficient' or 'lacking' in some way; that it contains too many speech errors, false starts and so on. This is missing the point. The point is that a learner who had no idea where to start would have an *infinite* number of possible hypotheses to consider, even if she heard nothing but full well-formed sentences. Of course, some of the more fundamentally wrongheaded hypotheses (e.g. the hypothesis that rules are formulated in terms of the relative volume of the words) will be quickly ruled out. But since there are an *infinite* number of such hypotheses, there can *never* be enough input data to rule them out, *no matter how much language the child hears*. This is why the input is said to be 'impoverished'; not because parents do not always produce full, grammatically correct sentences.

The generativist answer to this problem (we will meet a constructivist answer in Chapter 6) is to posit that children have some innate knowledge which means that they *do* know where to start when formulating hypotheses. The correct rule is 'move the auxiliary in the **main clause** (not the relative clause) to the front of the sentence':

> **The boy** [who is smoking] **is crazy** → **Is$_i$ the boy** [who is smoking] t_i **crazy?**
>
> **The girl is kissing the boy** [who is smoking] → **Is$_i$ the girl** t_i **kissing the boy** [who is smoking]?

Generativist accounts of acquisition posit that children's innate knowledge of language includes knowledge that **rules make reference to the phrase structure of the sentence**. Children are said to have the principle of **structure dependence**: they know in advance that the rules that they are trying to acquire will refer to things such as main clause and subordinate clause, CP and IP, Spec position, complement position and so on (*not* to linear order (e.g. first word, second word), volume, proximity to the word *the*, whether it is raining or sunny etc.).

Of course, children will still have to learn that the auxiliary moves from the main clause as opposed to the relative clause, but if the child knows (in effect) that it will be one of these two options, then she can learn the rule from a couple of examples (perhaps even solely from single-clause question/declarative pairs such as *The boy is crazy* → *Is the boy crazy?*).

4.1.8   Innate parameters

Clearly, innate knowledge that the rules of language make reference to phrase structure would be of no use if the child did not know anything about phrase structure in the first place. Generativist accounts therefore assume that children have knowledge not only of **principles** such as structure dependence, but also of some version of X-bar syntax (or one of its more recent descendents) itself. That is, generativist accounts assume that virtually all of the adult knowledge that we have described above (e.g. that all sentences contain a CP and an IP, that all phrases have the levels X, X′ and XP, that a VP contains a V head and its complement and so on) is also possessed by newborn infants.

Why do we say 'virtually all' and not 'all'? The answer is that some knowledge possessed by adult speakers cannot be innate, because it is specific to particular languages. For example, as we saw in Section 4.1.3, English-speaking adults know that heads (e.g. *kissed*) come before their complements (e.g. *Sue*) – e.g. *(John) kissed Sue* – whilst Korean-speaking adults know that heads come after their complements – e.g. *(John) Sue kissed* (where, in both cases, Sue is the one being kissed). Thus whilst generativist accounts assume that children's innate knowledge contains knowledge that a VP contains a VERB (e.g. *kiss*) and its complement (e.g. an NP such as *Sue*), they assume that this innate knowledge does not specify the order in which the two occur. If children's innate knowledge did specify an order (e.g. **head-first**), it would be the *wrong* order for children learning certain languages (in this case, Korean, and other **head-final** languages). The solution is to assume that children's innate knowledge includes (i) the fact that a phrase contains a head and its complement and (ii) the fact that every language is either head-first or head-final. Children's task is to learn from their input whether their language is head-first (e.g. English) or head-final (e.g. Korean). Technically, we say that children are born with a **head-direction parameter**, analogous to a 'mental switch' with two settings (head-first/head-final). Children then **set the parameter** (i.e. set the 'switch' to the correct position) on the basis of their input (the process is known as **parameter setting**). We will return to parameter setting in Chapters 5 (inflection) and 6 (syntax).

4.1.9   Universal Grammar: principles and parameters

Under generativist accounts then, children's innate knowledge of language (i.e. the knowledge of language with which they are born) consists of three things:

(1) Knowledge of phrase structure; i.e. syntactic categories and basic rules for combining them into phrases and sentences (as summarized in Section 4.1).
(2) Principles of language (e.g. structure dependence, Chapter 7; the binding principles, Chapter 8).
(3) Parameters for aspects of syntax that cannot be innate because they vary across languages (e.g. the head-direction parameter, Chapter 6; the *wh*-movement parameter, Chapter 7).

Together, these three elements constitute **Universal Grammar (UG)**. The term Universal Grammar refers to the knowledge of grammar with which children are born; a general grammar that is applicable to all the languages of the world (i.e. a grammar that is universal). For this reason, **generativist–nativist** theories are also known as **principles-and-parameters** theories. Phrase structure has been discussed extensively above. In the following sections we look more briefly at the second and third proposed elements of Universal Grammar: principles and parameters.

4.1.9.1 Universal Grammar principles   A problem facing principles-and-parameters approaches is that few theorists have attempted to posit an exhaustive list of either. Furthermore, on the few occasions when exhaustive lists have been proposed (e.g. Baker, 2001; Fodor, 2003; Wunderlich, 2007) there is often very little overlap, with some theorists explicitly rejecting principles or parameters proposed by others (Tomasello, 2007). The following principles should therefore not be taken as a set on which all (or even most) generativist researchers would necessarily agree, but simply as a list of principles that are frequently discussed in acquisition research.

- Language contains the lexical categories N, V, A, P, ADV and the functional categories CP, IP, DET (as discussed above; see also Chapter 6).
- The rules that are used to construct sentences (e.g. movement rules for question formation) make reference to phrases (e.g. the CP that is the main clause) and not to individual words (e.g. 'the first auxiliary in the sentence') (e.g. Chomsky, 1980; Crain and Nakayama, 1987). This is the principle of **structure dependence** as discussed above (see also Chapters 7 and 8).
- The possibility of **movement** (discussed above) is present in Universal Grammar. Some researchers argue that, in particular, 'the possibility for [subject–auxiliary] inversion [discussed above and in Chapter 7 with reference to question formation] is universal' (Santelmann *et al.*, 2002: 815). The possibility of *wh*-movement (see Chapter 7) may also be universal. However, whether and how individual languages make use of movement/inversion is a matter of parametric variation (see below).
- The **extended projection principle** (Chomsky, 1982) states that every sentence must have a SUBJECT (see Chapter 6).
- Sentences must obey the **theta criterion** (Chomsky, 1981). This states that for every semantic role (e.g. AGENT), there must be a syntactic role (e.g. SUBJECT), and vice versa (see Section 4.1.4 and Chapter 5.)
- Principles of **binding** (Chomsky, 1982; see Chapter 8) govern the interpretation of sentences such as *Mama Bear is washing her* (*her* cannot mean *Mama Bear*).
- Principles of **control** (Chomsky, 1982; see Chapter 8) govern the interpretation of sentences such as *John wants to leave* (this means *John wants JOHN to leave* and not, for example, *John wants Bill to leave*).

4.1.9.2 Universal Grammar parameters   Whilst, again, researchers
are not necessarily in agreement with regard to the set of parameters that
are present in Universal Grammar, the following are frequently discussed in
generativist acquisition research.

- The **head-direction** (complement-head) parameter (e.g. Chomsky, 1981), as
  discussed above (see Chapter 6).
- The **specifier–head** parameter (e.g. Chomsky, 1981; see Chapter 6).
- The **null-subject** parameter (e.g. Hyams, 1986). Some languages require a
  subject. In English, for example, it is grammatical to say *I play football* but
  not **Play football*, with the subject (*I*) omitted. In Spanish, for example, the
  subject (here *Yo*) would usually be omitted (or, more accurately, phonologically null; see Chapter 8), unless it is required for emphasis: *(Yo) juego el
  football.* (Not discussed in detail, but relevant in Chapters 6 and 8.)
- Many other parameters that specify the way in which a given principle
  applies in a particular language. For example, whilst the principle of syntactic
  movement in general (or even of *wh*-movement in particular) is present in
  UG, a ***wh*-parameter** is set corresponding to whether *wh*-movement occurs in
  that particular language (as in English; see Chapter 7) or not (as in Japanese).

4.2   Constructivist approaches

Constructivist approaches assume that the adult end-state (i.e. what children are
acquiring) does not constitute a generative grammar that is specified in terms of
X-bar syntax (or one of its descendents) but, rather, a set of constructions. The
theoretical approach presented here is largely based on Croft and Cruse (2004), a
textbook that summarizes a number of related **cognitive linguistics** approaches
(e.g. Langacker, 1987; Goldberg, 1995; Croft, 2001). The acquisition account
is based on that given in Tomasello (2003), which draws on many previous
proposals (e.g. Bowerman, 1973; Braine, 1976; Bates and MacWhinney, 1979;
Bybee, 1995; Peters, 1983; Pine and Lieven, 1993; Dąbrowska and Lieven,
2005).

4.2.1   Constructions and construction grammar

Most constructivist approaches to language acquisition (including that of
Tomasello, 2003) assume a construction grammar approach, under which
language is an inventory of **constructions** (utterance templates) of various
sizes and various levels of abstraction, each of which serves some **communicative** or **socio-pragmatic function.** For example the constructions *I want
it* (entirely **concrete**) and *I want X* (which has an **abstract slot**) both have
the function of requesting an object (or, in some scenarios, simply making a
comment).

The formal definition of a construction is a 'form–meaning pair such that some aspect of the form or some aspect of the function is not strictly predictable from the construction's component parts, or from other previously established constructions' (Goldberg, 1995: 4). To understand this definition, consider the (active) English transitive construction. This is a form (i.e. a pattern; NOUN1 VERB NOUN2) associated with a function (i.e. a meaning), roughly 'A acts upon B, causing B to be affected in some way'. Suppose we have the components *kicked*, *Bill* and *John*. From these components alone, it is not possible to tell who was the *kicker* and who the *kickee*. However, if these items are inserted into the NOUN1 VERB NOUN2 construction (e.g. *John kicked Bill*), the meaning is clear. Thus the constructional pattern in and of itself adds some meaning that is not available from the component parts. So the English transitive construction is a 'form–meaning pair such that some aspect of the function [i.e. who kicked someone and who got kicked] is not strictly predictable from the construction's component parts'.

4.2.2   Motivation for construction grammar

According to construction grammar approaches, then, adults form a sentence (e.g. *John kicked Bill*) by slotting appropriate items (e.g. *kicked*, *Bill* and *John*) into a construction: a pattern (e.g. NOUN1 VERB NOUN2) that is associated with some particular meaning ('A acts upon B, causing B to be affected in some way'). However, as we have already seen, there is an alternative to this account. Under generativist approaches, a speaker would form the same sentence by retrieving the verb *kick* from the lexicon and seeing that it selects a kicker and a kickee (theta-selection) expressed by a subject and object NP respectively (c-selection). The relevant items (*John* and *Bill*) would then be inserted into the subject and object positions of the tree respectively (under generativist accounts, constructions – such as the English transitive construction discussed here – do not have an independent existence, but are purely epiphenomenal, arising from the interaction between the selection properties of lexical items and general principles of phrase structure).

If the generativist approach can account for sentence formation, why did the alternative construction-based account emerge? One reason is that generativist accounts based on the notion of theta- and c-selection struggle to plausibly account for the formation of certain sentence types. For example, consider the sentence *He sneezed the napkin off the table* (Goldberg, 1995). Under a construction-based account, a speaker would form this sentence by inserting the relevant lexical items into the caused-motion construction: a pairing of the form NOUN1 VERB NOUN2 GOAL and the function 'A causes B to move to location C by performing some action on B' (e.g. *John brushed the leaves off the step*). Importantly, it is the caused-motion construction itself that imparts the caused-motion meaning to the verb *sneeze*. In contrast, a generativist account would have to posit that the verb *sneeze* itself contains a lexical entry with the meaning 'A causes B to move to C by sneezing' which theta- and c-selects a sneezer (SUBJECT), an object that is caused to move (OBJECT), and a location (PP). A problem for this latter approach is that it would seem odd to include a caused-motion meaning in one's lexical (mental dictionary) entry for *sneeze*, when it is unlikely to have ever been encountered with this meaning (or indeed in any context other than intransitive sentences such as *John sneezed*).

In fact, Goldberg (1995) argues that the positing of extra senses for *sneeze* would be not just odd but unprincipled and circular: generativist theory posits a different sense of a verb (e.g. solo action; caused motion) for each different configuration of arguments (e.g. SUBJECT sneeze; SUBJECT sneeze OBJECT PP). However, often – as in this case – there is no reason for positing a given verb sense independent of the fact that the verb occurs with a different configuration of arguments. The positing of additional senses seems particularly unwarranted in the case of verbs that can appear with a large number of different argument structures. For example, the verb *kick*, can appear with at least eight different argument structures, such *as kick the ball*, *kick black and blue*, *kick the ball into the goal*, *kick Bob the ball* (Goldberg, 1995: 11). It would seem implausible to posit the existence of eight different senses of *kick* (*X kicks Y*, *X causes Y to become Z by kicking*, *X kicks Y to location Z* and so on), each projecting a different argument structure, when the verb denotes essentially the same action in each. As we have already seen, construction grammar approaches seek to avoid this apparent problem by positing the independent existence of constructions (the first of three *essential principles of construction grammar* set out by Croft and Cruse, 2004): part of the meaning of an utterance such as *John kicked Bill* or *He sneezed the napkin off the table* is contributed by the meaning of the construction itself.

4.2.3   *Construction grammar and language acquisition*

An important attraction of construction grammar for the language acquisition theorist is that constructions (e.g. the transitive SUBJECT VERB OBJECT construction) – unlike rules of generative grammar (e.g. V′ contains V and an NP) – can, in principle, be learned on the basis of the input. What makes constructions learnable is the fact that each form (e.g. NOUN1 VERB NOUN2) is paired with a particular meaning ('A acts upon B, causing B to be affected in some way'). If the child is able to notice the correlation between this meaning and the pattern NOUN1 VERB NOUN2 in the input, then she can begin to learn the construction. Importantly, the fact that each form is paired with a meaning provides the child with motivation to learn the construction. For example, for the transitive construction, the motivation may be for the child to comment on her own actions or to request an activity (e.g. *I draw picture*). Because of its focus on the way that speakers **use** language to perform certain **functions** (e.g. describing an event, requesting an event, cajoling a listener, threatening a listener), the constructivist approach is also known as the **functionalist** or **usage-based** approach.

There is another, more important reason why a construction grammar can, in principle, be learned, whilst a generative grammar requires the assumption of innateness. Constructions such as the SUBJECT VERB OBJECT transitive construction do not need to be learned all in one go. Rather they can be learned in a **piecemeal** fashion, bit by bit. The child starts by learning a number of **frozen phrases** such as (for the transitive construction) *I'm kicking it*, *I'm hitting it* and *I'm eating it* directly from the input (again, note that the learnability of these strings will be aided by the fact that they express a simple, readily observable meaning). The child will then **schematize** across these strings to form an *I'm ACTIONing it* schema (a **lexically specific** or **item-based construction**), into which she can insert the name of any action that she is performing. Only later does the child analogize across these schema to arrive at an adultlike abstract construction (see Section 4.2.8.3).

Item-based constructions (sometimes called **patterns** or **schemas**) are also described as **partially productive**, **low-level** or **low-scope**. They may also be referred to as **slot-and-frame** or **variable+constant** (or **constant+variable**) **positional patterns**, where the **frame** or **constant** is the invariant material (e.g. *I'm . . . ing it*) and the **slot** or **variable** is the element that is varied to produce new utterances (e.g. ACTION in *I'm ACTIONing it*). Whatever terminology is used, the important points are that item-based patterns such as *I'm ACTIONing it* (a) can, in principle, be readily learned from the input and, (b) are paired with a meaning or **communicative function** that the child understands (e.g. describing an action performed by the speaker). Note, in relation to this last point, that the variable slot (e.g. ACTION) does not contain an adultlike syntactic category (e.g. VERB) but a simpler **functional** category (e.g. 'actions that I can perform'). Explaining how this category develops into an abstract adultlike category is, of course, a challenge for constructivist approaches (and one that remains problematic; see Chapter 6). However, the benefit in terms of acquisition theories is that a construction such as *I'm ACTIONing it* (where ACTION stands for any action that the child can perform and knows the name for) is semantically transparent, and hence presumably learnable.

Constructivist researchers argue that this piecemeal learning is more consistent with what we know about children's early language. It is uncontroversial that much of children's early utterances *look as if* they *could* have been generated by item-based schemas such as *I'm ACTIONing it*. The debate is whether these utterances *actually were* generated by such schemas (as constructivists would argue) or whether they were in fact generated by the more abstract rules of generative syntax, with which they are equally compatible.

4.2.4 Constructions at different levels of abstraction

Indeed, perhaps the most important difference between generativist and constructivist approaches is that the latter do not automatically assume that utterances are produced by the most abstract rule (or construction) possible. Consider the sentence *John kissed Sue*. As we have seen in Section 4.1, generativist accounts assume that this sentence is generated according to the maximally abstract (or general) rules (a) VP=NP+V', and (b) V'=V+NP (and also the movement of V to I to receive/check the *-ed* inflection).

Under a constructivist account, the sentence *could* also be formed by the most abstract (or general) 'rule' possible: the SUBJECT VERB OBJECT transitive construction. However, this account also allows for the possibility that the utterance could be formed by a lexically specific construction based around the verb form *kissed* (e.g. *KISSER kissed KISSEE*), around the items *John* and *kissed* (e.g. *John kissed KISSEE*), and many other alternatives. These constructions are said to be **item-based** or **lexically specific** because at least one component of the construction is a **specific lexical item** (i.e. a word or morpheme). Another possibility, under the constructivist account, is that the entire utterance could have been memorized, and produced as a **frozen-phrase** (or **fixed phrase** or **rote-learned unit**). These possibilities are summarized below:

Most abstract (most '**general**' or '**schematic**')	SUBJ VERB OBJ	Wholly abstract construction
	KISSER kissed KISSEE ⎫ John kissed KISSEE ⎬	Item-based/lexically specific construction
Most substantive (most '**concrete**' or '**specific**')	John kissed Sue	Frozen phrase

The constructions shown above represent only some of the possible constructions that could have been used to produce the utterance *John kissed Sue*. In principle, all combinations of abstract and concrete components are possible. In practice, the particular constructions that speakers store will depend on the sentences that they hear. If a speaker hears a number of highly similar sentences where just one item is different each time, she is likely to form an item-based construction around the invariant material:[9]

> I wanna play; I wanna eat; I wanna go → I wanna ACTION
>
> I'm kicking it; I'm hitting it; I'm eating it → I'm ACTIONing it

Conversely, if a speaker hears exactly the same utterance repeatedly with no variation, she is likely to acquire the utterance as a 'frozen phrase' with no variable slots. Bybee and Scheibman (1999) argue that this is the case for the phrase *I dunno* (which, in fact, is often pronounced as little more than a rising and falling pitch contour, with no speech sounds actually articulated). Generativist accounts also assume that at least some frequent phrases will be stored and produced by rote. In fact, this *has* to be the case for idiomatic phrases that are non-productive (e.g. *Be that as it may*; **Have that as she could*), and hence that are presumably not generated according to X-bar-type rules. However, no current generativist theories incorporate a role for partially abstract (i.e. lexically specific) schemas such as *I don't VERB* (as discussed in Section 4.2.6, this is potentially problematic for idioms such as *I wouldn't X, let alone Y* that appear to be neither rote-learned phrases nor sentences generated using standard phrase-structure rules; Fillmore, Kay and O'Connor, 1988).

Another important assumption of construction grammar approaches is that speakers store both more and less abstract forms of the same construction simultaneously. For example, in addition to a wholly concrete *I dunno* construction, speakers may have partially abstract, lexically specific constructions such as *I don't VERB* and SUBJECT DO-*n't* VERB, and a wholly abstract SUBJECT AUX NEG VERB construction. When producing a sentence, a speaker may use any one of the relevant constructions stored. For example, a speaker may produce *I don't know* as a concrete phrase on one occasion, and generate it using the fully abstract SUBJECT AUX NEG VERB construction on another.

4.2.5   Inflection and the uniform representation of semantic structures

In Section 4.1, we saw that, under generativist accounts, inflection (e.g. *John kissed Sue*) is accounted for by the functional category INLF (where the verb 'picks up' or 'checks' the past-tense *-ed* inflection). An essential principle of construction grammar (Croft and Cruse, 2004) is the 'uniform representation of semantic structures'. Traditionally (and, so far, in this chapter), the term 'construction' has been used to refer only to **argument structure** constructions (e.g. SUBJECT VERB OBJECT): constructions that specify where VERBs (e.g. *kiss*) appear in relation to their **arguments** (e.g. the SUBJECT argument – the kisser – and the OBJECT argument – the kissee).

Under construction grammar approaches, every semantic structure (that is, every form that is associated with a particular meaning) is considered to be a construction, regardless of its length. As we have already seen, since the form SUBJECT VERB OBJECT has a particular meaning (roughly 'A acts upon B, causing B to be affected in some way'), it is a construction (in this case a fully abstract construction, since it consists entirely of open slots). In the same way, since *I'm ACTIONing it* has a particular meaning, it too is a construction (in this case a lexically specific construction). Since a single word (e.g. *man*) is also a form that is associated with a particular meaning, every individual word is also a construction; in this case simply one that happens to have no slots, and consists entirely of fixed lexical material.

Why would one want to make this (seemingly somewhat odd) assumption? The reason is that, by assuming that an individual word (and any form associated with a particular meaning) is a construction, construction grammar approaches can deal with inflection in the same way that they deal with verb argument structure. For example, the individual verb form *kissing* can be considered an instantiation of the morphological (present-tense) construction VERB+*ing* (an item-based construction based not around a particular word, but the morphological item -*ing*). Thus a speaker could produce the form *kissing* either by retrieving the wholly specific construction (i.e. word) *kissing* directly from memory or by inserting the VERB *kiss* into the partially productive *VERB+ing* pattern.

In the previous two chapters, we noted that constructivist approaches, unlike generativist approaches, do not draw a sharp distinction between the grammar (the 'rules' for sentence formation and inflection) and the lexicon (the 'mental dictionary'). The reason for this should now be clear: under the constructivist approach, all learning consists of the acquisition of constructions of different sizes (from a single word to an entire sentence) at different levels of abstraction, from wholly concrete frozen-phrase constructions (e.g. *I'm kicking it*, or the word *kissing*), through partially productive lexically specific constructions (e.g. *I'm ACTIONing it*; *VERBing*), to wholly abstract constructions (e.g. SUBJECT VERB OBJECT).

Another consequence of the uniform representation of semantic structure is that recursion can be accounted for in much the same way as under generativist accounts: a construction simply serves as a variable in another construction. For example, a sentence that would be analysed, under a generativist account, as consisting of multiple CPs would be analysed as follows:

SUBJ VERB that [SENTENCE]   James hoped that
    [SUBJ VERB that [SENTENCE]]   Sarah knew that
        [SUBJ VERB OBJ]   John kissed Sue

Each sentence-level construction (*[SUBJ VERB that SENTENCE]* or *[SUBJ VERB OBJ]*) fills the SENTENCE slot in another sentence-level construction (*[SUBJ VERB that SENTENCE]*). Of course, there is a debate to be had over whether the generativist or the constructivist account of this phenomenon better explains the data. The point to note here is simply that it is untrue that, as some generativist accounts have assumed, non-generativist accounts cannot explain recursion in principle.

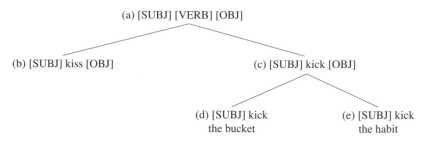

Figure 4.19 A taxonomic hierarchy of constructions

4.2.6   *A structured inventory of constructions (and non-'core' constructions)*

We noted at the outset of this section that construction grammar approaches take the adult end state to be a 'structured inventory of constructions'. Figure 1.19 shows a taxonomic hierarchy of constructions (illustrating Croft and Cruse's, 2004, third essential principle of construction grammar: *the taxonomic organization of constructions in the grammar*). Note that, as discussed in the previous section, this hierarchy includes more and less abstract versions of the same construction. Although this taxonomy resembles a generativist phrase structure tree, it actually represents something quite different; something more akin to a family tree, where 'daughters' inherit properties of their 'parents'.

Each construction not only inherits the properties of its parent construction(s), it is also an instantiation of its parent construction(s). In Figure 4.19, (d) *[SUBJ] kick the bucket* and (e) *[SUBJ] kick the habit* are both instantiations of the construction (c) *[SUBJ] kick [OBJ]* which, in turn, is an instantiation of the more general *[SUBJ] [VERB] [OBJ]* construction. What does 'inheriting the properties of (or being an instantiation of) a parent construction' actually mean, in terms of what is stored inside speakers' heads? It means that there is no need to repeatedly store the same information for different items. For example, when a speaker stores the word *kick*, there is no need for her to store the fact that the SUBJECT comes before the VERB and the OBJECT after (though she *may* do; unlike generative approaches, construction grammar does not rule out redundant representation). All she *need* store is the fact that *kick* is a daughter of the SUBJECT VERB OBJECT construction. The constructions (d) *[SUBJ] kick the bucket* and (e) *[SUBJ] kick the habit* will need to be stored separately (by all speakers), even though they are instantiations of the more general construction *[SUBJ] kick [OBJECT]*. This is because although they can inherit their word order from their parent construction, these constructions cannot inherit their meaning. The meanings of *kick the bucket* and *kick the habit* are not simply more specific versions of the general meaning of the *SUBJECT kick OBJECT* construction (A hits B with her foot). Rather, they have special idiomatic meanings of their own (i.e. *die* and *give up a habit*).

Proponents of construction grammar argue that this framework deals more satisfactorily than generativist accounts with such idioms, and also with semi-formulaic, semi-productive patterns as exemplified by the sentence pairs below:

> I wouldn't live in London, let alone New York.
>
> She isn't even fat, let alone obese.
>
> Him, be a doctor!
>
> Me, catch the bus!

The problem for generativist approaches is that 'normal' processes of sentence generation (using X-bar principles) cannot capture the idiosyncratic meanings behind the constructions. However, since the patterns appear to be productive, such utterances cannot be classed as rote-learned phrases (e.g. *How do you do?*). The generativist approach, then, simply classifies these items as peripheral (i.e. not part of 'core grammar') and argues that they are outside the scope of normal processes of language acquisition. Constructivist approaches see this as problematic, given that some 'core' processes (e.g. verb inflection) nevertheless apply (e.g. **She isn't/they aren't** *even fat, let alone obese*). The claim is that constructivist approaches can deal with these examples more easily by positing, for example, an 'incredulity construction' such as [SUBJECT-ACCUSATIVE] [VERB-NON-FINITE] ([OBJECT])!

4.2.7   *Differences between generative grammar and construction grammar*

Since construction grammar approaches allow speakers to store constructions at *any* possible level of abstraction, generativist and constructivist analyses of the same sentence sometimes appear, at first glance, to be mere notational variants (i.e. different ways of saying the same thing). Figure 4.20 shows a generative-grammar and construction-grammar analysis of the sentence *John kissed Sue*. Both assume that the sentence consists of a SUBJECT NP, a VERB and an OBJECT NP, in that order. Some construction grammar approaches (e.g. Kay and Fillmore, 1999; Lakoff, 1987) posit intermediate constructions that correspond to traditional syntactic phrases such as VP, making the two approaches look virtually indistinguishable. Despite their surface similarity, the generative and construction grammar approaches do differ in many important respects.

First, although the two accounts may broadly agree on one possible analysis of a given sentence, construction grammar always additionally allows the possibility that the sentence was generated on the basis of a less abstract lexically specific schema (e.g. *John kissed KISSEE*). This may be true not only for

Generativist analysis   Constructivist analysis

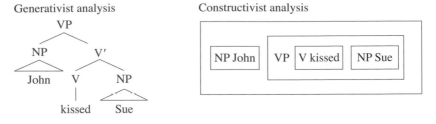

Figure 4.20 Generativist and constructivist analysis are sometimes (apparent) notational variants

children, but also (particularly for very high-frequency schemas such as *I think SENTENCE*) for adults.

Second, it is important to note that the generativist tree in Figure 4.20 shows only the starting point for the utterance (the VP), and not the functional projections that are additionally assumed (IP and CP). Thus the generative and construction grammar accounts differ in that the former requires the VERB to move to I to receive or check inflection, whereas the latter treats morphological constructions (e.g. VERB*ed*) in the same way as syntactic constructions, and hence does not posit INFL, or any other functional categories (although other problems may arise in terms of how such constructions are combined). Similarly, the VP shown in Figure 4.20 could, under generative accounts, be the starting point for a syntactic movement operation that would yield a passive (e.g. *Sue was kissed by John*) or a question (e.g. *Did John kiss Sue?*; *Who did John kiss?*). Construction grammar posits that passives, questions and so on are independent constructions (e.g. SUBJECT was VERBed by OBJECT; WH-WORD, AUX, NP, VERB?) that are not formed by movement, and that are acquired independently, in the same way as any other construction (though they may be related through meaning).

Third, whist the generative and construction grammar analyses use many of the same category labels (e.g. V, NP), this hides some very different assumptions. For generative accounts, syntactic categories such as NOUN and VERB are not only present from birth (with lexical learning required to 'fill in' the relevant categories with exemplars) but also universal: whilst not all languages have the same inventory of syntactic categories (e.g. many languages do not use determiners), all languages 'choose' from the same limited range of categories. Furthermore, where languages do share a given category (e.g. NOUN, VERB), there will be important similarities in the way that these categories operate across language. For constructivist accounts, syntactic categories such as NOUN and VERB are neither present from birth nor universal. Rather, they are constructed on the basis of the input, on a language-by-language basis. Construction grammar accounts (in particular Croft, 2001) point to languages that have syntactic categories that do not fit neatly in the UG-specified inventory of syntactic categories posited by generative grammar (which was drawn up essentially on the basis of English and related languages). For example, Mandarin Chinese has property words that are verb-like in some respects, but adjective-like in others (see Chapter 6). The claim is that, to the extent that there are syntactic categories that exist crosslinguistically, this is a function of the fact that speakers of different languages have similar communicative needs. For example, all languages have some kind of NOUN category, because all languages must provide a way to denote concrete objects, people and so on. Similarly (whether or not there is a crosslinguistic category of VERB), all speakers need some type of word that denotes a relationship between two entities (e.g. *X hit Y*; *X saw Y* etc.).

Indeed, under at least some versions of a construction grammar approach, speakers do not operate with 'free-standing' grammatical categories at all. Rather, novel utterances are generated online as they are needed, by analogy with previously encountered utterances, which is all that are stored. What does the term 'VERB category' actually mean under a construction grammar account? One possibility is that VERB denotes a category of items in the speaker's grammar that have been, in some way, stored with the label VERB. This **category-based** account treats the VERB category in the same way as the generative approach, except that the category is seen as language-specific and learned from the input. Under an **exemplar-based** account, however, the speaker generates a novel utterance by analogy with stored concrete strings, both full sentences (e.g. *John kissed Sue*; *The man kicked the ball*) and shorter strings (e.g. *cat*; *dog*). In this case, the label VERB is simply a convenient shorthand for something like 'every item that I have ever seen in this construction, and other items that are sufficiently semantically/phonologically/distributionally similar to such an item'. Under the category-based account, VERB is (like the category ANIMALS) a free-standing category that has independent existence before it is put to a particular purpose (such as generating an SVO sentence). Under the exemplar-based approach, VERB is (like the category THINGS I'D TAKE TO A DESERT ISLAND) a label for an online generalization that is made for some particular purpose (such as generating an SVO sentence). In the same way, a speaker producing a transitive utterance could be seen as (a) using a pre-existing SUBJECT VERB OBJECT construction that is stored in the minds of speakers or (b) generating the sentence online by analogy to every SUBJECT VERB OBJECT transitive sentence previously encountered.

4.2.8 *Constructivist approaches to acquisition*

So far, we have outlined the construction grammar approach to the adult grammar, but we have only touched on the constructivist approach to language acquisition that is based on this account. The constructivist account of acquisition set out in Tomasello (2003) is summarized below. We begin at the point at which the child has solved (or at least begun to solve) the problem of segmenting the continuous speech stream into words (e.g. *ball*), and utterances or clauses (e.g. *I'm kicking it*) (see Chapter 2). She has also developed some ability to monitor the focus of a speaker's **attention** (e.g. the speaker may be looking at a ball as opposed to a cake, which is also present) and to infer her **communicative intention** (e.g. to describe an action that she is currently performing on the ball) (see Chapter 3). Finally, the child also has acquired some knowledge and understanding of cultural routines (e.g. bedtime, mealtime etc.) (see Chapter 3).

4.2.8.1 Frozen phrases   First, the child uses these abilities and knowledge to rote-learn a number of whole utterances (e.g. *I'm kicking it*, *I'm eating it*; also known as *frozen phrases, fixed phrases or holophrases*) paired with their communicative function or meaning. For example, whilst taking part in the cultural routine of a mealtime, the child may hear her caregiver say *I'm eating it*. The child understands the cultural routine (i.e. mealtime) and so understands that the utterance is something related to this routine (and not to something else altogether). This understanding, together with the skill of intention reading, allows the child to understand what the caregiver intends by the utterance. For example, the child can tell by the fact that the caregiver is bringing the food towards her own mouth, as opposed to the mouth of the child, that her intention is to label her own action (rather than to persuade the child to eat, for example). Once the child has learned this phrase, she may use it to comment on her own actions (e.g. *I'm eating it*).

4.2.8.2 Lexically specific constructions   Second, by decomposing these stored utterances (e.g. *I'm hitting it*; *I'm kicking it*; *I'm eating it*) into their component parts and generalizing across utterances with shared lexical items and shared meaning, the child abstracts **partially productive, lexically specific construction schemas** (see above, and Chapters 5 and 6) each associated with a particular meaning or communicative function (e.g. *I'm ACTIONing it*, to describe the child performing some action on an object). However, note that the slots within these schemas are, at this stage, functional rather than formal (e.g. this schema contains an ACTION slot denoting 'actions that I can perform' rather than a more abstract VERB slot).

There are no well-specified proposals for exactly how this **schematization** process occurs. However, as outlined above, the claim is essentially that if a speaker hears a number of highly similar sentences where only one element varies (e.g. *I'm hitting it*; *I'm kicking it*; *I'm eating it*) she will form a slot-and-frame pattern with the recurring elements constituting the frame and the variable element the slot (e.g. *I'm ACTIONing it*). Although this constitutes only indirect evidence in support of this claim, constructivist studies (summarized in Chapter 7) have found that if a slot-and-frame pattern is attributed to the child whenever she produces three similar utterances with one variable element in this way, the resulting inventory of patterns can account for a reasonably large proportion of children's utterances (e.g. 60 per cent in the study of Lieven, Pine and Baldwin, 1997).

One factor that may affect schematization is the number of different items that appear in the variable position in the child's input (the **type frequency** of the slot position). Evidence for this claim comes from regular and irregular past-tense formation (in which the VERB stem constitutes the variable slot, and the morphology (shown in **bold**) the frame):

> Regular pattern: walk**ed**, play**ed**, listen**ed**, jump**ed**
> (One) irregular pattern: sl**ept**, w**ept**, cr**ept**

As noted by many authors (e.g. Bybee, 1995) the high type frequency of the slot position in the regular pattern (several hundred verbs form their past tense in this way) leads children to form a *VERBed* slot-and-frame pattern; evidence for which occurs in the form of **overgeneralization** errors, where a verb is incorrectly inserted into this schema (e.g. *runned*). However, the relatively low type frequency of the slot in the irregular pattern (only a handful of verbs form their past tense in this way) means that overgeneralizations with this pattern (e.g. *beep →* bept*) are virtually non-existent (though, as we will see in Chapter 5, phonological factors are also important here).

4.2.8.3 Abstract constructions and analogy   Third, having acquired an inventory of lexically specific constructions (e.g. *I'm ACTIONing it*), the child analogizes across these constructions (or particular stored utterances that instantiate them) to arrive at adultlike fully abstract constructions. Constructivist researchers would probably agree that this is the area of the theory that is most seriously underspecified. Nevertheless, some details of the process of analogy have been proposed. The basic idea is that children analogize across lexically specific schemas on the basis of functional and/or formal similarity between them (see Chapter 6). For example, the child might generalize across the schemas *I'm ACTIONing it* and *KISSER kiss KISSEE* (or actual stored utterances instantiating these schemas) on the basis of similar AGENT–ACTION and ACTION–PATIENT relations in the two ('**structure mapping**'). Additionally, she might generalize across the schemas *I'm ACTIONing* it and *He's ACTIONing it* (or sentences instantiating them) on the basis of shared invariant material (*-ing it*). Analogizing across utterances/schemas that share formal but not functional similarity (e.g. *The books cost money → The dogs chase cats*) in this way may allow children to acquire a syntactic SUBJECT VERB

OBJECT construction (as opposed to a semantic AGENT ACTION PATIENT construction).

4.2.8.4 Syntactic categories Fourth, at the same time as the processes above are ongoing, the child will also form syntactic categories such as VERB and NOUN (though, as discussed above, the categories that children form under constructivist approaches may initially be low-scope and/or idiosyncratic, only gradually converging on those of the adult grammar). Under the constructivist account, this occurs via the process of **functionally based distributional analysis**: the child groups together words that perform similar **function**s (e.g. words that denote events) and that appear in similar sentence **distributions**. For example, a child might group together *hit*, *kick* and *eat* (into an emerging VERB class) on the basis that (a) all denote ACTIONS and (b) all appear in the frames *I'm Xing it*, *He's gonna X it*, and so on. This process is discussed in more detail in Chapter 6.

4.2.8.5 Restriction of overgeneralization errors Via the processes outlined above, the child forms **generalizations**: (fully or partially) abstract constructions that allow her to generate novel utterances. However, children sometimes insert into an abstract construction items that may not appear in that construction in the adult grammar, producing an **overgeneralization error**. For example, **verb argument structure overgeneralization errors** occur when a child inserts a verb (for example the intransitive verb *laugh*) into a transitive construction (e.g. **The funny clown laughed Lisa* [meaning 'The funny man made Lisa laugh']). Full discussion of this topic is reserved for Chapter 6 (Section 6.3). Here, it will suffice to say that, under the constructivist account, children retreat from error not (of course) with the aid of innate rules of UG, but by probabilistic learning of patterns of usage of both construction and verb meaning.

4.3   Theoretical approaches to grammar acquisition: conclusion

In this chapter, we have outlined the adult endstate as it is seen under generativist and constructivist accounts respectively. We have also briefly outlined the claims of the two accounts with regard to the initial state and the transition to the adult grammar (see Sections 4.1.7–4.1.9 and 4.2.8). The remainder of the book sets out in more detail competing proposals regarding children's acquisition of the adult grammar (i.e. mature systems of morphology and syntax) and tests these proposals against the available empirical data.

5 Inflection

5.1 Introduction to inflection

Inflection is the process by which words (or phrases) are marked for certain **grammatical features**. Perhaps the most common way that languages accomplish this marking is by 'adding' a **morpheme** to the end of a word (in which case this morpheme is known as a **suffix**). For example, many languages (including English) add a particular marker (in this case, *-ed*) to denote past tense (e.g., *play-ed*). Similarly, many languages (though not English) attach a suffix to verbs to encode the grammatical feature of **gender**. In Russian, the verb form *igral* (= was playing) refers to a male, and *igrala* a female. The study of the way in which these morphemes are added to words to mark grammatical features is the study of **inflectional morphology**.

What other grammatical features are encoded by inflection? Although some languages encode features such as humanness, approximate distance, shape, whether or not the speaker actually witnessed the event discussed, and so on (Slobin, 1982), we will focus here on four grammatical features that – it is probably fair to say – are represented in the majority of the world's languages that use inflection: **Tense**, **Person**, **Number** (verb inflection) and **Case** (noun/pronoun inflection).

5.1.1 Verb inflection

- **Tense**. English (like most languages) distinguishes between present and past tense. English marks past tense (for 'regular' verbs) by adding the morpheme *-ed* to the **base** form (also known as the **root** or **stem**) of the verb (e.g. *play-ed*). Present tense is marked with (a) a combination of **auxiliary BE** and the **present progressive** morpheme *-ing* (e.g. *he is play-ing*, *they are play-ing* etc.); (b) with a **modal auxiliary** (e.g. *can*, *will*) and an infinitive form (e.g. *he can play*, *they will play etc.*); (c) with *-s* (e.g. *he play-s*); or (d) with a **null** or **zero** marker (e.g. *you play*).[1]
- **Person**. English (like most languages) distinguishes between the first person (the person/people speaking), the second person (the person/people being

addressed) and the third person (a person/group of people that is neither the speaker nor the addressee). For example, assuming present tense (see above) and singular number (see below), English distinguishes between third person (*He play-s*) and first/second person (*I play/You play*). However, as this example shows, English (unlike more richly inflected languages) does not always use different forms for different persons. Indeed, past-tense forms do not distinguish between person at all (e.g. *I/you/he played*).

- **Number.** To some extent, English marks the number of people. In the third person present tense, English distinguishes between singular (3sg; *He play-s*) and plural (3pl; *They play*). However, English (unlike more richly inflected languages) does not mark number in the first person (*I/we play*) or second person (*You/You play*) present tense, or on any past-tense forms (*I/we/he/they played*).

Thus in languages that make use of inflection, verbs are generally marked for **tense** and person+number **agreement**. The term *agreement* reflects the fact that a verb must **agree** with its subject. For example, if the subject is 3sg (e.g. *he*) the agreeing 3sg verb form (e.g. *plays*) must be used. If the subject is 3pl (e.g. *they*) the 3sg form would not agree with the subject (e.g. *they plays); instead the agreeing 3pl form *play* must be used (e.g. *they play*).

In fact, English is not a good language to choose when explaining (or studying) inflection. This is because English uses very few different morphemes (i.e. it has **impoverished inflectional morphology**). For example, when forming a simple present-tense form, there are only two morphemes available: *-s* (e.g. *plays*) or the null/zero marker (e.g. *play*). This means that a single form is used for a large number of different tense/person/number combinations (a high degree of **syncretism**). For example, the zero-marked form *play* is the present tense form for 1sg (*I play*), 2sg (*you play*), 1pl (*we play*), 2pl (*you play*) and 3pl (*they play*). Consequently, monolingual English speakers often find it difficult to understand agreement, as they are not used to using different verb forms for different person+number combinations.

A better choice is a language such as Russian, which, for the present tense, uses a different morpheme to mark each different person+number combination (see Table 5.1). Most European languages fall somewhere between the extremes of Russian (which uses a different morpheme for each person+number combination) and English (which uses the same morpheme for all but one person+number combination): a different morpheme is used for many different person+number combinations, but some serve two or more functions. This is illustrated in Table 5.1, which shows some different person+number present-tense forms for Dutch, German, French and Spanish, in each case, for the verb *to play* (note that the Spanish verb *jugar* additionally undergoes a stem change, from *jug-* to *jueg-* for some forms, reflecting the fact that stress falls on the stem).

Table 5.1 *Some examples of present-tense person+number (agreement) marking across six fusional languages*

Person	No.	Pronoun (English)	English (regular verb)	Russian (regular -t′ verb)	Dutch (regular -en verb)	German (regular -en verb)	French (regular -er verb)	Spanish (regular -ar verb)
Infinitive			play-Ø	igrat'	spelen	spielen	jouer	jugar
1st	Sing.	I	play-Ø	igraiu	speel-Ø	spiele	joue	juego
2nd	Sing.	You	play-Ø	igraiesh	speelt	spielst	joues	juegas
3rd	Sing.	He/she/it	plays	igraiet	speelt	spielt	joue	juega
1st	Plur.	We	play-Ø	igraiem	spelen	spielen	jouons	jugamos
2nd	Plur.	You	play-Ø	igraiete	spelen	spielt	jouez	jugáis
3rd	Plur.	They	play-Ø	igraiut	spelen	spielen	jouent	juegan

The languages shown in Table 5.1 (and, indeed, most Indo-European languages) are **fusional**, meaning that a *single* morpheme codes for a particular *combination* of tense, person and number (for example, the Russian morpheme *-esh* marks present tense, second person and singular number). Other languages (e.g. the Mayan languages) are not fusional but agglutinative, meaning that one (or more) morpheme is added to mark tense, one to mark person, and one to mark number (further morphemes may be added to mark other grammatical features). For example, the translation of the English sentence *You are hitting me* in K'iche' Mayan is a single word, *kinach'ayo*, consisting of five morphemes:

k-	in-	a-	ch'ay-	o.
present tense-	1sg OBJ (*me*)-	2sg SUBJ (*you*) –	hit –	present tense

To the **root** or **stem** *ch'ay* (*hit*) are added the **prefix** morphemes *k-* (marking present tense) *-in* (marking 1sg object: *me*) and *-a* (marking 2sg subject: *you*) and the **suffix** morpheme *-o* (also marking present tense).

We should acknowledge from the outset that some of the debates covered in this chapter are rather Anglocentric (or Indo-Europeancentric) in nature, simply as a consequence of the fact that most of the theory development and empirical research has been conducted in countries where these languages are spoken. Nevertheless, when evaluating theories of the acquisition of inflection, it is important to bear in mind that a successful theory will apply to all languages, fusional and agglutinative alike.

5.1.1.1 Finite, non-finite and infinitive verb forms

When a verb form is marked for tense it is said to be **finite**. For example, the forms *plays* and *played* are marked for present tense and past tense respectively. 'Finite' means 'bounded or limited in time' (i.e. the opposite of infinite). A verb that is marked for tense is known as 'finite' because it denotes an event occurring at a particular point in time (e.g. the present or past). When a verb form is not marked for tense, it is said to be **non-finite**. A non-finite form is used when tense marking is not required. Most often, this is because the job of tense marking is done by another verb in the sentence. The simplest case of this is where tense is marked on a **modal auxiliary** verb, and the **infinitive** form of the verb is used:

He	can	*play*
He	**will**	*play*
	modal auxiliary	*infinitive*

In English, tense may also be marked on the dummy auxiliary DO, in which case the infinitive form of the verb is again used:

He	**does**	*play*
He	**doesn't**	*play*
	dummy DO	*infinitive*

Another case where the infinitive form of the verb is used is when tense is marked on the main verb (e.g. *saw, watched, let*)

She	**saw**	him	*play*
She	**watched**	him	*play*
She	**let**	him	*play*
	main verb		*infinitive*

English is unusual in that it has two different infinitive forms: a bare form (e.g. *play*) and a form that is marked with the infinitival marker *to* (e.g. *to play*). Some main verbs (e.g. *want, like*) require this *to* form. Again, tense is marked only on the main verb:

She	**wants**	him	*to play*	(cf. *She wants him play*)
She	**likes**	him	*to play*	(cf. *She likes him play*)
	main verb		*infinitive*	

Most languages (e.g. all those shown in Table 5.1) are simpler in that they have a single infinitive form (e.g. *igrat', spelen, spielen, jouer, jugar*), as opposed to two (e.g. *play* and *to play*). Notice, too, that, these languages have an infinitival marker (shown in **bold**) that always clearly marks the verb as a non-finite form. As we will see later in this chapter, the fact that one of the two English infinitival forms is not marked in this way (e.g. *play*) can sometimes make children's errors difficult to interpret.

A somewhat confusing aspect of English is that in addition to the two infinitive forms (e.g. *play* and *to play*), it has a **present-participle** form that ends *-ing* (e.g. *playing*) and a **past-participle** form that (often) ends *-en* (e.g. *eaten*). These are both **non-finite** forms because they do not, by themselves, mark tense. The job of tense marking is done by an auxiliary verb (e.g. BE, HAVE):

She	**is**	*playing*		She	**has**	*eaten*
She	**was**	*playing*		She	**had**	*eaten*
	auxiliary verb	*non-finite*			**auxiliary verb**	*non-finite*
		present participle				*past participle*

A further complication is that some past-participle forms end in *-ed* as opposed to *-en*.

She	**has**	*played*
She	**had**	*played*
	auxiliary verb	*non-finite past participle*

This can be confusing, because *played* is also a past-tense form (e.g. *she played*). However, when used in conjunction with an auxiliary, it is the auxiliary that marks tense. Hence in the above examples, *played* is *not* a past-tense form, but a non-finite past-participle form.

In all the examples discussed above, a **non-finite form** (i.e. an **infinitive** or **participle**) is used because the job of tense marking is taken on by another verb in the sentence (either a main verb or an auxiliary verb). Less frequently, a non-finite form (again, either an auxiliary or participle) is used because the sentence makes reference to a state of affairs that is not bounded in time. For example, Alexander Pope's famous line ***To err** is human, **to forgive** divine* (*to err* is a somewhat archaic verb meaning 'to make a mistake') uses infinitive forms (in bold) because the reference is to making mistakes and forgiving *in general*; not to a specific occasion on which a mistake was made or forgiveness granted. More prosaically, a *No **smoking*** sign uses the participle form to indicate that what is forbidden is smoking in general, not a specific past, present or future act of smoking (the French equivalent *Ne pas **fumer*** uses the infinitive form for the same reason).

Although this discussion has been somewhat technical, a detailed understanding of finite versus non-finite forms is crucial for understanding the accounts of optional infinitive errors discussed in Section 5.2.

5.1.2   Noun inflection (Case)

Many languages mark nouns and pronouns for **case**. The case marking that a (pro)noun receives denotes its grammatical role in the sentence. For example, in the majority of the world's languages, a (pro)noun that is the SUBJECT (e.g. the AGENT of an active sentence) receives **nominative** case, with the (pro)noun that is the OBJECT (e.g. the PATIENT of an active sentence) receiving **accusative** case. For example:

- In Russian, if *Veronika hit Alexandra*, the AGENT takes nominative case (*Veronika*), whilst the PATIENT takes accusative case (*Alexandroo*). Because the listener can determine 'who did what to whom' from the nominative/accusative case marking, Russian speakers can change the order of the words in the sentence without changing the meaning. So *Alexandroo hit Veronika*[2] also means 'Veronika hit Alexandra.'
- In German, it is not the noun, but the determiner (equivalent of English *the* or *a*) that receives case marking. If *the woman hit the man*, then *the man* takes accusative case: *den Mann*. If *the man hit the woman*, then *the man* takes nominative case: *der Mann*. Again this allows German speakers to vary the word order without changing the meaning.
- English has almost no case marking and uses word order to convey 'who did what to whom'. Thus an English speaker cannot change the word order without altering the meaning. However, English does have case marking on some pronouns. If Sue hit John, we would say *She hit **him*** (not **She hit he*). If John hit Sue, we would say ***He** hit her* (not **Him hit her*). Thus ***him*** and ***he*** are the accusative and nominative forms of the 3sg masculine pronoun respectively. English also has an accusative/nominative contrast for ***her/she, us/we*** and ***me/I***. Although English is not, in general, an appropriate language in which to discuss children's acquisition of case marking (due to the fact that it does not occur on nouns), one of the theories of optional infinitive errors (see Section 5.2) makes a critical prediction regarding (pronoun) case-marking errors.

5.1.3   Generativist and constructivist approaches to inflection

As this brief discussion has shown, languages use a variety of means to mark inflection including (a) the 'addition' of a morpheme to a word (e.g. *play+ed*); (b) the selection of one of two alternative forms (e.g. *me/I*; *der/den*); (c) the inclusion of an auxiliary (e.g. *is playing*) and various combinations and/or intermediate strategies. Nevertheless, generativist approaches assume that – however inflection may be realized on the surface – it reflects movement (or checking) of the relevant items (e.g. NOUN, VERB, DETERMINER PHRASE) to the Inflectional Phrase (IP), or to the Agreement (AGRP) and Tense (TNSP) phrases (for one account discussed in Section 5.2, the distinction is crucial); see Chapter 4 for details.

Constructivist approaches assume that learners initially acquire utterance wholes (e.g. *I'm kicking it*; *I'm hitting it*) across which they then abstract, to form lexically specific morphological schemas (e.g. *I'm X-ing it*). Later in development, learners will abstract across these schemas (e.g. across *I'm X-ing it* and *He was X-ing*) to form more adultlike morphological constructions (e.g. [PRONOUN] [BE] [VERB]ing). Again, these assumptions (particularly the first two) are central to the theoretical accounts to be discussed in this chapter.

5.1.4   Debates in children's acquisition of inflection

Perhaps surprisingly, theoretical debates over children's acquisition of inflection have not tended to focus on the question of how children actually acquire the individual morphemes (e.g. 3sg -*s*; past-tense -*ed*). Presumably this is because, under any account, children must acquire morphemes by abstracting across individual inflected verb forms that contain them (e.g. *plays*, *runs*, *walks*), whether or not they have some kind of innate knowledge of a generativist-style system of inflection.

Much research on inflection has instead centred around three debates. First, we discuss rival generativist and constructivist explanations of root infinitives: children's erroneous utterances that lack tense and agreement marking (e.g. **John play football*). The debate here is between generativist–nativist accounts, which assume some version of the generativist account of morphology outlined in Chapter 4 and above, and constructivist accounts, based on the notion of learning strings from the input. Second, we investigate the issue of productivity. Generativist accounts predict that children will be productive with inflectional morphemes as soon as they are acquired (e.g. once children can add 3sg -*s* to *play*, they should be able to do this for all verbs that they know). Constructivist accounts assume that early correct performance may reflect rote learning, and that, when appropriate rote-learned forms are unavailable, children will make omission errors or use incorrectly inflected forms. Finally we investigate the most hotly contested debate in the area of inflectional morphology (and possibly child language acquisition in general): whether regular morphological forms (particularly English past-tense forms) are produced using a formal rule ('add -*ed*') or by analogy to stored exemplars. The debate here is between one broadly generativist account (though one that does not make particularly strong nativist assumptions) and one constructivist account (though we also consider a multiple-rules account that combines elements of both approaches).

5.2   Why do children fail to mark tense and agreement in obligatory contexts?

Children learning English often produce errors such as *John play football* or *John playing football* (e.g. Cazden, 1968). These would seem, at first glance, to be little more than simple omission errors, with the child omitting tense/agreement-bearing morphemes such as *-s* (*John plays football*), *can* (*John can play football*) or *is* (*John is playing football*). It would seem an over-interpretation to argue that the child was using a non-finite verb form (e.g. *play*) in a context where a finite verb form (e.g. *plays*) is required.

Yet children learning languages such as Dutch, German, Russian and Swedish make analogous errors that cannot be dismissed as simple omission errors. For example, if a German child says *John Fußball spielen* (instead of *John spielt Fußball*) it is clear that she is using a non-finite form (the infinitive *spielen*) as opposed to the correct finite form (*spielt*). Furthermore, she is respecting the rule of German that non-finite verb forms appear at the end of the utterance (e.g. *John kann Fußball spielen*), whilst finite verb forms appear in second position (e.g. *John spielt Fußball*); see Pierce (1992), Wexler (1998). Such forms are known as **root infinitives** or **RIs** (Rizzi, 1993/4). One of the main challenges facing generativist and constructivist theories of morphology acquisition is to explain why many languages show root infinitives – though often at very different rates – whilst others do not (or at least have very low rates).

5.2.1   Generativist accounts

5.2.1.1 The small-clause and truncation accounts   Radford (1996; see also Aldridge, 1989; Clahsen, 1991; Guilfoyle and Noonan, 1992; Meisel and Muller, 1992; Vainikka, 1994) proposes a theory under which children in the root-infinitive stage lack functional categories (e.g. Agreement and Tense) altogether. Thus all their utterances are Verb Phrases ('**small clauses**'). Although this would explain why children produce non-finite forms in finite contexts (i.e. because they cannot assign/check inflection at AGR or TNS), this theory cannot explain the fact that rates of root infinitives differ dramatically across different languages (e.g. Wexler, 1998; Freudenthal, Pine, Aguado-Orea and Gobet, 2007) nor the fact that individual children generally produce some root infinitives and some correctly inflected forms in the same developmental period (e.g. Cazden, 1968; Brown, 1973). In answer to this second criticism, Radford (1996) argues that apparently correct forms are produced only as part of rote-learned or semi-productive chunks (e.g. *He's playing*). Whilst plausible, this modification renders the theory untestable, as any utterances inconsistent with the theory can be dismissed as rote-learned.

Rizzi's (1993/4) **truncation** account suffers from similar problems. Rizzi argues that children in the root-infinitive stage can, in principle, project all the necessary functional categories (i.e. Agreement and Tense), but do not know that it is obligatory to do so (i.e. they optionally 'truncate' structures at the Verb Phrase level). This account can explain the general finding that children produce both root infinitives (when they truncate) and correctly inflected forms (when they do not) during the same period. However, it cannot explain particular patterns of tense/agreement omission and non-omission, such as the finding that – within a particular language – children tend to omit subjects more often for root infinitives than for finite verbs (e.g. Wexler, 1998). Neither can this theory explain why different languages show dramatically different rates of root infinitives. In summary, it is probably fair to say that, due to these problems, few current generativist theorists would advocate either the small-clause or truncation accounts.

5.2.1.2 The Agreement/Tense Omission Model (ATOM)   Far more successful has been Wexler's (Schütze and Wexler, 1996; Wexler, 1998) **Agreement/Tense Omission Model** (henceforth, **ATOM**). The ATOM is designed to explain (in addition to the basic root-infinitive phenomenon) the finding that, within a given language, root infinitives are more frequent with subjectless sentences than sentences with a subject; yet, crosslinguistically, root infinitives are *less* frequent in languages that allow subject omission (e.g. Spanish, Italian) than those that do not (e.g. English, German). It is also designed to explain why children sometimes produce non-nominative subjects (e.g. *I/*me play football*) and why this seems to correlate with the provision/omission of verb inflection.[3]

The basic claim of the ATOM is that whilst all functional projections are in place and all parameters correctly set 'from the earliest observation we can make' (Wexler, 1998: 30), during the root-infinitive stage, children optionally omit tense and/or agreement marking in finite contexts (Schütze and Wexler, 1996). In other words, the ATOM posits an **optional-infinitive** (**OI**) stage, where children optionally (i.e. sometimes but not always) use an infinitive (non-finite) verb form where a finite form is required.

The ATOM goes further than accounts such as Rizzi's (1993/4) truncation account in that it attempts to explain *why* children believe that tense and agreement marking is optional. According to Wexler (1998), young children are subject to a **Unique Checking Constraint** (**UCC**) which prohibits items from checking against more than one functional category. This means that an item can be checked at Agreement or Tense, but not both. How then, are children able to sometimes produce correct finite utterances (which require checking at both Agreement and Tense)? The answer, according to Wexler (1998), is that children can violate constraints, but always attempt to minimize the number

Table 5.2 *Patterns of error predicted under the Agreement/Tense Omission model (Wexler, 1998)*

Does child check...		Example resulting utterance	
TNS?	AGR?	English	German
YES	NO	*Him play *Him playing	*Er spielen
NO	YES	*He play *He playing	*Er spielen

of constraints violated for each utterance. For a child in the optional-infinitive stage, producing a finite utterance requires violation of the unique checking constraint, but producing a non-finite utterance requires violation of whatever pragmatic principle forces tense and agreement to be specified in finite contexts in the adult grammar. Thus finite and non-finite forms coexist, as each requires the violation of exactly one constraint. The ATOM also seeks to explain how children reach the adult state. The unique checking constraint 'withers away' due to 'UG-constrained maturation' (Wexler, 1998), meaning that the constraint that requires tense and agreement to be specified 'wins out', and errors gradually cease.

Let us now consider how children's failure to check either Agreement or Tense leads to the pattern of errors characteristic of the optional-infinitive stage (when they check both, a grammatical utterance results). We do not discuss the case where children check neither (resulting in an utterance with a genitive subject; e.g. *his playing) as such errors are relatively rare. Table 5.2 shows the error type that results when the child checks (a) Tense (TNS) but not Agreement (AGR) and (b) Agreement but not Tense. Note that, in English, whilst *SUBJECT play and *SUBJECT playing are both root infinitives (as both bare and -ing forms are non-finite; see Section 5.1), the former will be visible only for 3sg contexts (e.g. I play could be a root-infinitive or a grammatical 1sg present-tense form).

In the first case, TNS is specified but AGR is not. Since AGR is not present, and case is assigned (or checked) at AGR, the pronoun cannot receive (nominative) case. Under the ATOM, when an item cannot receive case, 'default case' is automatically assigned instead. In German (and most languages) nominative case is the default case. Thus the nominative form *er* (as opposed to the accusative form *ihn*) appears. In English, accusative case is the default case, thus the accusative form *him* (as opposed to the nominative form *he*) appears.[4] A question that remains is why, if TNS is present, a non-finite form of the verb (e.g. *play* instead of *plays*; *playing* instead of *is playing*) appears. The answer is that because the subject has not been checked for agreement (as AGR is not present), the system does not 'know' which form of the verb (e.g. 3sg vs 3pl) to use.[5] If a morpheme instantiating tense were chosen at random (e.g. present tense 3sg -*s*), the person and number features on this morpheme (third person, singular) could not be checked at AGR, causing the derivation to crash (see Chapter 4). In fact, since the past-tense morpheme -*ed* does not (in English) encode person and number, the ATOM correctly predicts that children will produce utterances such as *him played* (by specifying TNS but not AGR).

In the second case, AGR is specified but TNS is not. Since AGR is specified, nominative case is correctly assigned in both English (*he* as opposed to accusative *him*) and German (*er* as opposed to accusative *ihn*). If AGR is specified, why does a non-finite form of the verb (e.g. *play* instead of *plays*; *playing* instead of *is playing*) appear? The answer is that (in the converse scenario to that discussed above) the system cannot select a morpheme that instantiates agreement (e.g. 3sg -*s*) because it does not 'know' – in the absence of TNS – whether to select the present-tense morpheme (e.g. -*s*) or a past-tense morpheme (e.g. -*ed*). Again, if AGR 'took a guess' and selected 3sg -*s*, the derivation would crash when the tense feature (+present) could not be checked off, due to the absence of TNS.

5.2.1.2.1 Advantages of the ATOM   As outlined above, the Agreement/Tense Omission Model (ATOM) gives a good account of the crosslinguistic data. As predicted, children in the optional-infinitive stage produce utterances such as *Him play*, *Him played* and *He play* (English) and *Er spielen* (German). An apparent advantage (though one which we will subsequently raise as a disadvantage) is that it predicts – apparently correctly – that children will not produce non-nominative subjects with agreeing verb forms (e.g. *Him is playing*).

The ATOM also offers an explanation of the finding that, in languages where subjects cannot be omitted (e.g. English, French, Dutch, German), children seem to (erroneously) omit subjects more often for non-finite than finite verbs (e.g. Bromberg and Wexler, 1995). The explanation is that even languages in which subjects are obligatory do allow 'null subjects' for non-finite verbs, in some circumstances. Consider an utterance such as *John wants to play*. If this sentence is contrasted with a sentence such as *John wants Bill to play*, it is clear that, in the former case, the non-finite verb has a subject that is understood (i.e. *John wants **John** to play*) but that is absent from the surface utterance. As we will see in Chapter 8, the standard assumption is that the subject of the non-finite verb *play* is an abstract marker PRO (*John$_i$ wants PRO$_i$ to play*). According to the ATOM, children assume on the basis of exposure to such sentences that non-finite verbs can have PRO (i.e. null) subjects.

A final advantage of the ATOM is that it offers an explanation for the finding that, crosslinguistically, the opposite pattern seems to apply: Children learning languages that allow subjects to be omitted (Wexler, 1998: 55, lists Italian, Spanish, Catalan, Tamil and Polish) are argued not to go through an optional-infinitive stage. Children learning languages that do not allow subject omission (Wexler lists Danish, Dutch, English, Faroese, Icelandic, Norwegian, Swedish, French, Irish, Russian and Brazilian Portuguese) do. According to Wexler (1998), in null-subject languages, the role of the subject is – in some sense – taken on by the functional category of AGR itself. An intuitive way to think about this is that because – in null-subject languages – AGR unambiguously marks person and number on the verb (see the Spanish column of Table 5.1), there is no 'need' for a subject (i.e. the speaker can determine the subject just by looking at the person and number marking assigned by AGR). Thus, whilst children learning null-subject languages are still subject to the unique checking constraint, it does not cause root infinitives: they can check Tense, and do not need to additionally check Agreement.

5.2.1.2.2 Problems for the ATOM   One problem facing the Agreement/Tense Omission Model is that it seems to make an incorrect prediction regarding children's production of non-nominative subjects with correctly agreeing finite verb forms (e.g. *Her plays). As Table 5.2 shows, there is no pattern of AGR/TNS omission that would give rise to such utterances, and Schütze (2001: 508) explicitly states that the ATOM predicts that they will not occur.

Initially, this prediction appeared to be correct. In analyses of naturalistic corpora, Schütze and Wexler (1996), Loeb and Leonard (1991), Wexler, Schütze and Rice (1998) and Rispoli (1999) all found that the vast majority of non-nominative subjects (e.g. her) occurred with non-finite verb forms (e.g. play). However, Pine, Rowland, Lieven and Theakston (2005) argued that the scarcity of non-nominative subjects with agreeing verb forms (e.g. *Her plays) is a simple consequence of the scarcity of non-nominative subjects (e.g. her) and agreement-marked verb forms (e.g. plays) independently. During the developmental period in which they produce non-nominative subjects, the majority of children's verb forms are not marked for Tense and Agreement, but are non-finite. Pine et al. (2005) identified corpora in which children were producing a reasonable number of both non-nominative subjects (in every case her) and agreeing verb forms (e.g. plays or is playing) in the same time period (this amounted to only 3 corpora out of an initial sample of 12). The ATOM predicts that the rate of her+agreeing verb forms produced by these children should be 'essentially zero, modulo noise in the data' (Schütze, 2001: 508). In fact all three children produced these forms at a rate significantly greater than zero, and than an arbitrary upper bound of 'acceptable noise' set at

10 per cent. Most of these forms were of the form *her's* (e.g. **Her's playing football*), which are somewhat ambiguous: children may have been producing utterances such as **Her playing football* (consistent with the ATOM) but substituting the possessive pronoun *hers* (e.g. *that's hers*) for *her*. Ambridge and Pine (2006) addressed this issue in an elicited-imitation study which included target items with tense marked on the main verb (e.g. *She plays football*). A number of children produced sentences containing a non-nominative subject with an agreeing verb form (e.g. **Her plays football*), which do not suffer from this ambiguity.

Another problem for the ATOM is that it cannot account for the **modal reference effect**. Most non-finite utterances produced by children do not comment on the 'here and now' but refer to activities that the child (or someone she is talking about) *can* do, *should* do, *will* do, *wants to* do, and so on (though this effect is larger for other optional infinitive languages than for English, for which it has been argued to be non-existent; see Hoekstra and Hyams, 1998). In principle, the ATOM (or a similar account) could explain this pattern by arguing that children overgeneralize from unusual contexts in which a non-finite form is grammatically used to denote a hypothetical event (e.g. ***To know*** *him is* ***to love*** *him*; Hoekstra and Hyams, 1998). However, as we will see in more detail later, the distinction is not clear-cut, as certain verbs that are rarely used in modal contexts show high rates of optional-infinitive error.

Two remaining problems relate to the ATOM's ability to predict the crosslinguistic pattern of optional-infinitive data. First, whilst it is true that as predicted, children learning languages such as English and German erroneously omit subjects *more often* for non-finite verbs (e.g. **Play football*), they do nevertheless also omit subjects of finite verbs (e.g. **Plays football*; see Bromberg and Wexler, 1995). Wexler's (1998) explanation is that the latter are instances of 'topic drop': children may omit subjects that they (perhaps mistakenly) think are 'given' by the preceding discourse, as adults do in sequences such as *John plays tennis. Plays football too.* This is also the explanation offered for the finding that – counter to the prediction of the ATOM – some languages that apparently allow null subjects (e.g. Russian, Brazilian Portuguese) show the optional-infinitive phenomenon (Wexler, 1998: 55). The claim is that these are not 'INFL-licensed null subject' languages, but rather that all subjectless utterances are instances of 'topic drop'. However, this seems somewhat circular: Russian and Brazilian Portuguese are structurally very similar to (and indeed are historically related to) Polish and Spanish respectively, yet the non-existence of an optional-infinitive stage in Polish and Spanish ('INFL-licensed null-subject languages') is taken as support for the prediction.

In fact, even if one accepts arguments that Polish and Spanish are 'true' null-subject languages, whereas Russian and Brazilian Portuguese are not (Wexler, 1998, cites Franks, 1995), the ATOM struggles to explain the fine-grained nature of the crosslinguistic pattern of optional infinitives. Whilst the ATOM classifies languages as either OI or non-OI, languages in fact seem to lie on a gradient whereby optional infinitives are extremely frequent (e.g. English, Dutch), frequent (German), intermediate (French) or rare (Spanish, Italian, Japanese; see Hoekstra and Hyams, 1998; Legate and Yang, 2007; Freudenthal, Pine, Aguado-Orea and Gobet, 2010). An alternative generativist theory – the **variational learning model** (**VLM**) – is designed to explain this phenomenon.

     5.2.1.3 The variational learning model   Under the variational learning model (Yang, 2002) children are innately endowed with a set of parameters or 'mental switches' (e.g. whether or not a language has *wh*-movement or allows subjects to be dropped) that are then set on the basis of the input data. This approach differs from more traditional parameter-setting accounts (see Chapters 4 and 6) in that, at any one time, the learner has a number of different grammars – each specifying a particular setting for each parameter – that compete probabilistically: grammars that successfully parse input sentences are rewarded, thus increasing the likelihood of their being selected to parse subsequent sentences, whilst those that do not are punished. Eventually the learner arrives at a stable grammar (i.e. a set of parameter settings that allows any required utterance to be parsed or generated).

    Legate and Yang (2007) apply this approach to the root-infinitive phenomenon. The relevant parameter here is whether or not a VERB raises to Tense (i.e. receives TNS marking). Some languages (e.g. Mandarin Chinese) do not mark tense on verbs (the concept of tense may be expressed with an adjunct such as 'every day'). Children learning these language must set the parameter to the – TNS setting. Children learning languages that do mark tense on verbs (e.g. all the other languages discussed up to this point) must set the parameter to +TNS. Under the variational learning model, all children have some grammars where the TNS parameter is set to -TNS ('–TNS grammars') and others where the parameter is set to +TNS ('+TNS grammars'). These grammars compete to parse input utterances. Utterances with tense marking (e.g. *She plays football*) reward the +TNS grammars, whilst those with no overt tense marking (e.g. *I play football*; *Play football!*) reward the –TNS grammars. Note that whilst adult utterances such as *I play football* are assumed, under generativist accounts, to have a present-tense marker that happens to be null (i.e. *I play-Ø football*), the assumption is that children cannot distinguish such forms from those in which tense marking is genuinely absent (e.g. infinitival forms).

    The variational learning model predicts that, crosslinguistically, the greater the evidence for the +TNS grammars over the –TNS grammars, the lower the rate of root infinitives shown by that language, and the shorter the duration of

Table 5.3 *Predictions of the variational learning model for Spanish, French and English*

	Spanish	French	English
% Verbs rewarding +TNS grammar	80	70	53
% Verbs rewarding –TNS grammar	20	30	47
% Advantage for +TNS grammar	**60**	**40**	**6**
Duration of RI stage	**2;0**	**2;8**	**3;5**
% RIs (from Freudenthal et al., 2010; at MLU=2.0)	20 (Juan)	32 (Tim)	87 (Anne)

the root-infinitive stage in children. Legate and Yang (2007) provide support for this prediction with a naturalistic corpus analysis of speech directed to children learning Spanish, French and English (see Table 5.3).

5.2.1.3.1 Problems for the variational learning model   One disadvantage of the variational learning model as compared to the ATOM, is that it does not integrate non-nominative subject errors into accounts of the optional-infinitive stage. However, Legate and Yang's (2007) proposal discusses only TNS. Presumably it would be possible for the account also to assume an AGR parameter which is probabilistically set in the same way.

A more serious problem is that (like the parameter-setting accounts of word-order acquisition discussed in the following chapter), Legate and Yang's (2007) parameter-setting account is somewhat circular. In order to reward the +TNS grammar, the child has to recognize tense-marked forms when they appear in the input. Presumably, the child does this by noticing that there exist highly similar lexical items (e.g. *kick*, *kicks* and *kicked*) that denote the same action, but differ with respect to the semantic property of tense. The problem is that once the child has made this discovery, she already knows that her language contains tense-marked forms, and thus there is no need to entertain the possibility that she may be learning a –TNS language. In other words, as soon as the child has encountered a single tense-marked form, she can immediately and definitively set the TNS parameter to +TNS, without any possibility of making an error: A –TNS language will, by definition, contain no tense-marked forms.

There is another way in which the model's probabilistic nature – its strength in terms of describing the crosslinguistic data – is also its downfall. For at least some children learning a +TNS language (e.g. the Dutch child studied by Freudenthal *et al.*, 2010) –TNS forms marginally outnumber +TNS forms in the input. Thus without some additional assumption (such as the assumption that the child adjusts the parameter to a greater degree on the basis of encountering +TNS than –TNS forms), the learner risks never arriving at a +TNS grammar.

This problem, like the problem raised in the previous paragraph, could be solved by having the learner definitively set the parameter to +TNS as soon as a single (or handful) of +TNS utterances have been encountered. However, this model would lose the ability to explain the crosslinguistic pattern of data.

A final problem is that even the current probabilistic version of the variational learning model cannot explain why different verbs display different rates of optional-infinitive error. For example, in the Mattijs corpus (Bol, 1995) discussed in the study of Freudenthal *et al.* (2010), 18 verbs occur exclusively in root-infinitive errors (e.g. *wash, scrub, cut*) and 7 (e.g. *need, know, rain*) exclusively in correct finite form (Pine, p.c.). No account in which root-infinitive errors are a consequence of underspecification of Tense and/or Agreement across the board (e.g. the variational learning model or the ATOM) can explain this pattern. We now consider a constructivist proposal that aims to account for these two findings.

5.2.2   A constructivist account of root-infinitive errors: MOSAIC

The hallmark assumption of constructivist approaches is that children learn strings of language directly from the input (see Chapters 1 and 4). One possibility, then, is that children produce root-infinitive errors by omitting material (either at the learning or production stage) from adult utterances. A likely source for root-infinitive errors is adult **compound finites**: utterances in which tense and agreement are marked on another verb in the sentence such as an auxiliary verb (e.g. *is/has/does*), a modal verb (e.g. *can/will*) or a lexical main verb (e.g. *heard/made/let*):

Input utterance (compound finite)	→	Child's utterance (non-finite)
(What) can/will/does **he play**?		*He play
I saw **him playing**		*Him playing
Peut-**il jouer** ? (Can he play ?)		*Il jouer [French]
Wil **hij spelen**? (Can he play?)		*Hij spelen [Dutch]

For English, this account could also explain many (though not all) of children's non-nominative subject errors, particularly those with non-agreeing verb forms (e.g. **Him playing*). This account is similar in many ways to the null-modal hypothesis (Van Ginneken, 1917; Boser, Lust, Santelmann and Whitman, 1992; Kramer, 1993), except that this older (generativist) account posits that the modal verb (e.g. *can*) is present in the underlying representation but phonologically null (e.g. *He can play → *He play*).

A potential problem for the constructivist account is that languages that have similar rates of compound finites in child-directed speech (e.g. Dutch, German and Spanish; around 30% of all verb uses in each case) have very different rates of root-infinitive error (74%, 61% and 22% in the data reported by Freudenthal *et al.*, 2007). However, on the assumption that children show a **recency effect** (i.e. they are more likely to fail to store words from the beginning than the end of an input utterance), the claim that compound finites are the source of root-infinitive errors is more plausible. Across Dutch, German, Spanish and English there would seem to be a good correlation between the proportion of utterance-final non-finites in the input (87%, 66%, 26% and 76% respectively) and rates of root-infinitive errors in children (74%, 61%, 22% and 50%; data from Peter, Leo, Juan and Anne; Freudenthal *et al.*, 2007).

Freudenthal *et al.* (2007) implemented this account as a computer model: **MOSAIC (model of syntax acquisition in children)**. The precise details of how the model learns are not important for our purposes here. In brief, the model incrementally learns input utterances (taken from real child-directed speech) from the end of the utterance backwards, storing (at most) one extra word each time. For example, if *Can he play?* is presented ten times, the model may store *play* after the first, *he play* after the sixth and *can he play* only after the tenth (the actual numbers depend on the setting assigned to a learning-speed parameter). The model also has generative links that allow it to substitute words that have similar distributions for one another. For example, if *he* and *she* have occurred in similar contexts (e.g. *He is happy*; *She is happy*) the model will substitute *she* into *Can he play* to produce *Can she play*, even if it has never heard this utterance. At various points in training, the model is interrogated for its output, which consists of all the utterances that it has rote learned, plus any new utterances that it can create with its generative links. These are then compared to the real speech produced by the child who received this input (matched by **mean length of utterance (MLU)**). The model successfully simulates the proportion of non-finite and finite utterances across increasing MLU within a particular child (see Figure 5.1; from Freudenthal *et al.*, 2007: 326), and across particular languages (see Table 5.4; compiled from data presented in Freudenthal *et al.*, 2010).

In fact, MOSAIC and the variational learning model perform similarly well. Both predict the correct rank order of Dutch (most root-infinitive errors) > German > French > Spanish, with both incorrectly predicting a similar rate of root-infinitive errors for English and Dutch, or slightly lower rate for English. Is there any reason, then, to favour MOSAIC over the variational learning model?

Freudenthal *et al.* (2010) argue that there is, on the basis that only MOSAIC can account for lexical effects in the data. Within each language, a significant correlation was observed across verbs between the proportion of compound finites in the input and the proportion of root-infinitive errors produced by the child (ranging from $r = 0.35$ for English to $r = 0.71$ for Dutch). For example (Pine, p.c.), three of the seven verbs that the Dutch child (Matthijs) always produced in (correct) finite form were produced in only this form in his input corpus (e.g. *He needs it*; *He knows it*; *It rains [i.e. it's raining]*). Conversely,

Table 5.4 *Crosslinguistic rates of root infinitive errors and predicted error rates from MOSAIC and the variational learning model (NB: For the latter, the prediction does not relate to the absolute rate of RI errors, only the rank order of the languages)*

	Actual rate of RI errors at MLU = 2;0 (Child) (%)	Predicted rate of RI errors at MLU 2.0 (MOSAIC) (%)	Clauses rewarding MINUS TNS Grammar (VLM) (%)
English (Anne)	**87**	63	43
Dutch (Matthijs)	**77**	65	51
German (Leo)	**58**	49	38
French (Tim)	**32**	32	33
Spanish (Juan)	**20**	15	19

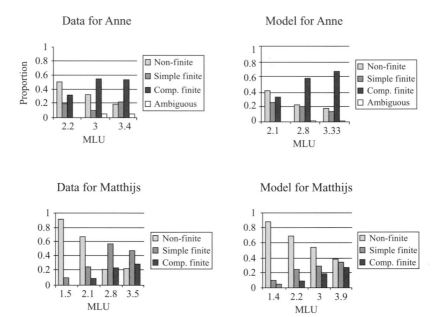

Figure 5.1 Actual (left-hand panel) and predicted (right-hand panel) rates of RI errors ('Non-finites'; e.g. *He go*), correct simple finites (e.g. *He goes*) and compound finites (e.g. *He is going*) for the English and Dutch children studied by Freudenthal *et al.* (2007: 326; reproduced by permission of the Cognitive Science Society)

many of the eighteen verbs that Matthijs produced only in root infinitives (e.g. *he wash/scrub/cut it*) appeared predominantly in compound-finite form in his input corpus (with the three verbs listed above appearing solely in this form; e.g. *Can he wash/scrub/cut it?*). It is difficult to see how this pattern of significant correlations between the rate at which individual verbs occur in compound finites in the input and root-infinitive errors in the output (for every language studied) could be explained by an account (such as the ATOM or variational learning model) that does not assume at least some rote learning of surface forms from the input.

A second advantage of MOSAIC is that it can explain the modal reference effect and a related phenomenon known as the **eventivity constraint** (see Freudenthal, Pine and Gobet, 2009). The modal reference effect (as we have already seen) is the phenomenon whereby most root-infinitive errors refer to future events that the child wants to occur. The eventivity constraint is the phenomenon whereby a larger proportion of utterances with **eventive verbs** (i.e. verbs that refer to events; e.g. *wash*, *scrub*, *cut*, *build*, *cook*) than utterances with **stative verbs** (i.e. verbs that refer to states; e.g. *need*, *be*) are root infinitives. MOSAIC explains this finding in terms of properties of the child's input: eventive verbs occur frequently in utterance-final compound finites, generally with a modal meaning (e.g. *Can/should/will he wash it?*). Stative verbs occur predominately in tensed form (e.g. *He needs it*) and, indeed, often cannot felicitously appear in compound finites (**Can he need it?*).

A final advantage for MOSAIC is that there is experimental evidence that supports its central claim that root-infinitive errors are a consequence of children learning non-finite strings from the ends of adult utterances. Theakston, Lieven and Tomasello (2003: study 1) taught children aged 2;6–3;0 ($M = 2;8$) novel verbs presented either as 3sg forms (*It VERBs*) or as utterance-final non-finites (*Will it VERB?*). Whilst children never produced root-infinitive errors for the verbs presented in 3sg -*s* form, the verbs presented as utterance-final non-finites displayed a root-infinitive rate of 64 per cent (verbs presented in both constructions during training displayed an root-infinitive rate of 52 per cent). A possible criticism of this finding is that the experimental scenario – whereby children were taught novel verbs in particular sentence contexts, then asked almost immediately to produce them – might have caused children to be more over-reliant on imitating strings from the input than they would be in a naturalistic setting. However, a very similar finding was observed from an analysis of naturalistic data based on seventeen children aged 1;10–2;8. Kirjavainen, Theakston and Lieven (2009) found that verbs that children produced with non-nominative subjects (e.g. **Me do X*; **Me have X*; **Me go*) appeared significantly more often in the input in utterance-final compound finite form (e.g. *Let me do X/have X/go*) than verbs that did not appear with non-nominative subjects (e.g. *I found*; *I fetch*; *I want*).

5.2.2.1 Problems for MOSAIC   One potential problem for MOSAIC is that it does not give a plausible account of the transition to the adult state. The model does show increasingly adultlike performance throughout development, but this is largely due to the simple fact that ever-longer rote-learned utterances can be stored, reducing the rates of root-infinitive error. The generalization mechanism means that the model simulates the ability to generate novel utterances, but this ability is limited by the fact that the model operates only at the whole-word level. All accounts of the acquisition of inflection assume, in one way or another, that children can generalize across forms such as *play-s*, *walk-s* and *run-s* to form a *VERB-s* rule or schema. MOSAIC cannot 'see' the internal structure of forms, and hence cannot abstract the pattern. This also means that MOSAIC cannot currently simulate the data from agglutinative languages, in which words are formed by joining many morphemes together. On the other hand, these are limitations only of the current version of MOSAIC, not of the model in principle. It remains to be seen whether a version that operated at the morpheme level could account for these phenomena.

Another problem is that, although MOSAIC gives reasonably accurate quantitative crosslinguistic predictions of the rates of root-infinitive error, it appears to somewhat underestimate the very high rates found in English, Dutch and German (see Table 5.4). This suggests that there may some other factor driving root-infinitive errors that is not simulated by MOSAIC. One possibility is that when children are unsure which form to use (or unable to recall the correct form) they 'default' to the most frequent form in their language (either the form that is most common in terms of tokens in the input, or the form that is appropriate in the most different person/number/tense combinations). As Table 5.1 shows, the (apparently) non-finite form (i.e. the bare form in English; the *-en* form in Dutch/German) fits at least this second criterion (and most likely the first, too). Indeed, English – the language for which an (apparently) non-finite form (e.g. *play*) fills the most cells in the inflection paradigm – is the language for which MOSAIC underestimates the rate of root-infinitive errors by the biggest margin.

A final problem is that although MOSAIC can explain some non-nominative subject errors as truncations of adult utterances (e.g. *let me play football* → **me play football*), many of children's non-nominative subject errors cannot be explained in this way (Kirjavainen *et al.*, 2009; Ambridge and Pine, 2006). In this respect, non-nominative utterances with agreeing verb forms (e.g. **Her plays football*) are as problematic for MOSAIC as they are for the ATOM. Presumably at least part of the reason that children produce these errors is that they have yet to solidly learn the full case-marking paradigm (e.g. that *she* is the nominative form and *her* the accusative form) for each pronoun. The *she/her* distinction is particularly problematic (Pine *et al.*, 2005; Ambridge and Pine, 2006), which may be due to the fact that *her* also serves as the possessive pronoun (e.g. *That's her book*), which is not the case for other accusative forms such as *me* or *him* (Rispoli, 1994).

5.2.3   Why do children fail to mark tense and agreement in obligatory contexts? Conclusion

Whilst early generativist accounts (e.g. Radford, 1996; Rizzi, 1994) failed to satisfactorily account for the apparent optionality of root-infinitive errors, more recent accounts (e.g. Wexler, 1998; Hoekstra and Hyams, 1998) generally explain the data far more successfully. These accounts are lacking, however, in that they do not offer a satisfactory account of quantitative crosslinguistic differences in error rates. The variational learning model's (Legate and Yang, 2007) success in this regard means that it is almost certainly the leading current generativist account, yet it struggles to explain lexical effects (and – to some extent – crosslinguistic effects) in the data. The constructivist alternative, MOSAIC (Freudenthal *et al.*, 2007), explains these effects but tends to underestimate the rate of root-infinitive errors (particularly for English) and has not yet been implemented for more agglutinative languages.

Given this state of affairs, it seems that the best way for generativist accounts to proceed would be to build in some role for lexical learning. There is no reason why children could not initially learn and reproduce individual strings from their input (as under MOSAIC), but at the same time use these to set a TNS parameter (as under the VLM). Constructivist theorists should refine MOSAIC to operate additionally at the sublexical level, which may allow for a better account of English, and for an account of agglutinative languages. At the same time, constructivist researchers could consider possible sources of optional-infinitive errors (other than repeating forms from the input), in order to better explain the extremely high rate of errors in some languages (particularly English).

5.3   Are children less productive with morphology than adults?

5.3.1   Generativist and constructivist predictions regarding productivity

As outlined at the beginning of this chapter, according to generativist accounts, the production of all tense- and agreement-marked forms is governed by the abstract functional categories of TNS (Tense) and AGR (Agreement). What this means, in simple terms, is that children inflect verbs by using a general rule or procedure that operates over every VERB stored in their vocabulary (roughly VERB STEM + appropriate AGR/TNS-marked ending), not by learning a different rule for each verb (e.g. *plays+s*). Generativist accounts (e.g. Wexler, 1998; Hoekstra and Hyams, 1998; Legate and Yang, 2007) therefore predict

Summary table 5.1 *Why do children produce root-infinitive errors (e.g. *He play)? (☑ = supports theory; ☒ = counts against theory)*

Issue/phenomenon	Agreement/Tense omission model (generativist); Wexler (1998)	Variational learning model (generativist); Legate and Yang (2007)	Model of syntax acquisition in children (constructivist); Freudenthal et al., 2007
Summary of theory	Children are unable to check verbs for TNS and AGR (Schütze and Wexler, 1996; Wexler, 1998)	Children initially assume they are learning a language that does not mark TNS (Legate and Yang, 2007)	Strings containing non tense-marked verbs are learned directly from the input (Freudenthal et al., 2007, 2010)
Subject omission more common for non-finite than finite verbs	☑ Explains this phenomenon (Bromberg and Wexler, 1995), but ☒ arguably not why omission also occurs for finite verbs.	Not discussed.	Not discussed in detail, but model does yield this effect (Freudenthal, Pine and Gobet, 2005a).
Languages differ with regard to rates of RI error	☒ Only crude division into RI/non-RI (Wexler, 1998: 55)	☑ Correct crosslinguistic order (Legate and Yang, 2007). ☒ Any +TNS form unambiguous evidence for +TNS grammar. ☒ Underestimates RIs in English (Freudenthal et al., 2010)	☑ Good quantitative crosslinguistic predictions but ☒ Underestimates RI error rate, particularly for English (but also Dutch and German); Freudenthal et al., (2010).
Non-nominative subjects + agreeing verb forms (predicted not to occur by ATOM)	☒ Observed in naturalistic (Pine et al., 2005) and experimental study (Ambridge and Pine, 2006).	Not discussed. Account could possibly be extended to include a +AGR parameter.	☑ Explained, to some extent, by learning of input strings (Kirjavainen et al., 2009), but ☒ cannot explain all errors in this way (Pine et al., 2005; Ambridge and Pine, 2006; Rispoli, 1994)
Modal reference/lexical effects (different rates of RIs for different verbs)	☒ No explanation	☒ No explanation	☑ Verbs appear in bare/agreeing forms at different rates in surface strings that child acquires (Freudenthal et al., 2009, 2010; Theakston et al., 2003).
Transition to adult state	☒ Withering of unique checking constraint difficult to verify independently	☒ Possible problem for languages with <50% +TNS forms (e.g. Dutch).	☑ Some ability to generalize, but ☒ Decrease in error rate mostly due to increased rote-storage.

that, although children will continue to produce root-infinitive errors long after they have begun to produce inflected forms, they should not reliably provide Tense and Agreement marking for some contexts and omit it for others. For example, one would not to expect to find an English child who virtually always supplied auxiliary *is* (e.g. *He is playing*), but virtually always omitted auxiliary *are* (e.g. **They playing*) or 3sg *-s* (e.g. **He play*). Neither would one expect to find a child who reliably produced correct marking in some contexts, but incorrect Tense and Agreement marking in others (e.g. a Spanish child who reliably provided 3sg *-a* in all 3sg contexts (e.g. *juega*), but incorrectly also used this form in 3pl contexts (e.g. in place of *juegan*)). In other words, children should demonstrate **full productivity** with all Tense/Agreement-bearing morphemes. Of course, this prediction of full productivity applies only *provided that the child knows the relevant form.*

Constructivist accounts are also known as **lexical learning** accounts because they assume that children learn lexical strings (i.e. strings of words and morphemes; e.g. *He's playing*; *He's running*) directly from the input, and abstract across them to form **lexically specific schemas** (e.g. *He's X-ing*). These are also known as **slot-and-frame**, **constant+variable** or **partially productive patterns/constructions/schemas**. Thus constructivist accounts do not predict full productivity. In fact, they predict precisely the opposite: children will show correct use of inflectional morphology in contexts where they are able to use a well-learned string (e.g. *He's playing*) or schema (e.g. *He's X-ing*) but may produce non-finite forms (see Section 5.3.2) or finite forms with incorrect tense and agreement marking (see Section 5.3.3) when a relevant string/schema is rare in the input and thus has yet to be learned (e.g. *They are X-ing*).

5.3.2 Do children omit different morphemes at different rates (constructivist prediction) or show full productivity (generativist prediction)?

Wilson (2003) provided evidence that children omit different tense/agreement-bearing morphemes at different rates. Wilson (2003) coded five of the largest English child corpora available on CHILDES for provision of copula BE (e.g. *I'm a good boy*), auxiliary BE (e.g. *I'm coming*) and 3sg present-tense agreement (e.g. *He plays*). These morphemes were chosen because all unambiguously encode both tense and agreement (unlike, for example, past-tense *-ed* which does not overly encode agreement). All children showed different rates of provision for the three morphemes, with at least two of the three comparisons significant for each child. Error rates also differed by the particular pronoun+auxiliary combination required. For example, Nina produced auxiliary BE for 82 per cent of sentences where the subject was *He* (e.g. *He's* *coming*) but for only 9 per cent of sentences where the subject was *I* (e.g. *I'm coming*). Wilson argued that this provides evidence for the assumption of the lexical learning account that children are acquiring strings such as *He's* and *I'm* directly from the input.

However, Wilson's (2003) analysis suffers from the failure to control for knowledge of the relevant morphemes. This problem also applies to studies that found little or no overlap in children's use *-ing*, *-s* and *-ed* (Pine, Lieven and Rowland, 1998; and similar studies looking at Spanish (Gathercole, Sebastián and Soto, 1999) and Italian (Pizzuto and Caselli, 1992). Pine *et al.* (2008) therefore repeated Wilson's analysis, counting contexts only from the point at which the child had produced the relevant morpheme in two different utterances (and including utterances with non-nominative subjects – e.g. **Me do it* – that were excluded by Wilson, 2003). In general, this analysis replicated the findings of Wilson (2003), including differences in rates of auxiliary omission for different pronouns (e.g. *He's* > *I'm* for auxiliary BE). Similar findings were also reported by Theakston, Lieven, Pine and Rowland (2005), who found uneven rates of provision for auxiliary BE and HAVE in the corpora of eleven children aged 2;0–3;0. A longitudinal elicited production study with twelve children aged 2;10–3;6 (Theakston and Rowland, 2009) also found that the different forms of auxiliary BE (*is*, *are*) showed a different developmental time course.

However, unlike Wilson (2003), Pine *et al.* (2008) found few individual differences between children, with virtually all showing the pattern copula BE > auxiliary BE > 3sg *-s*. Whilst a constructivist account would argue that this is due to similarities in the input to which children are exposed, the finding of a similar pattern across children means that it may also be possible for a generativist account to explain the data. For example, Rice, Wexler and Hershberger (1998) argue that properties such as whether or not morphemes are freestanding (e.g. auxiliaries and the copula) or attached to verbs (e.g. 3sg present *-s*), and whether or not they are contractible, will affect rates of provision. However, this could not account for findings such as the difference in rates of auxiliary omission for different pronouns (e.g. *He's* > *I'm* for auxiliary BE).

Rice *et al.* (1998) would have difficulty explaining the finding of Freudenthal *et al.* (2007) that within the data of each of five children learning different languages (English, Dutch, German, French and Spanish) a significant correlation was observed across verbs between the proportion of utterance-final compound finites in the input (e.g. *Can he play?*) and the proportion of root-infinitive errors (e.g. **He play?*) produced by the child. Thus a generativist account would have to explain not only why rates of TNS/AGR omission differ according to the identity of the pronoun subject and the lexical verb but also why they seem to do so in a way that correlates with what the child hears in her input.

5.3.2.1 Are apparent lexical-learning effects an artefact of sampling?

The children whose data are reported by Pine *et al.* (2008) were recorded for one hour twice every three weeks (over a period of twelve months), with the Spanish and Italian data of Gathercole *et al.* (1999) and Pizzuto and Caselli (1992) thinner still. Theakston *et al.* (2005) sampled for two hours every three weeks, but this still represents a tiny fraction (perhaps 2 per cent) of the speech produced in the relevant period.

Thin sampling regimes are problematic because they are likely to make children's speech look more lexically specific than is in fact the case (Aguado-Orea, 2004; Rowland and Fletcher, 2006; Tomasello and Stahl, 2004; Valian, Solt and Stewart, 2009). Consider, for example, the finding of Pine *et al.* (1998) that many children never used the progressive *-ing* and the present *-s* marker on the same verb. Some of these children may have used both (for example) *playing* and *plays* on the same day, with only the latter captured by the recording regime. Thus thinly sampled naturalistic data may unfairly provide support for the constructivist claim of gradual lexical learning over the generativist claim of full productivity. This is particularly true for studies that fail to control for lexical knowledge of the relevant morphemes. A related problem is that many studies (e.g. Pine *et al.*, 1998) fail to take into account the number of different verbs that the child used in the period studied. If a child uses a handful of verbs that tend to occur only in progressive contexts (e.g. *He is eating the cake > He eats the cake*) and a handful that tend to occur only in simple present-tense contexts (e.g. *He likes cake > He is liking cake*) then there would be virtually no opportunity for overlap (i.e. for the child to use *-ing* and *-s* with the same verb) even if she did have productive use of these morphemes.

On the other hand, it is equally likely that thinly sampled naturalistic data may unfairly provide support for the generativist over the constructivist position by making a child look *more* productive than in fact is the case (Rowland and Fletcher, 2006). Although this may seem counterintuitive, suppose – for example – that in a monthly one-hour recording, the child used only two different verbs, but used each of them with both *-ing* and *-s*. This would give a productivity rate of 100 per cent (100 per cent of verbs were used with both morphemes). Over the remainder of the month, however, the child could have produced many other verbs with *-ing* but not *-s* and/or vice versa. Indeed, this is likely to be the case: most verbs that are sampled in a given recording will be highly frequent verbs for which both the *-ing* and *-s* forms are common in the input. Rarer verbs, for which the child is less likely to have heard both the *-s* and *-ing* forms in the input, are less likely to be produced by the child in the recording session, so the child's system may look more productive than is actually the case.

5.3.2.2 *Addressing the sampling problem: using the caregiver's speech as a control*   The heart of the problem outlined above is that simply by looking at a corpus of spontaneously produced speech it is not possible to determine how lexically specific the data would look, as a result of sampling constraints, even if it had been produced by a speaker with full productive knowledge and a full inventory of the relevant verbs and inflections. One way to address this issue is to compare a child corpus with a corpus produced by a speaker who is assumed to have full productive knowledge of the inflectional system: the child's caregiver. If, having controlled for vocabulary knowledge, knowledge of the relevant inflectional morphemes and the size and sampling frequency of the data, the child's speech still appears to be more lexically specific than the caregiver's, then this is good evidence that the child's system is less than fully productive at that point in development. For example, if, when looking at verb stems and morphological markers that are used by both the child and the caregiver in a given time period, the child uses fewer different markers with a particular verb than the caregiver, one can conclude that the child has less than full productivity.

Aguado-Orea (2004) conducted such an analysis using data collected from two Spanish children. Spanish is an ideal language in which to conduct such an analysis for this because the large number of different tense/agreement-bearing morphemes (over forty) means that (unlike an English-speaking child) a Spanish child is unlikely to have rote-learned all the different forms of a given verb, and thus has an excellent opportunity to show productivity. The analysis was restricted to verbs (30 for one child, 62 for the other) and morphemes (1sg, 2sg, 3sg and 3pl) used by both the child and the caregiver. Utterances were randomly deleted from the caregiver's data to ensure an equal corpus size. With these controls in place, the mean number of different inflections per verb was significantly smaller for the child (e.g. Lucia: 1.87 out of a possible maximum of 4) than either the mother ($M = 2.17$) or father ($M = 2.48$). See also Krajewski (2007) for an analogous analysis of Polish data.

Whilst these findings provide some support for the constructivist lexical learning approach, two problems remain. First, it is impossible to rule out the possibility that children showed less apparent productivity simply because they were less inclined than their parents to use a range of sentence subjects (for example, children may prefer to talk mostly about themselves). One way to address this issue is to look for converging evidence from error data (as we will do in Section 5.3.3): if a child is attempting to produce (for example) a 3pl form (i.e. is using a 3pl context) but incorrectly produces a 3sg form, this suggests a lack of productivity with the 3pl form, rather than mere avoidance of 3pl contexts. Second, the findings highlight the inherent difficulty in determining whether or not an individual is 'productive' with an inflection on the basis of corpus data. The adults studied used only around two inflections with each verb *on average* (meaning that for many they used only one), yet one would not wish to conclude they were not operating with a productive system of morphology. One way to address both of these issues is to elicit particular tense/agreement-marked forms (especially those that are rare in spontaneous speech) in experimental studies.

5.3.2.3 Addressing the sampling problem: experimental elicited-production studies   In a typical elicited-production study focusing on morphology, children are asked to complete a sentence by supplying a particular tense/agreement-marked form (e.g. *Yesterday John blicked. Every day he...*). A novel verb is used to avoid the possibility that children may have simply rote-learned the relevant inflected form (e.g. *plays*). For this reason, studies that use real as opposed to novel items (e.g. Rice and Wexler, 1996) cannot be taken as compelling evidence for morphological productivity.

In the training study of Theakston *et al.* (2003) discussed above, only half (12/24) of the children (aged 2;6–3;0; $M = 2;8$) were able to produce the 3sg *-s* form of a novel verb that had not been presented in this form during training. Yet these children clearly knew the morpheme on some level, with 23/24 children producing a 3sg *-s* form of a familiar verb (see also Theakston and Lieven, 2005, for an elicitation study with auxiliaries BE and HAVE, Theakston and Rowland, 2009, for auxiliary BE and Rowland and Theakston, 2009, for DO and the modal auxiliaries).

Again, English is a poor language in which to conduct such a test, as the number of different morphemes that must be learned is very limited. Dąbrowska and Szczerbiński (2006) conducted a study designed to investigate children's knowledge of case-marking morphology in Polish, a language with rich morphology. Although most 2 and 3-year-olds demonstrated some productivity with novel nouns, performance was not at ceiling, even for reasonably common morphemes. For example, 3-year-olds produced the singular feminine dative marker correctly on only 35 per cent of trials with novel nouns. It is difficult to argue that this is a simple consequence of not knowing the morpheme, as children produced it correctly in 69 per cent of trials with familiar nouns (see Leonard, Caselli and Devescovi, 2002, for a similar study in Italian). Of course, this could be a consequence of rote learning of familiar forms. However, if one is to make this argument, then one has to accept that successful production of such forms (in either naturalistic or experimental studies) does not constitute strong evidence for productivity.

Studies investigating children's comprehension of morphological markers with novel nouns (and verbs) are notable by their absence. Useful evidence could come from studies using the act-out paradigm in which children are given two toys and asked – for example – to *make the cat+ACC hit the dog+NOM*. If children understand the nominative and accusative morphological markers, they should enact the dog hitting the cat, even if this conflicts with the usual word order of their language (e.g. in German). Whilst many act-out studies of this nature have been conducted (see Chapter 6 for a review), virtually all have used familiar verbs and nouns (Chan, Lieven and Tomasello's, 2009, study of English, German and Mandarin used novel verbs – though not nouns – but neutralized the cue of case marking in German; the only one of these languages that uses such morphology). The use of familiar nouns is problematic as it is impossible to rule out the possibility that children know (for example) that the individual form *cat+ACC* denotes an activity where *the cat* is the PATIENT, but do not know that the accusative marker can be added to any noun to denote PATIENT status.

The study of Krajewski, Lieven, Theakston and Tomasello (in press) is an exception. In this study novel nouns were used to investigate the ability of Polish children (aged 2;6 and 3;6) to switch from one case-marked ending to another. Results showed that even the older group were not at ceiling and that the level of success depended on (a) the precise form of the source and target forms and (b) the direction of transfer from one case to the other. Given the centrality of the issue to the generativist–constructivist debate, more studies along these lines should be conducted.

5.3.3   Do children produce incorrectly agreeing verb forms (e.g. *I likes)?

As discussed earlier, constructivist accounts predict that children will some-times use incorrect agreement/tense-marked verb (or noun) forms if they have not yet either rote learned the correctly marked form or achieved productiv-ity with the required morpheme. Generativist accounts explicitly predict that, provided they have learned the required morpheme, children will not make **agreement errors** (Hoekstra and Hyams, 1998; Poeppel and Wexler, 1993; Wexler, 1998: 41). That is, they will not, for example use a verb marked for 3sg (e.g. *likes*) with a 1sg pronoun (e.g. *I*, to give *I likes*).

At a broad level, there seems to be good support for this prediction. Hoek-stra and Hyams (1998: 84) summarize naturalistic data from German, Italian, Spanish and Catalan showing that overall rates of agreement error are typically around 2 per cent. However, overall error rates are misleading because they largely reflect children's use of forms that are highly frequent in the input, and hence could well have been rote learned. For example, Rubino and Pine (1998) showed that, for a child learning Brazilian Portuguese, an overall error rate of around 3 per cent was made up of an error rate of close to zero for 2sg and 3sg forms, but 25 per cent for 3pl forms (counting from the point at which the child first used a 3pl form correctly). Similarly, in a study of two Spanish children, Aguado-Orea (2004) found 3pl error rates of 68 and 34 per cent for Lucia and Juan respectively (again counting from the first correct production of a 3pl form). It is important to stress that these are errors where the child uses an incorrect tense/agreement-marked morpheme. Whilst a lack of productivity with a particular morpheme (e.g. 3pl) could be a consequence of nothing more than a child's reluctance to use 3pl contexts, this explanation does not apply to these errors: these are errors in which children are producing 3pl contexts (i.e. they are using a 3pl subject) but supplying an inflection that does not have the correct 3pl features.

Even children's apparently excellent performance with some parts of the paradigm (e.g. 1sg) largely reflects the use of individual verb forms that are highly frequent in the input, and hence could well have been rote learned. One of the children studied by Aguado-Orea (Juan), displayed an error rate of 5 per cent for 1sg forms. However, when just the two most frequent forms (*quiero*, 'I want' and *puedo*, 'I can') were excluded, the error rate doubled to 10 per cent.

5.3.3.1 Why do children sometimes produce agreement errors?

There is good evidence, then, that children do produce incorrectly marked verb forms, particularly for individual verbs and individual parts of the paradigm (e.g. 3pl) that are relatively infrequent. This finding holds even when we count only from the point at which the child has used the relevant morpheme correctly. Why, then, do children make such errors? Generativist accounts seem to have painted themselves into a corner with their insistence that children do not make such errors (e.g. Hoekstra and Hyams, 1998; Wexler, 1998). However, this insistence is almost certainly unnecessary. Neither of the constructivist explanations for these errors discussed below are, in principle, incompatible with a generativist account.

One likely source of errors is the child's repetition of a preceding adult form. For example, the mother and child studied by Rubino and Pine (1998: 45) engaged in the following exchange:

> MOT: Quer isso tambien?   Do you want (2sg) this too?
> CHI: Quer.   Want (2sg).

Here, the child uses the 2sg form of want (*you want*), most likely because he is repeating it from his mother's utterance, when he presumably intends the 1sg form (*I want*). Of course, it would be possible to dismiss such errors as simple 'parrot-fashion' utterances that are not produced by the child's grammar. However, if one were to apply this objection fairly, one would also have to rule out a good number of correct forms that – under standard assumptions – are taken as evidence of knowledge of inflection. For example, every 1pl form (e.g. *Vamo*, 'Let's') produced by the child studied by Rubino and Pine (1998) was an immediate repetition of an adult form.

Experimental evidence that children repeat forms recently produced by adults comes from the study of Theakston *et al.* (2003). These authors found that children were more likely to produce a correct 3sg form (e.g. *goes* as opposed to *go*) when it had been recently produced by the experimenter (see also Farrah,

Table 5.5 *Instances of incorrect inflection provided by Juan (from Aguado-Orea, 2004)*

Actual production	Target inflection					
	1sg	2sg	**3sg**	1pl	2pl	3pl
1sg		1	7			
2sg	8		3			
3sg	**24**	**14**				**75**
1pl						1
2pl						
3pl			1		1	

1992, for similar evidence regarding past-tense *-ed*, progressive *-ing* and noun plural *-s*).

Another likely source of agreement errors is the child 'defaulting' to the most frequent inflected form of the verb when she is unable to retrieve or generate the correct form. Table 5.5 (adapted from Aguado-Orea, 2004: 245) shows the forms that Juan used in place of the correct inflection (blank cells indicate zero).

The eight 2sg for 1sg errors could be a consequence of Juan repeating an adult form addressed to him (as discussed above). However, many more errors appear to be a consequence of the child defaulting to the most frequent form: 3sg (see highlighted row).

Theakston *et al.* (2005) provided evidence that English-speaking children also acquire the tense/agreement-marked forms that are most frequent in their input. These authors used a longitudinal study of eleven children aged between 1;8 and 2;8, to investigate their use of subject+auxiliary BE/HAVE combinations (e.g. *we're*; *we've*). Across nine subject+BE combinations (*they're, we're, I'm, that's, she's, it's, he's, [proper noun]'s* and *[NP]'s*), the frequency of the combination in the mothers' speech was significantly negatively correlated with the mean age of acquisition ($r = 0.7$).[6]

Apart from frequency, another possible reason for the apparent 'default' status of 3sg may be that it is phonologically prototypical of the paradigm (see Table 5.1). For example, for an *-ar* verb (e.g. *jugar*) the 3sg form (*juega*) ends in the *-a* sound that is shared by all finite forms (except 1sg) and the infinitive. It could also be considered to be a phonologically reduced version of the longer plural forms.

An alternative possible generativist account would be that 3sg is a 'default' not in the sense of the most frequent or phonologically prototypical form, but in a more technical sense of a form that can be used even when its features (i.e. third person, singular) are not licensed by the subject (e.g. Radford and Ploennig-Pacheco, 1995; Hoekstra and Hyams, 1998). Aguado-Orea (2004) argues against this possibility on the basis that, if 3sg really were a grammatical 'default', it would be expected to replace all other forms at equal rates. However, this is not necessarily the case. Most definitions of a default form (e.g. Pinker and Ullman, 2002) include the notion that it is a form that steps in when another form is unavailable due to memory failure. There is no reason why this should not be more common for certain forms (particularly less frequent forms) than others. More problematic is the finding that children do not always 'default' to the same form. For example, although the vast majority of Juan's errors involve 'defaulting' to 3sg, there are twenty-two separate occasions on which the form that is incorrectly substituted is not 3sg. In order to settle the issue of whether 3sg is a grammatical, frequency-based, or phonological default, one would have to investigate a language where 3sg is taken to be the default form in some grammatical sense, but is not the most frequent or phonologically prototypical form. However, because speakers of different languages presumably discuss similar situations, it may prove difficult to find a language in which 3sg is not the most frequent form.

A strong effect of children 'defaulting' to the highest frequency form was found in the Polish experimental elicitation study of Dąbrowska and Szczerbiński (2006). Children aged between 2;4 and 4;8 were asked to inflect novel nouns in genitive, dative and accusative contexts. Polish has a masculine, feminine and neuter ending for each of these three cases, with the masculine the most frequent in each case. For datives, children incorrectly used the high-frequency masculine inflection in place of a lower-frequency feminine inflection ten times as often as the reverse. For accusatives, children incorrectly used the high-frequency masculine inflection in place of the neuter ending on 57 trials, but never made the converse error.

5.3.4   *Are children less productive with morphology than adults? Conclusion*

Even when counting from the point at which they have correctly used the relevant morphemes, children are less productive with inflectional morphology than adults, supplying different morphemes at different rates in both naturalistic contexts and experimental studies (including those with novel verbs). Looking at lower-frequency verb forms and inflectional morphemes, children also use the wrong tense/agreement-marked morpheme at reasonably high rates (sometimes >50 per cent). This seems to be a consequence of the immediate repetition or overuse of forms that are frequent in the input. Whilst all of these findings are predicted by the constructivist approach, they are problematic for current generativist accounts.

Yet there is no reason, in principle, why generativist accounts could not build in the assumption that – in addition to the learning procedures posited by the

Summary table 5.2 *Do children show full productivity (generativist prediction) or not (constructivist prediction)? (☑ = supports theory; ☒ = counts against theory)*

Issue/phenomenon	Generativist approaches (e.g. Wexler, 1998; Hoekstra and Hyams, 1998; Rice et al., 1998; Legate and Yang, 2007)	Constructivist approaches (e.g. Theakston et al., 2005; Pine et al., 2008).
Summary of theory	Children can apply procedure of checking at TNS/AGR for all verbs. Hence – once relevant morpheme has been learned – children predicted not to use wrong morpheme, nor to reliably omit it in some contexts but not others.	Children form slot-and-frame patterns around individual morphemes and other invariant material (e.g. *He's VERBing*). Hence may omit/use wrong morpheme until relevant pattern learned.
Are different morphemes instantiating TNS/AGR (copula BE, auxiliary BE, 3sg -s) omitted at different rates? (constructivist prediction)	☒ Yes, though ☑ Certain properties (e.g. being attached to verbs) may make omission more likely for some morphemes than others (Rice et al., 1998). ☒ Same morpheme shows different omission rates with different subjects (see right-hand column).	☑ Yes (Wilson, 2003; Pine et al., 1998; Gathercole et al., 1999; Pizzuto and Caselli, 1992). ☑ Correlation between utterance final bare stems in input and children's production (Freudenthal et al., 2010).
Failure to control for knowledge of morpheme and/or thin sampling may make children look less productive than is the case	☒ Valian et al. (2006) show how this can arise (for determiners). ☒ Thin sampling may also *over*-estimate productivity (Rowland and Fletcher, 2006).	☑ Effects above remain when controlling for knowledge of the relevant morphemes (Pine et al., 2008; Theakston et al., 2005; Theakston and Rowland, 2009; Aguado-Orea, 2004; Krajewski, 2007).
Naturalistic vs experimental studies	☑ Children may simply be less motivated than adults to use a range of subjects, which would necessitate the use of a range of different morphemes. Indeed, even (Spanish) adults, who have full productivity under any account, typically use only 2–3 inflections per verb (Aguado-Orea, 2004).	☑ Experimental studies looking at a single morpheme find production at different rates in different contexts (Theakston et al., 2003; Theakston and Lieven, 2005; Theakston and Rowland, 2009; Rowland and Theakston, 2009; Dąbrowska and Szczerbiński, 2006; Leonard et al., 2002; Krajewski et al., in press).
Do children produce agreement errors (incorrectly agreeing verb forms; e.g. *I likes)?	Generativist account predicts low error rate. In fact, though overall rates of these errors are low (Wexler, 1998; Poeppel and Wexler, 1993; Hoekstra and Hyams, 1998), they are sometimes high (50%++) for low-frequency target forms (Rubino and Pine, 1998; Aguado-Orea, 2004), perhaps due to repetition of adult forms (Theakston et al., 2003; Farrar, 1992) or 'defaulting' to most frequent/most phonologically prototypical form (Aguado-Orea, 2004; Theakston et al., 2005; Dąbrowska and Szczerbiński, 2006). ☒ Some errors could be explained as children substituting a default form (e.g. 3SG), permitted even when its features do not match those of the subject (e.g. Radford and Ploennig-Pacheco, 1995; Hoekstra and Hyams, 1998), though ☒ see right-hand column.	☑ Children do not always 'default' to one particular form (Aguado-Orea, 2004).

particular theory – children learn and repeat strings of language from the input. Indeed, for certain domains of language acquisition (e.g. noun learning) all theories share this assumption. Why are generativist theories happy to make this assumption for object names (e.g. *dog*) but not morphologically marked verbs (e.g. *play-s*) or even nouns (e.g. *dog+ACC*)? Presumably the reason for the reluctance of generativist theorists to incorporate considerable input-driven learning is that it would then be difficult to tease apart the forms that are rote learned and those that should be taken as evidence regarding the state of the child's grammar. Whilst this is clearly a high price to pay, the undeniable lexical effects observed in the data mean that this is an assumption that future generativist theories will most likely have to make.

5.4   Rules versus analogies in inflectional morphology (with special reference to the English past-tense debate)

When given a novel verb such as *rick*, children are able to supply *ricked* as the past tense (Berko, 1958). Further evidence that children have learned an add *-ed* 'rule' comes from spontaneous overgeneralization errors (e.g. **I sitted down*) that are a hallmark of child language. How children acquire the ability to generalize the *-ed* form to novel verbs (and overgeneralize it to irregular verbs) is perhaps the most fiercely contested issue in child language acquisition. At first glance, this may seem surprising: the *-ed* regular past-tense morpheme is only one of a number of inflectional morphemes that English-speaking children must acquire (amongst 3sg *-s* and present progressive *-ing*, as well as auxiliary and modal forms), and many languages do not have an equivalent regular morpheme (or, in some cases, tense-marking morphology at all). Why, then, is this debate so central to the issue of children's acquisition of morphology (and to language-acquisition debates in general)?

The answer is that children's mastery of the past-tense *-ed* morpheme (and other 'regular' morphemes such as the noun plural *-s* in English, German and Dutch) constitutes an ideal test case for the wider debate over whether language – and its acquisition – is best characterized in terms of formal rules that act on variables or analogy across stored exemplars. Generally, these two positions are associated with the generativist–nativist and constructivist approach respectively: The constructivist approach assumes that children can acquire the entire system by forming analogies across items stored in memory, whereas the generativist–nativist approach assumes that this process is not sufficient, and that a formal rule (possibly with an innate basis) is required. However, pigeonholing the two approaches as generativist–nativist and constructivist respectively may be counterproductive in this case. In principle, it would presumably be possible for children to set up a formal rule with no innate basis, and analogy across stored exemplars plays an important role in both accounts.

Accordingly, we present this debate not as one between generativist–nativist and constructivist approaches *per se*, but between the **dual-route** (rule+analogy) and **single-route** (analogy-only) accounts (we will also consider, more briefly, a third account: the **multiple-rules** account).

5.4.1   The dual-route model

According to (traditionally generativist) 'words and rules' accounts (e.g. Pinker and Prince, 1988; Marcus *et al.*, 1992; Marcus, 1995), irregular past-tense forms (stored *words*) and regular past-tense forms (generated by a default *rule*) are produced by different mechanisms (or via different *routes*).

Irregular past-tense forms (e.g. *threw*) are stored in the lexicon (the 'mental dictionary'). However, forms are stored not as a simple list, but clustered into **phonological neighbourhoods** (also called **families** or groups of **friends**), such as *throw/threw*, *blow/blew*, *know/knew* or *sleep/slept*, *weep/wept*, *creep/crept*. The forms in each cluster share **associative links** to one another. This assumption is necessary to account for that fact that, if introduced to novel verbs that are phonologically similar to (i.e. sound similar to) existing irregulars (e.g. *clow*, similar to *throw/blow/know*), adults are able to generate a novel 'irregular' past tense form (e.g. *clew*) by analogy with the members of this phonological neighbourhood (*throw/threw*, *blow/blew know/knew*) (e.g. Prasada and Pinker, 1993).

Regular past-tense forms are not stored in the lexicon.[7] The stem (e.g. *walk*) is stored, and the past tense formed by the application of a **default rule** 'add -*ed*'. This default rule steps in whenever a stored irregular past-tense form is unavailable, either because the verb does not have an irregular past-tense form (i.e. is regular), or the speaker is unable to remember the irregular past-tense form. Importantly, the default rule is 'capable of operating on any verb, regardless of its sound' (Prasada and Pinker, 1993: 2). However, if an irregular form is retrieved (or generated by analogy with phonologically similar forms), this blocks application of the default rule.

Whilst (as discussed above) it may be possible to imagine a non-nativist dual-route account, traditionally, the account does make a number of nativist assumptions (and its leading proponent, Steven Pinker, is certainly a prominent generativist–nativist theorist). First, it assumes that VERB STEM and PAST-TENSE MORPHEME are psychologically real categories that are present from birth, before children have 'filled' them with the relevant items (as opposed to simply descriptive categories used by linguists to identify regularities in the language, or categories that learners construct on the basis of experience). Second, the regular-route mechanism is assumed to be innate (though, presumably, it lies dormant for morphological systems and languages that do not have a regular system). Third, the dual-route account assumes a distinction between the lexicon (*words*) and the grammar (*rules*) that is innate, and it is often claimed that the two systems reside in different parts of the brain (e.g. Ullman, 2001).

5.4.2   The single-route model

Whereas the dual-route model claims that irregular, but not regular, past-tense forms are stored in the associative memory system, the single-route model (e.g. Bybee and Moder, 1983) claims that *all* past tense forms (regulars and irregulars alike) are stored in an associative memory system (like the system posited under the dual-route model for irregulars): generalizations are formed by phonological analogy to stored forms. The difference is that (unlike under the dual-route model) stored regular forms are also available for phonological analogy. For example, if asked to generate a past-tense form for the novel verb *clow*, a speaker may produce *clew* by analogy with *throw/threw*, *blow/blew*, *know/knew* (as can also happen under the dual route model), or *clowed* by analogy with *show/showed*, *crow/crowed* (and by a more distant analogy with all forms ending *-ed*). Which of these two outcomes will occur depends on how many forms of each type are stored, and how 'available' for analogy (i.e. easy to recall) each one is. This is related to frequency in the input (e.g. *know/knew* is likely to be more available than *crow/crowed*). The second outcome is ruled out by the dual-route model: a speaker could produce *clowed* using the default rule, but not by phonological analogy to stored regular forms.[8]

The single-route model is constructivist in its orientation because it does not posit a default rule or innate knowledge. Whilst a 'rule' such as 'add *-ed* to the verb stem' may be a useful *description* of the process of regular past-tense formation (which one might give to a non-native speaker learning English), the claim of the single-route model is that children learning English do not acquire formal rules of this nature. Rather, the all-purpose process of analogy is argued to be sufficient to generate both irregular and regular forms.

Box 5.1 Examples of past-tense formation under the two models

Example 1: *walk* (regular verb phonologically similar to regulars only)

Dual-route model (assuming that the form *walked* is not stored)
1. Search the lexicon for an irregular past-tense form of *walk*. None found.
2. Attempt to generate a past-tense form by analogy with phonologically similar irregulars. None found.
3. Default rule steps in to produce *walk+ed*.

Single-route model
1. Search memory for a past-tense form of *walk*. If *walked* is found, output it. If not . . .
2. Attempt to generate a past-tense form by analogy with *all* phonologically similar verbs, regular and irregular. No irregulars found. If enough regulars (e.g. *talk/talked, squawk/squawked*) are sufficiently available *walked* will be generated. If not, no past-tense form will be generated (child may simply produce *walk*).

Example 2: *show* (regular verb phonologically similar to regulars and irregulars)

Dual-route model (assuming that the form *showed* is not stored)	**Single-route model**
1. Search the lexicon for an irregular past-tense form of *show*. None found. 2. Attempt to generate a past-tense form by analogy with phonologically similar irregulars (e.g. *throw/threw, know/knew, blow/blew*). If enough are sufficiently available, *shew will be generated. If not . . . 3. Default rule steps in to produce *show+ed*.	1. Search memory for a past-tense form of *show*. If *showed* is found, output it. If not . . . 2. Attempt to generate a past-tense form by analogy with *all* phonologically similar verbs, regular (e.g. *flow/flowed, mow/mowed*) and irregular (e.g. *throw/threw, know/knew, blow/blew*). Depending on which are most available for analogy, either *showed* or *shew will be generated.

Example 3: *sing* (irregular verb phonologically similar to irregulars only)

Dual-route model	**Single-route model**
1. Search the lexicon for an irregular past-tense form of *sing*. If *sang* is found, output it. If not . . . 2. Attempt to generate a past-tense form by analogy with phonologically similar irregulars (e.g. *ring/rang*). If enough are sufficiently available, *sang* will be generated. If not . . . 3. Default rule steps in to produce **sing+ed*.	1. Search the lexicon for a past-tense form of *sing*. If *sang* is found, output it. If not . . . 2. Attempt to generate a past-tense form by analogy with *all* phonologically similar verbs, regular and irregular. No regulars found. If enough irregulars (e.g. *ring/rang*) are sufficiently available, *sang* will be generated. If not, no past-tense form will be generated (child may simply produce *sing*).

Example 4: *sleep* (irregular verb phonologically similar to regulars and irregulars)

Dual-route model	**Single-route model**
1. Search the lexicon for an irregular past-tense form of *sleep*. If *slept* is found, output it. If not . . . 2. Attempt to generate a past-tense form by analogy with phonologically similar irregulars (e.g. *creep/crept, weep/wept*). If enough are available, *slept* will be generated. If not . . . 3. Default rule steps in to produce **sleep+ed*	1. Search memory for a past-tense form of *sleep*. If *slept* is found, output it. If not . . . 2. Attempt to generate a past-tense form by analogy with *all* phonologically similar verbs, regular (e.g. *beep/beeped*) and irregular (e.g. *creep/crept*). Depending on which are most available for analogy, either *sleeped or *slept* will be generated.

5.4.3 Computer simulation studies   There is no room here to discuss in detail the debate over computer simulation studies of past-tense inflection (which could fill a book on its own). Our goal in this section is to highlight some of the major theoretical issues that have arisen from such studies.

Rumelhart and McClelland (1986) conducted a **neural-network** (or **pattern-associator**) simulation designed to implement the single-route account. The model has a set of 406 input units, each of which represents a particular sound (e.g. nasal stop, consonant cluster). A verb stem (e.g. *sleep*) is input to the model by switching on the units for the sounds that make up the word. The model also has a set of 406 output units, representing the same sounds as the input units. The model outputs past-tense forms by switching on the units for the sounds that make up the form. Every input unit is connected to every output unit. The task of the model is to learn which output units to switch on in response to which input units (e.g. the model must learn that when the input units representing *sleep* are switched on, it should switch on the output units representing *slept*). The model learns by changing the strength of the connections between the relevant input and output units on the basis of a teacher signal. For example, if the model outputs *slept* in response to *sleep* it is given a 'correct' signal and increases the strength of the connections that led to this output. If it outputs *sleeped*, it is given an 'incorrect' signal and reduces the strength of the relevant connections.

Rumelhart and McClelland's (1986) model proved extremely controversial. The model was reasonably successful at learning the training set, could generalize to regular and irregular verbs that it had not seen during training, and also produced some childlike overgeneralization errors (e.g. *sitted*). However, the model also produced some garbled unrealistic errors (e.g. *membled* as the past tense of *mailed*), which critics (e.g. Pinker and Prince, 1988) took as evidence that the model does not show humanlike default behaviour (adding *-ed* to novel verbs that are not similar to any stored regulars). In fact, the model gave an incorrect response for 20 out of 72 irregular verbs.

Pinker and Prince (1988) raised a large number of problems for the model. Many of these problems were simply to do with the way in which words were represented. For example, the model cannot represent the word *algalgal* (from the Australian language Oykangand), as the model represents the *gal* sound as either present or absent; it cannot represent it twice. However, these problems are specific to Rumelhart and McClelland's (1986) model in particular, not to the account in general, and were addressed by a new simulation that used a more accurate phonological representation (MacWhinney and Leinbach, 1991).

Pinker and Prince (1988) also accused the model of 'cheating' to exhibit a phenomenon known as U-shaped learning, whereby irregular forms are initially produced correctly (e.g. *sang*), subsequently overgeneralized (e.g. *singed*) and then produced correctly again. Rumelhart and McClelland (1986) achieved this by first presenting the model with almost exclusively irregular forms, for which it learned the correct mappings (e.g. *sang*) and then swamping it with a large number of regulars, causing the model to overgeneralize (e.g. *singed*) on the basis that the *-ed* mapping was now correct for the majority of trials. Even researchers sympathetic to the approach generally concede that this constitutes illegitimate 'fiddling with the data' (MacWhinney and Leinbach, 1991).

In any case, although subsequent studies have found that it is sometimes possible to achieve this pattern without any such 'fiddling' (e.g. MacWhinney and Leinbach, 1991), the kind of **macro-U-shaped learning** that Rumelhart and McClelland (1986) were attempting to model – whereby the *-ed* ending is rapidly overgeneralized to all irregular verbs – does not seem to exist. What is in fact seen is **micro-U-shaped learning**, whereby each verb undergoes a different pattern of overgeneralization then retreats; some verbs showing a high rate of overgeneralization, some a very low (or even zero) rate (Plunkett and Marchman, 1991, 1993; Marcus *et al.*, 1992; Maslen, Theakston, Lieven and Tomasello, 2004). As we will see, whether a particular irregular verb undergoes a high or low rate of over-regularization is dependent on its phonological properties such as the number of **friends** (phonologically similar verbs that form the past tense in the same way).

The remainder of Pinker and Prince's (1988) criticisms relate in some way to the relatively poor performance of the model. Generally speaking, later single-route learning models (e.g. MacWhinney and Leinbach, 1991; Forrester and Plunkett, 1994; Hare and Elman, 1995; Hare, Elman and Daugherty, 1995; Plunkett and Nakisa, 1997; Hahn and Nakisa, 2000) have performed much better. Nevertheless, dual-route theorists (e.g. Pinker and Ullman, 2002) maintain that these models bring in rules 'by the back door'. For example, some include a connection which copies the stem from the input to the output units, to ensure that the output is always an inflected form of the stem (to reduce odd errors such as *membled*). Others build in knowledge of the relevant inflections, with the task of the model to select the correct one in each case. Rather than attempting to adjudicate in this (often very heated) debate, we will instead focus on two interesting issues that have arisen from Pinker and Prince's (1988) review of the model.

5.4.3.1 The denominal verb debate   A particularly interesting problem for the Rumelhart and McClelland (1986) model is that it has difficulty producing the correct forms for verbs such as *ring*. The correct past-tense form is *rang* when the meaning is 'to telephone' but *ringed* when the meaning is 'to form a ring around' (this is known as the **homophony problem** as the two 'rings' are **homophones**; words that sound the same). Of course, it is possible to build semantic inputs into the model such that it learns that *ring+[telephone]→rang*, whilst *ring+[encircle]→ringed*, thus apparently solving the homophony problem (MacWhinney and Leinbach, 1991).

However, the actual problem goes much deeper than this. According to Kim, Pinker, Prince and Prasada (1991), the two past-tense forms are not arbitrary; there is a reason why the past-tense form of *ring* is *ringed* when it means 'to form a ring', but *rang* in other cases. To see why, we need to look more generally at the process of novel-word formation. When a new verb is derived from another verb (e.g. *overtake* is derived from *take*) it inherits its properties, including having an irregular past-tense form (e.g. *take* → *took* so *overtake* → *overtook*). However, when a new verb is derived from a *noun* (e.g. *to ring* [= encircle] is derived from the noun *ring*) it cannot inherit the property of having an irregular past-tense form, because it makes no sense for a noun to *have* a past-tense form. Because the new verb *ring* has no past-tense form, the default marker steps in, generating *ringed*.

If Kim *et al.*'s (1991) claim is correct, then this would be very damaging for the single-route model. Of course, proponents of the single-route model could simply argue that children learn that, when two verbs are homophonous, the one that is related to a noun takes the regular past-tense form. However, whilst the single-route model has no explanation for why this is in fact the case, an explanation is already built in to the dual-route model. *Ringed* is regular for the same reason that children produce errors such as **sitted* when they cannot remember the correct form: the 'add -*ed*' rule steps in when an irregular past-tense form is unavailable.

There is some evidence for the claim of Kim *et al.* (1991) that adults consider all denominal verbs to take regular past-tense forms. In a grammaticality judgment study conducted by these authors (see also Berent, Pinker and Shimron, 1999; Marcus *et al.*, 1995) adults rated novel denominal verbs as more acceptable in regular than irregular form, but showed the opposite pattern for novel verbs created from other verbs (deverbal):

> Denominal: *Gretzky [an ice-hockey player]* **high sticked/*high stuck** *the goalie* (i.e. hit him with a high stick).

> Deverbal: *Pete* ***resticked/restuck** *the tape on the wall* (i.e. repeatedly tried to stick the tape onto the wall).

Similar findings were observed in production studies with children (Kim *et al.*, 1991, 1994).

An alternative explanation is that it is not denominal status *per se* that determines whether a verb is regular or irregular in the past tense, but semantic distance from the usual meaning of the verb (Lakoff, 1987; Harris, 1992). When coining a new verb (e.g. *to stick* [= 'to hit with a stick']), speakers may seek to prevent possible confusion by avoiding assigning to it a past-tense form that already exists with a different meaning (e.g. *stuck*). In order to compare the denominal verb and semantic-distance accounts, Kim *et al.* (1991) asked their adult participants to rate the extent to which each novel verb was 'extended' from its usual meaning. In support of Kim *et al.*'s (1991) approach, the denominal/deverbal status of the verb accounted for 23 per cent of the variance in participants' acceptability ratings (preference for the regular over the irregular form), with semantic-extendedness accounting for less than 1 per cent.[9]

Ramscar (2002) objects that Kim *et al.*'s (1991) classification of verbs as denominal was subjective and risked circularity. For example, the verb *lie*, which is regular, was classified as denominal, because one can tell *a lie*. However, the verb *drink*, which is irregular, was not classified as denominal, even though one can have *a drink*. In a modified version of the study (Ramscar, 2002: 70) participants' acceptability ratings were not significantly predicted by their judgments of denominal status ($r = 0.06$), but were significantly predicted by their semantic-extendedness judgments. It may be useful for future studies to replicate this method on children, using the paradigm outlined in Ambridge (in press) to obtain ratings of novel past-tense forms from children.

Plunkett and Juola (1999) demonstrated that a connectionist network can generalize the *-ed* ending to verbs that are homophonous with irregulars on the basis of semantic distance. These authors trained a standard connectionist network to map from stem to past-tense form (e.g. Rumelhart and McClelland, 1986). The innovation was that the network had an additional input set of fifty pseudo-semantic units (i.e. each verb was associated with a random set of weightings of these units). Once the model had learned to map irregular stems onto the correct irregular past-tense forms, it was presented with the familiar irregular stems, but with different 'semantics' (i.e. a different pattern of random weightings for the pseudo-semantic units). Although the model was not presented with any grammatical information (i.e. denominal versus non-denominal status), it learned to map the novel forms that were homophonous with semantically different irregulars onto the regular *-ed* ending.

Nevertheless, a semantic-extendedness account (and Plunkett and Juola's, 1999, implementation of such an account) would seem to incorrectly predict that verb senses that are far removed from their conventional uses (e.g. *bought the farm* [= 'died'] or *blew away* [= 'impressed' or 'assassinated']) should be regular in the past tense (Pinker and Ullman, 2002). Of course, one can always think of a post-hoc explanation for such anomalies (e.g. one theory is that a solider dying in combat really did 'buy the farm' as the compensation received would be sufficient for his wife to pay off the mortgage), but at present it seems that neither account can explain the entire pattern of results without some circularity.

5.4.3.2 The minority-default debate Despite the absence of a hard-wired 'default rule', models such as that of Rumelhart and McClelland (1986) are able to show apparent default-like behaviour, adding *-ed* to verbs that they have not previously encountered. Marcus *et al.* (1995) argue that this is simply because such models have been trained on far more regular than irregular verbs, with the consequence that the connections that yield the *-ed* ending are always strongly activated. According to these authors, connectionist models will have difficulty in simulating **minority-default** behaviour. A candidate for a system with a minority default is the German noun plural system, which has five different plural morphemes: *-s -n, -en, -er* and *-Ø*. The claim is that, whilst *-s* is by far the least frequent marker, it is the default in the sense that it applies in all situations where an irregular plural form is not stored in the lexicon. This is the case for unassimilated foreign borrowings (e.g. *cappuccinos*), eponyms (e.g. *3 Mickey Mouses* [= idiots]; surnames and products (e.g. the plural of *Kadett* [= cadet] is *Kadetten* when it refers to actual cadets [soldiers] but *Kadetts* when it refers to the *Opel Kadett*, a German car).

In order to test this claim, Marcus *et al.* (1995) asked German adults to rate each of the different plural forms (e.g. *Kachen, Kachs, Kacher* and *Kach*) for a novel noun (e.g. *Kach*) when presented as a native German word (e.g. a cold tablet), a name and a foreign borrowing. When presented as a native word (e.g. cold tablet) one of the 'irregular' (though majority) forms was always preferred to the 'regular' *-s* form (presumably simply as a result of the very low frequency of this latter pattern). When presented as a name, the *-s* form was always preferred over the best 'irregular' form. The results from the foreign-borrowing condition were less clear: Although speakers did not significantly prefer the *-s* form over the 'irregular' endings, the preference for an irregular over an *-s* form shown for native words did at least disappear.

Whilst Marcus *et al.* (1995) take these findings as support for their claim, Hahn and Nakisa (2000) argue that if *-s* really were a true default, it should apply equally to all categories for which the irregular form is blocked (Marcus *et al.*, 1995, attribute their anomalous finding to some assimilation of foreign borrowings). In an extended replication of the study of Marcus *et al.*, Hahn and Nakisa (2000) found that for some apparently default-requiring categories (first names and acronyms) one of the irregular endings was preferred over *-s* for some items.

Whether or not human speakers in fact show minority-default behaviour, a number of computer simulation studies (Forrester and Plunkett, 1994; Hare, Elman and Daugherty, 1995; Plunkett and Nakisa, 1997) have attempted to demonstrate that connectionist networks are capable of doing so. These studies show that an item can receive a minority inflection if either (a) it is phonologically very similar to a class of items that takes this inflection or (b) the forms that do not take this inflection form coherent phonological clusters, with the items that do widely distributed throughout phonological space. In reply, Berent *et al.* (1999) argued that the Hebrew plural system displays default behaviour, even though irregular and regular nouns are 'intermingled in the same phonological neighbourhoods' (p.459). Again, however, the human data are open to different interpretations with raters preferring the 'default' form more for names than foreign borrowings.

5.4.4   Naturalistic data studies

Whilst these findings are informative, one could argue that the most relevant data are children's actual productions. Naturalistic data from English-speaking children have been used to compare the dual- and single-route models on two key predictions.

The first issue is the rate of overgeneralization shown by children. According to the dual-route model, the error rate will be very low as, once a particular irregular form (e.g. *came*) has been learned, overgeneralization errors with that verb (e.g. **comed*) will cease virtually immediately, as a consequence of the irregular form 'blocking' the default rule (Marcus *et al.*, 1992). The single-route model argues that errors will persist as the correct and overgeneralized form will remain in competition (e.g. Ramscar and Yarlett, 2007). Marcus *et al.* (1992) argue that an overall overgeneralization rate of 4 per cent (averaging across 83 children in the literature) counts as support for the dual-route prediction of a low error rate. However, Maslen *et al.* (2004; see also Maratsos, 2000) showed that some individual verbs (e.g. *come, eat* and *throw*) displayed high overgeneralization rates (25%, 50% and 75%), despite the irregular form being attested hundreds (or in the case of *came*, thousands) of times in the recorded input sample (which represented perhaps 10% of all the input). Whilst neither model predicts a specific error rate, it would be difficult to argue that these rates are 'low'.

The second issue relates to zero-marking errors (e.g. supplying *come* as the past tense of *come*). According to the dual-route model, these should disappear suddenly at around the point of the child's first over-regularization. This is because the first over-regularization constitutes evidence that the child has acquired the *-ed* marker and begun to use it in the pre-existing default route (i.e. whenever no stored past-tense form is available). Under the single-route model, the rate of zero-marking errors will decline slowly as the child gradually builds a *VERB+ed* construction. A difficulty here is deciding what a sudden versus a gradual change looks like. For example, Marcus *et al.* (1992: 103) state that 'Adam's first over-regularization error occurred during a 3-month period in which regular marking increased from 0 to 100%', whilst McClelland and Patterson (2002), talking about the same data, state that 'Adam's first over-regularization occurred during a six-month period in which the probability of using the regular gradually rose from 24–44%' (these statements are both true, because the rate of 100 per cent represents a spike in the rate of correct regular marking). Hoeffner (1996) analysed the same data (from Cazden, 1968) statistically, demonstrating that age was a statistically significant (negative) predictor of the rate of zero marking error. This finding provides evidence for the claim that rates of zero marking decrease gradually.[10]

5.4.5   Experimental studies

5.4.5.1 Elicitation studies with real English verbs

5.4.5.1.1 Zero-marking errors   Elicitation studies conducted with children generally use a simple paradigm where the child is asked to complete a sentence such as *Every day John sings. Today he is singing. Yesterday he...* (usually with accompanying pictures). We first consider the predictions of the two models with regard to zero-marking errors (e.g. giving *knit* as the past tense of *knit*). Under the dual-route model, the majority of zero-marking errors occur before the child has acquired the default *-ed* marker and so outputs a bare stem. However, even after the rule has been acquired, zero-marking errors can be produced by phonological analogy with genuine no-change verbs (e.g. *knit → knit* by analogy with *hit → hit*). Furthermore, verb stems that end in *-t* or *-d* (e.g. *knit*, *read*), and thus have the appearance of being past-tense forms, may be erroneously stored as irregular past-tense forms, with their retrieval blocking application of the default rule.

The single-route model does not posit that children produce a stem form as such, as the account does not posit the existence of a separate stem. However, children could produce zero-marking errors for verbs that end in *-t* or *-d* (e.g. *knit*, *read*) as a consequence of the use of what Bybee and Slobin (1982: 273) term a **goal-based schema** ('verbs that end in t/d amount to acceptable past-tense forms'), particularly as present- and past-tense forms (e.g. *knit*, *knitted*) compete in memory (e.g. Cottrell and Plunkett, 1994). The single-route model shares with the dual-route model the assumption that zero-marking errors can also be produced by analogy with genuine no-change verbs (i.e. on the basis of a **source-based schema**). This means that both models predict higher rates of zero-marking error for verbs (e.g. *knit*) that have a large number of and/or highly frequent no-change irregular enemies (verbs that have a similar present-tense form but that do not change in the past tense; e.g. *hit/hit*).

However, there is one important prediction of the single-route model that is not shared by the dual-route model: the single-route model predicts that zero-marking errors should be rare for regular past-tense forms that have a large number of regular 'friends' (phonologically similar verbs that form the past tense in the same way). For example, zero-marking errors for *try* should be rare because, if *tried* cannot be retrieved, the child is likely to be able to generate this form on the basis of a phonological analogy with *die/died*, *sigh/sighed*, *lie/lied* and so on. In contrast, zero-marking errors should be more frequent for *mend* which has fewer friends (though one is *end/ended*). The dual-route model does not share this prediction, as past-tense forms are never generated by analogy with stored regulars, only stored irregulars (see Box 5.1).

In an elicitation study with 74 children aged 3;8–13;5, Marchman (1997; see also Marchman, Wulfeck and Weismer, 1999) elicited past-tense forms for

11 regular verbs and 38 irregulars. Collapsing across regulars and irregulars, zero-marking errors were more common for verbs with fewer friends. Unfortunately, regular verbs were not analysed separately[11] but the number of friends (high/low) did not interact with the variable of regular/irregular. Thus although (consistent with both models) irregular friends helped irregular verbs to resist zero-marking errors, regular friends helped regular verbs to resist zero-marking errors *to a similar extent*, which Marchman (1997) takes as evidence for the single-route model. Matthews and Theakston (2006) conducted a similar elicitation study designed specifically to examine zero-marking errors (in both verb past-tense and noun-plural formation). Whilst this study did not examine friend/enemy effects, a number of interesting frequency effects were observed. For example 5-year-olds showed a *relative* frequency effect, such that they were significantly more likely to supply a plural form for nouns that are at least as common in plural as singular form (e.g. *teeth, feet*) than nouns that are more common in singular than plural form (e.g. *mouse, knife*). An overall frequency effect was only marginally significant (though significant when looking only at regulars). The relative frequency effect would seem to provide support for the single-route model, under which singular and plural forms compete in memory. However, since modern versions of the dual-route model do allow rote storage of high-frequency regular forms (e.g. Alegre and Gordon, 1999; Hartshorne and Ullman, 2006), frequency effects can never provide compelling evidence against this account.

5.4.5.1.2 Over-regularization errors   In most respects, the models make similar predictions with regard to over-regularization errors. Both agree that low-frequency irregular past-tense forms will be less likely to be retrieved than higher-frequency forms, and hence more susceptible to error (though the mechanism generating the error differs between the models). Both agree that irregulars with a large number of and/or high-frequency phonologically similar friends (e.g. *sleep/slept*, with friends *creep/crept, weep/wept*) will be protected from over-regularization, as these friends provide the basis for generating the irregular form using a phonological analogy, if it cannot be retrieved directly from memory (see Box 5.1).

The two models differ, however, with regard to their predictions regarding regular enemies. Because, under the single-route model, past-tense forms are produced by analogy with stored irregular *and regular* forms, irregular verbs like *throw* that have a large number of regular enemies (*throw* has thirteen, including *show/showed, flow/flowed* and *sew/sewed*) are predicted to be more likely to be over-regularized (e.g. **throwed*) than irregular verbs with fewer irregular enemies (e.g. *hit*). In contrast, because the dual-route model does not allow past-tense forms to be generated by phonological analogy to stored regulars, the number of regular enemies that an irregular verb has cannot affect the likelihood of that verb erroneously receiving regular inflection (again, see Box 5.1 for examples).

In this respect, the findings of Marchman (1997) provided support for the dual-route model. Over-regularization errors were equally likely for irregular verbs with a high and low number of regular enemies. On the other hand, the study of Marchman *et al.* (1999) did find an effect of regular enemies, as predicted by the single-route model. These contradictory findings are probably, in part, caused by the fact that other factors (e.g. number of friends, verb frequency, presence or absence of stem-final *-d* and *-t*) also influence the likelihood of over-regularization error, and, in some cases, interact with the number of enemies. One way to remove such confounds is to run studies with novel, experimentally created verbs. Such studies are discussed in the following section.

5.4.5.1.3 Correctly inflected forms   The final elicited production study that we will consider here (Kidd and Kirjavainen, in press) investigated past-tense inflection (of both real and novel verbs) by native learners of Finnish. This study was designed to test the single-route accounts against a version of the dual-route account known as the **declarative/procedural** model (Ullman, 2001). Under this model, irregular forms are stored in **declarative memory**, the part of memory that stores facts (e.g. 3 is an odd number). Because (at least some) regular forms are not stored, they are instead formed using **procedural memory**, the part of memory that stores, for example, knowledge of how to drive a car. Thus the declarative/procedural model predicts that children's score on a test of declarative memory will predict rates of correct performance with irregular verbs, whilst children's score on a test of procedural memory will predict rates of correct performance with regular verbs.[12] To test this prediction, Kidd and Kirjavainen (in press) elicited past-tense forms of 120 verbs (both real and novel) from Finnish children aged 4;0–6;0 (*M* = 5;2), and had each child complete a test of declarative memory (word-pair recall) and procedural memory (children implicitly learned a button-press sequence corresponding to the position of a cartoon character on a screen).

Counter to the predictions of the declarative/procedural model, there was no correlation between the procedural-memory measure and performance on regular verbs. As predicted by the model, significant (though small) correlations were observed between the declarative-memory measure and performance on irregular verbs. However, by far the best predictor – for regulars and irregulars alike – was vocabulary size (as measured by an adapted version of the *Peabody Picture Vocabulary Scale*). This finding is consistent with the single-route account, as it suggests that the key factor in correct past-tense inflection is having a large number of 'friends' (whether regular or irregular) that are the basis for phonological analogy. Further evidence against the declarative/procedural model comes from a similar study conducted with native learners of English (Kidd and Lum, 2008). This study found no support for the prediction of the declarative/procedural model that girls will display higher rates of over-regularization error than boys (Hartshorne and Ullman, 2006).

   5.4.5.2 Elicitation and judgments with novel verbs   Nevertheless, it is hard to draw firm conclusions on the basis of studies with real verbs because both models allow for rote storage of past-tense forms. Therefore when a child produces (for example) a correct form, it is not possible to tell whether she has done so using the default-rule (dual-route model) or analogy to phono-logically similar regulars (single-route model), or simply retrieved the form as a whole. The most informative studies are therefore those that use novel verbs.

   The predictions of the dual- and single-route models are the same for novel verbs as for real verbs: as we saw in the previous section, both models predict that the closer – in phonological terms – a novel verb is to an existing class of irregular verbs (e.g. *spling* is similar to *ring/rung, sing/sung* etc . . .), the more likely the novel verb is to be inflected as an irregular of this type (e.g. *splung*). That is, the greater the number of (and/or the higher the frequency of) irregular friends (for a pseudo-irregular) or irregular enemies (for a pseudo-regular), the greater the likelihood of irregular inflection. This is because when no past-tense form can be retrieved from memory (as will always be the case for novel verbs), both models posit that one is generated by analogy with stored irregulars. However, only the single-route model additionally predicts that the closer a novel verb is to existing regulars, the more likely it is to receive regular inflection, as novel past-tense forms are generated by analogy with stored irregulars *and regulars*. The dual-route model holds that past-tense forms are not generated by analogy with stored regulars, and hence that 'the goodness of the suffixed [i.e. regular – BA] past-tense forms does not decline as a function of distance from known suffixed forms' (Prasada and Pinker, 1993: 22).

   These predictions were tested in a series of studies by Prasada and Pinker (1993) in which adult participants both produced past-tense forms and rated such forms for grammatical acceptability on a Likert-type scale. As predicted, under both accounts, novel verbs that were phonologically similar to existing irregulars (e.g. *spling*, similar to *string, sling* etc . . .) received higher irregular past-tense form ratings (e.g. *splung*) than novel verbs less similar to existing irregulars (e.g. *blip* → *blup*). Seemingly in support of the single-route model, participants also gave higher ratings of acceptability for novel regulars that were similar to (e.g. *plipped*, similar to *slipped, dripped* etc . . .) than distant from (e.g. *ploamphed*) existing regulars. However, Prasada and Pinker (1993) argue that this is simply because 'the sounds of [verbs such as] *ploamph* themselves are bad to an English speaker', and show that this effect disappears when ratings of the acceptability of the stem form (e.g. *plip* vs *ploamph*) are partialled out (i.e. controlled for statistically).

Albright and Hayes (2003) raised two methodological concerns with the study of Prasada and Pinker (1993). The first relates to the fact that Prasada and Pinker's novel 'regulars' that were dissimilar to all existing regulars (e.g. *ploamph*) also violated rules of English phonology (and hence were rated as relatively unacceptable in stem form). Albright and Hayes (2003) argue that partialling out the rating of stem-acceptability may preclude the possibility of observing any similarity effect for novel regulars that may exist. The second problem is that Prasada and Pinker designed novel verbs simply by finding verbs that rhymed with existing English regulars and irregulars, and manipulated phonological distance by changing one or more phonemes. This means the novel verbs were not controlled for the number of existing verbs that they were (dis)similar to (or – in Marchman's terms – the number of 'friends' and 'enemies').

In order to address these concerns, Albright and Hayes (2003) asked adult participants to rate the acceptability of both regular and irregular past-tense forms (and also to produce their own past-tense forms) for novel verbs that were:

a. Similar to both an existing class of regulars and an existing class of irregulars; e.g. *dize (dized/doze), fro (froed/frew), rife (rifed/rofe)*
b. Similar to an existing class of regulars only, e.g. *bredge (bridged/broge), gezz (gezzed/gozz), nace (naced/noce)*
c. Similar to an existing class of irregulars only; e.g. *fleep (fleeped/flept), gleed (gleeded/gled), spling (splinged/splung)*
d. Not similar to either an existing regular class or an existing irregular class; e.g. *gude (guded/gude), nung (nunged/nang), preak (preaked/proke)*

That is, the variables of similarity-to-regulars (similar/not similar) and similarity-to-irregulars (similar/not-similar) were fully crossed in a 2×2 within-subjects design.

All the test items were generated by a computer simulation of past-tense learning that builds 'micro-rules' for both irregular and regular English verbs (which we will consider in more detail below). Importantly, the model operates on the basis of phonological features (e.g. 'voiceless fricative' rather than individual phonemes (e.g. *-f, -th, -s* or *-sh*). This allows the model to generate novel verbs that vary in their similarity to subtypes of English verbs, without being either too similar to individual verbs or too non-English-like (e.g. *ploamph*). Because the model forms its micro-rules on the basis of exposure to a real input corpus, this allows it to compute a measure of precisely *how* similar a novel past-tense form is to existing regular and irregular forms. These measures can then be used as a prediction of the human acceptability rating for each form (e.g. *fleeped, flept*).

Albright and Hayes' (2003) results were in striking contrast to those of Prasada and Pinker (1993). Effects of phonological similarity to both irregulars and, crucially, regulars were observed: as predicted by the single-route model (but as explicitly ruled-out by Prasada and Pinker's, 1993, dual-route model), the more similar a novel verb was to an existing regular verb, the more likely it was to receive regular inflection (in the production task), and the better the regular form was rated (in the judgment task). Importantly, the effect of similarity-to-regulars was – if anything – greater in magnitude than the effect of similarity to irregulars. A dual-route model which allows storage of regulars but assumes that *at least some* regulars are not stored (e.g. Alegre and Gordon, 1999; Hartshorne and Ullman, 2006) would appear to predict the opposite.

Ambridge (in press) replicated the judgment component of Albright and Hayes (2003) with children aged 6–7 and 9–10. An effect of similarity to irregulars (predicted by both models) was found for both age groups. An effect of similarity to regulars (predicted by the single-route model only) was found only for the older group. This suggests that phonological families of irregular verbs are learned relatively early in development (probably because the majority of early forms are irregular; see references in Rumelhart and McClelland, 1986), with regular families acquired later.

Whilst the findings of Albright and Hayes (2003) would seem to favour a single-route over a dual-route account, these authors in fact interpret their findings as providing support for their own **multiple-rules** model. Under this account, learners set up an individual rule for each particular phonological context (i.e. each stem → past-tense mapping type), whether notionally irregular (e.g. *-ing* → *-ang*) or regular (*-sh* → *-shed*). Albright and Hayes argue that such an approach is necessary to account for the fact that so-called 'regular' verbs also form phonological neighbourhoods of similarly inflected friends. The 'add *-ed*' orthographic rule actually abstracts over three different phonemes: *-d* (as in *rubbed*), *-t* (as in *jumped*) and *-əd* (as in *voted* or *needed*), each of which applies to different phonologically defined groups of verbs. Whereas a traditional 'one-size-fits-all' default rule requires additional assumptions to prevent forms such as **jump-əd* (as opposed to *jumpt*) being produced, Albright and Hayes' (2003) account simply assumes that a separate micro-rule is set up for each.

Albright and Hayes (2003) show that a computational model that explicitly builds a different phonological rule for each pattern outperforms a connectionist network of the type previously discussed in this chapter. However, this finding depends crucially on the particular implementation of the single-route model used, with some versions outperforming the multiple-rules model (Keuleers and Daelemans, 2007; Keuleers, 2008). Even if the multiple-rules model does provide the best coverage of the human rating data, theoretically speaking it loses the advantages of both the dual-route and single-route models. The advantage of the dual-route model is that it is simple and parsimonious, with a single (perhaps innate) default rule dealing with all cases of regular inflection (including memory failure, denominal verbs etc.). The advantage of the single-route model is that the domain-general psychological process of analogy can account for all inflection, without the need to posit a rule. In contrast, it is not clear how an account such as that of Albright and Hayes (2003) would be implemented in the minds of learners. On the one hand, it would not be plausible to claim that a set of micro-rules can be present in advance. On the other hand, if, as Albright and Hayes (2003) claim, the rules are deduced from the input, then there is little to differentiate the model from single-route approaches. Indeed, the multiple-rules model could be said to 'characterize an underlyingly connectionist processing system at a higher level of analysis, with rules providing descriptive summaries of the regularities captured in the network's connections' (McClelland and Patterson, 2002: 471).

5.4.6   Crosslinguistic considerations

Finally, it is important to note that a number of authors have raised the objection that the dual-route model cannot account for languages or morphological systems that do not seem to have any kind of default. One such system is the paradigm of genitive noun inflection in Polish. In a naturalistic-data analysis, Dąbrowska (2001) found that the three children studied (aged between 1;4 and 4;11) overgeneralized all three different genitive singular markers at similar rates, with no evidence to suggest that one was being treated as the default. Presumably, however, the dual-route account does not insist that every morphological system has a default. Perhaps the Polish genitive has three 'irregular' morphemes and no default.

Potentially more problematic is the case of Dutch, where there are two different noun-plural markers, -en and -s, each of which is considered the default marker for a particular 'fiefdom' (Pinker, 1999) which is, in the main, defined phonologically. Thus, in contrast with the claims of Marcus et al. (1995) for German, there does not seem to be a default that applies universally for names, foreign borrowings and so on: A Dutch 'toy store may have a supply of Bob de Bouwers (Bob the Builders) . . . and Piet Piraten (Pete-Pirates)' (Keuleers et al., 2007: 315). This means that, if one is to reject the single-route model that operates on the basis of phonological analogy, one must instead accept a 'dual-route model that prohibits phonological analogy, yet must include phonological rules to determine which default marker applies in each case' (see Keuleers et al., 2007: 315). Another problem is that, for some individual nouns, either 'default' plural marker is acceptable.

5.4.7   Rules versus analogies in inflectional morphology: conclusion

A successful model of the English past tense (and of morphological systems more generally) must be able to explain the following findings:

(1) Verbs that are homonymous with irregulars but have very different meanings to those irregulars and/or are derived from nouns receive regular inflection (e.g. *ring → rang/ringed*).

(2) Speakers will apply minority mappings to some novel items, but whether these items are defined grammatically, semantically or phonological remains controversial.

(3) Naturalistic data studies show high rates of over-regularization error even for some high-frequency irregular verbs.

(4) Naturalistic data also suggest that zero-marking errors do not cease suddenly at the point of the first over-regularization, but disappear more gradually.

(5) Both zero-marking and over-regularization errors are more common for items that (a) are low in frequency (especially in relation to the present-tense/stem form), (b) have few/low-frequency friends, and/or (c) many/high-frequency enemies, and (d) have the characteristics of past-tense forms (e.g. the verb stem ends in *-d* or *-t*).

(6) Children's vocabulary is a good predictor of their performance with both regular and irregular past-tense forms. However, tests of declarative and episodic memory do not specifically predict performance on irregular and regular forms respectively.

(7) The inflection that a novel verb will receive is determined by phonological similarity to stored irregulars and regulars.

Together, these findings (in particular points 6 and 7) suggest that a successful model will involve the storage of both regular and irregular forms in an analogical memory system. One such model is the single-route model (or the multiple-rules model which, we have argued, is largely indistinguishable from the single-route model). Another option would be to retain the dual-route model, but additionally posit that children store regular forms and use them as the basis for phonological analogy in memory. Whilst this is a direction that some dual-route models are taking (e.g. Alegre and Gordon, 1999; Hartshorne and Ullman, 2006), a problem that arises is that the predictions of such a model would be, for the most part, identical to those of a single-route alternative (e.g. both would predict effects of similarity to stored regulars when subjects are asked to produce or judge past-tense forms of novel verbs). Presumably, however, if *at least some* regulars are not stored, one would expect to see larger effects of similarity to irregulars than similarity to regulars. This does not seem to be the case (Albright and Hayes, 2003; Ambridge, in press). If all regulars *are* assumed to be stored, then, on the grounds of parsimony, it would seem wise to avoid positing an additional default rule, unless there is compelling evidence that it is required in some special circumstances (e.g. inflection of surnames that are homophonous with irregular nouns). Showing that this is the case, must therefore be the goal for dual-route theorists.

This is not to say that single-route models have 'won the day'. Even the best simulations still typically achieve below 90 per cent 'correct' classification of English or novel past-tense forms, clearly far short of the level of competence that children achieve. However, most current simulations leave out at least one factor (e.g. semantics, direct-mapping to past-tense form) that has been shown to be important. The goal of future experimental and modelling work should be to investigate the interaction of these factors in children, adults and computer models.

5.5   Learning inflectional morphology: conclusion

This chapter has discussed root infinitives, the emergence of productivity, incorrect morphological marking and the debate surrounding regular inflection (in the main, English past-tense inflection). Although we have approached these as separate issues (and, indeed, they have traditionally been seen as different research areas), they are all tightly interrelated. A child utterance such as *He come* could be analysed as a root infinitive, as reflecting a lack of productivity with the 3sg morpheme, a person-marking error (e.g. 1sg for 3sg) or an attempt at a past-tense form by a child yet to master the -ed rule or schema. An important goal for both generativist and constructivist approaches, then, must be to build a model of the acquisition process that can explain all the phenomena associated with the learning of inflectional morphology discussed in this chapter.

If one common finding has emerged from our consideration of the research evidence, it is that it is impossible to give a coherent account of any of these phenomena without assuming that children store strings (both individual items and longer chunks) from the language they hear. This assumption lies at the heart of the constructivist approach, but it is one that many generativist researchers seem extremely resistant to. This is surprising as this assumption would not undermine the generativist enterprise. On the contrary, it could allow generativist researchers to better explain the data by attributing otherwise-problematic utterances to rote learning (although, of course, it would be necessary to build in some criteria for identifying rote-learned chunks to guard against circularity). Indeed, a number of leading generativist theories do make this assumption (e.g. Marcus et al., 1992; Radford, 1996; Pinker, 1999). In the past-tense literature, for example, Marcus et al. (1992) do not attribute productivity with the -ed marker until the point at which the child has produced an over-regularization error, on the conservative assumption that any previously produced -ed forms could have been rote learned. Yet researchers from essentially the same

Summary table 5.3 *Rules versus analogies in inflectional morphology* (☑ = *supports theory*; ☒ = *counts against theory*)

Issue/phenomenon	Dual-route (Pinker and Prince, 1988; Marcus, 1995; Marcus *et al.*, 1992; Prasada and Pinker, 1993).	Single-route (e.g. Bybee and Moder, 1983; Rumelhart and McClelland, 1986)
Summary of theory	Novel forms are generated by analogy to stored *irregular forms only* or – if no irregular family has sufficient strength – generated by a default rule ('add *-ed*').	Novel forms are generated by analogy to stored irregular and regular forms; outcome depends on relative strength of relevant irregular vs regular families.
Computer simulation studies of single-route model	☑ Computer models sometimes make unrealistic errors and, in some cases, can achieve macro-U-shaped learning only via unrealistic manipulations of training set (Pinker and Prince, 1998). More recent modelling studies (see right-hand column) argued to bring in rules by the back door (Pinker and Ullman, 2002).	☑ Can simulate some aspects of children's performance (Rumelhart and McClelland, 1986) and achieve U-shaped learning without unrealistic manipulations of training set (MacWhinney and Leinbach, 1991; Hare *et al.*, 1995; Hare and Elman, 1995; Hahn and Nakisa, 2000; Forrester and Plunkett, 1994; Plunkett and Nakisa, 1997). ☑ Macro-U-shaped learning probably a myth (Plunkett and Marchman, 1991, 1993; Marcus *et al.*, 1992; Maslen *et al.*, 2004).
Denominal verb debate	☑ When new verbs are created from nouns (denominal verbs), adults prefer regular > irregular past-tense form, even when controlling for semantic extendedness (Kim *et al.*, 1991, 1994; Berent *et al.*, 1999; Marcus *et al.*, 1995).	☑ Semantic extendedness may be better predictor than denominal status when more appropriately controlled (Ramscar, 2002), though ☒ some exceptions may remain.
Minority-default debate	☑ Irregular > regular noun plural preferred for native-like novel words, but not names, foreign borrowings etc. (Marcus *et al.*, 1995). ☑ Some evidence of this effect even when irregulars and regulars intermingled in phonological space (Berent *et al.*, 1999), though perhaps not for all cases.	☑ Irregular > regular noun plural, in fact, preferred for first names and acronyms (Hahn and Nakisa, 2000). ☑ Connectionist networks show minority default behavior if items that take 'default' widely distributed phonologically (Hare *et al.*, 1995; Forrester and Plunkett, 1994; Plunkett and Nakisa, 1997).
Rate of over-regularization in naturalistic data	Generativist account predicts low error rate, as errors 'blocked' as soon as competing irregular form learned. In fact, though *overall* rate is low (e.g. 4%; Marcus *et al.*, 1992), this hides a high rate (50%+) for some individual verbs, even after irregular form has been learned (Maratsos, 2000; Maslen *et al.*, 2004).	

Zero-marking errors in naturalistic data	Debate over whether same data pattern constitutes rapid decline as soon as regular rule learned (Marcus, *et al.* 1992; Hoeffner, 1996; ☑ single-route). ☑ dual-route) or gradual decline (McClelland and Patterson, 2002;	
Zero-marking errors in experimental studies	Findings in right-hand column may be compatible with current versions of dual-route model that assume storage of high-frequency regular forms (e.g. Pinker and Gordon, 1999; Alegre and Gordon, 1999).	☑ Zero-marking errors rare for verbs with many regular friends (Marchman, 1997; Marchman *et al.*, 1999) and ☑ for nouns that rarely appear in plural form (Matthews and Theakston, 2006).
Over-regularization in experimental studies (real English verbs)	☑ Marchman (1997) does not find effect reported by Marchman *et al.* (1999; right-hand column). In any case, this effect may be compatible with version of dual-route model that assumes storage of high-frequency regulars.	☑ Over-regularization errors more common for irregular verbs with many regular enemies (Marchman *et al.*, 1999).
Over-regularization in experimental studies (novel verbs)	☑ No effect of similarity to regulars on acceptability of regular forms, controlling for stem acceptability (Prasada and Pinker, 1993, for adults). Any such effect (see right-hand column) may be predicted under a version in which large number of regulars are stored.	☑ Correlation between similarity to regulars and acceptability of regular forms with better controlled stimuli (Albright and Hayes, 2003, for adults; Ambridge, in press, for children).
Declarative-procedural model	☑ Naturalistic study suggests girls make more over-regularization errors than boys (Hartshorne and Ullman, 2006); Some evidence girls show advantage on declarative memory, so may store more regular forms.	☑ Experiment found no correlation between declarative memory and performance on irregulars, or procedural memory and performance on regulars (Kidd and Kirjavainen, in press) and no sex difference on any measure (Kidd and Lum, 2008).
Crosslinguistic considerations	Presumably does not predict that every morphological system has a default marker. Concedes that some systems have multiple 'defaults' (Pinker, 1999), which may be problematic (see right-hand column).	☑ Many systems have no default (e.g. Dąbrowska, 2001) or ☑ several 'defaults', choice of which is phonologically conditioned (Keuleers *et al.*, 2007).

theoretical standpoint who approach the topic from the direction of the root-infinitives literature (e.g. Wexler, 1998; Hoekstra and Hyams, 1998) assume that every verb form produced by the child was generated using a full productive grammar. In our view, this is a mistake.

Whilst generativist researchers tend to focus on the end state (full adultlike productivity), perhaps at the expense of explaining early child utterances, constructivist researchers display the opposite pattern. Lexical-learning theories (and computer simulations such as MOSAIC that instantiate them) may be able to give a good account of children's errors, but there are no sufficiently detailed proposals for how children acquire an adultlike system of morphology. There are not, as generativist accounts sometimes imply *no* constructivist proposals of this nature. For example, Tomasello (2003) discusses how a child moves from rote-learned holophrases (e.g. *I'm playing*; *I'm running*), through morphological slot-and-frame patterns that instantiate tense and agreement marking (e.g. *I'm ACTIONing*) to fully abstract adultlike morphological constructions (*[SUBJ] [AUX] [VERB]ing*). Fine-grained constructivist accounts of morphological acquisition have also been outlined by Peters and Menn (1990, 1993), Slobin (1973; Shirai, Slobin and Weist, 1998) and Dressler, Mayerthaler, Panagl and Wurzel (1988). Importantly these accounts all depend on looking at a range of languages other than English. Nevertheless, it remains fair to say that (aside from very restricted domains such as past-tense acquisition) there are no constructivist proposals that are sufficiently detailed to allow them, for example, to be implemented as a computer simulation.

In summary, if generativist researchers focus more on explaining early errors as a function of the input (rather than simply seeking to dismiss them) and constructivist researchers focus more on explaining how children achieve adultlike productivity (rather than simply emphasizing the lexically specific nature of early utterances), the field will be able to move closer to a complete understanding of the domain of inflectional morphology, and all the research phenomena contained therein.

6   Simple syntax

A sentence is not simply a set of words (e.g. *cat*, *dog*, *bit*), but also contains the grammatical information necessary to allow the listener to determine 'who did what to whom' (and also whether the utterance is a statement or a question, and so on). As we saw in the previous chapter, many languages convey this information by means of morphology (e.g. nominative and accusative noun markers). Many languages, with English being a prime example, instead rely primarily on word order. For example, basic declarative English sentences use SUBJECT–VERB–OBJECT word order to mark the AGENT, ACTION and PATIENT of an event respectively (e.g. *The dog bit the cat* means something different to *The cat bit the dog*). Although some languages (arguably) exhibit entirely 'free' word order (i.e. all word orders are possible, equally common and convey the same meaning), most retain a 'default' word order that is used for the majority of basic declarative sentences (and which guides interpretation when case marking is not present), even when case marking makes word-order information redundant.

Our main focus in this chapter is the question of how children learning **word-order languages** acquire the word-order 'rules' of their language. However, we will also discuss data from languages in which morphological cues to meaning override word-order information. We focus here on **simple sentences**: sentences with only one clause (e.g. *The dog bit the cat*). **Complex sentences** – those with a main and a dependent (or subordinate) clause (e.g. *John said [that the dog bit the cat]*) – are discussed in Chapter 7. Although, in Section 6.3, we also discuss constructions such as the **dative** and **locative**, we generally focus on **transitive** and **intransitive** sentences (e.g. *The dog bit the cat*; *The dog barked*); those that contain only a SUBJECT, VERB and (for transitive sentences) OBJECT. Finally, we restrict ourselves, in this chapter, to discussion of **canonical (basic) declarative sentences** (as opposed to questions and passives, which are discussed in Chapter 7).

The set of word-order 'rules' in a given language (and, under some definitions, its morphology) is known as the **grammar** or **syntax** of that language. As we saw in Chapter 4, these 'rules' apply not to individual words (e.g. *cat*, *dog*, *bit*) but to **syntactic categories** of words such as NOUN and VERB;

(also known as **word-class**, **lexical** or **part-of-speech** categories) and **grammatical functions** (also known as **grammatical relations**) such as SUBJECT and OBJECT. Consequently, in order to put together simple sentences, children must accomplish three tasks: (1) identifying or constructing syntactic categories such as NOUN and VERB; (2) identifying or learning the correct ordering of these categories into phrases, and phrases into sentences (e.g. SUBJECT VERB OBJECT in English); (3) learning the appropriate restrictions on verbs (e.g. some verbs are restricted to intransitive or transitive sentences only, whilst some may appear in both types).

This chapter discusses generativist and constructivist proposals for how children accomplish each of these tasks. Whereas, in previous chapters, the various theoretical positions taken have not always been straightforwardly characterizable as generativist or constructivist, for each of these three issues (in particular the first two), there is a straightforward debate between nativist, generativist accounts on the one hand and non-nativist, constructivist accounts on the other.

6.1   Identifying/constructing syntactic categories

Even if the child is assumed to have solved the problem of parsing the continuous speech stream into words (see Chapter 2), assigning these words to syntactic categories presents a significant challenge. Generativist theories make the nativist assumption that newborn children are already in possession of syntactic categories (both **lexical categories** such as NOUN and VERB and **grammatical relations** such as SUBJECT and OBJECT). However, words do not come labelled with their syntactic category. The challenge facing the child, then, is to assign each incoming word to a pre-existing category. Once this is done (and relevant parameters have been set; see Section 6.2) the child can use her innate knowledge of syntax (e.g. VP = NP + VP) to produce sentences. Constructivist theories posit neither innate syntactic categories nor innate knowledge of syntactic structures. Thus the child must simultaneously acquire both the categories themselves and the 'rules' for combining them into sentences, from scratch.

6.1.1   Identifying syntactic categories: generativist approaches

6.1.1.1 Semantic bootstrapping   The problem facing children is that the definition of each syntactic category is circular. For example, *ball* is a NOUN only because it shares distributional, morphological and syntactic properties with other NOUNS (e.g. it can appear with a determiner, be marked for number etc . . .). Children therefore need some way to break (or **bootstrap**) into this circular system. Pinker's (1984, 1987, 1989a) proposal is that children bootstrap into this system using semantics: whilst words (e.g. *dog*, *bite*) do not come labelled with their syntactic category (e.g. NOUN, VERB), their semantic category (e.g. PERSON/THING, ACTION/CHANGE OF STATE) is observable from the world. Pinker (1984) proposed that children's innate knowledge consists not only of an inventory of syntactic categories, but also an inventory of semantic categories and a set of **linking rules** linking the two. These apply at the level of lexical categories (e.g. PERSON/THING → NOUN, ACTION/CHANGE OF STATE → VERB) and grammatical relations (e.g. AGENT → SUBJECT, PATIENT → OBJECT).

Many NOUNS are not people or things (e.g. *happiness, terror*), and many VERBS do not denote actions or state changes (e.g. *see, hear*). Pinker's (1984) proposal is therefore that children use the linking rules to build a syntactic tree for a basic sentence (e.g. *The dog bit the cat*), and then 'read off' rules which can be used to understand or produce less prototypical sentences. For example, using the linking rules described above (plus another that links DEFINITE-NESS MARKER → DETERMINER) the child can build the following tree for *The dog bit the cat*:

$$[[NP_{SUBJ} \text{ The dog}][VP [V \text{ bit}] [NP_{OBJ} \text{ the cat}]]]$$

The child can then use this tree – $[[NP_{SUBJ}][VP [V] [NP_{OBJ}]]]$ – to parse non-prototypical sentences such as *The situation justified the measures* and assign each word to the relevant category (e.g. *situation, measure* → NOUN; *justify* → VERB), even if she does not know the meaning of these words.

An important, but often overlooked, aspect of Pinker's (1984) proposal is that once the child has used the linking rules to break into the system, they are largely abandoned in favour of **distributional analysis**: items that share the same distribution (i.e. that occur in the same position) are grouped into the same category. For example, once the child has used the linking rules to assign a few words to the NOUN category, she will notice that nouns are often preceded by *the* (e.g. *the dog*; *the situation*; *the measures*) and will subsequently assign other words that are preceded by *the* to this category.

A problem for Pinker's theory is that some words and sentences violate the linking rules. At the level of lexical categories, a NOUN (e.g. *spanking*) or ADJECTIVE (e.g. *noisy*) may be used to refer to an ACTION. For example 'if a child heard *you will get a spanking from me* in his or her first inputs, the child might conclude that English is an OVS language with *from* as a nominative case marker and *a* as a verb phrase complementizer or modifier' (Pinker, 1984: 61). At the level of grammatical relations, a child could take a sentence such as *Eats a lot of pizza, that guy!* as evidence that English is a VERB OBJECT SUBJECT language.

As a solution, Pinker (1984) originally proposed that caregivers or children (or both) filter out such non-basic sentences, before later conceding that this is probably implausible (Pinker, 1987). In a later version of the theory, Pinker

(1987) instead proposed that linking rules are used probabilistically rather than in a one-shot fashion. For example, a child hearing *The dog bit the cat* would simply increase the probability that *dog* and *cat* are nouns rather than irrevocably assigning them to that category. An additional modification is that linking rules, at all stages, compete with other information such as distributional information. For example, whilst linking rules would push the learner in the direction of assigning *noisy* to the VERB category, the fact that it is distributionally similar to ADJECTIVES such as *tall* or *silly* (e.g. all occur before a noun) will push the learner in the direction of assigning it to this category.

The aim of these modifications is to ensure that occasional erroneous inferences made on the basis of non-basic sentences (e.g. *you will get a spanking from me*) will soon be overridden. However, it may be that these modifications raise more problems than they solve. What happens, for example, when the linking rules suggest one category assignment and distributional information another? Does the learner compute and keep in mind all possible parses, narrowing the options when further information becomes available (like the unsupervised tree-parsing algorithm of Bod, 2009)? If so, what happens in the meantime? (i.e. how does the child interpret the incoming utterance, or produce her own utterances?). Until these questions are answered (for example, by implementing the proposal as a computational model) Pinker's account does not appear to make testable predictions regarding the state of the child's grammar at any particular stage.

A second problem is that some languages seem to at least partially violate the grammatical function linking rules. In morphologically ergative languages (e.g. Dyirbal), AGENTS (*The man opened the door*) receive one type of marking (ergative case), whilst ACTORS (*The man danced*), THEMES (*The door opened*) and PATIENTS (*The man opened the door* receive another (absolutive case), presumably because such languages are 'impressed by the similarity' between THEMES and PATIENTS in contexts such as the above (Pinker, 1989a: 252). Ergativity is a complex phenomenon, and there is no room for a detailed discussion here. Suffice it to say that a linking rule that linked both AGENTS and ACTORS to SUBJECT (as is required to yield the correct pattern for languages such as English) risks yielding an incorrect pattern of linking for languages such as Dyirbal. Thus, whilst the multiple-competing-cues version of Pinker's proposal (Pinker, 1987) would presumably allow children to arrive at the correct pattern via some combination of linking rules and distributional cues, it remains possible, for at least some languages, that innate linking rules would make the child's task more difficult rather than easier.

A related problem for Pinker's theory is that even the probabilistic version would seem to predict – apparently incorrectly – that children should find it easier to acquire prototypical than non-prototypical items. Using diary data collected from two children (the relevant period being 1;9–2;1), Bowerman (1990) showed that prototypical AGENT–ACTION–PATIENT verbs (e.g. *open*, *close*, *push*, *drink*) did not seem to be acquired earlier than less prototypical verbs that do not denote an action or state change (e.g. *have*, *get*, *got*, *see*, *need*, *watch*, *want*, *scare*, *hold*). However, it is possible to argue against this objection, on the basis that many of these verbs may have denoted prototypical ACTIONS for the child (e.g. *have*, *get*, *got* and *want* were mostly used to denote a 'getting' action, rather than states of affairs).

There is one final problem for Pinker's theory that, despite being seldom discussed, is probably the most serious (Bowerman, 1990). Whether or not certain languages or items violate the linking rules, it is unclear how children can determine which nouns (or noun phrases) in a sentence are actually arguments of the verb, and hence should be used as the input to linking rules. Consider the English sentence *Johnny hit Tommy with a stick*. *Tommy* as PATIENT is linked to OBJECT and *Johnny* to SUBJECT. *The stick* is not an argument of the verb at all (the prepositional phrase *with a stick* is an optional adjunct) and so does not participate in linking. In the equivalent sentence in Chechen-Ingush, however, *the stick* is the direct object of the verb *hit* (*Johnny hit a stick to Tommy* would be a rough paraphrase), and so must be linked to OBJECT position. Here we have a situation where precisely the same event is being described in two languages, yet the learner of one (Chechen-Ingush) must include in the linking process an NP (*the stick*) that the learner of another must exclude. If the Chechen child behaved like an English child and assumed that *the stick* was not an argument of the verb, she would incorrectly link *Tommy*, rather than *the stick*, to OBJECT position. Again, it may be the case that probabilistic semantic bootstrapping, operating across many different sentence types, would be sufficient to overcome this problem. However, unless a probabilistic account is specified in more detail (ideally sufficient detail to enable it to be implemented as a computational model), it is virtually impossible to determine whether or not this is the case.

All of these problems relate to the fact that languages seem to be too flexible (i.e. there are too many ways of saying the same thing, both within and across languages) for a rigid set of linking rules to be useful (except perhaps if they are relegated to probabilistic cues, in which case their value is less certain). The trend for more recent generativist theories, then, has been to abandon the notion of innate linking rules and to investigate other ways in which children can break into the circular system of syntactic categories.

6.1.1.2 Prosodic bootstrapping The claim of the **prosodic boot-strapping** hypothesis (e.g. Christophe, Millotte, Bernal and Lidz, 2008) is that children can use prosodic information (e.g. pauses, syllable lengthening, pitch contours) to split an utterance into clauses, and clauses into syntactic phrases. They can then use knowledge of **function words** to label the phrases. For example, imagine that a child hears *John said the boy is running*. Prosodic information can be used to split the utterance into the clauses *John said X* and *the boy is running*, and this second clause into its component syntactic phrases: [*The boy*] [*is running*]. The child then uses the 'flags' of determiner *the* and auxiliary *is* to label the phrases as a Noun Phrase and Verb Phrase respectively – [NP *The boy*] [VP *is running*] – finally allowing her to classify *boy* as a NOUN and *running* as a VERB (example adapted from Christophe *et al.*, 2008: 70).

In Chapter 2, we evaluated evidence regarding the claims (a) that prosodic cues to clause and syntactic phrase boundaries are available and reliable in child-directed speech (in all languages) and (b) that children are not only sensitive to these cues, but know that they *are* cues to clause and phrase boundaries and use them to divide up speech accordingly. We concluded that that, whilst there is good evidence in support of these claims with regard to clauses, the evidence with regard to syntactic phrases is more mixed. A particular problem is that for sentences with unstressed pronoun subjects (e.g. *He kissed the dog*) – which constitute 84 per cent of input sentences in the study of Fisher and Tokura (1996) – prosodic cues would incorrectly place the NP/VP boundary after *kissed* as opposed to *he* (see 2.4.2.1.1).

Nevertheless, even working on the assumption that children can parse (at least some of) the utterances that they hear into syntactic phrases, evidence that they can use function words to label these phrases, and ultimately to assign the component words to syntactic categories, is thin. Consider, for example, the claim that if the child has parsed a sentence into the phrases [*The boy*] [*is running*], 'the first unit would be identified as a Noun Phrase because it starts with the determiner *the*, whilst the second unit would be identified as a Verb Phrase because it starts with the auxiliary *is*' (Christophe *et al.*, 2008: 70).

A problem for this proposal is that it is unclear how a child could learn that *the* signals an NP and *is* a VP without having previously identified some NPs and VPs and observed that many begin with *the* and *is* respectively. Of course, this is not possible, because the claim is that children use function words to identify NPs and VPs in the first place. What is needed to break into this circularity is a way for children to learn which function words are associated with which phrases without having to first identify the phrases. Christophe *et al.* (1997: 596) propose that 'Babies . . . may be helped by some universal properties of language' such as (paraphrasing roughly) the property that a clause can contain only one VP, but more than one NP. Thus function words and morphemes that sometimes appear in more than one phrase can be attributed to NPs, whilst those that always appear only once can be attributed to VPs. For example, *the* appears twice in the clause *The boy kicked the girl*, and thus must signal an NP in each case; *kicked* appears only once, and so signals a VP (which contains the second NP: *the girl*).

Presumably, Christophe *et al.* (1997) are claiming that children are innately endowed with such principles (though they do not state this directly). However, even if one accepts this claim in principle, it is far from clear that there exists a set of properties that would allow children to label particular items as prepositions, pronouns, auxiliaries, complementizers and so on. Furthermore, this set of properties would have to be sufficient to allow children learning all the languages of the word to identify 'flags' to syntactic categories. This may well be problematic (for example, the universal principle that allows English children to infer that determiners flag NPs would be of no use to children learning languages that lack determiners, such as Russian). Indeed, even in English, sentences with two NPs, each containing a determiner (e.g. *The boy kicked the ball*) are presumably extremely rare (recall that Fisher and Tokura, 1996, found that 84 per cent of sentences had pronoun subjects).

Of course, nobody would deny that when children have identified some NPs beginning with *the* and VPs beginning with *is*, they will be able to use these flags to identify further instances of NPs and VPs (this is the process of distributional analysis as assumed by generativists and constructivists alike). The difficulty lies with the claim that children can use function words to directly identify instances of syntactic phrases in the first place.

In conclusion, support for the prosodic bootstrapping hypothesis is weak. Whilst children as young as 0;6 show some sensitivity to cues to syntactic boundaries in the laboratory (e.g. Soderstrom *et al.*, 2003; see Chapter 2), the evidence suggests that such cues are only rarely available in the actual speech to which children are exposed. Even if children are able to use such cues to split clauses into syntactic phrases, there is little reason to suppose that children will be able to label these phrases (e.g. NP, VP) without having previously identified some example of the relevant phrases. It would seem that what is needed to break into this circularity is an account whereby children can use words (presumably content as well as function words) to form syntactic classes of other words without knowing anything about these words other than their surface form (information which is available from the speech stream). Such accounts are termed **distributional** as syntactic categorization is based on surface distribution. Distributional accounts have been proposed within both the generativist and constructivist frameworks; it is to the first of these that we now turn.

6.1.1.3 Distributional analysis: generativist approaches Distributional analysis is a very simple idea: The child groups together words that appear in similar **distributional contexts**. For example, if the child hears the strings *the dog is* and *the cat is* she may group *dog* and *cat* into a single category. For constructivist approaches (see Section 6.1.2), these emergent categories will be used directly in production. For generativist approaches, 'the problem then becomes one of labelling ... distributionally derived categories with the innately specified system' (Mintz, 2006: 46).

Three a priori objections to distributional analysis are often made. The first (the **ambicategory problem**) is that multiple-category words would lead to incorrect categorizations, as in the following famous example from Pinker (1987):

> John ate fish.   John ate rabbits.
> John can fish.   *John can rabbits.

Certainly, if this was the entire corpus to which a child was exposed, such errors could occur. However, as long as category assignment is probabilistic (i.e. words are only grouped together when they have been observed to share a large number of distributional contexts) they will quickly be ruled out (e.g. *rabbits* will join a noun category on the basis of appearing in contexts such as *There are the_*), as demonstrated empirically by Mintz, Newport and Bever (2002: 417), amongst others. The second objection is that the child cannot know which distributional properties to pay attention to. In principle, the child could group together all words that appear as the seventh word in a sentence, all words that occur in the same sentence as the word *mouse* and so on (Pinker, 1987). Again, this is true in principle, but it does not seem implausible that contexts such as the immediately preceding and following word (e.g. Mintz, 2003) which give reasonably successful classifications, are more salient and easier to track than, for example, the seventh-word position. In addition, many real-world distributional contexts (e.g. appearing after *I wanna*) will be associated with a particular meaning, whereas 'appearing in the same sentence as the word *mouse*' will not. Finally, it is sometimes objected that calculating distributional statistics would require too much computational capacity to be plausible (e.g. Pinker, 1979). The problem with this objection is that we have no way of knowing either how much computational capacity is available to a child learner or whether whatever learning procedure is posited instead of distributional analysis would require less or more.

Mintz (2003) proposed a distributional learning procedure whereby the learner groups together words that appear in a **frequent frame**. A frame was defined as 'an ordered pair of words with any word intervening' (p. 95), with the main analysis (study 1) focusing on the 45 most frequent frames of a given corpus. For example, some frames that were frequent in all six corpora studied (speech to Eve, Peter, Naomi, Nina, Anne and Aran up to age 2;6) were *you _ it* (a VERB frame), *what_you* (an AUX frame) and *the_in* (a NOUN frame). By definition, for a given corpus, the learning procedure yielded 45 separate categories (one for each frame). Whilst these scored high for **accuracy** (e.g. the frame *the_in* yielded a cluster made up exclusively of NOUNS), they scored low for **completeness** (e.g. the frame *the_in* grouped together only a low proportion of all NOUNS in the corpus). Because words can appear in more than one frame, a potential solution to this is to collapse together frame-defined categories that share a certain percentage of words. For example, Peter's seventeen VERB clusters were grouped together to form a single frame with over 90 per cent accuracy and completeness, whilst his two NOUN clusters were joined to form a single category containing 88 nouns and just one incorrect item (a pronoun).

Whilst these accuracy and completeness scores are impressive, it is important to note that both were calculated only over the items that were actually classified by the frequent-frames procedure. Approximately half of the word types in each corpus were not classified at all, since they never occurred in one of the 45 most frequent frames. This is problematic as increasing the number of frames included in the analysis to improve coverage would seem likely, at some point, to reduce accuracy and completeness.

In general, however, the frequent-frames procedure performs well (and better than the majority of distributional learning procedures discussed here). The procedure also works well for French (Chemla, Mintz, Bernal and Christophe, 2009), a language with more word-order variation than English (and that therefore might be expected to yield less useful frames). It remains to be seen whether the procedure would work for languages where word order is much more variable than either French or English. Since such languages generally make considerable use of inflectional morphology, it would seem feasible that a frequent-frames procedure could operate successfully at a sublexical level (indeed, frames such as *I'm-ing* would presumably be useful for English).

Furthermore, there is some evidence that frames are not only useful for categorization in principle, but are actually used in this way by real learners. In a study by Mintz (2002), adults heard sets of fifteen sentences, each consisting of one of three frames plus a target word. For example, participants in one counterbalance group heard (in addition to various filler and control sentences):

Bool_jiv	Zim_noof	Poz_fen	Sook_runk
Bool nex jiv	Zim nex noof	Poz nex fen	Sook nex runk
Bool kwob jiv	Zim kwob noof	Poz kwob fen	Sook kwob runk
Boll zich jiv	Zim zich noof	Poz zich fen	Sook zich runk
Bool pren jiv	Zim pren noof	Poz pren fen	- **'Missing' sentence**

Although the 'missing' sentence *Sook pren runk* was never actually presented, participants judged the sentence as familiar, presumably because they had used the other frames to create a category containing *nex*, *kwob*, *zich* and *pren*, and had heard the other items used in the *Sook_runk* frame (as a control, Mintz, 2002, showed that participants judged sentences *choon pren wug* to be significantly less familiar, though this frame had also been presented during training).

However, such effects are notoriously difficult to obtain in children. Although Mintz (2006) reported similar results from a listening time study with children aged 1;0, real English words were used as the frames (e.g. *to deeg it*), meaning that children may simply have assimilated the novel items to existing categories, rather than forming new categories during the study. Despite numerous attempts, no studies have unequivocally demonstrated that children show this type of generalization in studies that use only novel items, and even adults seem to require additional phonological cues to category membership (e.g. Gómez, 2002; Peña, Bonatti, Nespor and Mehler, 2002; Newport and Aslin, 2004; Onnis, Monaghan, Richmond and Chater, 2005; and papers reviewed in Braine, 1987).

Perhaps the most serious problems facing Mintz's proposal relate to linking the distributionally defined categories to innately specified categories such as VERB and NOUN. Mintz (2003) sets out (though seems to stop short of explicitly advocating) a possible account for how this could be accomplished. First, the child labels the category that contains concrete objects NOUN (using an innate linking rule such as that proposed by Pinker, 1989a), then labels as VERB either the next largest category or, if this turns out not to be viable crosslinguistically, the category of items that take nouns as arguments.

The first problem with this proposal is that it is not clear how the child could determine which word in a sentence (e.g. *John kicked the ball yesterday*) takes the nouns as its argument (it could be *the*, or *yesterday*). Of course, one could argue that the child uses semantics to identify the word type that takes nouns as arguments (i.e. VERB) but, as we have seen in relation to the semantic bootstrapping hypothesis, this would raise problems for non-actional verbs. The second problem is that this proposal says nothing about how children would assign the innately specified labels to all the other categories yielded by the frequent frames process (e.g. ADJECTIVE, AUXILIARY, COMPLE-MENTIZER, WH-WORD). The third problem (which applies to any theory that posits innately specified syntactic categories) is that many languages seem to have parts of speech that cannot be straightforwardly classified as one of the apparently universal categories. For example, Mandarin Chinese, under some analyses, has property words that are verb-like in some respects but adjective-like in others (McCawley, 1992; Dixon, 2004). Even the apparently straightforward case of the NOUN/VERB distinction has been disputed for languages such as Salish (Jelinek and Demers, 1994) and Samoan (Rijkhoff, 2003), leading some authors (e.g. Maratsos and Chalkley, 1980; Croft, 2001) to argue that the only category that all languages share is some kind of NOUN category that includes all concrete objects.

Constructivist approaches (see the following section) argue that such problems are insurmountable, and therefore that children use distributionally acquired categories directly, rather than linking them to innately specified categories. Generativist approaches view the problem of explaining precisely how children could become productive with these distributionally acquired categories as more serious than the linking problem.

6.1.2   *Constructing syntactic categories: constructivist approaches*

Whilst constructivist and generativist approaches use syntactic category labels in a way that is, on the surface, indistinguishable, the underlying assumptions are rather different. For constructivist accounts, labels such as VERB and AUXILIARY are not innately specified categories but simply useful mnemonics for clusters of items that behave in a similar way. Everything that a child knows about the behaviour of a particular word has been learned from observing the behaviour of that word directly (though children may also generalize to words that are distributionally and/or semantically similar). This means that the inventory of items that constitutes a particular syntactic category is an empirical matter. For example, if a child (or even an adult) showed zero overlap in her use of *the* and *a* (given sufficient contexts) constructivist accounts would not credit her with a DETERMINER category (see the debate between Pine and Martindale, 1996/Pine and Lieven, 1997, and Valian, Solt and Stewart, 2009).

6.1.2.1 Semantic assimilation   In a proposal somewhat similar to that of Pinker (1984), Schlesinger (1988) proposed that children's SUBJECT, VERB and OBJECT categories emerge out of the semantic categories of AGENT, ACTION and PATIENT. For Schlesinger (1988), however, children's earliest grammar is semantic in its entirety. The child produces and interprets transitive sentences using an AGENT–ACTION–PATIENT schema (e.g. *The woman hit the man*). Events that are not true actions (e.g. *see*) and entities that are not true agents (e.g. *The woman* in *The woman saw the man*) are **assimilated** into the ACTION and AGENT category on the basis of their similarity to real ACTIONS and AGENTS (e.g. *seeing* is semantically similar to *looking*; thus a *seer* is semantically similar to a *looker*). In this way, the AGENT, ACTION and PATIENT categories gradually develop into the adult SUBJECT, VERB and OBJECT categories. Finally, entities that are not at all semantically similar to members of the relevant category (e.g. *The situation* in *The situation justified the measures*) will be assimilated to the relevant category (here, SUBJECT) on the basis of purely distributional similarity to other members of the category. In this respect, the theory is almost identical to that proposed by Pinker (Braine, 1992).

An advantage of the Braine–Schlesinger version of Pinker's (1984) theory is that it can explain why the adult categories retain a 'flavour' of the semantic categories from which they are derived. For example, many sentence types require a SUBJECT to be an AGENT (e.g. *The man carved the statue* vs *The knife carved the statue*). An account under which semantic categories are abandoned in favour of syntactic categories as soon as possible (i.e. Pinker, 1984) would not capture this finding.

Ultimately, however, the semantic assimilation account fails for the same reasons as the semantic bootstrapping account. Children do not seem to show an advantage for prototypical AGENT–ACTION–PATIENT verbs (e.g. *open*, *close*) over less prototypical verbs (e.g. *see*, *need*); arguably a stronger prediction of the assimilation than the bootstrapping account. Neither does the assimilation account address the problem of how the child can determine which elements of the sentence are (semantic) arguments of the verb (e.g. the stick is a PATIENT argument of *John hit Tommy with a stick* in Chechen-Ingush, but not English; Bowerman, 1990).

As we will see later in this chapter, modern constructivist accounts (e.g. Tomasello, 2003) combine elements of this proposal with distributional learning, discussed below (hence, **functionally based distributional analysis**). Children form syntactic categories as a by-product of the processes of schematization and analogy that allow for the generation of novel utterances. For example, a child might generalize across the sentences *I can kick you* and *I can see you* to form an *I can X you* construction schema, where X represents a developing VERB category that includes both actional verbs such as *kick* and non-actional verbs such as *see*. Similarly, a child might generalize across the schemas *I'm ACTIONing it* and *KISSER kiss KISSEE* on the basis of similar AGENT–ACTION and ACTION–PATIENT relations in the two ('**structure mapping**'). This allows the child to move towards a NOUN(SUBJECT) VERB NOUN(OBJECT) construction and, as a by-product, abstract NOUN and VERB categories. An advantage of this approach is that it does not incorrectly predict that children will necessarily show an advantage for AGENT–ACTION–PATIENT sentences (Bowerman, 1990): children acquire the schemas that occur frequently in the input and that suit their communicative intentions, whether they are AGENT–ACTION–PATIENT schemas or not (e.g. *I want X*). Neither is there a problem of knowing which NPs or semantic entities are expressed as verb arguments (Bowerman, 1990). Children form constructions on the basis of the input to which they are exposed, without regard to the syntactic status of the individual words. The experimental evidence that pertains to this account is discussed in Section 6.2 (see, in particular, Summary table 6.2).

6.1.2.2 Distributional learning The clustering algorithm of Redington, Chater and Finch (1998) groups together words on the basis of the number of contexts that they share, where context is defined as the immediately preceding and following word (e.g. *the dog is*; *the cat is*). Categories are iteratively collapsed on this basis until the algorithm reaches a predetermined cut-off point, designed to maximize **accuracy** (e.g. a NOUN category should contain only NOUNS) and **completeness** (e.g. a NOUN category should contain all the NOUNS in the set of target words). This is a difficult trade-off: The categories yielded are typically accurate but not complete (e.g. NOUN: 90 per cent accuracy, 53 per cent completeness; VERB: 72 per cent accuracy, 24 per cent completeness) or vice-versa (ARTICLE: 10 per cent accuracy, 100 per cent completeness; p. 455).

Whilst this study demonstrates that information that would yield (reasonably) successful categorization is present in the input, it is not intended as a simulation of a learning process that a child could actually use (for one thing, the algorithm requires the learner to parse the entire corpus in one go). Cartwright and Brent (1997) attempted to propose a more psychologically realistic model under which sentences are processed one at a time and then 'forgotten'. The model uses a learning mechanism based on the notion of **minimum description length.** Any corpus of sentences can be described using a set of **categories** and a set of **templates (derivations)** that specifies how the category members are combined into sentences. Together these make up the **description**. For example, a description of one toy corpus (containing four sentences) is as follows (example adapted from Cartwright and Brent, 1997: 136–7):

Sentence	Template
this is a kitty	A B C D1
this is a doggie	A B C D2
what a nice kitty	E C F1 D1
what a cute doggy	E C F2 D2

Category	Members
A	(A1) *this*
B	(B1) *is*
C	(C1) *a*
D	(D1) *kitty*; (D2) *doggie*
E	(E1) *what*
F	(F1) *nice*; (F2) *cute*

When the learner encounters an utterance, each word is assigned to a new category, even if that word has been encountered before. Thus if the first utterance that the model hears is *This is a kitty* and the second, *This is a doggy*, words will be assigned to categories as follows.

> *This* → A, *is* → B, *a* → C, *kitty* → D.
>
> *This* → E, *is* → F, *a* → G, *doggy* → H.

The algorithm then inspects each pair of groups in turn to see whether merging them would maximize the coverage of the corpus whilst minimizing the **description length**. That is, the aim of the model is to have as few categories and templates as possible, whilst retaining the ability to generate each sentence in the corpus. In the above example, merging A&E, B&F, C&G and D&H would reduce both the number of categories and the number of templates, and so is desirable. Note that, as shown in this example, repeated instances of 'the same' word are not *automatically* grouped together (but may subsequently be grouped if they are sufficiently similar). This means that instances of multiple-category words (e.g. *fish*) can be separately assigned to developing NOUN and VERB classes independently. Cartwright and Brent (1997) assessed their model using the Berstein-Ratner (1984) corpus of child-directed (mean age 1;6) speech. Although the model learns in a more plausible way than those based on clustering algorithms, the results were similar, with average accuracy and completeness scores (collapsing across all categories) of around 70 per cent and 20 per cent respectively (token scoring, experiment 4).

Freudenthal, Pine and Gobet (2005c: 18) raise a problem with the way that Cartwright and Brent's (1997) model (and every other model discussed up to this point) was evaluated. Since a model's VERB category (for example) typically contains verbs in a variety of tenses, verbs that can and cannot be used in certain constructions (e.g. the imperative) and verbs that can be used as both auxiliaries and main verbs (e.g. *do, have*), the category does not in fact constitute a set of items that could be substituted for one another in particular sentences. Thus not only does such a 'category' fail the standard linguistic definition of a syntactic category, it is also of little use for producing novel utterances. For example, Mintz's (2003) simulation grouped *put* and *do* into a VERB category – 'correctly' according to the scoring system – but *put* cannot be substituted for *do* in utterances such as *What do you want?*, and children do not seem to make such errors (e.g. **What put you want?*).

Freudenthal *et al.* (2005c) argue that the only way to fairly evaluate a model that constructs syntactic categories is to incorporate a production component that allows the model's output to be compared to speech produced by children exposed to the same input. Freudenthal *et al.*'s (2005c) MOSAIC model (introduced in the previous chapter) meets this criterion. The model incrementally learns input utterances (taken from real child-directed speech) from the end of the utterance backwards. Two aspects of the model are particularly important here. First, the model probabilistically sets up generative links that allow it to substitute words that have similar distributions for one another. For example, if *he* and *she* have occurred in a sufficient number (determined by the setting of an overlap parameter) of similar contexts (e.g. *He is happy*; *She is happy*) the model will substitute *she* into *Can he play?* to produce *Can she play?*, even if it has never heard this utterance. Second, the model incorporates a chunking mechanism that 'chunks up' word sequences (e.g. *do you*) that have occurred a large number of times (the number is determined by the setting of a chunking parameter). A chunk is, in effect, treated as a single word (e.g. *do+you*), meaning that it is no longer possible to substitute words for the individual words that make up the chunk (though the chunk as a whole can be substituted by other chunks such as *can+you*, or single words). Thus, if *do+you* is a chunk, the model will not substitute *put* for *do* to give unrealistic errors such as **What put you want?* (an earlier version of the model that did not incorporate the chunking mechanism did make such errors; Jones, Gobet and Pine, 2000).

Freudenthal *et al.* (2005c) assessed their model by inputting maternal speech addressed to Anne and Becky from the Manchester corpus (Theakston *et al.*, 2001) and having it generate a sample of 500 novel utterances using substitution. Independent raters then coded the utterances for whether they were grammatically acceptable (semantically anomalous sentences such as *Cut it with the puzzle* [substituted for *knife*] were allowed) or contained incorrect substitutions (e.g. **What put you want?*). Whilst error rates were high (7 per cent for Anne's data, 18 per cent for Becky's), and presumably higher than those for real children, it is difficult to compare the performance of this model with those that do not produce output. Indeed, Freudenthal *et al.* (2005c) note that many of the errors observed were 'precisely the kinds of errors that are likely to be hidden by the kind of evaluation metrics used in previous research'. For example, MOSAIC sometimes substituted *a* for *the* with a mass noun (e.g. **in a mud*), scoring an error, whilst a traditional clustering algorithm would be credited for 'successfully' grouping *a* and *the* into the same category. The model also made some interesting childlike errors such as substituting *don't want to* for *want to*, to give utterances such as **Do you don't want to* (an error produced by children in the study of Ambridge and Rowland, 2009).

6.1.3 *Phonological cues to syntactic categories*

Finally, there is one potential learning strategy that is consistent with both generativist and constructivist approaches. Words from different syntactic categories tend to differ in a number of phonological properties (e.g. Kelly, 1992, for a review). For example, English bisyllabic (two-syllable) words tend to be nouns if they have initial-syllable (trochaic) stress (e.g. *monkey*, *tractor*) and verbs if they have final-syllable (iambic) stress (e.g. *undo*, *repeat*). This is often true for words that are otherwise ambiguous between noun and verb readings (e.g. *contrast, record, contest, rebel* and *permit*; Cassidy and Kelly, 2001). Once children have begun to form a particular syntactic category, it is possible that they could notice the phonological properties that are typical of its members and assign new words to the category on this basis. Indeed, one study (Cassidy and Kelly, 1991) found that children aged 3;8–5;4 ($M = 4;8$) generally assume longer and shorter novel words to be nouns and verbs respectively.

Christiansen and Monaghan (2006), in an analysis of the 1,000 most frequent words addressed to children (in the CHILDES corpus), found that, together, 16 phonological cues could be used to predict whether a particular item was a verb or non-verb with 66 per cent accuracy, and a noun or non-noun with 62 per cent accuracy.[1] The corresponding scores for prepositions, pronouns, conjunctions and interjections were over 85 per cent with only articles (47 per cent) failing to show above-chance performance (50 per cent).

It may even be possible for children to use phonological cues to solve (or bypass) the ambicategory problem. In both adult- and child-directed English, nouns are generally longer in duration and have greater pitch changes than verbs (Sorenson, Cooper and Paccia, 1978; Shi and Moisan, 2008) even for noun and verb uses of 'the same' word (e.g. *call, drink, hug, kiss, walk*; Conwell and Morgan, 2010). This raises the intriguing possibility that children may be able to maintain two phonologically distinct versions of the same word (e.g. *drink-VERB* and *drink-NOUN*), thus bypassing the ambicategory problem altogether.

6.1.4   Identifying/constructing syntactic categories: conclusion

The question of how children assign words to syntactic categories has proved to be a difficult one to answer. Accounts based on the notion that children exploit correlations between semantics and syntax (both Pinker's generativist account and the Schlesinger/Braine constructivist formulation) incorrectly predict that children should have difficulties with languages and utterances that violate the linking rules. The main difficulty facing the prosodic bootstrapping hypothesis is a lack of evidence that cues to syntactic structure are reliable and available in child-directed speech (though there is some evidence that children are sensitive to them). There is also little evidence to support the claim that children can label phrases using knowledge of function words. This means that, for generativist and constructivist approaches alike, some form of distributional analysis is the most likely solution. For generativist approaches, the challenge is to come up with a mechanism for linking distributional and innately specified categories that is valid crosslinguistically. For constructivist approaches, the challenge is to come up with a more detailed account of how the distributionally defined clusters are used in comprehension and production. The MOSAIC model represents a step in the right direction (particularly its

Summary table 6.1 *How do children assign words to (generativist approaches) or construct (constructivist approaches) syntactic categories?* (☑ = *supports theory*; ☒ = *counts against theory*)

Semantics-based approaches

Summary of theory / Issue/phenomenon	Semantic bootstrapping (Generativist); Pinker (1984, 1987, 1989a)	Semantic assimilation (Constructivist; Schlesinger, 1988; Braine, 1992) / functionally based distributional analysis (Tomasello, 2003).
	Children identify the words labelling the AGENT, ACTION, PATIENT of a sentence and use innate linking rules to identify SUBJ, VERB and OBJ.	Children begin with AGENT, ACTION, PATIENT categories and assimilate other items on the basis of semantic/distributional similarity.
Input may contain ACTION words that are not VERBS, and sentences that violate linking rules (particularly for ergative languages)	☒ Claim parents filter out such utterances improbable (Pinker, 1987). ☒ Probabilistic-rule version (Pinker, 1987) hard to test.	☑ Will not cause learning of wrong word-order rules, as initial schemas semantic not syntactic (also ☑ explains why syntactic categories have certain semantic properties).
Unclear how children know which NPs/semantic entities expressed as verb arguments	☒ Issue is problematic for both semantics-based approaches (Bowerman, 1990), but not for functionally based distributional analysis (see Section 6.2; in particular Summary table 6.2).	
Do children show advantage for prototypical AGENT–ACTION–PATIENT sentences?	☒ Both predict advantage for sentences of this type. Some evidence against this prediction (Bowerman, 1990), but data are difficult to interpret without knowledge of children's verb meanings. Functionally based distributional analysis does not necessarily predict such an advantage (see Section 6.2; in particular Summary table 6.2).	

Prosodic bootstrapping (generativist); Christophe et al., 2008

Summary of theory / Issue/phenomenon	
	Children use pauses, syllable lengthening and pitch contours to split input sentences into phrases, then use flags to label phrases (e.g. *the* = Noun Phrase).
Input speech may not contain prosodic cues to phrase boundaries	☑ Children are sensitive to these cues from 0;6 (e.g. Soderstrom et al., 2003). ☒ Low reliability/availability of cues in input (Fisher and Tokura, 1996). ☒ Unclear how children acquire 'flags' to categories.

(cont.)

Summary table 6.1 (*cont.*)

Summary of theory / Issue/phenomenon	Distributional analysis (generativist or constructivist)			
	Frequent frames (Mintz, 2003)	Clustering (e.g. Redington et al., 1998)	Minimum distance length (e.g. Cartwright and Brent, 1997)	MOSAIC production model (Freudenthal et al., 2005c)
	Items that appear in the same position relative to another word/frame (e.g. *the_is*) grouped together. Clusters then linked to innate categories such as NOUN and VERB (generativist version; e.g. Mintz, 2003) or used directly in production (constructivist version).			
Does the procedure lead to correct classifications in a computational model?	☑ Better accuracy and completeness scores than clustering/MDL (Mintz, 2003; Chemla et al., 2009); but ☒ only if categories are collapsed (to some degree, arbitrarily). ☒ 50 per cent of all words in corpus (those that do not appear in frequent frames) left unclassified.	☒ Generally scores high on accuracy but low on completeness, or vice versa.		☑ Good performance in production, but difficult to compare with other models as does not produce comparable accuracy/completeness scores.
Is the procedure plausible for real learners?	☑ Shown to work with adults (Mintz, 2002), but ☒ not yet children, without some additional cue (e.g. Mintz, 2006; Braine, 1987; Gómez, 2002; Newport and Aslin, 2004; Onnis et al., 2005; Peña et al., 2002). ☒ Struggles to explain linking from distributional to innate categories.	☒ No, as parses entire corpus each pass.	☑ More psychologically plausible, but ☒ see below.	☑ Most realistic, and gives (mostly) childlike errors. ☒ Higher error rate than real learners but ☑ probably lower than other approaches; (difficult to compare).
	☒ Groupings that are 'correct' on standard measures (e.g. accuracy and completeness) would yield errors of a type that children do not make in production (Freudenthal et al., 2005c).			
	☒ Generativist approach struggles to explain how these distributionally defined categories could be linked to innate syntactic categories.			☑ Categories used directly in production; no need to link to innate categories.

inclusion of a production front-end), but still suffers from unrealistically high error rates (a situation that may be ameliorated by adding semantic and sub-lexical information to the model). Finally, it is likely that once some items have been assigned to a syntactic category, children will notice the phonological properties that are typical of category members and use this information to assign further words to the category. Thus the incorporation of phonological (and semantic) information would be a useful step for generativist and constructivist theories of syntactic category acquisition alike.

6.2   Acquiring basic word order

This section is concerned with children's acquisition of the ability to produce and comprehend basic declarative sentences consisting of a SUBJECT (e.g. *The man*), VERB (e.g. *kicked*) and OBJECT (e.g. *the ball*) (or, for intransitive sentences, such as *The man laughed*, a SUBJECT and a VERB). Word-order languages (of which English is a prime example) mark the **SUBJECT Noun Phrase** (NP) and the **OBJECT Noun Phrase** (NP) using word order: in basic declarative sentences (i.e. not questions, passives etc.) the NP that appears before the verb is the SUBJECT and the NP that appears after the verb, the OBJECT. In this section, we discuss generativist and constructivist accounts of how children acquire this knowledge and apply it in both comprehension and production.

After briefly considering Pinker's (1984, 1987, 1989a) **semantic bootstrapping** account (discussed above), as it applies to the acquisition of word order, we investigate more recent generativist approaches based on the notion of **parameter setting**. Having next briefly outlined the constructivist approach to the acquisition of word order, we spend the remainder of the chapter on a detailed comparison between a constructivist account, under which word-order rules are acquired gradually on a piecemeal basis (e.g. Tomasello, 2003), and a generativist account under which word-order rules are acquired rapidly and across-the-board (e.g. an account such as that proposed by Wexler, 1998: 25, under which 'basic parameters are set correctly at the earliest observable stages, that is, at least from the time that the child enters the two-word stage around 18 months of age').

6.2.1   Generativist accounts

6.2.1.1 Semantic bootstrapping   In Section 6.1, we saw how, under Pinker's (1984) semantic bootstrapping hypothesis, the child can identify the SUBJECT, VERB and OBJECT of a sentence using the semantics–syntax linking rules AGENT $\rightarrow$ SUBJECT, ACTION $\rightarrow$ VERB and PATIENT $\rightarrow$ OBJECT. This procedure would not only allow children to assign individual words to syntactic categories (as discussed in Section 6.1), but also to acquire the word-order rules of their language. Consider the example discussed previously where the child uses these linking rules to build the following syntactic tree for the utterance *The dog bit the cat*:

[[NP$_{SUBJ}$ The dog][VP [V bit] [NP$_{OBJ}$ the cat]]]

The child can then 'read off' from the tree the word-order rules that English sentences (or VPs or CPs) consist of a SUBJECT NP followed by a VP in which the VERB appears before the OBJECT NP (if present). In other words, using the semantic–syntax linking rules to parse the sentence allows children to acquire the SUBJECT VERB OBJECT word order of English.[2]

Whilst it is probably the most explicit generativist account to date of how children could acquire word order, few current generativist theories of language acquisition include a place for Pinker's (1984) proposal. Presumably, the reason for this is that all the problems for Pinker's theory with regard to syntactic category learning (see Section 6.1.1.1) apply equally to the theory as an account of the acquisition of basic word order.

6.2.1.2 Parameter-setting accounts   The probabilistic parameter-setting account of Yang (2002) was introduced in the previous chapter. The more traditional parameter-setting accounts to be discussed here differ in that a parameter is analogous to a switch that is set to one value or another (e.g. +TNS for a language that has tense marking, −TNS for a language that does not) rather than (under Yang's account) something more analogous to a Left/Right stereo 'pan' knob that is incrementally turned towards one of the two settings. Under these older accounts, parameters are set – in the idealized scenario – on the basis of a single relevant piece of input data or, at least, as soon as possible.

6.2.1.2.1 Word-order parameters   For the acquisition of basic word order, three parameters are particularly important (Gibson and Wexler, 1994). The most important is the **complement–head** parameter (sometimes known simply as the **head-direction parameter**). Under standard generativist assumptions, children's innate knowledge of Universal Grammar includes the knowledge that a VERB PHRASE (like all V″ phrases) contains a head (in this case the VERB) and complement (in the case an NP) (see Chapter 4). However, the order of the head and complement (here the VERB and the NP) cannot be specified in UG because it is different for different languages. In head-first languages (such as English) the head (VERB) comes before the complement (NP). In head-final languages (such as Turkish) the head (VERB) comes after the complement (NP). Thus the setting of the head-direction parameter determines whether a language uses VERB–OBJECT (**VO**) order (e.g. English) or OBJECT–VERB (**OV**) order (e.g. Turkish).

```
English:  The man.... [VP [V kicked]        [NP the ball]
          (SUBJECT)           VERB          OBJECT
                              HEAD          COMPLEMENT
Turkish:  The man.... [VP [NP the ball]     [V kicked]
          (SUBJECT)        OBJECT           VERB
                           COMPLEMENT       HEAD
```

In the same way, the setting of the **specifier–head** parameter determines whether the specifier (here, the SUBJECT NP) appears before or after the head (here, the VERB). This parameter has attracted far less attention than the complement–head parameter because the vast majority of languages (including English and Turkish) have the SUBJECT–VERB (**SV**) setting (**VS** languages include Classical Arabic and Hebrew, Gaelic and related languages, Welsh, Hawaiian and Maori).

The third parameter relevant to basic word order is the **V2 parameter**. In V2 languages (e.g. German, Swedish) a finite verb (i.e. a verb marked for tense) must always be the second constituent of all declarative main clauses (though not necessarily of subordinate clauses), as illustrated by the following examples (from Gibson and Wexler, 1994).

1	2	3
Hans (S)	kauft(V)	das Buch
Hans (S)	buys(V)	the book

Consequently, if tense is marked not on the main verb but an auxiliary, it is the auxiliary that must appear in this second position:

1	2	3	4
Hans (S)	hat(AUX)	das Buch(O)	gekauft(V)
Hans (S)	has(AUX)	the book(O)	bought(V)

Another consequence of the V2 'rule' is that if the subject is displaced from first position (e.g. by a prepositional phrase), it will appear after the verb. This is because to appear before the verb, the subject would have to occupy second position, but this is always reserved for the verb:

1	2	3	4
Gestern(PP)	kaufte (V)	Hans (S)	das Buch (O)
Yesterday(PP)	bought (V)	Hans (S)	the book (O)

A fourth parameter that is not a word-order parameter *per se* is nevertheless relevant here. The **null-subject parameter** determines whether subjects are obligatory, as in English, or may be omitted, as in Spanish (indeed, it would not be usual to include the pronoun subject – in this case, *Yo* – unless it is required for emphasis):

> English: I play football/*Play football
> Spanish: (Yo) juego al fútbol

This parameter is also known at the **pro-drop** or **AG/PRO** parameter (techni- cally, the subject is not 'dropped'; rather the phonologically null **PRO** serves as the subject; see Chapter 8). Whilst the setting of this parameter does not actually determine the ordering of the SUBJECT, VERB and OBJECT, it will indirectly affect the learning process, in that sentences with no overt subject cannot be used to set the specifier–head parameter.

6.2.1.2.2 Can multiple parameters be set simultaneously?   Together, the settings of the complement–head (VO/OV), specifier–head (SV/VS) and V2 (+V2/−V2) parameters determine the ordering of the SUBJECT (if present) VERB and OBJECT. The basic idea is that as soon as a child can parse (in the idealized case) a single input utterance into SUBJECT, VERB and OBJECT she will be able to set one or more parameters. For example, hearing *The man (S) kicked (V) the ball (O)* would allow the child to set the specifier–head and complement–head parameters to SV and VO.

A problem for this account is that many input sentences will not provide unambiguous evidence with regard to the settings of a particular parameter unless the child has previously correctly set another parameter, and knows this setting to be correct. For example, suppose that a child hears *Gestern, kaufte (V) Hans (S) das Buch (O)*. If the child had not correctly set the V2 parameter to +V2 (and consequently 'knows' that this is why the subject appears after the verb) this utterance would constitute evidence for the incorrect VS setting of the specifier–head parameter. In fact, Gibson and Wexler (1994) proved mathematically that a **triggering learning algorithm (TLA)** that, in the face of an ambiguous sentence, sets one parameter at random (so long as this allows the sentence to be parsed) will, in some circumstances,[3] never arrive at the correct settings for all three parameters. Whilst a system under which some parameters start out with default settings and others are unset can, in principle, always converge on the correct grammar, such a system cannot recover from mis- settings. One way to solve the problem is to prohibit a learner from attempting to set certain parameters until others have been set, by imposing a maturational constraint. A problem with this solution is that it would leave the learner essentially without a grammar (and thus unable to parse incoming utterances) until the relevant maturational point had been reached.

Another way in which the TLA can be made to work is if it is allowed to randomly change the setting of more than one parameter at once, or keep changes that do not allow for a parse of the incoming sentence (Gibson and Wexler, 1994; Niyogi and Berwick, 1996). A problem with this solution is that it would seem to incorrectly predict that children will produce a large number of word-order errors (or incorrectly interpret sentences that they hear) whilst they try out various combinations of settings. Even a system that tried to deduce the settings by holding one or more parameters constant whilst varying the others (much like a scientific experimenter) would presumably make a large number of non-childlike errors (e.g. *Kicked the man the ball*) until the correct settings have been reached.

An alternative solution (Fodor, 1998) is to posit that learners' knowledge of UG includes knowledge of which input structures are potentially ambiguous. Learners would then avoid setting parameters on the basis of ambiguous utterances and await unambiguous 'triggers'. Sakas and Fodor (2001) demonstrate mathematically that, in most circumstances, this learning mechanism will require exposure to far fewer input sentences than that of Gibson and Wexler (1994) to arrive at the target grammar. A potential problem is that there may be certain parameters in certain languages which can be set only on the basis of potentially ambiguous utterances. Though this is not the case for the parameters studied by Gibson and Wexler (1994), Fodor (1998: 24) acknowledges that 'every parametric domain . . . needs to be checked' and that 'outcomes cannot be anticipated'.

6.2.1.2.3 Can word-order parameters be set before syntactic categories can be identified? The parameter-setting accounts discussed above ignore an important paradox (Mazuka, 1996). Children cannot set (for example) the head-direction (complement–head) parameter until they can determine which word in an input utterance is the head (e.g. the VERB *kicked*) and which is the complement (e.g. the OBJECT NP *the ball*). However, as we saw in Section 6.1, generativist theory has yet to arrive at a non-problematic account of how children can assign words in an input sentence to the syntactic categories of SUBJECT, VERB and OBJECT (the semantic bootstrapping, prosodic bootstrapping and distributional learning accounts all suffering from various shortcomings). Indeed, under the prosodic bootstrapping account, parameter setting (as described above) puts the cart before the horse: children do not identify the VERB and the NP and use these to determine the syntactic structure of the sentence (parameter setting). Rather, they first determine the syntactic structure of the sentence (using prosodic cues and knowledge of function words) and use this to identify the VERB and the NP.

What is needed to overcome this paradox is some way for children to set the head-direction parameter without having to know the syntactic categories of the words in the trigger sentence. Whilst this may seem impossible, there are in fact two proposals for how this could be done. Mazuka's (1996) proposal is based on the fact that there is a strong correlation crosslinguistically between the setting of the head-direction parameter and the **branching-direction parameter**. The setting of the branching-direction parameter (left- or right-branching) corresponds to the position of subordinate clauses relative to the main clause. For example, English (a VO language) is **right-branching** in that each successive clause is added to the right of the sentence, whilst Japanese (an OV language) is **left-branching** in that each successive clause is added to the left:

> English: [**I met the teacher**] → [who called the student] →
>   [who had an accident]
> Japanese: [who an accident had] ← [who to the student called] ←
>   [**I to the teacher met**]

Mazuka's (1996) claim is that children can set the branching-direction parameter on the basis of prosodic information, then exploit this correlation (knowledge of which would be specified in UG) to set the head-direction parameter. As evidence that children can set the branching-direction parameter on the basis of prosodic information, Mazuka (1996) presents evidence that pitch changes are greater for subordinate/main clause boundaries than main/subordinate boundaries. At present, however, this proposal remains mere speculation. There is no evidence that this prosodic cue is present in naturalistic adult–adult or adult–child speech (Mazuka analysed utterances that were recorded by a professional radio announcer specifically for the study), let alone that children are aware of the cue and able to exploit it. Furthermore, evidence reviewed in the following chapter suggests that young children have great difficulty parsing multiple-clause sentences. In any case, there are some languages (e.g. German, Chinese) that do not follow the predicted pattern for at least some sentence types, meaning that children would be at risk of setting the head-direction parameter incorrectly.

Christophe *et al.* (2003) propose that children make use of another prosodic correlate of head direction. Within a phonological phrase, prominence generally falls on the right for VO languages (e.g. English) and on the left for OV languages (e.g. Turkish). A **phonological phrase** generally corresponds to a syntactic phrase. Phonological **prominence** corresponds to raised pitch, syllable lengthening and stress. For example, consider the English NP [*The man*] and VP [*kicked the ball*]. If you say each phrase out loud, you will hear that you naturally emphasize the right-hand constituents (in **bold**). To investigate whether infants (with a mean age of just 63 days) are sensitive to phonological prominence, Christophe *et al.* (2003) conducted a study using a sucking paradigm, under which infants trigger the playback of sentences by increasing their rate of sucking on a dummy (pacifier). After listening to sentences[4] with prominence on the left of each phrase, infants increased their sucking rate in response to sentences with prominence on the right of each phrase (or vice versa). This finding demonstrates that children are able to detect phonological prominence. However, the study does not address the issue of whether children know that prominence is correlated with head direction, or (assuming that they do) are able to use prominence to set the head-direction parameter. A potentially problematic finding is that when adult French speakers were asked which of the stimulus sentences sounded more like French, they correctly picked the right-hand prominence sentences on only 65 per cent of trials (despite completing a twenty-trial training session during which feedback was given for each sentence). Another concern is whether the correlation between phonological prominence and the setting of the head-direction parameter exists across all languages. Though Christophe *et al.* (2003: 12) cite evidence that the correlation is widely accepted in the literature, there do not appear to be any systematic reviews that take in a variety of language families.

6.2.2   *Constructivist accounts*

In Chapter 4, we summarized the constructivist approach to language acquisition (in particular, the account proposed by Tomasello, 2003). Three aspects of this account are most relevant to the question of how children acquire basic word order. First, many of children's earliest utterances are assumed to be rote-learned holophrases (e.g. *I'm kicking it*; *I'm eating it*). Second, many early utterances are generated using partially productive, lexically specific slot-and-frame patterns or schemas (e.g. *I'm ACTIONing it*) formed by abstracting across stored phrases. Importantly, both rote-learned holophrases and slot-and-frame patterns specify the appropriate word order. Third, only later in development do children analogize across stored holophrases and slot-and-frame patterns to arrive at fully abstract adultlike constructions (e.g. SUBJECT VERB OBJECT).

6.2.3   *Comparing generativist and constructivist accounts of the acquisition of basic transitive word order*

In this section, we evaluate evidence for the constructivist claim that children's earliest knowledge of basic word order consists of **holophrases** (e.g. *I'm kicking it*) and **lexically specific schemas** (e.g. *I'm ACTIONing it*), and the rival generativist claim that children are operating with **adultlike syntactic categories** and **knowledge of phrase structure** from their earliest multiword utterances. Because the constructivist account assumes that an abstract [SUBJECT] [VERB] [OBJECT] **transitive construction** is acquired only relatively late in development, it predicts that young children will not be able to produce or comprehend transitive sentences for which they do not have a suitable lexically specific schema. Because the generativist account assumes that much of children's knowledge of phrase structure (e.g. the knowledge that a sentence can have the structure [NP][VP [V] [NP]]) is innate, it predicts that children will be able to produce and comprehend transitive sentences with any item, as soon as the word-order parameters have been set (e.g. for English, yielding [NP$_{SUBJ}$][VP [V] [NP$_{OBJ}$]]). Evidence that the word-order parameters have been set is usually taken to be any utterance that conforms to adult word order (e.g. Radford, 1996; Wexler, 1998). Thus the generativist account predicts that once a child can produce or comprehend (in principle) a single transitive sentence, she should be able to produce or comprehend any other transitive sentence (provided, of course, that she has learned the relevant lexical items).

6.2.3.1 Naturalistic data studies   Constructivist studies of naturalistic data have aimed to demonstrate that a large proportion of children's utterances could, in principle, have been produced using lexically specific slot-and-frame patterns, rather than the abstract phrase-structure operations assumed by generativist theory.

Pine and Lieven (1993; see also Lieven, Pine and Dresner-Barnes, 1992) conducted an analysis based on Braine's (1976) notion of **positional patterns**. Braine (1976: 4) argued, on the basis of an analysis of English, Finnish, Samoan and Swedish corpora that the majority of children's multiword utterances could have been produced using a small number of 'formulae of limited scope for realizing specific kinds of meanings' (e.g. *X+gone*). Under Pine and Lieven's (1993) analysis, any pattern that appeared three times with the same word in one position and a different word in another (e.g. *Daddy gone*; *Mummy gone*; *Cat gone*) was classified as a productive **variable+constant** (e.g. *X+gone*) or a **constant+variable** (e.g. *The+X*) pattern (these are also known as **slot-and-frame** or **lexically specific** or **partially productive patterns/constructions/schemas**). Using diary and monthly audio recordings from seven children aged 0;11–1;8, Pine and Lieven (1993) identified the ten most frequently occurring patterns for each child. For example, for the most productive child (Leonard) these were (p. 566):

1. Oh don't + X
2. X + stairs
3. Oh + X
4. It's a + X
5. Wanna + X
6. Daddy + X
7. Me got + X
8. X + shoe
9. The + X
10. X + in there

For the five children who were attributed with 10 patterns by the end of the study, a mean of 77 per cent of utterances could have been produced using one of these productive patterns (or an 'intermediate' **variable+variable** pattern in which two words previously attested as single word utterances are combined in a novel way).[5] Evidence for the psychological reality of these patterns comes from the finding that between 50 and 100 per cent (depending on the child) were apparently used to produce further novel utterances before the end of the study. Consistent with Tomasello's (2003) proposal, two-thirds of the patterns appeared to have their roots in **frozen phrases** (utterances consistent with neither a productive or an intermediate pattern). For example, Leonard produced several instances of *It's a car*, before apparently forming a more abstract *It's a + X* pattern.

One problem with this study (see Lieven, Pine and Baldwin, 1997: 197) is that since a potential positional pattern had to occur at the least three times to be classified as such, 30 multiword utterances per child are consistent with such a pattern by definition. To address this issue, Lieven *et al.* (1997) replicated this analysis over a larger time frame (1;0–3;0) with a group of eleven children, looking at the first 25 positional patterns for each child. On average, children produced 300 utterances consistent with one of the 25 most frequent patterns (only 75 of which were inevitable as a result of the coding scheme). A mean of 60.3 per cent of all multiword utterances could potentially have been produced by one of the 25 lexical positional patterns, and a mean of 81 per cent of these patterns had at least one further instance in the recording session after the 25-pattern point was reached.

However a problem with this study lies with the 31 per cent of utterances that were classified as frozen. The criterion for an utterance to be classified as frozen was that the component words had not previously appeared independently. However, since there was no requirement for a putative 'frozen phrase' to appear more than once in the same form, it remains possible that many 'frozen' utterances were in fact produced using a generativist style fully abstract system, with the sampling regime failing to catch independent uses of the component words that the child had, in fact, produced.

A similar analysis was conducted by Tomasello (1992), who kept a diary of his daughter's verb- (and other predicate-) based utterances between the ages of 1;0 and 2;0. Tomasello (1992: 177) concluded that the data showed evidence of 'verb islands', as word-order rules seemed to be restricted to particular verbs rather than applying to a VERB category in general. For example, whilst the verb *draw* was used in the construction *PERSON draw* (e.g. *I draw*), the verb *cut*, which was learned at the same time was never used in the construction *PERSON cut*, with all uses of the form *cut THING CUT*. A shortcoming of this study, however, is that (unlike in the studies of Pine and Lieven) no statistical criteria were used when attributing productive patterns to the child.

Whilst the verb-island hypothesis has attracted much attention in the litera-ture, it is almost certainly incorrect with regard to the privileged status accorded to verbs (as admitted by Childers and Tomasello, 2001: 746). When 'islands' (i.e. productive positional patterns) are defined using purely distributional cri-teria, only a small minority have a verb as the invariant element (see, for example, Leonard's patterns which include *It's a+X*, *The+X* and *Daddy+X*). On the other hand, it may be that when semantics is also taken into considera-tion, verb islands retain a central role. An important aspect of the constructivist approach is that each schema is associated with a particular meaning or com-municative function. Most verb islands (e.g. *got+X*), would meet this criterion, whilst many distributionally defined patterns (e.g. *X+stairs*; *X+shoe*) would not.

An important consideration in this debate is that to posit schemas where the variable position is occupied by some subset of the VERB category (e.g. *Wanna + X*) is actually to attribute knowledge to that child that is – to some degree – verb general. The slot is not completely general (or abstract), as it is not taken to represent a generativist style VERB category. However, it is abstract to the extent that various items can appear in this position (including items that have not been attested in this position, but are sufficiently semantically similar to items that have). The point is illustrated by the study of McClure, Pine and Lieven (2006), in which children's production data from the Manchester corpus (Theakston *et al.*, 2001) were divided into two stages by MLU (1.0–1.99 and 2.0–2.99). Transitive-only verbs that appeared for the first time at Stage II appeared with a mean of 1.25 arguments, whereas those that had also appeared in Stage I appeared with significantly more (1.41). This is evidence for verb-specific knowledge as children did not transfer knowledge from their Stage I transitive verbs (i.e. that they must appear with two arguments) to the transitive verbs that were new at Stage II. On the other hand, verbs that were new at the start of Stage II appeared with significantly more arguments (1.25) than verbs that were new at the start of Stage I (1.13). This shows that children were acquiring, during Stage I, some verb-general knowledge that allowed them to perform better with verbs that were new at Stage II than with those that were new at Stage I. These findings can be reconciled by proposing that children form both schemas that are verb-specific (e.g. *cut [THING CUT]*) and – to some degree – verb-general (e.g. *Wanna [ACTION]*).

An alternative approach is to use a 'trace-back' methodology whereby the researcher attempts to account for all of the utterances produced in a short test corpus (e.g. the final session of recording) using lexically specific schemas and holophrases attributed to the child on the basis of previous sessions. The first study of this type (Lieven, Behrens, Speares and Tomasello, 2003) suffered from the drawback that the caregiver's speech was also used as a source for schemas, meaning that the child was almost certainly credited with schemas that she showed no evidence of possessing. A follow-up study (Dąbrowska and

Lieven, 2005) was restricted to wh-questions, and is hence of limited relevance for our purposes here (i.e. investigating acquisition of basic declarative word order). Most relevant is the study of Lieven, Salomo and Tomasello (2009), who studied four children recorded using a relatively dense sampling regime (five hours per week for six weeks, from age 2;0). Depending on the child, 58–78 per cent of utterances in the test corpus were either verbatim repetitions of previous utterances (25–45 per cent) or could be derived from a previous utterance using a single 'operation' (around 33 per cent). The operations allowed were (a) the substitution of a previously attested word or phrase into a semantically appropriate schema (e.g. *I can't PROCESS it*), posited whenever two or more instances of the pattern occurred (e.g. *I can't see it*; *I can't do it*) and (b) the addition of a previously attested string (e.g. *now*) onto the beginning or end of a previously attested utterance (e.g. *I want it → I want it now*).

A contentious issue is the status of 'syntactic fails', observed at a rate of 5–16 per cent (depending on the child). These occur when a target utterance cannot be derived, even by using multiple operations, from a previous schema (excluding 'lexical fails' due simply to the lack of a necessary slot-filler in the source corpus). It is unclear whether these occur simply because the sampling happens to have missed suitable schemas in the source corpus or because children were, in fact, using more abstract (i.e. generativist-style) rules to produce such utterances. Indeed, for all naturalistic data studies, it remains possible that many utterances that *could have* been produced using low-level lexically specific construction schemas were in fact produced by adultlike rules. One way to address this issue would be to run a comparable analysis on adult speech. If adults – who uncontroversially have abstract knowledge of syntax – show high levels of lexical specificity, this would suggest that children's apparent reliance on low-level schemas may be an illusion caused by thin sampling. Such a comparison was conducted by Lieven *et al.* (2003), looking at the child's mother. Although these researchers found that the mother's speech required many more multi-operation tracebacks than the child's, findings remain inconclusive since sample size, vocabulary and utterance length were not controlled.

A particularly thorough study using a variant on this paradigm (a 'trace-forward' paradigm) was conducted by Bannard, Lieven and Tomasello (2009). These authors used a Bayesian computer model to construct an entire grammar (an inventory of strings and slot and frame patterns) for each child on the basis of the source corpus. Patterns could be recursively embedded such that (for example) a REFERENT slot (e.g. *kick REFERENT*) could be filled by another slot and frame pattern (e.g. *the REFERENT*). Consequently, many thousand possible grammars per child were generated. The model then attempted to generate the utterances in the test corpus using each of a random sample of different grammars (1,000 per child). At 2;0, averaging across all grammars, 60 per cent (Annie) and 80 per cent (Brian) of all utterances could be generated by inserting either one or two strings into a slot-and-frame pattern. Interestingly, a traditional context-free grammar which forms probabilistic rules on the basis of the distribution of individual lexical items (and posits no slot-and-frame patterns) did not outperform the frame-based grammar (even when the analyses were performed at 3;0). This study also addressed the issue of whether the children could, nevertheless, have been operating with more abstract adultlike categories. If so, then replacing all nouns and verbs with a single category marker (NOUN or VERB) should increase the coverage of the model. For the less advanced child (Brian), adding the NOUN category led to a small (6 per cent) increase in coverage at 2;0 and a much larger (14 per cent) increase at 3;0. Adding the VERB category led to no significant increase at 2;0, but a 7 per cent increase at 3;0. This study, then, constitutes perhaps the best evidence yet (at least from naturalistic data studies) that children's knowledge of syntax is initially tied to individual lexical items, but eventually generalizes as abstract constructions, containing (amongst others) NOUN and VERB slots, are formed.

6.2.3.2 Elicited production   Another way to investigate the abstractness of children's knowledge of syntax is to use experimental **elicited production** studies. Children are taught a novel verb (e.g. *meek*) whose semantics are consistent with the SVO transitive construction (e.g. a novel bouncing, rolling or spinning action). During training, the verb is presented with **no arguments** (e.g. *Look! Meeking*) or in an **inchoative intransitive** construction (e.g. *Ernie is meeking*), an **agent-only** intransitive construction (e.g. *Bert is meeking*, to describe a scene where Bert is meeking Ernie), a **patient-only** construction (e.g. *meeking Ernie*, to describe the same scene) or a **passive** construction (e.g. *Ernie got meeked by Bert*). At test, the child is asked to describe a scene with different characters in which (for example) *Big Bird is meeking Cookie Monster* to see whether she is capable of using a verb in the abstract SUBJECT VERB OBJECT construction in which it has never been attested (the experimenter often uses a prompt that 'pulls' for a transitive response such as 'What's Big Bird doing?'). If so, this constitutes evidence for verb-general knowledge of the SVO transitive construction. The findings of some of the major elicited production studies of this type are summarized in Table 6.1.

As far as we are able to tell, all of the studies listed included patient-only utterances (e.g. *tamming Cookie Monster*) and – in some cases – agent-only utterances (e.g. *Big Bird is tamming*) in their counts of productive transitives (as such utterances are grammatical as a response to certain prompt questions). Thus the majority of the children who were scored as 'productive' with the transitive did not in fact provide a full SVO utterance with a novel verb that had not been attested in that construction (as a control, Tomasello and Brooks, 1998, showed that 11/16 younger children and 16/16 older children (see Table 6.1 for ages) would use a novel verb trained in the SVO transitive to produce an SVO transitive with a different AGENT and PATIENT).

Table 6.1 *Elicited production studies investigating productivity with the SVO transitive construction*

Study	Construction used during training	Age of children	Children generalizing novel verb into SVO transitive construction at least once	
			%	No.
Pinker *et al.* (1987: ex3)	Passive	7–8 (*M* = 7;11)	100	
Maratsos *et al.* (1987)	Inchoative intransitive	4;6–5;6 (*M* = 5;0)	89	25/28
Pinker *et al.* (1987: ex3)	Passive	5–6 (*M* = 6;1)	88	
Pinker *et al.* (1987: ex2)	Passive	4;6–5;6 (*M* = 5;1)	88	
Akhtar and Tomasello (1997: ex2)	No-argument ('This is called *chamming*')	3;5–3;11 (*M* = 3;8)	80	8/10
Brooks and Tomasello (1999a: ex1)	Passive (2 verbs)	3;3–3;8 (*M* = 3;5)	55	11/20
Tomasello and Brooks (1998)	Inchoative intransitive	2;4–2;8 (*M* = 2;6)	44	7/16
Pinker *et al.* (1987: ex2)	Passive	3;0–4;6 (*M* = 3;10)	38	
Olguin and Tomasello (1993)	No argument (2 verbs), Agent only (2 verbs), Patient only (2 verbs)	1;10–2;1 (*M* = 1;11)	28	2/7
Dodson and Tomasello (1998)	No argument ('Look what Ernie's doing to the stove. This is called *keefing*')	2;5–3;1 (*M* = 2;9)	25	6/24
Akhtar and Tomasello (1997: ex2)	No-argument ('This is called *chamming*')	2;9–2;11 (*M* = 2;9)	20	2/10
Brooks and Tomasello (1999a: ex1)	Passive (2 verbs)	2;9–3;0 (*M* = 2;10)	20	4/20
Tomasello and Brooks (1998)	Inchoative intransitive	1;11–2;1 (*M* = 2;0)	19	3/16
Akhtar and Tomasello (1997: ex1)	No argument (1 verb), Agent only (1 verb), Patient only (1 verb)	2;9–3;8 (*M* = 3;1)	10	1/10

Again, as far as we are able to tell, all the studies listed above included utterances with pronouns (e.g. *he/him/it*) in subject and/or object position. Dodson and Tomasello (1998) found that over 90 per cent of all agents and patients were pronouns. These authors also reported that all eleven productive transitive sentences produced by children aged under 2;6 in a no-argument training condition (across the studies by Braine *et al.*, 1990; Olguin and Tomasello, 1993; Akhtar and Tomasello, 1997; Tomasello, Akhtar, Dodson and Rekau, 1997) contained

I (or, for one child, *me*) as the subject. These findings provide support for the constructivist claim that children's earliest verb-general knowledge consists of knowledge of lexically specific frames with a VERB as the variable slot (e.g. *I'm ACTIONing him*).

This issue was investigated more directly in the study of Childers and Tomasello (2001; see also Abbot-Smith, Lieven and Tomasello, 2004). Childers and Tomasello (2001) taught children (aged 2;4–2;10) novel verbs in intransitive and passive constructions. During training, children also heard transitive sentences with English verbs which included either exclusively full NPs (e.g. *The cow's pulling the car*) or full NPs and pronouns (e.g. *The cow's pulling the car. He's pulling it*). In the pronoun group, 17/20 children produced a full SVO transitive sentence with a novel verb at test (with 71 per cent of all arguments pronouns), as opposed to only 9/20 children who heard full NPs only (with no child producing a single pronoun argument).

Summarizing these studies, Tomasello (2000) concludes that until about 3 years of age, children do not have an abstract transitive construction into which they can assimilate novel experimentally taught verbs. This conclusion has been challenged, most notably by Fisher (2002). One objection raised by Fisher (2002) is that children may fail to produce transitive utterances with novel verbs because they are too shy, or subject to performance limitations. Tomasello and Abbot-Smith (2002) counter that many of the studies include control conditions that rule out such factors. For example, children appear willing and able to freely substitute nouns and, indeed, produce transitive utterances with novel verbs when they have heard such utterances modelled by the experimenter (e.g. Tomasello and Brooks, 1998).

Fisher also objects that children should not automatically assume that verbs that have been presented in presentational or intransitive constructions can necessarily be used in the transitive construction as many intransitive verbs (e.g. *giggle*) are ungrammatical in the transitive construction (e.g. **The funny clown giggled the man*). As we will see in detail in Section 6.3, the main determinant of whether or not a particular intransitive verb may also appear in the transitive construction is verb semantics (Pinker, 1989a; Ambridge *et al.*, 2008, 2009). Tomasello and Abbot-Smith (2002) point out that the novel verbs used were chosen to be semantically compatible with both the intransitive and transitive constructions. However, it is not clear that this aim was always achieved. Consider, for example, one action used by Tomasello and Brooks (1998: 383).

The first action (*meeking*) involved a puppet pulling a small object up a ramp (the object was inside a clear jar attached to a string and was pulled up through a clear tube affixed on the ramp). The novel verb *meek* was used to describe . . . the action of the object moving up the ramp (when modelled in an intransitive construction).

If children interpreted the novel verb as meaning something like 'go up' or 'ascend', they would assume that the verb should **not** be used in the transitive construction (e.g. *The puppet went up/ascended the car*) and presumably avoid doing so during the test phase of the study. However, as Tomasello and Abbot-Smith (2002) point out, studies in which the two-argument nature of the verb is already 'given' – elicitation studies where the passive form is used during training, and weird word-order studies (discussed in the following section) – are not subject to this criticism. Evidence discussed in Section 6.3 also suggests that it is unlikely that young children have acquired these semantic restrictions on the transitive construction. Fisher's final criticism is that young children may have knowledge of the transitive construction that is sufficient for comprehension but not production. Whilst Tomasello and Abbot-Smith (2002) discuss evidence against this claim, subsequent preferential looking studies (discussed later in this chapter) provide support for Fisher's claim.

6.2.3.3 Weird word order   In **weird-word-order** studies, children are taught a novel transitive verb in a construction with two arguments. However, the training sentences presented do not use conventional SVO word order. Instead, a non-English word order is used for each verb (e.g. SOV: *Elmo the car gopping* or VSO: *Tamming Elmo the car*). The sentences are enacted with puppets, so that the intended meaning (e.g. *Elmo knocking the car down a chute*) is clear. The rationale is that if children's word-order knowledge is stored on a verb-by-verb basis (e.g. *KICKER kick KICKEE*), then they will have no trouble learning and using a different word order for a novel verb (e.g. *GOPPER GOPPEE gop*). If, on the other hand, children are in possession of an SVO transitive construction that is verb-general (i.e. that applies to *all* verbs) then they should resist novel word orders, 'correcting' to SVO even for novel verbs.

The first weird-word-order study was conducted by Akhtar (1999) with children aged 2;1–3;1 ($M = 2;8$), 3;2–3;11 ($M = 3;6$) and 4;0–4;9 ($M = 4;4$). Each child was taught three verbs, each with a different word order: SVO (e.g. *Elmo dacking the car*), SOV (*Elmo the car gopping*) and VSO (*Tamming Elmo the car*). Children also completed a control condition in which a familiar verb was presented in a weird word order (e.g. *Elmo the car pushing*) to investigate whether they would follow a word order that they (presumably) knew to be incorrect to please the experimenter (in fact, this happened on less than 10 per cent of trials). The experimenter produced a total of eighty models of each verb (in the relevant word order). For some trials, a new agent and patient (i.e. not those that appeared in the training sentences) enacted the novel verb with the child being asked to describe the action (for a total of twenty elicitation trials per novel verb). Unlike in many of the elicited production studies discussed above, the child had to produce an agent and a patient for the trial to be counted.

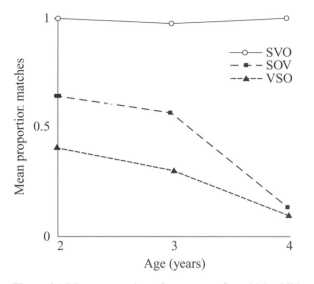

Figure 6.1 Mean proportion of utterances for which children matched the experimenter's weird word order (SOV/VSO) or – in a control condition – conventional SVO word order (from Akhtar, 1999: 346; reproduced by permission of Cambridge University Press)

The findings of this study are summarized in Figure 6.1. The Y-axis shows the proportion of trials for which children reproduced the word order used by the experimenter for the relevant verb ('matches'). All 'mismatches' in the SOV and VSO conditions were corrections to SVO order.

These results can be interpreted in two ways. One interpretation provides support for the verb-island (or lexical-specificity) hypothesis: the 2-year-old children clearly did not have a complete and verb-general understanding of SVO word order, as they were prepared to use other word orders (SOV and VSO) for about 50 per cent of trials with the novel verbs. As predicted by this account, children's knowledge of the SVO construction becomes increasingly verb-general with age, with the oldest children correcting to this construction on around 90 per cent of trials. On the other hand, the results clearly demonstrate that even the youngest children have *some* verb-general knowledge of the SVO construction. If, as a strong version of the verb-island hypothesis predicts, young children's knowledge is entirely verb-specific, then they should have adopted the novel word order for virtually all trials. Instead, they corrected to SVO on around 50 per cent of SOV and VSO trials; a response that is only possible if children have some verb-general knowledge of the SVO construction.

Discussing these data in response to Fisher's (2002: 210) challenge, Tomasello and Abbot-Smith (2002) concede that 'young 2-year-olds have . . . a weak transitive schema – one that enables certain kinds of linguistic operations but not others'. What might a 'weak transitive schema' look like? As we have already seen, one proposal (McClure *et al.*, 2006) is that it takes the form of a collection of lexically-specific patterns organized around material other than verbs (e.g. *He's X-ing it*). In support of this view, Akhtar (1999) found that when the younger children corrected SOV or VSO orders to SVO, they often did so by using pronouns. In fact, over half of all arguments in SVO utterances (but no arguments in SOV or VSO utterances) were pronouns, providing support for the suggestion that children may have been using lexically specific schemas such as *He's X-ing it*.

A number of studies have replicated and extended Akhtar's (1999) findings. Matthews, Lieven, Theakston and Tomasello (2004), in a study with children aged 2;3–3;2 ($M = 2;9$) and 3;3–4;3 ($M = 3;9$), used English (as opposed to novel) verbs in order to investigate frequency effects. Another modification is that two animal puppets (as opposed to one puppet and one inanimate object) were used to remove animacy cues to meaning. The results for the younger children were consistent with the lexical-learning approach: these children never followed the weird word order (SOV) for high-frequency verbs (*push/pull/throw/wipe*), for which they had had considerable opportunity to form lexically specific schemas (e.g. *PUSHER push PUSHEE*). However, for medium- (e.g. *shove/drag/flip/rub*) and low-frequency verbs (e.g. *ram/tug/hurl/dab*), for which they had less opportunity to form lexical schemas, the younger children followed SOV order on around 20 and 55 per cent of trials respectively. The older children showed no significant frequency effects, presumably because overall rates of correction to SVO were always high (never less than 70 per cent).

Abbot-Smith, Lieven and Tomasello (2001) adapted the paradigm for use with younger children (2;2–2;6; $M = 2;4$) and a control group (3;6–4;0; $M = 3;9$). Since young 2-year-olds have difficulty producing three-word utterances, inchoative intransitives – in correct (SV) and weird (VS) word order – were used with novel verbs. As in Akhtar's study, children showed some evidence of 'verb-island' behaviour and some evidence of generalization. On the one hand, the younger group corrected from VS to SV on only around 20 per cent of trials, showing evidence for verb-specific learning. On the other hand, the fact that they corrected from VS to SV at a rate of 20 per cent as opposed to zero (the approximate rate of SV to VS switches) constitutes some evidence for verb-general knowledge. The older children showed more evidence of verb-general knowledge, correcting on around 75 per cent of VS trials, but virtually never switching on SV trials. Abbot-Smith *et al.*'s (2001) study also highlights the importance of frames based around subject+auxiliary combinations (e.g. *He's Xing*). Whilst the experimenter never used auxiliaries (e.g. *the cat meeked*), children frequently (above 70 per cent of trials for both age groups) inserted an auxiliary when using a pronoun subject in an SV utterance (e.g. *He's meeking*), but never inserted an auxiliary into a VS utterance.

Finally, one study has extended the weird-word-order paradigm into another language.[6] French children show a similar pattern of frequency effects to English children (Matthews, Lieven, Theakston and Tomasello, 2007), but appear to be delayed in their acquisition of the abstract SVO construction. Matthews *et al.* (2007) attribute this finding to the fact that, in French, utterances with pronoun objects do not follow SVO word order but SoV; e.g. *Renard le pousse*, 'Fox him pushes'. Thus French children cannot – as English children seem to do – begin to acquire the abstract SVO pattern on the basis of pronoun-based frames (e.g. *He's Xing him*).

6.2.3.4 Syntactic priming Some authors (e.g. Shimpi, Gámez, Huttenlocher and Vasilyeva, 2007: 1340) have argued that syntactic-priming studies can be used to investigate children's 'abstract syntactic knowledge of the transitive structure'. In fact, whilst we agree that this may be possible in principle, we will argue that no suitable paradigm for doing so has yet been devised.

The concept of **syntactic priming** (see Pickering and Ferreira, 2008 for a review) can be illustrated with the following example from Bock (1986). In this study, participants were presented with a **prime** sentence: either a prepositional-object (PO) or double-object (DO dative):

> PO: The lifeguard tossed a rope to the struggling child.
> DO: The lifeguard tossed the struggling child a rope.

Participants were then asked to describe a semantically unrelated picture that can be described using either a PO-dative (*The man read a book to the boy*) or a DO-dative (*The man read the boy a book*). Adults typically show a tendency to describe the sentence using the same syntactic structure that they encountered in the prime sentence (i.e. they show **syntactic priming**), even though the prime and target sentences share no lexical items (except *the* and *a*). The claim is that syntactic priming operates by the prime sentence activating a stored representation of the relevant construction (e.g. DO-dative: [SUBJECT] [VERB] [INDIRECT OBJECT] [DIRECT OBJECT], which is hence more available than the alternative construction (here the PO-dative) at the time of production. Thus the rationale is that if an individual shows syntactic priming for a particular structure, then this constitutes evidence for abstract knowledge of this structure.

Savage, Lieven, Theakston and Tomasello (2003; see also 2006) applied this logic to investigate abstract knowledge of the active transitive (SVO) and passive constructions by children aged 2;11–3;7 ($M = 3;2$), 3;10–4;6 ($M = 4;2$) and 6;1–7;1 ($M = 6;2$). The experimenter described an animation using either an active (e.g. *The digger pushed the bricks*) or a passive sentence (e.g. *The bricks got pushed by the digger*) before inviting the child to describe an animation also consistent with either construction (e.g. a hammer breaking a vase). In this low-lexical-overlap condition (designed to investigate abstract knowledge of the constructions) only the oldest group showed evidence of syntactic priming, producing more active sentences after active than passive primes.[7] Similarly, active → active priming was found for children aged 4;5–5;8 ($M = 4;8$) and 3;9–4;6 ($M = 4;2$), but not 2;7–3;7 ($M = 3;10$; Huttenlocher, Vasilyeva and Shimpi, 2004; Shimpi *et al.*, 2007) or 2;11–3;6 ($M = 3;2$; Bencini and Valian, 2008).

Why do syntactic-priming studies fail to demonstrate knowledge of the transitive construction until age 4;0, when most other paradigms suggest that children have certainly acquired this knowledge by 3;0 (and quite possibly considerably younger)? The problem is most likely to do with the way that (active) transitives and passives are pitted against one another. If children have learned the active construction, but not the passive (a likely scenario at 3;0), they are likely to produce an active sentence on every trial, regardless of whether the prime sentence was active or passive. If this is the case, then presenting an active prime will not boost the number of actives compared to a passive prime (the only outcome that could provide evidence for abstract knowledge of the [active] transitive construction). Even for older children who know both constructions, it is difficult to tell which is driving any priming effect: are active primes boosting the number of actives, or are passive primes indirectly reducing the number of actives by boosting the number of passives? Since children can only produce either an active or a passive each time they choose to say anything at all, it is impossible to tell.

The way around this issue is to compare production of active SVO transitives not to passives but to something else. But to what? Shimpi *et al.* (2007) showed that their youngest group ($M = 3;1$) produced significantly more active SVO transitives after hearing active SVO transitive primes than when they were simply asked to describe the pictures. However, this is not very compelling. The prime sentences may have primed nothing more than the idea that simply naming the characters is not a suitable response. Ambridge (2007) found that children were quicker to repeat an SVO sentence (e.g. *Fox kicked him*) after hearing an SVO prime sentence (e.g. *Bear saw him*) than a control NP string (e.g. *Bear and him*). However, the study was never submitted for publication because (echoing the active/passive problem discussed above) it turned out that production of the target SVO sentence was not *facilitated* by the prime SVO sentence but *inhibited* by the control NP string (hence yielding the difference between the prime and control conditions). One way to overcome this problem may be to adapt comprehension paradigms that have been successfully used to study dative constructions (Thothathiri and Snedeker, 2008) for use with the SVO transitive.

Even if this problem can be overcome, studies using the syntactic-priming paradigm cannot provide evidence for abstract knowledge of a particular construction unless a simple, but important, additional control condition is also included. The rationale behind the paradigm is that if hearing a construction (e.g. active SVO) makes children more likely to produce a subsequent instance of the construction, then this constitutes evidence for prior knowledge of this construction. However, as we have seen in the discussion of weird-word-order studies, hearing a completely novel construction (e.g. SOV) *also* makes children more likely to produce subsequent instances of this construction, despite the fact that they *cannot* have had prior knowledge of it. In principle, then, children could be learning the SVO construction during the study – just like they do the novel SOV construction – as opposed to using their prior knowledge. Of course, nobody would argue that this is what 4-year-old children are actually doing in these studies, as other studies suggest that children of this age are certainly in possession of the construction. However, if the goal is to use this method to investigate abstract knowledge of the construction in much younger children – the focus of the theoretical debate – syntactic-priming studies must include a weird-word-order control condition to rule out 'on-task' learning.[8]

It is also worth noting that current priming studies (including weird-word-order studies) have investigated only knowledge of AGENT–ACTION–PATIENT word order, not true abstract SVO order. When children have genuinely abstract knowledge of the SVO transitive construction, an utterance such as *Books cost money* should prime a completely unrelated utterance (with no lexical overlap) such as *The man kicked the ball*. Until this has been shown to be the case (with suitable control and comparison conditions in place) syntactic-priming studies will not have shown 'fully abstract' knowledge of the SVO transitive construction.

Returning to the study of Savage *et al.* (2003), these authors reported one finding (supporting the constructivist approach) that holds regardless of the criticisms raised above. Savage *et al.* found that, in a high-lexical-overlap condition, where the prime sentence contained material that could be reused in the target sentence (active, *It is _ing it*; passive *It got_by it*), even the youngest group showed priming. For the reasons outlined above, it is impossible to tease apart the effects of active → active and passive → passive priming, or to tell whether children had prior knowledge of these lexically specific schemas, or learned them 'on task'. Nevertheless, either way, this finding constitutes evidence for the general claim of the constructivist approach that all constructions (active and passive included) are initially based around lexical frames.

6.2.3.5 Act-out studies and the competition model   All the studies discussed above suffer from the shortcoming that children may have abstract knowledge of the SVO transitive construction that they are able to use in comprehension, but not production (e.g. Fisher, 2002). Act-out studies are designed to overcome this problem. Children are given appropriate toys and asked (for example) to 'make Mickey Mouse keef Big Bird' (with the novel action denoted by the novel verb having previously been demonstrated using other characters). If children have knowledge of word order that is abstract and verb-general (i.e. that extends to novel verbs), then they should enact these sentences correctly. If children's knowledge of word order is not verb-general but tied to specific verbs, they will essentially perform at random.

Akhtar and Tomasello (1997: study 2) showed that for a novel verb presented with no arguments during training (*Keefing!*) only 4/10 younger children (2;8–2;11; $M = 2;10$), as compared to 10/10 older children (3;5–3;11; $M = 3;8$) performed at above-chance levels (8/10 correct enactments or better). The poor performance of the young children did not seem to be attributable to failure to understand the task as they achieved a mean of 84 per cent correct enactments for a novel verb presented with both arguments (though different characters) during training. A further study (study 3) showed that children (aged 2;8–2;11; $M = 2;10$) performed no better when the actional nature of the novel verbs was highlighted with statements such as *Look what Big Bird's going to do to Cookie Monster* before the novel verb was introduced (again with no arguments). However, since these children also performed poorly with a familiar verb (*push*), their poor performance can plausibly be attributed to difficulties with the task.

As for the production paradigms discussed in this chapter, children perform better when they are able to make use of (presumably familiar) pronoun-based frames (Childers and Tomasello, 2001: study 2). When asked to enact events featuring one animate character and one inanimate object, children (aged 2;4–2;9; $M = 2;6$) performed significantly better after hearing pronouns (e.g. *He's meeking it*) than full NPs (e.g. *The dog's meeking the car*) at training and test (despite the fact that the entities were named only in the latter condition).

Most other languages use a greater variety of word orders than English (even in basic declarative sentences). For such languages, the question becomes not 'how do children learn to use word order to mark SUBJECT and OBJECT?' but 'how do children balance the (probabilistic) cue of word order and other cues to SUBJECT and OBJECT status (e.g. case marking)?' This question has been addressed by a large number of studies that are designed to test the constructivist **competition model** (Bates and MacWhinney, 1987; MacWhinney and Bates, 1989). Under this model, when interpreting a sentence, children will rely on whichever cues have most **validity**. A cue's validity is a function of its availability and reliability. **Availability** 'represents the extent to which a cue is there when you need it' (MacWhinney and Bates, 1989: 41) and is defined as 'the percentage of time that it is present over all exemplars' (McDonald,

Table 6.2 *Order of importance of cues to actor assignment across languages (from Tomasello, 2003: 138, based in turn on MacWhinney and Bates, 1989)*

English	Adults	SVO > Animacy > Agreement > Stress
	Under 5	SVO > Animacy > Stress > Agreement
Italian	Adults	SV Agreement > Clitic Agreement > Animacy > SVO
	Under 7	Animacy > SVO > SV Agreement > Clitic Agreement
French	Adults	SV Agreement > Clitic Agreement > Animacy > SVO
	Under 6	SVO > Animacy (others not tested)
Dutch	Adults	Case > SVO > Animacy
	Under 10	SVO > Case > Animacy
Serbo-Croatian	Adults	Case > Agreement > Animacy > SVO, VSO, SOV
	Under 5	Animacy > Case > SVO, VSO, SOV > Agreement
Hungarian	Adults	Case > SV Agreement > Animacy > VO Agreement
	Under 3	Animacy > Case > SVO > Stress (agreement not tested)
Turkish	Adults	Case > Animacy > Word order
	Under 2	Case > Word order (animacy not tested)
Hebrew	Adults	Case > Agreement > Order
	Under 10	Case > Order > Agreement
Warlpiri	Adults	Case > Animacy > Order
	Under 5	Animacy > Case > Order

1989: 376). For the example of trying to identify the AGENT and PATIENT in a NOUN VERB NOUN utterance, the cue of word order is 100 per cent available (i.e. whenever two nouns and a verb are mentioned, they will be placed in some order). The cue of case marking in German is less than 100 per cent available, as NOM/ACC case marking appears on the determiner (*der/den*) only for masculine singular nouns. **Reliability** 'represents the extent to which a cue leads to the correct interpretation when you count on it' (MacWhinney and Bates, 1989: 41) and is defined as 'the percentage of time the cue correctly indicates that classification on the cases that it is present' (McDonald, 1989: 376). For example, whilst German case marking may not always be available, it approaches 100 per cent for reliability: if one noun appears with *der* and the other with *den*, the former will almost always[9] be the subject, regardless of word order.

Table 6.2 shows the weightings that children and adults attach to various cues when asked to enact NOUN VERB NOUN sequences (as in the Akhtar and Tomasello, 1997, study with English-speaking children). Several cues listed here have not yet been discussed. The cue of **animacy** is that animate entities (people or animals) are more likely to be AGENTS than inanimate entities. For example, if an Italian child hears 'The pencil kicks the horse' she will generally make the horse kick the pencil (the cue of word order is easily overridden as

Italian is quite flexible with regard to word order). An English child presented with this sentence would be more likely make the pencil 'kick' the horse (as word order is a highly reliable cue to meaning in English). **Agreement** also serves as a cue to AGENT/PATIENT relations. For example, whilst the word order of '*John are hitting the monkeys' suggests John as AGENT, the fact that the auxiliary *are* agrees with *monkeys* suggests this NP as AGENT. **Stress** is a somewhat more complex cue. Most languages do not stress either the AGENT or PATIENT by default; rather, if one or more NPs are stressed, this is a cue that the sentence uses an unusual word order. For example, 'The pencil kicked the cow' is more likely to prompt an enactment with the cow as AGENT than 'The pencil kicked the cow' (e.g. Grünloh, Lieven and Tomasello, 2009).

Whilst adults (almost by definition) act-out sentences on the basis of the most valid cues, young children (as Table 6.2 shows) do not. Early in development, children may over-rely on cues that are highly available, at the expense of those that are more reliable (but less available). For example, in a study using novel verbs, Dittmar, Abbot-Smith, Lieven and Tomasello (2008a) showed that, when word order and case marking were placed in conflict, only the oldest German children that they studied (aged 7;0–7;11; $M = 7;3$) correctly based their decisions on case marking, with younger children (aged 2;6–2;8; $M = 2;7$ and 4;6–5;3; $M = 4;10$) over-relying on the more available – but less reliable – cue of word order (although, as discussed below, it is not always clear exactly how to calculate reliability). This finding held even when an easier pointing task was used (see below for discussion of this method). Sokolov (1988) reported a similar finding (though with familiar verbs) for Hebrew.

Cue cost is another factor that seems to affect children's performance (MacWhinney and Bates, 1989). For example, whilst subject–verb agreement may score highly on availability and reliability, it is also a relatively 'difficult' cue to use, because the child has to keep in mind the subject while waiting for an agreeing verb form.

The competition model faces a number of criticisms. One problem is that the model implicitly assumes that the (sometimes very young) children studied are already operating with categories such as SUBJECT and OBJECT, AGENT and PATIENT. It would be more consistent with the model's constructivist theoretical origins to assume that children are constructing these categories as they learn, and leave open the question of which are available at any particular point in development (Rispoli, 1991; Tomasello, 2003). This relates to the more general problem that the competition model is really an account only of sentence comprehension, and not of language acquisition in general. In particular, whilst it seeks to explain how children and adults balance different cues to meaning, it offers no account of how the different cues are acquired in the first place (Tomasello, 2003).

A final problem is that there is no principled way to decide what counts as a relevant case when calculating a cue's validity, or to decide precisely how a cue should be formulated. For example, in English, word order is a (virtually) 100 per cent reliable cue to meaning if basic declarative sentences are held to be the only relevant cases, but drops sharply if one also considers object questions (e.g. *Who did you see?*), passives (e.g. *The man got run over by a bus*) and so on. With regard to cue formulation, Bates *et al.* (1984) found that English-speaking children did not reliably enact VERB–NOUN–NOUN sentences with the first NOUN as agent, which they should do if they use a word-order cue formulated as 'assume that the first NOUN is the AGENT'. Bates *et al.*'s (1984) explanation was that the word-order cue should in fact be formulated as 'assume that the very first item in the sentence is the AGENT'. The danger is that by redefining cues and validity, one could potentially explain away any result that would otherwise constitute evidence against the competition model.

All the 'competition-model' studies summarized above (except the German study of Dittmar *et al.*, 2008a) used familiar (as opposed to novel) verbs. Whilst this is not a problem when the goal is to investigate how children balance conflicting cues, in order to address the more central question of when and how fully abstract constructions are acquired, studies with novel verbs are needed. In fact, for languages in which case marking appears on nouns (e.g. Russian or Polish), studies with novel nouns are also needed (to check that children understand, for example, the accusative marker in general and not just the accusative form of a particular word; e.g. cat+ACC).

Unfortunately, few act-out studies using novel verbs (e.g. Akhtar and Tomasello, 1997) have been conducted on languages other than English (though see Krajewski, Lieven and Tomasello, 2010, for Polish). Dittmar *et al.* (2008a: study 1) found that German children aged 2;6–2;8 ($M = 2;7$) failed to show above-chance performance using an act-out task (similar to Akhtar and Tomasello's, 1997, finding for English 2-year-olds). Perhaps surprisingly, the German children performed no better when an additional cue to SVO order (case-marked determiners) was given. An older group (aged 4;6–5;3; $M = 4;10$) performed at significantly above-chance levels with or without the additional cue of case marking, but were at chance when case marking and word order were in conflict.

Chan, Lieven and Tomasello (2009), however, replicated this study with somewhat different findings. This time, both German and English children ($M = 2;6$) correctly enacted sentences with two animate characters at above-chance levels, choosing the first noun as AGENT on 67 and 78 per cent of trials respectively (no case-marking information was present). A possible reason for the apparent conflict between the findings of this study and that of Dittmar *et al.* (2008a) is that, when split into narrower age bands, only Chan *et al.*'s (2009) older German 2;6-year-olds were above-chance (72 per cent).[10]

Similarly, for English children, Chan, Meints, Lieven and Tomasello (in press) found marginally ($p = 0.06$) above-chance performance for older 2-year-olds (2;7–2;10; $M = 2;9$) but not younger 2-year-olds (1;11–2;1; $M = 2;0$). Chan *et al.* (2009) found that Cantonese children did not choose the first noun as agent at above-chance levels until 3;6 (81 per cent). Presumably this is due to the facts that (1) non-SVO orders are used for various pragmatic functions and (2) both subject and object arguments are frequently omitted when they are recoverable from discourse. Again, this raises the issue of how to accurately calculate validity (e.g. in a VO sentence, is the cue of word order 'available' or not?).

All in all, the crosslinguistic act-out findings suggest that, for most languages, young 2-year-olds do not have an adultlike general understanding of the way that word order and case marking are used to mark the AGENT and PATIENT of a transitive sentence.

6.2.3.6 Preferential looking/pointing Although they may seem extremely simple from an adult perspective, even act-out studies may be relatively demanding for young children. Indeed, recall that the children studied by Akhtar and Tomasello (1997), with a mean age of 2;10, had difficulty correctly enacting sentences with the familiar (and relatively frequent) verb *push*. **Preferential-looking** and **pointing** studies follow the same logic as act-out studies, but seek to reduce task demands. Children hear a NOUN–VERB–NOUN sentence containing a novel verb (e.g. *The duck is gorping the bunny*) but, instead of having to enact this sentence themselves, 'choose' one of two possible enactments shown on adjacent screens (e.g. the duck tipping the bunny in a rocking chair or the bunny wheeling the duck back and forth in a wagon), either by looking longer at or pointing at the relevant screen. Typically, training trials with familiar verbs are used to introduce children to the idea that only one of the two displays will match the sentence presented. For example, a child might hear *The duck is feeding the bunny* with one screen showing this event and the other showing the duck tickling the bunny (Gertner, Fisher and Eisengart, 2006).

Gertner *et al.* (2006) used a preferential-looking paradigm to investigate whether children aged 2 and younger would show any evidence of abstract knowledge of the transitive SVO construction. Using the **comparison-to-chance** measure (see Chapter 3), Gertner *et al.* (2006) found evidence for such knowledge in children aged 2;0–2;3 ($M = 2;1$; study 1) and 1;8–1;10 ($M = 1;9$; study 3) with 56 and 70 per cent of looking time towards the matching screen for the older and younger children respectively (a possible reason for the younger children's better performance is that more familiar NPs – *the boy* and *the girl* – were used in place of *the duck* and *the bunny*). Two further studies provided evidence that children are capable not only of linking the first

NP to AGENT but also the second NP to PATIENT. In these studies, children who heard sentences such as *He is meeking the bunny* looked longer than would be expected by chance at the scene featuring the bunny as PATIENT, with mean looking-rates at this screen of 56 per cent (study 2) and 65 per cent (study 4) for the older and younger children respectively.

In a modified replication of Gertner *et al.*'s (2006) main study with children aged 1;1–2;1 ($M = 2;0$), 2;7–2;10 ($M = 2;9$) and 3;4–3;7 ($M = 3;5$), Chan, Meints, Lieven and Tomasello (2010) found that removing the training component of the study detrimentally affected children's performance. The youngest group did not succeed at this task (or an act-out task; see above) when assessed with either a comparison-to-baseline or number-of-children measure (see Chapter 3), with the middle group succeeding on both measures. For the older children, only those who had not previously completed an act-out task succeeded on the number-of-children measure, with the comparison-to-baseline effect narrowly missing significance. Whilst this failure may seem surprising, preferential-looking methods are seldom used for children this old because, if they find the task too easy, children are likely to fail to pay attention (as seems to have happened in this case). One possible reason for the discrepancy between the findings of Gertner *et al.* (2006) and Chan *et al.* (2010) is that, in the latter study, the actions shown on each screen were identical, with the agent and patient reversed. Gertner *et al.* (2006) used different actions on each screen. Whilst, in principle, if children really are in possession of abstract knowledge of SVO word order, this should make no difference, in practice, using the same action may make the videos less discriminable.

Another possibility is that children's success at this task may be contingent upon their completing prior training with familiar verbs (Chan *et al.*, 2010; Dittmar, Abbot-Smith, Lieven and Tomasello, 2008b: 580). If, during this training, children were learning a *general* association between first-mention and AGENT (and/or last-mention and PATIENT), this would not count against the claim that children aged 2;0 are capable of acquiring verb-general word-order rules. However, since the same characters were used during training and test, Gertner *et al.*'s (2006) findings are compatible with the explanation that children were learning a *character-bound* association (e.g. when *the frog* is mentioned first, *the frog* is the AGENT) that does not transfer to other nouns.

Whilst this objection may seem somewhat implausible, it offers a possible explanation for a set of findings obtained in another replication of Gertner *et al.*'s (2006) study (Dittmar *et al.*, 2008b). Although this study was conducted with German-speaking children, since German uses SVO word order for the vast majority of single-clause declarative utterances, the issues are the same. Children (aged 1;8–1;10; $M = 1;9$) who completed a familiar-verb training session similar to that of Gertner *et al.* (2006) performed at significantly above-chance levels (55 per cent looking time to the matching screen), whilst those whose training session used different characters to those used at test did not (51 per cent).

A problem with all of these studies is that they are based on the measure of looking time to the correct screen. This is true both for studies in which looking time is compared to chance or a baseline measure and for those in which looking time is used to classify children as passing (i.e. looking longer at the correct screen) or failing the task (for use in a subsequent binominal analysis). However, looking-time measures may be problematic, as once children have 'chosen' one particular screen over another, there is little motivation for them to continue to look longer at that screen (indeed, this is the likely reason for the failure – on some measures – of many of the 3-year-olds studied by Chan *et al.*, 2010). A pointing paradigm, where the child simply points to one of the two screens, does not suffer from this shortcoming.

Noble, Rowland and Pine (in press) conducted a modified replication of the main study of Gertner *et al.* (2006) using a pointing paradigm. Noble *et al.* (in press) found that 2-year-olds (1;11–2;4, $M = 2;3$), 2½-year-olds (2;5–2;10, $M = 2;7$), 3-year-olds (2;11–3;10, $M = 3;4$) and 4-year-olds (3;11–4;10, $M = 4;3$) all pointed to the matching scene at above-chance levels.[11] However, as in the study of Gertner *et al.* (2006), the same characters were used at training and test, meaning that it is not possible to rule out Chan *et al.*'s (2010) objection that children could have succeeded at the task using a character-bound strategy acquired during training.

There are, however, two similar studies that are not subject to this shortcoming, as the novel verbs were presented only in neutral frames (e.g. *That's called weefing*) or intransitive sentences (e.g. *Greenbean is dacking* [as Bunny dacks Greenbean]) during training. Whilst Fernandes, Marcus, Di Nubila and Vouloumanos (2006) found that children as a group showed above-chance performance, a problem is that the results were not broken down by age, even though the authors describe the study as containing two age groups: 2;3–2;6 ($M = 2;4$) and 2;9–2;11 ($M = 2;10$). Contrasting findings were obtained in a study conducted with learners of German (which uses the same word order as English for the relevant sentence types). Dittmar *et al.* (2008a: study 3) found that even relatively old 2-year-olds (2;6–2;8; $M = 2;7$) failed to show above-chance performance, even when an additional cue to SVO order (case-marked determiners) was given. Four-year olds (4;6–5;2; $M = 4;10$) performed at above-chance levels with these stimuli, but only the oldest group (aged 7;0–7;11; $M = 7;3$) correctly weighted case marking above word order when the two cues were placed in conflict.

Thus, whether young 2-year-olds can succeed at a preferential-looking or pointing version of this task without a training session that involves the same characters as the test session remains an open question. However, the suggestion that children could be succeeding purely on the basis of character-bound strategy formed during the training trials (Chan *et al.*, 2010) seems a little far-fetched. For this to be the case, one would have to assume that children learn, from a single trial, that 'when the duck is mentioned first, the duck is the AGENT', yet have failed to notice a correlation between first mention and agenthood in the thousands of utterances to which they have been previously exposed in everyday life.

On balance, then, findings from preferential-looking and pointing studies suggest that, from around 2;0, children have at least some abstract knowledge of the transitive construction. As we saw earlier, however, findings from production studies suggest that this knowledge does not emerge until around 3;0. This discrepancy was investigated in a computer simulation study by Chang, Dell and Bock (2006). Having learned pairings between syntactic frames and event semantics for a number of verbs, the model attempts (a) to generate a sentence given the event semantics of a novel verb (elicited production task) and (b) to identify which of two possible sets of event semantics best predicts the structure of a target novel-verb sentence (preferential-looking/pointing task). As for children, success occurs earlier in development for the comprehension task than for production task. Although implementation of the model and tasks requires certain assumptions that may or not be realistic for actual learners, this study demonstrates that – in principle at least – a learner can show different performance on two tasks that tap into exactly the same underlying knowledge.

6.2.4   How do lexically specific constructions become more abstract?

Unlike those discussed in the previous section, the studies discussed in this section do not directly compare the predictions of the constructivist and generativist approaches. Rather, they test predictions of the constructivist account regarding children's transition to the adult state. However, because specifying how children reach this endstate is an important goal for both approaches, the studies discussed here bear directly on the issue of which approach gives the best overall explanation of the acquisition of abstract knowledge of word order. In this sense, this section is a counterpart to Section 6.2.1, which investigated the generativist account of how children acquire this knowledge (via semantic bootstrapping or parameter setting).

Perhaps for rhetorical reasons, constructivist studies have tended to focus on demonstrating that early knowledge is lexically-specific (i.e. tied to particular verbs or subject+auxiliary frames such as *I'm X-ing it*) at the expense of testing proposals for how children eventually acquire fully abstract constructions. Nevertheless, the constructivist approach (in particular the theory of Tomasello, 2003) contains a proposal for how this could be accomplished. The claim is that children analogize across lexically specific schemas on the basis of functional and/or formal similarity between them. For example, the child might generalize across the schemas *I'm ACTIONing it* and *KISSER kiss KISSEE* (or actual stored utterances instantiating these schemas) on the basis of similar AGENT–ACTION and ACTION–PATIENT relations in the two ('**structure mapping**'). Additionally, she might generalize across the schemas *I'm ACTIONing* it and *He's ACTIONing* it (or sentences instantiating them) on the basis of shared invariant material (*-ing it*). Analogizing across utterances/schemas that share formal but not functional similarity (e.g. **The** books cost money → **The** dogs chase cats) in this way may allow children to acquire a syntactic SUBJECT VERB OBJECT construction (as opposed a semantic AGENT ACTION PATIENT construction).

However, very few studies to date have investigated these possibilities experimentally. In one study (Gentner and Medina, 1998), children were shown a picture of *a car towing a boat* and another of *a truck towing a car*, and then asked to indicate which item in the second picture was 'the same' as the car in the first. Children ignored the literal match (the car) and chose the truck, providing evidence for **structure mapping**: children aligned the two *tower–towee* structures and noticed the similarity between items playing the same role (*tower*). Tomasello's (2003) claim is that children do something very similar when analogizing across lexically specific constructions (as in the linguistic example above). However, this study does not demonstrate that children actually perform structure mapping in a linguistic context (neither does any other study of which we are aware).

In fact, one study that did investigate the roles of semantic similarity and shared syntactic distribution in the acquisition of an abstract SVO transitive construction with children aged 2;6 found no evidence for either. Abbot-Smith, Lieven and Tomasello (2004) adapted the NOUNS-only condition of the study of Childers and Tomasello (2001). Recall that in this previous study, children heard transitive SVO sentences with familiar verbs during training and were prompted to produce such sentences with novel verbs at test. To investigate the role of semantic similarity, Abbot-Smith *et al.* (2004) used familiar and novel verbs from different semantic classes (verbs of emission and verbs of caused motion). The prediction was that these children would consequently perform worse than those in Childers and Tomasello's (2001) study who heard familiar and novel verbs from the same class (caused motion). To investigate the role of shared syntactic distribution, Abbot-Smith *et al.* (2004) taught children two novel verbs: one shared a number of distributional similarities with the training verbs (e.g. both appeared in the intransitive frame *this toy VERBs*), whilst the other did not. Neither of these modifications seemed to affect children's performance. The proportion of children who produced a transitive utterance with the novel verb was identical to that observed in the study of Childers and Tomasello (2001) where the familiar and novel verbs were semantically related.

Neither did the number of productive transitives differ for the novel verbs that did and did not share distributional similarities with the familiar training verbs.

However, although it is the most relevant study of which we are aware, the study of Abbot-Smith *et al.* (2004) does not directly test the claims of Tomasello's (2003) account outlined above. One problem is that, whilst the novel test verbs and familiar training verbs were from different semantic classes, both were AGENT–ACTION–PATIENT verbs. As Abbot-Smith *et al.* acknowledge (2004: 53), a better semantic manipulation would be to investigate whether children can assimilate a non-actional novel verb into their emerging SVO construction. Neither did the study directly address the question of whether children can analogize across lexically specific constructions on the basis of purely formal similarity between them: children could have succeeded on the generalization task due to prior knowledge of the SVO construction, or by forming a semantic analogy between the training and test verbs. One way to address this question more directly may be to teach children an entirely novel construction. This would allow the researcher to manipulate the semantic and formal similarity between the lexically specific constructions that children would be expected to form on the basis of the input.

The few construction-learning studies that have been conducted have generally focused on investigating which factors seem to help children to acquire constructions (rather than directly testing theoretical proposals for how they are acquired). For example, Ambridge, Theakston, Lieven and Tomasello (2006: study 1) found that 20/24 children (aged 3;6–4;6; $M = 4;3$ and 4;10–5;10; $M = 5;4$) were able to produce a novel instance of an unfamiliar construction (*It was the PATIENT that the AGENT VERBed*) when training was spread over five days, as opposed to only 10/24 who received the same amount of training in a single sitting. Investigating another factor, Casenhiser and Goldberg (2005: experiment 1) found that children aged 5–7 ($M = 6;4$) were best able to acquire the semantics of a novel construction (*The ACTOR the LOCATION VERB-o-ed*), where the construction denotes the ACTOR appearing at a particular LOCATION, when a single verb appeared in the majority of the training sentences. (The task was to identify which of two scenes was correctly described by a novel instance of the construction.) When the training sentences used a more even spread of verbs, children did not identify the correct scene at above-chance levels.

Whilst these studies do not directly test the predictions of Tomasello's (2003) account with regard to the formation of abstract constructions, they demonstrate that experimental studies in which children are taught a novel (or unfamiliar) construction are feasible, and thus that this paradigm may be useful for testing these predictions in future work.

6.2.5   Acquisition of basic transitive word order: conclusion

The preferential-looking and pointing studies reviewed in the previous section suggest that, by 2;0, children almost certainly have at least some abstract, verb-general knowledge of the basic word-order rules of English (i.e. the SUBJECT VERB OBJECT transitive construction). At the same time, there is very strong evidence that much of children's word-order knowledge consists of knowledge of lexically specific schemas based around verbs (e.g. *cut THING CUT*), subject+auxiliary+pronoun combinations (e.g. *He's X-ing it*), and so on. What do these findings mean for generativist and constructivist accounts of the acquisition of basic word order?

Generativist researchers may wish to argue that the finding that children have some knowledge of word order from 2;0 constitutes evidence for the view that important aspects of this knowledge are innate. Although, logically speaking, this is a weak argument (children could have acquired this knowledge between birth and 2;0), it is difficult to see how one could demonstrate abstract knowledge of word order in much younger children, even if it were present. Furthermore, on the generativist account, what is innate is not knowledge of word order itself (it cannot be, as it differs between languages) but word-order parameters. One could feasibly claim that children do not set the word-order parameters until around 2;0, shortly after which they begin to produce three-word utterances.

Problematic for such an account, however, would be the finding that, long after this age, much of children's word-order knowledge appears to be tied to particular lexical items. If the parameters have been set at 2;0, then children should presumably be able to produce SVO utterances with familiar and novel verbs, pronouns and full NPs alike. One way to resolve this problem may be to posit that the word-order parameters are not set until much later (perhaps 3;0), with early success attributed to knowledge of low-level schemas. One can imagine an account along the lines of Legate and Yang's (2007) account of inflection (see Chapter 5) under which children store lexically specific schemas, using these to probabilistically set word-order parameters as they go (though, so far as we are aware, no such account has actually been proposed).

Constructivist researchers will almost certainly have to concede that there is evidence for at least some abstract knowledge of word-order at 2;0 (and perhaps younger). In fact, if as the account assumes, children (a) have been understanding adult utterances from 1;0 or younger and (b) are adept at noticing distributional regularities, it would be odd if they remained entirely unaware of such a frequent and reliable correlation as the tendency for the first-mentioned entity to be the AGENT. A potential problem for a constructivist account under which the relevant learning has taken place by 2;0 is that two

Summary table 6.2 *Acquiring basic word order ([☑] = supports theory; [☒] = counts against theory). Note that the position of the columns in this table (constructivist on the left, generativist on the right) is reversed with respect to the other summary tables that contrast a generativist and constructivist position. This reflects the fact that the studies discussed have generally been taken as support for the constructivist position; thus the table is naturally read from left to right, with the constructivist interpretation on the left, and a possible generativist refutation on the right.*

Issue/phenomenon	Constructivist approach (lexical learning): e.g. Tomasello, 2003	Generativist approach (parameter setting): e.g. Wexler, 1998
Summary of theory	Children abstract across lexically specific constructions (e.g. *I'm X-ing it* *He X-ed her*) to gradually acquire an abstract SUBJECT VERB OBJECT construction.	Children have abstract knowledge of phrase structure and set parameters determining the relative order of the SUBJECT, VERB and OBJECT.
Naturalistic data studies	[☑] Approx. 60–80 per cent of children's utterances could have been produced using one of a few high-frequency lexical schemas (Pine and Lieven, 1993; Lieven *et al.*, 1992, 1997, 2003, 2009; Bannard *et al.*, 2009). Longitudinal study (McClure *et al.*, 2006) suggests knowledge not entirely verb general ([☑] constructivist account), but not entirely verb specific ([☑] generativist account, or 'early abstraction' constructivist account).	[☑] All utterances also consistent with adultlike system. Remaining 20–40 per cent could constitute evidence for abstract rules, but [☒] adding a VERB category does not improve coverage until 3;0 (Bannard *et al.*, 2009).
Elicited production studies	[☑] Most children < 3;0 cannot produce a transitive sentence with a novel verb (Table 6.1; see also Tomasello, 2000). [☒] Preferential-looking results (below) suggest this may be a production problem [☑] Good evidence for schemas such as *He's X-ing it* (Table 6.1; Childers and Tomasello, 2001; Abbot-Smith *et al.*, 2004)	[☑] In some cases, verb semantics may preclude such utterances (Fisher, 2002), but [☒] not true for studies where passive is source construction/weird-word-order studies (Tomasello and Abbot-Smith, 2002).
Weird-word-order studies	Children's tendency to use non-English word orders declines with increasing age (Akhtar, 1999; Abbot-Smith *et al.* 2001) and verb frequency (Matthews *et al.*, 2004, 2007) ([☑] constructivist account) but even youngest children 'change' a WWO to English order more often than vice versa, demonstrating some abstract knowledge as young as 2;4 ([☑] generativist account, or 'early abstraction' constructivist account).	

Syntactic priming studies	Methodological problems mean that current studies are uninformative with regard to children's acquisition of an abstract SVO construction. However, lexical effects support the constructivist approach (Savage et al., 2003, 2006)	
Act-out studies	☑ Children learning English do not appear to have verb-general knowledge of SVO word order until close to 3;0 (Akhtar and Tomasello, 1997; Chan et al., 2009, 2010). ☑ In other languages, knowledge of cues to agenthood may develop even later (Dittmar et al., 2008a; Sokolov, 1988; Chan et al., 2009). ☑ Good evidence for schemas such as He's X-ing it (Childers and Tomasello, 2001).	☒ These findings count against the generativist approach, though one could argue that children's difficulties are in part due to task demands (as preferential-looking studies – see below – suggest knowledge at a younger age).
Preferential-looking/pointing	☒ Findings count against strong claim of no abstract knowledge before around 3;0 but ☑ not against more general claim that this knowledge is acquired from the input.	☑ Children show some abstract knowledge from 1;9 in preferential-looking studies (Gertner et al., 2006) and 2;3 in pointing studies (Noble et al., in press) but ☒ some evidence children may be using a task-dependent strategy (Chan et al., 2010; Dittmar et al., 2008b).
Transition to the adult state	☒ Very little direct evidence for the account of how children analogize across constructions to reach the adult state (Gentner and Medina, 1998; Abbot-Smith et al., 2004).	☒ No non-problematic account of how multiple parameters can be set simultaneously (Gibson and Wexler, 1994; Niyogi and Berwick, 1996; Fodor, 1998; Sakas and Fodor, 2001). ☑ Possible, in principle, that children could use phonological prominence to set head-direction parameter (Christophe et al., 2003) but ☒ adult speakers may not be aware of the relevant correlation and ☒ correlation may not hold crosslinguistically.

preferential-looking studies (Gertner *et al.*, 2006; Dittmar *et al.*, 2008b) found no correlation between success at the task and children's vocabulary level. If children's knowledge of the SVO construction emerges from verb-by-verb learning, such a correlation would be expected. However, it may be that the measures used were not appropriate, as they measured total vocabulary as opposed to verb vocabulary. It is also possible that there was too little variation in vocabulary between children for a significant correlation to be observed. Nevertheless, the constructivist account would seem to predict, in principle, that such a correlation should, at some level, be observable.

The challenge for constructivist accounts is to explain precisely what the 'weak transitive schema' (Tomasello and Abbot-Smith, 2002) that is held to underlie early success in comprehension tasks consists of, and how it develops – via the acquisition of lexically specific frames – into a fully abstract SVO transitive construction. A particular challenge is to explain how children acquire an SVO construction that applies to non-actional verbs, non-agentive subjects, and so on: none of the experimental studies described in this chapter have provided evidence for the existence of anything more general than a semantic AGENT ACTION PATIENT construction (this also means that generativist accounts cannot take the findings from, for example, preferential-looking studies as evidence for early knowledge of a syntactic SUBJECT VERB OBJECT construction, as opposed to a semantic schema).

Finally, the constructivist account of how children analogize across lexically-specific frames to form abstract syntactic constructions remains speculative at this point: we are aware of no studies that address this question directly. Implementing Tomasello's (2003) verbal account as a computer simulation may prove a useful way to generate hypotheses that can be investigated experimentally.

6.3   The retreat from overgeneralization error

As we have seen in Chapters 1 and 4, a key aspect of human language is that speakers can produce utterances that they have never heard before (if this were not the case, language acquisition would be nothing more than the rote learning of a set of utterances, as proposed by Skinner, 1957). An important aspect of this ability is the ability to use **verbs** in **argument structure constructions** in which they have not been encountered in the input. Suppose, for example, that the child hears the **intransitive** utterance *The ball rolled* and the **transitive** utterance *The man rolled the ball*.[12] On the basis of hearing these utterances (and other similar intransitive–transitive pairs), the child will form a generalization or rule that generates transitive utterances for verbs that have appeared in intransitive utterances. The precise way in which this rule is formulated will differ under generativist and constructivist approaches. However, in simple terms, we can assume that the 'rule' looks something like this:

Intransitive			Transitive		
[NP1]	[VERB]	→	[NP2]	[VERB]	[NP1]
The ball	rolled		The man	rolled	the ball

A verb that can appear in two different constructions (e.g. the intransitive and the transitive) is said to **alternate** between the two constructions. For reasons that will become clear later, we find this term somewhat misleading, and so avoid it whenever possible (however, purely for convenience, we will sometimes refer to **alternating** and **non-alternating verbs**). This rule allows the child to produce utterances that she has not previously heard. Suppose for example, that the child now hears *The cup broke* and wants to say that her mother broke the cup. Although the child has never heard the utterance *Mummy broke the cup*, she can generate it using this rule, as follows:

Intransitive			Transitive		
[NP1]	[VERB]	→	[NP2]	[VERB]	[NP1]
The cup	broke		Mummy	broke	the cup

How do we know that children are forming such generalizations? One piece of evidence comes from experimental studies with novel verbs. As we saw in Section 6.2, when presented with a novel verb in an intransitive sentence (e.g. *Ernie is meeking*), virtually all children aged 4;6 and above are able to produce a transitive sentence with this verb (e.g. *Bert is meeking Ernie*; Maratsos *et al.*, 1987). Because the verb is novel, we know that children have never heard it used in a transitive sentence. Therefore, they must have generated one using something like the rule set out above.

Another piece of evidence comes from children's **overgeneralization errors**. Not all intransitive verbs can appear in the transitive construction. For example, whilst one can say *Mummy giggled*, it is ungrammatical to say *The clown giggled Mummy* (meaning 'The clown made Mummy giggle'). Some examples of **transitive overgeneralization errors**[13] produced by real children are as follows (from Bowerman, 1988; see also Pinker, 1989a: 23). In each case a grammatical intransitive use is shown in brackets:

*She came it over there (cf. It came over there)
*I'm just gonna fall this on her (cf. This is gonna fall on her)
*You cried her (cf. She cried)
*Do you want to see us disappear our heads? (cf. Do you want to see our heads disappear?)
*Don't giggle her (cf. She giggled)

Since adults do not produce such utterances, children must have generated them using some kind of general rule of the type outlined above. (All the errors listed above involve the overgeneralization of intransitive-only verbs into the transitive construction. Other types of verb argument structure overgeneralization error attested in the literature are listed in Box 6.1.)

Box 6.1 Different types of argument-structure overgeneralization error

Note: All the errors (from Bowerman, 1988; Pinker 1989a) listed here have been produced by children. However, in some cases, the utterances have been simplified (in a manner that does not affect the issue at hand) to make the examples easier to follow.

Thus far, all the **errors** listed have involved the overgeneralization of intransitive-only verbs into the transitive construction; for example:

Intransitive			Transitive		
[NP1]	[VERB]	→	[NP2]	[VERB]	[NP1]
The ball	rolled		The man	rolled	the ball
Mummy	**giggled**		***The clown**	**giggled**	**Mummy**

Occasionally (though less often), children also make the opposite error, overgeneralizing a transitive-only verb (e.g. *lose*) into an intransitive construction (e.g. Lord, 1979)

Intransitive			Transitive		
[NP1]	[VERB]	←	[NP2]	[VERB]	[NP1]
The ball	rolled		The man	rolled	the ball
*It	**lost**		**I**	**lost**	**it**

The intransitive/transitive pair is not the only pair of constructions with which children make argument structure overgeneralization errors. Children also sometimes generalize verbs that may appear only in the **prepositional-object (PO) dative into the double-object (DO) dative** (e.g. Bowerman, 1988):

PO dative						DO dative			
[NP1]	[VERB]	[NP2]	to	[NP3]	→	[NP1]	[VERB]	[NP3]	[NP2]
John	gave	the ball	to	Sue		John	gave	Sue	the ball
I	**said**	**something**	**to**	**her**		***I**	**said**	**her**	**something**

The **prepositional object** dative is so called because the indirect object (the recipient; in this case *Sue*) is marked by the preposition *to* (*to Sue*). The **double-object dative** is so called because there are two objects – the indirect object (the recipient; in this case *Sue*), and the direct object (the thing being given; in this case *the ball*) – that appear in this order (with no additional marking)

With this construction pair, children do not seem to make overgeneralization errors in the opposite direction, presumably because verbs that may appear in the double-object dative only are relatively infrequent, and are virtually never used by young children:

PO dative						DO dative			
[NP1]	[VERB]	[NP2]	to	[NP3]	←	[NP1]	[VERB]	[NP3]	[NP2]
John	gave	the ball	to	Sue		John	gave	Sue	the ball
*I	**denied**	**a drink**	**to**	**him**		I	**denied**	**him**	**a drink**

A pair of constructions for which children make overgeneralization errors in both directions is the **contents-locative/container locative**. In the following error, the child uses contents-locative-only verb in a container-locative construction:

Contents-locative						Container-locative			
[NP1]	[VERB]	[NP2]	in(/on)to	[NP3]	→	[NP1]	[VERB]	[NP3]	with [NP2]
Lisa	sprayed	water	onto	the roses		Lisa	sprayed	the roses	with water
I	**spilled**	**juice**	**onto**	**the rug**		*I	**spilled**	**the rug**	**with juice**

Perhaps more common are errors in the opposite direction, whereby a container-locative-only verb is used in a contents-locative construction:

Contents-locative						Container-locative			
[NP1]	[VERB]	[NP2]	[PREP]	[NP3]	←	[NP1]	[VERB]	[NP3]	with [NP2]
Lisa	sprayed	water	onto	the roses		Lisa	sprayed	the roses	with water
*I	**filled**	**salt**	**into**	**the shaker**		I	**filled**	**the shaker**	**with salt**
*I	**covered**	**a screen**	**over**	**myself**		I	**covered**	**myself**	**with a screen**

The **contents-locative** (e.g. *The man poured **coffee** into the cup*) is so called because the speaker first mentions the **contents** (e.g. *coffee*) and then the container or location into which they are transferred (e.g. *the* *cup*). The container-locative (e.g. *The man filled **the cup** with coffee*) is so called because the speaker first mentions the container or location (e.g. *the cup*) and then the contents which are transferred into it (e.g. *the coffee*). The contents- and container-locative are more technically known as the **figure-object** and **ground-object locative** respectively. These terms are based on the idea that the contents (e.g. the coffee) are like a 'figure' that moves in relation to a '(back)ground' (e.g. the cup).

Finally, also relevant here are overgeneralization errors involving reversative *un*-prefixation (although technically this is an overgeneralization of involving morphology, not verb argument structure). The prefix *un*- can be attached to many verbs to specify the reversal of an action (e.g. *fold →*
unfold). However, some verbs cannot be prefixed with *un*-, even though, in principle, they denote reversible actions (e.g. *bend/*unbend*; *close/*unclose*; *freeze/*unfreeze*; *squeeze/*unsqueeze*). Children occasionally over-apply this rule to produce ungrammatical forms such as **unsqueeze.*

This leaves us with a paradox: in order to be able to generate novel utterances, children must (and clearly do) form some generalizations that allow verbs to be used in argument structure constructions in which they have not appeared in the input. Yet, once that have begun to use this rule to produce overgeneralizations, children need some way to **cut back** or **retreat** from overgeneralization errors. Children clearly do this at some point, as all become adult speakers who consider such overgeneralizations to be unacceptable. But how? The paradox is that children cannot take the non-appearance of a verb in a particular construction as evidence that the verb is not permitted in this construction, as the phenomenon that we are trying to explain is that children *do* use verbs in non-attested constructions (e.g. **Don't giggle her*).

The solution to the paradox does not seem to lie with caregiver feedback. Despite earlier evidence to the contrary (e.g. McNeill, 1966; Demetras, Post and Snow, 1986), a recent systematic longitudinal analysis of naturalistic data (Chouinard and Clark, 2003) suggests that parents do reformulate many ungrammatical utterances (e.g. *Child: *I filled salt into it. Caregiver: You filled it with salt?*), with children often repeating the corrected form in their next conversational turn. Whilst such feedback no doubt aids in the retreat from overgeneralization, some additional mechanism is almost certainly required: adults are able to reject overgeneralization errors for which they have almost certainly never received corrective feedback (e.g. errors with low-frequency verbs such as **The joke chortled me*), and, indeed, rate as ungrammatical overgeneralization 'errors' with novel verbs (e.g. **The joke tammed Lisa*; where *tam* is a novel verb meaning to laugh in a particular way). Because of the putative lack of evidence that particular utterances are ungrammatical (i.e.

'negative evidence'), the problem is sometimes known as the **no-negative-evidence problem** (Bowerman, 1988). This term is somewhat misleading, as children *do* receive, and take account of, negative evidence (e.g. Chouinard and Clark, 2003). However, the more general implication of the term, that children cannot retreat from error on the basis of negative evidence alone, seems to be accurate.

This problem turns out to be very difficult to solve. Although some progress has been made, forty years after it was first highlighted (Braine, 1971), this problem remains one of the biggest facing language acquisition researchers. It is sometimes assumed that a lack of negative evidence is particularly problematic for a generativist 'child-as-hypothesis-tester' position, under which children formulate linguistic rules which they subsequently test against incoming data. However, since, under any account, children must form some kind of generalizations that allow for the production of novel utterances, the no-negative-evidence problem in fact represents a challenge for generativist and constructivist approaches alike (see MacWhinney, 2004; Pinker, 2004). Indeed, this debate does not generally polarize generativist and constructivist approaches to anything like the extent of the other debates covered in this chapter. Although we will discuss some 'strong' generativist–nativist approaches, the leading account of this type (Pinker, 1989a) does not depend crucially on any strong nativist assumptions and, indeed, its general approach has been adopted by several constructivist proposals.

6.3.1 Generativist approaches

6.3.1.1 Conservatism   Baker (1979; see also Berwick and Weinberg, 1984) proposed that children are constrained by an innate principle of Universal Grammar not to formulate rules that cannot be corrected without some form of negative evidence (i.e. evidence that an utterance is ungrammatical). However, this solution cannot possibly be correct, as it incorrectly predicts that children will not make verb argument structure overgeneralization errors at all; numerous examples of which we have already seen.

6.3.1.2 Principles of Universal Grammar   Randall's (1990) proposed solution also lies with innate principles of Universal Grammar. Unlike Baker (1979) Randall does not propose one overarching principle that rules out all overgeneralization errors, but smaller-scale principles that rule out particular errors. For overgeneralizations of **PO-dative**-only verbs into the **DO-dative** construction (e.g. **I said her something*; see Box 6.1 for definition and examples of PO- and DO-datives) the relevant principle is that 'an optional argument may not intervene between a head and an obligatory argument' (Randall, 1990: 1391).

Sentences such as *I said her something* are ruled out because the head (the VERB *said*) and its **obligatory argument** (the NP *something*) are divided by an **optional argument** (the NP *her*). The (direct object) NP *something* is an obligatory argument of *say* because utterances such as *I said* (without an argument expressing *what* was said) are ungrammatical. The (indirect object) NP (*Sue*) is optional, because it is perfectly grammatical to omit this argument (e.g. *I said something*). Verbs that may appear in either construction (e.g. *give*) have two obligatory arguments. For example, one cannot (normally) say *John gave something* (omitting the argument that expresses the recipient) or *John gave to Sue* (omitting the argument that expresses what was given). Because *both* arguments are obligatory, they can appear in either order (e.g. *John gave a book to Sue/John gave Sue a book*) without violating the principle that an optional argument may not intervene between a head and an obligatory argument.

A potential problem is that some verbs do seem to allow an optional argument to appear in between the verb and an obligatory argument in a double-object dative sentence. For example, the sentence *John read Sue a story* is grammatical, even though *Sue* is an optional argument (it is grammatical to say *John read a story*). In fact, **positive exceptions** (verb uses that are allowed when they should not be) are not particularly problematic, because children can learn them on a verb-by-verb basis. Children simply need to avoid placing an optional argument between a head an obligatory argument, *unless they have heard the particular verb used in that way*. Problematic **negative exceptions** (verb uses that are not allowed when they should be) do not seem to exist. That is, there seem to be no double-object dative sentences which are ungrammatical despite the obligatory argument coming first.

If children are in possession of this principle from birth, why do they sometimes produce utterances that contravene it (e.g. *I said her something*). Randall's proposal is that children produce errors for verbs that they mistakenly believe to have two obligatory arguments. For example, if children think that the argument of *say* that expresses the hearer is also obligatory, they can produce an utterance such as *I said her something* without violating the principle. Errors will cease when the child realizes that the relevant argument is optional (for example, when she hears an utterance such as *I said something*, with no hearer argument).

A problem for Randall's (1990) theory is that children who produce such errors do not, in fact, seem to mistakenly believe that the relevant verb has two obligatory arguments. For example, the child who produced the error *I said her something* had previously produced sentences without the optional hearer argument, such as *She said hello* (Bowerman, 1988). A more serious problem is that this proposal is specific to overgeneralizations into the DO dative, and to English (Bowerman, 1988). It is not clear what principles of UG could be evoked to account for the retreat from overgeneralization for errors using different constructions, or for the equivalent constructions in other languages.

6.3.1.3 The semantic verb class hypothesis   A more successful generativist proposal was put forward by Pinker (1989a). Pinker's proposal is based on the observation that verbs that may appear in certain constructions do not form an arbitrary list. Rather, verbs that may appear in a particular construction cluster into a number of **semantic verb classes** (i.e. classes of verbs that have similar meanings). For example, two classes of verbs that may appear in both the intransitive and the transitive construction (Pinker, 1989a: 130) are verbs that denote 'extrinsic change of physical state' (e.g. *open, melt, shrink*) and 'contained motion taking place in a particular manner' (e.g. *roll, bounce, skid*).

Pinker proposes a three-stage learning process based on the notions of **broad-range rules** and **narrow-range semantic verb classes**. First, the child sets up a broad-range rule that allows any intransitive verb that denotes an ACTION to also appear in the transitive construction. This is essentially the rule that we outlined above (i.e. [NP1] [VERB] → [NP2] [VERB] [NP1]) except that it excludes verbs that denote states as opposed to actions (thus children are predicted never to produce overgeneralization errors with state verbs such as *stay*; e.g. **The shopkeeper stayed the shop open all night*).

Second, the child forms narrow-range semantic classes of verbs (e.g. *motion in a particular manner*) that she has witnessed undergoing the broad range rule; i.e. that she has heard in both the intransitive construction (e.g. *The ball rolled*; *The ball bounced*) and the transitive construction (e.g. *The man rolled the ball*; *The man bounced the ball*). Importantly, verbs that share a 'grammatically relevant semantic structure' (Pinker, 1989a: 279) with class members (e.g. *spin* shares relevant semantic properties with *roll* and *bounce*) will also be assimilated into the class (here, *motion in a particular manner*), even if they have not been encountered in the target construction (here the transitive) in the input.

Third at some 'maturationally determined critical point, presumably around puberty' (Pinker, 1989a: 349) the broad-range rule is essentially abandoned in favour of the narrow-range classes. After this point, only verbs that are a member of one of the relevant narrow-range classes (e.g. *motion in a particular manner*; *extrinsic change of physical state*) will be used in the relevant construction (here the transitive). However, subsequently encountered verbs that are consistent with a particular narrow-range class will still be assimilated into it. For example, if the child does not encounter the verb *twirl* until after this critical period has been reached, she will still assimilate *twirl* into the class of verbs of *motion in a particular manner* and hence be able to use it in a transitive construction (e.g. *The cheerleader twirled the baton*).

Some overgeneralization errors (e.g. **I'm just gonna fall this on her*) will be produced by application of the broad-range rule, before the child has begun to form the narrow-range semantic classes. Others will be produced because the child has yet to 'fine tune' the meaning of particular verbs and/or particular classes. For example, the above error could be produced because the child incorrectly believes that *fall* specifies a particular manner of motion (in fact, it specifies a direction but not a manner) or has yet to identify the precise set of semantic properties shared by the emerging *manner of motion* class. One final source of overgeneralization 'error' is possible. When the broad-range rule is abandoned in favour of the narrow-range classes, it is not discarded entirely. Adults may use the broad-range rule to create 'one shot innovations' (Pinker, 1989a: 350) for dramatic or comic effect, or to fill a particular lexical gap. For example, although *disappear* is not a member of a semantic class of verbs that can appear in the transitive construction (hence one cannot say **The magician disappeared the rabbit*), it can be used in one-shot innovations such as *Stalin 'disappeared' his opponents* (with inverted commas sometimes used to denote an 'ungrammatical' or special usage). Children, too, may produce such one-shot innovations, thought they too would be expected to regard them as less than fully acceptable. The reader may be wondering what is 'generativist' about Pinker's (1989a) proposal. In fact, one of its strengths is that the proposal is potentially consistent with both generativist and constructivist approaches to acquisition. Although the theory does make some generativist assumptions (e.g. the existence of a maturationally determined critical point, and discrete as opposed to probabilistic semantic classes), these would not seem to be central to the theory.[14]

Before discussing the evidence regarding Pinker's (1989a) theory, it is important to briefly mention an issue about which there has been some confusion in the literature. Pinker's (1989a) theory is often described as proposing that children form classes of verbs that do *not* appear in particular constructions. For example, the class of intransitive verbs of 'emotional expression' (e.g. *laugh, cry, frown*) cannot appear in the transitive construction (e.g. **The woman laughed/cried/frowned the man*). Although Pinker (1989a) sometimes refers in passing to non-alternating classes, he clearly does not mean to propose that children literally form classes of verbs that do *not* alternate, as such classes would not be learnable: the very problem that we are trying to address is that there is no straightforward way for a child to learn that a particular verb does not alternate. Rather, Pinker's (1989a) proposal is that children form classes of verbs that *do* alternate. Any verb that is not a member of an alternating class at the maturationally defined cut-off point is assumed not to alternate. When we refer to classes of verbs that do not appear in a particular construction (or non-alternating verbs), we (presumably like Pinker, 1989a), use the term purely descriptively.

Evidence supporting Pinker's (1989a) semantic verb class hypothesis comes from a study conducted by Ambridge, Pine, Rowland and Young (2008). These authors taught children (aged 5–6 and 9–10) and adults three novel verbs, each consistent with one (descriptive) intransitive-only verb class: 'directed motion' (a novel type of falling action), 'going out of existence' (a novel type of disappearing action) and 'semivoluntary expression of emotion' (a novel type of laughing action). Because these verbs are not semantically consistent with any semantic class of verbs that can appear in the transitive construction, Pinker's (1989a) theory predicts that participants should rate transitive uses (e.g. *The funny clown meeked Lisa*) as ungrammatical (relative to intransitive uses). Participants watched computer animations depicting the novel verbs and indicated their judgments using a five-point 'smiley face' acceptability scale. In support of Pinker's (1989a) proposal, the two older groups showed the predicted pattern for all three verb classes. The younger group showed the predicted pattern only for the novel *laughing* verb.

Similar findings were observed in an earlier study that used an elicited production paradigm. Brooks and Tomasello (1999b) taught children two novel verbs presented in intransitive constructions only. One verb was semantically consistent with the class of verbs of 'motion in a particular manner' (e.g. *spin/bounce*) which may appear in both the intransitive and the transitive construction. The other was consistent with the (descriptive) non-alternating (i.e. intransitive only) class of 'motion in a particular direction' (e.g. *ascend/go up*). Children aged 4;5 and older (though not a younger group aged 2;5) produced more transitive sentences for the novel *spinning* than the novel *ascending* verb, suggesting some sensitivity to the narrow-range classes relevant to the transitive construction. However, the use of a production methodology is less than ideal here, as it is impossible to tell whether children in fact considered transitive uses of the novel *ascending* verb to be 'ungrammatical'.

Ambridge, Pine, Rowland and Clark (2010b) extended the findings of Ambridge *et al.* (2008) to overgeneralizations of PO-dative-only verbs into the DO dative (e.g. *I said her something*; see Box 6.1). Although semantic verb class effects were found, they were less pervasive than for overgeneralizations involving the transitive causative construction (as discussed above), with effects observed only for 9–10-year-olds and adults but not 5–6-year-olds. In a similar study using an elicited production paradigm, Gropen *et al.* (1989) found that children (aged 5–6 and 7–8) showed evidence of possessing the broad-range rule for the DO dative (this study did not investigate the narrow-range classes). The relevant broad-range rule is that the DO-dative construction can be used only to describe events involving successful transfer of possession (e.g. one can say *John sent Bill a package*, but not *John sent London a package* because only Bill is capable of possessing the package).

Finally, Clark, Ambridge, Pine and Rowland (2010) extended the judgment paradigm to overgeneralizations involving the locative constructions (e.g. *I spilled the rug with juice/*I filled salt into the shaker*; see Box 6.1). Again, only older children and adults showed evidence of having acquired the relevant narrow-range semantic verb classes. This may be because, compared to the other constructions, the semantic criteria that define these classes are extremely fine-grained (and perhaps less readily apparent from seeing the relevant events). For example, according to Pinker's (1989a) classes, what distinguishes verbs like *spray* and *splash* (which may appear in the container locative) and verbs like *drip* and *dribble* (which may not) is that the former involve the application of force, whilst the latter involve merely the enabling of motion caused by gravity. Again, however, a production study conducted by Gropen and colleagues (Gropen, Pinker, Hollander and Goldberg, 1991a, b) found evidence for knowledge of the relevant broad-range rule (discussed in more detail below) in children as young as 3–4; $M = 3;11$.

Although the semantic verb class hypothesis enjoys some support in the literature, it faces two potential problems. The first is that it seems somewhat implausible to posit that learners form such precisely defined semantic verb classes as (for example) verbs denoting *manner* of motion which may appear in the transitive construction (e.g. *John rolled the ball*), and verbs denoting *direction* of motion which do not (e.g. *John fell the ball*). Bowerman (1988) asks why a child would bother forming narrow-range classes when the broad-range rule allows her to understand all relevant adult utterances and produce novel utterances herself (of course, the child does not know that her errors *are* errors). Nevertheless, since the experimental findings reviewed above suggest that adults are sensitive to such fine-grained semantic distinctions, it seems that they are indeed acquired at some point. A more serious problem is that the account does not, in its present form, account for effects of verb frequency that are widespread in the literature (discussed in the following section).

6.3.2   Constructivist approaches

6.3.2.1 *Entrenchment*   The **entrenchment hypothesis** (e.g. Braine and Brooks, 1995; Ambridge *et al.*, 2008) is that repeated presentation of a particular verb (e.g. *giggle*) in a particular construction (e.g. the intransitive *Mummy giggled*) constitutes ever-strengthening probabilistic evidence that the verb cannot be used in constructions in which it has not appeared in the input (e.g. the transitive *The clown giggled Mummy*). An intuitive way to think about the entrenchment hypothesis is to imagine the child reasoning (not consciously, of course) 'I've heard *giggle* used many times, but never in transitive construction. Surely if this were allowed, I would have heard it by now', with this assumption growing stronger every time she hears *giggle*.[15]

The study of Ambridge *et al.* (2008) discussed above also provides support for the entrenchment hypothesis (see also Theakston, 2004; Ambridge, Pine, Rowland *et al.*, 2009). Children and adults rated overgeneralizations of high-frequency verbs (e.g. *The funny clown laughed Lisa*), lower-frequency verbs (e.g.*The funny clown giggled Lisa*) and novel (i.e. 'zero-frequency') verbs (e.g. *The funny clown tammed Lisa*, where *tam* denotes a novel laughing action), all with similar meanings. The entrenchment hypothesis predicts that overgeneralization errors should be rated as least acceptable for the high-frequency verbs, for which considerable entrenchment will have occurred (e.g. the child will have heard *laugh* used thousands of times, but never in a transitive construction). Errors are predicted to be rated as somewhat more acceptable for the lower-frequency verbs, for which less entrenchment will have occurred (e.g. *giggle* may have been encountered only a few hundred times). Finally, errors should be most acceptable for the novel (zero-frequency) verbs which, prior to the experiment, had never been encountered. This prediction was confirmed for all three age groups studied (5–6, 9–10 and adults), and for all semantically matched groups of verbs (*laugh/giggle/novel*; *fall/tumble/novel*; *disappear/vanish/novel*).

Similar findings were observed in a study conducted by Wonnacott, Newport and Tanenhaus (2008) in which the verb frequency was manipulated experimentally using novel verbs. Again, these findings corroborate those of an elicited production study (Brooks, Tomasello, Dodson and Lewis, 1999) in which children (aged between 3;4 and 9;0) produced fewer transitive overgeneralizations for high-frequency verbs (e.g. *The man disappeared the ball*) than semantically matched verbs of lower frequency (e.g. *The man vanished the ball*).

The judgment paradigm was also used to demonstrate frequency effects for overgeneralizations involving the DO dative construction (see also Stefanowitsch, 2008) and the contents/container locative constructions (Clark *et al.*, 2010; Ambridge *et al.*, 2010a). However, for these constructions, the frequency effects observed were less pervasive than those observed for overgeneralizations into the transitive construction (i.e. they were observed only for some verb classes and some age groups). This may be because the dative and locative constructions (and the verbs that typically appear in them) are less frequent than the intransitive and transitive constructions (and their associated verbs), meaning that there is less opportunity for entrenchment to occur.

Whilst the entrenchment hypothesis enjoys considerable support in the literature, a problem for the account is that it cannot explain the effects of verb semantics (discussed above) that have also been frequently observed in experimental studies. One approach is simply to posit that both processes – entrenchment and the formation of semantic verb classes – are operational, perhaps with entrenchment operating earlier, before all of the classes have been formed (e.g. Tomasello, 2003). However, this explanation is less than fully satisfactory, as it does not explain *how* the two processes work together. What happens, for example, if the child hears a verb that is semantically consistent with a class of verbs that appears in the transitive construction, but has appeared very frequently without ever appearing in this construction? The semantic verb class hypothesis predicts that the child should use the verb in the transitive construction, whilst the entrenchment hypothesis predicts that she should not. In fact, counter to the predictions of the entrenchment hypothesis, uses of high-frequency verbs in constructions in which they have never been attested are often perfectly acceptable (as in Goldberg's, 1995, famous example *Fred sneezed the napkin off the table*).

6.3.2.2 Pre-emption   The claim of the **pre-emption** hypothesis (Clark and Clark, 1979) is that overgeneralization errors (e.g. **sitted*) cease when the child learns an adult form that expresses the desired meaning (e.g. *sat*), with this form then out-competing the error (see also MacWhinney and Bates, 1989; MacWhinney, 2004). Braine and Brooks (1995) and Goldberg (1995) argued that this notion can be extended to verb argument structure over-generalization errors. For example, **periphrastic causative** uses of a particular verb (e.g. *The magician made the rabbit disappear*) could pre-empt **transitive** overgeneralization errors (e.g. **The magician disappeared the rabbit*). Similarly, **passive** uses (e.g. *The book was lost*) could pre-empt **intransitive** overgeneralization errors (e.g. **The book lost*).

Brooks and Tomasello (1999b) investigated pre-emption of transitive and intransitive overgeneralization errors with children aged 2–3, 4–5 and 6–11. Children were taught one semantically alternating novel verb (similar in meaning to *roll/bounce*) and either a (semantically) intransitive-only novel verb (similar in meaning to *ascend/go up*) or a (semantically) transitive-only verb (similar in meaning to *pull/hoist*). A 'no pre-emption group' heard 88 presentations of each verb in exclusively intransitive or exclusively transitive sentences. For the pre-emption group, the novel intransitive verb was presented in 44 intransitive sentences (e.g. *The car is tamming*) and 44 periphrastic causative sentences (e.g. *The doll is making the car tam*). The novel transitive verb was presented in 44 transitive sentences (e.g. *The mouse is meeking the flower*) and 44 passive sentences (e.g. *The flower is getting meeked*). This is because periphrastic causative and passive sentences (e.g. *The doll is making the car tam*; *The flower is getting meeked*) are hypothesized to 'pre-empt' or block transitive and intransitive overgeneralizations respectively (**The doll is tamming the car*; **The flower is meeking*). As predicted by the pre-emption hypothesis, children in the pre-emption group produced fewer utterances that mismatched the experimenter's models (i.e. intransitive uses of transitive verbs, or vice versa) than the no pre-emption group (except the youngest children who showed no such effect).

However, there are two potential problems with the conclusion that the results obtained support the pre-emption account. First, the children aged 4–5 did not show this pre-emption effect for the fixed transitivity verbs. That is, periphrastic causative and passive sentences blocked transitive and intransitive utterances only for the verbs for which such generalizations were in fact acceptable (the novel *slide/roll/bounce* verb), based on their semantics. Periphrastic causative and passive sentences did not, in fact, block transitive or intransitive overgeneralizations of the fixed transitivity verbs (e.g. *The mouse tammed the flower* [where tam means 'ascend'] or *The flower meeked* [where meek means 'pull']). In other words, the 'pre-empting' sentences did not block or 'pre-empt' the very errors that they are hypothesized to prevent. Whilst the older children did show a pre-emption effect, they did so indiscriminately. Periphrastic causative and passive sentences blocked not only overgeneralization errors (as in the two previous examples) but also perfectly acceptable transitive and intransitive sentences containing the novel alternating (*slide/roll/bounce*) verbs. All in all, then, pre-emption served not to selectively reduce the number of *over*generalizations, but simply to reduce the number of generalizations across the board. It is therefore difficult to see how pre-emption could allow children to retreat from overgeneralization errors whilst maintaining the capacity to form novel utterances.

The second problem is that it is impossible to rule out the possibility that children in the pre-emption group produced fewer overgeneralizations than children in the no pre-emption group simply because they produced more passive and periphrastic causative sentences. Given that each child generally produced only one utterance to describe each enactment, every periphrastic causative or passive utterance that a child produces necessarily reduces the number of transitive or intransitive utterances that he or she produces. One possible interpretation of the results, then, is that children learned nothing about the ungrammaticality of particular overgeneralizations, with the pre-emption group simply using the constructions that they had been taught to use during training.[16] In support of this view is the previously discussed finding that that the pre-emption group produced more periphrastic causative and passive sentences across the board, not just in place of overgeneralization errors.[17] The problem here is the use of an elicited-production methodology. In order to provide support for the pre-emption hypothesis it is necessary to show not only that presenting a verb in a periphrastic causative construction causes children to produce fewer uses of that verb in a transitive construction (and more in the periphrastic causative), but also – crucially – to consider such uses to be ungrammatical. A similar study using a grammaticality-judgment paradigm would therefore constitute a better test of the pre-emption hypothesis.

Certainly, some form of pre-emption or competition explains the retreat from morphological overgeneralization errors such as *goed* (pre-empted by *went*). Similarly, *a-adjective* overgeneralizations such as *the afraid man* seem to be pre-empted by complex NPs such as *the man who was/is afraid* (Boyd and Goldberg, in press). However, a problem for the pre-emption hypothesis is that certain overgeneralizations (e.g. *un*-prefixation errors such as **unbend, *unclose, *unfreeze, *unsqueeze*)[18] do not seem to have a suitable pre-empting form that could block the error (Bowerman, 1988). For pre-emption to work, one would have to posit that a particular form (e.g. **unsqueeze*) can be pre-empted by virtually any other utterance that expresses the same idea (e.g. *ease up, release, let go* etc.). However, languages do not seem to work like this; there are normally many different grammatically acceptable ways of expressing a given idea. If a given form (e.g. *take-off*) pre-empts even distant alternative formulations of the same idea (*unbutton*), it is difficult to see how a child could produce any non-attested *un*-prefixed forms at all (which they do; see Bowerman, 1988; Clark, Carpenter and Deutsch, 1995).

An empirical problem is that adults are able to reject ungrammatical (based on their semantics) uses of novel verbs (e.g. **The funny clown giggled Lisa*) that have *never* been encountered in the relevant pre-empting construction (here, the periphrastic causative). One possibility (Boyd and Goldberg, in press) is that pre-emption may extend to semantically related verbs (so *The man made X laugh* may pre-empt both **The funny clown laughed Lisa* and **The funny clown giggled Lisa*). However, in order for such an account not to incorrectly predict that pre-emption of related items would block perfectly grammatical generalizations, an account that integrates pre-emption with verb-semantics information is required.

6.3.2.3 The fit between item and construction properties   Here (see also Ambridge, Pine, Rowland *et al.*, 2009; Ambridge, Pine and Rowland, in press) we propose a unitary learning account designed to yield effects of verb semantics, entrenchment and pre-emption (based in part on the account of Langacker, 2000).

The account begins from the observation that 'semantic verb classes' are not arbitrary, but relate in some way to the semantics of the relevant constructions (Pinker, 1989a; Ambridge, Pine, Rowland *et al.*, 2009). For example, the intransitive construction describes events where a single entity performs some internally caused action (e.g. *The woman laughed*), whereas the transitive construction describes events where one entity causes another to perform an action or undergo a state change (e.g. *The man rolled the ball; The man cleaned the clothes*), prototypically by means of direct physical contact (for example, one cannot say *The man washed the clothes* if he simply took them to a laundrette). This would explain why (classes of) verbs that denote an internally caused event require the intransitive construction, with the transitive construction not permitted (e.g. *The woman laughed* vs **The funny clown* *laughed the woman*). Conversely, verbs that denote an externally caused event require the transitive construction, with the intransitive construction not permitted (e.g. *The man cleaned the clothes* vs **The clothes cleaned*). Verbs that participate in both constructions (e.g. *The man rolled the ball/The ball rolled*; *The gardener grew the flowers/The flowers grew*; *The secretary broke the photocopier/The photocopier broke*) can be seen, to some degree, as denoting both internal and external causation. For example, whilst one can cause something to *roll/grow/break* (external causation), this is only possible if some property internal to the relevant entity (e.g. *the ball/the flowers/the photocopier*) allows it to undergo this action (one cannot roll a box, grow a desk or break a pillow); i.e. there must be some degree of internal causation as well.

Our goal here is to outline a theory that could potentially be applied to *all* types of overgeneralization error, as opposed to simply argument-structure overgeneralizations. Central to this proposal is the claim that all overgeneralization errors involve the use of an **item** in a **construction template** with which it is less than optimally compatible in terms of its **semantic** and/or **phonologic** and/or **pragmatic** properties. That is, all overgeneralization errors involve an unacceptably high degree of **extension** or **coercion**. Because the account is based on the notion of the **fit** between **items** and (construction) **templates**, it is termed the **FIT** account. We illustrate the proposal with an example where the relevant properties are semantic, as in the discussion above (see Table 6.3 for constructions where the relevant properties are all or partly phonological or pragmatic).

When forming a novel string (for this example, a sentence-level string), the speaker begins with a **message** that she wishes to convey (for this example, that a joke caused a man to laugh). The message consists of a set of **items** (here JOKE, MAN and LAUGH) and an **event-semantics** that specifies the relationship between them. Informally, we can say that, for this example, the event-semantics is simply that the JOKE indirectly caused the MAN to LAUGH (this causation is relatively indirect, compared to a case of direct physical causation such as a man cleaning clothes). To produce an utterance, a speaker must choose an appropriate word (or phrase) to label each item in the message (e.g. *the+joke* for JOKE, *the+man* for MAN and *laugh* for LAUGH) and insert them into an appropriate **construction template**. A construction template is an ordered pattern of **slots** which, as a whole, is associated with a particular event-semantics (i.e. meaning). For example, the transitive causative [AGENT] [ACTION] [PATIENT] construction is associated with the event-semantics of the AGENT directly causing the PATIENT to perform the ACTION. Evidence that constructions themselves are associated with particular meanings comes from sentences such as *The man sneezed the foam off the cappuccino* (Goldberg, 1995), where the 'caused motion' meaning is provided by the construction itself.

Table 6.3 *Examples of grammatical and ungrammatical novel strings produced by (over)generalization. The claim is that all overgeneralization errors reflect the use of an **item** in a construction **slot** with which it is less than optimally compatible. For all the examples here, compatibility is defined in terms of* semantic *and/or* phonological *and/or* pragmatic *properties of the item and slot. It is likely that, for other constructions not considered here, compatibility will be partly or solely determined by other properties (e.g. stress).*

Construction template **[slot under consideration]** (relevant properties of slot; references)	Novel (assuming the **item** is unattested in this construction for the speaker) grammatical utterance	*Novel ungrammatical utterance (**item** overgeneralized into this construction)
Single-word-level (morphological) generalizations		
Regular past-tense **[VERB STEM]**-*ed* (Phonological; Albright and Hayes, 2003; Ambridge, in press)	**show**ed	*grow**ed
-*ew* irregular past-tense **[VERB ONSET]**-*ew*] (Phonological; as above)	**gr**ew	*sh**ew
Reversative *un*-prefixation *Un*-**[VERB]** (Semantic; Li and MacWhinney, 1996)	un**button**	*un**squeeze**
Present progressive **[VERB]**ing (Semantic)	(He is) **walk**ing	*(The book is) **cost**ing $10
Phrase-level generalizations		
Adjectival Phrase **[ADJ]** [NP] (Etymological/(morpho) phonological /semantic; Boyd and Goldberg, in press)	(The/a/an) **scared/astute** man	*(The/an) **afraid/alive** man
Determiner phrase with *a* A **[NP]** (Phonological)	A **ball**	*A **aardvark**
Determiner phrase with *an* An **[NP]** (Phonological)	An **aardvark**	*An **ball**
Monoclausal sentence-level generalizations		
Transitive causative [AGENT] **[ACTION]** [PATIENT] (Semantic; Ambridge, Pine, Rowland *et al.*, 2009; Pinker, 1989a)	The man **cleaned** the clothes	*The man **laughed** the woman
Inchoative intransitive [PATIENT/ACTOR] **[ACTION]** (Semantic; as above)	The woman **laughed**	*The clothes **cleaned**

Table 6.3 *(cont.)*

Construction template [slot under consideration] (relevant properties of slot; references)	Novel (assuming the **item** is unattested in this construction for the speaker) grammatical utterance	*Novel ungrammatical utterance (**item** overgeneralized into this construction)
Periphrastic causative [AGENT] make [PATIENT] **[ACTION]** (Semantic; as above)	The man made the woman **laugh**	*The man made the clothes **wash/clean** (ungrammatical if *clean* is a VERB, not an ADJ).
Double-object dative [AGENT] **[ACTION]** [RECIP] [OBJECT] (Semantic; phonological; Pinker, 1989a)	The man **gave/denied** the boy the book	*The man **shouted** the boy the answer/*suggested** the woman the trip
Prepositional-object dative [AGENT] **[ACTION]** [OBJECT] to [RECIP] (Semantic; as above)	The man **shouted** the answer to the boy/**suggested** the trip to the woman	*The man **denied** the book to the boy
Container locative [AGENT] **[ACTION]** [CONTAINER/ LOCATION] with [CONTENTS] (Semantic; Gropen *et al.*, 1989)	The man **filled** the box with pens	*The man **poured** the floor with water
Contents locative [AGENT] **[ACTION]** [CONTENTS] into [CONTAINER/ LOCATION] (Semantic; as above)	The man **poured** water onto the floor	*The man **filled** pens into the box
Caused-motion [AGENT] **[ACTION]** [OBJ] off/onto/into etc. [CONTAINER/ LOCATION] (Semantic; Goldberg, 1995)	Fred **sneezed** the napkin off the table	*Fred **liked/cost** the napkin off the table
Passive [PATIENT] **[ACTION]** by [AGENT] (Semantic; Pinker, Lebeaux and Frost, 1987)	The girl was **kicked** by the boy	*$10 was **cost** by the book
Multiple-clause sentence-level generalizations		
Wh-extraction question [[WH] [AUX] **[VERB]**] [that . . .] (Pragmatic; Ambridge and Goldberg, 2008)	What did John **claim** that Bill liked?	*What did John **stammer** that Bill liked?
Forward anaphora into main clause [[PRONOUN$_i$] [VP]] [that **NP$_i$** . . . (Pragmatic; Van Hoek, 1997; see Ch 8).	She$_i$ said that **she**$_i$ likes poetry	*She$_i$ said that **Sarah**$_i$ likes poetry

Every construction in the speaker's inventory competes for selection to convey the message (though, in practice, most will have an activation level close to zero). The winner is the most highly activated construction, where the activation of each candidate construction is determined by:

(1) **Relevance**. A highly relevant construction will match the message perfectly in that it contains an appropriate **slot** for each item and has a meaning (event-semantics) that closely matches that of the message. For the present example, the most **relevant** construction is the periphrastic causative (yielding *The joke made the man laugh*), which has a slot for each item ([AGENT] make [PATIENT] [ACTION]) – with no unfilled or missing slots – and the event-semantics of the AGENT indirectly causing the PATIENT to perform an ACTION. One competing, but less relevant, construction is the transitive causative construction ([AGENT] [ACTION] [PATIENT]) which has all the right slots, but not quite the right event-semantics: the AGENT *directly* (as opposed to indirectly) causing the PATIENT to perform the ACTION. Another is the inchoative intransitive construction (or patient intransitive) – [PATIENT] [ACTION] but this is missing both a slot for the AGENT and the event-semantics of causation.

(2) **Fit**. Each slot in a construction is associated with particular semantic properties (and, in many cases, pragmatic, phonological and other properties – see Table 6.3) that relate to the event-semantics of the construction. For example, the [ACTION] slot in the [AGENT] [ACTION] [PATIENT] transitive-causative construction has the semantic property of denoting direct, prototypically physical causation. The key assumption of the present account is that grammaticality is determined by fit. When there is a good fit between the semantic (or – in other cases – pragmatic, phonological etc.) properties of the item (e.g. *smash*) and the slot ([ACTION]), a grammatical utterance results (e.g. *The man smashed the vase*). Where there is a poor fit (e.g. *laugh*), an ungrammatical utterance results (e.g. *The joke laughed the man*). The [ACTION] slot in the [AGENT] [ACTION] [GOAL] [PATIENT] double-object dative construction is an example of a slot with particular phonological (as well as semantic) properties: the item (verb) that fills this slot must be monosyllabic, or have stress on the first syllable (e.g. *The man suggested the woman the trip*).

(3) **Construction frequency**: the overall frequency of the construction in the input. More frequent constructions (e.g. the transitive causative) will be more highly activated than less frequent constructions (e.g. the periphrastic causative). **Prior activation** will also be relevant here. Constructions that have been recently produced or encountered will be most available in memory.

(4) **Item-in-construction frequency**: the frequency with which each individual item has previously appeared in that construction. Items in the message

will activate constructions in which they have frequently appeared. For *laugh*, for example, the inchoative intransitive construction will be the most highly activated.

Which utterance is actually produced will depend on the relative weightings of these factors. For example, if a speaker wants to emphasize the directly causal nature of some event, he may choose to use a transitive-causative construction over a periphrastic causative, even if this produces a borderline ungrammatical utterance (e.g. ?*The water deteriorated the sockets*; Pinker, 1989a; ?*Stalin 'disappeared' his enemies*). Similarly, a child might produce an error such as *The joke laughed the man* if the periphrastic-causative construction is too low-frequency to be available (and the intransitive construction is insufficiently relevant). Note that, since constructions compete for activation, a particular construction may lose not because relevance, fit (and so on) are low *per se*, but because it is out-competed by a construction that scores more highly on these factors. Thus the account yields the **pre-emption** phenomenon without having to specify in advance which constructions pre-empt one another.

Before we discuss the cause of overgeneralization errors, we must outline how learning and generalization take place under the account. Children acquire constructions – formal patterns (e.g. [AGENT] [ACTION] [PATIENT]) paired with particular meanings (e.g. direct causation) – by abstracting across instances of those constructions in the input (e.g. *The man broke the plate*; *Sue rolled the ball*; *The duck is spinning the bunny*). Thus a particular slot is a generalization over every item that has appeared in that position. Slots derive their semantic (phonological/pragmatic etc.) properties probabilistically from all the items that have appeared in that position. Properties shared by all items that appear in that position will be taken on by the slot (this is how, for example, the [ACTION] slot in the transitive-causative construction comes to be associated with the meaning of direct external causation). If the items that appear in a particular slot are dissimilar on some dimension (e.g. phonology), the slot will not take on any particular (here, phonological) properties. To understand this generalization process, suppose, for example, that – in some imaginary language – only the words *lion* and *tiger* ever appeared in a particular slot. The slot would come to be associated with the meaning of 'big cats'. If the word *rabbit* also appeared in the slot, it would take on a more general meaning such as 'mammal' (i.e. a property shared by all the items that have appeared in this position). If many different words (e.g. *table*, *complaint*, *hope*, *screwdriver*) appeared in the slot, it would not be associated with any particular semantic properties (see Suttle and Goldberg, in press). It should be clear from this discussion that slots in different constructions that have the same label (e.g. [ACTION]) will in fact be associated with different sets of properties (in Table 6.3 we sometimes, for convenience, label slots with syntactic as opposed to semantic labels, though neither is really accurate). Were it not too cumbersome, all slots in all constructions would be given unique names.

In this way, the learning account yields **type-frequency** effects (the effect that slots in which many different items have appeared are more productive – i.e. will accept a wider range of novel items), without having to posit type frequency as a separate variable (see Suttle and Goldberg, in press). If many different items have appeared in a particular slot but they are all highly similar on some dimension, then (despite the high 'type frequency' of the slot) new items that are not similar on that dimension may not appear in this slot. On the other hand, if only a handful of items have appeared in a particular slot but they are *not* particularly similar, then the slot will be open to new items. At the limit, even if only one item has appeared in a particular slot, a new item may appear in this slot, provided that it is extremely similar to the attested item (Suttle and Goldberg, in press). As we saw in Chapter 5 (Section 5.3) morphological constructions behave in this manner with respect to phonological properties: a low-type-frequency construction (like the German *[NOUN]s* plural construction) can nevertheless be open to many new items, provided that the items that have previously appeared in this slot are phonologically dissimilar to one another (e.g. Hare, Elman and Daugherty, 1995; Forrester and Plunkett, 1994; Plunkett and Nakisa, 1997).

The semantic (phonological, pragmatic etc.) properties of particular items (e.g. *laugh*) are learned in exactly the same way: by generalizing across all encountered instances. For example, *laugh* will be associated with all the micro-properties of every event that the verb has been used to describe (e.g. the noise made, the physical movements of the mouth, instigation of the action by the laugher etc . . .). In exactly the same way as outlined above (with regard to slots), properties that are not shared by all events referred to with *laugh* (e.g. the identity of the laugher, what particular amusing stimulus was responsible, and so on) will not become part of the meaning of the item. Importantly, in this way, the speaker will learn which particular elements of laughing events the verb *laugh* picks out or lexicalizes (e.g. the actions of the laugher, *not* the actions of another entity responsible for indirectly causing the laughter). Because constructions are associated with particular meanings, encountering verbs used in particular constructions (e.g. *The man laughed*) will aid in this process (Landau and Gleitman, 1985; Gleitman, 1990).

This generalization process allows learners to produce utterances that they have not previously encountered: by inserting items into (semantically/phonologically/pragmatically) appropriate slots in a construction that expresses the meaning of the intended message. Overgeneralization errors occur when the child inserts into a slot an item that is a poor fit for that slot. Thus the cause of overgeneralization errors is the child's failure to have acquired an adultlike understanding of the (semantic/phonological/pragmatic) properties of a particular slot or a particular item *and/or* an alternative construction which contains a slot that is a better fit for that item. For example, adults would not insert the item *laugh* into the transitive-causative construction (e.g. *The joke laughed the man*) because there is a poor **fit** between the semantic properties of the item (e.g. instigation by the laugher) – and the [ACTION] slot (direct, external, prototypically physical causation). If children have not yet learned the fine-grained semantic properties of the item and/or the [ACTION] slot, the **fit** between the two may be high (or at least sufficiently high that this construction wins out over a less **relevant** construction such as the intransitive, or a less frequent construction such as the periphrastic causative).

As children gradually acquire the semantic properties of the item and slot, the construction will be out-competed by another construction that constitutes a better fit (provided that it also scores highly on relevance, construction-frequency and item-in-construction frequency). For this example, possible 'winners' will be the periphrastic causative (high in relevance but low on the frequency measures) or the intransitive (vice versa). Note that, because constructions compete for the right to express the message, the child does not have to 'notice' the poor fit between an item (e.g. *laugh*) and a particular construction (e.g. the transitive causative) and somehow resolve to 'avoid' mismatches. Rather, constructions which constitute a poor fit for the item will (usually) simply be out-competed by others (though not always, as adult speakers will also occasionally produce overgeneralizations).

In this way, the account implements verb frequency (**entrenchment**) effects: semantic (or phonological/pragmatic etc.) properties will be better learned for high-frequency than low-frequency verbs. Thus, for high-frequency verbs (e.g. *laugh*), both (a) the good **fit** between this verb and compatible constructions (e.g. periphrastic causative) and (b) the poor **fit** between this verb and competing incompatible constructions (e.g. transitive causative) will be readily apparent; less so for lower-frequency verbs. Furthermore, high-frequency verbs (e.g. *laugh*) will have appeared more often in permissible constructions than lower-frequency verbs (e.g. *giggle*), and hence more strongly activate these constructions, at the expense of competitor constructions (an effect of **verb-in-construction frequency**). Note that, unlike the standard entrenchment account, this account does not suffer from the empirical problem that high-frequency verbs can often be extended to constructions into which they have never appeared (e.g. *Fred sneezed the napkin off the table*[19]). This account also yields (apparent) **semantic verb class** effects (though no classes themselves are actually posited): verbs that have similar semantic properties (e.g. *laugh* and *giggle*) will inevitably have a similar degree of **fit** with particular constructions (e.g. high with the intransitive and periphrastic causative; low with the intransitive), and thus cluster together into 'semantic classes'.

Preliminary evidence in support of this proposal comes from studies involving the locative and dative constructions, and the *un*-prefixation morphological construction. For the **container-locative** construction [AGENT] [ACTION] [CONTAINER/LOCATION] with [CONTENTS] (e.g. *Lisa filled the box with paper*), the [ACTION] slot is associated with the semantic properties of the container/location being completely affected or undergoing a change of state (e.g. going from empty to full). For the **contents-locative** construction [AGENT] [ACTION] [CONTENTS] into/onto [CONTAINER/LOCATION], the [ACTION] slot is associated with the semantic properties of the contents moving in a particular manner. Hence one can say *Lisa filled the box with paper* but not **Lisa filled paper into the box* and *Lisa spilled juice onto the floor* but not **Lisa spilled the floor with juice*. In an experimental study (Ambridge 2009a; Ambridge *et al.*, 2010a), participants rated 142 verbs for fine-grained semantic features thought to be relevant to the [ACTION] slot in each construction. In another part of the study, (different) participants rated contents and container-locative uses of each of the verbs for grammatical acceptability. It was found that these semantic ratings could predict not only which verbs could appear in each of the two constructions, but also the relative ungrammaticality of overgeneralization errors.

Similar findings were observed for the double-object and prepositional-object dative constructions (see Box 6.1), for which the [ACTION] slots are probabilistically associated with the meanings of possession-transfer and caused-motion respectively (Ambridge *et al.*, 2010a). The double-object dative construction (e.g. *John sent Sue a present*) is particularly interesting for two reasons. First, the recipient slot (filled here by *Sue*) is associated with the semantic property of denoting a 'potential possessor' of the direct object (e.g. **John sent Chicago a present*). Second, the ACTION slot is associated with the phonological properties of monosyllabicity and first-syllable stress (e.g. *John gave/*donated the library the book*). Findings suggest that adults are sensitive to these properties. Finally, Ambridge, Freudenthal, Pine *et al.* (2009) reported similar findings for the morphological *un*-prefixation construction (*un-VERB*). Although the semantic properties of verbs that may and may not appear in this slot are not easily characterized (*enclosing, covering, surface attachment* and *circular motion*; Whorf, 1956; Li and MacWhinney, 1996), participants' ratings of these properties could again predict the relative unacceptability of particular errors (e.g. **unbend, *unclose, *unfreeze*). So far, however, these studies have been conducted only on adults, and it remains to be seen whether children show a growing sensitivity to the semantic and phonological properties of particular construction slots. Furthermore, since this account contains a large number of interacting factors, it will probably require implementation as a computational model for its predictions to be testable.

6.3.3   *The retreat from overgeneralization error: conclusion*

The debate over children's retreat from overgeneralization errors is somewhat different from the other debates in this chapter (and many of the debates in the book) in that it does not generally split generativist and constructivist researchers along what we might call 'party lines'. Whether the problem is conceptualized as learning how to predict the c-selection properties of novel verbs (as under a generativist account) or as learning which verbs are consistent with which argument-structure constructions (as under a constructivist account), the issues remain largely the same. Equally, both sides would now seem to agree that the solution cannot lie with innate properties of Universal Grammar that somehow constrain children's generalizations, as it would not seem possible to propose principles that would allow the observed errors to be produced before they are then recognized as errors.

That said, there has perhaps been a slight tendency for generativist researchers to emphasize the role of verb semantics (e.g. Pinker, 1989a) and for constructivist researchers to emphasize the roles of entrenchment and pre-emption (e.g. Tomasello, 2003), sometimes actively seeking to downplay the role of verb semantics (e.g. Braine and Brooks, 1995; Bowerman and Croft, 2007). In fact, whether or not the proposal we have outlined here turns out to be correct, it is almost certain that a successful account will need to incorporate all three factors. Computational modelling studies (e.g. Alishahi and Stevenson, 2008; Chang *et al.*, 2006) are likely to be crucial to our understanding of how these factors interact.

6.4   Simple syntax: conclusion

We end by summarizing the main conclusions from this chapter, many of which will be taken up in Chapter 9.

In Section 6.1, we demonstrated that although parameter-setting accounts of syntax acquisition begin from the assumption that children can identify instances of categories such as NOUN and VERB in their input, assigning words to syntactic categories is a problem that is far from trivial, even if the categories themselves are assumed to be innate. Universal semantics–syntax linking rules are unlikely to be the solution, simply because languages vary greatly with regard to how (and which) semantic roles are mapped onto syntactic arguments. Phonological bootstrapping is also problematic because – whilst children may well be sensitive to such cues – evidence for the existence of

Summary table 6.3 *The retreat from overgeneralization error (☑ = supports theory; ☒ = counts against theory)*

Issue/phenomenon	Generativist approaches	Constructivist approaches
Summary of theory	Various different proposals	Children use a combination of verb semantics, entrenchment and pre-emption to retreat from error (e.g. Ambridge et al., in press).
Overgeneralization errors are attested	☒ Counts against approaches where children are constrained by Universal Grammar not to make such errors (Baker, 1979; Berwick and Weinberg, 1984).	Errors are predicted before sufficient entrenchment/ pre-emption/learning of verb semantics has taken place.
Can small-scale UG principles rule out particular errors?	☒ Randall's (1990) proposal makes incorrect predictions and applies only to the English dative constructions (Bowerman, 1988).	N/A
Do children form semantic classes of verbs that are restricted to particular constructions?	☑ Evidence for Pinker's (1989a) proposal from production (Brooks and Tomasello, 1999b; Gropen et al., 1989, 1991a, b) and judgment studies (Ambridge et al., 2008, 2010a, b). ☒ Does not account for verb frequency effects (see below).	☑ Constructivist proposals (e.g. Theakston, 2004; Ambridge et al., 2008) also include a role for verb semantics (though do not assume discrete classes with an innate basis).
Overgeneralization errors least acceptable for high-frequency verbs.	☒ Inconsistent with a strong version of semantic verb class hypothesis whereby classes are discrete (not probabilistic) and fixed at maturationally-determined critical point (Pinker, 1989a).	☑ Evidence for entrenchment hypothesis (Theakston, 2004; Ambridge et al., 2008, 2009, 2010a, b; Wonnacott et al., 2008; Brooks et al., 1999; Stefanowitsch, 2008). ☒ Entrenchment alone cannot explain verb-semantics effects.
Do adult utterances pre-empt overgeneralizations?	Not explicitly proposed as part of any generativist account, but existence of pre-emption effects is compatible with above proposals (including Pinker, 1989a).	☑ Evidence for pre-emption hypothesis (Brooks and Tomasello, 1999b; Brooks and Zizak, 2002; Boyd and Goldberg, in press) but ☒ Brooks' findings somewhat unclear. ☒ May not work for some error types (e.g. un-prefixation) (Bowerman, 1988).

phonological cues to phrase boundaries in actual child-directed speech is weak. This leaves distributional information as the most plausible basis upon which to proceed, whether the distributionally defined categories are later hooked up to innately specified syntactic categories (generativist approach) or used directly in production and comprehension (constructivist approach). Although which of these is more plausible remains an open question, it is important to note that positing innate syntactic categories does not, in and of itself, necessarily make the problem easier to solve.

Similarly, in Section 6.2, with regard to the acquisition of basic word order, we found that positing the existence of word-order parameters does not necessarily make the task easier. The problem of how children could learn word-order rules directly from the input is simply replaced with two new problems. The first is the problem of how children can identify heads and complements, which they can only begin to do once they can recognize instances of syntactic categories (see above). It is possible, in principle, that children could use phonological prominence to set the head-direction parameter (though this has not actually been demonstrated empirically). However, it seems unlikely that every word-order parameter has a phonological correlate that is valid across all languages. The second is the problem of how multiple parameters can be set simultaneously, when the setting of one determines the way in which a particular input 'trigger' is used to set another.

For the constructivist approach, explaining how the acquisition of word-order rules gets underway is simpler: children's earliest utterances are produced using schemas in which word order is already specified (e.g. *I want X*). However, this shifts the burden of explanation to later in development, where the constructivist account still owes an explanation of precisely how the child moves from these low-level patterns to abstract word-order constructions. With regard to the empirical data, evidence increasingly suggests that children have at least some abstract knowledge of word order as young as they can feasibly be tested using the preferential-looking paradigm (2;0 or slightly younger). Of course, this does not tell us whether this knowledge is innate or learned. Either way, the existence of lexical effects in the data is virtually undeniable (and is uncontroversial in adult psycholinguistics), meaning that generativist approaches must not only acknowledge such effects, but find a way to incorporate them into their accounts.

Whether children achieve productivity by setting word-order parameters or gradually acquiring constructions from the input, they must somehow appropriately restrict this productivity to avoid producing ungrammatical utterances, as discussed in Section 6.3. Although the problem is generally framed as one of retreating from error (e.g. how do children stop producing utterances such as *The joke giggled me*?), it is perhaps more appropriate to ask whether it is possible to arrive at an account whereby a single mechanism is responsible both for generalization, and for restricting these generalizations to items with particular semantic, pragmatic, phonological (and no doubt other) properties. It would also be desirable to have an account that can explain (over)generalization in *all* domains (e.g. not just argument structure, but also morphology, see Chapter 4; pronoun coreference, see Chapter 8, and so on) as opposed to proposing different accounts for each. Whatever this account looks like, and whether a generativist or constructivist standpoint is adopted, it would seem uncontroversial that children form and restrict their generalizations on the basis of some kind of input-driven learning.

7   Movement and complex syntax

The previous chapter dealt with children's acquisition of sentences that use canonical (basic) declarative word order and that are 'simple', in the sense that they contain a single clause expressing a single proposition or idea (e.g. *The boy kicked the ball*). The present chapter investigates children's acquisition of sentences that use different word orders (passives and questions; e.g. *The ball was kicked by the boy*; *What did the boy kick?*; Section 7.1) and multiple-clause sentences (e.g. *The boy who is smoking is crazy*; Section 7.2).

The four debates covered here – on the acquisition of **passives, questions, relative clauses** and **sentential complement clauses** – are each a debate between generativist accounts on the one hand, and constructivist accounts on the other. On the generativist side, although we cover a number of different proposals, most modern approaches share an important similarity in assuming that children have the competence necessary to produce and comprehend these structures from birth. Thus generativist research has generally attempted to show that, when various task demands are minimized, children show adultlike performance with these structures from a very early age. Constructivist approaches assume that children are not born with the necessary syntactic knowledge, but must acquire these constructions on the basis of the input. Thus, as for the acquisition of basic word order (Chapter 6), constructivist research has generally attempted to show that early knowledge of these constructions is restricted to low-scope frames built around certain items, that gradually increase in abstraction with age.

7.1   Non-canonical word orders (passives and questions)

As we saw in the previous chapter, many languages make use of word order to convey the 'who did what to whom' of the sentence. For example, English uses SUBJECT VERB OBJECT (SVO) order for basic declarative utterances (e.g. *The boy kicked the ball*). The word order that is used in such circumstances is known as 'basic' or 'canonical' word order. Many constructions, however, do not use canonical word order. The non-canonical constructions that have attracted most research are passives and questions. English passives use the same SUBJECT (*was/got*) VERB (*by*) OBJECT word order as declarative utterances. However, the link between semantic (AGENT / PATIENT) and syntactic roles (SUBJECT / OBJECT) is non-canonical:

Canonical utterance			Passive utterance		
AGENT	ACTION	PATIENT	PATIENT	ACTION	AGENT
SUBJ	VERB	OBJ	SUBJ	VERB	OBJ
The boy	kicked	the ball	The ball	was kicked	by the boy

Why do we say that passives have the same word order as declaratives with non-canonical linking, as opposed to saying that they use the opposite word order (i.e. OBJECT VERB SUBJECT)? The answer is that the patient of a passive action has other grammatical properties that are associated with subjects, for example receiving nominative as opposed to accusative case (e.g. *He/*Him was run over by a bus*), agreeing with the verb (e.g. *He was/They were run over by a bus*) and **controlling** omitted arguments (e.g. if *John was hit by Bill and went to hospital*, it is the subject – John – and not the object – Bill – who went to hospital). Control is discussed in the following chapter.

English *wh*-questions, on the other hand, respect canonical linking. Subject questions also respect canonical word order with the *wh-* or 'question' word (e.g. *who*) simply replacing the queried element. Object *wh*-questions (i.e. questions where the *wh*-word replaces an object as opposed to a subject) use a different word order:

Canonical declarative utterance		
AGENT	ACTION	PATIENT
SUBJ	VERB	OBJ
The boy	kicked	the ball

Subject question			Object question			
AGENT	ACTION	PATIENT	PATIENT	(AUX)	AGENT	ACTION
SUBJ	VERB	OBJ	OBJ	(AUX)	SUBJ	VERB
Who	kicked	the ball?	What	did	the boy	kick?

Section 7.1 investigates generativist and constructivist accounts of children's acquisition of these structures.

7.1.1   Acquisition of passives

7.1.1.1 Acquisition of passives: generativist approaches   Figure 7.1 shows how a passive sentence such as *The ball was kicked* is generated under

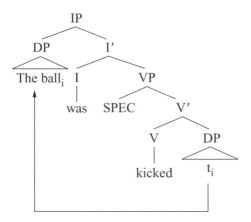

Figure 7.1 Formation of the passive sentence *The ball was kicked* under a generativist account

modern generativist approaches (e.g. Guasti, 2004: 246). Note that, unlike under older approaches, passives are *not* generated from actives. Rather, the starting point for the derivation is the Verb Phrase [V *kicked*][DP *the ball*]. The Determiner Phrase that starts out as the OBJECT (*the ball*) moves to the **A(rgument)-position** SPEC IP, where it is assigned the syntactic role SUBJECT. (Recall than an argument position is a position that can contain an argument – i.e. a subject or an object complement – but not a non-argument such as an adjunct). Here, it triggers insertion or agreement of the auxiliary (e.g. *was* not **were*) at the head I(nflection). Movement of *the ball* to an A-position leaves an **A(rgument)-chain**. This A-chain is assigned a thematic (*theta* or *θ*) role (patient) by the verb *kicked*.

So far, something is missing from this account. The verb *kicked* theta-selects not only a patient (the thing kicked) but an agent (the person doing the kicking). The theta criterion states that each theta role (AGENT and PATIENT) must be assigned to one (and only one) argument. Whilst the patient role has been assigned to the A-chain formed by *the ball*, the agent role appears not to have been assigned to an argument. In fact, it is assumed that the agent role is assigned to the passive morphology (e.g. *was/got -ed/-en*). This assumption is designed to capture the fact that it is not obligatory, in English, to express the agent (e.g. *the boy*) overtly. If, however, the speaker does choose to specify the agent, this would potentially create a problem, as the agent role has already been assigned to the passive morpheme, and each theta role can be assigned to only one argument. The solution is to assume that the passive morphology 'transmits' the agent role to an optional prepositional phrase headed by *by* (e.g. *by the boy*).

In principle, since A-movement is specified as part of Universal Grammar, children should able to produce and comprehend passives as early as they can be tested. However, early comprehension studies (e.g. Horgan, 1978; Sudhalter and Braine, 1985; Maratsos, Fox, Becker and Chalkley, 1985) revealed that this was not the case. Although children performed reasonably well with actional verbs (e.g. *drop, hold, shake, wash*), comprehension of non-actional passives (e.g. *watch, know, hear, see*) was significantly below chance until age 5 (i.e. children would interpret *The cat was watched by the dog* as *The cat watched the dog*), and did not reach adultlike levels until around age 9–11 (Maratsos *et al.*, 1985). A similar pattern was observed in production studies (e.g. Horgan, 1978), which also revealed that children (even those aged 11–13) rarely produced a *by*-phrase (though adults did). Similar findings were reported for German (Mills, 1985) and Hebrew (Berman and Sagi, 1981).

An early influential generativist proposal (Borer and Wexler, 1987; 1992) accounted for these findings by arguing that the ability to form A-chains does not mature until later in development (apparent correctly formed passives such as *The car was broken* were argued to be adjectival in nature; i.e. equivalent in structure to sentences such as *The car was red*). However, this approach has fallen out of favour as it incorrectly predicts that children should have difficulty producing simple intransitive sentences with **unaccusative** verbs. Under the unaccusative hypothesis (Perlmutter, 1978), intransitive **unergative** verbs (e.g. English *laugh, run, talk, dance*) – like transitive verbs such as *kick* – have subjects that are generated in SPEC VP and move to SPEC IP. Unaccusative verbs (e.g. English *die, disappear, fall, arrive*) have a single argument that is generated in object position within V′ but moves to subject position (SPEC IP), creating an A-chain.[1] Counter to the A-chain maturation hypothesis, many unaccusative verbs (e.g. *die, fall*) are acquired early (e.g. Pierce, 1992); certainly before children have mastered passives.

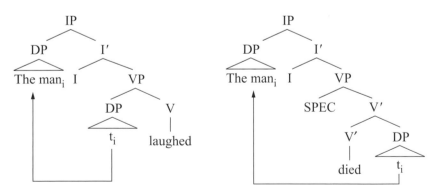

Figure 7.2 Unergative and unaccusative intransitive verbs

More recent generativist studies have therefore aimed to show that young children do have the syntactic machinery to produce and comprehend passives, and that poor performance in these earlier studies was due largely to methodological issues. For example, picture description tasks (e.g. Horgan, 1978) are likely to be unsuccessful at eliciting passives for non-actional verbs such as *see* or *hear*, which are difficult to represent pictorially. Perhaps counterintuitively, studies with familiar, English verbs (particularly high-frequency verbs) may be especially difficult for children, as they must override the AGENT VERB PATIENT order that they have frequently encountered for the relevant verb.

These issues were addressed in a novel verb act-out and production study by Pinker, Lebeaux and Frost (1987). Overall, children performed better than in previous studies, with 4-year-old children (experiment 1) showing near-ceiling performance on comprehension tasks with both novel action and perception verbs. However, a younger group (mean age 3;10) showed only 53 per cent correct performance on novel spatial verbs (similar to *suspend/contain*) as compared with 72 per cent for novel action verbs. Performance on the production task was also lower for the novel spatial verb (18.5 per cent correct) than the novel action verb (31.5 per cent).

A final problem with previous studies relates specifically to children's apparent inability to produce full *by*-passives (this problem also applies to Pinker *et al.*'s study, although passives without a *by*-phrase were scored as correct). The problem is that simply asking children to describe a picture or event where (for example) one girl chases one boy (e.g. Horgan, 1978) places them in a situation where there is no communicative need to use a *by*-phrase: a sentence such as *The boy is getting chased* describes the sentence unambiguously (indeed, Svartvik, 1966, found that only 20 per cent of adult passives included a *by*-phrase; presumably for this reason). To address this problem, Crain and Fodor (1993) developed a paradigm designed to encourage the use of a *by*-phrase (p. 167):

> Experimenter: The Incredible Hulk is hitting one of the soldiers … Darth Vader is also hitting one of the soldiers [a different one]. Ask Keiko which one.
>
> Child (to Keiko): Which soldier is getting hit by Darth Vader?

This set-up discourages the use of a passive question without a *by*-phrase (*Which soldier is getting hit?*) as such a question is ambiguous and hence could not elicit the desired answer (which the child knows). Children (aged 3;4–4;9) showed much improved performance with 29/32 producing full passives with a *by*-phrase (for a total of 50 per cent of all responses). Nevertheless, this study does not address children's apparent difficulty with non-actional passives (as far as it is possible to determine, only action verbs were used in the study).

One reason why performance in this study (and most of the studies discussed above) may have remained relatively poor is that children were asked to produce sentences with two animate Noun Phrases (e.g. a soldier and Darth Vader), which may cause children to become confused as to which is the agent and which the patient. Studies in which children show better performance (e.g. Bencini and Valian, 2008; Fox and Grodzinsky, 1998; Brooks and Tomasello, 1999a; Tomasello, Brooks and Stern, 1998; discussed below) generally involve an inanimate NP (the surface subject) being acted upon by an animate agent NP. Such sentences offer less opportunity for confusion, and, in addition, are presumably more typical of those that children encounter in their input.

Bencini and Valian (2008) used a priming methodology to demonstrate that children as young as 3 (2;11–3;6; $M = 3;2$) have at least some abstract knowledge of full passives (see the previous chapter for a discussion of the rationale behind the priming methodology). In a picture-description task, children who had previously heard and repeated passive primes (e.g. *The milk is stirred by the spoon*) produced significantly more full passives when describing a subsequent picture (e.g. a knife slicing lemons) than children who had previously been exposed to active primes (e.g. *The wagon is carrying the presents*). However, this does not constitute evidence for completely abstract knowledge of the passive, as children could have been using a lexical frame based on the prime (e.g. *The X is ACTIONed by the Y*) to produce the target sentence (note that all priming and target sentences used actional verbs).

These more recent studies leave generativist accounts with a puzzle. If children's success is indicative of adultlike syntactic knowledge, it is unclear why they should consistently perform poorly with non-actional passives and – in many studies – have difficulty supplying a *by*-phrase. One possible answer is offered by Fox and Grodzinsky (1998). These authors argue that children are initially unable to 'transmit' the agent role from the passive morphology to the NP in the *by*-phrase. For actional passives, children can overcome this difficulty by using another route: the agent role is assigned to the NP by the preposition *by* itself. This route is available because an actional verb necessarily has an agent role for the *by* preposition to assign (all actions have an agent). However, this 'direct assignment' route is not available for non-actional verbs, as they do not have an agent in their semantic representation. In support of this view, Fox and Grodzinsky (1998) point to Crain and Fodor's (1993) finding that the majority of children's full passives are with GET (Fox and Grodzinsky also describe a comprehension study demonstrating that children aged 3;6–5;6 show better comprehension of GET than BE passives). For GET passives, the direct assignment route is always available, as GET passives (unlike BE passives) are only possible for actional verbs:

Actional: The window was broken by the ball / The window got broken by the ball.

Non-actional: The boy was seen by the girl / *The boy got seen by the girl.

A problem for Fox and Grodzinsky's (1998) account, however, is that there does not seem to be a clear split whereby children show adultlike performance with all actional verbs but poor performance with all non-actional verbs. In a comprehension study with children aged 3;0–5;6 (Gordon and Chafetz, 1990) performance for some actional verbs (e.g. *hold*, 47% correct; *shake*, 48%) was little better than for non-actional verbs (*M* = 39%), whilst other actional verbs (e.g. *carry*, 82%) were associated with almost double the level of correct responses. Similarly, in both a comprehension and priming study, Messenger, Branigan, McLean and Sorace (2009) found that non-actional verbs such as *frighten, scare, shock, surprise* and *annoy* (where the surface subject is clearly affected in some way) showed no disadvantage as compared to action verbs (*pat, bite, pull, hit, carry, squash*).

A possible solution to this problem is offered by Pinker, Lebeaux and Frost (1987). Their proposal is based on the notion of broad-range rules and narrow-range classes (see Pinker, 1989a; and Chapter 6, Section 6.3) that classify verbs as consistent with particular constructions; in this case the passive. Pinker *et al.*'s (1987: 249) broad-range rule (or 'thematic core') for the passive specifies that

X (mapped onto the surface subject) is in a state or circumstance characterized by Y (mapped onto the *by*-object or an understood argument) having acted upon it.

This **affectedness constraint** explains why passives such as *Shampoo is contained by the bottle* are ungrammatical for adults (the bottle does not act upon the shampoo). Non-actional passives where the surface subject has clearly been affected by some action performed upon it (e.g. *frighten, scare, shock, surprise* and *annoy*) are – as predicted by this account – non-problematic for children (Messenger *et al.*, 2009). Non-actional passives where the surface subject is not affected (e.g. *see*) are more problematic as children must learn on a verb-by-verb (or class-by-class) basis that passives are possible. This proposal is also consistent with the FIT account outlined in the previous chapter (see also Ambridge, Pine and Rowland, in press). Having acquired the meaning of the construction (X [the surface subject] is affected in some way by Y [the surface object]), children readily learn that passives are possible for verbs that are highly semantically consistent with this construction (e.g. *hit, frighten, annoy*) and impossible for verbs that are highly semantically inconsistent (e.g. *cost, seem, contain*). In cases where X is somewhat or indirectly affected by Y (e.g.

see, *hear*, *surround*), the situation is less clear, and children may struggle to produce and comprehend passives.[2]

One finding counts against this view, however: Gordon and Chafetz (1990) asked adult participants to rate the verbs used in their study for 'affected-ness' (on a 7-point scale). Looking only at the nine actional verbs (which received mean affectedness ratings of between 1.8 and 6.3), no correlation with children's correct performance was observed. However, it would seem premature to reject Pinker *et al.*'s (1987) hypothesis purely on this basis, given that the non-actional verbs, on which children performed poorly, did receive uniformly low affectedness ratings ($M = 1.1$), exactly as Pinker *et al.* (1987) would predict (these verbs were not included in the correlation). A finer-grained test of Pinker *et al.*'s (1987) account (and the FIT account) would be to see whether these semantic ratings can predict the relative (un)grammaticality of passive sentences with a range of actional and non-actional verbs.

7.1.1.2 Acquisition of passives: constructivist approaches

7.1.1.2 *Acquisition of passives: constructivist approaches*   Whereas Pinker *et al.* (1987) argue that children learn passivization, at least for some verbs, on a class-by-class basis, constructivist accounts go further still. Under constructivist accounts, passive utterances are not formed by transformation or movement. Rather, the passive construction – like any other construction – is initially learned on an item-by-item basis: children begin with holophrases (e.g. *The car's broken*), moving gradually through low-scope lexically spe-cific formulas (e.g. *The X was broken by the Y*) towards an adultlike abstract construction (*X BE/GET VERB by Y*).

Interestingly, this account (e.g. Israel, Johnson and Brooks, 2000) shares with the generativist proposal of Borer and Wexler (1987) the assumption that children's earliest passives are adjectival (e.g. *The car's broken*). The differ-ence is that, under constructivist approaches, these utterances do not represent a dead-end that is abandoned when a system for forming 'real' passives becomes available; rather, they are the building blocks from which an abstract pas-sive construction emerges. Under Israel *et al.*'s (2000) 'constructional ground-ing' account, children first learn stative participle forms (e.g. *broken, finished, cooked*) without necessarily associating them with verbs at all. Later, children learn to understand and produce stative utterances (e.g. *The spinach is cooked*). Israel *et al.* (2000) argue that these are easily acquired as they reliably co-occur with the situations they describe. The next stage involves utterances such as *The spinach needs to be cooked* which have both a stative (i.e. we require cooked as opposed to raw spinach) and eventive (i.e. somebody needs to cook the spinach) reading. The claim is that these utterances represent a 'bridge' between earlier-acquired statives (e.g. *The spinach is cooked*) and the fully eventive passives learned later (e.g. *The spinach was cooked by Mommy*). Israel *et al.* (2000) do not discuss the acquisition of non-actional passives (e.g. *The boy was seen by the girl*); presumably the idea is that (as proposed for other constructions under the constructivist approach) these are produced by analogy with these more concrete exemplars as children develop a syntactic VERB class.

Israel *et al.* (2000) conducted a naturalistic data analysis of seven children from the CHILDES database (mostly from around 2;0 to 4;6). As predicted, all children appeared to go through the stages stative (e.g. *it's broken*; 2;6) > equivocal (e.g. *that's gonna be broken too,* 2;7) > eventive (e.g. *a monarch butterfly was killed by a bird*, 3;7) in the predicted order (examples from Abe). A problem for this analysis, however, is that it is difficult to rule out the possibility that this apparent effect was an artefact of sampling. If stative (adjectival) passives are the most common and fully eventive passives the least (as may well be true for adults), this apparent progression could be observed even if children were actually producing all three types of passives from the earliest stages. Neither do the data constitute strong evidence against generativist accounts which argue that children initially have difficulty with the *by*-phrase (e.g. Fox and Grodzinsky, 1998). It would also be possible to argue that children have the competence to produce all types of passives from early in development but are subject to some kind of memory or production constraint which limits the length (or number of arguments) in their passives (although we are not aware of any specific generativist claims to this effect).

Another argument put forward in support of the constructivist viewpoint that passives are learned on an independent timetable (as opposed to being produced by syntactic movement) is that there appears to be a rough crosslinguistic correlation between the age at which passives are acquired and the frequency of such utterances in the input. Children learning languages in which passives are more frequent in the input – though not always syntactically simpler – produce passives earlier than learners of English[3] (e.g. Inuktitut, Allen and Crago, 1996; K'iche' Mayan, Pye and Quixtan Poz, 1988; and the Bantu languages Sesotho, Demuth, 1990; and Zulu, Suzman, 1999). However, in support of the generativist account, one could argue that this may be an artefact of sampling: the more frequently passive utterances occur in a language in general (i.e. in both adult and child speech), the greater the likelihood of one being picked up in early speech. A comprehensive programme of crosslinguistic elicitation/comprehension studies would help to address this issue. Intriguingly, however, one recent study of English-speaking adults found evidence for an effect of the input. Dąbrowska and Street (2006) demonstrate that adults who read only infrequently, and hence have little experience with the full-passive construction (which is rare in spoken discourse), perform poorly on a comprehension picture-selection task with reversible passives (only 19/31 participants performed at significantly above-chance levels).

More direct evidence in support of this input-based proposal comes from studies which demonstrate that English-speaking children produce passives earlier than is normally the case if their input is manipulated to contain a large number of exemplars of the construction. Brooks and Tomasello (1999a: study 1) presented children (aged 2;9–3;0 and 3;3–3;8) with 96 passive constructions (both full and truncated passives) for each of two novel verbs. Children then completed a task designed to elicit passives (e.g. *What happened to the PATIENT?*) with new characters (to ensure that they could not simply repeat training sentences verbatim). Brooks and Tomasello (1999a) found that 80 per cent of the younger group and 90 per cent of the older group were able to produce at least one novel full passive with a *by*-phrase. In a follow-up study (Tomasello, Brooks and Stern, 1998: study 2) one group of children (aged 3;0–3;2) were presented with truncated passives (e.g. *The car got meeked*) questions (e.g. *The car got meeked by who?*) and *by*-phrases (e.g. *by Big Bird*) that 'added up' to a full passive, without ever actually hearing a full passive. Children in this scaffolding condition produced a mean of only 0.2 full passives per child (two utterances) as compared with 7.2 (seven utterances) produced by a full-passives training group. Together, these studies provide support for the view that the passive construction is learned from the input; most likely as a whole construction rather than in a piecemeal fashion. On the other hand, one could also use these findings to argue for the generativist claim that children have innate knowledge of the syntactic processes involved in passive formation, but require an experimental scenario in which the use of passives is strongly encouraged or primed to display this competence.

Under constructivist accounts, all constructions are initially acquired in the form of lexically specific frames. A priming study conducted by Savage, Lieven, Theakston and Tomasello (2003: study 1) provided evidence in support of this view with respect to the passive construction. Children aged 2;11–3;7 ($M =$ 3;2), 3;10–4;6 ($M = 4;2$) and 6;1–7;1 ($M = 6;2$) described computer animations (e.g. a hammer smashing a vase) after repeating a passive (or, in a control condition, active) prime sentence produced by the experimenter. For half of the children, the passive prime (*It got VERBed by it*) was designed to allow for high lexical overlap between the prime and the target (i.e. the child could essentially repeat the prime sentence, substituting the verb). For the remainder, the passive prime (e.g. *The ball got caught by the net*) was designed to allow for lower lexical overlap (i.e. the child would have to replace both nouns and the verb to produce the target sentence). The youngest two groups displayed priming (i.e. more passives were produced following passive than active primes) in the high lexical overlap condition only (overlap did not matter for the oldest children).

The finding that the younger children did not display priming in the low lexical overlap condition is surprising, given that many 3-year-olds are able to produce full passives with novel verbs (e.g. Brooks and Tomasello, 1999a). Indeed, subsequent priming studies using an almost identical condition have found priming for 3- and 4-year-olds (Huttenlocher, Vasilyeva and Shimpi,

2004; Bencini and Valian, 2008). Nevertheless, the finding of a difference between the high and low lexical overlap condition lends support to the constructivist view that lexically based frames (e.g. *It got VERBed by it*) are important in children's acquisition of the passive. Of course, generativist accounts would be free to assume that children acquire a repertoire of lexically specific constructions of this type that are used alongside the movement rules assumed for more abstract passives, though we are not aware of any proposals along these lines.

7.1.1.3 Acquisition of passives: conclusion   In conclusion, the two sides – generativist and constructivist – are essentially in agreement with regard to the data. English-speaking children first acquire adjectival stative passives (e.g. *It's broken*), then full actional passives (e.g. *It got broken by the hammer*), and finally non-actional passives (e.g. *The boy was seen by the girl*). Furthermore, both sides agree that, given the right experimental circumstances, children aged as young as 3 demonstrate at least some abstract knowledge of the full passive (e.g. Brooks and Tomasello, 1999a; Bencini and Valian, 2008).

Where the two sides differ is with respect to the question of how children come to attain this knowledge. The generativist view is that it is essentially innate (perhaps after some maturation; e.g. Borer and Wexler, 1987, 1992), with early poor performance attributed to task demands (e.g. Crain and Fodor, 1993) or specific problems with the *by*-phrase (Fox and Grodzinsky, 1998). The constructivist view is that the passive construction is learned from the input: children begin with lexically specific – often stative – frames (e.g. *it's broken*) that become increasingly abstract (e.g. → *it got VERBed by it* → *NP BE/GET VERB by NP*). In fact, whilst the studies discussed here provide some evidence that is consistent with one viewpoint, rarely do they provide conclusive evidence against the other.

In many areas of child language acquisition (e.g. acquisition of questions, discussed in the following section) researchers have sought to distinguish between generativist and constructivist accounts by looking for effects of lexical specificity. This approach could also be applied to the passive. If it turns out that children are excellent at forming passives with some verbs (e.g. *kill*) and – whilst holding actionality constant – worse with others (e.g. *kick*) then this may constitute evidence for the constructivist claim that children begin by acquiring lexically specific constructions (e.g. *X got killed by Y*), particularly if the verbs for which children show good performance are frequent in passive constructions in the input. Conversely, if it turns out that children are equally good at forming passives with verbs that differ along dimensions such as frequency, this would provide support for the generativist approach. This, then, may be a profitable avenue for future research into children's acquisition of the passive. Finally, it is important to note that accounts of how children become productive with

Summary table 7.1 *Acquisition of passives* (☑ = *supports theory*; ☒ = *counts against theory*)

Issue/phenomenon	Generativist full-competence approach (e.g.Crain and Fodor, 1993)	Constructivist approaches (e.g. Israel et al., 2000)
Summary of theory	Children have syntactic machinery to form passives (A-chains); 'poor' performance due to design of experiment/inability to transmit agent role to by-phrase (Fox and Grodzinsky, 1998).	Children move from holophrases (e.g. *The car's broken*), via lexical frames (e.g. *The X was broken by the Y*), to an adultlike abstract construction (*X BE/GET VERB by Y*), learning from input.
Comprehension studies	☒ Poor comprehension of non-actional passives until at least 5;0 (Horgan, 1978; Sudhalter and Braine, 1985; Maratsos et al., 1985; Mills, 1985; Berman and Sagi, 1981)	☑ Since passives are rare in the input, account predicts poor performance, improving with age, though ☒ even some adults show poor performance (Dąbrowska and Street, 2006).
Production studies	☒ Poor performance with non-actional passives (Horgan, 1978). Could argue studies in right-hand box 'prime' underlying knowledge.	☑ Boosting passives in input improves performance in novel verb studies (Brooks and Tomasello, 1999a; Tomasello et al., 1998).
Crosslinguistic studies	Could argue correlation (see right-hand box) is an artefact of sampling.	☑ Rough negative correlation between % passives in input and age of acquisition (Allen and Crago, 1996; Pye and Quixtan Poz, 1989; Demuth, 1990; Suzman, 1999).
Novel verb act-out/ comprehension study	☑ Near-ceiling performance for 4-yr-olds but ☒ 3-yr-olds still poor at non-actional passives (Pinker et al., 1987).	☑ Account predicts age-related improvement (and perhaps non-actional/actional effect – see two cells down).

Children rarely produce a *by*-phrase (all production studies listed).	But ☑ 3–4-yr-olds can do so, given suitable experimental design (Crain and Fodor, 1993).	☑ Predicted to rarely produce *by*-phrase as this is rare in the input (Svartvik, 1966; Gordon and Chafetz, 1990).
Are any difficulties with *by*-phrase linked to non-actional passives?	☑ Some support for Fox and Grodzinsky's (1998) proposal (see also Crain and Fodor, 1993), but see below.	
Do children go through stages eventive → equivocal → stative?	Not specifically predicted by account.	☑ Some evidence for claim (Israel *et al.*, 2000) but ☒ descriptive study, not yet backed up experimentally
Affectedness constraint: Surface subject must be affected in some way (Pinker, 1989a)	☑ Good performance for non-actional verbs when subject is affected (Messenger *et al.*, 2009) but ☒ no significant correlation with affectedness (Gordon and Chafetz, 1990).	☒ Does not directly predict affectedness effect but ☑ early eventive passives (e.g. *broken, finished cooked*) denote affected subject (Israel *et al.*, 2000). ☑ Constraint consistent with account under which fit between item and construction properties (here affectedness) determines grammaticality (Ambridge *et al.*, in press; see Chapter 6, Section 6.3).
Priming studies	☑ Even 2–3 yr-olds have some knowledge of the passive (Huttenlocher *et al.*, 2004; Bencini and Valian, 2008), but ☒ see right-hand column.	☑ . . . best performance when children can use lexical frame (*The X is ACTIONed by the Y*) (Savage *et al.*, 2003).

the passive construction will have to incorporate an account of how children avoid over-applying the constructions to verbs that do not passivize (e.g. *£30 was cost by the book). As Pinker et al. (1987) argue, such an account will most likely need to make reference to acquisition of the fine-grained semantics of the construction and individual verbs. Research into this aspect of acquisition of the passive has barely begun.

7.1.2   Acquisition of questions

7.1.2.1 Acquisition of questions: generativist approaches   Under generativist approaches, non-subject questions – like passives – are formed by movement. However, whereas passives are formed by NP-movement, questions are formed by movement of the auxiliary[4] from I to C (**subject–auxiliary inversion**) and – for *wh*-questions – by movement of the *wh*-word from within VP to SPEC CP (***wh*-movement**), as shown in Figure 7.3.

Interestingly, a preferential-looking study (Seidl, Hollich and Jusczyk, 2003) has shown that children aged as young as 1;8 are able to respond appropriately (i.e. differentially) to subject and object *wh*-questions (e.g. *What hit the book?* vs *What did the book hit?*), suggesting early knowledge of (from a generativist perspective) inversion.

The challenge for generativist accounts is therefore to explain why, given that knowledge of subject–auxiliary inversion is acquired early (or, indeed, is innate), errors are relatively common amongst learners of English. Most

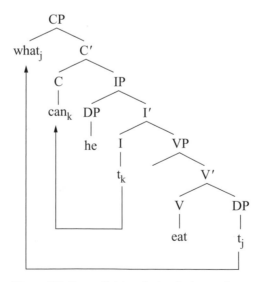

Figure 7.3 Generativist analysis of *wh*-questions

common are **non-inversion** (or **uninversion**) **errors** (e.g. *What she can eat?*; *What she doesn't like?*) where the auxiliary appears in post-subject position. Various types of **auxiliary-doubling errors** are also observed, particularly for negative questions (e.g. *What does she doesn't like?*) and questions with long subjects (e.g. *What can the boy who is smoking can do?*). Many different studies (see Ambridge, Rowland, Lieven and Tomasello, 2006, for references and a more comprehensive review) have investigated how these errors pattern by *wh*-word, auxiliary and the presence or absence of negation. Although the studies are often not directly comparable, and sometimes produce contradictory results, a number of consistent findings emerge:

- Auxiliary DO is typically associated with more errors (particularly double-marking errors in negative questions) and lower rates of correct use than all other auxiliaries.
- Both copula and auxiliary BE (the two are not always distinguished) generally display very low rates of error and high rates of correct use. Where the two are distinguished, copula BE generally shows higher error rates.
- *What* is the first *wh*-word to be acquired and is typically associated with the lowest error rate, and highest rate of correct use (and overall use) of any *wh*-word. *Why* is typically the latest acquired and shows the highest error rates (though this may at least in part reflect the fact that spontaneous *why* questions are more likely than other questions to be negative).
- Negated *wh*-questions (and *yes/no* questions) typically attract extremely high rates of error (often 100 per cent for a certain period), particularly auxiliary-doubling error (indeed such errors occur almost exclusively with negative questions).
- It is sometimes suggested that *wh*-questions display higher rates of inversion error than *yes/no* questions, but findings are contradictory, and the picture is complicated by the fact that non-inverted *yes/no* questions are not always counted as errors as they are permissible in certain contexts (e.g. *She can't do it?*).

To account for non-inversion errors with *wh*-questions (e.g. *Why she can't do it?*), Stromswold (1990) and de Villiers (1991) argue that children initially mis-analyse *wh*-questions such that the *wh*-word is analysed as an unmoved element, generated in place at the start of the sentence (adjoined to IP). This misanalysis persists longer for adjunct (e.g. *how* and *why*) than argument *wh*-words (e.g. *what* and *who*), as certain adjunct *wh*-questions (e.g. *How come he is leaving?*) do not require movement.

This prediction is not well supported in the literature. Although naturalistic data studies often find a high error rate for *why* (e.g. Labov and Labov, 1978; Kuczaj and Brannick, 1979; Rowland and Pine, 2000), this may largely reflect the fact that many *why* questions are negative questions (e.g. *why can't . . . why doesn't . . .*), which children seem to find problematic in general (e.g. Maratsos and Kuczaj, 1978; Stromswold, 1990; Guasti, Thornton and Wexler, 1995). In elicited production studies, children show good performance with *why* in positive questions (e.g. Ambridge, Rowland, Theakston and Tomasello, 2006) but poor performance in negative questions (e.g. Ambridge and Rowland, 2009). There is little evidence of poor performance on adjunct *how* questions from either naturalistic or elicited production studies (e.g. Rowland and Pine, 2000; Ambridge, Rowland, Theakston and Tomasello, 2006).

More successful have been generativist accounts that have sought to locate the source of children's non-inversion errors with particular auxiliaries, rather than particular *wh*-words. Errors are argued to occur only for two auxiliaries that display idiosyncratic properties: copula BE and the dummy auxiliary DO (Santelmann *et al.*, 2002; see also Stromswold, 1990; Hattori, 2003). Copula BE is unique in that it is the only main verb in English that displays inversion in questions:

> Minnie is a mouse. → What is Minnie?
>
> Minnie Mouse likes cake. → *What likes Minnie Mouse?

Since children learn that, in English, main verbs do not invert, they are predicted to have difficulty in forming questions with copula BE until they learn to 'override their grammatical knowledge that main verbs do not raise . . . for their language' (Santelmann *et al.*, 2002: 837) for this particular item. The dummy auxiliary DO is also unique in that, unlike all other auxiliaries, it is not present in the underlying declarative sentence, unless added for emphasis or negation, but is added for questions to bear tense and agreement:

> Minnie Mouse likes cake.
>
> Minnie Mouse *does* (not/n't) like cake.
>
> What does Minnie Mouse like?

Thus this process of *DO-support* in questions does not fall naturally out of children's UG knowledge of inversion, but is a historical accident of the development of English (specifically that main verbs may no longer invert). Thus children's documented difficulties in forming questions with DO (e.g. Stromswold, 1990; Santelmann *et al.*, 2002; Hattori, 2003) are argued to be a result of the difficulty of integrating their UG knowledge of inversion with their language-specific knowledge of the process of DO-support.

To test this hypothesis, Santelmann *et al.* (2002) conducted a study in which children (aged 2;1–5;3) were asked to repeat declaratives and corresponding *yes/no* questions. As predicted, children performed worse for questions than declaratives with copula BE (e.g. *Is Miss Piggy a movie star?*) and the dummy auxiliary DO (e.g. *Does Mickey Mouse open a present?*), but not auxiliary BE and the modal auxiliary CAN (which follow the UG-specified movement rule). However, this pattern of results depends crucially on a particular interpretation of statistical significance testing. Children did perform (marginally) worse on questions than declaratives for auxiliary BE ($p = 0.06$) and (under a conventional definition) modal CAN ($p = 0.03$). However, because a stricter standard of $p < 0.01$ was arbitrarily adopted, these findings were taken as positive evidence for *no* difference. Although particularly high error rates for DO have been found in both naturalistic (e.g. Rowland and Pine, 2000) and experimental studies (e.g. Ambridge and Rowland, 2009), in both cases this largely reflects performance with negative questions, which are problematic across the board.

This brings us to the question of why both non-inversion errors (e.g. *What she doesn't like?*) and auxiliary-doubling errors (e.g. *What does she doesn't like?*) are particularly frequent for negative questions. A related finding is that almost all auxiliary-doubling errors are of the type AUX . . . AUX+NEG (as in the example above), as opposed to AUX+NEG . . . AUX (e.g. *What doesn't she does like?*) or AUX+NEG . . . AUX+NEG (e.g. *What doesn't she doesn't like?*). Guasti *et al.* (1995) proposed a generativist parameter-setting account designed to explain both of these phenomena. In some language dialects (e.g. Paduan Italian) the negation marker *not* (or the clitic form *n't*) may not raise out of IP. Guasti *et al.* (1995) argue that children must set a parameter that determines whether the negation marker does (e.g. English) or does not (e.g. Paduan Italian) raise out of IP, and that English children initially mis-set this parameter to the 'do not raise' setting.

This creates a problem when the child uses the abbreviated *-n't* form of the negation marker cliticized onto the auxiliary at I (e.g. *doesn't*). In the adult grammar, both the auxiliary and the negation marker are moved to C, as per the normal process of subject–auxiliary inversion (e.g. *What doesn't she like?*). In the child grammar, the auxiliary is moved but the negation marker (because of the mis-set parameter) remains at I (e.g. *What does she n't like?*). Since the *n't* marker requires a host, the child spells out the trace of the moved auxiliary, to give an AUX . . . AUX+NEG error (e.g. *What does she doesn't like?*). Non-inversion occurs when the child chooses to keep the negation marker within IP not by moving the auxiliary and stranding the *n't* marker, but by keeping the whole AUX+NEG form within IP (e.g. *What she doesn't like?*). The simple prediction of this theory is that AUX . . . AUX+NEG and non-inversion errors will be essentially the only types of error produced for negative questions. In an elicited production study with children aged 4–5, Guasti *et al.* (1995) found that 60 per cent of all negative questions involved one of these two errors. Whilst this finding is generally taken as support for Guasti *et al.*'s (1995) theory, it is worth noting that, of the ten children who produced such errors, six produced adultlike questions as well; a finding somewhat at odds with the notion that the errors reflect a mis-set parameter. Similarly, the finding that 8 per cent of questions constituted either AUX+NEG . . . AUX+NEG or AUX+NEG errors (the type that are predicted not to occur) can be taken as evidence either for or against the theory, depending on whether or not this rate is considered sufficiently low as to constitute noise.

7.1.2.2 Acquisition of questions: constructivist approaches
Under constructivist accounts, questions are not formed by movement. Rather, questions are independent constructions and undergo the same acquisition process as any other: children begin with rote-learned holophrases (e.g. *What is he doing?*; *What is he eating?*) and gradually schematize across these to form low-level lexically specific slot-and-frame patterns (e.g. *What is [THING] [PROCESS]?*). Finally, children analogize across these schemas (or instances of these schemas in the form of actual utterances) to yield fully abstract constructions (e.g. *Wh-word AUX SUBJECT VERB?*).

The prediction of this account is that children will show effects of lexical-specificity: they will show good performance with questions that can be formed using a well-learned schema, but poor performance for questions where a ready-made schema is unavailable and a more creative strategy is acquired. To test this prediction, it is, of course necessary to specify in advance the schemas with which children are assumed to be operating. Rowland and Pine (2000: 164) argue that 'the child's lexically specific knowledge is likely to centre round wh-word+auxiliary[5] combinations, rather than auxiliary+subject combinations'. This is because the range of *wh*-words and auxiliaries is relatively narrow (perhaps especially in speech to young children), whereas the range of subjects is potentially infinite.

Rowland and Pine (2000) investigated rates of correct *wh*-question production and non-inversion errors (e.g. **What she is eating?*) in the naturalistic data of a single child aged between 2;3 and 4;10. Whilst many question types (e.g. *What are . . .*; *What do*) were associated with 100 per cent correct production, a number of others (e.g. *Why is . . .*; *How can . . .*; *What's . . .*) were produced only in the incorrect non-inverted form (e.g. **Why he is going to the shops? *What he's eating?*). These errors are analysed as 'groping patterns' where, in the absence of a suitable frame, children follow a strategy such as adding a *wh*-word to a declarative form (e.g. *Why + he is going to the shops?*). Furthermore, the *wh*-word+auxiliary combinations that occurred in correctly formed questions were shown to be significantly more frequent in the child's input than the *wh*-word+auxiliary combinations with which the child made errors. This finding in particular provides support for the constructivist view that children learn schemas based around particular *wh*-word+auxiliary combinations (e.g. *What is [THING] [PROCESS]?*) from the input.

Similar results were obtained in an elicited production study in which children (aged 3;6–4;6) produced questions using each combination of four wh-words (*what, who, how* and *why*) and three auxiliaries (BE, DO and CAN) in 3sg and 3pl form (Ambridge, Rowland, Theakston and Tomasello, 2006). Non-inversion errors (e.g. **What Mickey is eating?*) did not pattern either by *wh*-word or by auxiliary type alone (i.e. no main effect of either was observed). Rather, a three-way interaction of *wh*-word by auxiliary by number was revealed, indicating that error rates differed according to the particular *wh*-word+lexical auxiliary combination required.

Further studies have attempted to investigate in more detail the particular lexical frames that, under this approach, children use to produce correct questions and errors. Dąbrowska and Lieven (2005) applied the trace-back procedure discussed in Section 6.2 of the previous chapter to a corpus of questions produced by two children. Even for the more productive of the two children, at age 2, 66 per cent of questions could be derived from previous utterances or schemas by just one operation (91 per cent with multiple operations, though this drops to 75 per cent when only the child's questions – as opposed to the child's and the mother's – were used as the source corpus). However, as we concluded with reference to the trace-back studies in Chapter 6, since adult speech is also rather lexically restricted, future studies should investigate whether children are indeed less productive than adults after controlling for vocabulary, corpus size and so on. Nevertheless, in support of this approach, a further corpus analysis based on data from ten children aged 2–5 (Rowland, 2007) found that questions that could have been produced by a single operation (e.g. the superimposition of a filler into a schema *What does THING PROCESS?*) were associated with a lower error rate than questions for which no such schema was attested.

Rowland (2007) and Ambridge and Rowland (2009) investigated whether the use of operations on schemas could also give rise to errors. For example, an error such as *Why does he doesn't like peas?* could have been produced by super-imposing an inappropriate filler (e.g. *He doesn't like peas*) into a schema (e.g. *Why does THING PROCESS?*). As findings from a naturalistic data analysis (Rowland, 2007) were inconclusive, Ambridge and Rowland (2009) conducted a study in which positive and negative *what, why* and *yes/no* questions were elicited from children aged 3;3–4;3 ($M = 3;10$). Schemas were attributed to children on the basis of their performance with positive questions. For example, a child who produced *What does she like?* was credited with having a *What does THING PROCESS?* schema, whereas a child who produced an error (e.g. *What she does like?*) was not. The prediction was that children who possessed a question frame such as *What does THING PROCESS?* would sometimes produce AUX ... AUX+NEG doubling errors for the corresponding negative question (e.g. *What does she doesn't want?*) by incorrectly superimposing a declarative chunk (here, *she doesn't want*).[6] Children who showed no evidence of possessing the relevant question frame (on the basis of their positive question performance) were predicted not to make this error.

Consistent with this prediction, of the 69 AUX ... AUX+NEG errors produced in the study overall, only two were produced by a (single) child who did not show evidence of having acquired the relative positive question frame. Furthermore, the question types that showed the highest rates of

AUX . . . AUX+NEG errors were those for which the frequency of the relevant schema (e.g. *What does THING PROCESS?*; 402 occurrences in a representative input corpus) and declarative chunk (e.g. *she does*; 37 occurrences) were high relative to the frequency of a more-useful negative schema (e.g. *What doesn't THING PROCESS;* 1 occurrence). Conversely, the error **Why can she can't . . .* was rarely observed, presumably because the negative schema (*Why can't THING PROCESS?*; 48 occurrences) is more frequent than the positive schema that would give rise to the error (*Why can THING PROCESS?*; unattested).

Ambridge and Rowland (2009) also found that the question types that showed the highest error rates (and lowest rates of correct performance) were the least frequent in a representative corpus of child-directed speech. Nevertheless, children do appear to show some difficulty with negative questions, beyond that which is attributable to their (generally) low frequency. This suggests that learning of high-frequency frames cannot be the whole story, and that negative questions are problematic for an additional reason (perhaps cognitive complexity).

However, a recent study of *yes/no* (as opposed to *wh-*) questions provides further support for the claim that children's earliest questions are strings that are learned directly from the input. Estigarribia (2010) analysed the productions and input of five English-speaking children aged 1;3–5;1. In fact, caregivers produce not only full inverted questions (e.g. *Are you coming?*), but also truncated questions consisting simply of a verb (e.g. *Coming?*) or a subject+verb combination (e.g. *You coming?*). Using break-point analysis, Estigarribia (2010) showed that, as development proceeds, children's questions follow a process of right-to-left elaboration (e.g. *Coming?* → *You coming?* → *Are you coming?*) with shorter, simpler strings scaffolding the production of full questions.

7.1.2.3 Acquisition of questions: conclusion   The constructivist studies discussed above appear to provide good evidence that children's earliest questions – both correctly formed questions and errors – are produced using low-level lexically specific construction schemas. Since errors appear to pattern by *wh-*word+lexical-auxiliary combination, as opposed to by *wh-*word or by auxiliary, it is difficult to see how generativist accounts that do not include some role for lexical learning of individual construction schemas could account for the data. The obvious solution for generativist accounts is to posit some role for lexical learning. One approach would be simply to posit that, in addition to generating questions using the UG-specified movement rules, children acquire some holophrases (e.g. *What's that?*) and lexically specific construction schemas (e.g. *What is he VERBing?*) that can be used as 'short-cuts' to question production (indeed, few generativist theories would deny rote learning of 'formulaic' questions such as *How are you?* e.g. Radford, 1996). However, such a compromise position would be distinguishable from the constructivist approach only if it is possible to specify the circumstances in which such short cuts will be used (e.g. in situations of cognitive overload, or for very high-frequency questions). An alternative approach may be for generativist theories to build in the assumption that, whilst movement is specified as part of UG, children initially believe that it is optional for all questions. Children have to learn that it is obligatory for all non-subject questions on a question-type by question-type basis (where question-type is defined in terms of the *wh*-word and lexical auxiliary, and possibly even the subject).

For constructivist accounts, the challenge (as for simpler constructions) is to explain precisely how children move from lexically specific construction schemas to a fully abstract *wh*-question construction. This will involve specifying not only the processes by which this occurs, but also the precise nature of the early schemas themselves. In their current form, constructivist accounts of question acquisition are open to the charge that they can be manipulated to fit the data post hoc, simply by assuming whatever criterion for a schema seems to best fit the observed pattern of data. One way to address this criticism may be to use computer models to extract schemas from spontaneous production data on the basis of factors such as the interaction between type and token frequency, without any prior specification of the size or composition of schemas (e.g. Bannard, Lieven and Tomasello, 2009; Solan, Horn, Ruppin and Edelman, 2005).

7.2 Multiple-clause sentences

Thus far, we have been concerned with children's acquisition of **simple** sentences such as *The boy ate the cake* (previous chapter) and related forms such as passives and questions. These sentences are termed 'simple' not because they are 'easy' but because they contain one clause that expresses a single proposition (idea). **Complex** (or **multiple-clause**) sentences contain two or more propositions and so require two or more clauses; one for each proposition. In this section, we investigate children's acquisition of two types of multiple-clause sentence:

(a) **Sentence containing a relative clause**
    [The boy [who John saw] ate the cake]
(b) **Sentence containing a sentential complement clause**
    [John knew [that the boy ate the cake]]

Both of these sentences contain two propositions (two ideas). The first contains the propositions (1) 'the boy ate the cake' (**main clause**) and (2) 'John saw the boy' (**relative clause**) The second contains the propositions (1) 'John knew X' (main clause) and (2) 'the boy ate the cake' (**sentential complement clause**). Relative and complement clauses are both types of **subordinate** clause. There is no limit, in principle, to the number of propositions that a sentence can contain,

Summary table 7.2 *Acquisition of questions* (☑ = *supports theory*; ☒ = *counts against theory*)

	Generativist approach (e.g. Stromswold, 1990; Santelmann et al., 2002)	Constructivist approach (e.g. Rowland and Pine, 2000; Ambridge and Rowland, 2009)
Summary of theory	Syntactic machinery required to form questions is available as part of UG; errors due to specific problems with adjunct wh-words/copula BE/auxiliary DO/negation.	Children move from holophrases (e.g. *What is he doing?*) via lexical frames (e.g. *What is [THING] [PROCESS]?*) to an adultlike abstract construction (e.g. *Wh-word AUX SUBJECT VERB?*), learning from input.
Issue/phenomenon		
Do children have particular difficulties with adjunct wh-words (e.g. *how, why*)?	Claim (Stromswold, 1990; de Villiers, 1991) supported by naturalistic data studies for ☑ *why* (Labov and Labov, 1978; Kuczaj and Brannick, 1979; Rowland and Pine, 2000) though ☒ mostly for negative questions and ☒ not *how*. ☒ Good performance for both in experimental study (Ambridge, Rowland, Theakston and Tomasello, 2006)	☑ Correctly predicts children's good performance with (high-freq.) positive *why/how* questions but ☒ doesn't explain problems with some frequent negative *why* questions.
Do children have particular difficulties with Aux DO?	☑ Claim supported by some naturalistic studies (Stromswold, 1990; Hattori, 2003; Rowland and Pine, 2000) and arguably (see below) one experimental study (Santelmann et al., 2002), but ☒ mainly due to problems with negative questions (Ambridge and Rowland, 2009)	☑ Problems with DO not across the board, but for some particular question types (Ambridge, Rowland, Theakston and Tomasello, 2006; Rowland, 2007; Ambridge and Rowland, 2009) but ☒ Doesn't explain problems with some frequent negative *why* questions.

Do children have particular difficulties with copula BE?	☑ Arguably supported by Santelmann *et al.* (2002), though problem with statistical analysis.	☑ Problems with copula BE not across the board, but for some particular question types (Ambridge, Rowland, Theakston and Tomasello, 2006).
Do children have particular difficulties with negative questions?	☑ Claim supported by one experimental study (Guasti *et al.*, 1995) but ☒ see right-hand column.	☑ Problems not across the board, but for some particular negative questions, but ☒ still more errors than would expected purely on the basis of frequency (Ambridge and Rowland, 2009).
Do questions associated with frequent frames show low error rates / high rates of correct use?	☒ No explanation for these findings, other than to acknowledge that certain questions are rote-learned (e.g. Radford, 1996).	☑ Prediction supported by naturalistic (Rowland, 2007; Dąbrowska and Lieven, 2005) and experimental (Ambridge and Rowland, 2009) studies
Do some errors appear to reflect schema combination?		☑ Prediction supported by Rowland (2007) and Ambridge and Rowland (2009)
Are individual question strings learned directly from the input?		☑ Prediction supported by naturalistic data study of *yes/no* questions (Estigarribia, 2010).

as long as each is expressed by a clause. For example, the sentence *Claire said that John knew that the boy who was hungry ate the cake* contains four propositions, and hence four clauses (two sentential complement clauses and one relative clause). Although such sentences are rare (particularly in spoken as opposed to written language), accounts of acquisition must explain how learners are (eventually) able to produce and comprehend them.

7.2.1   Acquisition of relative clauses

A **relative clause** (e.g. *who John saw*) gives some information about the NP (or DP) that **it relates** (i.e. refers back) to (e.g. *The boy*), known as the **antecedent**. Under a generativist analysis, both subject and object relative clauses (see Figure 7.4) are CPs, and are generated by *wh*-movement to SPEC CP (exactly as occurs for *wh*-questions; see Figure 7.3). Note that English allows the relative pronoun (e.g. *who*) to be null for object relatives.

Most research conducted in English (and related languages) has focused on the four types of relative clause shown below[7] (examples adapted from Sheldon, 1974).

Centre-embedded relative clauses
(1) **SS:**   [The dog$_i$ [CP that$_i$ t_i jumps over the pig]] bumps into the lion
(2) **SO:**   [The dog$_i$ [CP that$_i$ the pig jumps over t_i]] bumps into the lion

Right-branching relative clauses
(3) **OS:**   The lion bumps into [the dog$_i$ [CP that$_i$ t_i jumps over the pig]]
(4) **OO:**   The lion bumps into [the dog$_i$ [CP that$_i$ the pig jumps over t_i]]

The four sentence types are known as SS, SO, OS and OO. The first letter of each label identifies whether the antecedent (the NP that is modified by

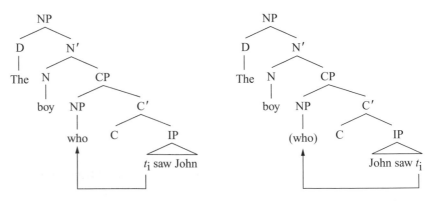

Figure 7.4 *Wh*-movement in subject (left) and object (right) relative clauses

Table 7.1 *Summary of findings from early studies of relative-clause comprehension with children aged 3–5. The greater than (>) sign indicates a higher rate of successful enactments (adapted from Kidd and Bavin, 2002: 601)*

Study	Finding
Sheldon (1974)	SS, OO > SO, OS
Smith (1974)	OS > SS > OO > SO
de Villiers, Flusberg, Hakuta and Cohen (1979)	OS, SS > OO > SO
Tavakolian (1981)	SS > OO, SO > OS
Corrêa (1982, 1995)	OS > SS > OO > SO

the relative clause) is the **subject or *object of the main clause*** (i.e. of the verb *bump*). The second letter identifies whether the antecedent is the **subject or object *of the relative clause*** (i.e. whether it is a subject relative or object relative as defined in Figure 7.4). As for *wh*-questions, generativist accounts assume that relative clauses are generated by movement, whilst constructivist accounts assume that they are directly generated in their surface form. Both types of account require children to have some understanding of **recursion** (i.e. that relative clauses can be embedded within a main cause).

7.2.1.1 Relative clauses: generativist accounts Since all types of relative clause require knowledge of movement and recursion, both of which are argued to be present as part of UG, generativist accounts would seem to predict that, in principle, children should be equally adept at understanding or producing all types. In fact, early comprehension studies revealed that children have considerably more difficulty with some types of relative clause than others. In a typical comprehension study, children are asked to act out sentences such as (1)–(4) using animal toys. For (1), for example, the correct response is to make the dog jump over the pig and then bump into the lion. As shown in Table 7.1, early comprehension studies generally revealed inconsistent results, as well as relatively low levels of correct performance (though a criticism that we will encounter later is that these are actually rather far removed from the types of relative-clause sentences that children typically encounter).

Consequently, many early generativist accounts assumed that children lack knowledge of either *wh*-movement (e.g. Labelle, 1990) or recursion (e.g. Sheldon, 1974; Tavakolian, 1981). Under Sheldon's (1974) **parallel process-ing hypothesis** children assume, for SX sentences, that the subject of the main clause is additionally the subject of the relative clause, leading to better perfor-mance for SS sentences (where this happens to be the case) than for SO sen-tences (where it does not). Similarly, for OX sentences, children assume that the object of the main clause is additionally the object of the relative clause, leading to better performance on OO than OS sentences. This pattern was observed in Sheldon's (1974) study. Under Tavakolian's (1981) **conjoined-clause hypothesis,** because children do not understand the grammar of relative clauses, they treat the relative clause as a conjoined clause; in effect treating *that* as if it were *and*. This accounts for Tavakolian's findings that children performed particularly badly with OS sentences:

> The lion bumps into the dog **that** jumps over the pig (= dog jumps).

misinterpreted as:

> The lion bumps into the dog **and** jumps over the pig (= lion jumps).

Hamburger and Crain (1982) (see also Corrêa, 1995; Crain, McKee and Emiliani, 1990) argued that the act-out paradigm used in these previous studies underestimates children's competence. The only situation in which it would make sense for a speaker to produce a sentence such as *The lion bumps into the dog that jumps over the pig* (as opposed to simply *The lion bumps into the dog*) is when there are two dogs present, only one of whom had jumped over a pig. It would then make sense for this speaker to use the relative clause construction to pick out *which* of the two dogs present the lion should bump into. In the studies summarized in Table 7.1, however, this was not the case (i.e., only one of each animal was present). Corrêa (1982, 1995) modified the procedure such that children (aged 3, 4 and 5) learning English and Brazilian Portuguese (the languages are structurally similar in relevant respects)[8] first heard two simple sentences such as *A dog jumps over a pig. Another dog pushes a cow* before being asked to enact the relevant sentence (e.g. *The lion bumps into the dog that jumped over the pig*). Studies using this modified paradigm have produced not only higher overall levels of correct performance, but – in general – consistent findings with regard to the relative difficulty of the four sentence types (OS > SS > OO > SO, see Table 7.1). Indeed, Corrêa (1982, 1995) observed this pattern across all age groups and both languages, as well as increasing correct performance with age.

Although children approach adultlike performance at around age 5, the finding that younger children struggle with certain sentence types (despite the fact that they generally have little difficulty with *wh*-movement in questions) is potentially problematic for generativist accounts. The solution (e.g. Goodluck and Tavakolian, 1982) is to propose that children's knowledge is essentially adultlike, but that they are subject to two specific processing difficulties. First, children have difficulty keeping in mind the NP that the relative clause will later modify (always *the dog* in (1)–(4) so that it is available to fill the 'gap' that appears in the relative clause (e.g. Wanner and Maratsos', 1978, **filler–gap hypothesis**). This gap appears later in SO and OO sentences (*The dog* *[that the pig jumps over_]*) than SS and OS sentences (*That dog [that_jumps over the pig*); hence children show worse performance on the former than the latter.

Second, children have difficulty keeping in mind a complex NP that appears at the start of an SS or SO sentence (*The dog that jumps over the pig . . . /The dog that the pig jumps over . . .*) until it can be analysed as the subject of the main verb (*. . . bumps into the lion*) (e.g. Slobin's, 1973, **non-interruption principle**). Complex NPs that appear at the end of an OS or OO sentence (e.g. after *The lion bumps into . . .*) can be analysed as the object of the main verb (*bump*) as soon as they occur (*. . . the dog that jumps over the pig./ . . . the dog that the pig jumps over . . .*).

These two factors conspire to make OS sentences the easiest and SO the hardest to process. SS and OO sentences are both 'easy' with respect to one of the factors and 'difficult' with respect to another. This means that whether children are predicted to perform better with SS > OO sentences (e.g. Corrêa, 1995) or vice versa (e.g. Kidd and Bavin, 2002) depends on the relative weighting attributed to these two processing problems). Studies in which children are asked to produce, as opposed to act out, sentences with relative clauses (discussed in more detail below) have also found that – all other things being equal – children experience the most difficulty with SO sentences (Diessel and Tomasello, 2005; Arnon, 2010).

In conclusion, the essential claim of generativist theories is that when it is possible to 'pull apart processing effects from underlying competence, [children demonstrate] an ability in interpreting relative clauses comparable to the adult's, which may be overridden by pressure on the language processor' (Goodluck and Tavakolian, 1982: 22).

7.2.1.2 Relative clauses: constructivist accounts Constructivist approaches to relative clauses generally begin from the observation that the types of relative clause that children (and indeed adults) produce do not generally take the form of the 'textbook' examples illustrated in (1)–(4). Diessel and Tomasello (2000) analysed all the relative clauses in the speech of four English-speaking children aged between 1;9 and 5;2 (a total of 329 sentences). Approximately half (47 per cent) modified the NP in a **presentational** copula clause (e.g. *Here's a tiger that's gonna scare him*, p. 135) with a further 22 per cent modifying an isolated NP that does not form part of a complete sentence (e.g. *The girl that came with us*). Diessel and Tomasello (2000: 136) conclude that '70% of all sentences including a relative clause express a single proposition and could thus be paraphrased by a simple clause'. The same is true, though to a lesser extent, for adult speech (perhaps especially speech to children), in which around 50 per cent of utterances have this status (p. 143).

Many of the children's earliest attempts at relative-clause sentences appeared to use what Diessel and Tomasello (2000: 139) called an **amalgam construction**; an amalgam of a prefabricated slot-and-frame pattern (e.g. *That's X, There's X, It's X*) and a bare untensed VP (as opposed to a full relative clause):

'Amalgam' form	Full (adultlike) presentational relative
*That's my doggy [turn around]	That's my doggy [that turns around]
*Here's a mouse [go sleep]	Here's a mouse [that's going to sleep]
*That's the rabbit [fall off]	That's the rabbit [that fell off]

Diessel and Tomasello (2000) therefore propose a developmental account whereby children begin with amalgam constructions (e.g. *That's my doggy turn around*) before moving onto adultlike presentational relatives (e.g. *That's my doggy that turns around*). In the final stage of development, both the main and relative clause become more complex. For example, in place of presentational main clauses (e.g. *That's my doggy*), children will be able to produce full clauses in which the NP serves as (for example) the object of a transitive verb (e.g. *The cow pushed the doggy*). The relative clause too will become more complex, with the 'moved' NP serving not only as subject of an intransitive verb (e.g. *that turns around*) but as (for example) the object of a transitive verb (e.g. *that the bear hit*). By this process, children gradually move towards the 'textbook' examples discussed above (e.g. *The cow pushed the doggy that the bear hit*).

A shortcoming of this account is that does not provide an explanation of precisely how children move from the simpler to the more complex clauses. Elaboration of the main clause (e.g. *That's my doggy* → *The cow pushed the doggy*) will presumably occur as a simple consequence of the acquisition of basic word order (see previous chapter). However, it is more difficult to see how (for example) a relative clause in which the relativized NP is an intransitive subject (e.g. *that turns around*) can 'turn into' a relative clause in which the NP is a transitive object (e.g. *that the bear hit_*).

Diessel and Tomasello (2005) conducted a study in which English- and German-speaking[9] children aged 4;3–4;9 ($M = 4;7$) were asked to repeat relative-clause sentences similar to those common in early speech (e.g. *There's the boy who played in the garden yesterday*). The only 'textbook' type sentences were of the form OS; generally found to be the easiest for young children to process (e.g. *Peter saw the woman who sat on the bench this morning*). Children showed the best performance on presentational constructions where the relative clause modified the subject (e.g. *There's the boy who played in the garden yesterday*) and, indeed, often modified other sentence types to fit this pattern (e.g. *This is the girl who the boy teased* → *This is the girl who teased the boy*).Whilst these findings are certainly compatible with Diessel and Tomasello's (2000) constructivist approach, they do not constitute strong evidence against generativist accounts. That is, they are consistent with the view that even young children have adultlike syntactic competence but can demonstrate this competence only when task demands are minimized (e.g. by the use of presentational relatives, or sentences with short filler-gap dependencies).

Somewhat more problematic for generativist accounts are studies showing that children perform best with the types of relative clause that they hear most often, even if they would be expected to be more complex in processing terms. The studies reviewed above suggest that, all other things being equal, children have more difficulty processing sentences where the relative clause modifies the object (e.g. *This is the dog that the cat chased*) than the subject (e.g. *This is the dog that chased the cat*) of the main clause. In naturally occurring speech, however, all other things are not equal. In most sentences with object relatives (e.g. *The car that she borrowed had a flat tyre*) the main-clause object (*the car*) is inanimate, whilst the relative-clause subject (*she*) is most often animate, 'discourse-old' (i.e. it has been mentioned previously) and expressed with a pronoun. This is true in both adults' (Fox and Thompson, 1990) and children's speech. For example, Kidd, Brandt, Lieven and Tomasello (2007) found that 75 per cent of children's object relatives had inanimate main-clause objects, with the pronouns *I*, *we* and *you* accounting for 87 per cent of relative-clause subjects.

In an elicited imitation study, based on that of Diessel and Tomasello (2005) (with children aged 3;1–3;9; $M = 3;5$ and 4;3–4;9; $M = 4;5$), Kidd *et al.* (2007) found that the previously reported subject/object asymmetry disappeared when the object relatives elicited respected these distributions. In fact, object relative clauses with inanimate main-clause objects and pronouns as relative-clause subjects (e.g. *There is the book that you read in the front room last night*) were associated with higher levels of correct performance than many subject relatives (e.g. *Here is the plant that grew in the garden last summer*). This finding holds across English, German and Hebrew, and across repetition and act-out tasks (Kidd *et al.*, 2007; Brandt, Kidd, Lieven and Tomasello, 2009; Arnon, 2010).

7.2.1.3 Relative clauses: conclusion   This section has investigated how children come to have the ability to comprehend and produce sentences with relative clauses. The generativist answer is essentially that children have the necessary syntactic competence from birth, as it is specified as part of Universal Grammar. However, various processing limitations, such as the ability to keep a filler in memory until a gap is encountered, prevent children from displaying this ability until around age 5. The constructivist answer is essentially that children acquire relative-clause constructions on the basis of the input, moving from simple amalgams (**That's my doggy turn around*) via presentational relatives (e.g. *That's my doggy that turns around*) to full relative clauses (e.g. *The cow pushed the doggy that the bear hit*).

None of the major findings discussed in this chapter provide conclusive support for one view over the other. The finding that children have difficulty with sentences that violate the non-interruption principle and/or have long-range filler-gap dependencies would be expected regardless of the linguistic framework assumed. The finding that children are best at producing and comprehending the relative-clause sentence types that they hear most often seems to constitute support for the constructivist claim that children learn lexically specific slot-and-frame patterns for complex constructions (e.g. *There's the [THING] that you [VERB]ed*), just as they are held to do for simpler constructions (e.g. *There's a [THING]*). However, it would also be possible to argue that children do have adultlike competence (as claimed under the generativist account), and that processing limitations are reduced for sentences that are similar to those that have been parsed many times before. One way to attempt to mediate between the two approaches may be to investigate whether children show better production of relative clause sentences that are frequent in terms of the actual combinations of lexical items that they contain (e.g. *There's the X that you VERBed*) – which would provide more direct evidence for lexically based frames. A profitable approach, for both sides, may be to use computer models that are trained on real child-directed speech and subject to memory/processing limitations to generate predictions regarding children's performance on individual sentence types at a fine-grained (i.e. lexical) level.

7.2.2   *Relative clauses in* yes/no *questions (structure dependence)*

So far in this chapter, we have discussed children's acquisition of *yes/no* questions (e.g. *Is the boy crazy?*) and relative clauses (e.g. *The boy [who is smoking] is crazy*). This section is concerned with *yes/no* questions that include a relative clause (e.g. *Is the boy who is smoking crazy?*). Despite (or, rather, because of) the rarity of this structure, children's apparent success with *yes/no* questions with a relative clause is often taken as the single best argument in favour of generativist approaches to language acquisition, for reasons discussed below.

7.2.2.1 Relative clauses in yes/no *questions (structure dependence): generativist accounts*   Recall from Section 7.1.2 that, under generativist accounts, questions are formed by moving the auxiliary from I to C ('subject–auxiliary inversion'):

The boy is crazy → Is the boy crazy?

On the basis of hearing such utterances, the child could in principle formulate a rule such as 'move the first auxiliary to sentence-initial position'. However, this rule would generate ungrammatical utterances when there is more than one auxiliary in the sentence (i.e. when the child is attempting to generate **complex questions**: questions with more than one clause):[10]

The boy who is smoking is crazy? → *Is the boy who smoking is crazy?

The adult rule, which the child must somehow acquire, is 'move the auxiliary *in the main clause* to sentence-initial position'. This rule is **structure dependent** because it is expressed in terms of the syntactic *structure* of the sentence ('move *the auxiliary in the main clause*') as opposed to linear order ('move the *first* auxiliary').

How could children learn that the structure-dependent rule is the correct one? The obvious answer is that they learn from the input. However, according to Chomsky (1980: 114–15) 'a person might go through much or all of his life without ever having been exposed to relevant evidence' (presumably 'relevant evidence' means complex questions, or even complex declarative/question pairs). Chomsky (1980: 145) famously went on to argue that children 'nevertheless unerringly employ the structure-dependent generalization on the first relevant occasion' because they are innately constrained to consider only structure-dependent rules – and not rules based on linear order – when formulating the grammar (i.e. children have the innate principle of 'structure dependence'). Thus when hearing a declarative/question pair such as *The boy is crazy/Is the boy crazy?*, children will never entertain a rule based on linear order ('move the first auxiliary'), but will hypothesize the correct structure-dependent rule ('move the auxiliary in the main clause').

Chomsky's (1980) two empirical claims (a) that children almost never hear complex questions and (b) that children never produce 'structure-dependence errors' (e.g. *Is the boy who smoking is crazy?*) both seem to be well supported. Whilst some authors (e.g. Pullum and Scholz, 2002) have identified complex questions in adult corpora, the entire corpus of child-directed speech in the CHILDES database (some 3 million utterances) contains just one example (MacWhinney, 2004). Naturalistic data are uninformative with regard to the question of whether children ever make structure-dependence errors as none of the children in the CHILDES database makes a single apparent attempt at a complex question (MacWhinney, 2004). Crain and Nakayama (1987) used an elicited production paradigm to elicit a range of complex *yes/no* questions with two instances of copula/auxiliary BE (experiment 1), or with one instance of copula *is* and one modal auxiliary (experiment 2), from thirty children aged 3;2–4;7 ($M = 4;3$). Although overall rates of correct performance were low (60 per cent and 21 per cent in experiments 1 and 2 respectively), no structure-dependence errors were observed. Perhaps surprisingly given that no negative questions were elicited, auxiliary-doubling errors (e.g. *Is the boy who is smoking is crazy?*) were relatively common (these can be analysed either as 'copying without deletion', or as reflecting a processing error whereby the long NP causes children to 'forget' that they have already produced copula *is* at the beginning of the sentence).

In summary, then, Chomsky (1980) appears to be correct in claiming that children (almost) never (a) hear 'relevant evidence' (if this is taken to constitute complex questions) or (b) produce structure-dependence errors. Most generativist researchers would therefore concur with Crain (1991) that structure dependence is the 'parade case' of an innate constraint.

7.2.2.2 *Relative clauses in* yes/no *questions (structure dependence): constructivist accounts*   In a larger modified replication of the study of Crain and Nakayama (1987), Ambridge, Rowland and Pine (2008) found that children aged 6;3–7;9 (experiment 1) and 4;7–5;7 (experiment 2) did, in fact, occasionally produce structure-dependence errors (e.g. *Can the boy who run fast can jump high?*) Although such errors were never produced at high rates (e.g. children in experiment 1 produced 16 errors; a rate of 8 per cent), over a quarter of the children made at least one such error. One possible reason for the discrepancy between the two studies is that this latter study used questions with two instances of the modal auxiliary CAN, which may have been more confusing for children.

Whilst these errors obviously count as evidence against Chomsky's (1980) famous claim that they never occur, from a constructivist viewpoint, the question of whether children might 'move' the wrong auxiliary simply does not arise. This is because, on this view, questions are not formed by movement at all. Rather, both simple and complex *yes/no* questions are constructed using a constructional template such as [AUX] [NP] [ADJECTIVE] (e.g. *[Is][the boy][crazy]?*; *[Is] [the boy who is smoking] [crazy]?*) or [AUX] [NP] [VERB] (e.g. *[Is][the boy][singing]?*; *[Is] [the boy who is smoking] [singing]?*). Of course, this proposal itself is not a solution, as it is still necessary to explain how children know that simple NPs (e.g. *the boy*) and complex NPs (e.g. *the boy who is smoking*) are structurally equivalent (i.e. they are both NPs). Accounts of how this might be done have been proposed by (amongst others) Tomasello (2003), MacWhinney (2004) and Ambridge, Rowland and Pine (2008). Essentially, children learn from their input both the structure of complex NPs (e.g. *the boy who is smoking*) and the fact that simple and complex NPs share the same distributional properties (i.e. they can be substituted for one another in utterance pairs such as *The boy is crazy* and *The boy who is smoking is crazy*). The fact that simple and complex NPs will often denote the same referent (as in this example) is also assumed to help children 'notice' their distributional similarity. In most cases, the complex NP (e.g. *The boy who is smoking*) will refer to an entity that is already discourse-old (i.e. under discussion), meaning that it would be odd if children did not treat it as a single unit that cannot be broken up (as a structure-dependence error would require).

Importantly, all this can, in principle, be acquired on the basis of exposure to declarative sentences with and without complex NPs. Once the child has acquired a simple *yes/no* question construction such as [AUX] [NP] [ADJ/VERB]? – on the basis of hearing simple questions such as *Is the boy crazy?* – she can form a complex question by substituting a complex NP (e.g. *the boy who is smoking*) into the NP slot. This account reconceptualizes Chomsky's (1980) notion of 'relevant evidence': children do not need to (and, indeed, probably do not) hear *any* complex *yes/no* questions (e.g. **Is the boy who is smoking crazy?*) to acquire this structure. Rather, the construction can be built up on the basis of exposure to more basic (and more common) utterances.

The only experimental evidence for this account, however, is indirect, consisting of two computer modelling studies. Lewis and Elman (2001) trained a simple recurrent network model to successively predict the next word in an input sentence. The input to the model was simply a string of words: No semantic or syntactic information was present. In a training phase, the input consisted of questions containing a single auxiliary (e.g. *Is Mummy beautiful?*) and declarative statements (e.g. *Mummy is beautiful*), around 2 per cent of which contained a relative clause (e.g. *The boy who is smoking is crazy*). Importantly, no complex questions (e.g. *Is the boy who is smoking crazy?*) were presented during training. At test, the model was presented with successive words of complex questions and interrogated for its predicted next word at each pass. The model did not make predictions corresponding to structure-dependence errors. For example, after a string such as *is the boy who* . . . the model always predicted an auxiliary (e.g. *is*) more strongly than a verb (*smoking*). More importantly, the model also appeared to have acquired the correct structure of complex questions: after hearing a string such as *Is the boy who is smoking*, the model most strongly predicted an adjective (e.g. *crazy*) (or occasionally an auxiliary, as occurs in children's attested auxiliary-doubling errors; e.g. **Is the boy who is smoking is crazy?*).

A possible objection is that Lewis and Elman's (2001) model did not in fact learn the structure of complex questions at all; rather, it simply avoided errors by learning that the crucial bigrams (e.g. *who+smoking*) virtually never occur (or, at least, occur significantly less often than *who+is*). Indeed, another computer simulation (trained on real child-directed speech from the Bernstein Ratner, 1984, corpus) explicitly *does* make use of bigram information to predict correctly formed questions with a higher probability than structure-dependence errors (Reali and Christiansen, 2004). However, the type of model used by Lewis and Elman (2001) – a simple recurrent network – has been shown to be capable of predicting the correct structure of relative-clause sentences, even when it can only do so by *overriding* bigram frequency information (Elman, 1990, 1993). For example, when presented with the string *boys who chase (the) girl* . . . , the model correctly predicts *walk* – agreeing with the plural *NP boys who chase the girl* – with a higher probability than *walks* – agreeing with girl. This occurs despite the fact that (as one would expect) the bigram *girl+walk* is less frequent in the corpus than *girl+walks*. It is important to note that this result is only obtained if the model is trained on simple sentences before complex sentences (or has a limited 'memory' to mimic this effect). Furthermore, this study used a 'toy' grammar, as opposed to real child-directed speech.

Whilst it therefore remains to be seen whether a computer simulation exposed to real child-directed speech can learn the correct structure of complex questions *in practice* (and this question should be investigated in future research), the studies reviewed above demonstrate that such learning is not impossible *in principle*. At this point, then, it is premature to conclude that the fact that children can produce complex questions without being exposed to this structure necessarily implies innate, rather than learned, knowledge of structure dependence.

7.2.2.3 Relative clauses in yes/no *questions (structure dependence): conclusion* Despite the often heated nature of the structure-dependence debate, both sides are essentially in agreement with regard to the empirical facts: children almost never hear complex *yes/no* questions and almost never produce structure-dependence errors (or, at least, produce them far less often than correctly formed questions). Where the two sides disagree is with regard to two background assumptions of the generativist position that are rarely made explicit. The first is the assumption that questions are generated by movement. Generativist researchers must accept that if one does not accept this hypothesis (as is probably the case for approximately half of the field), Chomsky's (1980) argument cannot even be formulated, let alone evaluated. The second is the assumption that the only sentences that can provide evidence with regard to the correct structure of complex *yes/no* questions are sentences that are exemplars of this construction. In fact, this seems an odd assumption for generativist acquisition theorists to make. If children know that NPs can contain other NPs nested within a CP (e.g. *[NP The boy [CP who is smoking]]*) and that *yes/no* questions have the (simplified) structure [CP[C AUX][IP [NP] [VP]]] – both of which would seem to be standard generativist assumptions – then they know the structure of complex questions 'for free'. Constructivist accounts, of course, make the opposite assumptions: questions are not generated by movement and utterances that are not complete complex *yes/no* questions can still provide evidence with regard to the form of this structure.

If the debate is to move forward, both sides must acknowledge their assumptions and seek to provide independent experimental evidence for them. Generativist researchers must provide empirical evidence (and not merely theoretical arguments) for the claim that questions are generated by movement (e.g. Roberts, Marinis, Felsen and Clahsen, 2007), and hence that Chomsky's

Summary table 7.3 *Acquisition of relative clauses* (☑ = *supports theory*; ☒ = *counts against theory*)

Issue/phenomenon	Generativist full-competence approach (e.g. Goodluck and Tavakolian, 1982)	Constructivist approach (e.g. Diessel and Tomasello, 2000)
Summary of theory	Syntactic machinery required is available as part of UG, but children are subject to processing difficulties and/or confused by pragmatically inappropriate tasks	Children move from amalgam constructions (e.g. *That's the X turn around*) via presentational relatives (e.g. *That's the X that turns around*), to full relative clauses, learning from input.
Act-out tasks (with full 'textbook' relative clauses)	☑ Children show good performance when task is pragmatically appropriate (Hamburger and Crain, 1982; Corrêa, 1982, 1995; Crain *et al.*, 1990)	☑ Improvements with age (e.g. Corrêa, 1995) consistent with lexical learning (but also decreasing processing difficulty).
Filler–gap hypothesis / non-interruption principle predict best performance for OS; worst for SO	☑ Prediction supported (Correa, 1995; Kidd and Bavin, 2002; Diessel and Tomasello, 2005; Arnon, 2010) but ☒ see right-hand column.	☑ Object relatives show good performance when children tested on relative-clause types they typically encounter (Kidd *et al.*, 2007; Brandt *et al.*, 2009; Arnon, 2010). Processing difficulties equally consistent with this account.
Do children move from presentational → amalgam → full relative clauses?	Findings in right-hand column consistent with account, particularly as these types of sentences typically have lower processing demands.	☑ Support for prediction from naturalistic (Diessel and Tomasello, 2000) and experimental study (Diessel and Tomasello, 2005).
Is there evidence of input-based learning?	Not explicitly predicted by the account, but could argue that frequent sentence types are associated with lower processing demands.	☑ Experimental studies (Kidd *et al.*, 2007; Brandt *et al.*, 2009; Arnon, 2010) show best performance for sentence types that are frequent in the input (e.g. Fox and Thompson, 1990).

(cont.)

Summary table 7.3 (*cont.*)

Summary of theory / Issue/phenomenon	Relative clauses in *yes/no* questions (structure dependence)	
	Generativist approach (Chomsky, 1980)	Constructivist approach (Tomasello, 2003; Ambridge, Rowland and Pine, 2008)
	Principle of structure dependence is innately specified.	Children learn from the input that simple and complex NPs are distributionally similar.
Are complex questions available in the input?	☑ Not in child-directed speech (MacWhinney, 2004), though in some adult corpora (Pullum and Scholz, 2002)	No requirement for complex questions to be present in input.
Do children make structure-dependence errors?	☑ No (Crain and Nakayama, 1987). ☒ Yes (Ambridge, Rowland and Pine, 2008).	Irrelevant, as questions (whether or not 'SD errors') not assumed to be formed by movement rules.
Could children avoid SD errors without knowledge of structure dependence?	Implicit assumption is that they could not (Chomsky, 1980; Crain and Nakayama, 1987)	☑ Yes, in principle, using bigram statistics (Reali and Christiansen, 2004)
Could children learn structure of complex questions from input?	Remains to be seen (for computer model and children) if this is possible in practice.	☑ Yes, in principle (Lewis and Elman, 2001)

(1980) structure-dependence argument is relevant to acquisition. Constructivist researchers must provide empirical evidence (and not merely theoretical arguments) that children can learn the structure of complex *yes/no* questions on the basis of hearing simple *yes/no* questions and declaratives with and without a relative clause. One way to test this latter claim would be to see if it is possible to teach children to produce complex *yes/no* questions (perhaps at a younger age than has been done previously) by exposing them to these hypothesized 'source' constructions (as Tomasello *et al.*, 1998, did for passives), with control groups exposed to (a) full complex *yes/no* questions and (b) no relevant structures.

7.2.3   Acquisition of sentential complement clauses

Before proceeding, it will be helpful to understand why **sentential complement clauses**[11] (sometimes abbreviated to 'complement clauses') are so called. As we saw in Chapter 2, a complement is an obligatory argument of a verb. For example, the verb *know* must have a complement (e.g. *the answer* in *John knew the answer*), otherwise the sentence is ungrammatical (e.g. **John knew*). In simple sentences, this complement is a direct object Noun Phrase (e.g. *the answer*). Under traditional linguistic analyses, sentences such as *John knew that they boy ate the cake* have the same structure as their simpler equivalents, except that the complement is not a simple Noun Phrase (e.g. *the answer*) but a complete sentence (*the boy ate the cake*). So, a sentential complement clause is a complement that is a complete clause (or 'sentence'). Sometimes the complement clause will be introduced by a **complementizer** such as *that* (e.g. *John knew <u>that</u> the boy ate the cake*) but in English this is not obligatory (*John knew the boy ate the cake*).

> *7.2.3.1 Acquisition   of   sentential   complements: generativist approaches*   Young children do not, of course, produce sentences with sentential complements. The question for generativist and constructivist approaches alike, then, is how children come to have this ability. As far as generativist approaches are concerned, there are essentially two possible answers. The first is that children initially lack the functional category COMP (and its projection CP) that, under generativist approaches, is required for the formation of such sentences. The second is that children possess COMP (CP) all along, but do not produce utterances of this type for reasons connected with performance or processing limitations.

Radford (1996) proposed an acquisition theory based on the notion that children initially possess only lexical categories (e.g. VERB, NOUN), with functional phrases emerging later in development (first IP, then CP). At around 2;6, lexical acquisition of complementizers (e.g. *that, which*) causes the child to posit the category COMP and its projection CP. Radford (1996) argues that there is independent evidence that the acquisition of complementizers triggers the projection of CP. Around the time that complementizers first appear, children begin to produce correctly formed *wh*-questions (in which the *wh*-word and the auxiliary move to SPEC CP and C respectively). However, most modern generativist acquisition theorists reject Radford's claim that functional categories are not present from birth (see Chapter 5). The general claim is that the absence of lexical items in children's speech (here complementizers) does not necessarily reflect the absence of the necessary projection (here, CP) (e.g. Hyams, 1994; Wexler, 1998). More recent generativist research has therefore been designed to demonstrate that young children are able to both produce and comprehend utterances with sentential complement clauses.

In the main, generativist research in this area has focused not on complement clauses in declarative sentences (e.g. *Bill thought [that John ate the cake]*) but on questions where the *wh*-word is moved from either the subject (e.g. *Who$_i$ did Bill think [t$_i$ ate the cake]?*) or object position (e.g. *What$_i$ did Bill think [that John ate t$_i$]?*) of the complement clause (termed **long-distance *wh*-questions**). In an experimental elicitation study with children aged 3;0–4;8, Thornton and Crain (1994) found that 9 out of 15 children (all aged 3;8 or older) were able to produce questions of this type (e.g. *What$_i$ do you think [t$_i$ is in the box]?*). In support of the generativist movement analysis of such questions, children also made **medial *wh*-question errors** where the *wh*-word appears both at the beginning of the sentence and in its original position within the complement clause (i.e. 'in the middle' of the sentence; as in **What do you think what is in the box?*).

However, Dąbrowska, Rowland and Theakston (2009) argue that apparent medial *wh*-question errors may result simply from the juxtaposition of two independent questions (e.g. *What do you think?* and *What is in the box?*). These authors further argue that children may have succeeded in Thornton and Crain's (1994) study not because they possessed abstract knowledge of complementization, but because they were able to use a specific formula – *What do you think + X?* – learned from the input (all the long-distance questions in the study were of this type, as are the majority addressed to children). In a repetition study these authors found that changing the verb (from *think* to *hope*, *expect* or *believe*) resulted in significantly lower levels of performance for both children (aged 4;6–5;3; $M = 4;10$) and adults.[12]

Other studies have focused on children's comprehension of *wh*-questions with extraction from a sentential complement clause. For example, in a study conducted by de Villiers, Roeper and Vainikka (1990), children (aged 3;6–6;0) heard a story in which a little girl ripped her dress on a fence in the afternoon, telling her mother about it later that night. Children were then asked 'When did she say she ripped her dress?' There are two possible answers to this question. The answer 'at night' does not require analysis of the complement clause, and could be given even by a child who did not hear or understand this clause (*The little girl said XXX at night*). However, the other possible answer, 'in the afternoon', can be given only by a child who understands that the equivalent declarative sentence contains an embedded sentential complement clause specifying the time at which the dress was ripped:

> The little girl said [CP (that) she ripped her dress in the afternoon] at night.

Providing this second answer therefore constitutes evidence that the child understands the syntax of sentential complements. In fact, children gave both types of answer, which the authors take as evidence that children aged as young as 3 have this understanding. To rule out the alternative explanation that children are simply guessing which of the two possible times to give, de Villiers *et al.* (1990) included a control condition in which children were asked 'When did she say *how* she ripped her dress?' In this case, the correct answer ('at night') was given by virtually all children, even the youngest. The authors argue that because long distance *wh*-questions are rare, children cannot have learned the constraints on interpretation from hearing adults ask and answer these types of questions, and therefore that the relevant principles must be innately specified.

The claim that children understand these sentences is somewhat undermined by the fact that they often answer the 'medial' question (for example, in answer to the question 'When did she say how she ripped her dress?' many children aged 3–4 answer 'on the fence'). However, de Villiers *et al.* (1990) argue that children's understanding, whilst not adultlike, is consistent with Universal Grammar, as many languages do allow medial interpretations of *wh*-questions in this way.

Another problem for the claim that children understand the syntax of sentential complements is that when asked a question such as *What did the mother say she bought?* – where the mother bought oranges, but mistakenly said that she had bought apples – children aged 3–4 often incorrectly respond with what the mother actually bought (e.g. de Villiers and de Villiers, 1999). One could object, however, that children fail this task because they lack understanding not of syntax, but of **false belief**. In a typical false-belief test (e.g. Wimmer and Perner, 1983), a child sees a girl hide a toy in a box, with the toy then being moved to a drawer whilst the girl is absent. The child is then asked where the girl will search for her toy. If the child incorrectly answers 'the drawer' then this demonstrates a lack of false-belief understanding (i.e. the child does not understand that the girl has a false belief with respect to the location of the toy).

However, as de Villiers herself acknowledges (de Villiers and Pyers, 2002: 1039) answering a question such as *What did the mother say she bought?* does not actually require false-belief understanding. For one thing, children make the error not only with mental state verbs (e.g. *think*, *believe*) but also with verbs of communication (e.g. *say*, as in the present example). For another, children make the error even when information concerning what the mother said (or thought/believed etc.) is provided by the story: children are *told* that the mother said (or thought) that she bought apples; no computation of the mother's belief or state of mind is required.[13] Thus children's failure at such tasks cannot be dismissed as a product of a failure of false-belief understanding rather than syntax. If anything, acquisition of complementization appears to help children to succeed on false-belief tasks, not vice versa (de Villiers and Pyers, 2002; Lohmann and Tomasello, 2003).

This leaves generativist approaches without any detailed account of why, if the required syntactic structures are innately specified, children make errors when interpreting sentences with sentential complements. De Villiers and Pyers (2002: 1057) argue that 'mistakes in interpreting complementation would be seen as performance or processing errors rather than stages of incomplete grammatical representation', but provide no explanation for the cause of these errors. Few researchers would deny that performance limitations are at least part of the reason why young children do not produce utterances containing sentential complements. However, if they are to convince the field of the correctness of the view that children are innately equipped with the syntactic structures necessary for complementization, generativist researchers must endeavour to explain precisely what those limitations are, and how they yield the particular pattern of correct and incorrect interpretations observed (e.g. as Valian, 1991, attempts for subject-omission errors).

7.2.3.2 Acquisition of sentential complements: constructivist approaches Constructivist approaches to the acquisition of sentential complements generally begin from the observation that the types of utterances attested in child (and adult) speech do not appear to have the main clause/subordinate clause structure of 'textbook' examples such as *John knew that the boy ate the cake*, which contains two propositions. Rather, most utterances express a single proposition with a 'frozen phrase' added as a hedge (*I think, I bet, I guess*), attention-getter (*You know*) or clarification (*That means*). Diessel and Tomasello (2001) analysed sentential complement clauses in the speech of seven English-speaking children from the CHILDES database (aged 1;2–5;2). They found that over 75 per cent of the 2,807 utterances used one of five verbs *think*, *say*, *see*, *know* and *look*, whilst 85 per cent of utterances with *think* (and 98 per cent and 100 per cent of utterances with *bet* and *guess* respectively) had the subject *I*. Complementizers (e.g. *that*) were used with these verbs extremely rarely, particularly early in development. Nevertheless, some verbs (e.g. *tell* and *pretend*) showed greater flexibility, appearing with a range of subjects and different tense and agreement marking from early in development. In addition, children showed increased abstraction of the construction with age, with most producing some 'true' sentential complement utterances by the end of the study. Similar results were found in smaller corpus studies conducted by Limber (1973) and Bloom, Rispoli, Gartner and Hafitz (1989).

As we have seen many times elsewhere, the finding that the majority of children's utterances *could have* been produced by a small number of lexically specific formulas (e.g. *I think X*) does not necessarily preclude the presence of more abstract knowledge. Indeed, around half of all relevant adult utterances are of the form *I think X* (Thompson and Mulac, 1991). In such circumstances, it is useful to use production studies to investigate children's ability to produce sentential complement utterances that they would not ordinarily attempt of their own accord.

Kidd, Lieven and Tomasello (2006) asked children aged 2;10–4;2 and 4;3–5;9 to repeat grammatical and ungrammatical sentences containing verbs that occur with sentential complements with high (*think*, *bet*, *hope* and *see*) and low frequency (*pretend*, *say*, *know* and *hear*).[14] For example, children were asked to repeat *I think/pretend she is riding away on the horse* and **I think/pretend him running away from the dog* (all sentences had *I* as subject). Both accurate repetitions and – for ungrammatical sentences – corrections were produced significantly more often for high- than low-frequency complement-taking verbs. Indeed, on around a quarter of all trials, children substituted a high-frequency verb – most often *think* – for a lower-frequency verb (as in Dąbrowska *et al.*'s, 2009 study of questions). Similar findings were observed in a study using a priming paradigm (Kidd, Lieven and Tomasello, 2010). Again children often substituted *think* for less frequent verbs, despite the fact that this was never a 'target' verb (i.e. was never used by the experimenter).

Somewhat different findings were obtained from a similar study (Brandt, Lieven and Tomasello, in press) in which German speaking children (aged 4;0–4;2 and 5;0–5;5) were asked to produce 3sg forms of high- and low-frequency complement taking verbs (e.g. *glauben* 'believe' vs *vermuten* 'assume') in response to hearing the 1sg form (e.g. a talking dog toy says 'I believe that Emma is going to the circus' and the child reports 'He believes that Emma is going to the circus'). No overall effect of frequency was observed. Rather, children performed better on verbs that appear in a greater number of different person-marked forms (e.g. 1sg, 2sg, 3sg, pl) in a representative corpus (though this is somewhat confounded with frequency in the target 3sg form).

In some respects, these findings support the claim of Diessel and Tomasello (2001) that children's earliest sentential complement sentences are based around frequently used formulae such as *I think X*. On the other hand, the finding that children were able to substitute complement-taking verbs (Kidd *et al.*, 2006) and subjects (Brandt *et al.*, in press) for one another suggests that some abstract knowledge of the construction is present from as early as age 3–4. The finding that children generally substituted *think* for a lower-frequency verb (Kidd *et al.*, 2006, 2010) is consistent with Goldberg's (2006) claim that construction learning is easiest when one verb accounts for the majority of tokens of the construction. The finding that children produced more correct utterances with some verbs than others is more difficult (though – as we will see shortly – by no means impossible) to square with the generativist view that children have fully abstract knowledge of the syntax of complementation.

       7.2.3.3 Acquisition of sentential complements: conclusion   Despite the rhetoric produced by both sides of the generativist/constructivist debate, the empirical facts are not entirely consistent with the strong claims of either. The generativist claim that children have fully abstract knowledge of the syntax of sentential complements from the earliest age at which they can be tested is undermined by the finding that, in both comprehension and production, children (and in some cases adults) perform poorly with some verbs and/or subjects, though much better with others. On the other hand, the constructivist claim that young children's knowledge of complementization is tied to specific lexical frames (e.g. *I think X*) is undermined by the finding that even the youngest children that can be tested show some evidence of abstraction, substituting verbs and/or subjects for one another. Generativists would have to argue that performance factors prevent children from demonstrating their underlying competence and/or that children acquire some lexically based frames that can be used as 'short cuts' to production, in addition to more abstract knowledge. Constructivists would have to argue that some abstraction has already taken place before the age at which children's knowledge of complementization has so far been tested.

    These claims will be difficult to test. Researchers on the generativist side must seek to provide and test an account of the relevant performance limitations that explains why these limitations appear to affect performance differently on different tasks and with different lexical items. Researchers on the constructivist side must endeavour to investigate whether there is any evidence for a stage at which knowledge of complementization is entirely lexically specific, perhaps through methodologies suitable for use with younger children, such as preferential looking/pointing.

    Finally, it is worth noting that neither side offers a satisfactory account of how children reach the adult state. Under generativist accounts, adultlike performance will be observed when the relevant performance limitations are lifted (e.g. via age-related improvements in memory and processing). Under constructivist accounts, children reach the adult state by analogizing across stored utterances or constructions that have similar form and function (e.g. *I think that X*; *He said that X*). As even constructivist researchers working

Summary table 7.4 *Acquisition of sentential complement clauses* (☑ = *supports theory*; ☒ = *counts against theory*)

Issue/phenomenon	Generativist full-competence approach (e.g. de Villiers and Pyers, 2002)	Constructivist approach (e.g. Diessel and Tomasello, 2000)
Summary of theory	Necessary syntactic knowledge (e.g. functional category COMP) is present; Errors due to performance/processing limitations, or because children have yet to learn language-specific aspects of complementation.	Children begin with simple constructions (*I think* + *X*; *What do you think* + *X?*) built around high-frequency combinations, later analogizing across these to form more complex utterances.
Question-elicitation studies	☑ 3–4-yr-olds can produce long distance wh-questions (Thornton and Crain, 1994). ☑ Medial wh-question errors consistent with UG (though not the grammar of English).	☑ Performance improves with age (Thornton and Crain, 1994). ☑ Medial *wh*-question errors could result from juxtaposition and ☑ best performance for high-frequency question types (Dąbrowska *et al.*, 2009).
Comprehension studies	☑ Children's answers to long-distance *wh*-questions suggest knowledge of complementation (de Villiers *et al.*, 1990). ☒ Wrong answers also given, though ☑ Answering medial *wh*-question consistent with UG.	Answering wrong question does not necessarily constitute a medial *wh*-question error (see above).
Could errors in comprehension studies be due to lack of false belief understanding?	☒ Unlikely, as false-belief understanding not necessarily required (de Villiers and Pyers, 2002).	☑ Acquisition of complementation seems to aid false belief more than vice versa (de Villiers and Pyers, 2002; Lohmann and Tomasello, 2003).
Naturalistic data studies	Findings in right-hand box do not necessarily constitute evidence against the account, as same is true for adults (e.g. Thompson and Mulac, 1991) who do have abstract knowledge of complementation.	☑ Most of children's utterances use the frame *I think*+*X*) (Diessel and Tomasello, 2001; Limber, 1973; Bloom *et al.*, 1989).
Elicited imitation/priming studies	☑ Evidence that children can swap one complement taking verb for another constitutes evidence of abstract knowledge (Brandt *et al.*, in press).	☑ Children best at producing sentences with *I think*+*X*, and often alter other utterances to fit this template (Kidd *et al.*, 2006, 2010).

in this area acknowledge, currently 'the basis for analogy is far from clear' (Kidd *et al.*, 2006: 94). Rather than studying younger and younger children in an attempt to demonstrate either that children do (generativist researchers) or do not (constructivist researchers) have abstract knowledge of sentential complementization, a more productive research strategy may be to study older children and adults to investigate the developmental process by which children reach the adult state.

7.3   Movement and complex syntax: conclusion

In many ways, the key theoretical debate that emerges from this chapter is the same debate that we have already encountered in the chapters on inflectional morphology and basic syntax (Chapters 5 and 6): generativist researchers take the correct production of any sentence instantiating a particular construction type (e.g. passive, *wh*-question, relative-clause utterance) as evidence for knowledge of the construction that is fully abstract and acquired with the aid of innate principles. The possibility that such utterances could be rote-learned, or produced using a low-level formula (e.g. *What does NOUN want?*; *What do you think +X*) is rarely considered. Conversely, constructivist researchers typically focus on demonstrating that the majority of utterances could have been produced using such low-level formulas, at the expense of investigating how the more abstract knowledge that characterizes adult competence is actually acquired.

As in the domains of inflectional morphology and syntax (see Chapters 5 and 6), the existence of lexical effects is undeniable. Generativist researchers cannot afford simply to ignore such effects, but must seek to come up with an explanation that is compatible with this theoretical framework. For example, one could posit knowledge of lexical frames in addition to more abstract knowledge and/or that performance limitations are lower for utterances with familiar lexical items. Constructivist researchers must move beyond simply asserting that children can move from lexically specific schemas to wholly abstract constructions and endeavour to show precisely how this could be done (for example, by using computer simulation studies).

Finally, it is worth noting that some of the construction types that have been considered in this chapter (particularly questions, but also some relative- and complement-clause constructions) differ from more basic constructions (e.g. the transitive; Chapter 6) in that certain types of production error are relatively common (e.g. *What does she doesn't like?*; *Is the boy who is smoking is crazy?*). As we have seen elsewhere, looking only at correctly formed utterances may lead to a theoretical impasse, as such utterances could have been produced using either lexically specific schemas or more abstract knowledge. Because errors cannot have been learned imitatively from adults, they constitute a particularly good testing ground for competing theoretical accounts of how children acquire the relevant constructions (e.g. Guasti *et al.*, 1995 vs Ambridge and Rowland, 2009, for negative *wh*-questions). For both generativist and constructivist researchers alike, then, the analysis of errors will most likely constitute a profitable avenue for future research into children's acquisition of 'movement' constructions and complex syntax.

Up to this point, we have mainly been concerned with children's ability to produce and comprehend unambiguous sentences (e.g. *The man kicked the ball*; *The boy who is smoking is crazy*). In this chapter we investigate how children interpret sentences that are ambiguous, whilst ruling out non-adultlike interpretations, as in the examples below. Note the subscript notation used to show possible and impossible [*] interpretations (explained more fully below).

(a) Goldilocks$_i$ said that Mama Bear$_j$ is touching her$_{i/*j}$ (*her* = Goldilocks or somebody else, *but not* Mama Bear)
(b) Every dwarf ate a pizza (= Every dwarf ate a different pizza or Every dwarf ate the same pizza *but not* [necessarily] Every pizza was eaten by a dwarf)
(c) John$_i$ told Bill$_j$ [PRO $_{*i/j}$] to leave (= Bill – not John – should leave)
(d) John$_i$ promised Bill$_j$ [PRO $_{i/*j}$] to leave (= John – not Bill – should leave)

In doing so, we will investigate the phenomena of **binding** (e.g. sentence (a)) **quantification** (b) and **control** (c–d)).

For generativist accounts, all three phenomena require knowledge of the innately specified principle of **c-command** (Reinhart, 1983). Radford (2004: 75) defines c-command as follows:

> A constituent X c-commands its sister constituent Y and any constituent Z which is contained within Y.

A simpler way to think about c-command is to use the analogy of a train network: X c-commands any node which one can reach by 'taking a northbound train [from X], getting off at the first station, changing trains there and then travelling one or more stops south *on a different line*' (Radford, 2004: 75). From this definition, it is easy to see that, in Figure 8.1, B c-commands D, E and F. D c-commands B, whilst E and F c-command one another. A does not c-command any node.[1]

Generativist accounts explain the phenomena to be discussed here in terms of **binding**: X binds Y if (a) X c-commands Y AND (b) X and Y are **coindexed** (i.e. X and Y refer to the same entity).

For each of the three phenomena to be discussed – binding, quantification and control – there is a relatively straightforward debate between generativist–

Figure 8.1 B c-commands, D, E and F; D, c-commands B; E and F c-command one another

nativist and constructivist–social pragmatic accounts. In each case, the generativist position is that children are born with innate knowledge of the relevant syntactic principles, which are part of Universal Grammar (UG). Where children do not show adultlike performance, this is due to task demands, reliance on surface word order, failure to learn the relevant lexical items, or some other non-syntactic factor. In each case, the constructivist position is that children learn the relevant constructions – including their semantic and discourse-pragmatic properties – gradually, on the basis of the input. The constructivist approach also stresses the importance of social-pragmatic understanding: In many cases, children's interpretations (and even those of adults) may be guided more by assumptions regarding the speaker's intended meaning than by the syntax of the sentence. In general, there is little disagreement with regard to the empirical data: in each case, children's performance improves gradually with age. The issue is whether this reflects gradual input-based learning, as under the constructivist account, or a reduced tendency to be misled by non-syntactic factors, as under the generativist account.

8.1   Binding and coreference

8.1.1   *Generativist approaches: the binding principles*

Under generativist approaches, three innately specified **binding principles** determine the entities to which NPs such as *her* and *herself* can and cannot refer (as in example a, reproduced below):

> Goldilocks$_i$ said that Mama Bear$_j$ is touching her$_{i/*j}$ (*her* = Goldilocks or somebody else *but not* Mama Bear)

Before introducing the binding principles, we define four important terms (based on the definitions given in Carnie (2006):

- A **referring expression** (**R-expression**) (e.g. *Goldilocks*) is an NP (Noun Phrase) that gets its meaning by referring to an entity in the world (here, the girl Goldilocks, star of the children's story about the three bears). For clarity, we use *italics* for the referring expression (i.e. the WORD *Goldilocks*) and underlining for its referent (i.e. the PERSON Goldilocks).

- An **anaphor** (e.g. *herself*) is an NP that gets its meaning from another NP in the sentence. To see why this is the case, consider the two sentences below:

  Goldilocks$_i$ is touching herself$_i$ (*herself = Goldilocks = *Goldilocks)

  Goldilocks$_i$ said that Mama Bear$_j$ is touching herself$_{*i/j}$ (*herself = Mama Bear = *Mama Bear)

  In the first example, the NP *herself* gets its meaning from the NP *Goldilocks* (which, in turn, gets its meaning by referring to the real-world entity Goldilocks). In the second, *herself* gets its meaning from *Mama Bear* (which, in turn, gets its meaning by referring to the real-world entity Mama Bear). So, unlike for an R-expression, the real-world referent that is picked out by an anaphor changes depending on the rest of the sentence. Anaphors such as *herself, himself and yourself* are termed **reflexive pronouns** (or simply **reflexives**) (reciprocals such as *each other* are also anaphors, but we do not discuss these here).

- A **non-reflexive pronoun** (also termed a **pronominal**, or, more usually, simply a **pronoun**) (e.g. *her*) can get its meaning *either* from another NP in the sentence (like an anaphor) or by referring to an entity in the world (like an R-expression). Consider, again, the sentence *Goldilocks said that Mama Bear is touching her.* As we have already seen, *her* could refer to Goldilocks (getting its meaning from the NP *Goldilocks*), but it could equally well refer to another person present in the room such as Susan (i.e. getting its meaning by referring to an entity in the world).

- An **antecedent** is an NP that gives its meaning to another NP. In the following sentences the antecedent is shown in **bold**.

  Goldilocks$_i$ is touching herself$_i$ (*herself = Goldilocks = *Goldilocks)

  Goldilocks$_i$ said that **Mama Bear**$_j$ is touching herself$_{*i/j}$ (*herself = Mama Bear = *Mama Bear)

  Goldilocks$_i$ said that Mama Bear is touching her$_i$ (where *her = Goldilocks = *Goldilocks, not somebody else)

Note that the antecedent and the NP to which it gives its meaning are coindexed using a subscript letter $_{i,j}$ etc. (no movement is implied, unless stated). For consistency across different sentence types, the asterisk that is used to denote impossible interpretations is always shown as a subscript to the (reflexive/non-reflexive) pronoun (e.g. *her/herself*).

As the definitions above suggest, there is some discrepancy between different researchers with regard to the terms used. We will use the term **reflexive pronoun** to refer to NPs of the type *myself, himself, herself* and *yourself*, **non-reflexive pronoun** to refer to NPs of the type *I/me, he/him, she/her* and *you*,[2] and **pronoun** as a catch-all term for both types.

8.1.1.1 Principle A   **Principle A** states that **a reflexive pronoun** (e.g. *herself*) **must be bound in its local domain**. As we have just seen, a pronoun is **bound** if it is c-commanded by a coindexed antecedent (i.e. an NP such as *Mama Bear*). In 'core' cases, the **local domain** is the **clause**, but in some cases the local domain may be an NP (*Goldilocks_i saw [Mama Bear_j's picture of herself*_{i/j}]*).

Essentially, then, Principle A stipulates that for sentences such as *Goldilocks_i said that Mama Bear_j is touching herself*_{i/j}, the reflexive pronoun *herself* can refer only to the NP that c-commands it *in the local domain* (i.e. *Mama Bear*), not an NP that (a) c-commands it but is not in the local domain (e.g. *Goldilocks*, which is in a different clause), or (b) does not c-command it at all (e.g. another character previously mentioned in the story). In most cases, Principle A therefore requires that a reflexive pronoun refer back to an antecedent in the same clause. This is illustrated in Figure 8.2.

If Principle A is innate, children should show understanding of this principle as early as they can be tested. Chien and Wexler (1990: experiment 4) tested this prediction using a **yes/no judgment task**. In the crucial mismatch condition, children were shown a picture of Mama Bear touching Goldilocks (see Figure 8.3, left-hand panel) and asked 'This is Goldilocks. This is Mama Bear. Is Mama Bear touching herself?', to which the correct answer is 'no'. In fact, the findings (see Figure 8.3, left-hand panel) suggest that Principle A may be gradually acquired over development, with the proportion of correct rejections rising from approximately 30 per cent at 2;6–4;0 (G1) through 65 per cent at 4;0–5;0 (G2) and 90 per cent at 5;0–6;0 (G3) to virtually 100 per cent for older children (6;0–7;0) and adults (G3 and A).

Young children's poor performance did not seem be due to the fact that the sentence contains a proper name (*Mama Bear*), as they performed equally poorly (see Figure 8.3, right-hand panel) when the proper name was replaced with the quantified NP *Every Bear* (see Section 8.2 for discussion of quantification). Young children also performed poorly in an act-out version of the same studies (experiments 1–3), though this could be due to general difficulties with act-out tasks (see Chapter 6).

Another possibility is that younger children are in possession of Principle A, but perform poorly on the task because they find it difficult to process a mismatch (note from the 'match' data that even the youngest group were able to correctly answer 'yes' to the question 'Is Mama Bear touching herself?' when such an event was depicted). A related possibility is that children have a **yes-bias**; i.e. they are reluctant to give a negative answer to a question posed by an adult.

To address this potential problem, McKee (1992) conducted a similar study using a **truth-value judgment** paradigm. In this case, rather than having the experimenter directly put a question to the child, the picture (or, in this study,

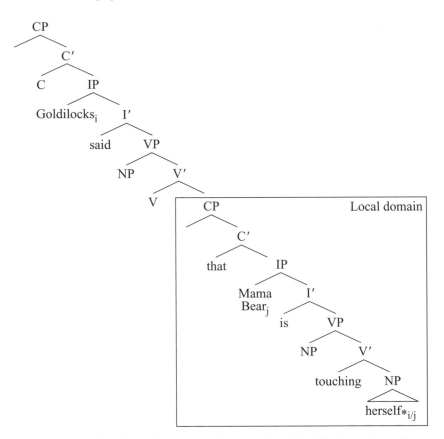

Figure 8.2 Principle A governs interpretation of *Goldilocks$_i$ said that Mama Bear$_j$ is touching herself$_{*i/j}$*

an action performed with toys) is described by a puppet (e.g. 'Mama Bear is touching herself'). The child then rewards or punishes the puppet by feeding it a cookie or a rag (whilst children may be reluctant to 'contradict' an adult experimenter, they apparently enjoy 'punishing' a puppet). For the crucial two-clause mismatch sentences (e.g. *While the clown$_i$ was sitting down, Roger Rabbit$_j$ covered himself$_{*i/j}$*), children (aged 3;7–5;4) achieved a mean of 81 per cent correct rejections. Again, however, children showed improvement with age: though separate data are not shown for each age group individually, when a median split was performed, older children significantly outperformed the younger group.

Another possibility is that young children are in possession of the syntactic principle, but have yet to acquire the lexical contrast between the **reflexive**

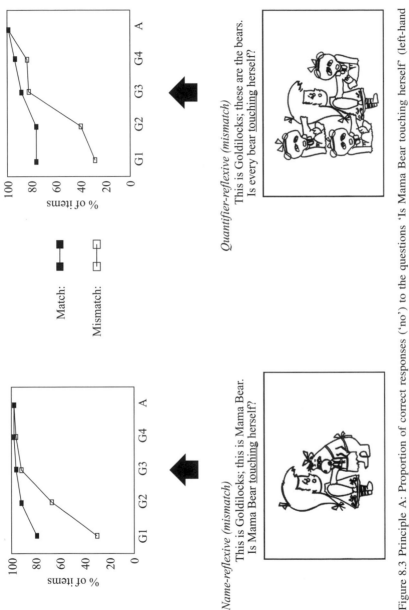

Name-reflexive (mismatch)
This is Goldilocks; this is Mama Bear.
Is Mama Bear touching herself?

Quantifier-reflexive (mismatch)
This is Goldilocks; these are the bears.
Is every bear touching herself?

Figure 8.3 Principle A: Proportion of correct responses ('no') to the questions 'Is Mama Bear touching herself' (left-hand panel) and 'Is every bear touching herself?' (right-hand panel) (from Chien and Wexler, 1990: 269; reproduced by permission of Taylor & Francis)

pronouns (e.g. *herself, himself, myself*) and the **non-reflexive pronouns** (e.g. *her, him, me*). This may be particularly difficult for learners of English, where the reflexive pronoun (e.g. *herself*) often contains the equivalent pronoun (e.g. *her*). In support of this claim, McKee (1992) found improved performance (91 per cent correct rejections) amongst a comparable group of children learning Italian; a language in which the reflexive pronoun (*si*) and non-reflexive pronoun (*lo/le*) are not similar.

8.1.1.2 Principle B   Principle B states that **a non-reflexive pronoun (e.g. *her*) must be free (i.e. NOT bound) in its local domain.** In informal terms, one can think of Principle B as the 'opposite' of Principle A: in a context where a reflexive pronoun (e.g. *herself*) must be used, one cannot substitute it with a non-reflexive pronoun (e.g. *her*) without changing the meaning. For example, for the sentence *Goldilocks$_i$ said that Mama Bear$_j$ is touching her$_{i/*j}$*, the pronoun (*her*) cannot take its meaning from *Mama Bear*. If it did, this would constitute a Principle B violation, since the non-reflexive pronoun (*her*) would be c-commanded in its local domain by *Mama Bear*. Note that Principle B stipulates only what the non-reflexive pronoun *cannot* refer to. The pronoun is free to take its meaning either from the NP *Goldilocks* or from an entity in the world (e.g. <u>Cinderella</u>; e.g. *Cinderella$_i$ was feeling lonely. Whilst Goldilocks read the book, Mamma Bear touched her$_i$ affectionately*).

Although Principle B is also held to be present from birth, the generativist literature acknowledges a phenomenon known as **Principle B Delay** whereby this principle does not seem to be operational for children until relatively late in development (later than Principle A). For example, Chien and Wexler (1990: study 4) found that even the oldest children tested (6;0–7;0) incorrectly allowed *her* to take its meaning from *Mama Bear* in sentences such as those illustrated in Figure 8.4 on 30% of trials (70% for the youngest group); see Figure 8.5.

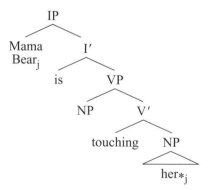

Figure 8.4 Principle B governs interpretation of *Mama Bear$_j$ is touching her$_{*j}$*

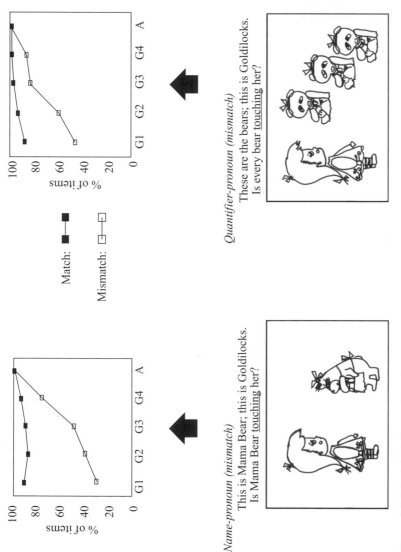

Name-pronoun (mismatch)
    This is Mama Bear; this is Goldilocks.
      Is Mama Bear touching her?

Quantifier-pronoun (mismatch)
    These are the bears; this is Goldilocks.
      Is every bear <u>touching</u> her?

Figure 8.5 Principle B. Proportion of correct responses ('no') to the questions 'Is Mama Bear touching her' (left-hand panel) and 'Is every bear touching her?' (right-hand panel) (from Chien and Wexler, 1990: 273; reproduced by permission of Taylor & Francis)

McKee (1992) found similar performance amongst English children, but again noted that Italian children showed much higher rates of correct performance. This again suggests that English children's difficulties with Principle B (and – to a lesser extent – Principle A) are due largely to failure to learn the lexical distinction between phonologically similar reflexive/non-reflexive pronoun pairs (e.g. *herself/her*; *himself/him*).

This being the case, it is perhaps surprising that generativist theorists have attempted to find alternative, more complex explanations for apparent Principle B delay. The accounts to be discussed here (Grodzinsky and Reinhart, 1993; McDaniel and Maxfield, 1992; Thornton and Wexler, 1999) all stem from the observation that whilst Principle B prevents a reflexive pronoun (e.g. *her*, in *Mama Bear is touching her*) from taking its interpretation from a c-commanding NP (i.e. the NOUN PHRASE *Mama Bear*), there is nothing to prevent it from taking its interpretation directly from an entity in the world (i.e. the actual person <u>Mama Bear</u>). In other words, whilst the NP *Mama Bear* may not be an **antecedent** of *her*, <u>Mama Bear</u> (just like <u>Cinderella</u> or <u>any other character present or under discussion</u>) can be chosen as a **plausible referent** for *her*. Indeed, adults allow such an interpretation in special pragmatic circumstances (so called Evans-style contexts; Evans, 1980).

> It's not true that nobody loves John. John loves him. (*him* = <u>John</u>)
>
> That must be John. At least, he looks like him. (*him* = John)
>
> I can understand a father wanting his daughter to be like himself, but I can't understand that ugly brute wanting his daughter to be like him. (Cantrall, 1974) (*him* = the 'ugly' father)

All three accounts share the assumption that children, in one way or another, fail to appreciate the special circumstances in which such uses are appropriate, and overgeneralize the reading to more everyday sentences. For example, Thornton and Wexler (1999) propose that adults create two separate guises for the referents (e.g. <u>a person who *may be* John</u>; <u>and a person who *is* John</u>), and that children extend this **guise creation** to the 'core' Principle B sentences of the type discussed here (e.g. <u>Mama Bear-as-toucher</u> and <u>Mama Bear-as-touchee</u>). Similarly, Reinhart's **Rule I** (Reinhart, 1983; Grodzinsky and Reinhart, 1993) effectively states that listeners expect speakers to use reflexive pronouns (e.g. *herself*) wherever this would give the correct meaning (i.e. in all contexts except Evans-style contexts), and so will not interpret a non-reflexive pronoun (e.g. *her*) reflexively (e.g. *Mama Bear$_j$ is touching her$_{*j}$*).

A problem with such accounts, however, is that they assume that children overgeneralize from the extremely rare Evans-style contexts to far more frequent contexts. The guise-creation hypothesis also incorrectly predicts that children should show good performance on universally quantified sentences such as *Every bear_j is touching her_{*j}*. This is because (as we will see in Section 8.2) a universally quantified NP such as *Every bear* always raises to a position where it c-commands the relevant pronoun. Although children do show much better performance with such sentences, rates of correct rejection remain low (e.g. less than 50 per cent for Chien and Wexler's youngest group; see Figure 8.5, right-hand panel).

8.1.1.3 Principle C   Principle C states that **A referential expression (R-expression) must be free (i.e. NOT bound) anywhere.** Recall that a referential expression is an NP (e.g. *The dog*, *Goldilocks*, *Cinderella*) that gets its meaning by referring to an entity in the world (as opposed to from another NP in the sentence). For the following single-clause sentences, a Principle C violation occurs because the (non-reflexive) pronoun subject *He* **binds** the R-expression *John* (i.e. *He* c-commands *John*, and both NPs refer to the same entity: <u>John</u>). Hence the R-expression (*John*) is not **free** (see Figure 8.6):

> He_{*i} saw John_i.
>
> He_{*i} saw John's_i mother.
>
> He_{*i} saw a snake next to John_i.

It is important to note that it is not linear order that is relevant here, but the hierarchical structure of the sentence. For example, if the sentence shown in Figure 8.6 is rearranged thus:

> Next to John_i, he_{*i} saw a snake.

exactly the same Principle C violation occurs: the pronoun that is the sentence subject (*he*) binds the R-expression (*John*). Conversely, when the R-expression

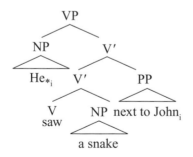

Figure 8.6 Principle C rules out the sentence interpretation *He_{*i} saw a snake next to John_i*

(e.g. *John*) is the sentence subject and hence c-commands the pronoun (e.g. *him*), no Principle C violation occurs, regardless of linear order:

John$_i$ saw a snake next to him$_i$ **(Forward anaphora)**
Next to him$_i$, John$_i$ saw a snake   **(Backward anaphora)**[3]

For multiple-clause sentences, a Principle C violation occurs when the pronoun is the subject of the main clause, and hence c-commands an R-expression in a subsequent subordinate clause:

[CP She$_{*i}$ listens to music [CP when Sarah$_i$ reads poetry]]

If the subordinate clause containing the R-expression occurs at the beginning of the main clause, the R-expression is not c-commanded by the pronoun (even if the pronoun is the subject of the main clause), and no Principle C violation occurs:

[CP [CP When Sarah$_i$ reads poetry] she$_i$ listens to music]

If the R-expression is the subject of the main clause, no Principle C violation will occur, regardless of the order of the main and subordinate clause:

[CP Sarah$_i$ listens to music [CP when she$_i$ reads poetry]]

[CP [CP when she$_i$ reads poetry] Sarah$_i$ listens to music]

Note that whilst (for the grammatical sentences) the pronoun and R-expression *may* corefer (i.e. refer to the same entity in the world), they do not have to. Indeed, in certain contexts, such an interpretation is relatively unlikely (e.g. *Unlike her sister Sarah, Claire$_i$ loves poetry. When she$_i$ reads poetry, Sarah listens to music*).

8.1.1.3.1 Experimental studies: backward anaphora   Early investigations into backward anaphora suggested that children have difficulty with Principle C. In act-out tasks (see Lust, Eisele and Mazuka, 1992, for a review) children correctly block the reading where the R-expression sends its interpretation backwards to a pronoun in the same clause (e.g. *She$_{*i}$ washes Sarah$_i$*), but also seem to block the legal reading where the R-expression sends its interpretation backwards to a pronoun in a subordinate clause (*When she$_i$ reads poetry, Sarah$_i$ listens to music*). That is, children interpret *she* as referring to somebody other than Sarah when enacting both sentences. This led some researchers (e.g. Solan, 1983) to propose that young children are in possession not of Principle C, but of a simpler constraint that blocks all backward anaphora.

In fact, act-out tasks cannot show that children *block* the legal reading, merely that this reading is dispreferred. Importantly, the reading that children prefer – where *she* is taken to mean another character (e.g. Sarah's poetry-loving sister, Claire) – is also legal. Crain and McKee (1986) therefore investigated this issue using a *yes/no* judgment task with children aged 4;2. In this study, children correctly accepted backward anaphora into a subordinate clause (e.g. allowing *When she$_i$ reads poetry, Sarah$_i$ listens to music*) for a mean of 73 per cent of trials (86 per cent for the seven youngest children tested; $M = 3;11$). Importantly, consistent with Principle C, children blocked backward anaphora into the same clause (e.g. they did not allow *She$_{*i}$ washes Sarah$_i$*) on a mean of 88 per cent of trials (79 per cent for the youngest seven children).

At the same time, even relatively old children do not seem to completely disallow sentence interpretations that are incompatible with Principle C. For example, in a similar *yes/no* judgment task, Grimshaw and Rosen (1990) found that children aged 4–5 accepted sentence interpretations such as *She$_{*i}$ washes Sarah$_i$* on over a third (38 per cent) of trials.[4] Similarly, Eisele (1988) found that children aged 4;1–7;11 ($M = 6;3$) accepted interpretations such as *She$_{*i}$ listens to music when Sarah$_i$ reads poetry* on 32 per cent of trials.

8.1.1.3.2 Experimental studies: forward anaphora

Neither do children categorically disallow Principle C violations in forward anaphora. Using an act-out task, Hsu, Cairns, Eisenberg and Schlisselberg (1989) found that 71/81 children (aged 3;1–8;0) would enact the violation *Under the zebra's$_i$ tail he$_{*i}$ drinks the water* (like *Next to John$_i$, he$_{*i}$ saw a snake*), with only 8-year-olds respecting the constraint (i.e. having a different animal drink the water). Note that, unlike for some of the act-out studies discussed above, children were not simply choosing one legitimate reading over another. Rather, children (and, on 22 per cent of trials, adults) were choosing an enactment that involved a Principle C violation over one that did not (for similar findings, see Ingram and Shaw, 1981; Taylor-Browne, 1983).

Other act-out studies have found much lower rates of Principle C violation in forward anaphora. For example, Lust and Clifford (1986) (see also Lust, Loveland and Kornet, 1980) found that even the youngest children they studied, aged 3;5–3;11, incorrectly enacted *On the top of Oscar's$_i$ head, he$_{*i}$ rubbed the donut* on only 13 per cent of trials (18 per cent for a larger group aged 3;5–7;11). Nevertheless, the finding that even relatively old children accept some Principle C violations is problematic for the claim that knowledge of the principle is innate. Furthermore, the very fact that the particular sentence type appears to have such a large effect on children's interpretations suggests that constraints on pronoun interpretation may be, at least in part, pragmatic rather than syntactic. This is the view taken by the constructivist approaches discussed in the following section.

8.1.2 *Constructivist approaches*

There is very little constructivist work on pronoun coreference, presumably because innate binding principles play no role in constructivist theory. However, given that developmental patterns of pronoun coreference are observed (e.g. young children accept interpretations such as *Mama Bear$_i$ washed her$_{*i}$* or *Next to Sarah$_i$, she$_{*i}$ saw a snake*, whereas older children and adults do not), an explanation of this phenomenon is required under any theoretical viewpoint.

8.1.2.1 A constructivist approach to Principle C   Although very little constructivist-oriented research has been conducted with children, there have been a number of attempts to provide a construction/cognitive grammar account of the binding principles. Primary amongst these is the account of Van Hoek (1997; see also Levinson, 1987; Roberts, 1987). Van Hoek (1997) begins with the observation that Principle C (in its traditional formulation) does not in fact rule out some coreference interpretations that speakers consider to be ungrammatical. Consider the following sentences

> She$_{*i}$ listens to music when Sarah$_i$ reads poetry.
>
> She$_{*i}$ listens to music and Sarah$_i$ reads poetry.
>
> She$_{*i}$ listens to music. Sarah$_i$ reads poetry.

Whilst coreference is not allowed (or at least odd) in each case, Principle C rules out only the first. For the second and third, *Sarah* is not c-commanded by *She* as they are in separate non-subordinated clauses (in the final case, entirely different sentences). Generativist accounts argue that the first example is ruled out by Principle C, whilst the second and third are ruled out by unrelated principles of discourse pragmatics (i.e. the question of whether or not the NP *Sarah* may send its interpretation backwards to *she* does not arise; speakers simply do not tend to use *she* to mean <u>Sarah</u> in such cases). This is somewhat unsatisfactory because it seems, intuitively at least, that what makes coreference impossible is essentially the same in each case.

Van Hoek (1997) argues that learned (as opposed to innate) principles of discourse pragmatics can account for all constraints on coreference (including cases not covered by the syntactic binding Principle C). It is uncontroversial that pronouns (e.g. *she*) are used when the referent is easily **accessible** (i.e. easy to infer or recover) from prior discourse, whilst full NPs (R-expressions) such as *Sarah* are used to begin a new topic of discourse. Indeed, the use of a full NP when a pronoun would have been appropriate (e.g. *Sarah said that *Sarah/she had seen the film*) is generally considered to be ungrammatical, or at least unnatural, except in special contexts. Van Hoek's (1997: 37) claim is that unacceptable coreference 'may be characterized as a configuration in which

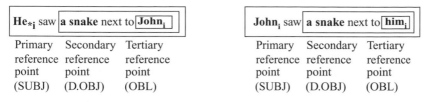

<table>
<tr><td>Primary
reference
point
(SUBJ)</td><td>Secondary
reference
point
(D.OBJ)</td><td>Tertiary
reference
point
(OBL)</td><td>Primary
reference
point
(SUBJ)</td><td>Secondary
reference
point
(D.OBJ)</td><td>Tertiary
reference
point
(OBL)</td></tr>
</table>

Figure 8.7 Nested reference point-dominion configurations within the clause

a full noun phrase, indicating low accessibility of the referent, is embedded in a context in which the referent is in fact highly accessible'. This straightforwardly accounts for the ungrammaticality of cases such as *She*i *listens to music when/and Sarah*i *reads poetry*. The speaker's use of the pronoun (*she*) indicates that she considers the referent to be highly accessible, meaning that the use of a full NP (*Sarah*) to refer to the same entity (Sarah) is pragmatically odd (as in the example *Sarah said that *Sarah/she had seen the film*). Why then, is it often permissible to use a pronoun and a full NP in close proximity to refer to the same referent (see examples above)?

Van Hoek's (1997: 57) proposal is that 'a full nominal [e.g. *Sarah*] cannot appear in the **dominion** of a **reference point** which it corresponds to'.[5] In simple terms, the reference point is the topic of discourse whilst the dominion is the part of the discourse that is understood within the context of the reference point, as illustrated by the following example (p. 54):

> *The final exam* (reference point) **is next week. The room will be different and I think we'll need three hours** (dominion).

The discourse in bold is within the dominion of the reference point, as a listener would clearly assume that these points relate to the final exam, not to any other possible topic. Thus the reference point is the entity that is **singled out for awareness** but that swiftly becomes part of the **background context**.

In fact, the assumption is that clauses have not a single reference point, but a nested hierarchy of reference point+dominion configurations. The primary reference point is the subject of the clause, with the direct object the secondary reference point, followed by the indirect and oblique object. This is illustrated in Figure 8.7, which shows the dominion (represented by a box) of each successive reference point (**bold**). Ungrammatical coreference (left-hand panel) is ruled out by the (learned) pragmatic principle that **it is anomalous for a full nominal [e.g. *John*] to appear in the dominion of a reference point which it corresponds to**. Coreference is permitted (right-hand panel) when this pragmatic principle is not violated.

Because reference points are defined in terms of sentence structure, not linear order, coreference is also blocked for *Next to John*i, *he*i *saw a snake* (*John* is in

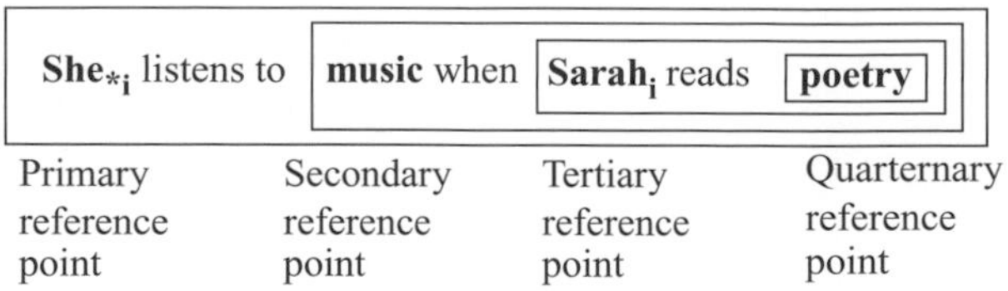

She$_{*i}$ listens to	**music** when	**Sarah**$_i$ reads	**poetry**
Primary reference point	Secondary reference point	Tertiary reference point	Quarternary reference point

Figure 8.8 Nested reference point-dominion configurations across clauses

the dominion of *he*) but allowed for *Next to him$_i$, John$_i$ saw a snake*, in exactly the same way (*John* is not in the dominion of *him*).

This may seem to the reader to be a restatement of Principle C. In one sense, this is precisely the point: Van Hoek's (1997) goal is to account for the Principle C facts. However, the claim is that the listener can identify the reference points and their dominions not by identifying the syntactic roles of SUBJECT, DIRECT OBJECT and so on, but by understanding what the sentence is 'about'. Van Hoek (1997) argues that Principle C gives good coverage of the coreferencing possibilities *precisely because* the syntactic structure of a sentence – on the basis of which the syntactic Principle C is formulated – is a reflection of its semantic structure.

When applied to multiple-clause sentences, this argument claims that syntactic subordination reflects semantic subordination (i.e. a sentence such as *The boy [who is washing the elephant] is tired* is 'about' the main clause subject – *The boy* – with the subordinate clause providing incidental information). Thus, embedded clauses are always in the dominion of the reference points that constitute the arguments of the verb in the main clause. Again, ungrammatical coreference (see Figure 8.8) is ruled out by the (learned) pragmatic principle that it is anomalous for a full nominal (e.g. *Sarah*) to appear in the dominion of a reference point which it corresponds to.

This correctly predicts that coreference will always be allowed when the full NP (e.g. Sarah) is the main clause subject (e.g. *Sarah$_i$ listens to music when she$_i$ reads poetry*; *When she$_i$ reads poetry, Sarah$_i$ listens to music*).

Potentially problematic are cases of permissible coreference where the pronoun is the subject of the main clause, with the full NP in the subordinate clause (e.g. *When Sarah$_i$ reads poetry, she$_i$ listens to music*). The claim here is that speakers may 'choose to rely on linear word order to determine reference point relations, just as in multiclausal discourse' (Van Hoeck, 1997: 68). In other words, coreference is allowed here for precisely the same reason that one can say *Sarah reads poetry. She listens to music, too.* Whilst this may seem somewhat unsatisfactory, note that omission of a role for linear order is precisely what causes the syntactic Principle C account to incorrectly fail to rule out examples such as *She**ᵢ *listens to music and Sarah*ᵢ *reads poetry* and *She**ᵢ *listens to music. Sarah*ᵢ *reads poetry.* It would seem then that the role of linear order is a factor which must be, but has yet to be, satisfactorily incorporated by syntactic and semantic/pragmatic theories of Principle C phenomena alike.

8.1.2.2 Differentiating the two accounts: a constructivist study of Principle C As we have seen, for most Principle C type sentences, the generativist and constructivist accounts make the same predictions. For example, both predict that a pronoun and full NP may not corefer when the full NP is in a subsequent clause (e.g. *She**ᵢ *listens to music when Sarah*ᵢ *reads poetry*) *unless* the clause containing the pronoun is subordinated syntactically (generativist account) or pragmatically (constructivist account), by being construed as providing only incidental information (e.g. *[When she*ᵢ *reads poetry] Sarah*ᵢ *listens to music*).

Harris and Bates (2002) propose a way to tease apart the two accounts. The constructivist account predicts that if it is possible to increase the extent to which the clause containing the pronoun is de-focused (i.e. is construable as providing only incidental information) – without changing the syntactic structure of the sentence – then the acceptability of coreference will increase; even to the extent of ameliorating a Principle C violation. For example, consider the following sentences:

He*ᵢ threatened to leave when Billyᵢ noticed that the computer had died.

He*ᵢ was threatening to leave when Billyᵢ noticed that the computer had died.

Whilst these sentences share identical syntactic structures, the information provided by the clause containing the pronoun appears more incidental in the second, due to the difference in aspect: *He threatened to leave* denotes an event that is part of the narrative, whilst *He was threatening to leave* constitutes 'scene-setting'. Accordingly, whilst both sentences constitute Principle C violations, the constructivist account predicts that coreference will be more acceptable for the second. This prediction was confirmed in a judgment study with adults (Harris and Bates, 2002: experiment 1). Participants allowed coreference for approximately 75 per cent of trials where the pronoun was presented in a 'scene-setting' clause (e.g. *He**ᵢ *was threatening to leave when Billy*ᵢ . . .) as compared to 60 per cent of control trials (e.g. *He**ᵢ *threatened to leave when Billy*ᵢ . . .).

Whilst generativist accounts have long acknowledged that pragmatic and discourse factors play a role in determining coreferencing possibilities (e.g. Reinhart, 1983), the finding that these factors can ameliorate sentences that are in violation of Principle C to the extent that they are judged as acceptable in the majority of cases would appear problematic. (Perhaps equally problematic is the finding that both Principle C-violating sentence types were accepted more often than not).

Nevertheless, in a third condition, syntactic subordination of the clause containing the pronoun was shown to have the biggest effect of all. Participants allowed coreference for sentences such as *When he$_i$ threatened to leave, Billy$_i$ noticed that the computer had died* (consistent with Principle C) on around 90 per cent of trials. This could be taken as support for the generativist view that the syntactic configuration is the primary determinant of coreferencing possibilities. However, it would also be possible to argue that the introduction of a *when* clause constitutes a higher degree of semantic subordination than the aspect manipulation. Future research should attempt to tease apart these possibilities by studying a wider range of Principle C sentence types in both adults and children. In particular, we are aware of no studies that have investigated constructivist functional-semantic accounts of Principle C acquisition in children.

8.1.2.3 Principles A and B   Van Hoek (1997) also offers a constructivist account of Principles A and B. Simplifying somewhat, the account assumes that children acquire two competing constructions: one is a reflexive construction (SUBJECT VERB REFLEXIVE PRONOUN), where the entity encoded by the item in the REFLEXIVE PRONOUN slot corresponds with the SUBJECT (e.g. *Mama Bear$_i$ is touching herself$_i$*). The other is a non-reflexive construction (SUBJECT VERB NON-REFLEXIVE PRONOUN) where the NON-REFLEXIVE PRONOUN slot corresponds with an entity other than the subject (e.g. *Mama Bear$_i$ is touching her$_{*i}$*). The two constructions have subtly different semantics in that the first describes events as seen from the point of view of the subject, the second from a more objective view, as succinctly illustrated by the example from Cantrall (1974) discussed above:

> I can understand a father wanting his daughter to be like himself [reflexive construction], but I can't understand that ugly brute wanting his daughter to be like him [non-reflexive construction].

When interpreting or producing relevant sentences, the two constructions compete in memory. Consequently, utterances such as *Mama Bear$_i$ is touching her$_{*i}$* are not so much ruled out as out-competed (or 'pre-empted') by utterances such as *Mama Bear$_i$ is touching herself$_i$*. Matthews, Lieven, Theakston and Tomasello (2009: 605) note that this formulation is very similar to Reinhart's rule I, with the difference that the constraint is held to be learned, rather than innate.

8.1.2.4 A constructivist study of Principle B We are aware of only one constructivist investigation of pronoun coreference conducted with children. Matthews *et al.* (2009) conducted a modified replication of the part of Chien and Wexler's (1990) study that investigated knowledge of Principle B (which blocks coreference for sentences such as *Mama Bear$_i$ is touching her*$_{*i}$) with children aged 4;3–4;10 ($M = 4$;7), 5;3–5;11 ($M = 5$;7) and 6;3–6;9 ($M = 6$;6).

The study contained two important modifications. First, Matthews *et al.* (2009) manipulated the frequency of the non-reflexive pronouns (*him/her/them*) and verbs (e.g. high: *tickling, washing*; low: *pinching, lassoing*). Under the constructivist account, children acquire the constructions that are relevant here (e.g. *[X] is [VERB]ing him/her/them*) – like all constructions – by abstracting across high-frequency exemplars of the construction (e.g. *Mum is tickling him*). Thus the account predicts that children should show the best performance for frequent items that will have appeared many times in this construction in their input. Provided children know the relevant (non-reflexive) pronouns, the generativist account has little room to explain any lexical effects, as ungrammatical coreference will be ruled out by the innately specified Principle B.

The second modification was that, after providing a *yes/no* judgment, children were asked to describe the picture themselves. This was implemented using a 'guessing game' procedure. An experimenter who could not see the picture 'guessed' what was shown (e.g. 'Mama Bear is washing her'). The child (who could see the picture) then told a second experimenter whether or not the first experimenter had guessed correctly. The second experimenter then asked the child to 'tell me what was in the picture so that I can write it down'. For example, if the above guess was produced in the mismatch condition, the child might say 'No, Mama Bear is washing herself'. As in the original study of Chien and Wexler (1990), the crucial case is the mismatch condition where children see a picture of (for example) Mama Bear washing herself and must reject the description *Mama Bear is washing her*. However, to correct for the *yes*-bias that is generally observed in such studies, Matthews *et al.* (2007) calculated a Receiver Operating Characteristic (ROC) score for each child that reflects both the rate of correct rejection and correct acceptance.

The findings observed by Matthews *et al.* (2009) were problematic for both the generativist and constructivist accounts. Counter to the prediction of the constructivist account, children actually performed better on the judgment task with low- than high-frequency verbs. Matthews *et al.* (2009) speculate that high-frequency verbs lead to a 'kindergarten path effect' (Trueswell, Sekerina, Hill and Logrip, 1999) whereby children quickly respond affirmatively to sentences that use familiar verbs (e.g. *Mama Bear is tickling her*), without waiting to check that the reflexive pronoun form (e.g. *herself*) has been used. Children generally showed the worst performance with *them* (the most frequent pronoun in the input of the children in the Manchester corpus), but worse performance with *him* (lowest frequency) than *her*. However, it may be difficult to obtain relevant frequency estimates as *them* is also used for inanimate objects, and *her* is also used as a possessive pronoun (e.g. *That's her book*).

The findings from the judgment task were also problematic for the generativist account. For sentences with illegal coreference such as *Mama bear$_i$ is touching her$_{*i}$* (when Mama bear was touching herself) all age groups failed to show significantly above-chance performance ($M = 39$ per cent correct rejections), even with quantifier sentences such as *Every bear is touching her* ($M = 54$ per cent). Interestingly, however, children at all ages showed significantly better performance in the production task, for both the noun ($M = 83$ per cent) and quantifier ($M = 80$ per cent) sentences. This means that children who incorrectly accepted *Mama bear$_i$ is touching her$_{*i}$* as a description of a picture where Mama bear was touching herself, correctly described the picture as 'Mama Bear is touching herself'.

On the one hand, one could argue that this finding supports the generativist claim that children are in possession of Principle B, with the production task a fairer test of their knowledge than the truth-value judgment task. On the other, one could argue that the finding that even 6-year-old children make production errors at a rate of around 20 per cent (e.g. actively describing a picture where Mama Bear is touching herself as 'Mama Bear is touching her') counts against this claim. Matthews *et al.* (2009) argue that these findings count against Thornton and Wexler's (1999) guise-creation hypothesis as, if erroneous responses in the truth-value judgment task were a result of children creating two guises (e.g. *Mama bear [toucher] is touching her [touchee]*), these errors should have persisted into the production task. However, one could argue that children may have been doing precisely this in the 20 per cent of production trials for which they gave an incorrect response.

8.1.3   Pronoun coreference: conclusion

As for many of the debates in this book, there is actually little disagreement between the two sides with regard to the data. Indeed, with regard to Principles A and B, even the accounts proposed are similar. Regardless of theoretical perspective, most researchers would probably agree that children make errors because (a) they have yet to learn the lexical contrast between reflexive pronouns (e.g. *herself/himself*) and the non-reflexive pronouns to which they are highly similar (e.g. *her/him*) and (b) they have yet to appreciate the particular contexts in which each is required (whether this is due to, for example, overextended guise-creation or the competition of two similar constructions in memory). The issue, of course, is whether children come to reject illegal coreference with the aid of innate rules, or through construction learning. Research designed to distinguish between these possibilities has barely begun. One profitable approach may be to use the production paradigm of Matthews *et al.* (2009) to study knowledge of Principles A and B in much younger children who have nevertheless acquired the relevant lexical contrast between reflexive and non-reflexive pronouns. A suitable group would be learners of a language such as Italian where the two forms are highly differentiated phonetically.

With regard to Principle C, generativist and constructivist theories also make similar predictions. This is not surprising, since (a) both must account for the same basic pattern of data and (b) the pragmatic/semantic subordination that is at the heart of the constructivist account invariably corresponds with the syntactic subordination at the heart of the generativist account. Yet the accounts do make some different predictions, which should be further investigated in adults and, crucially, children.

First, as we have already seen, the constructivist account predicts that semantic changes that do not affect syntactic structure may affect coreferencing possibilities. Second, this account predicts that precisely the same coreferencing possibilities obtain in discourse (i.e. across sentence boundaries) as within a sentence and clause. If either of these predictions turn out to be true, generativist accounts will have to specify precisely how and when discourse pragmatic factors interact with, and perhaps even over-rule, the binding principles. A third prediction of the constructivist account is that – as in every other domain of acquisition – widespread lexical effects will be observed. For example, given that 60 per cent of naturally occurring cases of backward anaphora involve possessive pronouns (e.g. *In his $_i$ ... radio series, Garrison Keillor$_i$ brought a remote part of Minnesota to life*; Van Hoek, 1997: 112) coreference ought to be judged as particularly acceptable in such cases. At a finer-grained level, if it turns out that – for example – naturally occurring violations occur considerably more frequently with *he* than *she* (or vice versa), then this too should be reflected in participants' judgments. Again, this would not constitute definitive evidence against the innate binding principles approach, but would constitute another factor that has to be taken into account by such theories.

Finally, constructivist approaches predict age effects as the pragmatic principles governing pronoun coreference possibilities are acquired. Many generativist studies appear to be designed simply to demonstrate that children show adultlike knowledge as early as they can be tested and downplay apparent effects of improvement with age (see, for example, Figure 8.3). Age effects, whereby children appear to be learning permissible patterns of pronoun coreference clearly count as evidence against innate binding principles *unless* it is possible to explain such effects in terms of well-specified and independently motivated performance limitations.

Summary table 8.1 *Binding principles A, B and C (☑ = supports theory; ☒ = counts against theory)*

Summary of theory / Issue/phenomenon	Generativist full-competence approach (e.g. Chien and Wexler, 1990)	Constructivist approach (e.g. Van Hoek, 1997)
Summary of theory	Children have innate knowledge of binding principles; Errors due to task demands or failure to learn relevant pronouns/reflexive pronouns or their properties.	Children learn constructions – including their semantic/discourse-pragmatic properties – gradually from the input.
Do children reject interpretations inconsistent with Principle A?	☑ Yes (Chien and Wexler, 1990), but ☒ not at adultlike levels until at least 5;0. ☑ Better performance in truth-value judgment tasks (McKee, 1992).	☑ Gradual improvement with age (in both studies) more consistent with learning than innate principles.
Do children reject interpretations inconsistent with Principle B?	Poor performance may be due to failure to learn (or appreciate importance of) contrast between reflexive and non-reflexive pronouns: (1) better performance in languages with clearer contrast (e.g. Italian; McKee, 1992); (2) children accept *her* for *herself* substitutions that they rarely produce themselves (Matthews *et al.*, 2009). ☒ No, not even 6–7-yr-olds (Chien and Wexler, 1990), though ☑ better performance in production task (Matthews *et al.*, 2009), though ☒ even 6-yr-olds show error-rate of 20%. ☒ Guise-creation hypothesis fails to account for poor performance on *every* sentences (Chien and Wexler, 1990; Matthews *et al.* (2009).	☑ Children show lexical-frequency effects (problematic for innate-principles account), though ☒ in opposite direction to that usually predicted by constructivist accounts (Matthews *et al.*, 2009).
	Constructivist account of Principle B/A possible in principle (Van Hoek, 1997), but difficult to distinguish from generativist accounts (e.g. Reinhart, 1983) empirically.	
Do children reject backward-anaphora interpretations inconsistent with Principle C?	☑ Data from act out tasks suggest yes, but ☒ children also block legal interpretations (Lust *et al.*, 1992). ☑ Better performance on judgment tasks (Crain and McKee, 1986), though ☒ illegal interpretations still accepted on 1/3 of trials.	☒ Linear-order explanation (Van Hoek, 1997) somewhat unsatisfactory, but syntactic Principle C account also fails to deal satisfactorily with linear order.
Do children reject forward-anaphora interpretations inconsistent with Principle C?	☒ Even 7-yr-olds (and sometimes adults) produce violations in act-out tasks (Hsu *et al.*, 1989; Ingram and Shaw, 1981; Taylor-Browne, 1983; Lust and Clifford, 1986; Lust *et al.*, 1980).	☑ Some evidence for a functional/pragmatic constructivist account (Harris and Bates, 2002) though ☒ syntactic subordination has bigger effect and ☒ study not conducted with children.

8.2   Quantification

Consider the sentence *John only kissed Sue*. This sentence has (at least) three possible interpretations, depending on the constituent over which *only* has **scope**.

(a)	John only **kissed** Sue	VERB (He didn't do anything else to her)
(b)	John only kissed **Sue**	OBJ NP (He didn't kiss Jane, or anyone else)
(c)	John only **kissed Sue**	V′ (He didn't drink, dance or do anything all night other than kiss Sue)

This notion of scope is relevant for understanding the possible interpretations of sentences containing quantifiers. As for the above examples, such sentences have different possible readings that differ in scope. Consider the sentence *Every dwarf ate a pizza* (example from Crain *et al.*, 1996).

(a) **Universal wide-scope reading: there is no dwarf who didn't eat a pizza.** This interpretation would be correct for a scenario in which every dwarf ate a different pizza, *or* a scenario in which every dwarf ate the same pizza (i.e. they shared a large pizza)

(b) **Existential wide-scope reading: there is a *single* pizza that every dwarf ate.** This interpretation would be correct for a scenario in which every dwarf ate the same pizza, but incorrect for a scenario in which every dwarf ate a different pizza.

A **quantifier** is a determiner that denotes a number or amount (e.g. *three, most*). A **universal** quantifier (e.g. *every, all*) is used when the speaker wants to talk about **every** item (in the context under discussion) of the type named by the following noun (e.g. *every dwarf*). An **existential** quantifier (e.g. *a, some*) is used when the speaker wants to talk about **at least one** item of the type named by the following noun (e.g. *a pizza, some pizzas*).

The two readings differ with regard to whether the NP (or DP) containing the universal quantifier (*every dwarf*), or the NP containing the existential quantifier (*a pizza*) has scope over the other (which has **wide scope**). On the first reading (a), the NP with the universal quantifier (**every dwarf**) has scope over the NP with the existential quantifier (*a pizza*).

(a)	**Every dwarf** ate *a pizza*	**universal wide scope reading**

On the reading where every dwarf ate the same pizza (b), the NP with the existential quantifier (**a pizza**) has scope over the NP with the universal quantifier (*every dwarf*)

(b)	(There is) **a pizza** (that) *every dwarf* ate	**existential wide scope reading**

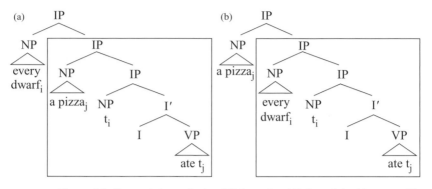

Figure 8.9 Generativist analysis of Universal and Existential wide scope. The NP that is highest in the tree has scope over the IP that it c-commands (boxed) (a) Universal wide-scope reading (there is no dwarf who did not eat a pizza), (b) Existential wide-scope reading (every dwarf ate *the same* pizza)

The questions for acquisition theorists are (a) when and how each interpretation becomes available to children and (b) when and how children come to reject non-adultlike interpretations (e.g. the interpretation of *Every dwarf ate a pizza* under which every pizza present must be eaten by a dwarf, with no pizzas left over).

8.2.1   *Generativist approaches*

Under a generativist analysis, sentences of this type are generated by movement of the two NPs. In addition to the usual IP that constitutes the sentence (e.g. *every dwarf ate a pizza*) two further IPs are projected, with one of the quantified NPs raising into the specifier position of each (a process termed **quantifier raising**). The NP with wide scope moves into the higher IP, where it c-commands the other. Thus the **universal wide-scope** and **existential wide-scope** readings of the sentence *Every dwarf ate a pizza* are as shown in Figure 8.9 (movement of the verb to I is not shown).

These phrase structure trees differ from the majority that we have seen up to this point, in that they do not correspond to the surface word order. However, this does not contravene the assumptions of the generativist approach: when all the relevant phrases have been selected and combined, a **spell-out** operation sends the structure to one system which outputs the **Phonological Form** (**PF**; i.e. the sentence as it is spoken) and another which outputs the **Logical Form** (**LF**; i.e. the meaning of the sentence as determined by its syntax). In each case, the structure shown above corresponds to the representation at LF (i.e. the one that determines the meaning of the sentence) not PF. It is in this way that two sentences with the same surface form (i.e. are that identical at PF) can have two different meanings (because they have a different underlying LF).

8.2.1.1 Acquiring adultlike interpretations

8.2.1.1 Acquiring adultlike interpretations Is there any evidence that children perform quantifier raising? In a truth-value judgment task, Crain *et al.* (1996) showed that children (aged 3;5–5;10; $M = 4;3$) accepted 'every skier drank a cup of hot apple cider' as a description of a story in which every skier drank *a different* cup of apple cider (universal wide-scope reading) on 88 per cent of trials. Similarly, 'every dwarf ate a pizza' was accepted as a description of a scenario in which every dwarf ate *the same* pizza (existential wide-scope reading) on 92 per cent of trials. However, these findings do not rule out the alternative possibility that children base their judgments on linear order and do not, in fact, perform quantifier raising. The problem is that children may have accepted the description 'every dwarf ate a pizza' simply because no dwarf went hungry (universal wide-scope reading), and would do so whether every dwarf happened to eat the same pizza (existential wide-scope reading) or not.

One way to avoid this problem is to use passive sentences where the existential quantifier comes first (e.g. *a pizza is being eaten by every dwarf*). If children will accept the universal wide-scope reading (e.g. every dwarf is eating a *different* pizza) that is incompatible with the existential wide-scope reading, this constitutes evidence that they have performed quantifier raising, moving the DP with the universal quantifier (*every dwarf*) to the highest SPEC IP position, where it has wide scope (see the left-hand tree in Figure 8.9).

Sentences of this type (though with the universal quantifier *each* as opposed to *every*) were used in a study conducted by Brooks and Braine (1996; though as non-generativist researchers, these authors were interested in the effects of surface order as opposed to quantifier raising *per se*). Children heard sentences such as *A boat is being built by every boy* and could choose a picture showing three boys each building his own boat (universal wide scope, conflicting with linear order) or one showing three boys building the same boat (existential wide scope). When given this picture-choice task, children mostly selected the existential wide-scope reading, as one would expect if children were operating mostly on the basis of surface word order (62 per cent of trials for 4-year-olds, decreasing steadily with age to 23 per cent for 9-year-olds and 18 per cent for adults). However, when asked if the description *A boat is being built by every boy* was a truthful description of the universal wide-scope picture (each boy building his own boat), 80 per cent of 4-year-olds agreed that it was, providing evidence for quantifier raising (or at least the ability to accept an interpretation that conflicts with surface word order). Although 9-year-olds and adults accepted this reading on around 95 per cent of trials, a somewhat anomalous finding was that 5-year-olds (45 per cent) and 6–7 year olds (around 72 per cent) were somewhere in between.

All in all, a fair conclusion would seem to be that the availability of sentence interpretations that require the overriding of linear order increases gradually with age. From a generativist perspective, one could argue that quantifier raising is available from the beginning of development, but that children need to learn to override their initial reliance on linear order where the two conflict. From a constructivist perspective, one could argue that children begin with a strategy whereby the first NP is always given the widest scope, but learn that cues such as those associated with the passive construction indicate that the opposite interpretation is available (and, eventually, that it is preferred). A similar type of learning is proposed for passive constructions in general. Children may initially misinterpret sentences such as *The mouse was eaten by the cat* as if the mouse were the AGENT, but learn, on the basis of exposure to passive sentences, that cues associated with the passive construction (e.g. the morphology *-en*) are associated with the reversal of usual roles.

8.2.1.2 Rejecting non-adultlike interpretations   As well as failing to access some adultlike interpretations of quantifier raising constructions, there is some evidence that children may also allow non-adultlike interpretations. In particular, many children seem initially to interpret sentences such as *Every dwarf is eating a pizza* **symmetrically** (e.g. as 'every dwarf is eating a pizza *and* every pizza is being eaten by a dwarf'). That is, children often reject 'every dwarf is eating a pizza' as a description of a scene in which every dwarf is eating a pizza, but there is an extra pizza that is not being eaten. For example, of 49 children tested by Philip (1995), 25 rejected *Every farmer is feeding a donkey* as a description of a picture such as that shown in Figure 8.10 (reproduced from Crain *et al.* 1996: 84). If asked to justify their answer, children point to unfed donkey. Similar findings were also reported by Roeper and de Villiers (1991) and Takahashi (1991) for English, Inhelder and Piaget (1964) for French, Lee (1991) for Chinese, and Philip and Verrips (1994) for Dutch.

Philip (1995) essentially argued that, for children, *every* refers not to individual participants (farmers) – as it does for adults – but to events (syntactically, children treat *every* as if it were an adverb – e.g. *always* – as opposed to a quantifier). This means that children interpret a sentence such as *Every farmer is feeding a donkey* as 'every event containing either a farmer or a donkey is an event in which a famer is feeding a donkey'. Thus children incorrectly reject *Every farmer is feeding a donkey* as a description of Figure 8.10 because, of the four 'events' depicted, only three show a farmer feeding a donkey. Philip (1995) provided support for this proposal by showing that if the *event* (feeding a donkey) was replaced with a *state* (being a 'donkey-feeder') the rate of non-adult responses, though still high, was significantly reduced: children incorrectly rejected *Every farmer is feeding a donkey* as a description of Figure 8.10 on 75 per cent of trials, but *Every farmer is a donkey-feeder* on only 50 per cent of trials.

Figure 8.10 As a description of this picture, children incorrectly rejected *Every farmer is feeding a donkey* on 75 per cent of trials, but *Every farmer is a donkey-feeder* on only 50 per cent of trials (from Crain *et al.*, 1996: 84; reproduced by permission of Taylor & Francis)

Crain *et al.* (1996) raise a problem for the symmetry account. Because this account argues that children interpret *every* as referring to events rather than to individuals, the position of *every* in the sentence should not matter. Thus the symmetry account predicts that children will reject *A man is feeding every donkey* as a description of Figure 8.11 (reproduced from Crain *et al.*, 1996: 105) because some events do not depict a man feeding a donkey. In fact, the children studied by Crain *et al.* (1996) correctly accepted this description on 72 per cent of trials, apparently recognizing that *every* refers to *donkey*, not to events. This does not appear to reflect a simple *yes*-bias, as children rejected *Every man is feeding a donkey* as a description of this picture on 87 per cent of trials (Takahashi, 1991).

Crain *et al.* (1996) further argue that experiments in which children perform poorly often use a task that makes little pragmatic sense. Speakers do not ask *yes/no* questions (or elicit truth-value judgments) when the answer is already available to both the speaker and the listener, or in situations where one possibility was never raised. Consider a possible scenario under which it would be reasonable to ask the question 'Is every farmer feeding a donkey?' Imagine a farm with several farmers, one of whom had mentioned that he might not have time to feed his donkey on a particular day, as he had some business to attend to in his office. Someone who wanted to round up all the farmers might

Figure 8.11 Children accept *A man is feeding every donkey* as a description of this picture (from Crain *et al.*, 1996: 105; reproduced by permission of Taylor & Francis)

ask 'Is every farmer feeding a donkey? (or do I need to go and look for one in the office?)'. On the other hand, if the speaker could *see* that every farmer was feeding a donkey, it would make no sense to ask the question. Thus a listener (or a child in an experimental study) might reason as follows: 'She can't have meant to ask whether every farmer was feeding a donkey as she can *see* that this is the case. Perhaps she meant "is every donkey being fed by a farmer?"' Indeed, Brooks and Sekerina (2006) found that 11 out of 22 *adult* speakers showed at-chance performance with comparable stimuli (e.g. *Every alligator is in a bathtub*).

Crain *et al.* (1996) conducted a modified version of the study of Philip (1995) using a truth-value judgment task in which a puppet attempted to remember a fact about a story. Children were then asked whether the puppet was correct or incorrect. The (four) stories were constructed such that both the *yes* and *no* possibilities were considered. In one story, three skiers found five bottles of soda and five cups of apple cider. Two of the skiers initially considered each drinking a bottle of soda, before deciding to each drink a cup of cider (leaving two cups undrunk). The puppet then guessed 'Every skier drank a cup of cider.' If children applied a symmetrical interpretation, they should have answered *no*, because two cups remained undrunk (in the same way that many rejected *Every farmer is feeding a donkey* for a scenario in which one donkey remained unfed). The participants in this study were fourteen children (aged 3–5;3;10; $M = 4;3$) who had already given symmetrical responses in a replication (Crain *et al.*, 1996: experiment 1) of Philip's (1995) farmer–donkey task. All fourteen children tested accepted the puppet's description of the story on all four trials (two seemed to reject the use of *every* for a small number of participants – i.e. three – but accepted the description when the number of participants was increased to five).

One problem with this study, however, is that Crain *et al.* (1996) did not vary the position of the quantifier. One cannot conclude that children show adultlike knowledge of quantification without demonstrating that they reject (for example) *A skier drank every cup of apple cider* as a description of this scenario. Another potential problem (Gordon, 1996; Drozd, 2001, 2004) is that children's improved performance in Crain *et al.*'s (1996) study could be due to the fact that whereas the un-fed donkey in Philip's (1995) study (and Crain *et al.*'s replication) is prominent, the extra items in Crain *et al.*'s (1996) scenarios (e.g. the undrunk cups of cider) are backgrounded, in that they are not directly relevant to the story. This would lead children who are operating on the basis of symmetry to reject *Every farmer is feeding a donkey* when a (salient) donkey is left unfed, but accept *Every skier drank a cup of cider* when two (relatively unimportant) cups of cider remain undrunk. Anticipating this possible objection, Crain *et al.* (1996) did attempt to make the left-over items salient in the story (e.g. the skiers discussed which cups of cider to drink, highlighting the fact that there were two left over). However, it is difficult to know how successful this manipulation was. The story was still very much 'about' the skiers as opposed to the apple cider, and contained a long lead-in, in which only the skiers were discussed (perhaps if the story had discussed a manufacturer of apple cider who was concerned over low sales a different pattern of results would have emerged).

In order to counter this objection, one would need to demonstrate that different pragmatic lead-ins differentially influence children's interpretations *of the same story*. For example, one could use the standard farmer–donkey scenario (*Every farmer is feeding a donkey*, as a description of Figure 8.10) with a lead-in in which one of the three farmers indicated that he might not feed his donkey. This would be expected to *reduce* the number of incorrect 'no' responses caused by the unfed donkey, by highlighting that the question in hand is whether or not all the farmers fed a donkey. On the other hand, a lead-in in which a donkey worried that he might not be fed would be expected to *increase* the number of incorrect 'no' responses, by incorrectly suggesting that the question in hand is whether or not every donkey is fed.

At present, the available data are consistent with two possibilities. The first (Crain *et al.*, 1996) is that children have essentially adultlike knowledge of quantification (which may be obscured by inappropriate experimental tasks).

The second is that children simply compute a rough parse of the sentence (i.e. it contains *farmer*, *donkey*, *feed* and *every*) and use the discourse context (in an experimental study, the picture and background story) to arrive at the most plausible interpretation (Bucci, 1978; Drozd, 2001; Geurts, 2003).

8.2.2   *Constructivist approaches*

Brooks and colleagues (Brooks and Braine, 1996; Brooks *et al.*, 1998; Brooks and Sekerina, 2006) argue for this latter view, additionally proposing that children (and adults) have a notion of a **prototypical scenario** for the use of a universal quantifier such as *every* or *each*: a scenario involving perfect one-to-one mapping between entities. For example, a prototypical scenario for the sentence *Every farmer is feeding a donkey* would contain the same number of farmers and donkeys, with one feeding each. Because this prototype scenario provides a 'good enough' way of understanding many common uses of *every*, children (and – as we will see – adults), often use this short-cut for interpreting all sentences involving *every*, and thus make mistakes for sentences that do not correspond to the prototype (see also Wason, 1966).

Brooks and Sekerina (2006) tested this prediction using a picture-matching task. Brooks and Sekerina argue that this provides a more accurate assessment of children's knowledge than the truth-value judgment task, as children may accept sentences due to a *yes*-bias, or reject sentences due to reasons unrelated to the syntax of quantification (as was the case for two children in the study of Crain *et al.*, 1996, who rejected any sentence where the puppet used the determiner *every* to refer to a small group of skiers). Children were presented with sentences such as *Every man is washing a bear* and *There is a man washing every bear* and asked to choose a matching picture for each. For example, each picture shown in Figure 8.12 is the target picture for one of these sentences and the foil picture for the other.

Children from five different age groups (mean ages 5;5, 6;6, 7;6, 8;6 and 9;6) participated in the study. Performance for the sentences of the form *Every man is washing a bear* was at chance for the 5-year-olds, but above chance (80 per cent and above) for all the other groups. However, performance for sentences of the form *There is a man washing every bear* was significantly above chance only for the oldest group (90 per cent correct). Brooks and Sekerina (2006) interpret this poor performance as evidence that children have difficulty with sentences that differ from the *every* prototype (an almost identical pattern of performance was observed for similar sentences with *each*). Indeed, only half of the adults tested showed above-chance performance for sentences such as *Every alligator is in a bathtub* (Figure 8.13).

Brooks and Sekerina (2006) argue that this constitutes evidence that listeners use 'quick and dirty' (Townsend and Bever, 2001) strategies (e.g.

Figure 8.12 *Every man is washing a bear / There is a man washing every bear*
(from Brooks and Sekerina, 2006: 183; reproduced by permission of Taylor
& Francis)

Figure 8.13 Which picture shows *Every alligator is in a bathtub?* Only half
of the adults studied correctly selected the left hand picture (from Brooks and
Sekerina, 2006: 192; reproduced by permission of Taylor & Francis)

every = one-to-one correspondence between alligators and bathtubs) that may
or may not be followed-up with a 'deeper' analysis (Sanford and Stuart, 2002).

Street and Dąbrowska (2010) conducted a very similar study with participants
defined as having 'low academic attainment'. As a group, these participants
were at chance with sentences of the form *Every basket has a cat in it* (43 per cent
correct choices). Although sentences of the form *Every cat is in a basket* were
associated with a higher overall level of correct performance (78 per cent), only
around 1/3 of the participants were above chance individually. These findings
have two implications. First, the fact that participants performed significantly
better for the construction that is more common in English (as confirmed by
a corpus analysis) suggests that speakers are gradually learning the correct

interpretation of these sentence types from the input, as opposed to relying on innate principles. Second, the finding that *most*[6] native speakers of English *never* achieve the idealized level of 'adult competence' posited under generativist accounts calls into question the assumption that arriving at an understanding of (formally defined) quantification is part of 'normal' language acquisition. If 'competence' is defined as showing a pattern of performance that would be considered correct by a logician or mathematician, perhaps quantification is better understood as being in the domain of formal mathematical instruction, rather than language acquisition.

8.2.3   Quantification: conclusion

Mediating between the generativist and constructivist accounts here is complicated by the fact that both agree that experimental findings will be heavily influenced by pragmatic and contextual findings, but disagree with regard to the adult state.

The generativist position is that adultlike knowledge of quantification consists of the UG-specified knowledge that a universally quantifying determiner (e.g. *every*) refers to the set of objects named by the noun with which this determiner combines (e.g. *every farmer*). Children's knowledge is essentially adultlike, but they may show non-adultlike performance if the experimental situation is pragmatically odd. Although some studies (e.g. Crain *et al.*, 1996) have demonstrated near-perfect performance with young children, this may be due to experimental confounds that help children arrive at the correct interpretation. For example, in the study of Crain *et al.* (1996), the set of items to which the quantifier referred (e.g. *skiers*) was highlighted in the story. Other studies (e.g. Brooks and Sekerina, 2006) have found much lower levels of correct performance, but it remains possible that the different paradigm used underestimated children's ability. The way forward for generativist approaches, then, must be to demonstrate that children show near-perfect performance whenever experimental confounds are reduced to a minimum (as opposed to actively working in support of the adult interpretation).

Constructivist accounts agree that experimental and contextual factors are important, but go further: much of children's (and adults') performance is held to be almost entirely a consequence of such factors. The constructivist position is that children have very little knowledge of the abstract syntax of quantification, and base their interpretation of such sentences on prototypical *every*-scenarios, overriding this default interpretation on the basis of contextual or pragmatic factors. For example, children may reject *Every farmer is feeding a donkey* as a description of a sentence in which one donkey remains unfed, as the prototypical *every*-scenario, when applied to this case, would involve every farmer feeding and every donkey being fed. On the other hand, whilst the

Summary table 8.2 *Quantification* (☑ = *supports theory*; ☒ = *counts against theory*)

Issue/phenomenon	Generativist full-competence approach (e.g. Crain et al., 1996)	Constructivist approach (e.g. Brooks and Sekerina, 2006)
Summary of theory	Children have innate knowledge of quantification; errors due to task demands or failure to override cue of surface word order.	Children learn quantification constructions from the input. Until (or even after) these have been learned, listeners use prototypical-scenario templates for interpretation.
Are adultlike interpretations available to children?	☑ Yes (Crain et al.'s, 1996, truth-value judgment task) but ☒ performance with passives suggest children initially use surface word-order strategy (Brooks and Braine, 1996).	☑ Improving performance with age supports input-based learning approach. Generativist account could argue children gradually learn to override surface word order.
Do children reject non-adultlike interpretations?	☒ No (Philip, 1995; Roeper and de Villiers, 1991; Takahashi, 1991; Inhelder and Piaget, 1964; Lee, 199; Philip and Verrips, 1994), but performance improves if task makes more pragmatic sense (Crain et al., 1996).	Crain et al.'s data equally compatible with suggestion that children compute a rough parse of the sentence and use discourse context to infer most plausible interpretation (Bucci, 1978; Drozd, 2001; Geurts, 2003; Townsend and Bever, 2001; Sanford and Stuart, 2002).
Do listeners use a prototypical one-to-one mapping scenario for interpretation (as opposed to syntactic principles)?	Many (though certainly not all) speakers do arrive at the idealized adult endstate assumed by the generativist approach (i.e. interpretations are in accordance with syntactic principles).	☑ Yes, both children and adults show difficulty with scenarios that differ from this prototype in picture-matching task (Brooks and Sekerina, 2006; Street and Dąbrowska, 2010).

default interpretation of *Every skier drank a cup of cider* would involve every skier drinking and every cup of cider being drunk, children can override this interpretation when the left-over entities (e.g. the cups of cider) are relatively incidental compared to the other entities (e.g. the skiers).

The challenge for constructivist accounts is to explain how some speakers (though, in reality, probably a minority) arrive at an interpretation that is consistent with the formal generativist analysis, whilst retaining 'quick and dirty' strategies for use in many everyday contexts. As discussed above, it may be that speakers acquire this understanding only through formal instruction in mathematics and logic. It is more likely, perhaps, that speakers attain knowledge of generativist-style quantification by exposure to formal written speech. It is clear that generativist and constructivist researchers alike can learn much by studying the performance of typical speakers, as opposed to restricting their experiments solely to high-academic-attainment groups.

8.3   Control

To an adult English speaker, the meaning of a sentence such as *John told Bill to leave* is so obvious that it scarcely seems possible that there could be another interpretation. Yet if the verb *promise* is used in exactly the same structure (e.g. *John promised Bill to leave*), the meaning is reversed: it is now John who is under the obligation to leave. Similarly, if *John spoke to Bill before/while/after leaving* or *John ignored Bill in order to leave*, John is the one who has left (or wants to leave). Children do not always interpret such sentences in an adultlike manner. In particular, a sentence such as *John spoke to Bill before leaving* is often incorrectly interpreted as if it is Bill who left. The questions for acquisition theorists, therefore, are 'why do children sometimes arrive at non-adultlike interpretations of such sentences?' and 'how do they subsequently reach the adult state?'

8.3.1   Generativist accounts

In this section, we will consider three different generativist accounts of children's difficulty with such structures (and subsequent adultlike performance). We begin by outlining the background assumptions that are shared by all three accounts. Non-finite clauses (e.g. *to leave*; *before/while/after leaving*; *in order to leave*) have an understood subject – termed **PRO** – that is phonologically null (i.e. not pronounced). In some sentences, there is only one possible referent for PRO:

John$_i$ wanted [PRO$_i$ to leave].

In other sentences, PRO has **arbitrary reference** (i.e. it can refer to anyone):

[PRO to smoke] is dangerous.

The sentences with which we are primarily concerned, however, are those where there are two possible referents for PRO (the adult interpretation is shown):

	Non-finite clause type	control
John told Bill$_i$ [PRO$_i$ to leave].	object complement	object
John$_i$ promised Bill [PRO$_i$ to leave].	object complement	subject
John$_i$ spoke to Bill [before/while/after PRO$_i$ leaving].	adjunct	subject
John$_i$ ignored Bill [in order PRO$_i$ to leave].	adjunct	subject

For sentences with non-finite object-complement clauses (the first two examples), the lexical properties of the main-clause verb (e.g. *tell/promise*) determine whether PRO is **controlled by** (i.e. receives its interpretation from) the main-clause object (as for *tell, ask, want* etc.) or the main-clause subject (as for *promise*[7]). When the non-finite clause is an adjunct clause (as opposed to an object complement), PRO is always controlled by the main-clause subject (regardless of the main-clause verb).

Interpretation of PRO is determined by c-command. The **controller** of PRO (i.e. the main clause NP to which PRO refers) is the closest NP that c-commands PRO. For a complement-clause sentence such as *John told Bill PRO to leave*, both NPs (*John* and *Bill*) c-command PRO, but *Bill* is closer, and hence controls PRO (an example of **object control**).[8] For adjunct sentences (e.g. *John spoke to Bill before PRO leaving*), only the subject NP (*John*) c-commands, and hence controls, PRO (an example of **subject control**).

8.3.1.1 The structure-changing hypothesis McDaniel, Cairns and Hsu (1990/1) propose a five-stage account for the acquisition of control structures. The basic assumption is that children have knowledge of PRO and the c-command relation that governs its interpretation throughout. However, children have difficulty assigning the correct syntactic structure to sentences with subordinate clauses. We outline this theory by setting out the experimental findings that formed the basis of the proposal.

McDaniel *et al.* (1990/1) asked children (aged 3;9–5;4, study 1 and 4;1–4;10, study 2) to enact sentences with an object-complement clause (requiring object control; no *promise*-type sentences were included) and with an adjunct clause (requiring subject control), for example:

> **Complement (object control):** Cookie Monster$_i$ tells Grover$_j$ to PRO$_{*i/j}$ jump into the water.

> **Adjunct (subject control):** The zebra$_i$ touches the lion$_j$ before/after/in order to PRO$_{i/*j}$ drink(ing) some water.

In addition to enacting (three) sentences of each type, children were asked about the possible referents of PRO. For example, for the second question, children were first asked who drank the water, and subsequently whether the sentence could mean that anybody else drank the water.

A number of children allowed PRO to refer to any entity – whether mentioned in the sentence or not – for both complement and adjunct sentences. For example, when presented with *The zebra touches the lion before drinking some water*, they answered that another character altogether (e.g. Bert) could be the one who drank some water. McDaniel *et al.* (1990/1) account for the behaviour of these **stage IA** children by arguing that they are unable to form (or analyse) subordinate clauses. Instead, children analyse the sentence as a co-ordinate structure (e.g. *[The zebra touches the lion] and [PRO (is) drinking some water])*. This means that PRO is analysed as if it were the subject of a single-clause sentence. As we have already seen, in these cases (e.g. *PRO to smoke is dangerous*) PRO can refer to anyone. As McDaniel *et al.* (1990/1) acknowledge, since subordination (i.e. the ability to form relative clauses; see previous chapter) is part of UG, it is somewhat anomalous to argue that children lack this ability. McDaniel *et al.* (1990/1) argue that, whilst children have knowledge of subordination in principle, subordination cannot occur until children acquire the necessary lexical and semantic knowledge: for complement sentences, children must learn that (for example) *tell* takes a subordinate object-complement clause. For adjunct sentences, children must learn that the adjunct clause is subordinate because of its semantic relationship with the main clause (it provides some additional, optional information).

At **stage IB** children show adultlike performance for complement sentences (e.g. *Cookie Monster_i tells Grover_j to PRO*_{i/j} jump into the water*) – with this continuing throughout subsequent stages – but still allow arbitrary reference for adjunct sentences (e.g. *The zebra touches the lion before PRO drinking some water*). McDaniel *et al.* (1990/1) argue that this is because the subordinating relationship between a verb and its complement clause is salient and learned early (e.g. *tell X [that] COMP*). In contrast, the difference between an adjunct clause (e.g. *before PRO drinking some water*) and a conjoined clause (*and PRO drank some water*) is subtle and later-acquired. Nevertheless, McDaniel *et al.* (1990/1) note that the theory does not *require* this ordering, and that it is possible that some children may disallow arbitrary reference for PRO sooner for adjuncts than for complements.

At **stage II** (actually the third stage), children no longer allow PRO in adjuncts to have arbitrary reference (i.e. they will not allow it to refer to a character who is not mentioned), but reliably incorrectly interpret such sentences as having object control (e.g. *The zebra_i touches the lion_j before PRO*_{*j} drinking some water*). Hsu, Cairns and Fiengo (1985) suggest that this is because children are misled by the similarity between object complements and adjuncts, and thus attach the adjunct at VP (as if it were a complement) as opposed to IP.[9] At **stage III**, children switch between the correct adultlike (subject-control) interpretation of adjunct sentences (e.g. *The zebra$_i$ touches the lion$_j$ before PRO$_{i/*j}$ drinking some water*) and the incorrect interpretation (object control) displayed at stage II. For McDaniel *et al.*, this is due to gradual lexical learning; specifically, that prepositions such as *before*, *after* and *in order to* introduce adjuncts (and therefore that such phrases must be attached at IP instead of VP). In support of this claim is the finding that three children studied displayed earlier adultlike performance with *before* and *after* than *in order to*. At **stage IV**, children show adultlike performance with all relevant structures.

Although the structure-changing hypothesis gives a plausible account of the experimental data, when analysed in detail, the motivation for many of the stages – and the transition between them – is weak. First, the only evidence which supports the claim that children allow PRO to have arbitrary reference (i.e. to refer to a character who is not mentioned in the main clause) – a characteristic of stage I performance – is the *judgments* of five children. Since all of these children first enacted object-control interpretations of sentences such as *The zebra$_i$ touches the lion$_j$ before PRO$_{*j}$ drinking some water*, it seems likely that they allowed an extra-sentential referent in the judgment task only as the result of a *yes*-bias. If an experimenter asks 'Could anybody else be drinking the water?', the strong implication is that the correct response is to answer *yes* and that the child should seek another possible drinker. Indeed, this sentence does not, in fact, preclude the possibility that the lion may *also* drink some water (Sherman and Lust, 1993).

Second, a longitudinal component of the experiment (study 2) investigated whether children actually pass through the stages in the predicted order. Of the fourteen children, half remained the same or (one child) 'regressed'. Whilst three children progressed through, or out of, stage I, this means little under the assumption that apparent 'stage I' performance reflects nothing more than difficulty with the judgment task. Whilst two children moved from stage II to stage III, in practice this means simply that the rate of incorrect object-control interpretations of adjuncts declined from 100 per cent to less than 100 per cent (on its way to 0 per cent at stage IV). The theory is also rather lenient in that children may 'skip' stages (one child did so) or disallow arbitrary reference for PRO sooner for adjuncts than complements (again, one child did so). This means that virtually any pattern of data that involves children getting better with age (as any theory would predict) can be explained (a similar objection applies to a follow-up longitudinal study conducted by Cairns, McDaniel, Hsu and Rapp, 1994).

A final problem is that it is far from clear that the theory constitutes an *explanation*, as opposed to simply a description of children's behaviour couched in formal terms. Consider the finding that children move from incorrect (object-control) interpretations of adjunct sentences (stage II) to mixed interpretations (stage III) to adultlike (subject-control) interpretations (stage IV). The claim is that children (II) incorrectly attach adjuncts at VP, (III) attach them both incorrectly at VP and correctly at IP, and (IV) attach them correctly at IP. This is simply a description of what children's enactments would look like if they were illustrated using phrase-structure trees; we still require an explanation of *why* children incorrectly attach adjuncts at VP, then alternate, then learn the correct attachment site.

McDaniel *et al.* (1990/1) do offer such an explanation: children treat adjuncts as if they were complements because they are superficially similar, and gradually learn to override this strategy on the basis of lexical learning. The problem with this explanation, as far as McDaniel *et al.*'s (1990/1) proposal is concerned, is that it is possible to restate it in terms that have nothing to do with attachment. In fact, if we accept the methodological objection raised with regard to the evidence for the existence of stage I, McDaniel *et al.*'s (1990/1) data can be summarized far more simply as follows: children initially interpret all relevant sentence types such that the main-clause object controls PRO (presumably because object-complement sentences are more frequent than adjunct sentences), gradually learning to override this interpretation when a preposition such as *before* or *after* introduces the subordinate clause. Indeed, given that all the sentence types used in this study had an equivalent structure, McDaniel *et al.*'s (1990/1) data cannot, in principle, rule out an explanation based solely on linear order (e.g. children initially interpret the second NP as controlling PRO in all circumstances, gradually learning to override this interpretation when a preposition such as *before* or *after* is present anywhere).

8.3.1.2 Children are in control   Sherman and Lust (1993) also argued that the findings of McDaniel *et al.* (1990/1) provide little evidence for a stage theory. These authors argued, on the basis of an act-out study (experiment 2), that children's interpretation of PRO is adultlike. This study focused on object complements. As well as non-finite object complements with PRO as subject (e.g. *John$_i$ told Tom$_j$ [PRO$_{*i/j}$ to leave]*), the study also included finite object complements with lexical pronoun subjects (e.g. *John$_i$ told Tom$_j$ that he $_{i/j}$ will leave*). Before hearing the target sentence, children were presented with a pragmatic lead-in that highlighted either the main-clause subject (e.g. *This is a story about John*) or object (e.g. *This is a story about Tom*). The prediction was that this would influence children's interpretation of the ambiguous subject pronoun *he* in finite object complements, but would not affect children's interpretation of PRO in non-finite object complements, which is determined by the principle of c-command (and is always the object; here *Tom*).

Broadly speaking, the results supported this prediction: for all age groups, the pragmatic lead-in affected children's interpretation of *he*, but not PRO. However, a problem for Sherman and Lust's (1993) claim that this reflects adultlike knowledge is that children did not unerringly interpret PRO as referring to the main-clause object. In fact, for around a quarter of trials with object-control verbs (*tell/remind*), the youngest group incorrectly interpreted PRO as referring to the main-clause subject (e.g. *John_i told Tom_j [PRO*_i to leave]*). Sherman and Lust (1993) also included a number of sentences with the subject-control verb *promise* (e.g. *John promised Tom to leave*). For sentences with *promise*, correct subject choices outnumbered object choices only for the oldest age group (mean age 7;4), who still displayed correct performance on only around 60 per cent of trials. However, late correct performance with *promise* is consistent with the view that children know the syntax of control, as it is precisely this knowledge that they must *override* to display correct performance with this item.

Although Sherman and Lust (1993) present their results as very different to those of McDaniel *et al.* (1990/1), a coherent developmental pattern emerges. Children initially perform well with object-control object complements (e.g. *John told Tom_i PRO_i to leave*), but overgeneralize this pattern to adjuncts and coordinate clauses (*The zebra touches the lion_i before PRO*_i drinking some water*; *The turtle tickles the skunk_i and PRO*_i bumps the car*), as well as the subject-control verb *promise* (e.g. *John promised Tom_i PRO*_i to leave*). Presumably, this happens because (a) object-control object complements are the most frequent relevant sentence type and/or (b) children initially interpret sentences on the basis of linear order, with the last-mentioned NP controlling PRO (possibly due to working-memory limitations). This pattern does not appear to constitute strong evidence for either a stage theory or a full-competence approach. Rather, children seem to initially overgeneralize the most frequent interpretation (object-control) to all relevant sentence types before gradually retreating from this error as they learn more about the relevant sentence types.

This does not mean, necessarily, that young children have no knowledge of the syntax of PRO. Indeed, children's early successful performance with sentences such as *John told Tom_i PRO_i to leave* requires an explanation. The generativist explanation would be that children are in possession of the UG-specified knowledge that the closet c-commanding NP (e.g. *Tom*) controls PRO. Whether or not a rival constructivist explanation that posits no such innate knowledge is feasible is a question to which we now turn.

8.3.2   *Constructivist approaches*

Like the other phenomena discussed in this chapter, control is an issue that has received very little attention from constructivist researchers. In particular, we are aware of no experimental studies that have explicitly attempted to test a constructivist account of control. Our approach here, then, will be to outline usage-based accounts of control phenomena in the adult grammar, and offer some suggestions for how such accounts could be investigated in young children.

8.3.2.1 The linear order and semantic role accounts   One relevant study is that of Maratsos (1974). This study investigated whether children's performance with object complements could be a consequence of a strategy based on linear order; specifically interpreting the second NP – i.e. the NP that is closest to the verb in the complement clause – as the subject of that verb. This simple strategy would explain the pattern of performance outlined above: early success with object-control verbs such as *ask* and *tell*, but failure with the subject-control verb *promise*:

> John asked/told Bill$_i$ PRO$_i$ to leave.
>
> John promised Bill$_i$ PRO$_{*i}$ to leave.

In order to test this account, Maratsos (1974) asked 4- and 5-year-old children to enact passive sentences with *ask* and *tell* (*promise*-type passives were not included). Passive sentences were used because a linear-order strategy would give the wrong interpretation:

Bill$_i$ was asked/told by John PRO$_i$ to leave.	Adult interpretation
Bill was asked/told by John $_i$ PRO$_{*i}$ to leave.	Incorrect linear-order interpretation

This study employed two important controls. First, passive screening trials (e.g. *The boy is pushed by the dog*) were used to ensure that only children who understood passive sentences completed the test trials. Second, children were trained to enact both the main clause (e.g. John leaving) and the complement clause (e.g. Bill asking John to do so) (so far as we can tell, most studies require children to enact only the complement clause).

Perhaps surprisingly, children were not misled by linear order, showing correct performance for 96 per cent of trials. Maratsos (1974) explained this finding in terms of a **semantic-role principle**. Children learn that the entity that receives the request (the *goal*; e.g. Bill) – and not the entity who is the *source* of that request (e.g. John) – is the one who must perform the relevant action. Presumably, children acquire this principle by hearing and understanding the meaning behind sentences such as *I told you to behave!* (indeed, it would be an odd child who took this utterance, when produced by a caregiver, to mean 'you told me to behave').

Maratsos (1974) asks how children avoid making the incorrect generalization based on surface word order. After all, it is likely that the vast majority of sentences children hear (e.g. *I told you to behave!*; *I asked you to be quiet!*) are consistent with the generalization that the second NP is to be interpreted as the referent for the missing subject. However, this is a slightly odd question to ask as children face exactly the same problem for conventional passive sentences (e.g. *The mouse was eaten by the cat*), for which they must override their knowledge that – in general – the first-mentioned entity is the one performing the action (e.g. *The cat ate the mouse*). Evidence reviewed in Chapter 7 shows that children initially misinterpret passives, presumably because they are misled by this surface-order generalization, before learning to override it, presumably on the basis of the presence of passive morphology (e.g. *BE/GET, -en, by*). Presumably, once they have learned that the presence of passive morphology requires the two semantic roles to be switched, children are able to apply this to object complements (e.g. sentences with *ask/tell*) as well as simple passives. Note that, by excluding children who could not enact passives with overt arguments (e.g. *The boy is pushed by the dog*), Maratsos (1974) included only children who have presumably moved beyond a linear-word-order strategy.

Thus although many of the details remained to be fleshed out, there is no reason, in principle, to rule out a possible semantics-based constructivist account under which children learn that the person receiving the request/order (however this is expressed syntactically) is the one who is to carry it out. After all, children can learn how the recipient is expressed syntactically in their language from simple sentences such as *John asked Bill a question* and *John told Bill a story*, before generalizing this knowledge to sentences with an object complement clause. Indeed, it would be bizarre for a child who understood <u>Bill</u> to be the listener in *John told Bill a story* to fail to understand <u>Bill</u> to be the listener – and hence the one who must leave – in *John told Bill to leave*.

Such an account could also potentially explain children's difficulties with *promise*. In many respects, *promise* is semantically very similar to verbs such as *ask/tell*: a speaker conveys some message regarding a potential action to a listener. Children may therefore treat *promise* as if it means something very similar to *ask/tell*, before learning the unusual semantic properties of this item. Anecdotal evidence for this proposal comes from interview data reported by Sherman and Lust (1993: 49):

Child: I promised him to make a wooden sword for me.
Experimenter: So did he promise to make a wooden sword for you?
Child: No, I can't make one! He did it with a saw.

A potential problem for the semantic-role account is that it does not explain why children initially have problems with adjunct sentences such as *The zebra$_i$ touches the lion$_j$ before PRO$_{i/*j}$ drinking some water.* One possible explanation is that there is in fact a stage where children follow the linear-order strategy discussed above (the second NP is always taken to be the missing subject), but that this stage was missed by Maratsos (1974), who studied only relatively old children (the youngest group are described as 4-year-olds, but no exact ages are given) and excluded those who misinterpreted standard passives on the basis of linear order.

8.3.2.2 A pragmatic account of subject control

Given that children do seem to initially misinterpret adjunct sentences such as *The zebra₍ᵢ₎ touches the lion before PRO₍ᵢ₎ drinking some water*, using a linear order (second NP strategy), the question is how they arrive at the adult interpretation (subject control). A useful place to start is to ask why adults interpret such sentences as they do. In languages that allow subject and object omission in main clauses (e.g. Italian, Spanish), subject omission is far more common than object omission. This is usually explained with reference to the principle of informativeness (e.g. Greenfield and Smith, 1976). The subject (or agent) is generally already under discussion (or discourse old) and thus 'is only spoken under unusual conditions, such as a conflict about agency or an actual change of agent' (1976: 184). The object generally represents new information, and thus is far less likely to be omitted (Bloom, 1990; Valian, 1991).

Although – in main clauses – English does not allow subjects to be omitted entirely, the same principle seems to govern the situations in which a noun is replaced with a pronoun. For example, if the zebra has been established as the topic (e.g. *The zebra went to the lake*), it would be usual to subsequently refer to this entity with a pronoun (e.g. *He drank some water*) (or, in languages that allow argument omission, to omit it altogether). Indeed, it would sound somewhat odd and stilted *not* to drop or pronominalize such a highly given subject (*The zebra went to the lake. The zebra drank some water*). All a child has to learn, then, to correctly interpret a sentence such as *The zebra₍ᵢ₎ touches the lion before PRO₍ᵢ₎ drinking some water* is the pragmatic principle that omitted arguments refer to the main topic of conversation, which is generally the subject of a previous clause. One way to test this account would be to use a pragmatic lead-in (as Sherman and Lust, 1993, did for object-control sentences). For this example, the prediction would be that the lead-in *This is a story about a zebra* would increase the number of correct responses, whilst *This is a story about a lion* would increase the number of errors.

8.3.2.3 A possible constructivist account of control

Under the potential constructivist account that we are sketching here, children initially interpret all relevant sentence types as if the second NP (or the NP that is closest to the subordinate clause) is the subject of the subordinate clause. As children come to understand the semantic roles of verbs of communication (e.g. *ask/tell*), and learn that conventional semantic role assignments must be reversed in the presence of passive morphology, they show correct performance with such verbs, in both active and passive sentences (e.g. *John asked/told Bill₍ᵢ₎ PRO₍ᵢ₎ to* *leave*; *Bill$_i$ was asked/told by John PRO$_i$ to leave*). Errors with *promise* (*John$_i$ promised Bill$_j$ PRO$_{*j}$ to leave*) occur until children realize that this verb has subtly different semantic roles to communication verbs such as *ask/tell*. For adjunct sentences, errors (e.g. *The zebra$_i$ touches the lion$_j$ before PRO$_{*j}$ drinking some water*) – which are also a consequence of children's early linear-order strategy – occur until children acquire the pragmatic principle that omitted arguments refer to salient, highly 'given' topics; usually the subject of a previous clause. Of course, children must override this pragmatic principle for *ask/tell* verbs (e.g. *John$_i$ asked/told Bill$_j$ PRO$_{*i/j}$ to leave*). One way in which they could do so is by learning the way in which these verbs mark their semantic roles on the basis of simple sentences (e.g. *John asked Bill a question*).

We must stress that this is only one possible constructivist account of control, and it is not one that – so far as we are aware – has been proposed in the literature. Clearly, any account along these lines will require experimental investigation; and we have outlined above some predictions of the account that could be tested. However, this account seems to be compatible in principle with the experimental evidence that we have discussed so far (though, of course, it is open to the charge that it covers the data at the expense of being vague and underspecified). Whether or not this account turns out to be correct, our goal in proposing it is simply to prompt researchers to consider the (largely ignored) possibility that a constructivist alternative that does not assume innate knowledge of PRO and c-command may be feasible.

8.3.3 Control: conclusion

As with the other topics discussed in this chapter, the data on control are relatively uncontroversial. Though they show good performance with object-control verbs (e.g. *ask/tell*), children initially make errors with subject-control verbs such as *promise* and subject-control adjunct sentences (e.g. *The zebra$_i$ touches the lion$_j$ before PRO$_{i/*j}$ drinking some water*). It seems likely that this is due, at least in part, to the use of a linear-order interpretation strategy. The challenge for generativist accounts is to offer a well-specified explanation of how children's UG-specified knowledge of control is obscured by performance and processing factors. The account should also make precise predictions regarding the pattern of correct performance and errors that will be observed as these limitations are lifted. For constructivist accounts, the challenge is to propose and test an explanation based on the acquisition of pragmatic and discourse principles. Such an account will also need to make precise predictions regarding the pattern of correct performance and error in studies with children.

Finally, it is important to note that the facts regarding control are not quite as straightforward as they have been portrayed up to this point. Although we have described subject vs object control as a property of the verb (e.g.

Summary table 8.3 *Control* (☑ = *supports theory*; ☒ = *counts against theory*)

Issue/phenomenon	Generativist full-competence approach (e.g. Sherman and Lust, 1993)	Constructivist semantic-role (e.g. Maratsos, 1974) / pragmatic principles (Greenfield and Smith, 1976) approach.
Summary of theory	Children have innate knowledge of PRO and c-command but – under some accounts (e.g. McDaniel *et al.*, 1990/1) – have difficulty with subordinate clauses	Children learn from understanding input sentences that entity that receives the request is the one who must perform the relevant action. Also learn pragmatic principle that omitted argument most likely current topic.
Are incorrect interpretations due to problems with subordinate clauses (McDaniel *et al.*, 1990/1)?	☑ Act-out/judgment data consistent with McDaniel *et al.*'s (1990/1) structure-changing account, but ☒ serious problems with methodology and interpretation of results.	N/A
Does syntactic knowledge of PRO override pragmatic cues to reference?	☑ Pragmatic lead-in affects children's interpretation of *he*, but not PRO, in act-out task (Sherman and Lust, 1993), but ☒ children still make errors on around 25% of trials.	Possibly predicts that pragmatic lead-in should affect interpretation, but could equally argue that children have learned semantic-role principle.
Is there evidence of gradual, input-based learning?	N/A	☑ Children perform well with the most frequent sentence type (object-control) and overgeneralize this interpretation to other sentence types (McDaniel *et al.*, 1990/1; Sherman and Lust, 1993).
Are children's initial interpretations on the basis of linear order?	☑ No, children show good performance when asked to act out passive sentences (Maratsos, 1974).	Possibly predicts that children should be misled on the basis of surface word order, but correct performance equally consistent with semantic-role account (Maratsos, 1974).

promise = subject control, *ask/tell* = object control), there are some situations in which the interpretation instead seems to be governed by the most probable scenario (see Levinson, 1987: 418).

John asked Bill$_i$ PRO$_i$ to leave.	BUT	John$_i$ asked Bill what PRO$_i$ to do.
John needed somebody$_i$ PRO$_i$ to clean.	BUT	John$_i$ needed somebody PRO$_i$ to blame.

Comrie (1985) notes that for German and Russian, even *promise*-type (i.e. subject-control) verbs vary in their interpretation in this way. This means that all accounts of control phenomena – whether or not they include a role for innate syntactic principles – will have to include some role for pragmatic and discourse factors.

8.4   Binding, quantification and control: conclusion

The existence of constraints on pronoun coreference (binding), quantification and control has long been seen as one of the strongest arguments for syntax that is innate, 'autonomous and independent of meaning' (Chomsky, 1957: 17). The claim is that, because these constraints operate (largely) without reference to surface order, semantics or pragmatics, they are too abstract to be acquired from the input. Four comments are in order here.

First, although the various syntactic principles discussed give good coverage of the data, there are some sentence types for which they make the wrong predictions (e.g. most people accept the Principle C violation *He$_{i*}$ was threatening to leave when Billy$_i$ noticed that the computer had died*). Furthermore, some languages (e.g. the Salish languages of North West America) appear to systematically violate certain binding principles (e.g. Davis, 2009). Second, the good coverage of the data is somewhat illusory, as it is achieved – to some extent – by dismissing as 'non-core' phenomena that would seem to require an explanation in terms of the relevant principles. For example, whilst Principle C is invoked to explain the impossibility of coreference in *She$_i$ listens to music when Sarah$_{*i}$ reads poetry*, cases such as *She$_i$ listens to music and Sarah$_{*i}$ reads poetry* – which are unacceptable despite the lack of any Principle C violation – are dismissed as irrelevant to the argument. Third – and relatedly – even the most purely syntactic theories are forced to include a role for pragmatic and discourse factors to explain these non-core cases (as in the Principle C example above, but also for Principles A and B (e.g. Evans-style contexts), as well as control phenomena). Finally, whether or not the constructivist accounts discussed in this chapter turn out to be correct, we have seen that it is possible *in principle* to provide an account of the relevant phenomena that does not assume innate knowledge of c-command or any other abstract constraints.

Of course, none of this necessarily means that children are not born with UG-specified abstract principles of syntax. At the same time, the implicit two-part claim that (a) there exists a generativist account that can explain all the relevant phenomena and (b) constructivist accounts cannot – in principle – explain these phenomena is wrong on both counts. Thus the very existence of constraints on pronoun coreference, quantification and control (and also complex-sentence formation; see Chapter 7) does not in and of itself constitute evidence for the generativist approach over a constructivist alternative. In both cases the question is an empirical one: which proposal offers the best coverage of the experimental data from adults and children?

9   Related debates and conclusions

In Chapters 1–8, we have looked at the leading debates in the core areas of first language acquisition by monolingual, typically developing children. Our goal in this final chapter, before summarizing our previous discussions and drawing some conclusions, is to briefly outline some relevant issues which we have not been able to consider elsewhere. All bear in one way or another on the debates between (broadly speaking) generativist–nativist and constructivist approaches (even if only to suggest that there may be other ways of framing the debate). We do not attempt to adjudicate between the competing proposals in detail, as we have in the rest of the book, but simply to make readers aware of the more recent research on these issues.

9.1   Related debates

9.1.1   Modularity, domain specificity and brain localization

A traditional nativist view is that children are born with an **innate language module**. A module, as defined by Fodor (1983), is a closed system (**encapsulation**) that is not available to conscious awareness (**unconscious**), is mediated by a dedicated neural system (**localization**) and – crucially for our purposes here – deals exclusively with one particular information type (**domain specificity**); in this case, language. Although it is perfectly possible, in principle, for a modular system to be acquired as opposed to innate (e.g. Bates, 1993; Elman *et al.*, 1996), the traditional view (e.g. Chomsky, 1957, 1965, 1988; Fodor, 1983) is that evidence for the domain specificity and localization of language constitutes evidence for an innate language module.

If language is an innate module (in the sense of Fodor, 1983) one would expect to find evidence that it is mediated by a dedicated neural system (as appears to be the case for other innate modules such as the face-recognition system). Thus whilst the language system could, in principle, be innate but not localized – or vice versa – evidence for localization has often been taken as evidence for the existence of an innate language module (e.g. Lenneberg,

1967). The claim is that there is a particular part of the brain that is hard-wired for language.

It is extremely well established that most adults are left lateralized for language, with a number of well-identified areas (e.g. Broca's and Wernicke's areas) involved in the comprehension and production of speech. Damage to these areas is associated with a variety of impairments to language function (Goodglass, 1993). fMRI studies with young infants (neonates and 3-month-olds) also show left lateralization for speech stimuli (Dehaene-Lambertz, Dehaene and Hertz-Pannier, 2002). ERP and fMRI studies of adult native signers show the same patterns of lateralization and localization, suggesting that many aspects of language processing take place independently of the input or output sensory system.

While it is clearly the case that there is relative encapsulation of language in the adult brain, two factors make understanding exactly what this entails in terms of modularity rather more complex than initially suggested (e.g. by Lenneberg, 1967). First, while patients with brain damage show considerable dissociations in particular language skills, scanning results do not always straightforwardly reflect clear and consistent localization across patients (Willems and Hagoort, 2007). Given the enormous complexity of working out how language is processed in the brain and that, in real life, language will always be interacting with many other environmental and internal factors, this is hardly surprising. But it does mean that conclusions about the encapsulation of language as a whole, or syntax in particular, from current knowledge of the brain are probably premature.

Second, studies of children with severe foetal or neonatal brain damage show that these children often learn language to a remarkably normal extent, though careful testing does show differences to non-brain-damaged children, particular for those children with left-hemisphere damage (MacWhinney, Feldman, Sacco and Valdés-Pérez, 2000; Feldman, MacWhinney and Sacco, 2002). While we know from fMRI scanning of young infants that there is already some sign of left lateralization for stimuli with speech-like properties, the research on early brain damage suggests that the infant brain has considerable flexibility and that the genetic basis for the localization of speech can be modified. Constructivists therefore argue that while 'domain-relevant' circuits are already present, domain-modularity is emergent and only fully arrived at during the developmental process (Elman et al., 1996, Karmiloff-Smith, 2007).

9.1.2   Atypical development

Dissociations in atypical development between language and other aspects of development have been cited by nativist researchers as evidence for an innate syntax module. If there is a domain-specific language module, one ought to be able to find individuals who show impairments in language but not in other cognitive and social abilities, and vice versa.

9.1.2.1 Specific Language Impairment (SLI) Children with **Specific Language Impairment** (SLI) are an example of a group who have been claimed to show impairments in language, but not in other cognitive abilities. Indeed, to qualify for a diagnosis of SLI a child must have non-verbal cognitive skills in the range of typically developing children of the same age, with language skills which are at least 1.25 standard deviations below the norm. Depending on diagnostic criteria, this is a relatively common disorder affecting 3–7 per cent of the population (Conti-Ramsden, Botting and Faragher, 2001; Leonard, 2000; Bishop and Leonard, 2000). Generativist researchers have argued that this dissociation between language and cognition supports the idea not only of a specific language module, but a specific module for inflection (e.g. Gopnik, 1990; Rice and Wexler, 1996), agreement (e.g. Clahsen, 1986) or structure-dependent relations (e.g. binding principles and movement, Van der Lely, 1997), that is impaired in children with SLI. Constructivist researchers generally see SLI as the result of more general impairments, such as impairments in working memory (e.g. Gathercole and Baddeley, 1990), or the processing of rapidly changing stimuli (e.g. Tallal *et al.*, 1996; Hayiou-Thomas, Bishop and Plunkett, 2004).

If SLI indeed reflects abnormalities in an innate language module – as opposed to more domain-general systems – it should show high genetic heritability. One particularly large-scale twin study (comparing monozygotic and dizygotic twins) found this to be the case (Bishop, 2000). Furthermore, although Bishop, Adams and Norbury (2006), in a study of 6-year-old children with SLI, found that performance on a test of inflection (a linguistic measure) and non-word repetition (a measure of memory/processing) were highly correlated, the two measures had different genetic origins in terms of heritability, supporting a modular view of SLI. On the other hand, Colledge *et al.* (2002), in a study of 4-year-olds with SLI, found a significant genetic influence on SLI, but little differentiation between linguistic and non-linguistic measures in terms of their genetic origin, supporting the idea of a more domain-general deficit.

It seems clear that children diagnosed with SLI come from a highly heterogeneous group, some perhaps at the extreme end of the normal distribution of language ability (Plomin and Kovas, 2005), others with more specific impairments, as indicated by the heritability on tests of grammatical inflection in the Bishop *et al.* (2006) study. These results challenge both a strong constructivist position that denies any domain-specificity to language and a strong nativist position under which language is an entirely modular system (though, in fact, such extreme positions probably do not exist; see Section 9.1.6).

9.1.2.2 Williams syndrome **Williams syndrome** is caused by the deletion of more than twenty-five genes on chromosome 7. This leads to a range of problems including cardiovascular and facial abnormalities as well as an abnormal behavioural phenotype. People with the syndrome score considerably better on standardized tests of language than would be predicted by their IQs. As a result, they are often described as showing the opposite profile to those with SLI, exhibiting severely impaired cognition but relatively spared (though still impaired) language (e.g. Rossen *et al.*, 1996). Generativist researchers have argued that this shows a separation between language and cognition (Pinker, 1994) or a separation between a syntax module and lexical memory (Clahsen and Almazan, 1998).

Again, the situation is more complex. Impairments are not exclusive to non-linguistic abilities but also affect some aspects of language, such as more complex syntax and semantics (Klein and Mervis, 1999). These authors suggest that, whilst language appears relatively fluent, this is a consequence of a good verbal memory which disguises underlying difficulties. Similarly while, as adults, these individuals often score better on language tests than predicted by their scores on IQ tests and other standardized cognitive tests, Donnai and Karmiloff-Smith (2000) argue that similar test scores obtained by different individuals may disguise different strategies used to approach the task. They argue for the importance of distinguishing scores on standardized tests from the processes by which individuals actually solve cognitive problems, and suggest that no aspect of language is 'intact' in either children or adults with the syndrome.

9.1.2.3 Autism People with **autism** show impaired social and communicative behaviour with no, or severely, limited language in a considerable number of cases. This could support the idea that the impairment in social cognition gives rise directly to the failure to learn language, supporting the constructivist position of the fundamentally social nature of language (see, for example, the discussion of word learning in Chapter 3). However, while most studies find that impairment in social-pragmatic understanding is definitive of people in the autistic spectrum range, language proficiency is extremely varied, ranging from none at all to normal (Kjelgaard and Tager-Flusberg, 2001). Happé and Plomin (2006) suggest that there is no single aetiology for autism but that it should be seen as a group of deficits.

9.1.2.4 Atypical development: summary The research so briefly summarized above seems to point towards a number of major cautions relating to the complexity of the issues involved. First, there is the question of the diagnostic unity of these disorders. Children diagnosed with SLI or autistic spectrum disorders show very varied profiles of abilities. For all of these disorders, research suggests that different deficits that are categorized under the same disorder can be underpinned by different genetic factors (e.g. Bishop, Adams and Norbury, 2006; Donnai and Karmiloff Smith, 2000; Happé, 2003). This means that any theory of – for example – SLI as a relatively pure deficit in inflection or grammatical relations will most likely fail to account for a substantial number of cases (which, of course, it would be circular to dismiss as not constituting SLI). Similarly, the linguistic difficulties of children with autism cannot be attributed solely to difficulties in social cognition, since many children who clearly have difficulties in social cognition attain normal language proficiency.

A second issue is that diagnosis, and more particularly, assignment to experimental groups, almost always involves standardized tests, and the same score on a test can be achieved through different strategies. Karmiloff-Smith (2007) points out that in all these cases, we need to be clear about exactly what aspects of language skills children show and, even more importantly, to have a developmental account of how they are arrived at. She emphasizes the importance of analysing the ways in which children can compensate in development by taking other routes.

Finally, with the sequencing of the human genome, research on the genetics of these conditions is developing very rapidly, but with conflicting results and explanations (Karmiloff-Smith, 2007; Bishop, 2009). Evidence on the heritability of particular language deficits and abilities should therefore be treated with caution, and not used to make wide-ranging theoretical claims.

9.1.3   A critical period for language learning?

Children who do not learn a first language until late in childhood often do not develop full language skills. This has led to the suggestion of a **critical period** for language acquisition. Some animals show **critical periods** (or **sensitive periods**) for certain types of learning. For example, if a chaffinch does not hear an adult song before it reaches sexual maturity, it will never learn the song correctly (Thorpe, 1958). Certain human systems such as binocular vision also seem to show a critical period (Banks, Aslin and Letson, 1975). Since a critical period must, by definition, be innately specified, strong evidence of a critical period for language acquisition would constitute evidence for an innate language system.

9.1.3.1 Early language deprivation   Evidence on the crucial importance of early language learning comes from studies of **hearing-impaired children** who do not learn a sign language or receive a cochlear implant until relatively late in childhood (e.g. Schauwers, Govaerts and Gillis, 2005;

Mayberry, 2009), and also of so-called **'feral' children** (e.g. Curtiss *et al.*, 1974; Jones, 1995). However, constructivists would argue that the implication of such findings is unclear, as children who have not been exposed to language have also missed out on a wide range of social, cultural and educational experiences with which language acquisition is presumably irrevocably intertwined. Hence, it is impossible in principle for there to be an ideal 'test subject' who was not exposed to language for the hypothesized critical period but otherwise developed normally.

9.1.3.2 Children 'inventing' a language   Other evidence relevant to this issue comes from situations where children who are not exposed to a language (e.g. **deaf children of hearing parents**) are said to 'invent' one. Goldin-Meadow (2003) found that such children develop a repertoire of referential gestures that can be used to communicate. The claim is that the invented language is fully linguistic, in that it contains categories such as NOUN and VERB, morphological and syntactic structures and possibly even complementation (i.e. complex syntax). The rapid development of **Nicaraguan Sign Language** (NSL) over the last thirty years has also been suggested as evidence of children's ability to invent a language 'from scratch'. NSL has developed into a fully fledged sign language since hearing-impaired children started to be brought together into schools for the deaf, having previously been isolated at home, communicating in a limited way with their **'home sign'**. Senghas (2003) found that each new generation of children coming into the school has made the language more grammatical and more like conventionalized sign languages (and, indeed, spoken languages).

Generativist researchers (e.g. Bickerton, 1981; Kegl, 2002) claim that this constitutes evidence for innate knowledge of language structure. The claim is that, because the development of NSL has been so rapid, it is not possible that abstract syntactic categories and rules evolved spontaneously; rather, these children must already have had some innate knowledge of categories and rules for combining them into phrases and sentences which they then 'filled out' with invented signs. Constructivist researchers would agree that the evolution of this language has been very fast, but would argue that this is a consequence of the need to communicate in a group, and that it has proceeded in essentially the same way as the evolution of spoken languages (e.g. Tomasello, 2008). Under this view, syntactic categories and relations are reflections of – and hence evolved to express – conceptual categories and conceptual relations that are important to speakers (e.g. Van Hoek, 1997; Langacker, 2000; Croft, 2001). The difficulty in this debate is that neither side has any idea just how 'slow' or 'fast' language evolution would be expected to be under generativist or constructivist assumptions.

9.1.3.3 Second language acquisition   There are differences, which increase with age, between children who learn one or two languages simultaneously during the normal period of language development and those who learn a **second language** later. The fact that a second language is more difficult to learn at later ages has been claimed to support the critical period hypothesis (Felser and Clahsen, 2009). For example, Johnson and Newport (1989) showed that, for a small group of Korean and Chinese immigrants to the USA, age at arrival was a significant predictor of proficiency (even when controlling for amount of exposure to English), but only for those who arrived before puberty. For those who arrived after puberty, thereby missing the hypothesized critical period, amount of exposure was not related to proficiency. These results have been challenged by a much larger analysis of US census data (Hakuta, Bialystok and Wiley, 2003) which found that the relationship between age-at-immigration and language proficiency did not differ between those who immigrated before and after puberty.

A problem in comparing first and second language acquisition is the difference in contexts in which they occur, and the fact that these contexts are more likely to be similar, the younger the learner. For example, in the studies discussed above, it may be that younger arrivals learned English in the same way that a first language is acquired (via contextual immersion and at the same time as cognitive and conceptual development), with older learners using different strategies (Clahsen and Muysken, 1996). The degree of interference from the learner's first language may also be important here (Bialystok and Hakuta, 1999). This most likely levels off after puberty, by which time systems such as grammar and morphology are largely adultlike.

9.1.4   The genetic basis of language and its evolution

Clearly, since language has evolved only in humans, it must have *some* genetic basis in evolution. However, this is trivially true of *all* exclusively human activities, such as driving, mathematics and reading. The question is precisely what is genetically specified and hence evolutionarily determined (Christiansen and Kirby, 2003). There are a wide range of possibilities, of which the following are a broad summary:

(1) There is no specific evolutionary basis for language *per se*, but for other aspects of human behaviour which then give rise to language, such as the **understanding of others' intentions** and the propensity for **categorization of symbols** into hierarchical and prototypical categories (Tomasello, 2008). Also innately specified, under this (and any) view, is the development of parts of the body essential for spoken or signed communication (e.g. vocal cords, lips, hands etc.). This is essentially the **constructivist** position, as we have characterized it throughout this book. Recent computational and

agent-based modelling studies (in which successive 'generations' attempt to learn a toy language and, in so doing, unconsciously introduce regularity), contribute to this position (Steels, 2006; Kirby, Dowman and Griffiths, 2007; Kirby, Cornish and Smith, 2008).

(2) Most aspects of language derive from general human cognitive skills but there is one specifically linguistic feature that is genetically and evolutionarily determined, and is 'the only unique component of the faculty of language' (Hauser, Chomsky and Fitch, 2002: 1569), namely **recursion** (see Chapters 4 and 6). This is a relatively recent (and somewhat marginal) **generativist–nativist** position.

(3) Universal Grammar, containing (a) knowledge of some version of X-bar syntax (or one of its more recent descendants) and the relevant lexical and functional categories, (b) principles of language (e.g. recursion, structure dependence, the binding principles) and (c) syntactic parameters (e.g. the head-direction parameter) is innately specified in the genes (Pinker and Bloom, 1990; Newmeyer, 1991). This is essentially the **mainstream generativist–nativist** position, as we have characterized it throughout this book.

(4) Language is a genetically determined dedicated system (module) that contains not only everything in (3), but also separate dedicated modules for particular aspects of language in domains such as phonology (e.g. the relation between acoustic and distinctive phonological features), word learning (e.g. constraints on word meanings) and morphology (e.g. the regular vs irregular distinction). This is a **strong generativist–nativist** position, that – on our reading of the literature – was previously popular, but appears to be losing ground to the more moderate generativist position (3) above.

In all the above cases, including the first, a plausible scenario needs to be developed which hypothesizes the selection pressure that was operating on the relevant expression of particular genes. Whilst nobody (except a creationist) would disagree with this statement, its implication for the field is rarely discussed. Let us spell it out here. It is legitimate to posit an innate principle or parameter only if one is prepared to claim that the presence of this parameter increases the organism's chances of reproduction (as argued by Newmeyer, 1991, with respect to the binding principles and subjacency; see Lightfoot, 1991b, for a sceptical response). This is true also, of course, for abilities that are assumed by the constructivist position to have emerged via natural selection (e.g. the ability to infer the intentions of others, to categorize stimuli and to perform rapid temporal order processing).

It is not difficult to see how the ability to infer others' intentions would confer a reproductive advantage. Abstract syntactic parameters (e.g. the head-direction parameter) may also be plausible if they can be shown to confer a clear advantage in communication that, in turn, increases the probability of reproduction (Pinker and Bloom, 1990, Newmeyer, 1991). The positing of increasingly fine-grained knowledge (e.g. of distinctive phonological features, parameters that apply to only a few languages and so on) becomes increasingly difficult to justify from an evolutionary perspective. Indeed, the desire to move away from positing knowledge that has only a 'tenuous connection to communicative efficacy' (Hauser, Chomsky and Fitch, 2002: 1574) seems to underlie Chomsky's recent claim that recursion is all that is innately specified. These authors go on to argue that 'by allowing us to communicate an endless variety of thoughts, recursion is clearly an adaptive computation' and, furthermore, speculate that it may have 'evolved to solve other computational problems such as navigation, number quantification, or social relationships' (p. 1574). Whilst this particular proposal has been controversial (e.g. Pinker and Jackendoff, 2005, argue that it neglects non-recursive domains such as phonology and morphology), it is clear that the field would do well to bear in mind considerations of evolutionary plausibility when positing theoretical accounts of acquisition.

So far only one gene has been unambiguously associated with the evolution of speech and language in humans. This is the FOXP2 gene identified from research with the KE family. Members of this family who have only one functioning gene have severe problems with language production and with orofacial movements (Vargha-Khadem, Watkins, Passingham and Fletcher, 1995). Two amino acids substitutions have taken place on the FOXP2 gene since the divergence of the human lineage from that of the chimpanzee (Enard *et al.*, 2002). Although almost all popular reports described FOXP2 as 'the language gene', Enard *et al.* in fact suggest that it may be involved in the neural control and coordination of the articulators that produce speech (see also Liégeois *et al.*, 2003; Vargha-Khadem, Gadian, Copp and Mishkin, 2005). However, the gene is involved in complex pathways involving many other genes and the extent to which it is specific to speech has still to be worked out (Marcus and Fisher, 2003). Note, for example, that the mutation on FOXP2 in the KE family has not been implicated in studies of SLI (Bishop, 2009).

9.1.5   Language change

As well as the variety of positions on the origins of language, constructivist and generativist–nativist researchers take opposing positions on the bases of **historical language change**. Languages are continually changing in their phonology, lexicon, morphology and syntax. For instance, English and German have both evolved from the West Germanic languages, spoken about 1,000 years ago, but English has lost most of its morphology and probably also had the 'verb-second' rule. German has retained both.

If grammar consists of an innate set of parameterized options, set in early childhood as the child encounters the input language, how can the fact that languages change be explained? One influential generativist approach is to maintain that language change results from changes in children's grammars (i.e. from **a change in the setting of parameters**; Lightfoot, 1979, 1991a). Two of the predictions that follow are, first, that children's errors (reflecting a changed parameter setting) should last into adulthood (so that the changed parameter setting can be passed on to the next generation; and, second, that speakers will have either the old grammar or the new, depending on which way the particular parameter is set. Non-generativists have challenged both these predictions: children's errors reduce and disappear, and the variable forms of adolescent and adult speech are not the same as the errors that children make; and individual speakers are variable in their usage, often using a number of possible variants of a linguistic form (for instance, as an expression of a particular group identity; Labov, 2001). While explanations for language change by non-nativists vary, they involve **sociolinguistic variation, communication pressure** and **language contact** operating on the actual utterances of speakers (rather than directly on their grammars; Slobin, 2001; Croft, 2000).

9.1.6   Conclusion

As this brief tour of the literature has shown, research on the underpinnings of language acquisition has moved rather far from the simplistic debate over whether or not humans have an innate, genetically specified language module. All researchers agree that there is clearly some genetic involvement in speech and language, which is neither completely domain-specific (since speakers are talking *about* something, it is not entirely clear what complete specificity would mean) nor completely domain general (again such a strong position would be nonsensical; clearly speech is not the same as – for example – vision). Rather we find dissociations between different aspects of speech and language development, continuities with variation in the normal population and differing strengths of genetic influence on language measures at different ages. Localization of language in the brain shows similar complexity: clear evidence of early lateralization for a particular type of acoustic stimulus related to speech, but also emergent modularity. Whilst it is clearly easier to learn a language in early childhood than adulthood, disentangling the biological and environmental factors involved to determine the existence or otherwise of a critical period will most likely prove to be impossible. Finally, we have seen that whilst there is (of course) a clear genetic involvement in speech and language, detailing this involvement is highly complex. Although specific deficits such as Williams syndrome and those experienced by the KE family are closely linked to particular genes, we are a long way indeed from understanding the complex genetic basis of language acquisition.

9.2   Conclusions and future directions

The previous section briefly highlighted some debates that we did not have room to consider elsewhere. In this final section, we revisit the debates that we have covered in detail throughout the book, drawing together a number of conclusions and suggesting some possible directions for future research and theoretical proposals.

9.2.1   Methodological conclusions

Throughout the book we have encountered many different methodological issues that can make the interpretation of results problematic. Whilst it would be tedious to summarize them all again here, the vast majority of methodological problems are instances of one of two general problems; namely (1) failure to code/analyse the data in a way that is fair to opposing theoretical viewpoints; and (2) failure to build in controls that allow reasonable alternative explanations to be ruled out.

With regard to the first problem if, for example, one wishes to test the constructivist prediction that the frequency of a particular item in a child's input will affect the child's proficiency with that item, it is clearly unfair to code and analyse the data at the level of lexical categories (e.g. VERB) – the level assumed by rival generativist theories – and not the level of individual lexical items (e.g. *plays*, *walking*) assumed by the (in this case, constructivist) position being tested. With regard to the second problem, the attempt to rule out alternative possible explanations is, of course, the whole motivation for doing experimental research. Yet throughout this book we have met studies that have failed to rule out alternative possible explanations of findings, due to particular shortcomings, of which the following are merely examples:

- In **corpus** studies (e.g. Chapter 5), apparent effects of either lexical-specificity or full productivity could arise as a failure to control for the corpus size, sampling regime, the size of the child's (or caregiver's) vocabulary and knowledge of the relevant morpheme or word.
- In **checklist** studies (e.g. Chapter 3), misleading findings could result from the failure to control for systematic report biases (e.g. under-/overestimation of vocabulary for certain types of words) and even the composition of the checklist (e.g. the fact that vocabulary checklists typically contain more nouns than verbs).
- The interpretation of **syntactic priming** studies (e.g. Chapter 6) is often problematic because it is difficult to rule out the possibility that priming may be occurring at the level of semantic roles, prosody, 'producing a full sentence' etc., or that children may be acquiring the relevant construction 'on task' (as indeed they do in weird-word-order studies).

- Similarly, **preferential-looking** studies (e.g. Chapters 3 and 6) often fail to control for the possibility that children may be learning task-specific strategies during training trials (the removal of which has been shown to disrupt previously observed effects). Some studies fail to control for children's baseline preference for one or other scene.
- **Elicited-production** studies on the retreat from overgeneralization (e.g. Chapter 6, Section 6.3) often fail to take into account the possibility that children may 'avoid' the production of a particular utterance not because they consider it ungrammatical, but because they prefer to use another form to express the same (or a close enough) meaning, particularly if they have been encouraged to use that form during training. More generally, elicited production studies usually cannot control for the fact that children may be unable to produce a given construction due to memory or processing limitations (but show knowledge of this construction in comprehension tasks).
- *Yes/no* **and truth-value judgmen**t tasks (e.g. Chapter 8) often fail to control for a simple *yes*-bias (all other things being equal, children are more likely to accept than reject particular picture descriptions or interpretations). Even when this is controlled for statistically, it is difficult to control for the possibility that children may accept descriptions that are 'close enough', even if they know them to be not quite accurate. Studies of binding often fail to take into account the possibility that children may have yet to learn the distinction between pronoun and reflexive forms that are semantically and phonologically similar (e.g. *her/herself*), whilst studies of quantification often fail to control for the fact that many adult speakers do not show the idealized pattern of judgments that is assumed to be the target for the child.

Of course, no study can rule out all possible alternative explanations. This highlights the importance of testing theoretical claims using a range of different techniques (see Chapter 1 for a summary of a range of techniques).

One problem is that, when this is done, different paradigms often yield different findings. A somewhat unfair (but not entirely inaccurate) caricature of what happens in this scenario is that generativists assume that children have full knowledge of the relevant structure (e.g. the SVO transitive) as soon as they demonstrate *some* knowledge on *any* task, whilst constructivists assume that children have not acquired the relevant structure until they show virtually adultlike performance by the most stringent measure. One way forward is for researchers from both sides to bear in mind that any experimental task is just that – a task – not a direct measure of children's linguistic knowledge. Results must be understood as arising from an interaction between the task and the child's knowledge. What this rather vague statement means, in practice, is that experiments that attempt to show that children do or do not have knowledge of a particular principle or structure at a particular age are often unhelpful. Generally, the better experiments are those that investigate the

conditions under which the same children display good or erroneous performance on a particular task. Another way forward is for constructivist theorists
to propose explanations of what 'partial' knowledge of a particular structure
might look like, and how it would be expressed in different experimental tasks.
The results outlined in Chapter 2 (Section 2.5.1), showing that infants' ability
to discriminate isolated phonological contrasts is not necessarily fully reflected
in their ability to use these contrasts in more complex tasks, are relevant here,
and computer modelling work (e.g. Chang *et al.*, 2006) will most likely also
be helpful. Generativist researchers should seek to develop models with underlying representations (e.g. categories and rules) that do not change, and show
how the gradual decreasing of particular performance limitations (e.g. memory,
processing speed) could give rise to the patterns of results observed.

9.2.2   *The poverty of the stimulus*

The **poverty-of-the-stimulus** argument holds that a finite set of utterances
generated by a grammar (i.e. the input to which the child is exposed) cannot,
in principle, be sufficient for the child to acquire that grammar (i.e. the target
language). As we saw in Chapter 1, the claim is not that the input is deficient
or lacking in some way (as if it *could* in principle be rich enough), but that a
learner who hypothesized every possible generalization that is consistent with
her experience would never converge on the target grammar, since there are an
infinite number of possible hypotheses. Thus many generativist arguments take
the following form: the child cannot acquire X – where X may be a category
(e.g. NOUN), a movement rule (e.g. move the auxiliary from the main clause),
a principle (e.g. structure dependence or the binding principles) and so on –
directly from the input, as there are too many possible generalizations that are
incorrect. Therefore X must be innate.

   The first part of the argument – that a learner who formed all possible generalizations would never arrive at the correct generalization – is correct. The
second part – that the generalization must therefore be innately given – is not.
The reason is that there is another possibility: the learner *does* have some idea of
where to begin when forming generalizations, but this comes not from innately
specified knowledge but through understanding of meaning. For example, the
reason that *the boy who is smoking* is a syntactic unit that cannot be split up
(e.g. **Is the boy who smoking is crazy?*) is because it is a semantic/conceptual
unit: it refers to an entity in the world (see Chapter 7). Similarly, when critics
of distributional analysis ask how children know how to perform distributional
analysis at the word level, as opposed to some other level, this ignores the fact
that words – because they refer to entities in the world – are meaningful units
for children. This, of course, is the constructivist approach. Another important
claim of this approach is that categories develop probabilistically rather than

being all-or-nothing and that – consequently – the child can begin to construct categories on the basis of partial information. Interestingly, even some generativist theorists have recently posited that children could develop syntactic categories (Mintz, 2003; see Chapter 6 above) and set morphosyntactic parameters (Yang, 2002; see Chapter 5 above) on the basis of a probabilistic statistical analysis of the input (whilst still assuming innate knowledge of the categories and parameters).

Whether or not the input in fact contains sufficient semantic and statistical regularity for children to form the generalizations necessary for adultlike productivity is an empirical question. As we have seen many times throughout this book, constructivist researchers frequently assume that this is the case, without actually demonstrating that it is so (i.e. showing the relevant generalization process in action). Of course, it may be that the information in the input is not sufficient to support such generalization. But simply to assert *a priori* that this is impossible in principle is surely premature.

9.2.3   The initial state

Given the argument from the poverty of the stimulus, generativist researchers must hypothesize an initial state that is sufficient to allow the child to learn any language (i.e. Universal Grammar or UG). One problem for testing the UG hypothesis is that what is proposed as the contents of UG varies from theorist to theorist (Tomasello, 2005). Nevertheless, there are many assumptions that would appear to be shared by most generativist theorists (e.g. that syntactic categories such as NOUN and VERB are innately specified). Furthermore, within a particular domain, there usually exist concrete proposals for innately specified knowledge (for example, the binding principles, see Chapter 8, or the subject–auxiliary inversion rule for question formation, see Chapter 7).

The idea is that this innate knowledge (e.g. of syntactic categories and rules for combining them into phrases and sentences) can account for children's productivity (once the relevant parameters have been set and lexical forms acquired, this is expected to be adultlike, subject to performance limitations). A problem here, however, is that innate knowledge does not automatically make the problems facing the language learner easier to solve. Take, for example, the problem of assigning items in the input to syntactic categories (see Chapter 6). Without additional assumptions (e.g. an innate rule linking the category NOUN to the largest distributionally formed category or the category that contains concrete objects), having a set of innately specified syntactic categories does not much help the learner identify instances of those categories in her input. Similarly, knowledge of phrase structure, the categories of SUBJECT, VERB and OBJECT, and the head-direction parameter is of little use, unless the learner has some independent way to set the parameter.

This is not to say that innate knowledge of rules and categories cannot be helpful. Provided that the learner has some way to link this knowledge to the input that she hears (and we have met several proposals along these lines; see, in particular, Chapter 6), it could greatly simplify the learning task. The point is simply that positing innate knowledge does not, in and of itself, necessarily solve any learnability (poverty-of-the-stimulus) problem.

Constructivists argue that the postulation of innate linguistic categories should be a last rather than a first resort. One approach has been to suggest that the initial state is one of an already developed ability of intention-reading which allows the child both to communicate and to understand communication. In this approach, language is analysed for form–meaning mappings: categories and abstractions are emergent (see Chapter 6). Early language use can, therefore, be a rote-learned association between words or strings identified in the input and child-interpreted meanings. Thus for constructivists, the challenges are to show how segmentation takes place, to identify the early form–meaning mappings and to explain the emergence of linguistic categories.

9.2.4 Development

Both generativist and constructivist theories face major issues in how development is theorized. For generativist theories, as noted above, there is the problem of how the highly abstract and universal categories, principles and parameters of UG are linked to the ambient language. A second issue is the order in which parameters are set. This appears to be little addressed in the literature, but is of potentially major consequence, since the outcome of setting one parameter may have consequences for another (see Chapter 6). A third is that generativist accounts often seek to explain the transition from the child to the adult grammar simply by assuming that the child is in possession of the adult grammar all along, but is affected by performance limitations (e.g. limitations on memory and processing) that decrease as development proceeds. Whilst all researchers agree that such processing factors are important, if they are to avoid the charge of non-falsifiability, generativist accounts must seek to explain precisely what those performance limitations are, and precisely what patterns of performance will be observed as they decrease.

Constructivist accounts are sometimes unfairly characterized as claiming that children 'have no grammar'. Whilst it is true that constructivist research often emphasizes the importance of early rote-learned phrases (perhaps chiefly in response to the generativist claim of full productivity), this is only a small (and relatively unimportant) part of the account. The more important aspects of the account relate to the hypothesized developmental progression whereby children move from these rote-learned phrases (e.g. *What are you doing?*), through low-scope slot-and-frame patterns (e.g. *What are [THING]*

[PROCESS]?) to fully abstract (productive) constructions (e.g. *[WH] [AUX] [SUBJ] [VERB]?*). Constructivists have not addressed in detail the processes by which a child moves from more lexically specific to fully abstract constructions. We have repeatedly met this problem in relation to (amongst others) the transitive construction (Chapter 6), *wh*-questions, and relative- and complement-clause constructions (Chapter 7). Again, if the account is to be falsifiable, constructivist researchers must define more precisely the types of generalizations with which children are assumed to be operating as development proceeds.

Somewhat parallel to the generativist question of the order in which parameters are set is the issue for constructivists as to how children learn to integrate knowledge from different constructions (see Chapter 4). If constructivists adopt some version of construction grammar as the end state, there is the question of how different constructions interact. For instance, while agreement or case marking may be learned initially in an item-based way, it is clear that partial generalization is occurring from early on and is presumably system-wide in the adult grammar. Thus, for example, the use of verb agreement (e.g. 3sg -*s*) in an SVO transitive construction (e.g. *John plays football*) somehow requires that the speaker's knowledge of the two constructions be integrated. So far, there are no concrete proposals for how this is done.

Finally, as we noted in Chapter 4, constructivist accounts have yet to address the question of whether the categories (e.g. VERB) and constructions (e.g. SVO) proposed are abstract entities that are somehow present in the language system 'at rest' (as under generativist accounts), or whether they are simply shorthand terms used to refer to online generalizations that are computed online as needed, by analogy with concrete exemplars stored in memory.

9.2.5   *Lexical effects, frequency effects and processing models*

In the sections on morphology (Chapter 5) and both simple and complex syntax (Chapters 6–7) we noted that generativist accounts could in principle (and occasionally, already do) accept that some degree of rote learning and lexical-specificity characterizes children's earliest productions, without necessarily abandoning their theoretical base. Indeed, we argued that, given that such effects are widely observed in all of these domains, they would be wise to do so. We also suggested two possible ways in which this could be done. First, generativist accounts could argue that all (or virtually all) utterances are constructed anew from scratch, but that the utterance-formation process will be easier and more fluent (and hence less prone to error) when it combines items in a way that it has done so many times in the past (e.g. to produce a high-frequency utterance like *What are you doing?*). Second, generativist accounts could accept the constructivist claim that children store some rote-learned utterances (as some already do) and low scope slot-and-frame patterns such as *What are [THING] [PROCESS]?* (which none currently do), but simply argue that these are 'short cuts' to the production of frequent utterance types. These 'short cuts' would be used when speakers are under cognitive pressure – or simply to reduce effort – but would essentially represent a 'dead-end' developmentally speaking, and have little to do with the processes involved in 'normal' sentence formation. The constructivist approach, of course, sees these low-scope formulas not as dead-ends, but as central to development.

Admittedly, these positions would be difficult to test. As we have seen, if performance limitations are to be invoked to explain lexical and frequency effects, this points to the need for a model that takes the hypothesized underlying knowledge and runs it through a variety of performance 'constraints' to see if the relevant features of children's language can be generated. In some cases, however, it may not be possible for a generativist theory to easily incorporate lexical effects. For example, once a parameter has been set (e.g. the TNS parameter has been set to +TNS), it would be difficult to explain why children appear to systematically violate this setting for some lexical items (e.g. **He cut*) but not others (e.g. *He needs*; see Chapter 5). From a constructivist point of view, models that can take the surface input and generate errors similar to those seen in children's language development (e.g. OI errors such as **He cut*) or that use a simpler input to generate a more complex output are, *prima facie*, important pieces of supporting evidence. This illustrates a point that we have made many times: errors are a good place to try to distinguish between the two approaches because, in the case of correct production, it may be difficult to determine whether this results from low-scope learning or from a fully abstract grammar.

9.2.6 What is the 'default' hypothesis?

One final issue that we have not mentioned up to this point is whether the generativist or constructivist account of language acquisition constitutes the 'default' hypothesis (i.e. the hypothesis that we should accept until, ideally, one is falsified).

Unsurprisingly, both sides have claimed their hypothesis as the default. For example, Pinker (1984: 7) famously argued for the continuity assumption that 'in the absence of compelling evidence to the contrary, the child's grammatical rules should be drawn from the same basic rule types, and be composed of primitive symbols from the same class, as the grammatical rules attributed to adults in standard linguistic investigations'. The motivation for this claim is essentially the argument from the poverty of the stimulus as discussed above: if we do not attribute to the child adultlike rules and categories, it is difficult to see how they could be acquired from the input. Tomasello (2003) argued that since all theories of acquisition must posit 'general purpose' learning processes to account for the acquisition of rote-learned phrases, semi-regular idioms and learning in non-linguistic domains, the default position should be *not* to posit an additional set of purely linguistic assumptions, unless subsequent experimental investigation shows this to be necessary. The argument for this position is simply that a theory should make as few assumptions as are necessary to understand the data.

We will not attempt to adjudicate between these positions here, but instead will suggest one way in which both generativist and constructivist theories could usefully develop. Whilst all scientific theories must be falsifiable, it is not clear that either of the major theories outlined in this book meet this criterion. Tomasello (2007) argues that if phenomena such as 'significant cross-linguistic variation in basic grammatical categories' cannot falsify the UG hypothesis (specifically the claim that children have an innate set of categories), it is difficult to see what kind of result possibly could. On the other hand, current constructivist theories are not yet sufficiently well specified as to be falsifiable. If one fails to find an effect that the account would seem to predict (e.g. if children do not show significantly better performance with a slot-and-frame pattern that is frequent in the input than one that is rare), there are still a number of 'escape hatches' for the theory (e.g. the hypothesized patterns may not be at the correct level of analysis, the child may have formed a more general construction, there may be a threshold rather than a linear-frequency effect and so on). In both cases, a falsifiable theory can arise only through a more detailed specification of the theory's assumptions. As we have noted throughout this book, computer-modelling studies may be useful in this regard, simply because they force theorists to make explicit all the relevant assumptions of the theory under investigation.

9.2.7   The final word

Our goal in this book has been to present the evidence for and against particular generativist–nativist and constructivist proposals regarding the central theoretical debates in child language acquisition. We hope that we have succeeded in our aim to be fair to – and appropriately critical of – these contrasting theoretical approaches. Finally, we hope that by setting out the evidence on these debates in a relatively systematic fashion we have inspired both generativist and constructivist researchers to further develop their own proposals and to test them experimentally, thus bringing the field closer to a complete understanding of children's language acquisition.

Notes

2 SPEECH PERCEPTION, SEGMENTATION AND PRODUCTION

1 Phonemic differences are written between //, phonetic differences between [ ].
2 A bilabial is a subgroup of labials involving only lip closure.
3 A glottalized, velar-uvular, place of articulation contrast (/kì/ versus /qì/) in Thompson, an indigenous, Salish language of British Columbia.
4 We are simplifying: in fact, allophonic regularities are sensitive to phonological words and these need not be isomorphic with grammatical words.
5 Capitals indicate the stressed syllable within the word.
6 As an analogy, you will probably find it easier to remember the arbitrary word sequence *green table* if you memorize a sentence where it is a syntactic unit (*The man sat on the green table*) than if you memorize a sentence where it straddles a phrase boundary (*The committee met on the village green. 'Table the first motion!' began the chairman*).
7 Note that children can only do the task at 14 months if the objects are moving. This debate between how to interpret the nature of children's representations when the results of discrimination tasks and more cognitively demanding tasks conflict is similar to the one raised in Chapter 6 in relation to the interpretation of preferential looking and comprehension/act-out tasks in children's understanding of the SVO transitive construction.

3 LEARNING WORD MEANINGS

1 Another obvious (though rarely discussed) problem for mutual exclusivity is that it can be of use only when the child has learned the words for *all* the other possible referents in the scene. Yet, in a real-world scenario (unlike word-learning studies) there will be very many possible referents for which the child has not yet learned a name (particularly early in development). In turn, the child could not have learned the names for *these* using mutual exclusivity without having previously learned the words for the other possible referents in each of the relevant scenes (and so on, ad infinitum). Far from being an early constraint that helps word learning 'get off the ground' then, mutual exclusivity can, almost by definition, only be helpful when the child has already learned quite a few words, presumably without much help from mutual exclusivity.
2 Thanks to Andrew Lampkin for this example.

3 However, the results of this study are not as conclusive as they are sometimes portrayed: 10/24 correct choices is, statistically speaking, only marginally significantly better than at-chance performance of 6/24 correct choices.

4 A number of studies have investigated the age at which children acquire the ability to track an adult's gaze. D'Entremont, Hains and Muir (1997) demonstrated that from around 3 months, children will look at whichever of two moving puppets an adult turns her head towards. However, until around 10 months, children will do this even if the adult's eyes are closed or blindfolded (Brooks and Meltzoff, 2002; 2005). Beyond this age, children begin to systematically check the adult's gaze, looking back and forth between the adult and the object to which she is attending (Franco and Butterworth, 1996).

5 Dogs also succeed at this task. Chimpanzees succeed only in a modified version where a 'competitive' experimenter reaches towards the baited container. Presumably they understand the intention of 'reaching for food' but not 'pointing to communicate' (Hare and Tomasello, 1999, 2004).

6 Given the difficulty in teasing these factors apart, it will be extremely difficult to test the emergentist coalition model's claim that '12-month-olds rely less on the cue of social eye gaze and relatively more on perceptual salience, whereas 24-month-olds rely more on social cues' (Hollich *et al.*, 2000: 61). The studies that Hollich *et al.* cite in support of this claim are problematic as they do not unambiguously show that children associate a novel word with a salient novel object in the absence of an eye-gaze cue.

7 The term *bootstrapping* (or *booting*) is used in many different fields to refer to a self-sustaining process that proceeds without external help (e.g. a computer starting up, cells differentiating or a new business starting from scratch without external investment). The metaphor here is 'pulling oneself up by the bootstraps'.

8 Pinker (1984, 1989a; see also 1989b) argues that linking rules of this type are innately specified, though raises doubts regarding whether they can be used for syntactic bootstrapping.

9 Although *squatting* is an English verb, it was chosen to be unfamiliar to the children and hence, in effect, novel.

10 Unlike in the study of Naigles (1990), children in the studies discussed in this paragraph did not actually have to perform syntactic bootstrapping to learn the meaning of a verb during the study. This is because, in effect, the training and test phases of Naigles' paradigm are reversed. In the training phase, the causative and non-causative actions are presented at the same time (i.e. one on each screen) with uninformative audio (e.g. 'Look, squatting!'). Thus children learn the meaning of the verb (either to force another to squat, or to squat) during training. At test, children are asked to find 'Big Bird squatting Cookie Monster' or 'Big Bird and Cookie Monster squatting' and 'choose' from the same scenes presented during training. Thus at test, children can demonstrate the *knowledge required* to perform syntactic bootstrapping (that transitive and intransitive sentences refer to causal and non-causal actions respectively), but do not actually perform syntactic bootstrapping to learn the meaning of the verb (which was given during training).

11 Fisher (2002: 57) uses the term 'bias', but rather avoids the issue of whether or not it is innate. If it is not innate, the account is somewhat circular: in order to observe

the correlation between two participants and transitive syntax, children will have
to understand at least some transitive verbs. This requires that children learn their
meanings without the aid of bootstrapping.

4 THEORETICAL APPROACHES TO GRAMMAR ACQUISITION

1 Our aim is to give an outline that is maximally compatible with the main generativist
  acquisition papers discussed in this book (Wexler, 1998; Legate and Yang, 2007;
  Radford, 1994; Rizzi, 1994; Hoekstra and Hyams, 1998; Christophe, Millotte, Bernal
  and Lidz, 2008; Pinker, 1984, 1987, 1989a; Fodor, 1998; Gibson and Wexler, 1994;
  Borer and Wexler, 1987, 1992; Fox and Grodzinsky, 1998; Santelmann *et al.*, 2002;
  Stromswold, 1990; Hattori, 2003; De Villiers, 1991; Guasti, Thornton and Wexler,
  1995; Sheldon, 1974; Tavakolian, 1981; Hamburger and Crain, 1982; Crain and
  Nakayama, 1987; Thornton and Crain, 1994; Radford, 1996; De Villiers, Roeper and
  Vainikka, 1990; Reinhart, 1983; Chien and Wexler, 1990; McKee, 1992; Grodzinsky
  and Reinhart, 1993; McDaniel and Maxfield, 1992; Thornton and Wexler, 1999;
  Lust, Eisele and Mazuka, 1992; Crain and McKee, 1986; Hsu, Cairns, Eisenberg
  and Schlisselberg, 1989; Lust and Clifford, 1986; Lust, Loveland and Kornet, 1980;
  Philip, 1995; Crain *et al.*, 1996; McDaniel, Cairns and Hsu, 1990/1; Sherman and
  Lust, 1993).
2 In this textbook (and most linguistics and child language literature) ungrammatical
  utterances are marked with an asterisk (∗). Utterances that are 'borderline' ungrammatical are marked with a question mark (?).
3 Note that, in a few very specialized contexts, *kick* may be used intransitively (i.e.
  with a subject but no object), as in *The baby kicked* or *Watch out, that horse kicks*.
  However, it is debatable whether such uses are, in fact, truly 'intransitive', as opposed
  to transitive with the object (e.g. 'her mother', 'people') understood, and hence
  omitted. For our purposes here, as in the majority of linguistics textbooks, *kick* is
  taken to be an obligatorily transitive verb.
4 Theories differ as to whether the intermediate single-bar level (X′) is present for every
  sentence, even when it is redundant (in which case it is not normally shown in tree
  diagrams, even if it is assumed to be present). Chomsky's more recent **minimalist**
  approach (e.g. Chomsky, 1995) avoids positing redundant levels (and also stipulat-
  ing positions such as specifier and head). Instead, each lexical item or phrase is
  successively combined with another in a binary branching procedure termed *merge*.
  Technically then, modern generativist approaches to adult syntax are not 'X-bar
  theory' approaches. However, the fundamental claim of the approach – that sentences
  are constructed from hierarchically structured phrases – remains.
5 If the tense feature on the verb's inflection (e.g. *-ed*) matches the tense feature at T
  (e.g. +past) then the derivation is said to **converge** (i.e. a grammatical sentence is
  produced). If the tense feature on the verb's inflection (e.g. *-ed*) does not match the
  tense feature at T (e.g. +present) then the derivation is said to **crash** (in the same
  way that a computer may crash when asked to perform an impossible operation).
  This notion is important for understanding the generativist theories of inflectional
  morphology discussed in Chapter 5.
6 Note that this is not the only possible solution (e.g. Carnie, 2006, has the inflection
  lower into the VP). However, it is the solution assumed by the leading generative

theories of children's acquisition of inflection, discussed in the following chapter (e.g. Wexler, 1998; Hoekstra and Hyams, 1998).

7 Checking can occur at the functional head itself (e.g. I) or at another position in the head's checking domain: Spec, or an adjunct, but not the complement.

8 The moved auxiliary leaves a trace, shown as t_i. The auxiliary that has moved (*is*) is **coindexed** with the same subscript letter (is$_i$) in order to show which element has moved, and from where (in cases where more than one element moves).

9 So, in fact, the item-based construction *John kissed KISSEE* is relatively unlikely, and would be formed only by a speaker who heard many sentences of this form with different entities in the KISSEE position (e.g. *John kissed Sue*; *John kissed Clare*; *John kissed Helen*).

5 INFLECTION

1 In (d) although no visible morpheme is present, the verb nevertheless *is* clearly marked for tense (i.e. *you play* must refer to the present, and not the past, tense). Thus the notation *play-Ø* is sometimes used to denote the fact that the verb is marked for tense, but that the marker happens to be zero (i.e. nothing).

2 Following convention, we will henceforth use NOM and ACC to represent the nominative (subject) and accusative (object) markers respectively, rather than writing them out in each language. Thus this sentence would be rendered *Alexandra-ACC hit Veronika-NOM* ('Veronika hit Alexandra').

3 The ATOM is also designed to explain why children learning English produce RIs in *wh*-questions as well as declaratives, whilst those learning other languages do not. For reasons of space (and because the *wh*-question data on many other languages are thin) we do not discuss this issue here.

4 There is some independent motivation for the claim that the default case is accusative in English but nominative in German. When a personal pronoun is used in 'standalone' form (e.g. as part of an exclamation such as *Me too!*), it appears in accusative form in English (*Me/*I too!*) but nominative form in German (*Ich/*Mich auch!*). Presumably, accusative case is also the default case in French (*Moi/*Je aussi!*), in which case, French children would be predicted to make errors such as **Moi jouer*. There is some evidence that they do (de Cat, 2002).

5 A reviewer raised the interesting question of whether it is the 'system' or the child who is attempting to come up with the correctly inflected verb form. As the relationship between the linguistic theory and the processing mechanism is unclear, we remain agnostic with regard to the issue of how particular forms come to be selected. Indeed, we attribute agency to 'the system', as opposed to the child, precisely to avoid the question of whether the checking of features at AGR and TNS is a psychologically real process that children undertake, or an abstract description of the linguistic system.

6 Findings using this methodology have demonstrated similar effects of input frequency on the order of acquisition of particular verbs (Theakston *et al.*, 2004), and the particular abstract constructions in which these verbs are used (e.g. transitive vs intransitive) (Theakston *et al.*, 2001, 2002).

7 In fact, more recent versions of the dual-route model assume that *some* regular past tense forms (e.g. highly frequent forms such as *played*) are stored in the lexicon

(e.g. Alegre and Gordon, 1999; Pinker and Ullman, 2002: 458; Hartshorne and Ullman, 2006). The point is that regular past-tense forms do not *have* to be stored (and *at least some* are not), as they can always be generated by the default rule.

8 At least, this is how the dual-route model has traditionally been presented. Hartshorne and Ullman (2006) propose a version of the dual-route model under which regular forms are stored and used as the basis for phonological analogy. However, given that this version of the dual-route model is essentially identical to a single-route model (save for the addition of a possibly redundant default rule) it is difficult to see how one could choose between the two accounts (though see Ambridge, in press, for one attempt to do so).

9 However, since the two predictors themselves were highly correlated ($r = 0.8$) these estimates of unique variance are somewhat unreliable. Indeed, the confounded effect of derivation and centrality accounted for almost 50 per cent of the total variance in ratings.

10 There is an additional question regarding the relative rates of overgeneralization for nouns and verbs. The two models make different predictions but the few studies that have looked at this (Marcus, 1995; Maslen *et al.*, 2004; Marchman, Plunkett and Goodman, 1997) are problematic for a variety of reasons (e.g. failure to compare rates statistically).

11 With only 11 regular verbs, comparing regular verbs with 'high' and 'low' numbers of regular friends would have resulted in comparing very small groups (5 or 6 members in each). However, this analysis was not performed in a larger study with 25 regular verbs (and 27 irregulars; Marchman *et al.*, 1999). Presumably because the number of friends did not interact with the variable of regular/irregular (in either study), Marchman *et al.* felt that a separate analysis of regular verbs was not necessary. However, given that this is the only area in which the two models unambiguously make opposing predictions, we consider this to be an oversight.

12 Although Finnish does not have a single 'default' default marker (equivalent to *-ed* in English), the distinction between verbs that undergo a stem change (e.g. *pelä-tä* → *pelkä-si* 'to be scared of') and those that do not (e.g. *halu-ta* → *halu-si* 'to want') parallels the irregular/regular distinction.

6 SIMPLE SYNTAX

1 These figures are generous because the choice at each stage is not between VERB and NOUN, ADJ etc., but simply between VERB and non-VERB.

2 Of course, this procedure will only work if (a) the sentence is accompanied by an ongoing/impending/imagined scene of a dog biting a cat and (b) the child understands all the words in the sentence. Similar assumptions are shared by all the acquisition theories discussed in this section.

3 For example, if the target grammar is SV, VO, −V2 (e.g. English) and the current settings are VS, OV and +V2.

4 The right-hand-prominence and left-hand-prominence sentences were modelled on French (VO) and Turkish (OV) respectively. However, the words themselves were nonsense words created by substituting consonants at random and rendering all vowels as a schwa (the sound at the end of the word *the*).

5 Lieven *et al.* (1992) found that 6% and 10% of the first 100 words and phrases of 12 low-SES children (aged 0;11–2;3) were consistent with positional- and intermediate-patterns respectively. Whilst these figures may seem low, the majority of the first 100 words/phrases were single words (63%) or frozen phrases (21%).

6 See Abbot-Smith, Lieven and Tomasello (2008) for a related 'weird linking' study in German.

7 In fact, if Savage *et al.*'s (2003) data are analysed in terms of the *proportion* of utterances that were actives (as opposed to the raw number), 4-year-olds do – numerically speaking – produce more actives after active primes (95%) than passive primes (85%). It is odd that the authors do not report these proportionalized figures, particularly given that they do so for a second study in the same paper.

8 In fact, the weird-word-order (WWO) studies discussed above *are* – to all intents and purposes – syntactic-priming studies with a WWO control condition. However, (to its detriment) the syntactic-priming literature seems to have developed largely independently of the WWO literature.

9 'Almost always' because *der* is also the feminine dative and genitive form.

10 On the other hand, the 'failure' of the younger 2;6-year-olds may be an artifact of reduced statistical power ($N = 12$), as these children nevertheless achieved a mean of 62% correct enactments. With a reasonable sample size, as few as 55% correct enactments can represent statistically above-chance performance size (as for several other studies discussed later in this chapter). To the extent that Chan's 2;6-year-olds do outperform Dittmar's, this may be a consequence of a small methodological difference: in the former study, both toys were placed on the apparatus for the child who had only to act on one to cause it to perform the novel action on the other. In the latter, the child was handed the toys and thus had additionally to arrange them on the apparatus.

11 The advantage of the pointing methodology is highlighted by the fact the same research group (in unpublished work) failed to find any effects for children aged 2;0 and 2;6 using a preferential-looking paradigm (Noble, 2009).

12 Recall than an **intransitive** utterance is one that describes an event involving one entity (e.g. *The ball rolled*), whereas a **transitive** utterance describes an event in which one entity does something to another (e.g. *The man rolled the ball*). The entities involved are **arguments** of the verb. Thus in a transitive sentence, the verb (e.g. *roll*) takes two arguments (e.g. *the man* and *the ball*), whereas in an intransitive sentence, the verb (e.g. *roll*) takes only one argument (e.g. *the ball*).

13 As should be clear from these examples, we are concerned here with *transitive causative* sentences (e.g. *The man rolled the ball*) in which one entity (e.g. *The man*) causes another (e.g. *the ball*) to perform some action (e.g. *rolling*). We are not concerned with non-causative transitive sentences such as *Books cost money*. Similarly, we are concerned with *inchoative intransitive* sentences in which a single entity (an ACTOR) performs some action (e.g. *The ball rolled*) as opposed to, for example, intransitives where an AGENT performs some action on a PATIENT, with the PATIENT omitted or understood (e.g. *The man ate [the food]*). However, we continue to use the simple terms *transitive* and *intransitive* as shorthand.

14 Another generativist assumption (obscured by the simplified presentation here) is that the broad-range rule operates on semantic structures (e.g. ACTOR ACTION → AGENT CAUSE [ACTOR ACTION], with the relevant syntax then spelt out by

innate linking rules (see Section 6.1). Again, however, the theory would not seem to hinge critically on this assumption.

15 The non-appearance of an otherwise-frequent verb in a particular construction is sometimes said to constitute **indirect negative evidence** that the non-attested form is ungrammatical (e.g. MacWhinney, 2004). However, we avoid this term as, confusingly, it is also sometimes used to refer to the evidence of ungrammaticality that is provided by adult reformulations, frowns, misunderstandings, and so on.

16 Indeed, 69% of passives produced by the 6–7 year olds and 85% of passives produced by the 4–5 year olds were produced by children in the pre-emption condition (see Brooks and Tomasello, 1999b: 731). No comparable figures are reported for the periphrastic causative construction.

17 Both of these problems also apply to a follow-up study conducted by Brooks and Zizak (2002). In this study, children were taught two novel verbs, both from the alternating 'manner of motion' class. Thus all overgeneralizations were in fact grammatical.

18 Whilst some of these *un*-forms may be acceptable as participles (e.g. *unbent/unbending/unfrozen*), utterances such as *The man unbent the bar* and *The sun unfroze the ice* are less than fully acceptable (and were rated as such in Ambridge, Freudenthal, Pine *et al.*, 2009).

19 The acceptability of this sentence, under the current account, is explained by the fact that the [ACTION] slot here will have been filled – on previous occasions – with a wide range of items such as *blow*, *push*, *shove*, *brush* and *wipe*. Consequently, this slot will be associated with a fairly broad meaning – any type of motion, including of air – with which *sneeze* is compatible. Of course, no dictionary definition of *sneeze* would include 'motion', but every event labelled with the word *sneeze* will have involved motion of air. Note that verbs that are inconsistent with even the fairly broad semantics associated with the slot (e.g. *Fred cost the napkin off the table*) may not appear in it. Further, there would seem to be a sliding scale of acceptability where the greater the degree of motion associated with the verb, the more grammatical the utterance (*Fred pushed > blew > sneezed > coughed > thought > liked > cost the napkin off the table*).

7 MOVEMENT AND COMPLEX SYNTAX

1 Semantically, the unergative/unaccusative distinction can be seen as the distinction between verbs describing 'something you do' (e.g. *laugh, run, talk, dance*) and those describing 'something that happens to you' (e.g. *die, disappear, fall, arrive*). The person that an unaccusative event (e.g. *dying*) 'happens to' is seen as the (underlying object) OBJECT, just like the PATIENT of a transitive event (e.g. *killing*).

2 Conversely, when a child wishes to emphasize that the surface subject *is* affected, she may ungrammatically coerce a verb into this construction (e.g. I don't want to be dog-eared today [the child does not want to have her hair put into 'dog ears'; Bowerman, 1988).

3 For English, Gordon and Chafetz (1990) identified only four full passives and 52 truncated passives in 86,655 child-directed utterances.

4 As is usual in the relevant literature, the term auxiliary (AUX) is used here to refer to genuine auxiliary verbs (BE, HAVE), the copula (BE), modals (CAN, SHOULD

etc.) and the dummy auxiliary (DO), unless specifically stated otherwise. Upper case is used to refer to a lexical auxiliary type (e.g. BE), lower case to refer to particular lexical auxiliary forms (e.g. *is*, *are*).

5 It is important to note that the term 'auxiliary' when used in the context of this study (and constructivist theories in general) refers to a specific lexical auxiliary form (e.g. *is*, *does*, *doesn't*) and not to an auxiliary type (e.g. BE, DO).

6 An issue that is sometimes raised (e.g. Dąbrowska and Lieven, 2005) is how children 'know' – when inserting a declarative chunk (e.g. *she doesn't want peas*) into a question schema (e.g. What does [THING][PROCESS]?) – to leave a 'gap' for the object that is replaced by the *wh*-word. That is, why doesn't the child say **What does she doesn't want peas?*. The first point to note is that the existence of a string such as *she doesn't want peas* does not preclude the existence of a shorter string such as *she doesn't want*: speakers are assumed to store strings of different lengths. To explain how the child knows to insert the shorter string, not the longer one, one has only to assume that the child knows that it makes no pragmatic sense to ask a question, but to include the answer in the question.

7 We do not discuss **genitive relatives** (e.g. *Here is the boy whose girlfriend ran away*).

8 Children learning languages with more case marking than English such as Italian (e.g. Crain, McKee and Emiliani, 1990; Bates, Devescovi and D'Amico, 1999) and French (Dasigner and Toupin, 1994) consistently perform better with relative-clause sentences than English-speaking children, presumably because case marking makes it easier to keep track of the subject and object of the relative and main clause.

9 English and German differ in two important respects. In German, the relativizer (= *that*) is, in the masculine Gender, marked for the syntactic role of the NP that it modifies (e.g. *der* for subject, *den* for object). However, when the relativizer is not marked (e.g. subjects and objects are not distinguished for feminine and neuter forms), German's relatively free word order means that clauses are often ambiguous (e.g. between *the girl who knows Peter* and *the girl who(m) Peter knows*). The fact that, despite these differences, children learning the two languages showed similar performance lends support to the view that factors such as conceptual complexity and activation of common constructions are important in determining which sentence types are easy/difficult to produce.

10 Another possible movement rule based on linear order – move the final auxiliary to sentence initial position – outputs an ungrammatical question from statements such as *The girl is kissing the boy who is smoking*.

11 Due to space considerations, we restrict our discussion to the acquisition of sentences with finite object complements (e.g. *John knew [that the boy ate the cake]*). Sentences of this form are known as object complements because the complement clause (*the boy ate the cake*) replaces the object of the equivalent simple transitive sentence (e.g. the NP *the answer* in *John knew the answer*). We do not discuss subject complements, where the subject in the equivalent simple sentence (e.g. *The report* in *The report was crazy*) is replaced by a complement clause (e.g. *[That the report was written in German] was crazy*). Neither do we consider acquisition of non-finite complements; those where the complement clause is not marked for tense (e.g. *John wanted [Sue to eat the cake]*).

12 Elsewhere, Dąbrowska (2008) argues that even adults may not have an abstract long-distance *wh*-question construction, and may produce all such questions by analogy with formula *What do you think X?* and/or *What did you say X?* (though see Ambridge and Goldberg, 2008, for evidence against this view).

13 A similar criticism (Dąbrowska *et al.*, 2009) applies to a comprehension study conducted by Thornton and Crain (1994) in which a puppet incorrectly guessed which of two items was hidden under a cloth. Although all children (aged 3;0–4;1) responded correctly to both the questions 'What did he say is under there?' (e.g. 'the baby') and 'What is under there?' (e.g. 'a bear'), this does not demonstrate understanding of either the syntax of complementization or of false belief. Children could succeed at the task by ignoring the complement clause altogether and simply answering the question 'What did he say?'

14 The 'high-frequency' complement-taking verbs were not always of higher overall frequency, nor of higher frequency in sentences with sentential complement clauses. However, in every case a higher *proportion* of uses were in sentences with sentential complement clauses. Repeating the analyses described with raw frequency as the independent variable yielded none of the effects observed.

8 BINDING, QUANTIFICATION AND CONTROL

1 At least under the strict definition of c-command given above. Under a less strict definition, **non-branching nodes** (= stations where it is not possible to change trains) are disregarded; hence A c-commands D, E and F.

2 Note that some varieties of English (e.g. Irish English) use a reflexive pronoun in some contexts where more 'standard' dialects use a non-reflexive pronoun (e.g. *Myself and Sue went shopping;* as opposed to *Sue and I* or, more colloquially, *Me and Sue*). Some (non-Irish) speakers also seem to use reflexive forms in a 'hypercorrect' attempt at a formal register (e.g. *Sue and myself went shopping*). The discussion in this chapter deals only with 'standard' British/American English, and hence does not cover such uses.

3 Forward and backward anaphora are the terms used to describe situations in which an R-expression sends its interpretation forward or backward to a pronoun respectively, as in these examples.

4 These errors are also potentially compatible with Thornton and Wexler's (1999) extended guise creation hypothesis, discussed above with reference to Principle B.

5 One might enquire precisely what, in the absence of any innate constraints, causes speakers to consider the use of a full nominal in the dominion of a reference point (e.g. *She$_{*i}$ listens to music when Sarah$_i$ reads poetry*) to be ungrammatical. Van Hoek (1997: 44) notes that, in such cases, there is a mismatch between the semantics/pragmatics of the individual item and the construction slot. For example, the NP slot in the construction *She$_i$ VERB when NP$_i$* will have the pragmatic properties of referring to a discourse-old referent. Hence inserting into this slot a full NP (e.g. *Sarah*), which usually has the pragmatic properties of introducing a new referent, yields a mismatch (poor fit) between the item and construction properties. This is similar to the account of argument structure overgeneralization errors (Ambridge

et al., in press) discussed in Chapter 6 (with **fit** defined in terms of discourse-pragmatic as opposed to semantic/phonological properties).

6 The inclusion criterion was not having attended university. Since the majority of people do not attend university, we can assume the LAA group are fairly representative of speakers at the modal level of the general population.

7 *Promise* seems to be unique (in English) in that it exhibits subject control even when an object is also present. Subject control can also occur when there is no object (e.g. *John$_i$ tried/wanted/asked PRO$_i$ to leave*).

8 Subject-control sentences with *promise* are an exception, presumably learned on a one-off basis.

9 McDaniel *et al.* (1990/1) argue that children in fact attach the VP in a way that is consistent with their preferred interpretation of such sentences at stage I, but since all but one stage I child enacted object-control readings of such sentences, the difference is of little consequence.

References

Abbot-Smith, K., Lieven, E. and Tomasello, M. (2001). What preschool children do and do not do with ungrammatical word orders. *Cognitive Development*, 16(2): 679–92.

(2004). Training 2;6-year-olds to produce the transitive construction: the role of frequency, semantic similarity and shared syntactic distribution. *Developmental Science*, 7(1): 48–55.

(2008). Graded representations in the acquisition of English and German transitive constructions. *Cognitive Development*, 23(1): 48–66.

Aguado-Orea, J. J. (2004). The acquisition of morpho-syntax in Spanish: implications for current theories of development. Unpublished PhD thesis, University of Nottingham.

Akhtar, N. (1999). Acquiring basic word order: evidence for data-driven learning of syntactic structure. *Journal of Child Language*, 26: 339–56.

Akhtar, N. and Montague, L. (1999). Early lexical acquisition: the role of cross-situational learning. *First Language*, 19: 347–58.

Akhtar, N. and Tomasello, M. (1996). Two-year-olds learn words for absent objects and actions. *British Journal of Developmental Psychology*, 14: 79–93.

(1997). Young children's productivity with word order and verb morphology. *Developmental Psychology*, 33(6): 952–65.

(2000). The social nature of words and word learning. In R. Golinkoff (ed.), *Becoming a Word Learner: A Debate on Lexical Acquisition* (pp. 115–30). Oxford University Press.

Akhtar, N., Carpenter, M. and Tomasello, M. (1996). The role of discourse novelty in early word learning. *Child Development*, 67(2): 635–45.

Albright, A. and Hayes, B. (2003). Rules vs analogy in English past tenses: a computational/experimental study. *Cognition*, 90: 119–61.

Aldridge, M. (1989). *The Acquisition of INFL*. Bloomington: Indiana University Press.

Alegre, M. and Gordon, P. (1999). Frequency effects and the representational status of regular inflections. *Journal of Memory and Language*, 40(1): 41–61.

Alishahi, A. and Stevenson, S. (2008). A computational model of early argument structure acquisition. *Cognitive Science*, 32(5): 789–834.

Allen, S. E. and Crago, M. B. (1996). Early passive acquisition in Inuktitut. *Journal of Child Language*, 23(1): 129–55.

Ambridge, B. (2007). Tapping into children's knowledge: The Totally Abstract Production Priming paradigm. Unpublished MS.

(2009a). 'Retreat' from argument-structure overgeneralization errors as a consequence of the acquisition of verb and construction semantics. Paper presented at the biennial meeting of the Society for Research in Child Development, April 2009, Denver, CO, USA.

(2009b). Review of Hirsh-Pasek, K. and Golinkoff, R. M. (2005). *Action Meets Word: How Children Learn Verbs. Infant and Child Development*, 18: 99–101.

(in press). Children's judgments of regular and irregular novel past tense forms: new data on the English past-tense debate. *Developmental Psychology*.

Ambridge, B. and Goldberg, A. E. (2008). The island status of clausal complements: evidence in favor of an information structure explanation. *Cognitive Linguistics*, 19(3): 349–81.

Ambridge, B. and Pine, J. M. (2006). Testing the Agreement/Tense Omission Model using an elicited imitation paradigm. *Journal of Child Language*, 33(4): 879–98.

Ambridge, B. and Rowland, C. F. (2009). Predicting children's errors with negative questions: testing a schema-combination account. *Cognitive Linguistics*, 20(2): 225–66.

Ambridge, B., Freudenthal, D., Pine, J. M., Mills, R., Clark, V. and Rowland, C. F. (2009). Un-learning un-prefixation errors. Paper presented at the International Conference on Cognitive Modelling 2009, Manchester, UK.

Ambridge, B., Pine, J. M. and Rowland, C. F. (in press). Children use verb semantics to retreat from overgeneralization errors: a novel verb grammaticality judgment study. *Cognitive Linguistics*.

Ambridge, B., Pine, J. M., Rowland, C. F. and Clark, V. (2010a). Verb semantics and the retreat from overgeneralization errors. Unpublished MS.

(2010b). Restricting dative argument-structure overgeneralizations: a grammaticality-judgment study with adults and children. Unpublished MS.

Ambridge, B., Pine, J. M., Rowland, C. F. and Young, C. R. (2008). The effect of verb semantic class and verb frequency (entrenchment) on children's and adults' graded judgements of argument-structure overgeneralization errors. *Cognition*, 106(1): 87–129.

Ambridge, B., Pine, J. M., Rowland, C. F., Jones, R. L. and Clark, V. (2009). A semantics-based approach to the 'No negative evidence' problem. *Cognitive Science*, 33(7): 1301–16.

Ambridge, B., Rowland, C. F. and Pine, J. M. (2008). Is structure dependence an innate constraint? New experimental evidence from children's complex question production. *Cognitive Science*, 32(1): 222–55.

Ambridge, B., Rowland, C. F., Theakston, A. L. and Tomasello, M. (2006). Comparing different accounts of inversion errors in children's non-subject wh-questions: 'What experimental data can tell us?' *Journal of Child Language*, 33(3): 519–57.

Ambridge, B., Theakston, A. L., Lieven, E. V. M. and Tomasello, M. (2006). The distributed learning effect for children's acquisition of an abstract syntactic construction. *Cognitive Development*, 21(2): 174–93.

Arnon, I. (2010). Rethinking child difficulty: the effect of NP type on children's processing of relative clauses in Hebrew. *Journal of Child Language*, 37(1): 27–57.

Aslin, R. N. and Newport, E. L. (2009). What statistical learning can and can't tell us about language acquisition. In J. Colombo, P. McCardle and L. Freund (eds.), *Infant*

Pathways to Language: Methods, Models and Research Disorders (pp. 169–94). New York: Psychology Press.

Aslin, R. N. and Pisoni, D. B. (1980). Some developmental processes in speech perception. *Child Phonology*, 2: 67–96.

Aslin, R. N., Pisoni, D. B., Hennessy, B. L. and Perey, A. V. (1981). Discrimination of voice onset time by human infants: new findings and implications for the effect of early experience. *Child Development*, 52: 1135–45.

Aslin, R. N., Saffran, J. R. and Newport, E. L. (1998). Computation of conditional probability statistics by 8-month-old infants. *Psychological Science*, 9: 321–4.

Aslin, R. N., Werker, J. F. and Morgan, J. L. (2002). Innate phonetic boundaries revisited (L). *Journal of the Acoustical Society of America*, 112: 1257–60.

Au, T. K. F., Dapretto, M. and Song, Y. K. (1994). Input vs constraints – early word acquisition in Korean and English. *Journal of Memory and Language*, 33(5): 567–82.

Baker, C. L. (1979). Syntactic theory and the projection problem. *Linguistic Enquiry*, 10: 533–81.

Baker, M. (2001). *The Atoms of Language*. New York: Basic Books.

Balaban, M. T. and Waxman, S. R. (1997). Do words facilitate object categorization in 9-month-old infants? *Journal of Experimental Child Psychology*, 64(1): 3–26.

Baldwin, D. A. (1991). Infants' contribution to the achievement of joint reference. *Child Development*, 62(5): 875–90.

(1992). Clarifying the role of shape in children's taxonomic assumption. *Journal of Experimental Child Psychology*, 54(3): 392–416.

(1993a). Early referential understanding – infants ability to recognize referential acts for what they are. *Developmental Psychology*, 29(5): 832–43.

(1993b). Infants' ability to consult the speaker for clues to word reference. *Journal of Child Language*, 20(2): 395–418.

Baldwin, D. A., Markman, E. M., Bill, B., Desjardins, R. N., Irwin, J. M. and Tidball, G. (1996). Infants' reliance on a social criterion for establishing word–object relations. *Child Development*, 67(6): 3135–53.

Banks, M. S., Aslin, R. N. and Letson, R. D. (1975). Sensitive period for the development of human binocular vision. *Science*, 190: 675–77.

Bannard, C. and Lieven, E. (2009). Repetition and reuse in child language learning. In R. Corrigan, E. Moravcsik, H. Ouali and K. Wheatley (eds.), *Formulaic language*, vol. 2: *Acquisition, Loss, Psychological Reality, Functional Explanations* (pp. 299–318). Amsterdam and Philadelphia: John Benjamins.

Bannard, C. and Matthews, D. (2008). Stored word sequences in language learning: the effect of familiarity on children's repetition of four-word combinations. *Psychological Science*, 19: 241–48.

Bannard, C., Lieven, E. and Tomasello, M. (2009). Modelling children's early grammatical knowledge. *Proceedings of the National Academy of Sciences of the United States of America*, 106(41): 17284–9.

Baron-Cohen, S., Baldwin, D. A. and Crowson, M. (1997). Do children with autism use the speaker's direction of gaze strategy to crack the code of language? *Child Development*, 68(1): 48–57.

Barr, D. (2008). Analyzing 'visual world' eyetracking data using multilevel logistic regression. *Journal of Memory and Language*, 59(4): 457–74.

Bates, E. (1993). *Modularity, Domain Specificity and the Development of Language.* Technical Report 9305. Center for Research in Language, UCSD. [AEG]
(1994). Modularity, domain specificity and the development of language. *Discussions in Neuroscience*, 10(1/2): 136–49.
Bates, E. and MacWhinney, B. (1979). A functionalist approach to the acquisition of grammar. In E. Ochs and B. Schieffelin (eds.), *Developmental Pragmatics* (pp. 167–209). New York: Academic Press.
(1987). Competition, variation and language learning. In B. MacWhinney (ed.), *Mechanisms of Language Acquisition*. Hillsdale, NJ: Erlbaum.
Bates, E., Camaioni, L. and Volterra, V. (1975). The acquisition of performatives prior to speech. *Merrill-Palmer Quarterly*, 21: 205–24.
Bates, E., Devescovi, A. and D'Amico, S. (1999). Processing complex sentences: a cross-linguistic study. *Language and Cognitive Processes*, 14(1): 69–123.
Bates, E., MacWhinney, B., Caselli, C., Devescovi, A., Natale, F. and Venza, V. (1984). A crosslinguistic study of the development of sentence interpretation strategies. *Child Development*, 55: 341–54.
Bavin, E. L. and Growcott, C. (2000). Infants of 24–30 months understand verb frames. In S. Perkins and S. Howard (eds.), *New Directions in Language Development and Disorders* (pp. 169–77). New York: Kluwer.
Beckman, M. E. (1986). *Stress and Non-Stress Accent* (Netherlands Phonetic Archives no. 7). Dordrecht: Foris. (Second printing, 1992, by Walter de Gruyter.)
Behne, T., Carpenter, M., Call, J. and Tomasello, M. (2005). Unwilling versus unable: infants' understanding of intentional action. *Developmental Psychology*, 41(2): 328–37.
Behne, T., Carpenter, M. and Tomasello, M. (2005). One-year-olds comprehend the communicative intentions behind gestures in a hiding game. *Developmental Science*, 8: 492–9.
Behrend, D. A. (1990). The development of verb concepts: children's use of verbs to label familiar and novel events. *Child Development*, 61(3): 681–96.
Bellagamba, F. and Tomasello, M. (1999). Re-enacting intended acts: comparing 12- and 18-month-olds. *Infant Behavior and Development*, 22(2): 277–82.
Bencini, G. M. L. and Valian, V. V. (2008). Abstract sentence representations in 3 year-olds: evidence from language production and comprehension. *Journal of Memory and Language*, 59: 97–113.
Berent, I., Pinker, S. and Shimron, J. (1999). Default nominal inflection in Hebrew: evidence for mental variables. *Cognition*, 72(1): 1–44.
Berko, J. (1958). The child's learning of English morphology. *Word*, 14: 150–77.
Berman, R. and Sagi, I. (1981). On word formation and word innovations in early age. *Balshanut Ivrit Xofshit* 18.
Bernstein Ratner, N. (1984). Patterns of vowel modification in mother–child speech. *Journal of Child Language*, 11(3): 557–78.
Bernstein Ratner, N. (1996). From 'signal to syntax': but what is the nature of the signal? In J. L. Morgan and K. Demuth (eds.), *Signal to Syntax: Bootstrapping From Speech to Grammar in Early Acquisition* (pp. 135–50). Mahwah, NJ: Erlbaum.
Berwick, R. and Weinberg, A. (1984). *The Grammatical Basis of Linguistic Performance*. Cambridge, MA: MIT Press.

Best, C. T., McRoberts, G. W. and Sithole, N. N. (1988). The phonological basis of perceptual loss for non-native contrasts: maintenance of discrimination among Zulu clicks by English-speaking adults and infants. *Journal of Experimental Psychology: Human Perception and Performance*, 14: 345–60.

Bialystok, E. and Hakuta, K. (1999). Confounded age: linguistic and cognitive factors in age differences for second language acquisition. In D. Birdsong (ed.), *Second Language Acquisition and the Critical Period Hypothesis* (pp. 161–81). Mahwah, NJ: Erlbaum.

Bickerton, D. (1981). *Roots of Language*. Ann Arbor: Karoma.

Bishop, D. V. M. (2000). Pragmatic language impairment: a correlate of SLI, a distinct subgroup, or part of the autistic continuum? In D. V. M. Bishop and L. B. Leonard (eds.), *Speech and Language Impairments in Children: Causes, Characteristics, Intervention and Outcome* (pp. 99–113). New York: Psychology Press.

(2009). Genes, cognition and communication: insights from neurodevelopmental disorders. *The Year in Cognitive Neuroscience: Annals of the New York Academy of Sciences*, 1156: 1–18.

Bishop, D. V. M. and Leonard, L. B. (eds.). (2000). *Speech and Language Impairments in Children: Causes, Characteristics, Intervention and Outcome*. New York: Psychology Press.

Bishop, D. V. M., Adams, C. V. and Norbury, C. F. (2006). Distinct genetic influences on grammar and phonological short-term memory deficits: evidence from 6-year-old twins. *Genes, Brain and Behavior*, 5: 158–69.

Blevins, J. (2004). *Evolutionary Phonology*. Cambridge University Press.

Bloom, L. (1973). *One Word at a Time: the Use of Single Word Utterances Before Syntax*. The Hague: Mouton.

Bloom, L., Rispoli, M., Gartner, B. and Hafitz, J. (1989). Acquisition of complementation. *Journal of Child Language*, 16(1): 101–20.

Bloom, L., Tinker, E. and Margulis, C. (1993). The words children learn – evidence against a noun bias in early vocabularies. *Cognitive Development*, 8(4): 431–50.

Bloom, P. (1990). Subjectless sentences in child language. *Linguistic Enquiry*, 21: 491–504.

(2000). *How Children Learn the Meaning of Words*. Cambridge, MA: MIT Press.

(2004). Myths of word learning. In D. G Hall and S. R. Waxman (eds.), *Weaving a Lexicon* (pp. 205–24). Cambridge, MA: MIT Press.

Bloom, P. and Markson, L. (2001). Are there principles that apply only to the acquisition of words? A reply to Waxman and Booth. *Cognition*, 78: 89–90.

Bock, J. K. (1986). Syntactic persistence in language production. *Cognitive Psychology*, 18: 355–87.

Bod, R. (2009). From exemplar to grammar: a probabilistic analogy-based model of language learning. *Cognitive Science*, 33: 752–93.

Bol, G. W. (1995). Implicational scaling in child language acquisition: the order of production of Dutch verb constructions. In M. Verrips and F. Wijnen (eds.), *Papers from the Dutch-German Colloquium on Language Acquisition*. Amsterdam Series in Child Language Development, 3. Amsterdam: Institute for General Linguistics.

Booth, A. E. and Waxman, S. R. (2002). Word learning is 'smart': evidence that conceptual information affects preschoolers' extension of novel words. *Cognition*, 84(1): B11–22.

Borer, H. and Wexler, K. (1987). The maturation of syntax. In T. Roeper and E. Williams (eds.), *Parameter Setting* (pp. 123–72). Dordrecht: Reidel.

(1992). Bi-unique relations and the maturation of grammatical principles. *Natural Language and Linguistic Theory*, 10(2): 147–89.

Bornstein, M. H. (1987). Perceptual categories in vision and audition. In S. Harnad (ed.), *Categorical Perception: The Groundwork of Cognition* (pp. 287–300). Cambridge University Press.

Bortfeld, H., Morgan, J. L., Golinkoff, R. M. and Rathbun, K. (2005). Mommy and me – familiar names help launch babies into speech-stream segmentation. *Psychological Science*, 16: 298–304.

Boser, C., Lust, B., Santelmann, L. and Whitman, J. (1992). The syntax of CP and V2 in early child German (ECG): the strong continuity hypothesis. *NELS 22: Proceedings of the Twenty-Second Annual Meeting of the North East Linguistic Society* (pp. 51–66). Amherst, MA: GLSA.

Bowerman, M. (1973). *Early Syntactic Development: A Cross-linguistic Study with Special Reference to Finnish.* Cambridge University Press.

(1985). What shapes children's grammars? In D. I. Slobin (ed.), *The Crosslinguistic Study of Language Acquisition*, vol. 2: *Theoretical Issues* (pp. 1257–1319). London: Erlbaum.

(1988). The 'no negative evidence' problem: how do children avoid constructing an overly general grammar? In J. A. Hawkins (ed.), *Explaining Language Universals* (pp. 73–101). Oxford: Blackwell.

(1990). Mapping thematic roles onto syntactic functions: are children helped by innate linking rules? *Linguistics*, 28: 1251–89.

Bowerman, M. and Croft, W. (2007). The acquisition of the English causative alternation. In M. Bowerman and P. Brown (eds.), *Crosslinguistic Perspectives on Argument Structure: Implications for Learnability.* Hillsdale, NJ: Erlbaum.

Boyd, J. K. and Goldberg, A. E. (in press). Learning what not to say: the role of categorization and statistical pre-emption in the production of *a*-adjectives. *Language*.

Boysson-Bardies, B. and Vihman, M. (1991). Adaptation to language: evidence from babbling and first words in four languages. *Language*, 67(2): 297–319.

Boysson-Bardies, B., Vihman, M. M., Roug-Hellichius, L., Durand, C., Landberg, I. and Arao, F. (1992). Material evidence of infant selection from the target language: a cross-linguistic study. In C. Ferguson, L. Menn and C. Stoel-Gammon (eds.), *Phonological Development: Models, Research, Implications.* Timonium, MD: York Press.

Braine, M. D. S. (1963). The ontogeny of English phrase structure. *Language*, 39: 1–14.

(1971). On two types of models of the internalization of grammars. In D. I. Slobin (ed.), *The Ontogenesis of Grammar* (pp. 153–86). New York: Academic Press.

(1976). Children's first word combinations. *Monographs of the Society for Research in Child Development*, 41(164): 1–104.

(1987). What is learned in acquiring word classes: a step toward an acquisition theory. In B. MacWhinney (ed.), *Mechanisms of Language Acquisition* (pp. 67–87). Hillsdale, NJ: Lawrence Erlbaum.

(1992). What sort of innate structure is needed to 'bootstrap' into syntax? *Cognition*, 45(1): 77–100.

Braine, M. D. S. and Brooks, P. J. (1995). Verb argument structure and the problem of avoiding an overgeneral grammar. In M. Tomasello and W. E. Merriman (eds.), *Beyond Names for Things: Young Children's Acquisition of Verbs* (pp. 352–76). Hillsdale, NJ: Erlbaum.

Braine, M. D. S., Brody, R. E., Brooks, P. J., Sudhalter, V., Ross, J. A., Catalano, L. *et al.* (1990). Exploring language-acquisition in children with a miniature artificial language – effects of item and pattern frequency, arbitrary subclasses and correction. *Journal of Memory and Language*, 29(5): 591–610.

Braine, M. D. S., Brody, R. E., Fisch, S. M., Weisberger, M. J. and Blum, M. (1990). Can children use a verb without exposure to its argument structure. *Journal of Child Language*, 17(2): 313–42.

Brandt, S., Kidd, E., Lieven, E. and Tomasello, M. (2009). The discourse bases of relativization: an investigation of young German and English-speaking children's comprehension of relative clauses. *Cognitive Linguistics*, 20(3): 539–70.

Brandt, S., Lieven, E. and Tomasello, M. (in press). Development of word order in German complement-clause constructions: effects of input frequencies, lexical items and discourse function. *Language*.

Brent, M. R. (1999). An efficient, probabilistically sound algorithm for segmentation and word discovery. *Machine Learning*, 34: 71–105.

Brent, M. R. and Cartwright, T. A. (1996). Distributional regularity and phonotactics are useful for segmentation. *Cognition*, 61: 93–125.

Brent, M. R. and Siskind, J. M. (2001). The role of exposure to isolated words in early vocabulary development. *Cognition*, 81: 33–44.

Bromberg, H. S. and Wexler, K. (1995). Null subjects in child wh-questions. In C. T. Schütze, J. Ganger and K. Broihier (eds.), *Papers in Language Processing and Acquisition* (MIT Working Papers in Linguistics 26) (pp. 221–47). Cambridge, MA: MIT.

Brooks, P. J. and Braine, M. D. (1996). What do children know about the universal quantifiers all and each? *Cognition*, 60(3): 235–68.

Brooks, P. J. and Sekerina, I. A. (2006). Shortcuts to quantifier interpretation in children and adults. *Language Acquisition*, 13(3): 177–206.

Brooks, P. J. and Tomasello, M. (1999a). Young children learn to produce passives with nonce verbs. *Developmental Psychology*, 35(1): 29–44.

(1999b). How children constrain their argument structure constructions. *Language*, 75(4): 720–38.

Brooks, P. J. and Zizak, O. (2002). Does pre-emption help children learn verb transitivity? *Journal of Child Language*, 29: 759–81.

Brooks, P. J., Tomasello, M., Dodson, K. and Lewis, L. B. (1999). Young children's overgeneralizations with fixed transitivity verbs. *Child Development*, 70(6): 1325–37.

Brooks, P. J., Xiangdong Jia, Braine, M. D. S. and Da Graca Dias, M. (1998). A crosslinguistic study of children's comprehension of universal quantifiers: a comparison of Mandarin Chinese, Portuguese and English. *First Language*, 18(52): 33–79.

Brooks, R. and Meltzoff, A. N. (2002). The importance of eyes: how infants interpret adult looking behavior. *Developmental Psychology*, 38: 958–66.

(2005). The development of gaze following and its relation to language. *Developmental Science*, 8: 535–43.

Brown, P. (1998). Children's first verbs in Tzeltal: evidence for an early verb category. *Linguistics*, 36: 713–55.

Brown, R. (1973). *A First Language: The Early Stages*. Cambridge, MA: Harvard University Press.

Bruner, J. S. (1975). The ontogenesis of speech acts. *Journal of Child Language*, 2: 1–20.

  (1978). Berlyne Memorial Lecture: 'Acquiring the uses of language'. *Canadian Journal of Psychology*, 32(4): 204–8.

Bucci, W. (1978). The interpretation of universal affirmative propositions: a developmental study. *Cognition*, 6: 55–77.

Bybee, J. (1995). Regular morphology and the lexicon. *Language and Cognitive Processes*, 10(5): 425–55.

Bybee, J. L. and Moder, C. L. (1983). Morphological classes as natural categories. *Language*, 59: 251–70.

Bybee, J. and Schiebmann, J. (1999). The effect of usage on degrees of constituency: the reduction of *don't* in English. *Linguistics*, 37: 575–96.

Bybee, J. L. and Slobin, D. I. (1982). Rules and schemas in the development and use of the English past tense. *Language*, 58(2): 265–89.

Cairns, H., McDaniel, D., Hsu, J. R. and Rapp, M. (1994). A longitudinal study of principles of control and coreference in child English. *Language*, 70: 260–88.

Cantrall, W. (1974). *Viewpoint, Reflexives and the Nature of Noun Phrases*. The Hague: Mouton.

Carey, S. and Bartlett, E. (1978). Acquiring a single new word. *Papers and Reports on Child Language Development [Stanford University]*, 15: 17–29.

Carnie, A. (2006). *Syntax: A Generative Introduction*. New York: Blackwell.

Carpenter, M., Akhtar, N. and Tomasello, M. (1998). Fourteen through 18-month-old infants differentially imitate intentional and accidental actions. *Infant Behavior and Development*, 21(2): 315–30.

Carpenter, M., Call, J. and Tomasello, M. (2002). Understanding 'prior intentions' enables two-year-olds to imitatively learn a complex task. *Child Development*, 73(5): 1431–41.

Carpenter, M., Nagell, K. and Tomasello, M. (1998). Social cognition, joint attention and communicative competence from 9 to 15 months of age. *Monographs of the Society for Research in Child Development*, 63(4): i–vi, 1–143.

Cartwright, T. A. and Brent, M. R. (1997). Syntactic categorization in early language acquisition: formalizing the role of distributional analysis. *Cognition*, 63(2): 121–70.

Casenhiser, D. and Goldberg, A. E. (2005). Fast mapping between a phrasal form and meaning. *Developmental Science*, 8(6): 500–8.

Cassidy, K. W. and Kelly, M. H. (1991). Phonological information for grammatical category assignments. *Journal of Memory and Language*, 30(3): 348–69.

  (2001). Children's use of phonology to infer grammatical class in vocabulary learning. *Psychonomic Bulletin and Review*, 8(3): 519–23.

Cazden, C. B. (1968). The acquisition of noun and verb inflections. *Child Development*, 39(2): 433–48.

Chan, A., Lieven, E. and Tomasello, M. (2009). Children's understanding of the agent–patient relations in the transitive construction: cross-linguistic comparisons between Cantonese, German and English. *Cognitive Linguistics*, 20(2): 267–300.

Chan, A., Meints, K., Lieven, E. V. M. and Tomasello, M. (2010). Young children's comprehension of English word order in act-out and intermodal preferential looking tasks. *Cognitive Development*, 25: 30–45.

Chang, F., Dell, G. S. and Bock, K. (2006). Becoming syntactic. *Psychological Review*, 113(2): 234–72.

Chemla, E., Mintz, T. H., Bernal, S. and Christophe, A. (2009). Categorizing words using 'frequent frames': what cross-linguistic analyses reveal about distributional acquisition strategies. *Developmental Science*, 12(3): 396–406.

Chien, Y. and Wexler, K. (1990). Children's knowledge of locality conditions in binding as evidence for the modularity of syntax and pragmatics. *Language Acquisition*, 1: 225–95.

Childers, J. B. and Tomasello, M. (2001). The role of pronouns in young children's acquisition of the English transitive construction. *Developmental Psychology*, 37(6): 739–48.

   (2002). Two-year-olds learn novel nouns, verbs and conventional actions from massed or distributed exposures. *Developmental Psychology*, 38(6): 867–978.

Childers, J. B., Vaughan, J. and Burquest, D. A. (2007). Joint attention and word learning in Ngas-speaking toddlers in Nigeria. *Journal of Child Language*, 34(2): 199–225.

Chomsky, N. (1957). *Syntactic Structures*. Berlin: Mouton de Gruyter.

   (1959). A review of B. F. Skinner's *Verbal Behavior*. *Language*, 35(1): 26–58.

   (1965). *Aspects of the Theory of Syntax*. Cambridge, MA: MIT Press.

   (1980). In M. Piatelli-Palmarini (ed.), *Language and Learning: The Debate between Jean Piaget and Noam Chomsky*. Cambridge, MA: Harvard University Press.

   (1981). *Lectures on Government and Binding*. Dordrecht: Foris.

   (1982). *Some Concepts and Consequences of Government and Binding Theory*. Cambridge, MA: MIT Press.

   (1986). *Barriers*. Cambridge, MA: MIT Press.

   (1988). *Language and Problems of Knowledge: The Managua Lectures*. London: MIT Press.

   (1993). A minimalist program for linguistic theory. In K. Hale and S. J. Keyser (eds.), *The View from Building 20* (pp. 1–52). Cambridge, MA: MIT Press.

   (1995). *The Minimalist Program*. Cambridge, MA: MIT Press.

Chomsky, N. and Halle, M. (1968). *The Sound Pattern of English*. New York: Harper & Row.

Chouinard, M. M. and Clark, E. V. (2003). Adult reformulations of child errors as negative evidence. *Journal of Child Language*, 30(3): 637–69.

Christiansen, M. and Kirby, S. (eds.) (2003). *Language Evolution*. Oxford University Press.

Christiansen, M. H. and Monaghan, P. (2006). Discovering verbs through multiple-cue integration. In K. Hirsh-Pasek and R. Golinkoff (eds.), *Action Meets Word: How Children Learn Verbs* (pp. 544–64). Oxford University Press.

Christophe, A., Guasti, T., Nespor, M., Dupoux, E. and Van Ooyen, B. (1997). Reflections on phonological bootstrapping: its role for lexical and syntactic acquisition. *Language and Cognitive Processes*, 12(5–6): 585–612.

Christophe, A., Millotte, S., Bernal, S. and Lidz, J. (2008). Bootstrapping lexical and syntactic acquisition. *Language and Speech*, 51: 61–75.

Christophe, A., Nespor, M., Guasti, M. T. and Van Ooyen, B. (2003). Prosodic structure and syntactic acquisition: the case of the head-direction parameter. *Developmental Science*, 6(2): 211–20.

Cimpian, A. and Markman, E. M. (2005). The absence of a shape bias in children's word learning. *Developmental Psychology*, 41(6): 1003–19.

Clahsen, H. (1986). Verb inflections in German child language, acquisition of agreement markings and the functions they encode. *Linguistics*, 24(1): 79–121.

   (1991). Constraints on parameter setting: a grammatical analysis of some acquisition stages in German child language. *Language Acquisition*, 1: 361–91.

Clahsen, H. and Almazan, M. (1998). Syntax and morphology in Williams syndrome. *Cognition*, 68(3): 167–98.

Clahsen, H. and Muysken, P. (1996). How adult second language learning differs from child first language development. *Behavioral and Brain Sciences*, 19(4): 721–3.

Clark, E. V. (1973). What's in a word? On the child's acquisition of semantics in his first language. In T. E. Moore (ed.), *Cognitive Development and the Acquisition of Language* (pp. 65–110). New York: Academic Press.

   (1978). Awareness of language: some evidence from what children say and do. In A. Sinclair, R. J. Jarvella and W. J. M. Levelt (eds.), *The Child's Conception of Language* (pp. 17–43). New York: Springer.

   (1987). The principle of contrast: a constraint on language acquisition. In B. MacWhinney (ed.), *Mechanisms of Language Acquisition* (pp. 1–33). Hillsdale, NJ: Erlbaum.

   (1988). On the logic of contrast. *Journal of Child Language*, 15(2): 317–35.

   (1993). *The Lexicon in Acquisition*. Cambridge University Press.

Clark, E. V. and Clark, H. H. (1979). When nouns surface as verbs. *Language*, 55: 767–811.

Clark, E. V. and Grossman, J. B. (1998). Pragmatic directions and children's word learning. *Journal of Child Language*, 25(1): 1–18.

Clark, E. V., Carpenter, K. L. and Deutsch, W. (1995). Reference states and reversals: undoing actions with verbs. *Journal of Child Language*, 22(3): 633–62.

Clark, E. V. and Svaib, T. A. (1997). Speaker perspective and reference in young children. *First Language*, 17(51): 57–74.

Clark, V., Ambridge, B., Pine, J. M. and Rowland, C. F. (2010). Locative overgeneralization errors: the effects of verb semantics and verb frequency. Unpublished MS.

Colledge, E., Bishop, D. V. M., Koeppen-Schomerus, G., Price, T., Happé, F., Eley, T., Dale, P. and Plomin, R. (2002). The structure of language abilities at 4 years: a twin study. *Developmental Psychology*, 38: 749–57.

Comrie, B. (1985). Reflections on subject and object control. *Journal of Semantics*, 4(1): 47–65.

Conti-Ramsden, G., Botting, N. and Faragher, B. (2001). Psycholinguistic markers for specific language impairment (SLI). *Journal of Child Psychology and Psychiatry*, 42: 741–48.

Conwell, E. and Morgan, J. L. (2010). When parents verb nouns: resolving the ambicategory problem. Unpublished MS.

Cooper, W. E. and Sorenson, J. M. (1977). Fundamental frequency contours at syntactic boundaries. *Journal of the Acoustical Society of America*, 62(3): 683–92.

Cooper, W. and Paccia-Cooper, J. (1980). *Syntax and Speech*. Cambridge, MA: Harvard University Press.

Corrêa, L. M. (1982). Strategies in the acquisition of relative clauses. In J. Aitchison and N. Harvey (eds.), *Working Papers of the London Psycholinguistic Research Group*, 4: 37–49.

(1995). An alternative assessment of children's comprehension of relative clauses. *Journal of Psycholinguistic Research*, 24: 183–203.

Cottrell, G. W. and Plunkett, K. (1994). Acquiring the mapping from meanings to sounds. *Connection Science*, 6(4): 379–412.

Crain, S. (1991). Language acquisition in the absence of experience. *Behavioral and Brain Sciences*, 14: 597–650.

Crain, S. and Fodor, J. D. (1993). Competence and performance. In E. Dromi (ed.), *Language and Cognition: A Developmental Perspective*. Norwood, NJ: Ablex.

Crain, S. and McKee, C. (1986). Acquisition of structural restrictions on anaphora. *NELS 16: Proceedings of the Sixteenth Annual Meeting of the North East Linguistic Society* (pp. 94–110). Amherst, MA: GLSA.

Crain, S., McKee, C. and Emiliani, M. (1990). Visiting relatives in Italy. In L. Frazier and J. de Villiers (eds.), *Language Processing and Language Acquisition* (pp. 355–6). Dordrecht: Kluwer.

Crain, S. and Nakayama, M. (1987). Structure dependence in grammar formation. *Language*, 63: 522–43.

Crain, S., Thornton, R., Boster, C., Conway, L., Lillo-Martin, D. and Woodams, E. (1996). Quantification without qualification. *Language Acquisition*, 5(2): 83–153.

Croft, W. (2000). *Explaining Language Change: An Evolutionary Approach*. Harlow: Longman.

(2001). *Radical Construction Grammar: Syntactic Theory in Typological Perspective*. Oxford University Press.

Croft, W. and Cruse, A. (2004). *Cognitive Linguistics*. Cambridge University Press.

Crystal, T. H. and House, A. (1988). Segmental duration in connected speech signals: current results. *Journal of the Acoustical Society of America*, 83: 1553–73.

Curtin, S. and Werker, J. F. (2007). The perceptual foundations of phonological development. In G. Gaskell (ed.), *The Oxford Handbook of Psycholinguistics* (pp. 579–99). Oxford University Press.

Curtiss, S., Fromkin, V., Krashen, S., Rigler, D. and Rigler, M. (1974). The linguistic development of Genie. *Language*, 50(3): 528–54.

Cutler, A. and Carter, D. M. (1987). The predominance of strong initial syllables in the English vocabulary. *Computer Speech and Language*, 2: 133–42.

Dąbrowska, E. (2001). Learning a morphological system without a default: the Polish genitive. *Journal of Child Language*, 28: 545–74.

(2008). Questions with long-distance dependencies: a usage-based perspective. *Cognitive Linguistics* 19(3): 391–42.

Dąbrowska, E. and Lieven, E. (2005). Towards a lexically specific grammar of children's question constructions. *Cognitive Linguistics*, 16(3): 437–74.

Dąbrowska, E. and Street, J. (2006). Individual differences in language attainment: comprehension of passive sentences by native and non-native English speakers. *Language Sciences*, 28: 604–15.

Dąbrowska, E. and Szczerbiński, M. (2006). Polish children's productivity with case marking: the role of regularity, type frequency and phonological diversity. *Journal of Child Language*, 33(3): 559–97.

Dąbrowska, E., Rowland, C. and Theakston, A. (2009). The acquisition of questions with long-distance dependencies. *Cognitive Linguistics*, 20(3): 571–97.

Dasinger, L. and Toupin, C. (1994). The development of relative clause functions in narratives. In A. Berman and D. I. Slobin (eds.), *Relating Events in Narrative: A Crosslinguistic Developmental Study* (pp. 457–514). Hillsdale, NJ: Erlbaum.

Davis, H. (2009). Cross-linguistic variation in anaphoric dependencies: evidence from the Pacific Northwest. *Natural Language and Linguistic Theory*, 27(1): 1–43.

de Boer, B. (2000). Self-organization in vowel systems. *Journal of Phonetics*, 28(4): 441–65.

de Cat, Cécile (2002). Apparent non-nominative subjects in L1 French. In J. Paradis and P. Prévost (eds.), *The Acquisition of French in Different Contexts: Focus on Functional Categories* (pp. 53–88). Amsterdam and Philadelphia: Benjamins.

de Léon, L. (1999). Why Tzotzil children prefer verbs over nouns. Paper presented at the Fourth International Conference for the Study of Child Language. San Sebastian, Donostia, Spain.

de Villiers, J. G. (1991). Why questions? In T. Maxwell and B. Plunkett (eds.), *Papers in the Acquisition of 'Wh'* (pp. 155–71). Amherst, MA: University of Massachusetts.

de Villiers, J. G. and Pyers, J. (2002). Complements to cognition: a longitudinal study of the relationship between complex syntax and false-belief-understanding. *Cognitive Development*, 17(1): 1037–60.

de Villiers, J. G. and de Villiers, P. A. (1999). Linguistic determinism and the understanding of false beliefs. In P. Mitchell (ed.), *Children's Reasoning and the Mind*. Hove: Psychology Press.

de Villiers, J. G., Flusberg, H. B., Hakuta, K. and Cohen, M. (1979). Children's comprehension of relative clauses. *Journal of Psycholinguist Research*, 8(5): 499–518.

de Villiers, J., Roeper, T. and Vainikka, A. (1990). The acquisition of long-distance rules. In L. Frazier and J. de Villiers (eds.), *Language Processing and Language Acquisition* (pp. 257–97). Dordrecht: Kluwer.

Deak, G. O. (2000). Hunting the fox of word learning: why 'constraints' fail to capture it. *Developmental Review*, 20: 29–80.

Deak, G. O. and Maratsos, M. (1998). On having complex representations of things: preschoolers use multiple words for objects and people. *Developmental Psychology*, 34(2): 224–40.

Dehaene-Lambertz, G., Dehaene, S. and Hertz-Pannier, L. (2002). Functional neuroimaging of speech perception in infants. *Science*, 298: 2013–15.

Demetras, M. J., Post, K. N. and Snow, C. E. (1986). Feedback to first language learners: the role of repetitions and clarification questions. *Journal of Child Language*, 13(2): 275–92.

Demuth, K. (1990). Subject, topic and Sesotho passive. *Journal of Child Language*, 17(1): 67–84.

D'Entremont, B., Hains, S. and Muir, D. (1997). A demonstration of gaze following in 3- to 6-month-olds. *Infant Behavior and Development*, 20: 569–72.

Diesendruck, G. (2005). The principles of conventionality and contrast in word learning: an empirical examination. *Developmental Psychology*, 41(3): 451–63.

Diesendruck, G. and Markson, L. (2001). Children's avoidance of lexical overlap: a pragmatic account. *Developmental Psychology*, 37(5): 630–41.

Diesendruck, G., Markson, L., Akhtar, N. and Reudor, A. (2004). Two-year-olds' sensitivity to speakers' intent: an alternative account of Samuelson and Smith. *Developmental Science*, 7(1): 33–41.

Diessel, H. and Tomasello, M. (2000). The development of relative clauses in spontaneous child speech. *Cognitive Linguistics*, 11(1–2): 131–51.

  (2001). The acquisition of finite complement clauses in English: a corpus-based analysis. *Cognitive Linguistics*, 12(2): 97–141.

  (2005). A new look at the acquisition of relative clauses. *Language*, 81(4): 882–906.

Dittmar, M., Abbot-Smith, K., Lieven, E. and Tomasello, M. (2008a). German children's comprehension of word order and case marking in causative sentences. *Child Development*, 79(4): 1152–67.

  (2008b). Young German children's early syntactic competence: a preferential looking study. *Developmental Science*, 11(4): 575–82.

Dixon, R. M. W. (2004). Adjective classes in typological perspective. In R. M. W. Dixon and A. Y. Aikhenvald (eds.), *Adjective Classes: A Cross-linguistic Typology* (pp. 30–83). Oxford University Press.

Dockrell, J. and Campbell, R. N. (1986). Lexical acquisition strategies in the preschool child. In S. A. Kuczaj II and M. D. Barrett (eds.), *The Development of Word Meaning: Progress in Cognitive Development Research* (pp. 121–54). New York: Springer.

Dodson, K. and Tomasello, M. (1998). Acquiring the transitive construction in English: the role of animacy and pronouns. *Journal of Child Language*, 25: 555–74.

Donegan, P. J. and Stampe, D. (1979). The study of natural phonology. In I. Dinnsen (ed.), *Current Approaches to Phonological Theory* (pp. 126–73). Bloomington: Indiana University Press.

Donnai, D. and Karmiloff-Smith, A. (2000). Williams syndrome: from genotype through to the cognitive phenotype. *American Journal of Medical Genetics: Seminars in Medical Genetics*, 97(2): 164–71.

Dressler, W. U., Mayerthaler, W., Panagl, O. and Wurzel, W. U. (1988). *Leitmotifs in Natural Morphology*. Amsterdam and Philadelphia: Benjamins.

Dromi, E. (1987). *Early Lexical Development*. Cambridge University Press.

Drozd, K. (2001). Children's weak interpretation of universally quantified sentences. In M. Bowerman and S. C. Levinson (eds.), *Conceptual Development and Language Acquisition*. Cambridge University Press.

  (2004). Learnability and linguistic performance. *Journal of Child Language*, 31: 431–57.

Duez, D. (1993). Acoustic correlates of subjective pauses. *Journal of Psycholinguistic Research*, 22: 21–39.

Eimas, P. D., Siqueland, E. R., Jusczyk, P. W. and Vigorito, J. (1971). Speech perception in infants. *Science*, 171: 303–6.

Eisele, J. (1988). Meaning and form in children's judgments about language: a study of the truth-value judgment test. Unpublished master's thesis, Cornell University, Ithaca, New York.

Elman, J. L. (1990). Finding structure in time. *Cognitive Science*, 14: 179–211.

(1993). Learning and development in neural networks: the importance of starting small. *Cognition*, 48(1): 71–99.

Elman, J. L., Bates, E., Johnson, M. H., Karmiloff-Smith, A., Parisi, D. and Plunkett, K. (1996). *Rethinking Innateness: A Connectionist Perspective on Development*. Cambridge, MA: MIT Press.

Enard, W., Przeworski, M., Fisher, S. E., Lai, C. S. L., Wiebe, V., Kitano, T., Monaco, A. P. and Pääbo, S. (2002). Molecular evolution of FOXP2, a gene involved in speech and language. *Nature*, 418: 869–72.

Estigarribia, B. (2010). Facilitation by variation: right-to-left learning of English yes/no questions. *Cognitive Science*, 34(1): 68–93.

Evans, G. (1980). Pronouns. *Linguistic Inquiry*, 11: 337–62.

Feldman, H. M., MacWhinney, B. and Sacco, K. (2002). Sentence processing in children with early unilateral brain injury. *Brain and Language*, 83: 335–52.

Felser, C. and Clahsen, H. (2009). Grammatical processing of spoken language in child and adult language learners. *Journal of Psycholinguistic Research*, 38: 305–19.

Fenson, L., Dale, P. S., Reznick, J. S., Bates, E., Thal, D. J. and Pethick, S. J. (1994). Variability in early communicative development. *Monographs of the Society for Research in Child Development*, 59(5).

Fernald, A. and McRoberts, G. (1996). Prosodic bootstrapping: a critical analysis of the argument and the evidence. In J. Morgan and K. Demuth (eds.), *Signal to Syntax: Bootstrapping from Speech to Grammar in Early Acquisition* (pp. 365–88). Mahwah, NJ: Erlbaum.

Fernald, A., Pinto, J. P., Swingley, D., Weinberg, A. and McRoberts, G. W. (1998). Rapid gains in speed of verbal processing by infants in the 2nd year. *Psychological Science*, 9(3): 228–31.

Fernald, A., Zangl, R., Portillo, A. L. and Marchman, V. A. (2008). Looking while listening: using eye movements to monitor spoken language comprehension by infants and young children. In I. A. Sekerina, E. M. Fernández and H. Clahsen (eds.), *Developmental Psycholinguistics: On-line Methods in Children's Language Processing* (pp. 97–135). Amsterdam and Philadelphia: Benjamins.

Fernandes, K. J., Marcus, G. F., Di Nubila, J. A. and Vouloumanos, A. (2006). From semantics to syntax and back again: argument structure in the third year of life. *Cognition*, 100(2): B10–20.

Fikkert, P. (2007). Acquiring phonology. In P. de Lacy (ed.), *Handbook of Phonological Theory* (pp. 537–54). Cambridge University Press.

Fikkert, P. and Levelt, C. (2008). How does place fall into place? The lexicon and emergent constraints in the developing phonological grammar. In P. Avery, B. E. Dresher and K. Rice (eds.), *Contrast in Phonology: Perception and Acquisition* (pp. 231–68). Berlin: Mouton.

Fillmore, C. J., Kay, P. and O'Connor, M. C. (1988). Regularity and idiomaticity in grammatical constructions: the case of *let alone*. *Language*, 64(3): 501–38.

Fisher, C. (1996). Structural limits on verb mapping: The role of analogy in children's interpretations of sentences. *Cognitive Psychology*, 31(1): 41–81.

(2000). From form to meaning: a role for structural alignment in the acquisition of language. *Advances in Child Development and Behavior*, 27: 1–53.

(2002). The role of abstract syntactic knowledge in language acquisition: a reply to Tomasello (2000). *Cognition*, 82(3): 259–78.

Fisher, C. and Tokura, H. (1996). Acoustic cues to grammatical structure in infant-directed speech: cross-linguistic evidence. *Child Development*, 67(6): 3192–218.

(1996). Prosody in speech to infants: direct and indirect acoustic cues to syntactic structure. In J. L. Morgan and K. Demuth (eds.), *Signal to Syntax: Bootstrapping from Speech to Grammar in Early Acquisition* (pp. 343–63). Mahwah, NJ: Erlbaum.

Fodor, J. (2003). Evaluating models of parameter setting. Handout, LSA Summer Institute. (cited in Tomasello, 2007)

Fodor, J. A. (1983). *Modularity of Mind: An Essay on Faculty Psychology*. Cambridge, MA: MIT Press.

Fodor, J. D. (1998). Unambiguous triggers. *Linguistic Enquiry*, 29(1): 1–36.

Forrester, N. and Plunkett, K. (1994). Learning the Arabic plural: the case of minority default mappings in connectionist networks. *Proceedings of the Sixteenth Annual Conference of the Cognitive Science Society*. Hillsdale, NJ: Erlbaum.

Fowler, C. A., Best, C. T. and McRoberts, G. W. (1990). Young infants' perception of liquid coarticulatory influences on following stop consonants. *Perception and Psychophysics*, 48: 559–70.

Fox, B. A. and Thompson, S. A. (1990). A discourse explanation of the grammar of relative clauses in English conversations. *Language*, 66: 297–316.

Fox, D. and Grodzinsky, Y. (1998). Children's passive: a view from the by-phrase. *Linguistic Inquiry*, 29: 311–32.

Franco, F. and Butterworth, G. (1996). Pointing and social awareness: declaring and requesting in the second year. *Journal of Child Language*, 23(2): 307–36.

Franks, S. (1995). *Parameters of Slavic Morphosyntax*. New York: Oxford University Press.

Fremgen, A. and Fay, D. (1980). Overextensions in production and comprehension: a methodological clarification. *Journal of Child Language*, 7(1): 205–11.

Freudenthal, D., Pine, J. M., Aguado-Orea, J. and Gobet, F. (2007). Modelling the developmental patterning of finiteness marking in English, Dutch, German and Spanish using MOSAIC. *Cognitive Science*, 31(2): 311–41.

(2010). Explaining quantitative variation in the rate of Optional Infinitive errors across languages: a comparison of MOSAIC and the Variational Learning Model. *Journal of Child Language*, 37(3): 643–69.

Freudenthal, D., Pine, J. M. and Gobet, F. (2005a). Simulating Optional Infinitive errors in child speech through the omission of sentence-internal elements. In B. G. Bara, L. Barsalou and M. Buchiarelli (eds.), *Proceedings of the Twenty-Seventh Annual Meeting of the Cognitive Science Society* (pp. 708–13). Mahwah, NJ: Erlbaum.

(2005b). Simulating the cross-linguistic development of Optional Infinitive errors in MOSAIC. In B. G. Bara, L. Barsalou and M. Buchiarelli (eds.), *Proceedings of the Twenty-Seventh Annual Meeting of the Cognitive Science Society* (pp. 702–7). Mahwah, NJ: Erlbaum.

(2005c). On the resolution of ambiguities in the extraction of syntactic categories through chunking. *Cognitive Systems Research*, 6(1): 17–25.

(2009). Simulating the referential properties of Dutch, German and English Root Infinitives in MOSAIC. *Language Learning and Development*, 5: 1–29.

Friederici, A. D. (2009). Neurocognition of language development. In E. Bavin (ed.), *The Cambridge Handbook of Child Language* (pp. 51–67). Cambridge University Press.

Gambell, T. and Yang, C. D. (2003). Scope and limits of statistical learning in word segmentation. *NELS 34: Proceedings of the Thirty-Fourth Annual Meeting of the North East Linguistic Society Meeting* (pp. 29–30). Amherst, MA: GLSA.

(2005). Mechanisms and constraints in word segmentation. Unpublished MS, Yale University.

Ganger, J. and Brent, M. R. (2004). Re-examining the vocabulary spurt. *Developmental Psychology*, 40(4): 621–32.

Gathercole, S. E. and Baddeley, A. D. (1990). Phonological memory deficits in language disordered children: is there a causal connection? *Journal of Memory and Language*, 29: 336–60.

Gathercole, V. C. M., Sebastián, E. and Soto, P. (1999). The early acquisition of Spanish verbal morphology: across-the-board or piecemeal knowledge? *International Journal of Bilingualism*, 2 and 3: 133–82.

Gee, J. and Grosjean, F. (1983). Performance structures: a psycholinguistic and linguistic appraisal. *Cognitive Psychology*, 15: 411–58.

Gentner, D. (1982). Why nouns are learned before verbs: linguistic relativity versus natural partitioning. In S. A. Kuczaj (ed.), *Language Development*, vol. 2: *Language, Thought, and Culture* (pp. 301–34). Hillsdale, NJ: Erlbaum.

(2006). Why verbs are hard to learn. In K. Hirsh-Pasek and R. Golinkoff (eds.), *Action Meets Word: How Children Learn Verbs* (pp. 544–64). Oxford University Press.

Gentner, D. and Boroditsky, L. (2001). Individuation, relativity and early word learning. In M. Bowerman and S. Levinson (eds.), *Language Acquisition and Conceptual Development* (pp. 15–256). Cambridge University Press.

Gentner, D. and Medina, J. (1998). Similarity and the development of rules. *Cognition*, 65: 263–97.

Gergely, G., Bekkering, H. and Király, I. (2002). Rational imitation in preverbal infants. *Nature*, 415: 755.

Gerken, L., Jusczyk, P. W. and Mandel, D. R. (1994). When prosody fails to cue syntactic structure: 9-month-olds' sensitivity to phonological versus syntactic phrases. *Cognition*, 51(3): 237–65.

Gertner, Y., Fisher, C. and Eisengart, J. (2006). Learning words and rules: abstract knowledge of word order in early sentence comprehension. *Psychological Science*, 17(8): 684–91.

Geurts, B. (2003). Quantifying kids. *Language Acquisition*, 11: 197–218.

Gibson, E. and Wexler, K. (1994). Triggers. *Linguistic Inquiry*, 25: 407–54.

Gillette, J., Gleitman, H., Gleitman, L. and Lederer, A. (1999). Human simulations of vocabulary learning. *Cognition*, 73(2): 135–76.

Gleitman, L. (1990). The structural sources of verb meanings. *Language Acquisition*, 1: 3–55.

Gnanadesikan, A. (2004). Markedness and faithfulness constraints in child phonology. In R. Kager, J. Pater and W. Zonneveld (eds.), *Constraints in Phonological Acquisition* (pp. 73–108). Cambridge University Press.

Godden, D. R. and Baddeley, A. D. (1975). Context-dependent memory in 2 natural environments – land and underwater. *British Journal of Psychology*, 66 (Aug): 325–31.

Goldberg, A. E. (1995). *Constructions: A Construction Grammar Approach to Argument Structure*. University of Chicago Press.

(2006). *Constructions at Work: The Nature of Generalization in Language*. Oxford University Press.

Goldin-Meadow, S. (2003). *The Resilience of Language: What Gesture Creation in Deaf Children Can Tell Us About How All Children Learn Language*. New York: Psychology Press.

Goldman-Eisler, F. (1972). Pauses, clauses, sentences. *Language and Speech*, 15: 103–13.

Golinkoff, R. M., Mervis, C. and Hirsh-Pasek, K. (1994). Early object labels: the case for a developmental lexical principles framework. *Journal of Child Language*, 21: 125–55.

Golinkoff, R. M., Suff-Bailey, M., Olguin, R. and Ruan, W. J. (1995). Young children extend novel words at the basic level – evidence for the principle of categorical scope. *Developmental Psychology*, 31(3): 494–507.

Gómez, R. L. (2002). Variability and detection of invariant structure. *Psychological Science*, 13(5): 431–36.

Gómez, R. L. (2007). Statistical learning in infant language development. In M. G. Gaskell (ed.), *The Oxford Handbook of Psycholinguistics* (pp. 601–15). Oxford University Press.

Goodglass, H. (1993). *Understanding Aphasia*. San Diego: Academic Press.

Goodluck, H. and Tavakolian, S. (1982). Competence and processing in children's grammar of relative clauses. *Cognition*, 11(1): 1–27.

Gopnik, A. and Choi, S. (1995). Names, relational words and cognitive development in English and Korean speakers: nouns are not always learned before verbs. In M. Tomasello and W. Merriman (eds.), *Beyond Names for Things: Young Children's Acquisition of Verbs* (pp. 63–80). Mahwah, NJ: Erlbaum.

Gopnik, A. and Meltzoff, A. N. (1992). Categorization and naming – basic-level sorting in 18-month-olds and its relation to language. *Child Development*, 63(5): 1091–1103.

Gopnik, M. (1990). Feature-blind grammar and dysphasia. *Nature*, 344: 715.

Gordon, P. C. (1996). The truth value judgment task. In D. McDaniel, C. McKee and H. S. Cairns (eds.), *Methods for Assessing Children's Syntax* (pp. 211–32). Cambridge, MA: MIT Press.

Gordon, P. and Chafetz, J. (1990). Verb-based versus class-based accounts of actionality effects in children's comprehension of passives. *Cognition*, 36(3): 227–54.

Grassmann, S. and Tomasello, M. (2007). Two-year-olds use primary sentence accent to learn new words. *Journal of Child Language*, 34(3): 677–87.

Grassmann, S., Stracke, M. and Tomasello, M. (2009). Two-year-olds exclude novel objects as potential referents of novel words based on pragmatics. *Cognition*, 112(3): 488–93.

Greenfield, P. M. and Smith, J. H. (1976). *The Structure of Communication in Early Language Development*. New York: Academic Press.

Grieser, D. and Kuhl, P. K. (1989). Categorization of speech by infants: support for speech-sound prototypes. *Developmental Psychology*, 25: 577–88.

Grimshaw, J. and Rosen, S. T. (1990). Knowledge and obedience: the developmental status of Binding Theory. *Linguistic Inquiry*, 21: 187–222.

Grodzinsky, Y. and Reinhart, T. (1993). The innateness of binding and coreference. *Linguistic Inquiry*, 24: 69–101.

Gropen, J., Pinker, S., Hollander, M. and Goldberg, R. (1991a). Affectedness and direct objects – the role of lexical semantics in the acquisition of verb argument structure. *Cognition*, 41(1–3): 153–95.

(1991b). Syntax and semantics in the acquisition of locative verbs. *Journal of Child Language*, 18(1): 115–51.

Gropen, J., Pinker, S., Hollander, M., Goldberg, R. and Wilson, R. (1989). The learnability and acquisition of the dative alternation in English. *Language*, 65(2): 203–57.

Grünloh, T., Lieven, E. V. M. and Tomasello, M. (2009). German children's use of prosodic cues in resolving participant roles in transitive constructions. Poster presented at the Boston University Conference on Language Development 34, Boston, MA.

Guasti, M. T. (2004). *Language Acquisition: The Growth of Grammar*. Cambridge, MA: MIT Press.

Guasti, M., Thornton, R. and Wexler, K. (1995). Negation in children's questions: the case of English. *Proceedings of the Nineteenth Annual Boston University Conference on Language Development* (pp. 228–39). Somerville, MA: Cascadilla Press.

Guilfoyle, E. and Noonan, M. (1992). Functional categories and language-acquisition. *Canadian Journal of Linguistics – Revue Canadienne de Linguistique*, 37(2): 241–72.

Gussenhoven, C. and Jacobs, H. (1998). *Understanding Phonology*. London: Arnold.

Hahn, U. and Nakisa, R. C. (2000). German inflection: single route or dual route. *Cognitive Psychology*, 47(4): 313–60.

Hakuta, K., Bialystok, E. and Wiley, E. (2003). Critical evidence: a test of the critical period hypothesis for second language acquisition. *Psychological Science*, 14(1): 31–8.

Hall, D. G., Waxman, S. R. and Hurwitz, W. M. (1993). How two- and four-year-old children interpret adjectives and count nouns. *Child Development*, 64: 1651–64.

Hamburger, H. and Crain, S. (1982). Relative acquisition. In S. Kuczaj (ed.), *Language Development: Syntax and Semantics*. Hillsdale, NJ: Erlbaum.

Happé, F. (2003). Cognition in autism: one deficit or many? *Novartis Foundation Symposium*, 251: 198–207.

Happé, F. and Plomin, R. (2006). Time to give up on a single explanation for autism. *Nature Neuroscience*, 9: 1218–20.

Hare, B. and Tomasello, M. (1999). Domestic dogs (Canis familiaris) use human and conspecific social cues to locate hidden food. *Journal of Comparative Psychology*, 113(2): 173–77.

(2004). Chimpanzees are more skilful in competitive than in cooperative cognitive tasks. *Animal Behaviour*, 68: 571–81.

Hare, M. and Elman, J. L. (1995). Learning and morphological change. *Cognition*, 56(1): 61–98.

Hare, M., Elman, J. L. and Daugherty, K. G. (1995). Default generalisation in connectionist networks. *Language and Cognitive Processes*, 10(6): 601–30.

Harris, C. L. and Bates, E. A. (2002). Clausal backgrounding and pronominal reference: a functionalist approach to c-command. *Language and Cognitive Processes*, 17(3): 237–69.

Harris, M. (1992). *Language Experience and Early Language Development: From Input to Uptake*. Hove: Erlbaum.

Hartshorne, J. K. and Ullman, M. (2006). Why girls say 'holded' more than boys. *Developmental Science*, 9(1): 21–32.

Hattori, R. (2003). Why do children say 'did you went?' The role of do-support. Poster presented at the Twenty-Eighth Boston University Conference on Language Development, Boston, MA.

Hauser, M., Chomsky, N. and Fitch, W. T. (2002). The language faculty: what is it, who has it and how did it evolve? *Science*, 298: 1569–79.

Hayiou-Thomas, M. E., Bishop, D. V. M. and Plunkett, K. (2004). Simulating SLI: general cognitive processing stressors can produce a specific linguistic profile. *Journal of Speech Language and Hearing Research*, 47(6): 1347–62.

Heath, S. B. (1983). *Ways with Words*. New York: Cambridge University Press.

Hirsh-Pasek, K., Golinkoff, R. M. and Naigles, L. (1996). *The Origins of Grammar: Evidence from Early Language Comprehension*. Cambridge, MA; London: MIT Press.

Hirsh-Pasek, K., Kemler Nelson, D., Jusczyk, P. W., Cassidy, K. W., Druss, B. and Kennedy, L. (1987). Clauses are perceptual units for young infants. *Cognition*, 26: 269–86.

Hoeffner, J. (1996). A single mechanism account of English past tense acquisition and processing. Unpublished PhD thesis, Carnegie Mellon University.

Hoekstra, T. and Hyams, N. (1998). Aspects of root infinitives. *Lingua*, 106(1–4): 81–112.

Hoff, E. (2001). *Language Development* (2nd edn). Belmont, CA: Wadsworth/Thomson Learning.

(in press). *The Guide to Research Methods in Child Language*. New York: Wiley-Blackwell.

Hollich, G. J., Hirsh-Pasek, K., Golinkoff, R. M. and Bloom, L. (2000). *Breaking the Language Barrier: An Emergentist Coalition Model for the Origins of Word Learning*. Malden, MA: Blackwell.

Horgan, D. (1978). Development of full passive. *Journal of Child Language*, 5(1): 65–80.

Houston-Price, C., Plunkett, K. and Duffy, H. (2006). The use of social and salience cues in early word learning. *Journal of Experimental Child Psychology*, 95(1): 27–55.

Houston-Price, C., Plunkett, K. and Harris, P. (2005). 'Word-learning wizardry' at 1;6. *Journal of Child Language*, 32(1): 175–89.

Hsu, J. R., Cairns, H. S., Eisenberg, S. and Schlisselberg, G. (1989). Control and coreference in early child language. *Journal of Child Language*, 16(3): 599–622.

Hsu, J., Cairns, H. and Fiengo, R. (1985). The development of grammars underlying children's interpretation of complex sentences. *Cognition*, 20: 25–48.

Huttenlocher, J., Vasilyeva, M. and Shimpi, P. (2004). Syntactic priming in young children. *Journal of Memory and Language*, 50(2): 182–95.

Hyams, N. (1986). *Language Acquisition and the Theory of Parameters*. Dordrecht: Reidel.

(1994). Non-discreteness and variation in child language: implications for principle and parameter models of language development. In Y. Levy (ed.), *Other Children, Other Languages* (pp. 11–40). Hillsdale, NJ: Erlbaum.

Imai, M., Gentner, D. and Uchida, N. (1994). Children's theories of word meaning – the role of shape similarity in early acquisition. *Cognitive Development*, 9(1): 45–75.

Ingram, D. and Shaw, C. (1981). The comprehension of pronominal reference in children. Unpublished MS, University of British Columbia, Vancouver, British Columbia.

Inhelder, B. and Piaget, J. (1964). *The Early Growth of Logic in the Child*. London: Routledge & Kegan Paul.

Israel, M., Johnson, C. and Brooks, P. J. (2000). From states to events: the acquisition of English passive participles. *Cognitive Linguistics*, 11: 1–2.

Jakobson, R. ([1941] 1968). *Child Language, Aphasia and Phonological Universals*. The Hague: Mouton. (Translated into English by A. R. Keiler, originally published in 1941 as *Kindersprache, Aphasie und allgemeine Lautgesetze*.)

Jelinek, E. and Demers, R. (1994). Predicates and pronominal arguments in Straits Salish. *Language*, 70: 697–736.

Johnson, E. K. and Jusczyk, P. W. (2001). Word segmentation by 8-month-olds: when speech cues count more than statistics. *Journal of Memory and Language*, 44: 548–67.

Johnson, J. S. and Newport, E. L. (1989). Critical period effects in 2nd language-learning – the influence of maturational state on the acquisition of English as a 2nd language. *Cognitive Psychology*, 21(1): 60–99.

Johnston, C. J., Durieux-Smith, A. and Bloom, K. (2005). Teaching gestural signs to infants to advance child development: a review of the evidence. *First Language*, 25: 235–51.

Jones, G., Gobet, F. and Pine, J. M. (2000). A process model of children's early verb use. *Proceedings of the Twenty-Second Annual Conference of the Cognitive Science Society* (pp. 723–28). Mahwah, NJ: Erlbaum.

Jones, P. E. (1995). Contradictions and unanswered questions in the Genie case: a fresh look at the linguistic evidence. *Language and Communication*, 15(3): 261–80.

Jusczyk, P. W. (1997). Perception of syllable-final stop consonants by two-month-old infants. *Perception and Psychophysics*, 21: 450–4.

(1998). *The Discovery of Spoken Language*. Cambridge, MA: Bradford Books, MIT Press.

Jusczyk, P. W. and Aslin, R. N. (1995). Infants' detection of the sound patterns of words in fluent speech. *Cognitive Psychology*, 29: 1–23.

Jusczyk, P. W. and Thompson, E. J. (1978). Perception of a phonetic contrast in multi-syllabic utterances by two-month-old infants. *Perception and Psychophysics*, 23: 105–9.

Jusczyk, P. W., Friederici, A. D., Wessels, J., Svenkerud, V. Y. and Jusczyk, A. M. (1993). Infants' sensitivity to the sound patterns of native language words. *Journal of Memory and Language*, 32: 402–20.

Jusczyk, P.W., Hirsh-Pasek, K., Kemler Nelson, D. G., Kennedy, L., Woodward, A. and Piwoz, J. (1992). Perception of acoustic correlates of major phrasal units by young infants. *Cognitive Psychology*, 24(2): 252–93.

Jusczyk, P. W., Hohne, E. A. and Bauman, A. (1999). Infant's sensitivity to allophonic cues for word segmentation. *Perception and Psychophysics*, 61: 1465–76.

Jusczyk, P. W., Houston, D. M. and Newsome, M. (1999). The beginnings of word segmentation in English-learning infants. *Cognitive Psychology*, 39: 159–207.

Jusczyk, P. W., Pisoni, D. B. and Mullenix, J. (1992). Some consequences of stimulus variability in speech processing by two-month-old infants. *Cognition*, 43: 253–91.

Kager, R., Pater, J. and Zonneveld, W. (2004). *Constraints in Phonological Acquisition*. Cambridge University Press.

Karmiloff-Smith, A. (2006). Modules, genes and evolution: what have we learned from atypical development? *Processes of Change in Brain and Cognitive Development: Attention and Performance*, 21: 563–83.

(2007). Atypical epigenesis. *Developmental Science*, 10: 84–8.

Kay, P. and Fillmore, C. J. (1999). Grammatical constructions and linguistic generalizations: the What's X doing Y? construction. *Language*, 75: 1–33.

Kegl, J. (2002). Language emergence in a language-ready brain. In G. Morgan and B. Woll (eds.), *Directions in Sign Language Acquisition* (pp. 207–54). Amsterdam and Philadelphia: Benjamins.

Kelly, M. H. (1992). Using sound to solve syntactic problems: the role of phonology in grammatical category assignments. *Psychological Review*, 99(2): 349–64.

Keuleers, E. (2008). Memory-based learning of inflectional morphology. Unpublished PhD thesis, University of Antwerp.

Keuleers, E. and Daelemans, W. (2007). Memory-based learning models of inflectional morphology: a methodological case study. *Lingue e Linguaggio*, 6(2): 151–74.

Keuleers, E., Sandra, D., Daelemans, W., Gillis, S., Durieux, G. and Martens, E. (2007). Dutch plural inflection: the exception that proves the analogy. *Cognitive Psychology*, 54(4): 283–318.

Kidd, E. and Kirjavainen, M. (in press). Investigating the contribution of procedural and declarative memory to the acquisition of past tense morphology: evidence from Finnish. *Language and Cognitive Processes*.

Kidd, E. and Bavin, E. L. (2002). English-Speaking children's comprehension of relative clauses: evidence for general-cognitive and language-specific constraints on development. *Journal of Psycholinguistic Research*, 31(6): 599–617.

Kidd, E. and Lum, J. A. G. (2008). Sex differences in past tense over-regularization. *Developmental Science*, 11(6): 882–9.

Kidd, E., Bavin, E. L. and Rhodes, B. (2001). Two-year olds' knowledge of verbs and argument structure. In M. Almgren (ed.), *Research on Child Language Acquisition* (pp. 1368–82). Somerville, MA: Cascadilla Press.

Kidd, E., Brandt, S., Lieven, E. and Tomasello, M. (2007). Object relatives made easy: a cross-linguistic comparison of the constraints influencing young children's processing of relative clauses. *Language and Cognitive Processes*, 22(6): 860–97.

Kidd, E., Lieven, E. and Tomasello, M. (2006). Examining the role of lexical frequency in the acquisition of sentential complements. *Cognitive Development*, 21: 93–107.

(2010). Lexical frequency and exemplar-based learning effects in language acquisition: evidence from sentential complements. *Language Sciences*, 32(1): 132–42.

Kim, J. J., Marcus, G. F., Pinker, S., Hollander, M. and Coppola, M. (1994). Sensitivity of children's inflection to grammatical structure. *Journal of Child Language*, 21(1): 173–209.

Kim, J. J., Pinker, S., Prince, A. and Prasada, S. (1991). Why no mere mortal has ever flown out to center field. *Cognitive Science*, 15(2): 173–218.

Kirby, S., Cornish, H. and Smith, K. (2008). Cumulative cultural evolution in the laboratory: an experimental approach to the origins of structure in human language. *Proceedings of the National Academy of Sciences*, 105(31): 10681–6.

Kirby, S., Dowman, M. and Griffiths, T. L. (2007). Innateness and culture in the evolution of language. *Proceedings of the National Academy of Sciences*, 104(12): 5241–5.

Kirjavainen, M., Theakston, A. and Lieven, E. (2009). Can input explain children's me-for-I errors? *Journal of Child Language*, 36(5): 1091–114.

Kirkham, N. Z., Slemmer, J. A. and Johnson, S. P. (2002). Visual statistical learning in infancy: evidence for a domain general learning mechanism. *Cognition*, 83: B35–B42.

Kjelgaard, M. M. and Tager-Flusberg, H. (2001). An investigation of language impairment in autism: implications for genetic subgroups. *Language and Cognitive Processes*, 16: 287–308.

Klatt, D. (1976). Linguistic uses of segmental duration in English: acoustic and perceptual evidence. *Journal of the Acoustical Society of America*, 59: 1208–21.

Klein, B. P. and Mervis, C. B. (1999). Contrasting patterns of cognitive abilities of 9- and 10-year-olds with Williams syndrome or Down syndrome. *Developmental Neuropsychology*, 16(2): 177–96.

Kõrgvee, K. (2001). Lapse sõnavara areng vanuses 1;8–2;1 [A child's lexical development, aged 1;3–2;1]. Unpublished undergraduate thesis, Tartu University.

Krajewski, G. (2007). Constructivist investigation into the development of Polish noun inflections in children between two and three-and-a-half years of age. Unpublished PhD thesis, University of Manchester.

Krajewski, G., Lieven, E. V. M. and Tomasello, M. (2010). The role of word order and case marking in Polish children's comprehension of transitives. Unpublished MS.

Krajewski, G., Theakston, A. L., Lieven, E. V. M. and Tomasello, M. (in press). How Polish children switch from one case to another when using novel nouns: challenges for current models of inflectional morphology. *Language and Cognitive Processes*.

Kramer, I. (1993). The licensing of subjects in early child language. *MIT Working Papers in Linguistics*, 19: 197–212.

Kuczaj, S. A. (1982). Young children's overextensions of object words in comprehension and/or production: support for a prototype theory of early object word meaning. *First Language*, 3: 93–105.

Kuczaj, S. and Brannick, N. (1979). Children's use of the wh-question modal auxiliary placement rule. *Journal of Experimental Child Psychology*, 28: 43–67.

Kuhl, P. K. (1979). Speech perception in early infancy: perceptual constancy for spectrally dissimilar vowel categories. *Journal of the Acoustical Society of America*, 66: 1668–79.

(1983). Perception of auditory equivalence classes for speech in early infancy. *Infant Behavior and Development*, 6: 263–85.

(1991). Human adults and human infants show a 'perceptual magnet effect' for the prototypes of speech categories, monkeys do not. *Perception and Psychophysics*, 50: 93–107.

Kuhl, P. K. and Padden, D. M. (1982). Enhanced discriminability at the phonetic boundaries for the voicing feature in macaques. *Perception and Psychophysics*, 32: 542–50.

Labelle, M. (1990). Predication, wh-movement and the development of relative clauses. *Language Acquisition*, 1: 95–119.

Labov, W. (2001). *Principles of Linguistic Change: Social factors*. Oxford: Blackwell.

Labov, W. and Labov, T. (1978). Learning the syntax of questions. In R. Campbell and P. Smith (eds.), *Recent Advances in the Psychology of Language*. New York: Plenum Press.

Lakoff, G. (1987). *Women, Fire, and Dangerous Things: What Categories Reveal about the Mind*. University of Chicago Press.

Landau, B. and Gleitman, L. R. (1985). *Language and Experience: Evidence from the Blind Child*. Cambridge, MA; London: Harvard University Press.

Langacker, R. W. (1987). *Foundations of Cognitive Grammar*, vol. 1. Stanford University Press.

(2000). A dynamic usage-based model. In M. Barlow and S. Kemmer (eds.), *Usage-Based Models of Language* (pp. 1–63). Stanford: CSLI.

Lederer, A., Gleitman, L. and Gleitman, H. (1995). Verbs of a feather flock together: structural properties of maternal speech. In M. Tomasello and W. Merriman (eds.), *Beyond Names for Things: Young Children's Acquisition of Verbs*. Mahwah, NJ: Erlbaum.

Lee, T. (1991). Linearity as a scope principle for Chinese: the evidence from first language acquisition. In D. Napoli and J. Kegl (eds.). *Bridges between Psychology and Linguistics*. Hillsdale, NJ: Erlbaum.

Legate, J. A. and Yang, C. (2007). Morphosyntactic learning and the development of tense. *Language Acquisition*, 14: 315–44.

Lehiste, I. (1972). The timing of utterances and linguistic boundaries, *Journal of the Acoustic Society of America*, 51: 2018–24.

Lenneberg, E. H. (1967). *Biological Foundations of Language*. New York: Wiley.

Leonard, L. (2000). *Children with Specific Language Impairment*. Cambridge, MA: Bradford Books; MIT Press.

Leonard, L. B., Caselli, M. C. and Devescovi, A. (2002). Italian children's use of verb and noun morphology during the preschool years. *First Language*, 3(66): 287–304.

Leonard, L. B., McGregor, K. K. and Allen, G. D. (1992). Grammatical morphology and speech perception in children with specific language impairment. *Journal of Speech and Hearing Research*, 35(5): 1076–85.

Leonard, L. B., Schwartz, R. G., Morris, B. and Chapman, K. (1981). Factors influencing early lexical acquisition: lexical orientation and phonological composition. *Child Development*, 52: 882–7.

Levin, B. (1985). Lexical semantics in review: an introduction. In B. Levin (ed.), *Lexical Semantics in Review. Lexicon Project Working Papers* no. I. Cambridge, MA: MIT Center for Cognitive Science.

Levinson, S. C. (1987). Pragmatics and the grammar of anaphora: a partial pragmatic reduction of Binding and Control phenomena. *Journal of Linguistics*, 23: 379–434.

Lewis, J. D. and Elman, J. L. (2001). Learnability and the statistical structure of language: poverty of stimulus arguments revisited. *Proceedings of the Twenty-Sixth Annual Boston University Conference on Language Development* (pp. 359–70). Somerville, MA: Cascadilla Press.

Li, P. and MacWhinney, B. (1996). Cryptotype, overgeneralization and competition: a connectionist model of the learning of English reversative prefixes. *Connection Science*, 8: 3–30.

Liberman, A. M., DeLattre, P. D. and Cooper, F. S. (1952). The role of selected stimulus variables in the perception of unvoiced stop consonants. *American Journal of Psychology*, 65: 497–516.

Liberman, A. M., Harris, K. S., Hoffman, H. S. and Griffith, B. C. (1957). The discrimination of speech sounds within and across phoneme boundaries. *Journal of Experimental Psychology*, 54: 358–68.

Liégeois, F., Baldeweg, T., Connelly, A., Gadian, D. G., Mishkin, M. and Vargha-Khadem, F. (2003). Language fMRI abnormalities associated with FOXP2 gene mutation. *Nature Neuroscience*, 6: 1230–7.

Lieven, E. V. M. (1994). Crosslinguistic and cross-cultural aspects of language addressed to children. In C. Gallaway and B. J. Richards (eds.), *Input and Interaction in Language Acquisition* (pp. 56–73). Cambridge University Press.

Lieven, E. V. M., Behrens, H., Speares, J. and Tomasello, M. (2003). Early syntactic creativity: a usage-based approach. *Journal of Child Language*, 30(2): 333–70.

Lieven, E. V. M., Pine, J. M. and Baldwin, G. (1997). Lexically-based learning and early grammatical development. *Journal of Child Language*, 24(1): 187–219.

Lieven, E. V. M., Pine, J. M. and Dresner-Barnes, H. (1992). Individual differences in early vocabulary development: redefining the referential-expressive distinction. *Journal of Child Language*, 19(2): 287–310.

Lieven, E. V. M., Salomo, D. and Tomasello, M. (2009). Two-year-old children's production of multiword utterances: a usage-based analysis. *Cognitive Linguistics*, 20(3): 481–507.

Lightfoot, D. (1979). *Principles of Diachronic Syntax*. Cambridge University Press.
  (1991a). *How to Set Parameters: Arguments from Language Change*. Cambridge, MA: MIT Press.
  (1991b). Subjacency and sex. *Language and Communication*, 11(1/2): 67–9.

Limber, J. (1973). The genesis of complex sentences. In T. E. Moore (ed.), *Cognitive Development and the Acquisition of Language* (pp. 169–85). New York: Academic Press.

Lisker, L. and Abramson, A. S. (1964). A cross-language study of voicing in initial stops: acoustical measurements. *Word*, 20: 384–422.

Liszkowski, U., Carpenter, M., Henning, A., Striano, T. and Tomasello, M. (2004). Twelve-month-olds point to share attention and interest. *Developmental Science*, 7(3): 297–307.

Liszkowski, U., Carpenter, M., Striano, T. and Tomasello, M. (2006). Twelve- and 18-month-olds point to provide information for others. *Journal of Cognition and Development*, 7: 173–87.

Locke, J. L. (1983). *Phonological Acquisition and Change*. New York: Academic Press.

Loeb, D. F. and Leonard, L. B. (1991). Subject case marking and verb morphology in normally developing and specifically language-impaired children. *Journal of Speech and Hearing Research*, 34: 340–6.

Lohmann, H. and Tomasello, M. (2003). The role of language in the development of false belief understanding: a training study. *Child Development*, 74: 1130–44.

Lord, C. (1979). Don't you fall me down: children's generalizations regarding cause and transitivity. *Papers and Reports on Child language Development (PRCLD) 17*. Stanford, CA: Stanford University Department of Linguistics.

Lust, B. (2006). *Child Language: Acquisition and Growth*. Cambridge University Press.

Lust, B. and Clifford, T. (1986). The 3-D study: effects of depth, distance and directionality on children's acquisition of anaphora. In B. Lust (ed.), *Studies in the Acquisition of Anaphora*, vol. 1: *Defining the Constraints* (pp. 203–43). Boston: Reidel.

Lust, B., Eisele, J. and Mazuka, R. (1992). The binding theory module: evidence from first language acquisition for Principle C. *Language*, 68: 333–58.

Lust, B., Loveland, K. and Kornet, R. (1980). The development of anaphora in first language: syntactic and pragmatic constraints. *Linguistic Analysis*, 6: 359–91.

Macken, M. A. (1979). Developmental reorganization of phonology. *Lingua*, 49: 11–49.

Macnamara, J., Cleirigh, A. O. and Kellaghan, T. (1972). The structure of the English lexicon: the simplest hypothesis. *Language and Speech*, 15(2): 141–8.

MacWhinney, B. (2004). A multiple process solution to the logical problem of language acquisition. *Journal of Child Language*, 31(4): 883–914.

MacWhinney, B. and Bates, E. (eds.). (1989). *The Cross-linguistic Study of Sentence Processing*. New York: Cambridge University Press.

MacWhinney, B. and Leinbach, J. (1991). Implementations are not conceptualizations: revising the verb learning model. *Cognition*, 40: 1–2.

MacWhinney, B., Feldman, H. M., Sacco, K. and Valdés-Pérez, R. (2000). Online measures of basic language skills in children with early focal brain lesions. *Brain and Language*, 71: 400–31.

Mandel, D. R. and Jusczyk, P. W. (1997). Infants' early words: familiar people and the changing nature of name representations. Paper presented at the biennial meeting of the Society for Research in Child Development, Washington, DC.

Mandel, D. R., Jusczyk, P. W. and Pisoni, D. B. (1995). Infants' recognition of the sound patterns of their own names. *Psychological Science*, 6: 315–18.

Maratsos, M. P. (1974). How preschool children understand missing complement subjects. *Child Development*, 45: 700–6.

   (2000). More overregularizations after all: new data and discussion on Marcus, Pinker, Ullman, Hollander, Rosen and Xu. *Journal of Child Language*, 27(1): 183–212.

Maratsos, M. and Chalkley, M. (1980). The internal language of children's syntax: the ontogenesis and representation of syntactic categories. In K. Nelson (ed.), *Children's Language*, vol. 2 (pp. 127–51). New York: Gardner Press.

Maratsos, M. P. and Kuczaj, S. (1978). Against the transformationalist account: a simpler analysis of auxiliary overmarking. *Journal of Child Language*, 5: 337–45.

Maratsos, M. P., Fox, D. E., Becker, J. A. and Chalkley, M. A. (1985). Semantic restrictions on children's passives. *Cognition*, 19(2): 167–91.

Maratsos, M. P., Gudeman, R., Gerard-Ngo, P. and DeHart, G. (1987). A study in novel word learning: the productivity of the causative. In B. MacWhinney (ed.), *Mechanisms of Language Acquisition* (pp. 89–112). Hillsdale, NJ: Erlbaum.

Marchman, V. A. (1997). Children's productivity in the English past tense: the role of frequency, phonology and neighborhood structure. *Cognitive Science*, 21(3): 283–304.

Marchman, V. A., Plunkett, K. and Goodman, J. (1997). Overregularization in English plural and past tense inflectional morphology: a response to Marcus (1995). *Journal of Child Language*, 24(3): 767–79.

Marchman, V. A., Wulfeck, B. and Weismer, S. E. (1999). Morphological productivity in children with normal language and SLI: a study of the English past tense. *Journal of Speech, Language and Hearing Research*, 42: 206–19.

Marcus, G. F. (1993). Negative evidence in language acquisition. *Cognition*, 46(1): 53–85.

  (1995). Children's overregularization of English plurals: a quantitative analysis. *Journal of Child Language*, 22(2): 447–59.

  (1995). The acquisition of the English past tense in children and multilayered connectionist networks. *Cognition*, 56(3): 271–9.

Marcus, G. F. and Fisher, S. E. (2003). FOXP2 in focus: what can genes tell us about speech and language? *Trends in Cognitive Sciences*, 7: 257–62.

Marcus, G. F., Brinkmann, U., Clahsen, H., Wiese, R. and Pinker, S. (1995). German inflection: the exception that proves the rule. *Cognitive Psychology*, 29(3): 189–256.

Marcus, G. F., Pinker, S., Ullman, M., Hollander, M., Rosen, T. J. and Xu, F. (1992). Overregularization in language-acquisition. *Monographs of the Society for Research in Child Development*, 57(4): R5–R165.

Markman, E. M. and Hutchinson, J. E. (1984). Children's sensitivity to constraints on word meaning: taxonomic versus thematic relations. *Cognitive Psychology*, 16: 1–27.

Markman, E. M. and Wachtel, G. F. (1988). Children's use of mutual exclusivity to constrain the meanings of words. *Cognitive Psychology*, 20: 121–57.

Markson, L. and Bloom, P. (1997). Evidence against a dedicated system for word learning in children. *Nature*, 385: 813–15.

Maslen, R. J. C., Theakston, A. L., Lieven, E. V. M. and Tomasello, M. (2004). A dense corpus study of past tense and plural over-regularization in English. *Journal of Speech, Language and Hearing Research*, 47: 1319–33.

Matthews, D. E. and Theakston, A. L. (2006). Errors of omission in English-speaking children's production of plurals and the past tense: the effects of frequency, phonology and competition. *Cognitive Science*, 30(6): 1027–52.

Matthews, D., Lieven, E., Theakston, A. L. and Tomasello, M. (2004). The role of frequency in the acquisition of English word order. *Cognitive Development*, 20: 121–36.

  (2007). French children's use and correction of weird word orders: a constructivist account. *Journal of Child Language*, 34(2): 381–409.

  (2009). Pronoun co-referencing errors: challenges for generativist and usage-based accounts. *Cognitive Linguistics*, 20(3): 599–626.

Mattys, S. L., Jusczyk, P. W., Luce, P. A. and Morgan, J. L. (1999). Phonotactic and prosodic effects on word segmentation in infants. *Cognitive Psychology*, 38: 465–94.

Mayberry, R. I. (2009). Early language acquisition and adult language ability: what sign language reveals about the Critical Period for Language. In M. Marshak and P. Spencer (eds.), *Oxford Handbook of Deaf Studies, Language and Education*, vol. 2 (ch. 19). Oxford University Press.

Maye, J. and Gerken, L. (2000). Learning phonemes without minimal pairs. In S. C. Howell, S. A. Fish and T. Keith-Lucas (eds.), *Proceedings of the Twenty-Fourth Annual Boston University Conference on Language Development* (pp. 522–33). Somerville, MA: Cascadilla Press.

Maye, J., Werker, J. F. and Gerken, L. (2002). Infant sensitivity to distributional information can affect phonetic discrimination. *Cognition*, 82: 101–11.

Mazuka, R. (1996). Can a grammatical parameter be set before the first word? Prosodic contributions to early setting of a grammatical parameter. In J. Morgan and K. Demuth (eds.), *Signal to Syntax: Bootstrapping from Speech to Grammar in Early Acquisition* (pp. 313–30). Mawah, NJ: Erlbaum.

McCarthy, D. (1954). Language development in children. In L. Carmichael (ed.), *Manual of Child Psychology* (pp. 492–630). New York: Wiley.

McCawley, J. (1992). Justifying part-of-speech assignments in Mandarin Chinese. *Journal of Chinese Linguistics*, 20(2): 211–46.

McClelland, J. L. and Patterson, K. (2002). 'Words or rules' cannot exploit the regularity in exceptions – reply to Pinker and Ullman. *Trends in Cognitive Sciences*, 6(11): 464–5.

McClure, K., Pine, J. M. and Lieven, E. V. M. (2006). Investigating the abstractness of children's early knowledge of argument structure. *Journal of Child Language*, 33: 693–720.

McDaniel, D. and Maxfield, T. L. (1992). Principle B and contrastive stress. *Language Acquisition*, 2: 337–58.

McDaniel, D., Cairns, H. S. and Hsu, J. R. (1990/1). Control principles in the grammars of young children. *Language Acquisition*, 1(4): 297–335.

McDonald, J. L. (1989). The acquisition of cue-category mappings. In B. MacWhinney and E. Bates (eds.), *The Cross-linguistic Study of Sentence Processing*. Cambridge University Press.

McKee, C. (1992). A comparison of pronouns and anaphors in Italian and English acquisition. *Language Acquisition*, 1: 21–55.

McKee, C., McDaniel, D. and Snedeker, J. (1998). Relatives children say. *Journal of Psycholinguistic Research*, 27: 573–96.

McNeill, D. (1966). Capacity for language acquisition. *Volta Review*, 68(1): 17–33.

McShane, J. (1980). *Learning to Talk*. Cambridge University Press.

Meisel, J. and Muller, N. (1992). Finiteness and verb placement in early child grammars: evidence from simultaneous acquisition of French and German in bilinguals. In J. Meisel (ed.), *The Acquisition of Verb Placement* (pp. 109–38). Dordrecht: Kluwer.

Meltzoff, A. N. (1995). Understanding the intentions of others: re-enactment of intended acts by 18-month-old children. *Developmental Psychology*, 31: 838–50.

Menn, L. (1983). Development of articulatory, phonetic and phonological capabilities. In B. Butterworth (ed.), *Language Production* (pp. 3–50). London: Academic Press.

Menyuk, P. and Menn, L. (1979). Early strategies for the perception and production of words and sounds. In P. Fletcher and M. Garman (eds.), *Language Acquisition: Studies in First Language Development* (pp. 49–70). Cambridge University Press.

Mervis, C. B., Golinkoff, R. M. and Bertrand, J. (1994). Two-year-olds readily learn multiple labels for the same basic-level category. *Child Development*, 65(4): 1163–77.

Messenger, K., Branigan, H., McLean, J. and Sorace, A. (2009). Semantic factors in young children's comprehension and production of passives. In J. Chandlee, M. Franchini, S. Lord and G.-M. Rheiner, (eds.), *Proceedings of the Thirty-Third Annual Boston University Conference on Language Development* (pp. 355–66). Somerville, MA: Cascadilla Press.

Mielke, J. (2008). *The Emergence of Distinctive Features*. Oxford University Press.

Miller, J. L. and Eimas, P. D. (1983). Studies on the categorization of speech by infants. *Cognition*, 13: 135–65.

Mills, A. E. (1985). Speech acquisition in childhood – a study on the development of syntax in small children – German. *Journal of Child Language*, 12(1): 239–44.

Mintz, T. H. (2002). Category induction from distributional cues in an artificial language. *Memory and Cognition*, 30(5): 678–86.

  (2003). Frequent frames as a cue for grammatical categories in child directed speech. *Cognition*, 90: 91–117.

  (2006). Finding the verbs: distributional cues to categories available to young learners. In K. Hirsh-Pasek and R. M. Golinkoff (eds.), *Action Meets Word: How Children Learn Verbs* (pp. 31–63). New York: Oxford University Press.

Mintz, T. H., Newport, E. L. and Bever, T. G. (2002). The distributional structure of grammatical categories in speech to young children. *Cognitive Science*, 26(4): 393–424.

Moll, H. and Tomasello, M. (2007). How 14- and 18-month-olds know what others have experienced. *Developmental Psychology*, 43(2): 309–17.

Moll, H., Carpenter, M. and Tomasello, M. (2007). Fourteen-month-olds know what others experience only in joint engagement. *Developmental Science*, 10(6): 826–35.

Moll, H., Koring, C., Carpenter, M. and Tomasello, M. (2006). Infants determine others' focus of attention by pragmatics and exclusion. *Journal of Cognition and Development*, 7(3): 411–30.

Moore, C., Angelopoulos, M. and Bennett, P. (1999). Word learning in the context of referential and salience cues. *Developmental Psychology*, 35(1): 60–8.

Morse, P. A. (1972). The discrimination of speech and non-speech stimuli in early infancy. *Journal of Experimental Child Psychology*, 14: 477–92.

Nagy, W. E. and Herman, P. A. (1987). Breadth and depth of vocabulary knowledge: implications for acquisition and instruction. In M. G. McKeown and M. E. Curtis (eds.), *The Nature of Vocabulary Acquisition* (pp. 19–35). Hillsdale, NJ: Erlbaum.

Naigles, L. (1990). Children use syntax to learn verb meanings. *Journal of Child Language*, 17(2): 357–74.

  (1996). The use of multiple frames in verb learning via syntactic bootstrapping. *Cognition*, 58(2): 221–51.

Naigles, L. G. and Kako, E. T. (1993). 1st contact in verb acquisition – defining a role for syntax. *Child Development*, 64(6): 1665–87.

Nazzi, T., Kemler Nelson, D., Jusczyk, P. W. and Jusczyk, A. M. (2000). Six-month-olds' detection of clauses embedded in continuous speech: effects of prosodic well-formedness. *Infancy*, 1: 123–47.

Nelson, K. (1974). Variations in children's concepts by age and category. *Child Development*, 45(3): 577–84.

  (1985). *Making Sense: The Acquisition of Shared Meaning*. New York and London: Academic Press.

Nelson, K., Hampson, J. and Shaw, L. K. (1993). Nouns in early lexicons – evidence, explanations and implications. *Journal of Child Language*, 20(1): 61–84.

Nespor, M. and Vogel, I. (1986). *Prosodic Phonology*. Dordrecht: Foris.

Newmeyer, F. (1991). Functional explanations in linguistics and the origins of language. *Language and Communication*, 11(1/2): 3–28.

Newport, E. L. and Aslin, R. N. (2004). Learning at a distance I. Statistical learning of non-adjacent dependencies. *Cognitive Psychology*, 48(2): 127–62.

Niyogi, P. and Berwick, R. C. (1996). A language learning model for finite parameter spaces. *Cognition*, 61: 161–93.

Noble, C. H. (2009). Comprehension of argument structure and semantic roles. Unpublished PhD thesis, University of Liverpool.

Noble, C. H., Rowland, C. F. and Pine, J. M. (in press). Comprehension of argument structure and semantic roles: evidence from infants and the forced-choice pointing paradigm. *Cognitive Science*.

Olguin, R. and Tomasello, M. (1993). 25-month-old children do not have a grammatical category of verb. *Cognitive Development*, 8(3): 245–72.

Oller, D. K. (2000). *The Emergence of the Speech Capacity*. Mahwah, NJ: Erlbaum.

Oller, D. K., Wieman, L., Doyle, W. and Ross, C. (1975). Infant babbling and speech. *Journal of Child Language*, 3: 1–11.

Onnis, L., Monaghan, P., Richmond, K. and Chater, N. (2005). Phonology impacts segmentation in speech processing. *Journal of Memory and Language*, 53(2): 225–37.

Oviatt, S. L. (1980). The emerging ability to comprehend language: an experimental approach. *Child Development*, 51(1): 97–106.

Peña, M., Bonatti, L. L., Nespor, M. and Mehler, J. (2002). Signal-driven computations in speech processing. *Science*, 298: 604–7.

Perlmutter, D. M. (1978). Impersonal passives and the unaccusative hypothesis *Proceedings of the Fourth Annual Meeting of the Berkeley Linguistics Society* (pp. 157–89). University of California, Berkeley.

Peters, A. M. (1983). *The Units of Language Acquisition*. Cambridge University Press.

Peters, A. M. and Menn, L. (1990). The microstructure of the development of grammatical morphemes: variation across children and across languages. *ICS Technical Report* no. 90-19. University of Colorado at Boulder.

  (1993). False starts and filler syllables: ways to learn grammatical morphemes. *Language*, 69(4): 742–77.

Philip, W. (1995). Event quantification in the acquisition of universal quantification. Unpublished PhD thesis, University of Massachusetts, Amherst.

Philip, W. and Verrips, M. (1994). Dutch preschoolers' *elke*. Paper presented at the 19th Annual Boston University Conference on Language Development, Boston, MA.

Pickering, M. J. and Ferreira, V. S. (2008). Structural priming: a critical review. *Psychological Bulletin*, 134(3): 427–59.

Pierce, A. E. (1992). *Language Acquisition and Syntactic Theory: A Comparative Analysis of French and English Child Grammars*. Dordrecht and London: Kluwer Academic Publishers.

Pierrehumbert, J. B. (2003). Phonetic diversity, statistical learning and acquisition of phonology. *Language and Speech*, 46: 115–54.

Pine, J. M. and Lieven, E. V. M. (1993). Reanalyzing rote-learned phrases – individual-differences in the transition to multi-word speech. *Journal of Child Language*, 20(3): 551–71.

  (1997). Slot and frame patterns and the development of the determiner category. *Applied Psycholinguistics*, 18(2): 123–38.

Pine, J. M. and Martindale, H. (1996). Syntactic categories in the speech of young children: the case of the determiner. *Journal of Child Language*, 23(2): 369–95.

Pine, J. M., Conti-Ramsden, G., Joseph, K. L., Lieven, E. V. M. and Serratrice, L. (2008). Tense over time: testing the Agreement/Tense Omission Model as an account of the pattern of tense-marking provision in early child English. *Journal of Child Language*, 35(1): 55–75.

Pine, J. M., Lieven, E. V. M. and Rowland, C. F. (1998). Comparing different models of the development of the English verb category. *Linguistics*, 36(4): 807–30.

Pine, J., Rowland, C. F., Lieven, E. V. M. and Theakston, A. L. (2005). Testing the Agreement/Tense Omission Model: why the data on children's use of non-nominative subjects count against the ATOM. *Journal of Child Language*, 32: 269–89.

Pinker, S. (1979). Formal models of language learning. *Cognition*, 7: 217–83.

  (1984). *Language Learnability and Language Development*. Cambridge, MA: Harvard University Press.

  (1987). The bootstrapping problem in language acquisition. In B. MacWhinney (ed.), *Mechanisms of Language Acquisition* (pp. 339–441). Hillsdale, NJ: Erlbaum.

  (1989a). *Learnability and Cognition: The Acquisition of Argument Structure*. Cambridge, MA, and London: MIT Press.

  (1989b). Resolving a learnability paradox in the acquisition of the verb lexicon. In M. L. Rice and R. L. Shiefelsbusch (eds.), *The Teachability of Language*. Baltimore: Paul H. Brookes.

  (1994a). How could a child use verb syntax to learn verb semantics? *Lingua*, 92: 377–410.

  (1994b). *The Language Instinct*. New York: Harper Collins.

  (1999). *Words and Rules*. London: Phoenix.

  (2004). Clarifying the logical problem of language acquisition. *Journal of Child Language*, 31(4): 949–53.

Pinker, S. and Bloom, P. (1990). Natural language and natural selection. *Behavioral and Brain Science*, 13: 707–84.

Pinker, S. and Jackendoff, R. (2005). The faculty of language: what's special about it? *Cognition*, 95: 201–36.

Pinker, S. and Prince, A. (1988). On language and connectionism: analysis of a parallel distributed processing model of language acquisition. *Cognition*, 28(1–2): 73–193.

Pinker, S. and Ullman, M. T. (2002). The past and future of the past tense. *Trends in Cognitive Sciences*, 6(11): 456–63.

Pinker, S., Lebeaux, D. S. and Frost, L. A. (1987). Productivity and constraints in the acquisition of the passive. *Cognition*, 26(3): 195–267.

Pisoni, D. B. (1977). Identification and discrimination of the relative onset time of two component tones: implications for voicing perception in stops. *Journal of the Acoustical Society of America*, 61: 1352–61.

Pizzuto, E. and Caselli, C. (1994). The acquisition of Italian verb morphology in a cross-linguistic perspective. In Y. Levy (ed.), *Other Children, Other Languages* (pp. 137–88). Hillsdale, NJ: Erlbaum.

Plomin, R. and Kovas, Y. (2005). Generalist genes and learning disabilities. *Psychological Bulletin*, 131: 592–617.

Plunkett, K. and Juola, P. (1999). A connectionist model of English past tense and plural morphology. *Cognitive Science*, 23(4): 463–90.

Plunkett, K. and Marchman, V. (1991). U-shaped learning and frequency effect in a multi-layered perceptron: implications for child language acquisition. *Cognition*, 38(1): 43–102.

(1993). From rote learning to system building: acquiring verb morphology in children and connectionist nets. *Cognition*, 48(1): 21–69.

Plunkett, K. and Nakisa, R. C. (1997). A connectionist model of the Arabic plural system. *Language and Cognitive Processes*, 12(5–6): 807–36.

Poeppel, D. and Wexler, K. (1993). The full competence hypothesis of clause structure in early German. *Language*, 69: 1–33.

Polka, L. and Werker, J. F. (1994). Developmental changes in perception of non-native vowel contrasts. *Journal of Experimental Psychology: Human Perception and Performance*, 20: 421–35.

Prasada, S. and Pinker, S. (1993). Generalisation of regular and irregular morphological patterns. *Language and Cognitive Processes*, 8(1): 1–56.

Prince, A. and Smolensky, P. (1993). Optimality Theory: constraint interaction in generative grammar. In J. McCarthy (ed.), *Optimality Theory in Phonology: A Reader* (pp. 3–71). Oxford: Blackwell.

(2004). *Optimality Theory: Constraint Interaction in Generative Grammar*. Oxford: Blackwell.

Pullum, G. K. and Scholz, B. C. (2002). Empirical assessment of stimulus poverty arguments. *Linguistic Review*, 19: 9–50.

Pye, C. and Quixtan Poz, P. (1989). Why functionalism won't function: the acquisition of passives and antipassives in K'iche' Mayan. *Working Papers in Language Development*, 4: 39–53. The Child Language Program, University of Kansas.

Quine, W. (1960). *Word and Object*. Cambridge, MA: Harvard University Press.

Radford, A. (1994). The syntax of questions in child English. *Journal of Child Language*, 21(1): 201–36.

(1996). Towards a structure building model of acquisition. In H. Clahsen (ed.), *Generative Perspectives on Language Acquisition* (pp. 43–90). Amsterdam and Philadelphia: John Benjamins.

(2004). *Minimalist Syntax: Exploring the Structure of English*. Cambridge University Press.

Radford, A. and Ploennig-Pacheco, I. (1995). The morphosyntax of subjects and verbs in child Spanish: a case study. *Essex Reports in Linguistics*, 5: 23–67.

Ramscar, M. (2002). The role of meaning in inflection: why the past tense does not require a rule. *Cognitive Psychology*, 45: 45–94.

Ramscar, M. and Yarlett, D. (2007). Linguistic self-correction in the absence of feedback: a new approach to the logical problem of language acquisition. *Cognitive Science*, 31: 927–60.

Randall, J. H. (1990). Catapults and pendulums: the mechanics of language-acquisition. *Linguistics*, 28(6): 1381–1406.

Reali, F. and Christiansen, M. H. (2004). Uncovering the richness of the stimulus: structure dependence and indirect statistical evidence. *Cognitive Science*, 29: 1007–28.

Redington, M., Chater, N. and Finch, S. (1998). Distributional information: a powerful cue for acquiring syntactic categories. *Cognitive Science*, 22(4): 425–69.

Reinhart, T. (1983). *Anaphora and Semantic Interpretation*. London: Croom Helm.

Rice, M. L. and Wexler, K. (1996). Toward tense as a clinical marker of specific language impairment in English-speaking children. *Journal of Speech and Hearing Research*, 39(6): 1239–57.

Rice, M. L., Wexler, K. and Hershberger, S. (1998). Tense over time: the longitudinal course of tense acquisition in children with specific language impairment. *Journal of Speech Language and Hearing Research*, 41(6): 1412–31.

Rice, M. L. and Wexler, K. (1996). A phenotype of specific language impairment: extended optional infinitives. In M. Rice (ed.), *Towards a Genetics of Language* (pp. 215–38). Mahwah, NJ: Erlbaum.

Rijkhoff, J. (2003). When can a language have nouns and verbs? *Acta Linguistica Hafniensa*, 35: 7–38.

Rispoli, M. (1991). The mosaic acquisition of grammatical relations. *Journal of Child Language*, 18(3): 517–51.

  (1994). Pronoun case overextension and paradigm building. *Journal of Child Language*, 21: 157–72.

  (1999). Case and agreement in English language development. *Journal of Child Language*, 26: 357–72.

Rizzi, L. (1993/4). Some notes on linguistic theory and language development: the case of root infinitives. *Language Acquisition*, 3: 371–93.

Roberts, C. (1987). Modal subordination, distributivity and anaphora. Unpublished PhD thesis, University of Massachusetts, Amherst.

Roberts, L., Marinis, T., Felser, C. and Clahsen, H. (2007). Antecedent priming at trace positions in children's sentence processing. *Journal of Psycholinguistic Research*, 36(2): 175–88.

Roeper, T. and de Villiers, J. (1991). The emergence of bound variable structures. In T. L. Maxfield and B. Plunkett (eds.), *University of Massachusetts Occasional Papers: Papers in the Acquisition of WH* (pp. 267–82). Amherst, MA: GLSA.

Rossen, M., Klima, E. S., Bellugi, U., Bihrle, A. and Jones, W. (1996). Interaction between language and cognition: evidence from Williams Syndrome. In J. H. Beitchman, N. J. Cohen, M. M. Konstantareas and R. Tannock (eds.), *Language, Learning and Behavior Disorders: Developmental, Biological and Clinical Perspectives* (pp. 367–92). Cambridge University Press.

Rowland, C. F. (2007). Explaining errors in children's questions. *Cognition*, 104(1): 106–34.

Rowland, C. F. and Fletcher, S. L. (2006). The effect of sampling on estimates of lexical specificity and error rates. *Journal of Child Language*, 33(4): 859–77.

Rowland, C. F. and Pine, J. M. (2000). Subject-auxiliary inversion errors and wh-question acquisition: 'what children do know!' *Journal of Child Language*, 27(1): 157–81.

Rowland, C. F. and Theakston, A. L. (2009). The acquisition of auxiliary syntax: a longitudinal elicitation study. Part 2: The modals and auxiliary DO. *Journal of Speech Language and Hearing Research*, 52(6): 1471–92.

Rubino, R. B. and Pine, J. M. (1998). Subject–verb agreement in Brazilian Portuguese: what low error rates hide. *Journal of Child Language*, 25(1): 35–59.

Rumelhart, D. E. and McClelland, J. L. (1986). Learning the past tenses of English verbs: implicit rules of parallel distributed processing? In B. MacWhinney (ed.), *Mechanisms of Language Acquisition*. Hillsdale, NJ: Erlbaum.

Saffran, J. R., Aslin, R. N. and Newport, E. L. (1996). Statistical learning by 8-month-olds. *Science*, 274: 1926–8.

Saffran, J. R., Johnson, E. K., Aslin, R. N. and Newport, E. L. (1999). Statistical learning of tone sequences by human infants and adults. *Cognition*, 70: 27–52.

Sakas, W. G. and Fodor, J. D. (2001). The structural triggers learner. In S. Bertolo (ed.), *Language Acquisition and Learnability*. Cambridge University Press.

Samuelson, L. K. and Smith, L. B. (1998). Memory and attention make smart word learning: an alternative account of Akhtar, Carpenter and Tomasello. *Child Development*, 1: 94–104.

Sanford, A. J. and Stuart, P. (2002). Depth of processing in language comprehension: not noticing the evidence. *Trends in Cognitive Sciences*, 6: 382–6.

Santelmann, L., Berk, S., Austin, J., Somashekar, S. and Lust, B. (2002). Continuity and development in the acquisition of inversion in yes/no questions: dissociating movement and inflection. *Journal of Child Language*, 29: 813–42.

Savage, C., Lieven, E., Theakston, A. and Tomasello, M. (2003). Testing the abstractness of children's linguistic representations: lexical and structural priming of syntactic constructions in young children. *Developmental Science*, 6(5): 557–67.

(2006). Structural priming as implicit learning in language acquisition: the persistence of lexical and structural priming in 4-year-olds. *Language Learning and Development*, 2: 27–50.

Schafer, G. and Plunkett, K. (1998). Rapid word learning by fifteen-month-olds under tightly controlled conditions. *Child Development*, 69(2): 309–20.

Schauwers, K., Govaerts, P. and Gillis, S. (2005). Language acquisition in deaf children with a cochlear implant. In P. Fletcher and J. Miller (eds.), *Developmental Theory and Language Disorders* (pp. 95–119). Amsterdam and Philadelphia: Benjamins.

Schieffelin, B. B. and Ochs, E. (1986). *Language Socialization Across Cultures*. Cambridge University Press.

Schlesinger, I. M. (1988). The origin of relational categories. In Y. Levy, I. M. Schlesinger and M. D. S. Braine (eds.), *Categories and Processes in Language Acquisition* (pp. 121–78). Hillsdale, NJ: Erlbaum.

Schütze, C. T. (2001). Productive inventory and case/agreement contingencies: a methodological note on Rispoli (1999). *Journal of Child Language*, 28(2): 507–15.

Schütze, C. T. and Wexler, K. (1996). Subject case licensing and English root infinitives. *Proceedings of the Twentieth Annual Boston University Conference on Language Development* (pp. 670–81). Somerville, MA: Cascadilla Press.

Schwartz, R. G. and Leonard, L. B. (1984). Words, objects and actions in early lexical acquisition. *Journal of Speech Language and Hearing Research*, 27(1): 119–27.

Scott, D. R. (1982). Duration as a cue to the perception of a phrase boundary. *Journal of the Acoustical Society of America*, 71: 996–1007.

Seidl, A. (2007). Infants' use and weighting of prosodic cues in clause segmentation. *Journal of Memory and Language*, 57: 24–48.

Seidl, A., Hollich, G. and Jusczyk, P. W. (2003). Early understanding of subject and object Wh-questions. *Infancy*, 4(3): 423–36.

Senghas, A. (2003). Intergenerational influence and ontogenetic development in the emergence of spatial grammar in Nicaraguan Sign Language. *Cognitive Development*, 18: 511–31.

Sethuraman, N., Goldberg, A. and Goodman, J. (1997). Using the semantics associated with syntactic frames for interpretation without the aid of non-linguistic context. In E. Clark (ed.), *Proceedings of the Twenty-Eighth Annual Child Language Research Forum* (pp. 283–94). Stanford, CA: CSLI.

Sheldon, A. C. (1974). *The Acquisition of Relative Clauses in English*. Bloomington: Reproduced by Indiana University Linguistics Club.

Sherman, J. C. and Lust, B. (1993). Children are in control. *Cognition*, 46(1): 1–51.

Shi, R. and Moisan, A. (2008). Prosodic cues to noun and verb categories in infant-directed speech. *Proceedings of the Thirty-Second Boston University Conference on Language Development* (pp. 450–61). Somerville, MA: Cascadilla Press.

Shi, R., Cutler, A., Werker, J. and Cruickshank, M. (2006). Frequency and form as determinants of functor sensitivity in English-acquiring infants. *Journal of the Acoustical Society of America*, 119: 61–67.

Shimpi, P. M., Gámez, P. B., Huttenlocher, J. and Vasilyeva, M. (2007). Syntactic priming in 3- and 4-year-old children: evidence for abstract representations of transitive and dative forms. *Developmental Psychology*, 43(6): 1334–46.

Shirai, Y., Slobin, D. I. and Weist, R. (1998). The acquisition of tense/aspect morphology. *First Language*, 18: 245–53.

Skinner, B. F. (1957). *Verbal Learning*. New York: Appleton-Century-Crofts.

Slobin, D. I. (1973). Cognitive prerequisites for the development of grammar. In C. A. Ferguson and D. I. Slobin (eds.), *Studies of Child Language Development* (pp. 175–208). New York: Holt, Rinehart and Winston.

(1982). Universal and particular in the acquisition of language. In E. Wanner and L. R. Gleitman (eds.), *Language Acquisition: The State of the Art* (pp. 128–70). Cambridge University Press.

(1997). The origins of grammaticizable notions: beyond the individual mind. In D. I. Slobin (ed.), *The Crosslinguistic Study of Language Acquisition*, vol. 5: *Expanding the Contexts* (pp. 265–323). London: Erlbaum.

(2001). Form-function relations: How do children find out what they are? In M. Bowerman and S. Levinson (eds.). *Language Acquisition and Conceptual Development* (pp. 406–49). Cambridge University Press.

Smith, L. B. (2000). Avoiding associations when it's behaviorism you really hate. In R. Golinkoff *et al.* (eds.), *Becoming a Word Learner: A Debate on Lexical Acquisition* (pp. 169–75). Oxford University Press.

Smith, L. and Yu, C. (2008). Infants rapidly learn word-referent mappings via cross-situational statistics. *Cognition*, 106(3): 1558–68.

Smith, M. (1974). Relative clause formation between 29–36 months: a preliminary report. *Papers and Reports on Child Language Development*, 8: 104–10.

Smith, N. V. (1973). *The Acquisition of Phonology: A Case Study*. Cambridge University Press.

Soderstrom, M., Seidl, A., Kemler Nelson, D. G. and Jusczyk, P. W. (2003). The prosodic bootstrapping of phrases: evidence from prelinguistic infants. *Journal of Memory and Language*, 49(2): 249–67.

Soja, N. N., Carey, S. and Spelke, E. S. (1991). Ontological categories guide young children's inductions of word meaning: object terms and substance terms. *Cognition*, 38(2): 179–211.

Sokolov, J. L. (1988). Cue validity in Hebrew sentence comprehension. *Journal of Child Language*, 15(1): 129–55.

Solan, L. (1983). *Pronominal Reference: Child Language and the Theory of Grammar*. Dordrecht: Reidel.

Solan, Z., Horn, D., Ruppin, E. and Edelman, S. (2005). Unsupervised learning of natural languages. *Proceedings of the National Academy of Sciences*, 102(33): 11629–34.

Sorenson, J. M., Cooper, W. E. and Paccia, J. M (1978). Speech timing of grammatical categories. *Cognition*, 6: 135–53.

Stager, C. L. and Werker, J. F. (1997). Infants listen for more phonetic detail in speech perception than in word-learning tasks. *Nature*, 388: 381–2.

Stampe, D. (1979). *A Dissertation on Natural Phonology*. New York: Garland.

Steels, L. (2006). Experiments on the emergence of human communication. *Trends in Cognitive Sciences*, 10(8): 347–9.

Steels, L. and de Boer, B. (2007). Embodiment and self-organization of human categories: a case study for speech. In J. Zlatev, T. Ziemke, R. Frank and R. Dirven (eds.), *Body, Language and Mind*, vol. 1, pp. 241–59. Berlin: Mouton de Gruyter.

Stefanowitsch, A. (2008). Negative evidence and pre-emption: a constructional approach to ungrammaticality. *Cognitive Linguistics*, 19(3): 513–31.

Street, J. A. and Dąbrowska, E. (2010). More individual differences in language attainment: how much do adult native speakers of English know about passives and quantifiers? *Lingua*, 120(8): 2080–94.

Streeter, L. A. (1976). Language perception of two-month-old infants shows effects of both innate mechanisms and experience. *Nature*, 259: 39–41.

(1978). Acoustic determinants of phrase boundary perception. *Journal of the Acoustical Society of America*, 64: 1582–92.

Stromswold, K. (1990). Learnability and the acquisition of auxiliaries. Unpublished PhD dissertation, MIT.

Sudhalter, V. and Braine, M. D. S. (1985). How does comprehension of passives develop – a comparison of actional and experiential verbs. *Journal of Child Language*, 12(2): 455–70.

Suttle, L. and Goldberg, A. E. (in press). The partial productivity of constructions as induction. *Linguistics.*

Suzman, S. M. (1999). Learn Zulu the way children do. *South African Journal of African Languages*, 19(2): 134–47.

Svartvik, J. (1966). *On Voice in the English Verb* (Janua Linguarum, Series Practica 63). The Hague: Mouton.

Swingley, D. (2005a). Statistical clustering and the contents of the infant vocabulary. *Cognitive Psychology*, 50: 86–132.

(2005b). 11-months-olds' knowledge of how familiar words sound. *Developmental Science*, 8: 432–43.

Takahashi, M. (1991). Children's interpretation of sentences containing *every*. In T. Maxfield and B. Plunkett (eds.), *Papers in the Acquisition of WH: Proceedings of the UMass Roundtable*, May 1990 (pp. 303–23). Linguistics Department, UMASS, Amherst, MA: Graduate Linguistics Students Association.

Tallal, P., Miller, S. L., Bedi, G., Byma, G., Wang, X., Nagarajan, S. S., *et al.* (1996). Language comprehension in language-learning impaired children improved with acoustically modified speech. *Science*, 271(5245): 81–4.

Tardif, T. (1996). Nouns are not always learned before verbs: evidence from Mandarin speakers' early vocabularies. *Developmental Psychology*, 32(3): 492–504.

Tavakolian, S. (1981). The conjoined clause analysis of relative clauses. In S. Tavakolian (ed.), *Language Acquisition and Linguistic Theory* (pp. 167–87). Cambridge, MA: MIT Press.

Taylor-Browne, K. (1983). Acquiring restrictions on forwards anaphora: a pilot study. *Calgary Working Papers in Linguistics*, 9: 75–99.

Theakston, A. L. (2004). The role of entrenchment in children's and adults' performance on grammaticality judgement tasks. *Cognitive Development*, 19(1): 15–34.

Theakston, A. L. and Lieven, E. V. M. (2005). The acquisition of auxiliaries BE and HAVE: an elicitation study. *Journal of Child Language*, 32(3): 587–616.

Theakston, A. L. and Rowland, C. F. (2009). The acquisition of auxiliary syntax: a longitudinal elicitation study. Part 1: Auxiliary BE. *Journal of Speech Language and Hearing Research*, 52(6): 1449–70.

Theakston, A. L., Lieven, E. V. M., Pine, J. M. and Rowland, C. F. (2001). The role of performance limitations in the acquisition of verb-argument structure: an alternative account. *Journal of Child Language*, 28(1): 127–52.

(2002). Going, going, gone: the acquisition of the verb 'go'. *Journal of Child Language*, 29(4): 783–811.

(2004). Semantic generality, input frequency and the acquisition of syntax. *Journal of Child Language*, 31(1): 61–99.

(2005). The acquisition of auxiliary syntax: BE and HAVE. *Cognitive Linguistics*, 16(1): 247–77.

Theakston, A. L., Lieven, E. V. and Tomasello, M. (2003). The role of the input in the acquisition of third person singular verbs in English. *Journal of Speech Language and Hearing Research*, 46(4): 863–77.

Thiessen, E. D. and Saffran, J. R. (2003). When cues collide: use of stress and statistical cues to word boundaries by 7- to 9-month-old infants. *Developmental Psychology*, 39: 706–16.

Thompson, S. A. and Mulac, A. (1991). The discourse conditions for the use of the complementizer *that* in conversational English. *Journal of Pragmatics*, 15: 237–51.

Thomson, J. R. and Chapman, R. S. (1977). Who is daddy revisited – status of 2-year-olds' over-extended words in use and comprehension. *Journal of Child Language*, 4(3): 359–75.

Thornton, R. and Crain, S. (1994). Successful cyclic movement. In T. Hoekstra and B. Schwartz (eds.), *Language Acquisition Studies in Generative Grammar* (pp. 215–53). Amsterdam and Philadelphia: Benjamins.

Thornton, R. and Wexler, K. (1999). *Principle B, VP Ellipsis and Interpretation in Child Grammar*. Cambridge, MA: MIT Press.

Thorpe, W. (1958). The learning of song patterns by birds, with special reference to the song of the Chaffinch, 'Fringilla coelebs'. *Ibis*, 100: 535–70.

Thothathiri, M. and Snedeker, J. (2008). Syntactic priming during language comprehension in three- and four-year-old children. *Journal of Memory and Language*, 58(2): 188–213.

Tincoff, R. (2001). Infants' attention to speech and non-speech vocalizations, and its relation to word-learning. *Poster presented at the Biennial Meeting of the Society for Research in Child Development*, Minneapolis, MN.

Tincoff, R. and Jusczyk, P. W. (1999). Some beginnings of word comprehension in 6-month-olds. *Psychological Science*, 10(2): 172–5.

Tomasello, M. (1992). *First Verbs: A Case Study of Early Grammatical Development*. Cambridge University Press.

  (1999). *The Cultural Origins of Human Cognition*. Cambridge, MA: Harvard University Press.

  (2000). Do young children have adult syntactic competence? *Cognition*, 74(3): 209–53.

  (2003). *Constructing a Language: A Usage-based Theory of Language Acquisition*. Cambridge, MA: Harvard University Press.

  (2005). Beyond formalities: the case of language acquisition. *The Linguistic Review*, 22: 183–97.

  (2007a). *The Origins of Human Communication*. Cambridge, MA: MIT Press.

  (2007b). What kind of evidence could refute the UG hypothesis? Commentary on Wunderlich. In M. Penke and Anette Rosenbach (eds.), *What Counts as Evidence in Linguistics?* (pp. 175–78). Amsterdam and Philadelphia: Benjamins.

  (2008). *Origins of Human Communication*. Cambridge, MA: MIT Press.

Tomasello, M. and Abbot-Smith, K. (2002). A tale of two theories: response to Fisher. *Cognition*, 83(2): 207–14.

Tomasello, M. and Akhtar, N. (1995). Two-year-olds use pragmatic cues to differentiate reference to objects and actions. *Cognitive Development*, 10: 201–24.

  (2000). Five questions for any theory of word learning. In R. Golinkoff and K. Hirsh-Pasek (eds.), *Becoming a Word Learner: A Debate on Lexical Acquisition* (pp. 115–35). Oxford University Press.

Tomasello, M. and Barton, M. (1994). Learning words in nonostensive contexts. *Developmental Psychology*, 30(5): 639–50.

Tomasello, M. and Brooks, P. J. (1998). Young children's earliest transitive and intransitive constructions. *Cognitive Linguistics*, 9(4): 379–95.

Tomasello, M. and Haberl, K. (2003). Understanding attention: 12 and 18 month olds know what is new for other persons. *Developmental Psychology*, 39(5): 906–12.

Tomasello, M. and Kruger, A. C. (1992). Joint attention on actions – acquiring verbs in ostensive and non-ostensive contexts. *Journal of Child Language*, 19(2): 311–33.

Tomasello, M. and Stahl, D. (2004). Sampling children's spontaneous speech: how much is enough? *Journal of Child Language*, 31(1): 101–21.

Tomasello, M., Akhtar, N., Dodson, K. and Rekau, L. (1997). Differential productivity in young children's use of nouns and verbs. *Journal of Child Language*, 24: 373–87.

Tomasello, M., Brooks, P. J. and Stern, E. (1998). Learning to produce passive utterances through discourse. *First Language*, 18: 223–37.

Tomasello, M., Strosberg, R. and Akhtar, N. (1996). Eighteen-month-old children learn words in non-ostensive contexts. *Journal of Child Language*, 23(1): 157–76.

Townsend, D. J. and Bever, T. G. (2001). *Sentence Comprehension: The Integration of Habits and Rules*. Cambridge, MA: MIT Press.

Trehub, S. E. (1973). Infants' sensitivity to vowel and tonal contrasts. *Developmental Psychology*, 9: 91–96.

(1976). The discrimination of foreign speech contrasts by infants and adults. *Child Development*, 47(2): 466–72.

Trueswell, J. C., Sekerina, I., Hill, N. M. and Logrip, M. L. (1999). The kindergarten-path effect: studying on-line sentence processing in young children. *Cognition*, 73(2): 89–134.

Ullman, M. T. (2001). The declarative/procedural model of lexicon and grammar. *Journal of Psycholinguistic Research*, 30(1): 37–69.

Vainikka, A. (1994). Case in the development of English syntax. *Language Acquisition*, 3: 257–325.

Valian, V. (1991). Syntactic subjects in the early speech of American and Italian children. *Cognition*, 40: 21–81.

Valian, V., Solt, S. and Stewart, J. (2009). Abstract categories or limited-scope formulae? The case of children's determiners. *Journal of Child Language*, 36(4): 743–78.

Van der Lely, H. K. J. (1997). Language and cognitive development in a grammatical SLI boy: modularity and innateness. *Journal of Neurolinguistics*, 10(2–3): 75–107.

Van Ginneken, J. (1917). *De roman van een kleuter (A Toddler's Novel)*. Nijmegen: Malmberg.

Van Hoek, K. (1997). *Anaphora and Conceptual Structure*. University of Chicago Press.

Vargha-Khadem, F., Gadian, D. G., Copp, A. and Mishkin, M. (2005). FOXP2 and the neuroanatomy of speech and language. *Nature Reviews Neuroscience*, 6: 131–8.

Vargha-Khadem, F., Watkins, K., Alcock, K., Fletcher, P. and Passingham, R. (1995). Praxic and nonverbal cognitive deficits in a large family with a genetically transmitted speech and language disorder. *Proceedings of the National Academy of Sciences*, 92: 930–3.

Vihman, M. M. (1996). *Phonological Development: The Origins of Language in the Child*. Cambridge, MA: Blackwell.

Vihman, M. M. and Croft, W. (2007). Phonological development: toward a 'radical' templatic phonology. *Linguistics*, 45: 683–725.

Vihman, M. M. and Velleman, S. L. (2000). The construction of a first phonology. *Phonetica*, 57: 255–66.

Vihman, M., Macken, M., Miller, R., Simmons, H. and Miller, J. (1985). From babbling to speech: a re-assessment of the continuity issue. *Language*, 61(2): 397–445.

Vihman, M., Nakai, S., DePaolis, R. and Hall, P. (2004). The role of accentual pattern in early lexical representation. *Journal of Memory and Language*, 50: 336–53.

Wanner, E. and Maratsos, M. (1978). An ATN approach to comprehension. In M. Halle, J. Bresnan and G. Miller (eds.), *Linguistic Theory and Psychological Reality* (pp. 119–61). Cambridge, MA: MIT Press.

Wason, P. (1966). Reasoning. *In New Horizons in Psychology* (pp. 135–51). Harmondsworth: Penguin.

Waterson, N. (1971). Child phonology: a prosodic view. *Journal of Linguistics*, 7: 179–211.

 (1979). The growth of complexity in phonological development. In N. Waterson and C. Snow (eds.), *The Development of Communication* (pp. 415–42). Chichester: Wiley.

Waxman, S. R. and Booth, A. E. (2000). Principles that are invoked in the acquisition of words, but not facts. *Cognition*, B33–B43.

 (2001). On the insufficiency of evidence for a domain-general account of word learning. *Cognition*, 277–79.

Waxman, S. R. and Braun, I. E. (2005). Consistent (but not variable) names as invitations to form object categories: new evidence from 12-month-old infants. *Cognition*, 95: B59–B68.

Werker, J. F., Cohen, L. B., Lloyd, V. L., Casasola, M. and Stager, C. L. (1998). Acquisition of word-object associations by 14-month-old infants. *Developmental Psychology*, 34(6): 1289–1309.

Werker, J. F. and Tees, R. C. (1983). Developmental changes across childhood in the perception of non-native speech sounds. *Canadian Journal of Psychology*, 37: 278–86.

 (1984). Cross-language speech perception: evidence for perceptual reorganization during the first year of life. *Infant Behavior and Development*, 7: 49–63.

Werker, J. F., Fennell, C. T., Corcoran, K. M. and Stager, C. L. (2002). Infants' ability to learn phonetically similar words: effects of age and vocabulary. *Infancy*, 3: 1–30.

Wexler, K. (1998). Very early parameter setting and the unique checking constraint: A new explanation of the optional infinitive stage. *Lingua*, 106(1–4): 23–79.

Wexler, K., Schütze, C. T. and Rice, M. (1998). Subject case in children with SLI and unaffected controls: evidence for the Agr/Tns Omission Model. *Language Acquisition*, 7(2–4): 317–44.

Whorf, B. (1956). *Language, Thought, and Reality*. Cambridge, MA: MIT Press.

Wightman, C., Shattuck-Hufnagel, S., Ostendorf, M. and Price, P. (1992). Segmental durations in the vicinity of prosodic phrase boundaries. *Journal of the Acoustical Society of America*, 91: 1707–17.

Willems, R. M. and Hagoort, P. (2007). Neural evidence for the interplay between language, gesture and action: a review. *Brain and Language*, 101: 278–89.

Wilson, S. (2003). Lexically specific constructions in the acquisition of inflection in English. *Journal of Child Language*, 30: 1–41.

Wimmer, H. and Perner, J. (1983). Beliefs about beliefs: representation and constraining function of wrong beliefs in young children's understanding of deception. *Cognition*, 13(1): 103–28.

Wonnacott, E., Newport, E. L. and Tanenhaus, M. K. (2008). Acquiring and processing verb argument structure: distributional learning in a miniature language. *Cognitive Psychology*, 56(3): 165–209.

Woodward, A. and Markman, E. M. (1998). Early word learning. In W. Damon, D. Kuhn and R. Seigler (eds.), *Handbook of Child Psychology*, vol. 2: *Cognition, Perception and Language* (pp. 371–420). New York: Wiley.

Wunderlich, D. (2007). Why assume UG? In M. Penke and A. Rosenbach (eds.), *What Counts as Evidence in Linguistics?* (pp. 147–74). Amsterdam and Philadelphia: Benjamins.

Yang, C. (2002). *Knowledge and Learning in Natural Language*. Oxford University Press.

(2004). Universal Grammar, statistics or both? *Trends in Cognitive Sciences*, 8: 451–6.

Zamuner, T. S. (2003). *Input-based Phonological Acquisition*. New York: Routledge.

Author index

Subject index